HOMILIES OF ÆLFRIC
A Supplementary Collection

EARLY ENGLISH TEXT SOCIETY

No. 260

1968

PRICE 84s.

þæra fixaþ. þhit hpæt hpæga bæþst;
And nubið eac spa spa fela manna
gebugað. miððam gecopenum tocpistes
geleafan. onhis gelaðunge. þhysume
yfele eft utabpecað· ⁊hyongeopyloü.
aðpeogað heopa lif. ⁊pa ⁊pa þa engli
scan men dod. þetoðam deniscum
gebugan, ⁊meapiciað hyðeopfle tohis
mann pædene. ⁊his peopc pypeað him
sylpum toforpypðe. ⁊heopa agene
leode. bespiken todeaðe; Þpæt bið æfre
pypse ænig þing onpoplde. þon spylc
dæd is. ongean his agene opihten. ⁊hine
sylfne besence. onðam ecum suslü.
ælfpemeð fpam gode. ⁊fpā eallü his
halgum; Spa dydon eac hpilon. su
me þacpistenan. onanginne cpisten

Trinity College, Cambridge, MS. B. 15. 34, p. 358. Homily XIV, 126 sqq., containing the reproach to traitors, with alterations by a scribe of the 12th or 13th century. Nearly constant half-line pointing by the original scribe.

Corpus Christi College, Cambridge, MS. 178, p. 156 (middle and upper left). Homily XXI, 443 sqq. In l. 3 the unexplained *velerā*, glossed *balles*. This and other glosses are in the 'tremulous' Worcester hand. Among other Worcester marks of alteration note *magon*, 6, with an imperfect *wyan* over the *g* to indicate *mawon*.

HOMILIES OF ÆLFRIC

A Supplementary Collection

BEING TWENTY-ONE FULL HOMILIES OF
HIS MIDDLE AND LATER CAREER
FOR THE MOST PART
NOT PREVIOUSLY EDITED

WITH SOME SHORTER PIECES

MAINLY PASSAGES ADDED TO THE
SECOND AND THIRD SERIES

Edited from all the known manuscripts
With Introduction, Notes, Latin Sources
and a Glossary by

JOHN C. POPE

VOLUME II

Published for

THE EARLY ENGLISH TEXT SOCIETY

by the

OXFORD UNIVERSITY PRESS

LONDON   NEW YORK   TORONTO

1968

PRINTED IN GREAT BRITAIN
AT THE UNIVERSITY PRESS, OXFORD
BY VIVIAN RIDLER
PRINTER TO THE UNIVERSITY

CONTENTS

XIII

DOMINICA V POST PENTECOSTEN

Luc. vi. 36–42

I

THE next four homilies, XIII–XVI, for the fifth, sixth, seventh, and tenth Sundays after Pentecost, fill gaps in the list of Sundays accounted for by Ælfric's first two series. Since they occur in the same two manuscripts, U and the interpolated portion of H, it is convenient to treat them as a group; and since U and the interpolations of H are derived from late texts, we may suppose that the four homilies were issued toward the end of Ælfric's career, having in all probability been composed not much earlier.[1] The period of Ælfric's abbacy, beginning in 1005, seems to be indicated.

The style of the homilies displays an easy mastery and a freedom in dealing with authorities that accords with a late date, though it can hardly be said to exclude the middle years. Two homilies, XIII and XIV, allude to contemporary evils, XIII in too general a way to be of much help for the chronology, XIV more specifically. These allusions are reviewed separately before each of the homilies, and before XIV I have suggested that the attack on English traitors, though we cannot know its exact occasion, may belong to a period as late as 1009 or 1010. Among the other three homilies we may notice a common emphasis on God's mercy and loving-kindness and his demand for the gentler virtues in man. Additional correspondences between XIII and XV, on which I have commented in the introduction to XV, suggest that these two were composed almost as a complementary pair and at very nearly the same time.

[1] The question is more fully discussed in the Introduction, p. 78, under the description of U; for U is the more reliable of the two witnesses, and its arrangement suggests that Ælfric first issued these homilies not as mere additions to the First and Second Series, but as parts of a Temporale that aimed at completeness for the church year. But U is incomplete at the end. Originally we may suppose that it included XVII (now in H only), for the thirteenth Sunday after Pentecost, and even Belfour III and IV (now in B only), for the twenty-second and twenty-third Sundays. These three homilies also are probably to be listed among Ælfric's latest compositions.

B

The two manuscripts, written close to the middle of the eleventh century, supply each other's defects at many points, though at a few they agree in what appears to be error (e.g. XV. 30, 179). U is better preserved and had always a somewhat more accurate text, but it has several small omissions that can be restored from H. On one occasion (XIV. 132–9) an important passage has been deliberately omitted from H. In spelling H conforms a little more consistently than U to the prevailing forms in the Ælfric manuscripts.[1]

II

By no means the whole of homily XIII is accounted for by the passages quoted as sources. Especially in the lines that glance at the contemporary scene—vaguely in the admonitions to masters and judges (56–66, 93–96), a little more precisely in the references to taxes (69), vaguely again in the summarizing instructions to the 'witan' (183–8)—Ælfric seems to be writing with considerable independence. In the background, certainly, of the admonitions to masters are St. Paul's words in *Ephes.* vi. 5–9, and for 56–61 I have quoted a Lenten homily of Rabanus Maurus (Migne, *PL* cx. 25–27), derived also from St. Paul and applied to the text from *Luke* that Ælfric is expounding. In Rabanus there is a comparable sense that current evils are under attack, and the general idea is the same, but the verbal expression is not close enough to Ælfric's to assure us of Rabanus's influence.

After the broad and partly contemporary comment on the opening verse of the gospel the other verses are treated more succinctly, and here traditional interpretations are easily recognized. Ælfric's chief guide appears to have been the corresponding section of Bede's commentary on *Luke*. Bede's main ideas are evident in many passages, and at 120–2 Ælfric is almost certainly dependent on him, for I have not found the relevant sentences (the last two in the passage quoted) in other commentators. At several other places I think Bede's language or sequence of ideas is closer to Ælfric than anything else I can find. But there are two

---

[1] U evidently attempts to follow the spelling of its exemplar and usually gives the normal spellings, but among the rare instances of deviation from Ælfric and normal LWS are, in XIII, 53 *ænde*, 69 *geldum*, 86 unsyncopated *sægeð*, 114 *ageldan*; in XIV, 82 *gewændon*, 201 *gelændon*; in XVI, 170 *forgeldon*, 223 unsyncopated *telest*, 228 *neddran*, 265 *awændað*. On U's probable connexion with Canterbury see the description in the Introduction, pp. 79–80.

homilies developed out of Bede's commentary that Ælfric probably consulted also. One is Haymo's homily CXV for the fifth
Sunday after Pentecost. Haymo so frequently echoes or merely
expands Bede that it is hard to tell which one to cite, but the passage
quoted at 141–5 appears only in Haymo and is clearly responsible
for Ælfric's comment. The other homily, assigned to the same
Sunday, is attributed to Hericus, a monk of Auxerre in the latter
part of the ninth century. It is included in Migne's edition of the
homiliary of Paulus Diaconus (*PL* XCV. 1363–9), a collection of
which some form was pretty certainly used by Ælfric.[1] The homily
is a painstaking development of Bede's ideas, making them more
explicit and simpler in expression but adding almost nothing.
Here and there, as at 113–16 and at 175–7, it has seemed to me that
Ælfric's sequence of thought was under Hericus's direct influence,
but of this it is hard to be certain.

There is also an earlier homily assigned to this Sunday in
Migne's edition of Paulus (*PL* XCV, Hom. CLXII), though it deals
with the parallel, much shorter text in *Matth.* vii. 1–5. This
homily, now attributed to Cæsarius of Arles (*Sermo* CXLVIII, ed.
Morin), is strongly influenced by Augustine's exposition of these
verses in the tract, *De Sermone Domini in Monte* (*PL* XXXIV.
1296 sqq.). Now Bede had incorporated verbatim in his commentary on *Luc.* vi. 36–42 all that was relevant in Augustine's
exposition of *Matth.* vii. 1–5. Consequently there is a strong resemblance between Cæsarius and Bede at the points where *Luke*
corresponds to *Matthew*. But at least one sentence in Cæsarius,
which I have quoted at 88–97, may have contributed to Ælfric's
insistence on the responsibilities of judges, and a bit of it seems to
have been directly translated at 186. I am the more inclined to
think these small resemblances significant in that a passage in XV
may well have been suggested to Ælfric by the same sermon.

Whether or not Ælfric made use of Cæsarius, he was mindful
of the relevance of *Matth.* vii. 1–5, for there is strong evidence that
he consulted Jerome's commentary on those verses and borrowed
from it an apt comparison that none of the other commentators
mentions: the comparison with *Matth.* xxiii. 24, in which the

---

[1] See Introduction, p. 156. Bede's commentary was in the *original* collection
(II. 37), but assigned to the first Sunday after Pentecost. After the third Sunday
the system of counting changed in the original collection so that there is nothing
to correspond exactly with the homilies for the fourth and fifth Sundays after
Pentecost in the Migne edition.

scribes and Pharisees are accused of straining out a gnat (as the Latin versions have it) and swallowing a camel. Ælfric gives the Latin at line 163 in a form that shows where he found it, for Jerome quotes the word *liquantes* from the Old Latin instead of the *excolantes* of his own version, and writes *et camelum* where both versions have *camelum autem.*[1]

Twice Ælfric makes extended use of Biblical passages that are not mentioned in the commentaries on the gospel-text in *Luke* or the related text in *Matthew*. At line 73 he introduces the first verse of the hundredth Psalm in the Vulgate, *Misericordiam et iudicium cantabo tibi, Domine*, and his interpretation of it corresponds to Augustine's in his *Enarratio* on that psalm. If he turned to Augustine directly he found him developing the theme of mercy with reference to the very verses in *Luke* and *Matthew* on which Ælfric builds lines 40–45, and perhaps furnishing a suggestion for line 46.

Secondly, Ælfric adds, as a highly effective *exemplum* for the close of his sermon, the story of Jesus and the woman taken in adultery from *John* viii. 1–11. His only elucidation of the text, the explanation of the motives of the scribes and Pharisees at 208–11, was probably common property, for it occurs in several writers including Jerome (*PL* xxx. 581) and Augustine (*PL* xxxv. 1648 sq.). Bede's phrasing in his Lenten homily on the text (I. 25 in Hurst's edition) seems as close as any. His words reappear in Alcuin's commentary on *John* (*PL* c. 853 sq.) and in Haymo (*PL* cxviii. 282).

Not only these Biblical additions but brief allusions to the Bible and quotations from it add richness to the homily. Among shorter passages the vigorous translation of *Matth.* xxiii. 24, already mentioned, at 164 and the adaptation of *II Peter* ii. 20, 22, at 230–4 may seem particularly striking.

[1] *PL* xxvi. 46 sq. For the older reading, see *Bibliorum Sacrorum Latinæ Versiones Antiquæ*, ed. P. Sabatier, 1743.

DOMINICA V POST PENTECOSTEN

Estote ergo misericordes, et *reliqua*

Lucas se godspellere, þe wæs læce on lífe,
and he manega gehælde fram mislicum coðum
mid his læcecræfte, ac he gelacnode swiðor
maneg'r'a manna sawla mid his lare on worulde,
he awrat be ðam Hælende þæt he her on life   5
on sumere tíde þus sæde on his godspelle
*to his halgum apostolum, and swa þurh hy to us: *p. 338
Estote ergo misericordes, et reliqua:
Beoð mildheorte eornostlice, eall swa eower Fæder is;
ne deme ge nateshwon, and ge ne beoð gedemede.   10
Ne fordeme ge, and ge ne beoð fordemede;

Text based on U (Trinity B. 15. 34), pp. 337–50. Collated with H (Cotton
Vitellius C. v), ff. 132ᵛ–4ᵛ. In the list of variants round brackets enclose portions
of the text as witnessed by U (including the modern punctuation) for which
there is approximately the right space, but no longer any reading in the
damaged H.
For Homilies XIII–XVI, where the manuscripts are the same, the following
variants are excluded: H regularly has *byð, gyf, hi, mann, menn, þiss, þuss* where
U has *bið, gif, hy, man, men, þis, þus*. But H usually has *man* for the indefinite
pronoun, 'one'. U's *hy* and *hym* were often written *hi* and *him* at first.
In H, the pointing is normally by half-lines; in U, intermittently so.

Sup.: V POST PENTECOSTEN] IVᵃ *POST* OCT*AVAS* PENTECOS-
TEN H.   6 sumere] sume *H.*

SOURCES. 9–33 [*Luc. vi. 36*] Estote ergo misericordes sicut et Pater vester
misericors est.
[*37*] Nolite iudicare, et non iudicabimini: nolite condemnare, et non con-
demnabimini. Dimittite, et dimittemini.
[*38*] Date, et dabitur vobis: mensuram bonam, et confertam, et coagitatam,
et supereffluentem dabunt in sinum vestrum. Eadem quippe mensura, qua mensi
fueritis, remetietur vobis.
[*39*] Dicebat autem illis et similitudinem: Numquid potest cæcus cæcum
ducere? nonne ambo in foveam cadunt?
[*40*] Non est discipulus super magistrum: perfectus autem omnis erit, si sit
sicut magister eius.
[*41*] Quid autem vides festucam in oculo fratris tui, trabem autem, quæ in
oculo tuo est, non consideras?
[*42*] Aut quomodo potes dicere fratri tuo: Frater sine eiiciam festucam de
oculo tuo: ipse in oculo tuo trabem non videns? Hypocrita eiice primum traben
de oculo tuo: et tunc perspicies ut educas festucam de oculo fratris tui.

forgifað oðrum mannum, and eow bið forgifen.
Dælað and doð gód, and eow bið gód forgifen.
Hy forgifað eft into eowrum bosme
swiðe gód gemet þam þe ge nu dælað,   15
and gecrammod gemet, and swiðe ge[h]rysed,
and oferflowende, eow to edleane.
On ðam gemete þe ge ametað eow bið eft ameten.
He sæde eac soðlice hym þis bigspell þus:
Hu mæg la se blinda lædan þone blindan,   20
and hu ne feallað hy begen on sumne blindne seað?
Ne bið na se leorningcniht furðor þonne his lareow;
ælc þæra bið fulfremed þe bið swa swa his lareow.
*Hu miht þu la geseon þæt mot to gewissan   *p. 339
on ðines broðor eagan, and þone beam ne gesihst   25
þe is soðlice on ðinum eag[an],
and hu miht þu secgan to þinum breðer þus:
geðafa, min broðor, þæt ic þæt mot at[eo]
of ðinum eagan nú, and þu nelt geseon
þe sylf þone beam þe bið on ðinum eagan?   30
Ac ateoh, þu hiwere, ærest þone beam
ut of ðinum eagan, and þu locast þonne
þæt þu of ðines broþor eagan þæt mot ut ateo.

Her syndon syllice word samlæredum mannum;
nu wylle we eow geopenian þæt andgit þærto,   35
and eow swutelicor sæcgan heora getacnunge.
Se Hælend us bebe'a'd on þisum halgan godspelle,
'Beoð mildheorte eornostlice, eal swa eower Fæder is.'
Her ge magon gehyran þæs Hælendes gódnysse,
þonne he cwæð swa be us, þæt we swylcne Fæder   40

12 forgyfen H.   14 forgyfað H.   bosmum H.   16 gerysed U; gehrised H.
19 him H.   23 full- H.   25 eagan] sic both MSS.   26 eagum U;
agenum eage H.   28 broðer H.   ateon U; ateo H.   29 (of) H.   eage H.
30 (ðin)um H.   eage H.   32 eage H.   (and þu loc)ast H.   þænne
H, followed by point.   33 eage H.   34 (syndon sylli)ce H.   35 wille H.
eow] om. H.   (þæt andgit þæ)rto H.   36 secgan H, followed by point.   37 (Se
hælend us bebea)d H.   38 (eornostlice, eal swa eower fæ)der H.
39 ge] we H.   þæs] f. 133, H.   godnesse H.

39–53 [Similar to Haymo and Hericus in emphasis on God's mercy but freely
developed.]
40–45 [Luc. vi. 35] Et eritis filii Altissimi, quia ipse benignus est super
ingratos et malos. [Matth. v. 44, 45] Diligite inimicos vestros, benefacite his qui
oderunt vos, . . . ut sitis filii Patris vestri qui in cælis est: qui solem suum oriri

us habban moton, þone heofenlican *God,   *p. 340
gif we mildheorte beoð, for ðan þe he is mildheort,
swa þæt he læt scinan his sunnan gelice
ofer þa gódan men and ofer ða yfelan,
and forgifð renscuras rihtwisum and unrihtwisum,   45
and eorð[lice] wæstmas eallum to fodan,
þam þe hine lufiað and þam þe hine hatigað.
Se hatað his Scyppend, se ðe forsihð his hæse,
and nele mid weorcum his word gefyllan,
ac swaðeah hine afet se heofonlica Fæder,   50
þæt he on sumne sæl gecyrre to Gode,
oððe he beo r`i´htlice þam reðan deofle
on his ænde betæht, gif he ær ne gecyrð.
He het us beon mildheorte oðrum mannum symble,
mid ealre gódnysse, swa swa God sylf is;   55
ac se ne bið na mildheort þe [oðre] men geswen`c´ð,
and hefige byrðene him on bæc behypð,
unforwandodlice, mid wælreownysse æfre,
and þa læssan berypð swiðe unrihtlice,
and wyle swaþeah habban him *sylfum softnysse,   *p. 341
and nyle geðencan hu he geswencð þa earman.   61
Ne sceolde he næfre softnysse brucan,

---

41 heofon- *H.*   42 þam *H.*   45 forgyfð *H.*   46 eorðlice] *sic*
H; eorð *U.*   47 hatiað *H.*   48 forsyhð *H.*   49 hys *H.*   53 ende *H.*
56 oðre] *sic H*; eowre *U.*   57 behypð] behefð *H.*   58 wælhreow-
nisse *H.*   60 wile *H.*   61 nele *H.*

---

facit super bonos et malos, et pluit super iustos et iniustos. [*These texts are
echoed or quoted in Haymo and Hericus.*]
    46 [*Psal. cxxxv. 25*] Qui dat escam omni carni. [*Act. xiv. 16*] . . . benefaciens
de cælo, dans pluvias et tempora fructifera, implens cibo et lætitia corda nostra.
[*Aug., En. in Psal. c, after quoting Matth. v. 44, 45*] Quando vides iustos et
iniustos eumdem solem intueri, . . . eadem pluvia saginari, iisdem fructibus
terræ repleri. . . .
    47–49 [*Ex. xx. 5, 6*] . . . qui oderunt me, . . . qui diligunt me, et custodiunt
præcepta mea. [*Ioan. xiv. 24*] Qui non diligit me, sermones meos non servat.
    50–53 [*Cf. infra, 76–81.*]
    56–61 [*Cf. Rabanus on same theme*] Nonnulli, peccata sua oblivioni tradentes,
. . . ita circa servos suos et subditos sibi potestatem dominationis exercent, ut
in his diebus non dubitent flagellis eos cædere, poenis afficere, compedibus
præpedire. . . . Quam absurdum est quod Christianus dominus Christiano in his
diebus servo non parcat, minime respiciens quod si servus est conditione, gratia
tamen frater est. . . . Et ideo, fratres, quicunque ex vobis aliis præsunt, per
charitatem illis imperent. [*Quotes Ephes. vi. 5–9.*]
    62–71 [*Apparently a free development of the preceding theme.*]

se ðe ne mæg geþafian his underþeoddum mannum
þæt hy [l]isse habban on heora lifes geswincum,
þonne he eaðe mihte him liðian foroft,   65
þæt he him sylf hæfde sume lisse his sawle.

God lufað þa liðnysse, þæt man lissige oðrum
on hefegum geswincum þe men habbað on gewunan,
on mislicum geldum and on manegum gesetnyssum,
and he ða m[an]nhatan swiðe micclum onscunað,   70
and þa mildheortan to his mildse becumað.

Be Godes mildheortnysse cwæð se witega þus:
Miscricordiam et iudicium cantabo tibi, Domine:
Ic singe þe, Drihten, soðe mildheortnysse,
and swiðe rihtne dóm þe ðu gedemest mannum;   75
for ðan þe he gemildsað mannum *her on life,   *p. 342
þæt hy gecyrran moton fram heora synnum to him,
and he ðam dom gedemeð þe hine dollice forseoð,
on ðam toweardan life, þe lyt his nu gymað,
for ðan þe nu is se tima on ðam þe he mildsað,   80
and þonne bið se ende, þæt he eallum deme.

Swiðe mildheort he is þam þe hihtað on hine,
ac swiðest þam welwillendum, and þam rihtgeðancedum,
þe nellað ʻunʼrihtlice oðre geswencan,
butan for rihtwisre steore and rihtum gesetnyssum.   85

---

64 lisse] *sic H;* blisse *U.*   66 *after* hæfde] on þam toweardan lífe eft *H.*
lisse] *corrected from* blisse *U.*   68 hefium *H.*   69 mistlicum gíldum *H.*
70 mann-] *sic H;* mán- *U.*   75 gedemst *H.*   76 þam *H.*   gemiltsað *H.*
78 gedemð *H.*   dwollice *H.*   79 lít *H.*   80 þam *H.*   (nu) *H.*
miltsað *H.*   81 dem(e) *H.*   83 swiþost *H.*   wel(willendum) *H.*
-þancodum *H.*   85 (butan for) rihtre *H.*

67–71 [*Cf. Luc. xi. 46*] Et vobis legisperitis væ; quia oneratis homines oneribus
quæ portare non possunt, et ipsi uno digito vestro non tangitis sarcinas. [*Rom.
xv. 1*] Debemus autem nos firmiores imbecillitates infirmorum sustinere, et non
nobis placere. [*Gal. vi. 2*] Alter alterius onera portate, et sic adimplebitis legem
Christi. [*Matth. v. 7*] Beati misericordes, quoniam ipsi misericordiam con-
sequentur.

73–75 *Psal. c. 1, as given.*]

76–81 [*Aug., En. in Psal. c*] Si temporibus distinguamus hæc duo, misericordiam et iudicium, . . . forte invenimus modo tempus esse misericordiæ,
futurum autem tempus iudicii. . . . Est ergo misericordiæ tempus, quando
patientia Dei ad pænitentiam adducit peccantes. . . . [*At end*] Sed qui non se
correxerint in isto tempore misericordiæ, interficientur.

82–85 [*Apparently independent.*]

þæt godspell sægeð gyt forð þus be endebyrdnysse:
'Ne deme ge nateshwón, and ge ne beoð gedemede.'
Ne forbead he mid ealle ælcne dom þam witan,
þam þe deman sceal, ac ða dyrstignysse,
þæt man ofaxxie ærest symble þæt riht.   90
Sume þing synd nu digle, þe God sylf demeþ eft,
and sume þing synd opene, be ðam man deman sceal,
and man ne sceal *mid gewille bewerian þone scyldigan, *p. 343
ne eft mid nanum wó þone unscyldigan fordon,
ne for nanum sceatte þæt soðe awægan,   95
ne for nanum ege þæt unriht drifan,
ac mid mildheortnysse þa men gerihtlæcan,
swa swa heræfter sægð on ðisum godspelle:
'Ne fordeme ge nænne, and ge ne beoð fordemede.'
Iacob se rihtwisa awrat on his pistole,   100
þam men bið dom geset butan mildheortnysse eft,
se ðe nu oðrum demeð butan mildheortnysse.
'Forgifað oðrum mannum, and eow bið forgifen.'

86 þæt] *cap. H, not U.*   segð (gyt forð þus) *H.*   87 (beoð gedemede) *H.*
88 Ne] *cap. H, not U.*   88–89 (witan . . . sceal) *H.*   90 ofac(si)ge *H.*
90–91 (ærest . . . þing) *H.*   91–92 (demeþ . . . ðam) *H.*   92 man] *f. 133ᵛ, H.*
93 gewille] wille *H.*   96 unriht ahwær drifan *H.*   97 -nesse *H.*
98 segð *H.*   101 þam] *cap. H, not U.*   gesett *H.*   102 demð *H.*
103 Forgyfað *H.*   forgyfen *H.*

88–97 [*Bede, In Lucam; from Augustine, De Sermone Domini in Monte, Matth.*
vii. 1, 2] Hoc loco nihil aliud nobis præcipi existimo, nisi ut ea facta quæ dubium
est quo animo fiant, in meliorem partem interpretemur. Quod enim scriptum
est, *Ex fructibus eorum cognoscetis eos (Matth. vii. 20)*, de manifestis dictum est,
quæ non possunt bono animo fieri, . . . de quibus nobis iudicare permittitur.
. . . Sunt ergo quædam facta media, quæ ignoramus quo animo fiant . . . de
quibus temerarium est iudicare, maxime ut condemnemus. Horum autem veniet
tempus ut iudicentur, cum Dominus illuminabit abscondita tenebrarum, et
manifestabit cogitationes cordis (*I Cor. iv. 5*). [*Similarly Haymo and Hericus.*
Haymo adds] Manifesta et aperta mala . . . a fidelibus non solum reprehendenda
sunt, sed et corrigenda ab illo qui locum regiminis tenet, atque iudicanda.
[*Similarly Cæsarius, Sermo CXLVIII*] De istis ergo rebus, quæ sunt Deo notæ,
et nobis incognitæ, periculose nostros proximos iudicamus. . . . De illis vero,
quæ aperta sunt et publica mala, iudicare et redarguere, cum caritate tamen et
amore [*cf.* 186], et possumus et debemus.
93–96 [*Not in immediate sources.*]
100–2 [*Iac. ii. 13*] Iudicium enim sine misericordia illi qui non fecit misericordiam. [*Quoted by Rabanus in passage from which excerpts are cited for lines*
56–61.]

God hat us forgifan ure teonan mannum,
þæt he us forgife ure synna þurh þæt.   105
'Dælað and doð gód, and eow bið gód forgifen.'
Se ðe dæleð for Gode, God geeacnað his þing,
and him eft be hundfealdum his ælmessan forgylt.
   'Hy forgyfað eft into eowrum bosme
swiðe god gemet, *þam þe 'ge' nu dælað,   *p. 344
and gecrammod gemet, and swiðe gehrisod,   111
and oferflowende, eow to edleane.'
He mænde þa þearfan, þe man nu deð gód,
þæt hy sceolon 'ageldan' us eft þæt gemet;
ac God sylf agylt for hyg swiðe glædlice us   115
eall þæt we him nu doð for his naman to góde,
swa þæt ure gemet bið swiðe wel getreden,
and on ælce healfe oferflewð þonne.
   'On ðam gemete þe ge ametað [eow] bið eft ameten.'
þis mæg beon gecweden be eallum urum dædum,   120
ge worda ge weorca, þæt God witodlice
ælcum men gylt eft be his agenum dædum.
   'He sæde eac soþlice hym þis bigspell þus:
Hu mæg la se blinda lædan þone blindan,
and hu ne feallað hy begen on sumne blindne seað?'   125

104 hat] het H.   105 ure] om. H.   107 dælð H.   ge-] om. H.
108 forgilt H.   110 swið H.   111 gehrised H.   113 deð nu H.
114 agildan H.   115 hi H.   116 heom H.   119 eow] sic H; þonne U.
122 forgylt H.   123 heom H.

104–5 [Bede] Dimittere nos iniuras . . . iubet, ut . . . nobis peccata dimittantur.
[Haymo quotes Matth. vi. 14 inexactly] Si dimiseritis hominibus peccata eorum,
et Pater vester dimittet vobis peccata vestra.
   107–8 [Bede, in same sentence as above] Dare beneficia iubet ut . . . vita detur
æterna. [Haymo] Ad dandam eleemosynam pertinet. . . . Mensura enim bona a
bonorum omnium remuneratore dabitur, quando pro minimis maiora rependet.
[But see note.]
   113–16 [Bede] Non enim pauperes ipsi, sed Christus mercedem his qui
eleemosynam fecere redditurus est. [Hericus's expansion suggests Ælfric's phrasing]
Qui sunt isti qui dabunt mensuram bonam, nisi pauperes quibus beneficia dede-
rimus? . . . Non enim pauperes ipsi mercedem reddent his qui eleemosynam
illis largiuntur, sed Christus, pro cuius dilectione hoc faciunt.
   120–2 [Bede] Et apostolus ad eleemosynam Corinthios hortans, inter alia
dicit: Hoc autem dico, Qui parce seminat, parce et metet. Et qui seminat in benedictionibus, de benedictionibus et metet (II Cor. ix. 6). Potest autem et de omnibus
quæ mente, manu, lingua gerimus, accipi. Quia tu reddes singulis, inquit, secundum opera eorum (Psal. lxi. 13).

Bispell getacnað on bocum gelome
oðer þing on wordum and oðer on getacnungum.
Nu 'ne' mæg nan lareow, butan he ða lare hæbbe,
*þa læwedan men gerihtlæcan to Godes rihtwisnysse,   *p. 345
ne se leahterfulla man ne mæg leahtras forbeodan,   130
ne ðam dysigan styran, buton he styre ærest
his agenum unðeawum fram eallum gedwyldum,
and góde bysne sylle symble þam læwedum.
    'Ne bið na se leorningcniht furðor þonne his lareow;
ælc þæra bið fulfremed þe bið swa swa his lareaw.'   135
Crist sylf 'is se lareaw', and he sealde us bysne,
þæt we sceolan mildsian, swa swa he mildsað us;
and we ne magon beon butan ehtnysse hér,
þe ma þe he sylf wæs, ac we sceolan forberan
fela for his naman, swa swa he gebysnode us.   140
Mænig leorningcild leornode foroft
þæt he mare cuðe on micclum andgyte
þonne his agen lareow, þe hine lærde æt fruman,
and forðig is se Hælend her gecweden lareow,
þæt we beon fulfremede, *gif we him folgiað.   *p. 346
    'Hu miht þu la geseon þæt mot to gewissan   146
on þines broðor eagan, and ðone beam ne gesihst

126 Bigspell *H.*   128 hæbbe þa lare *H.*   131 æror *H.*   132 gedwildum *H.*   133 (and) *H*   symle *H*   134 (fur)þor *H.*   135 ac
ælc *H.*   full- *H.*   (his lar)eow *H.*   136 lareow *H.*   137 sceolon *H.*
(mildsian) *H.*   miltsað *H.*   139 (þe ma þe he sylf wæ)s *H.*   sceolon *H.*
140 swa (swa . . . u)s *H.*   141 Menig *H.*   læring- *H.*   142–3 (cuðe . . .
þon)ne *H.*   143–4 fru(man . . . gecwede)n *H.*   145 full- *H.*
145–6 (gif . . . geseon) *H.*   147 broðor] *f. 134, H.*   eage *H.*   gesihð *H.*

126–7 [*Not in Ælfric's immediate sources.*]
128–33 [*Haymo*] Sunt enim nonnulli qui, antequam discipuli fiant, magistri
fieri appetunt: et quibus non est sanctitas in moribus, nec maturitas in ætate,
neque doctrina in sermonibus suffragatur, inverecunde locum regiminis appetunt. [*Bede*] Cæcum a cæco duci, id est peccantem a peccatore castigari non
posse præmonuit. [*Ælfric develops these suggestions independently.*]
136–40 [*Bede*] Si magister, qui utique quasi Deus potuit, non suas ultum ire
iniurias, sed ipsos maluit insecutores patiendo reddere mitiores, eandem necesse
est discipuli, qui puri homines sunt, regulam perfectionis sequantur. [*Haymo
repeats this in other words, and adds*] Pro modulo nostræ capacitatis humilitatem
et mansuetudinem illius imitari debemus.
141–5 [*Haymo*] Solet namque in humanis disciplinis contingere, ut discipulus
per acumen mentis antecellat magistrum. Magister ergo in hoc loco ille intelli-
gitur, qui alibi ait: *Vos vocatis me, Magister et Domine, et bene dicitis* (*Ioan.
xiii. 13*).

þe is soðlice on ðinum eagan,
and hu miht þu secgan to ðinum breðer þus:
geðafa, min broðor, þæt ic þæt mot ateo   150
of ðinum eagan nú, and þu nelt geseon
þe sylf þone beam þe bið on ðinum eagan?'
Ne mæg se langa beam licgan on þinum eagan,
ac se beam getacnað þa teonfullan hatunge,
þæt þu hatige þone man mid hetelum mode,   155
and þæt mot getacnað þæs mannes yrsunge;
þonne ne miht þu na þæt mot ut ateon
of ðæs mannes eagan, buton þu ærest awurpe
þa hatunge þe fram, þe is heafodleahter,
and ðu syððan swa miht þæs mannes yrre gestyran,   160
and gif ðu hine hatast, ne miht þu him styran.
Be ðam ylcan andgyte he cwæð on oðre stowe,
Liquantes culicem et glutientes camélum:
*Hy ahlyttriað þone stút of heora liðe mid seohhann,   *p. 347
and hy ealne forswelgað þone olfend gehalne.   165
þæt is, þæt hy tælað mid teonfullum mode
and mid modignysse, þe is gylta mæst,
þa lytlan gyltas, swylce hy 'h'luttrion þone stút,
and nellað þa micclan synna on hym sylfum gebetan,
ac wyllað mid hospe huxlice tælan   170
oðra manna misdæda, þonne hy maran sylfe habbað.

148 ys *H.*   (ðinum agenum) eage *H? (suggested by spacing and by line 26)*.
150 geþ(afa, min) *H.*   151 eage *H.*   152 s(ylf) *H.*   agenum ege *(sic) H.*
153 eage *H.*   154 hatun(ge) *H.*   156 þ(æs) *H.*   158 eage *H.*
erest *H.*   aweorpe *H.*   160 styran *H.*   162 andgite *H.*   164 ahlutt-
riað *H. U has faint Latin gloss in margin, perhaps* liquantes *for* ahlyttriað.
liðe] *followed by full stop U.*   seohhan *H.*   165 oluend *H.*   167 -nesse *H.*
mæ(st) *H.*   168 lyttlan *H.*   swilce *H.*   169 heom *H.*   170 willað
H.   huxl(ice) *H.*   171 silfe *H.*

154–61 [*Bede*] Hæc cum fratre agis, si (verbi gratia) quod ira ille peccavit, tu
odio reprehendis. Quantum autem inter festucam et trabem, quasi tantum inter
iram distat atque odium. Odium est enim ira inveterata. . . . Fieri autem potest,
ut si irascaris homini, velis eum corrigi. Si autem oderis hominem, non potes
eum velle corrigere. . . . Primo abs te expelle odium, et deinceps poteris iam
eum quem diligis emendare. [*Similarly Haymo and Hericus. Ælfric's 'heafodleahter' in* 159 *may have been suggested by Haymo*] Quantum inter festucam et
trabem, tantum inter peccatum maius et minus distat.
162–71 [*Jerome, In Matth. vii. 3–5*] De his loquitur, qui cum ipsi mortali
crimine teneantur obnoxii, minora peccata fratribus non concedunt: *culicem
liquantes, et camelum glutientes (Matth. xxiii. 24, inexactly recalling Old Latin;
Jerome's own Vulgate has,* excolantes culicem, camelum autem glutientes).

'Ac ateoh, þu hýwere, ærest þone beam
ut of þinum eagan, and ðu locast þonne
þæt þu of ðines broðor eagan þæt mot út ateo.'
Híwere bið se mann þe hogað ymbe þæt   175
þæt he oðerne gerihtlæce ær hine sylfne,
swylce he leahtras onscunige, and bið him sylf leahterfull;
ac Crist us gewissode, þe ne wandode nan þing,
hét us ærest adón ure dyrnan unðeawas
and þa yfelan hatunge fram ure heortan aweg,   180
and mid hluttrum mode syððan gerihtlæcan
þa eaðelican *gyltas on oðrum mannum swa.   *p. 348

þa men sceolon styran þe to styrene agon,
þæt syndon þa witan, þe ðone wisdom habbað
and fram Gode þone anweald þæt hy oðrum styron,   185
swaþeah mid liðnysse and mid lufe symble,
and hy heora agene unþeawas ne forgytan,
þæt God sy gehered on his halgum þegenum.

We willað eow secgan sume bysne be ðysum,
hu se Hælend sylf her on life dyde: 190
He becom to ðam munte þe men hatað Oliuéti
wið ða burh Hierusalem, on Iudea lande;

---

172 (a)teoh H.   hywere] *glossed* Hipocrit(a) U; hiwere H.   173 agenum
eage H.   174 eage H.   175 embe H.   177 onscunie H.   182 giltas
H.   183 styrenne H.   184 synd H.   186 mi(d) H.   simble H.
187 (for)giton. H.   188 si H.   geherod H.   189 will(að eow) H.
þisum H.   190 he(r on life) H.   dide H.   191–2 (oliueti . . . burh) H.

175–7 [*Bede*] Et est vere multum cavendum et molestum hypocritarum, id
est simulatorum, genus, qui cum omnium vitiorum accusationes odio et livore
suscipiant, etiam consultores videri se volunt. [*Hericus*] Et hypocrita vocatur non
solum qui aliud corde gerit et aliud opere agit, verum et ille qui, cum sit malus,
quærit reprehendere bonos.
178–82 [*Apparently Ælfric's own recapitulation.*]
183–8 [*Cf.* 88–97, *and quotations there given from Haymo and Cæsarius, esp.
Cæsarius for* 186: cum caritate tamen et amore.]
191–207 [*Ioan. viii. 1*] Iesus autem perrexit in montem Oliveti.
[*2*] Et diluculo iterum venit in templum, et omnis populus venit ad eum, et
sedens docebat eos.
[*3*] Adducunt autem scribæ et Pharisæi mulierem in adulterio deprehensam,
et statuerunt eam in medio.
[*4*] et dixerunt ei: Magister, hæc mulier modo deprehensa est in adulterio.
[*5*] In lege autem Moyses mandavit nobis huiusmodi lapidare. Tu ergo
quid dicis?
[*6*] Hoc autem dicebant tentantes eum, ut possent accusare eum.

þa eode he on ærnemergen into ðam temple,
and eall þæt folc sona in ðrang him to,
and he ða sittende him sylf hy lærde georne,   195
swa swa his gewuna wæs; and hit þa gelamp swa
þæt þa Sunderhalgan and þa sylfan boceras
gebrohton án wíf swa into ðam temple,
and heo wæs befangen on fúlum forligre,
and leton hy standan on his gesihðe, *and cwædon,   *p. 349
þu leof lareow,   201
þis wif wæs nu gelæht on openum forligre,
and on Moyses lage he bebead witodlice
þæt man mid stanum oftorfode swa forscyldegodne wifman;
hwæt sægest þu us nú be swylcere dæde?   205
þis hy sædon to him þæt hy his fandodon,
þæt hy mihton wyrcan sume wrohte be him,
gif he þurh his liþnysse heora lag[e] tobræce,
gif he ðam forlegenan wife lif 'þa' getæcan wolde,
oððe he wurde wælreow on heora gewitnysse,   210
gif he oftorfian hete þæt wif þa mid stanum.
He ða beah adún, and awrat mid his fingre
swa on ðære eorðan, and hy acsodon þa gyt.

193 ær(nemergen . . . ðam) H.   194 inn aþrang H.   194–5 (him . . .
sittende) H.   196 (swa swa . . . þa) H.   197–8 sund(erhalgan . . .
temple) H.   199 and heo] *first words visible f. 134ᵛ, H.*   199–200 for-
(ligre . . . leton) H.   201 leofa la(reow) H.   202 forligere H.   203 on]
om. H.   lagu H.   he bebead] (: : : :)ad H, *probably* he *om.*   204 for-
scylde(go)dne H.   205 segst H.   206 (s)ædon H.   hys fandedon H.
207 wircan H.   208 lage] *sic H; laga U; see note.*   209 tæcan H.
210 wælhreow H.   -nesse H.   212 beah þa H.   213 axodon H.

208–11 [*Bede, Hom. I. 25, ed. Hurst, lines 46–50*] Ut si et ipse hanc lapidandam
decerneret, deriderent eum quasi misericordiæ quam semper docebat oblitum;
si lapidare vetaret, striderent in eum dentibus suis, et quasi fautorem scelerum,
legisque contrarium velut merito damnarent.

212–27 [*Ioan. viii. 6*] Iesus autem inclinans se deorsum, digito scribebat in
terra.

[7] Cum ergo perseverarent interrogantes eum, erexit se, et dixit eis: Qui sine
peccato est vestrum, primus in illam lapidem mittat.

[8] Et iterum se inclinans, scribebat in terra.

[9] Audientes autem unus post unum exibant, incipientes a senioribus; et
remansit solus Iesus, et mulier in medio stans.

[10] Erigens autem se Iesus, dixit ei: Mulier, ubi sunt qui te accusabant?
nemo te condemnavit?

[11] Quæ dixit: Nemo, Domine. Dixit autem Iesus: Nec ego te condemnabo:
vade, et iam amplius noli peccare.

þa sæt se Hælend upp and sæde hym þus to:
Swa hwylc eower swa næfð nane synne on him,   215
awyrpe se ærest ænne stán on hy;
and he sylf þa eft on þære eorðan awrat.
Hwæt þa, ða heafodmen, þa hy þis gehyrdon,
eodon hym ealle ut *endemes hire fram,   *p. 350
and þæt wíf stód ána ætforan þam Hælende.   220
He sæt þa eft up and sæde to ðam wífe,
Hwær syndon nu, la wíf, [þa] þe ðe wregdon swa swiðe;
ne fordemde heora nán þe to deaðe for ðam?
þæt wif him andwyrde, mid afyrhtum mode,
Na, leofa Drihten, ne fordemde heora nán me.   225
Se Hælend hire cwæð to, Ne ic ðe ne fordeme;
gang þu nu aweg, and þu heonan forð ne synga.
On ða wisan he forgeaf þone gylt þam wífe,
þæt heo syððan sceolde wið swylc þing hy gehealdan,
for ðan þe ælc man bið, þe geandet his synna,   230
and þæt ylce eft deð his Drihtne on teonan,
þam hunde gelic, þe geet his spiweðan,
and ðam swine gelíc, þe hit besylað eft æfter his þweale,
and bið his ende wyrse þonne his angin wære.

    Gewissige us se Hælend to his willan æfre,   235
þam is wuldor and lóf a to weorulde, AMEN.

214 him H.   215 hwilc H.   218 heafod(men) H.   219 heom H.
220 (and) H.   221 upp H.   222 þa] sic H; om. U.   225 me heora
nan H.   226 Ne] cap. H, not U.   227 gang (þ)e H.   awegg H.
heonon H.   singa H.   228 (þ)one H.   229 sceolde syþþan H.   swilc H.
geheal(da)n H.   230 þam H.   geandett H.   231 (yl)ce H.   232 geett
H.   (s)piweþan H.   233 besilað H.   234 (and b)yð H.   anginn H.
235 (hæ)lend H.   236 worulde H.

230-4 [II Petr. ii. 20, 22] Si enim refugientes coinquinationes mundi in
cognitionem Domini nostri et salvatoris Iesu Christi, his rursus implicati
superantur, facta sunt eis posteriora deteriora prioribus (Matth. xii. 45: et fiunt
novissima hominis illius peiora prioribus). . . . Contigit enim eis illud veri
proverbii: Canis reversus ad suum vomitum; et, Sus lota in volutabro luti.

NOTES

13. doð god. Nearly always in Ælfric this expression has the concrete
sense, 'give (material) goods', though the wider modern sense of doing
good may not be wholly excluded.

21. In his earlier translation of the parallel verse, Matth. xv. 14, Ælfric
has the dative, on sumum blindum seaðe (CH II. 320/15), but plays on blind

in the same way. *Blind* in the sense 'dark' occurs also in Ælfric's life of
St. Agatha, *LS* VIII. 92, *on anum blindum cwearterne.*

26. *eagan.* This is the regular form of the dative singular in U, which
here has the plural *eagum* by mistake. In H, after the orthodox *eagan* at
25, we regularly encounter ds. *eage* (26, 29, 30, 32, 33, 147, 148, 151, 153,
158, 173, 174) and once *ege* (152), as if the word were a strong neuter.

54–66. This passage deals much more explicitly and feelingly with the
treatment of servants by their masters than the corresponding passage in
CH II. XXI, p. 326, where Ælfric merely reports St. Paul's advice.

57. *behypð*, 'heaps up'. Hitherto this meaning has been assigned to the
one recorded instance of *behypian* in a gloss, whereas the equally solitary
instance of *behypan* in the OE Bede translates *circumseptus* (*behyped*) and
is defined by Bosworth Toller as 'to heap' or 'cover over, surround, en-
compass'. The variation of meaning is readily explained by the range of
application of the prefix and the difference between the two constructions.
In the Bede, if we turn the passive into the active voice, a man is the direct
object of the verb. Here the encumbrance is the object. (See BT *behypan*,
BTS *behipian*, Hall–Meritt *behypan*, *behypian*.)

70. *mannhatan.* I adopt the spelling of H in order to avoid the presumably false etymology suggested by U's *mánhatan.* When the word
recurs at XXV (*a*). 19, spelled ambiguously *manhata*, a gloss interprets it
correctly, as I suppose, by *hodiosus hominum.* Hall–Meritt records, under
mannhata, one occurrence only as *monhatæ*, in Belfour IV, p. 38/32. The
Belfour sermon, which survives only in MS. B, is by Ælfric, on a text
normally assigned to the twenty-third Sunday after Pentecost.

67–69. *þæt man lissige oðrum on hefegum geswincum þe men habbað on
gewunan on mislicum geldum and on manegum gesetnyssum*: 'that one show
kindness to others in heavy afflictions to which men are accustomed in
various taxes and many ordinances.' Several words require comment. The
word *lissige*, a weak verb of the second class based on *liss* (*liþs*), 'kindness,
mercy, favour', though not recorded in BT or Hall–Meritt, presents no
difficulty of form or meaning. The word *geswincum* is used for both
actual labour and general hardship or affliction. The latter sense appears
preferable here in view of what follows, though doubtless a poor man
might often be required to pay in labour what he could not pay in goods
or money. The word *geldum* (H *gildum*) refers to taxes or enforced payments of any kind. In the course of Ethelred's reign, from 991 on, taxes
levied for payments to the Danes became increasingly heavy, but Ælfric's
generalization probably includes taxes of other sorts by which the ordinary
man was oppressed. Wulfstan's complaint in the *Sermo ad Anglos*, 'us
ungylda swyþe gedrehtan' (Bethurum, p. 269/58; Whitelock, line 59),
perhaps reflects a still more critical stage of the same evil. Miss Whitelock
in her notes on lines 59 and 31, and Miss Bethurum, p. 361, refer to the
Danegeld as the principal grievance.

91–102. There is a paragraph of Biblical quotations for the instruction of judges in *Letania Maiore*, *CH* II. xxi, pp. 320, 322. It includes the passage from *James* ii. 13, but altogether lacks the economy and comprehensive sweep of the present passage.

96. *þæt unriht drifan*. Since the reference is to a judge, I take *drifan* in the sense 'promote' or 'further' rather than 'practise' or 'carry on', which are the nearest approximations in BTS and Hall–Meritt. Indeed one of the examples in BTS might be interpreted as 'further'. It occurs at Assmann II. 8, 9, where Ælfric is qualifying his adverse judgement against a priest: 'me is lað to tælenne agenne Godes freond, gyf he Godes riht drifð.'

107 sq. *God geeacnað his þing, and him eft be hundfealdum his ælmessan forgylt*. These statements, which do not correspond to anything in the sources Ælfric is using for most of his exegesis, are Biblical in origin and repeat what Ælfric had said when he dealt with almsgiving in his homily for the first Sunday in Lent, *CH* II. vii:

> Dæl of ðam ðe ðe God forgeaf, and þin god beoð gemenigfylde (Thorpe 102/21). . . . Swa hwæt swa we be anfealdan Godes þearfum for his lufan syllað, he hit us forgylt be hundfealdum on ðam toweardan life (106/1–3).

The first of these statements might have been suggested by *II Cor.* ix. 10; Thorpe's punctuation mistakenly makes it part of a quotation from *Prov.* xxi. 13. The second is probably an extension of *Matth.* xix. 29. A good deal of Ælfric's doctrine on alms in the earlier homily corresponds to what is said in the pseudo-Augustinian *Sermo* cccx, *De Eleemosynis*, *PL* xxxix. 2340–2 (which is not among those now attributed to Cæsarius). With the first statement above, cf. col. 2341, 'Da, quid dubitas? quia si dederis, ego plura dabo'.

141. The *leorningcild* of U is probably correct. The word itself, though rare, occurs also at *CH* II. 164/10, and the element *leorning-* or *leornung-* is used by Ælfric with *mann* and especially with *cniht* in the same sense. The element *læring-* of H, on the other hand, is recorded only twice in BT (once with *mann*, from the Benedictine Rule, and once with *mæden*, from *Apollonius*) and appears to be non-Ælfrician. The play on *leorningcild* and *leornode* is of a sort not uncommon in Ælfric.

164. *Hy ahlyttriað þone stut of heora liðe mid seohhann*. Ælfric's expansion of the idea in the Latin (which differs from that in the Authorized Version) has a striking particularity. No doubt *stut*, *lið*, and *seohha* were everyday words, but they are rare in literature. Indeed *stut* and *seohha* appear elsewhere in Old English only in glosses. And the unusual *ahlyttrið* is used in an unrecorded sense.

193. *on ærnemergen*. The same phrase recurs at xxi. 225, 396, 411, and xxiii. 88, 93. The compound *ærnemergen* was perhaps originally accusative of *ær morgen* (*mergen*) and may still have been looked upon in this light by

Ælfric himself. In his *De Temporibus Anni*, III. 25 (ed. Henel), in a list of the seven divisions of night, we read, 'Seofoða is Diluculum, þæt is se ærmergen, betwux ðam dægrede and sunnan upgange.' Henel's basic manuscript is Thorpe's for the *Catholic Homilies*, our K, and its reading is supported by one other; but the remaining three (admittedly later than K) replace *ær* with *ærne*, and this, according to the evidence in BTS, s.v. *ærne*, is the usual treatment of the word in the eleventh century, *ærne* being an indeclinable member of the compound. If Ælfric, as is possible,, looked upon *ærne* as accusative singular masculine of the adjective *ær*, then he must have thought that *on* was governing the accusative in *on ærne mergen*, and he may have so interpreted the construction in *on mergen*, *on dæg*, and *on niht*, whereas historically *mergen* and *dæg* are thought to be endingless locatives and *niht*, perhaps, a survival of a mutated dative (see Glossary under these three words). From the same historical point of view, *on ærnemergen* should be an endingless locative and *ærne* therefore indeclinable. In the *OED* under *arne-morwe* and the *MED* under *erne-morwe* the development of the compound in OE is not recognized.

197. *þa sylfan boceras.* Aside from the alliteration I am not sure why Ælfric used *sylfan* here. If we take the usual meaning of the word in this position, 'very', we may wonder why the presence of the scribes should be more remarkable than that of the Pharisees. Perhaps we may understand it in a weakened sense, approximately as 'the scribes also'.

201. *Þu leof lareow.* These words seem to be extrametric, though their alliteration is picked up in 202. Were they added as an afterthought by Ælfric or another who realized that the Latin *Magister* had not been translated? We may wonder a little at the *leof* coming from the scribes and Pharisees, but probably the expression should be regarded as perfunctory. The strong *leof* of U is supported by v. 71, 226; VI. 10, 21; and XIV. 19; but the weak form, as in H, is attested in this very homily in the vocative *leofa Drihten* at 225. Evidently Ælfric used both forms, governing his choice perhaps by considerations of rhythm and emphasis.

208. *lage*, H, *laga* U. The context, the singular *legi* of the Latin, and Ælfric's normal usage all tend to confirm the singular *lage* of H. Moreover, the *laga* of U is probably not Ælfric's form for the plural. See note on XX. 34.

XIV[1]

DOMINICA VI POST PENTECOSTEN

Luc. v. 1-11

EARLY in his career Ælfric had commented on some features of
Luke's story of the fishing, to which he now gives full attention.
The homily for Wednesday in Easter Week, *CH* II. xvii, deals
primarily with *John* xxi. 1-14, which tells of the other fishing after
the resurrection. Ælfric's main authority, as Förster pointed out
(*Anglia* XVI. 6), was Homily xxiv of Gregory the Great's series
in Evangelia. In the midst of the exposition Ælfric follows Gregory
in drawing a comparison between John's account of the fishing
after the resurrection and Luke's of the fishing before the passion.
In a few sentences of one paragraph (Thorpe 290/5 sqq.) Ælfric
brings out certain differences between the two accounts that we
find him repeating here in very similar language: (1) After the
resurrection Christ told the disciples to throw out the net on the
right hand side, because the right stands for the good, the left for
the evil, and the fish caught on the right betokened the future
congregation of the elect in heaven. Before his passion Christ did
not specify which side, because the fish caught on that occasion
betokened the present congregation, made up of good and bad
members. (2) In the earlier fishing so many fish were caught that
the net burst, signifying that so many men are converted to the
faith in the present congregation that some, being perverse, break
out again. In the later fishing many and large fish were caught, but
the net did not burst, for no man will break out of the future congregation when he has come to God's kingdom.

In the main, however, since Gregory touches only incidentally
on the text in *Luke*, Ælfric relies on two detailed and closely
similar interpretations of it by other writers. One is the relevant
section of Bede's commentary on *Luke*; the other a homily by
Haymo—no. cxvii, assigned to the same Sunday as Ælfric's. For
the most part Haymo merely expands and simplifies Bede, only

---

[1] On the group XIII–XVI, see XIII, introduction, pp. 493–4.

occasionally introducing a different idea. Hence it is hard to tell which of the two Ælfric is following; but verbal correspondences indicate that he studied both, and chose Bede as his guide a little more often than Haymo.

Now Bede and Haymo made use of Gregory's homily on the other fishing, and Haymo incorporates most of what Gregory had said about the difference between the two, but with many variations in expression. When Ælfric comes to this passage in Haymo (at line 147 of his own exposition) he starts to paraphrase it, but after a sentence or two reverts to Gregory, or to his own earlier rendering of Gregory—for although I have quoted Gregory's Latin as a source I cannot be sure that Ælfric turned to it afresh.

One of Gregory's own authorities was evidently Augustine in *Sermo* CCXLVIII, which deals, like Gregory's homily, with *John* xxi. 1–14, and anticipates a good many of Gregory's points about the two fishings. In two short passages of Ælfric's homily (85–90 and 127b–131) certain details seem to have been suggested by Augustine rather than any of the other commentators. Hence I believe that Ælfric had consulted him also, though evidently the others better served his purpose most of the time.

One other source, decidedly tangential, has turned up. At line 171 Ælfric mentions, as Augustine and Gregory had done, that the left hand signifies the wicked. But at once he reassures his congregation with the reminder that, according to Scripture and learned expositors, the righteous man has no left hand, but both his hands serve him for right. The Biblical example at the basis of this doctrine is evidently the ambidextrous Aod of *Judges* iii. 15; and the most likely expositor, so far as I can discover, is Rabanus Maurus in his commentary on the passage. Ælfric had told the story of Aod in his homily on *Judges*, and he may have consulted Rabanus at the same time.

Two wholly original passages deserve special notice. In certain features of the traditional exposition Ælfric found sharp reminders of current evils. His measured reproof of English impiety in general and of English traitors in particular constitutes what is probably his severest and most sweeping indictment of his countrymen. The first passage, 98–107, comes as a sudden revulsion of feeling after the account of the triumphant establishment of the Christian faith among the nations. Ælfric finds the English congregation oblivious of its great inheritance, slack, insubordinate, frivolously newfangled, and for a sentence or two he issues such warnings as we expect from a Gildas or a Wulfstan. The second passage, 132–9, applies to a smaller part of the population but is more violent in expression. It denounces the Englishmen who submit to the Danes, putting themselves in the devil's power and betraying their own countrymen to death. What seems worst of all is that in bowing to the heathen they have been false to their own Lord. The passage was omitted from MS. H, doubtless because it had become so conspicuously out of date, but, as I have pointed out in the notes, it cannot properly be separated from the passage that follows on those who renounced the faith to save their lives in the time of the martyrs.

I am not sure how much we have a right to deduce from these striking passages about the date of the homily. In his *Sermo ad Anglos* Wulfstan complains of widespread betrayals of lords, 'and eac her syn on earde on mistlice wisan hlafordswican manege', but when he gives specific examples by way of climax, one is the murder of Edward the Martyr in 978, the other the expulsion of King Ethelred in 1013.[1] Ælfric's accusation may in a similar way have embraced instances of defection to the Danes over a considerable period of years. The Chronicle first mentions disloyal conduct on the part of the Ealdorman Ælfric in 992, and Professor Whitelock has called attention to an Essex conspiracy, as early as 994, to accept Swein as king.[2] The English reverses of the following years may have been accompanied by many more instances of betrayal than the highly selective account in the Chronicle mentions. Still it may be urged that, as Wulfstan did not speak his mind fully until the situation had become extreme, so Ælfric would hardly have made even this brief but sweeping charge until desertion had begun to seem alarmingly frequent. Unfortunately we do not know how many years Ælfric lived after 1005 when he became abbot of Eynsham. It would seem, however, that at least five or six years should be allowed for the completion of the letters and sermons that are to be assigned to the period of his abbacy. If we take 1005 and 1010 as reasonable limits for the composition of the homily, we may be inclined to favour the middle or end of this period. At the close of 1006, when the Danes ravaged the country near Eynsham, there may have been local instances of disloyalty. In 1009, after

---

[1] Ed. Whitelock, lines 73 sqq.; Bethurum, *Homilies of Wulfstan*, p. 257/65 sqq.
[2] See her note on *hlafordswican*, 73.

an intermission of two years, the Danish attack was renewed with a formidable army and Wulfnoth of Sussex led a large part of the fleet astray. And in the Chronicle for 1010 we read: 'Æt nextan næs nan heafodman þæt fyrde gaderian wolde, ac ælc fleah swa he mæst mihte; ne furðon nan scir nolde oþre gelæstan æt nextan.'[1] By that time the collapse of Ethelred's government was imminent and English demoralization was pretty surely widespread enough to account for both passages.

[1] The passage is in MSS. C, D, and E; the spellings are from C, as in *The Anglo-Saxon Chronicle*, ed. B. Thorpe (Rolls Series, London, 1861), I. 264, col. 1. Plummer prints from E (*Two of the Saxon Chronicles Parallel*, Oxford, I, 1892, pp. 140–1).

DOMINICA VI POST PENTECOSTEN

Cum turbe inruerent ad Iesum, et *reliqua*

On ðære tide íu hit getimode swa,
þa ða se Hælend wæs her on life mid mannum,
þæt he stod mid ðam folce swa wið ænne fixnoð,

Text based on U (Trinity B. 15. 34), pp. 350–63. Collated with H (Cotton Vitellius C. v), ff. 134ᵛ–6ᵛ. In the list of variants round brackets enclose portions of the text as witnessed by U (including the modern punctuation) for which there is approximately the right space but no longer any reading in the damaged H.

For Homilies XIII–XVI, where the manuscripts are the same, the following variants are excluded: H regularly has *byð*, *gyf*, *hi*, *mann*, *menn*, *þiss*, *þuss* where U has *bið*, *gif*, *hy*, *man*, *men*, *þis*, *þus*. But H usually has *man* for the indefinite pronoun, 'one'. For this homily only, H's regular *scyp* for *scip* is excluded after its first appearance in line 11. U's *hy* and *hym* were often written *hi* and *him* at first.

In H, the pointing is normally by half-lines; in U, intermittently so.

Sup.: VI POST PENTECOSTEN] V POST OCT*AVAS* PENTECOST*EN* H. inruerent] irruerent *H* 2 mannum] *What is not now legible in H is confirmed to this point by Wanley, Catalogus, p. 210. No variants in first two lines.* 3–4 (ænne fixnoð, þæt wæ)s *H*.

SOURCES. 1–40 [*Luc. v, 1*] Factum est autem, cum turbæ irruerent in eum, ut audirent verbum Dei, et ipse stabat secus stagnum Genesareth.

[*2*] Et vidit duas naves stantes secus stagnum: piscatores autem descenderant, et lavabant retia.

[*3*] Ascendens autem in unam navim, quæ erat Simonis, rogavit eum a terra reducere pusillum. Et sedens docebat de navicula turbas.

[*4*] Ut cessavit autem loqui, dixit ad Simonem: Duc in altum, et laxate retia vestra in capturam.

[*5*] Et respondens Simon, dixit illi: Præceptor, per totam noctem laborantes, nihil cepimus: in verbo autem tuo laxabo rete.

[*6*] Et cum hoc fecissent, concluserunt piscium multitudinem copiosam, rumpebatur autem rete eorum.

[*7*] Et annuerunt sociis, qui erant in alia navi ut venirent, et adiuvarent eos. Et venerunt, et impleverunt ambas naviculas, ita ut pene mergerentur.

[*8*] Quod cum videret Simon Petrus, procidit ad genua Iesu, dicens: Exi a me, quia homo peccator sum, Domine.

[*9*] Stupor enim circumdederat eum, et omnes, qui cum illo erant, in captura piscium, quam ceperant:

[*10*] Similiter autem Iacobum, et Ioannem, filios Zebedæi, qui erant socii Simonis. Et ait ad Simonem Iesus: Noli timere: ex hoc iam homines eris capiens.

[*11*] Et subductis ad terram navibus, relictis omnibus secuti sunt eum.

þæt wæs an brad mere Genesareð gehaten,
and he geseah twa scipu standan wið ðone mere,   5
and þæt folc efste eall swiðe wið his weard,
and woldon æt him gehyran his halgan lare,
and ða fisceras mid ðam þe ficsodon on ðam mere
eodon of ðam wætere and swyledon heora net.
Petrus wæs þa fiscere, þe is apostol nú;   10
þa stód his scip þærwið, on ðam astah se Hælend,
and het hine ascufan þæt scip hwon fram lande,
and sæt þa on ðam scipe gehende þam lande,
and he lærde þæt folc þe on ðam lande stód,
swa swa his gewuna wæs þæt he wissode mancynne.   15
þa æfter þære lare, he het alætan út
þone *halgan Petrum his scip on ðære dypan,   *p. 352
and het hy aweorpan heora net on fixnoðe.
Him andwyrde Petrus, Eala leof lareow,
ealle niht we swuncon, on idel wacigende,   20
and we naht ne gefengon; ac ic for ðinum worde
þæt net nu awurpe; and hy hit wurpon þá út.
þa sloh þæt net swa full sona þæra fisca
þæt hit hwæthwega bærst; ac hy bicnodon sona
heora geferan on ðam oðrum scipe,   25
þæt hy hraðe comon hym to fultumigenne.
Hy comon þa sona, and þa scipu buta
mid fixum afyldon, þæt hy fornean d'u'fan.
þa ða Petrus geseah swylcne fixnoð mid him,
þa feoll he sona to ðæs Hælendes cneowum,   30
and cwæð mid ege eadmodlice him to,
Gewit fram me, Drihten; ic eom synful man.
He wæs swiðe afyrht, and his geferan ealle,

---

4 genesareth H.   5 ge(seah twa scipu sta)ndan H.   6–7 (wið his
weard, and woldon æt) H.   8 and] And H.   (fisceras mid ðam þe ficsodon) H.   9 (and swyledon heora net) H.   10 Petrus . . . fiscere]
probably (Petrus wæs fiscere) þa H.   11 þa] *f. 135, H.*   scyp (*and regularly
hereafter*) H.   12 hin(e) a(scufan) H.   13 (lande) H.   15 (þæt) H.
wissode] wisode (*cf.* 80) H.   mann- H.   17 þo(ne) H.   18 awyrpan
H.   heo(ra) H.   nett H.   20 nih(t) H.   waciende H.   23 fixa H.
24 hwæthwega] æt hwega H; U has for neh (*partly erased*) over line.   bærst]
'to'bærst U (*late correction*); bærst H.   26 hym] heom H.   fultumienne
H.   27 butu H.   28 fornean] *altered to* forneahð U;
dufon H.   29 swylcne fixnoð] *altered to* swylche fixunge U; swilcne fixnoð H.
him] heom H.   32 synfull H.   33 afirht H.

and Iacob, and Iohannes, Zebedees suna,
wæron eac afyrhte for ðam fiscnoðe swiðe.   35
þa cwæð se Hælend þus to þam *halgan Petre: *p. 353
Ne ondræd þu ðe nan ðing for ðissere dæde.
þu fehst men heonan forð, swa swa þu fixas fenge.
Hy tugon þa to lande heora scipa gehladene,
and hy ealle þing forleton, and folgodon swa Criste.   40

Se fiscnoð þe we embe sprecað wæs swiðe fæger and myrige
on Iudea lande, Galileiscre scire,
and swiðe mycel mere, manegra mila lang,
þreo mile on bræde, mid ferscum wætere.

þæt wæter flewð eall of ðære miclan éá   45
þe men hatað Iordanén into ðam mere,
þær is myrige fiscnoð, and men hit heton sǽ,
for ðære micelnysse þæs micclan flodes.

Wið ðone mere stod se Hælend mid ðam folce þa,
and þæt folc genealæhte, his lare to gehyrenne,   50
for ðan þe ealle þeoda nu yrnað him to,
þurh soðne geleafan, his lare secende.

þa twa scipu getacniað, þe he geseah þær standan,
*þa men þe gelyfdon on Iudea lande   *p. 354
on þone halgan Hælend, and þæt hæðene folc   55
þe of eallum [landum] gelyfdon on hine.

---

34 Iohanne(s) *H.*   35 afirhte *H.*   ðam fiscnoðe] *altered to* þere fiscunge
U; þam fixnoðe *H.*   38 heonon *H.*   39 scipu *H.*   40 folgodan *H.*
41 fixnoð *H.*   w(æs) *H.*   42 scyre *H.*   43 and *om. H.*   micel *H.*
44 mile] mila *H.*   45 micclan *H.*   46 iordanē (iordanem?) inn to *H.*
47 þær] Ðær *H.*   fixnoð *H.*   48 þæ(re) *H.*   49 mi(d) *H.*   50 genea-
læhte] þa genealeahte *H.*   gehirenne *H.*   51 yrnað] yrnað a *H.*   52 hi(s)
H.   53 sta(ndan) *H.*   55 hæl(end, and þæt) *H.*   56 landu*m*] *sic H*;
þeodum *U.*

41–48 [*Bede, In Lucam*] Stagnum Gennesareth idem dicunt esse, quod mare
Galileæ, vel mare Tiberiadis: sed mare Galileæ ab adiacente provincia dictum.
. . . Neque enim in stagni morem sternitur aqua, sed frequentibus auris spiranti-
bus agitatur, haustu dulcis, et ad potandum habilis. Sed Hebrææ linguæ consuetudine omnis aquarum congregatio, sive dulcis, sive salsa, mare nuncupatur.
Qui lacus interfluente Iordane centum quadraginta stadiis in longitudinem, et
quadraginta extenditur in latitudinem.

51–52 [*Bede*] Turbarum conventus ad eum, gentium in fide concurrentium
typus est, de quibus Esaias: *Et fluent*, inquit, *ad eum omnes gentes* (*Is. ii. 2*).

53–56 [*Haymo, Hom. CXVII*] Duæ naves, duos ordines significant credituros,
unum ex Iudæis, alterum ex gentibus. [*Bede*] Duæ naves secus stagnum positæ,
circumcisionem et præputium figurant.

Of ægðrum folce God wát his gecorenan,
and of ægðrum mennisce he manega gebringð
of ðam deopum yðum þissere worlde
to staþolfæstnysse þæs toweardan lifes;   60
for ðan þe þæt flod getacnað þe hy on fixodon
þas andweardan woruld þe we on wuniað,
and se strand getacnað þa staðolfæstnysse
þæs toweardan lifes, to ðam us gelæt Crist,
gif we his lare folgiað on ures lifes þeawum.   65
þa fisceras þe eodon up of ðam ficsnoðe
and heora net swyledon, þæt syndon þa lareowas
þe us læran sceolon, þæt we gelyfon on God,
and us fram nytennysse mid heora nette ateon
to ðam halgan Hælende, þe us habban wyle   70
to þære stoðolfæstnysse þære stæþþian worulde.
þa fisceras swyledon heora *net on ðam wætere,   *p. 355
for ðan þe ða lareowas hwilon us læran sceolon,
and on sumne sæl heora sylfes gyman.
  'Petrus wæs ða fiscere, þe is apostol nu;   75
þa stod his scip þærwið. On ðam astah se Hælend,
and het hine ascufan þæt scip hwón fram lande,

---

57 Of] *cap. H, not U.*   ægð(rum folce) *H.*   58 (manega gebringð) *H.*
59 worlde] worulde *H.*   60 staþ(olfæstnysse þæs) *H.*   61–62 geta(cnað þe
hy on fixodon þas) *H.*   62 (wuni)að *H.*   63 (and se strand getacnað þa
sta)þolfæstnysse *H.*   64 towea(rdan) *last word visible f. 135, H.*   65 (þe)a-
wum *first word visible f. 135ᵛ, H.*   66 upp (of ðam) fixnoðe *H.*   67 nett
swiledon *H.*   þæt] *om. H.*   68 (læra)n *H.*   69 (nette) *H.*   70 wile *H.*
71 sta(þol)fæstnysse *H.*   stæððigan *H.*   72 swiledon *H.*   (net)t *H.*
73 'oþer' hwilon *U (ME corrector, 73–78).*   74 (and o)n *H.*   heora
sylfes] *sic both MSS originally; U altered to* heom sylfen.   75 (n)u *H.*
76 þærwið] *altered to* þærbi *U.*   77 ascufan] asceo(f)an *H.*   hwon fram
lande] *altered to* a lutel fram þan lande *U.*

---

57 [*Haymo*] Ex utroque populo . . . novit . . . Dominus qui sunt eius. Nam
videre, eligere est. [*A mere variation of Bede.*]

58–65 [*Bede*] Eorumque cor a fluctibus sæculi huius, ad futuræ vitæ tranquilli-
tatem quasi ad soliditatem litoris . . . provehit. [*Earlier*] Quia ergo stagnum sive
mare præsens sæculum designat, Dominus secus mare stat postquam . . .
stabilitatem perpetuæ quietis adiit.

66–71 [*Bede*] Piscatores sunt ecclesiæ doctores, qui nos rete fidei comprehensos, et de profundo ad lumen elatos, quasi pisces litori, sic terræ viventium
advehunt.

72–74 [*Bede*] Hæc retia modo laxantur in capturam, modo lota plicantur, quia
non omne tempus est habile doctrinæ, sed nunc exerenda lingua doctori, nunc
suimet cura gerenda.

and sæt ða on ðam scipe gehende þam lande,
and he lærde þæt folc þe on ðam lande stód,
swa swa his gewuna wæs þæt he wissode mancynne.' 80
Petrus scip getacnode, þe ðær stód gehende,
þæt Iudeisce folc þe gewændon to Criste
and on hine gelyfdon, þeah þe hy sume noldon,
on ðam wæs þæt anginn ealre gelaðunge.
þæt oðer scip getacnode eall þæt hæðene folc 85
of eallum mancynne þe mid geleafan oncnawað
þone leofan Hælend, and þæt is seo gelaðung
[þe is gecweden Ecclesia.]
þæt Iudeisce folc wæs gehaten Sinagoga,
þæt is gegaderung on Engliscere spræce. 90
Of Petrus scipe he lærde þæt folc on ðam *lande, *p. 356
and us becom seo lar of Iudea lande,
þurh þa halgan apostolas, þe ða hæðenan lærdon,
and men to geleafan of ælcum lande gebigdon,
and cyrican arærdon to Godes gesetnyssum 95
on his halgum þeowdome, swa swa hit man healt gyt
on ðam godum folcum, þe Godes willan cepað;
ac we healdað wace, her on Engla þeode,
Godes gesetnyssa, þe he gesette to steore,
and þam eallum to lare þe hine lufiað. 100

---

78 gehende] *altered to* neh *U.* 79 (and) *H.* 80 wis(s)ode (*the second*
s *clearly attested by spacing in spite of* 15) *H.* mann- *H.* 81 Petres *H.*
82 iudei(s)ce *H.* gewendon *H.* 86 mann- *H.* 87 þæne *H.*
88 þe is gecweden ecclesia *H*; *om. U*; *see note.* 89 synagoga *H.*
90 ys *H.* 91 petres *H.* 94 of] on *H.* 95 cyrcan *H.* 96 halgan
H. gyt] *U wrongly puts a full stop after this word and capitalizes the next. H
has only the half-line point.* 100 (l)are *H.*

81–84 [*Bede*] Navis Simonis est ecclesia primitiva, de qua Paulus ait: *Qui
enim operatus est Petro in apostolatum circumcisionis, operatus est et mihi inter
gentes* (*Gal. ii. 8*).

85–90 [*Already intimated by Bede and Haymo; cf. supra,* 53–56; *but the complication introduced by the distinction between Ecclesia and Synagoga apparently
stems from Augustine, Sermo CCXLVIII*] Duo autem illa navigia, duos
populos significabant, Iudæorum et Gentium, Synagogæ et Ecclesiæ, circumcisionis et præputii.

91–97 [*Perhaps suggested by Bede*] De qua [nave Simonis] docebat turbas, quia
de auctoritate ecclesiæ docet usque hodie gentes. [*But mainly an independent de-
duction from 82, anticipating* 112–14.]

98–107 [*Nothing in Bede or Haymo at this point to suggest the contemporary
application; but cf. infra* 127 *sqq.,* 152–7.]

We wyrcað us sylfe eall-níwe gesetnyssa
of ðam þe God sylf tæhte, ongean his gesetnyssum,
and ealra þæra witena þe wæron beforan us,
ongean hy ealle we gað mid ure anwilnysse;
ac se weg sceal beon swiðe earfoðe us,   105
þæt we hy fortredon mid teonfullum þeawum,
and God sylfne forseon, swa swa we to swiðe doð.

    'þ'a' æfter þære lare, he hét alætan út
þone halgan Petrum his scip *on ðære dypan,   *p. 357
and hét hy awurpan heora net on fiscnoðe.'   110
Wið þæt land he lærde, [and] hy leton uttor syððan,
for ðan þe he sylf lærde on Iudea lande,
and his lar becom syððan to gehwylcum landum,
swa swa hit fullcuð is, on Cristendome wide.

    'Him andwyrde Petrus, eala leof lareow,   115
ealle niht we swuncon, on idel wacigende,
and we naht ne gefengon; ac ic for ðinum worde
þæt net nu awurpe; and hy hit awurpon þa út.'
Se sealmwyrhta cwæð, þus singende be Gode:
*Nisi Dominus edificauerit domum, in uanum labórant qui ædi-
ficant eam:*   120

---

101 wyrceað *H.*   102 gesetnyssum] gesetnyssa *H.*   103 wæ(r)on *H.*
104 Ongean *H.*   hy] heom *over line U.*   105 (sc)eal *H.*   us] 'to' us *U.*
106 þea(wum) *H.*   107 forseon] forse'g'on *U*; na forseon *H.*   108 (lare,
he) *H.*   109 halgum (!) *H.*   on ðære dypan] on þone deope mere *over
line U.*   110 (and het hy aw)yrpan *H.*   nett *H.*   fixnoðe *H.*   111 and
H; þæt *U.*   *over* hy] id est apostoli *U.*   111–12 (uttor syððan, for)
H.   112 sylf] 'him' sylf *U.*   113 be(com syððan to gehw)ilcum *H.*
114–15 cristen(dome wide. Him andw)yrde *H.*   116–17 swun(con, on idel
wacigende, and we naht) *H.*   118 (net nu awurpe; and hy hit awurpon þa
ut) *H.*   119–20 (singende be gode: Nisi Dominus edificauerit domum, in)
H.   120 ædificant] *f. 136, H.*

111–14 [*Bede*] Quod primo rogavit Simonem navem a terra reducere pusillum,
significat . . . prius in proximis regionibus gentibus prædicandum, ut quod dicit
item Petro, *Duc in altum, et laxate retia vestra in capturam*, ad remotiores gentes
quibus postea prædicatum est, pertineat. [*Haymo substantially the same; Ælfric
substitutes the Saviour for the apostles at the beginning.*]
119–25 [*Bede*] *Nisi Dominus ædificaverit domum, in vanum laborant qui
ædificant eam* (*Psal. cxxvi. 1, Roman version*). Nisi Dominus cor illustraverit
auditorum, doctor in nocte laborat. [*Haymo, restating Bede*] Nisi Dominus
illuminet mentem auditoris interius, in vacuum laborat sermo doctoris exterius,
Scriptura dicente (*Psal. cxxvi. 1, as above, except that Migne gives only the first
clause and does not reveal whether Haymo had laborant or the Gallican labora-
verunt*).

Buton Drihten [s]ylf þæt hus getimbrige,
on idel hy swincað, þa ðe hit wyrcað.
Butan God sylf onlihte þara manna heortan
þe his lare gehyrað mid his halgan gife,
on idel swincð se lareow mid his lare wiðútan.   125
'þa sloh þæt net swa ful sona *þæra fixa   *p. 358
þæt hit hwæthwega bærst.' And nu bið eac swa.
Swa fela manna gebugað mid ðam gecorenum
to Cristes geleafan on his Gelaðunge,
þæt hy sume yfele eft ut abrecað,   130
and hy on gedwyldum adreogað heora líf,
swa swa þa Engliscan men doð þe to ðam Deniscum gebugað,
and mearciað hy deofle to his mannrædene,
and his weorc wyrcað, hym sylfum to forwyrde,
and heora agene leode be(læwað) to deaðe.   135
Hwæt, bið æfre wyrse ænig þing on worlde
þonne swylc dæd is ongean his agene Drihten,
and hine sylfne besence on ðam ecum suslum,
ælfremed fram Gode, and fram eallum his halgum?
Swa dydon eac hwilon sume þa Cristenan   140
on anginne Cristendomes: þa ða man acwealde

---

121 sylf] *sic H*; him sylf *U.*   121–2 ge(timbrige, on idel hy swincað) *H.*
123 Buton *H.*   123–4 þæra mann(a heortan þe) *H.*   124 gife] grace *over
line U.*   125 (l)ar(eow mid) *H.*   126 nett *H.*   full *H.*   þæra fixa]'of'
þæra fixaˋsˊ (!) *U.*   127 (hit hwæt)hwega *H.*   swa.] *punct. follows H*; *no
punct. U.*   128 (ðam) gecorenan *H.*   130 y(fele) *H.*   131 gedwildum *H.*
132–9 *om. H.*   132 doð] *crossed out,* dudend *over line U.*   gebugað]
altered to gebugan *U.*   133 mearciað hy deofle to his] *altered to* mear-
ˋchedand heom to deoflesˊ *U.*   134 wyrcað] *altered to* ˋwerðhtenˊ *U.*
forwyrde] *altered to* ˋpineˊ *U.*   135 be(læwað)] *altered after erasure to*
beswiken *U.*   137 agene] *sic U, for* agenne.   140 Swa] *Here H resumes.*
dydo(n eac) *H.*   141 ac(weal)de *H.*

127b–31 [*Bede, quoting Gregory, Hom. XXIV in Evang.*] Præ multitudine
piscium rete rumpebatur, quia nunc ad confessionem fidei etiam cum electis
reprobi tanti intrant, qui ipsam quoque Ecclesiam hæresibus scindant. [*Augustine, Sermo CCXLVIII*] Ibi premebantur navigia præ multitudine. Sic fit modo:
multi christiani qui male vivunt, Ecclesiam premunt. Parum est quia premunt:
et retia disrumpunt. Nam si non essent retia scissa, schismata non essent
commissa.
140–6 [*Haymo, adapting to this passage Bede's illustrations*] Ipsi Ecclesiam
variis hæresibus scindere conati sunt, qui in ea per fidem capti tenebantur;
qualis fuit Iudas proditor, et Simon Magus; et quales erant illi, de quibus Ioannes
apostolus ait: *Exierunt ex nobis, sed non erant ex nobis (I Ioan. ii. 19). [See note
on 132–9.]*

þa halgan martiras huxlice mid wítum,
for Cristes geleafan, þa cyddon wel fela
heora ungetrywðæ, and wiðsocon Criste,
*and hine forleton, þæt hy libban moston,   *p. 359
ac heora líf wæs syððan wyrse þonne deað.   146
  Tuwa het se Hælend her on ðissum life
mid nette fixian, and hy fengon sona
heora net full fixa, for micelre getacnunge:
æne ær his þrowunge, be ðam þe we nu secgað,   150
and oðre siðe eft, æfter his æriste.
Nu bærst heora net on ðisum fixnoðe,
for ðære getacnunge þe we ær sædon,
and þes fixnoð getacnað þa halgan Gelaðunge,
þæt is eall Cristen folc þe on God nu gelyfað,   155
on ðam syndon ægðer ge yfele ge góde,
and hy sume misfarað, swa swa we sædon ær.
Æt ðam oðrum cyrre, æfter his þrowunge,
he het awurpan þæt net on ða swiðran healfe,
and hy manega fixas [and] swiðe micele gefengon,   160
and heora net ne bærst for ðære getacnunge,
for ðan þe se fixnoð æfter his æriste
getacnode soðlice þa gesæligan Cristenan,

142 martyras H.   143 þ(a) H.   kyddon H.   144 ungetrywðe H.
145 þæt] wiþ þæt H.   lybban H.   146 wirse H.   147 Tuw(a) H.   þisum H.
149 heo(ra) nett H.   152 net(t) H.   155 gely(fað) H.   157 misfaran H.   158 his om. H.   159 awyrpan H.   nett H.   160 and]
sic H; om. U.   161 nett H.   162 fix(noð) H.

147–71 [*Haymo, revising Gregory, Hom. XXIV in Evang.*] Bis in sancto
Evangelio legimus, quod ad iussionem Domini laxata retia copiosam multitudinem piscium ceperunt, nunc ante passionem, et secundo post resurrectionem
(*Ioan. xxi. 1–14*). [*Gregory, from whom Haymo gradually diverges*] Sed priusquam
Redemptor noster pateretur et resurgeret, mitti quidem rete ad piscandum iubet,
sed utrum in dexteram, an in sinistram mitti debuisset, non iubet; post resurrectionem vero discipulis apparens, mitti rete in dexteram iubet. In illa piscatione
tanti capti sunt, ut retia rumperentur; in ista autem et multi capti sunt, et retia
rupta non sunt. Quis vero nesciat bonos dextera, et malos sinistra figurari? Illa
ergo piscatio, in qua specialiter in quam partem mitti rete debeat non iubetur,
præsentem Ecclesiam designat, quæ bonos simul ac malos colligit. . . . Hæc
autem piscatio post Domini resurrectionem facta, in solam dexteram missa est,
quia ad videndum claritatis eius gloriam sola electorum Ecclesia pertingit, quæ
de sinistro opere nihil habebit. In illa piscatione præ multitudine piscium rete
rumpitur [*etc., ut supra, 127b–131*]. In ista vero piscatione et multi pisces et
magni capiuntur, et rete non rumpitur, quia sancta electorum Ecclesia, in con-
tinua auctoris sui pace requiescens, nullis iam dissensionibus dilaniatur.

*þe to Godes rice þurh Godes sylfes fultum   *p. 360
eadige becumað to ðam ecan life,   165
þanan heora nan ne mæg syððan út aberstan;
and seo swiðre hand getacnode þa gecorenan halgan,
and for ðam hy awurpon þæt net on ða swiðran hand.
þis godspell ne sægð ná þe we nu secgað eow
on hwæðre healfe he hete hy awurpan þæt net;   170
ac seo wynstre hand swaþeah getacnað þa yfelan.
Ne wen þu na forðig þæt þin wynstre yfel beo,
for ðan þe Godes lár and lareowas us secgað
þæt se rihtwisa man næfð nænne wynstran,
ac buta his handa him beoð for swiðran.   175
    þis godspell us sægð her þæt 'hy sona gebicnodon
heora geferan on ðam oðran scipe,
þæt hy hraðe comon hym to fultumigenne.'
þæt oðer scíp getacnað, swa swa we ær sædon,
þæt hæðene folc on fyrlenum landum   180
þe on Crist gelyfað on Cristendome wide,
for ðan *þe se Hælend ne afunde nateshwón   *p. 361
on Iudea lande swa fela gelyfedra manna
'swa swa' he habban wolde to ðam heofonlican life.
þa geceas he us of eallum leodscipum,   185

165 lif(e) *H.*   166 þanon *H.*   168 nett *H.*   169 secgð *H.*
170 hwæðer(e) *H.*   nett *H.*   171 wynstre] luft *over line U*; winstre *H.*
172 forþi *H.*   wynstre] lufð hand *over line U*; winstre *H.*   173 for
(ðan) *H.*   174 næ(nne wyn)stran *H*; nane luft hand *over line U.*   175 *over*
swiðran] *id est* riðht hand *U.*   176 (us sægð) *H.*   177 oðre *H.*
177–8 scy(pe, þæt hy hra)þe *H.*   178 hym] heom *H.*   179 g(etacnað,
swa swa) *H.*   180 firlenum *H.*   181 (þe on crist gelyfað) *H.*
182 hæ(lend ne afunde nateshwon) *H.*   nateshwon] nawiðt *over line U.*
183–4 gelyfe(dra manna swa swa he habban wolde) *H.*   184 heo(fonlic)an *H.*
life] *last word visible f. 136, H.*   185 þa] *no cap. U.*

172–5 [*Iudic. iii. 15*] Aod . . . qui utraque manu pro dextera utebatur. [*Rabanus, Com. in Lib. Iudic.*] Ecce qualis est iste qui suscitatur ad salvandum Israel!
Nihil habet in se sinistrum, sed utramque manum dextram habet; hoc est enim
quod dicitur ambidexter. . . . Quod . . . præsumere puto, quod secundum spiritalem intelligentiam, et sancti omnes ambidextri dicantur, et e contrario diabolus
et principes eius, si dici potest, ambisinistri dicantur.
    179–87 [*Bede*] Alia navis (ut prædiximus) est ecclesia de gentibus, quæ et ipsa
non sufficiente una navicula piscibus impletur electis, quia *novit Dominus qui
sunt eius* (*II Tim. ii. 19*), et apud ipsum certus est suorum numerus electorum;
dumque tot in Iudæa credituros non invenit, quot ad fidem vitamque præ-
destinatos novit æternam, quasi aliæ navis receptacula piscibus quærens suis,
corda quoque gentium fidei gratia replet.

and he swa gefylð þæt fulle getel
þe he habban wyle to his ecan wuldre.
'Hy comon þa sona, and þa scipu butu
mid fixum afyldon, þæt hy fornean dufon.'
þa scipu he gefylð forð oð Domes-dæg,   190
and þeah þe hy frecednysse and fela costnunga þolion
on þissere worulde, hy ne wurðað swaþeah
nateshwon besencte, for ðan þe Crist sylf mæg
his halgan gehealdan, and heora gehelpan æfre.
'þa þa Petrus geseah swylcne fixnoð mid hym,   195
þa feol he sona to þæs Hælendes cneowum,
and cwæð mid ege eadmodlice him to,
Gewit fram me, Drihten; ic eom synfull man.'
Nolde se Hælend for his bene swaþeah
hym fram gewitan, ac wunode mid hym,   200
oððæt hy to lande gelændon mid ealle,
*for ðan þe ða lareowas þe Godes folc lærað,   *p. 362
bisceopas and mæssepreostas, ne moton forlætan
þa halgan Godes wícan þe God hym betæhte
for nanre costnunge, for ðan þe Crist hy ahret,   205
gif hy for his lufan ne forlætað his heorde.
'He wæs swiðe afyrht, and his geferan ealle,
and Iacob, and Iohannes, Zebedees suna,
wæron eac afyrhte for þam fixnoðe swiðe.'
Iacob and Iohannes wæron gebroðra,   210
and heora fæder wæs gehaten Zebedeus,

187 þe] *first word visible f. 136ᵛ,* H. wile H.   188 (Hy comon þa sona) *H.*
buta *H.*   189 afildon *H.*   189–90 (dufon. þa) *H.*   190 scypa *H.*
gefilð *H.*   191 frecednes(se and fela) *H*   þolian *H.*   193 (nate)shwon *H*;
nawiðt *over line U.*   mæg] *followed by point U; preceded by point H.*   194 (and
he)ora *H.*   heom *over* heora *U.*   195 swilcne *H.*   hym] heom *H.*
196 (þa) feoll *H.*   198 (Ge)wit *H.*   synnfull *H.*   199 (b)ene *H.*
200 hym fram] him swa fram *H (perhaps rightly).*   *second* hym] heom *H.*
201 gelendon *H.*   204 hym] heom *H.*   205 ahrett *H.*   206
lufon *H.*   208 suna] sunas *H.*

190–4 [*Bede*] Harum impletio navium usque in finem sæculi crescit. [*Haymo*]
Periclitantur autem naves, sed non merguntur, quia sæpe persecutionibus
hæreticorum Ecclesia concussa est, sæpe falsorum fratrum iniqua operatione
commota, sed mergi non potuit, quia Christum in fundamento habuit.

199–206 [*Bede*] Quod tamen quia non fecit Dominus (non enim recessit ab
eis, sed eos subductis navibus ad litus perduxit) significat in bonis et spiritalibus
viris non esse oportere hanc voluntatem, ut peccatis turbarum commoti, quo
quasi securius tranquilliusque vivant, munus ecclesiasticum deserant.

and heora modor wæs Cristes moddrige,
swa swa béc secgað be heora gebyrdum.
'þa cwæð se Hælend þus to ðam halgan Petre:
Ne ondræd þu ðe nan þing for ðissere dæde.   215
þu fehst men heonan forð, swa swa þu fixas fenge.'
Se Hælend gefrefrode swiðe fægere Petrum,
for ðan þe he wel wyle eallum welwillendum,
and sæde þæt he sceolde syððan men gefon;
nu dyde 'he' eac swa be his Drihtnes wordum,   220
þæt he manega *menn mid his lare gefeng,   *p. 363
and mid wundorlicum tacnum þe he geworhte on life,
swa swa he ær gefeng fixas mid his nettum;
and we gyt habbað his halgan lare mid us
on Cristenum bocum, us sylfum to beterunge.   225
  'Hy tugon þa to lande heora scipa ge'h'ladene,
and hy ealle þing forleton, and folgodon swa Criste.'
Crist geceas fisceras him sylfum to folgerum,
ungelærede men, and hy forleton ealle þing,
his lare folgiende, and him her on life,   230
and hy syððan wurdon swa swiðe gelærede
þæt eall se Cristendom on Cristes gelaðunge
wearð þurh hy ah'ræ'red mid þæs Hælendes fultume;
þam is wuldor and wurðmynt a to worolde, AMEN.

212 moder H.   modrige H.   215 Ne] cap. H, not U.   216 heonon H.
218 wile H.   219 syððan] followed by point U; preceded by point H.
220 drihtenes H.   223 (m)id H.   225 (b)ocum H.   226 ge(hla)dene H.
228 (fisce)ras H.   229 (ealle þ)ing H.   231 (swa swiðe) H.   233 (þurh
hi ar)æred H?   234 wyrð(mynt a to worold)e H.

212 [Ælfric habitually asserts this relationship. Cf. Hom. I. 5 and note.]
217–25 [Haymo] Imo in pavente Simone omnes pænitentes confortare videtur, ne de magnitudine peccatorum desperent. [Bede] Exponit enim ei Dominus,
quid hæc captura piscium significet. Quod videlicet ipse sicut nunc per retia
pisces, sic aliquando per verba sit capturus homines. Totusque facti huius ordo,
quid in ecclesia cuius ipse typum tenet quotidie geratur, ostendat.
228–34 [Ælfric's independent conclusion.]

NOTES

3, 18, 29. fixnoð. The three meanings of the word as it occurs at these
points (and elsewhere) in the homily were distinguished by Napier in his
'Contributions to Old English Lexicography', with appropriate quotations
from the text of U. See Glossary.

23, 126. *sloh*. This use of the verb *slēan*, though unrecorded, seems to be very clearly related to the meaning illustrated in BT, definition B III, '*to move rapidly, rush, dash, break, take* a certain direction'. In the present context *sloh* ought to mean 'became', with the added implication of great suddenness to reinforce the adverb *sona*. There is a close parallel to this meaning in the cognate Icelandic verb, *slá*, which has an impersonal use, as defined by Cleasby–Vigfussen, s.v., III, '*it strikes* or *breaks out to a thing*, i.e. *the thing happens*'.

44. *þreo mile* (*mila* H). Bede's forty stadia would come to five miles rather than three, and *fif* would alliterate with *ferscum*, whereas now we have only the weak alliteration of *mile* and *mid*. Or did Ælfric match the vague *manegra* of 43 with an equally vague *fea*?

56. *landum*. This reading, from H, supports the alliteration and by repeating the element of sameness in the phrase *Iudea lande* throws the emphasis on the contrast between *Iudea* and *eallum*. U's *þeodum* is probably just a careless reminiscence of *þeoda* in 51.

88. *þe is gecweden Ecclesia*. I have decided to include this clause from H, since the logic of the passage and Augustine's Latin point to its authenticity. Ælfric needs both *Ecclesia* and *Sinagoga* to balance *gelaðung* and *gegaderung* respectively, and the restrictive clause helps to distinguish *seo gelaðung*, 87, from *gelaðunge*, 84. The clause alliterates and is probably just long enough to make an admissible line, though I am tempted to add *on Leden* at the end of it.

98–107. *ac we healdað wace*, etc. Wulfstan is more specific, *Sermo ad Anglos*, ed. Whitelock, lines 37 sqq.; Bethurum's *Wulfstan*, p. 268/37 sqq.

132–9. *swa swa þa Engliscan men doð*, etc. That this passage was an original part of the sermon, not one of Ælfric's additions, is evident not only from the inadequacy of the preceding lines to support the comparison made in 140–6, but from Ælfric's deviation from Haymo in these last-mentioned lines. Haymo puts emphasis on Judas and Simon Magus; Ælfric, on the host of timorous nobodies who forsook the faith to save their lives when the martyrs were being persecuted. Thus he accents the theme of cowardice in both parts of the comparison and his final comment, 'ac heora lif wæs syððan wyrse þonne deað', may justly remind us of Wiglaf's remarks to the cowards in *Beowulf*. At lines 136 sq. the horror at betraying one's own *Drihten*, though clearly the word refers to Christ, draws strength from the implicit comparison with ordinary betrayals, of which indeed these offenders are concurrently guilty. Evidently the passage is omitted from H because someone considered it no longer appropriate. Many years elapsed before the text of U aroused sufficient uneasiness to cause a corrector to alter the tenses.

148 sq. *hy fengon . . . heora net full fixa*. I am uncertain how to explain this idiom, where it is clear that *full* is a complementary adjective, not the second member of a compound *net-full*. Perhaps *fengon* here unites the

ideas of grasping a net and catching a draught of fish. In any case we can hardly state the idea without a circumlocution: 'they caught a full draught of fish in their net.'

200. *hym fram gewitan, ac wunode mid hym.* U's revised spelling of the pronouns, with *y* from original *i*, indicates that the reviser took both to be plural, whereas H treats the first as singular (*him*) and the second as plural (*heom*). Ælfric himself seems to have spelled singular and plural alike, as *him*, and there is probably no way to tell what he intended here; but Bede has the plural in the loosely corresponding passage.

233. *ahrǽred.* That is, *arǽred*, 'raised up', 'established'. Perhaps the *h*, which is not needed for the alliteration, was nevertheless inserted by a scribe in an earlier manuscript, thus leading to *ahred*, past participle of *ahreddan*, 'to set free, rescue', the first reading of U. Since -*ǽred* survives in H, its reading was certainly not *ahred*. It may have been either *ahrǽred* or, more likely, the usual *arǽred*.

XV[1]

DOMINICA VII POST PENTECOSTEN

Matth. v. 20–24

THERE is a natural affinity of theme between the gospel-text of XIII, with its insistence on mercy, and that of XV, with its warnings against anger and vituperation. Ælfric has not only made much of mercy in both homilies but has developed other thematic correspondences. These secondary correspondences, though partially suggested, were not worked out in the Latin authors he consulted and their presence in Ælfric calls attention to a good deal of thoughtful planning on his part and suggests that he composed the two homilies at about the same time. Before entering into particulars about these correspondences, however, I must give some account of the main authorities behind the exegetical parts of XV.

In contrast to XIII, where Ælfric seems to have consulted half a dozen commentaries and exegetical homilies, I have found clear evidence in XV for his use of only two. The reason is not far to seek: these were apparently the only full treatments of the text that were available to him. One was the relevant portion of Augustine's tract, *De Sermone Domini in Monte*, which had been excerpted to represent the seventh Sunday after Pentecost in the collection of Paulus Diaconus. The other was the homily for that Sunday by Haymo, no. CXVIII. Neither Gregory nor Bede had composed a homily on this text, and Smaragdus merely repeats Augustine with a few bits from Jerome's commentary on *Matthew*. In fact Jerome's rather sparse commentary and the seldom helpful pseudo-Bede (here containing only snippets from Jerome and Augustine) are the only other treatments of the text I can find among authors available to Ælfric. Since Ælfric consulted Jerome's commentary for other homilies, including XIII, he very probably consulted it for XV also; but if so he found nothing he cared to use. Indeed at one point (164 sqq.) he accepts from Augustine an interpretation that Haymo

---

[1] On the group XIII–XVI, see XIII, introduction, pp. 493–4.

and pseudo-Bede, following Jerome, expressly reject. And at another (203 sqq.), where Augustine and Jerome are in basic agreement in contrast to Haymo, Ælfric follows the details of Augustine's explanation, probably finding Jerome's less helpful.

At the crucial spots I have just mentioned it is Augustine rather than Haymo by whom Ælfric is guided; but usually he follows Haymo rather than Augustine, or more closely than Augustine. This is understandable enough, for Haymo has developed a comprehensive and well organized homily on the five verses of the gospel-text for the day, whereas Augustine is commenting on these verses only as a part of the whole Sermon on the Mount. When Haymo is interpreting the greater part of the text he is saying the same thing as Augustine, sometimes more clearly and succinctly, the chief exceptions being the two passages I have mentioned, in one of which he follows Jerome, in the other his own fancy. But at the beginning he comments on the difference between the old law and the new, and on the shortcomings of the scribes and Pharisees, in a broadly introductory exposition of the first verse of the text, drawing certain details from later passages of the Sermon on the Mount, others from more distant parts of the gospel. This portion of Haymo, which has no parallel in Augustine, was of great service to Ælfric and underlies a good deal of the even broader introduction that Ælfric composed.

The two subordinate themes that Ælfric develops, in complementary fashion, in both XIII and XV are, first, the theme of the scribes and Pharisees, and secondly, that of legitimate judgement and reproof by persons in authority. The scribes and Pharisees are mentioned in the gospel-text of XV and their significance is carefully explained by Haymo; but the only hint of their relevance to the text of XIII among Ælfric's authorities is Jerome's quotation of the verse about the gnat and the camel. Their hypocrisy, however, is obviously relevant, and Ælfric makes them a significant part of XIII by not only calling vivid attention to the verse cited by Jerome but by adding at the conclusion of the homily the story of their discomfiture with respect to the woman taken in adultery.

The problem of legitimate judgement belongs very obviously to the treatment of the text of XIII, where Jesus seems to forbid judgement altogether. Augustine touches on the problem, Bede repeats his words, Cæsarius and Haymo develop the theme with particular vigour, though none, I think, devotes quite as much space to the matter as Ælfric himself. Moreover, Cæsarius especially links with the problem of judgement that of rebuke and correction on the part of persons in authority, and in support of his argument that Christ did not mean to forbid any such exercise of authority when it is properly directed, he quotes St. Paul's injunction, *Argue, obsecra, increpa, in omni patientia et doctrina*, from *II Tim.* iv. 2.

Now Ælfric mentions correction and guidance in XIII, 183 sqq., as the duty of the 'witan', to whom he has previously assigned the duty of judging (88 sqq.), and it may have been Cæsarius who put it into his head to do this, because Ælfric appears to be translating Cæsarius directly in line 186. But if he was struck by the quotation from St. Paul, he decided that it would be much more useful in XV, where at any rate we find it at line 170, near the beginning of a long and important passage on the duties of teachers and counsellors— *lareowas* and *witan*, apparently representing the ecclesiastical and civil authorities respectively. The excuse for the passage is furnished by Augustine, who points out that St. Paul can hardly be supposed to have acted contrary to Christ's doctrine when he called the Galatians fools; but Ælfric has developed the idea independently in such a way as to make it an extension of the principle enunciated in XIII. There the emphasis is on the operation of public justice; here, on correction and guidance by means of stern reproof.

As in XIII, Ælfric's independent expansions of his themes are full of Biblical reminiscences. So far as I know, his quotations from the *Psalms* at 181 and 223 are of his own choosing. The first adds to the discussion of the responsibility of the religious teacher; the second provides a closing reminder of the theme of mercy.

DOMINICA VII POST PENTECOSTEN

Amen, dico uobis, nisi abundauerit, et reliqua

Matheus se godspellere, þe wæs mid Criste on life,
and his lare gehyrde, on his hirede wuniende,
*he awrat be Criste þæt he gecwæð hwilon þus   *p. 364
to his halgum apostolum, and þurh hy eac to us:
Soð ic eow secge, þæt ge sylfe ne becumað   5
into heofonan rice, butan eower rihtwisnys
beo eallunga mare ætforan minum Fæder
þonne þæra bocera is and ðæra Sunderhalgena.
Ge gehyrdon þa bebodu þe God bebead gefyrn
þam ealdan Israhele under Moyses lage,   10
and hym þus sæde: Ne ofsleh þu mannan;

Text based on U (Trinity B. 15. 34), pp. 363–76. Collated with H (Cotton
Vitellius C. v), ff. 136ᵛ–9. In the list of variants round brackets enclose portions
of the text as witnessed by U (including the modern punctuation) for which
there is approximately the right space but no longer any reading in the
damaged H.
For homilies XIII–XVI, where the manuscripts are the same, the following
variants are excluded: H regularly has *byð, gyf, hi, mann, menn, þiss, þuss* where
U has *bið, gif, hy, man, men, þis, þus.* But H usually has *man* for the indefinite
pronoun, 'one'. U's *hy* and *hym* were often written *hi* and *him* at first.'
In H, the pointing is normally by half-lines; in U, intermittently so.

Sup.: Dom*inica* .VI. post OCT*AVAS* pente*costen.* (Amen dico uobis) quia
nisi abundauerit. ET RELIQVA *H.*   Amen (amen), *the second erased U.*
     1 (Matheus se godspe)llere *H. Wanley (Catalogus, p. 210) confirms readings of
H to end of line 1, but wrongly inserts* his *before* life   2 la(re gehyrde, on his
hirede wu)nigende *H.*   3–4 (þæt he gecwæð hwilon þus to his halgum) *H.*
4 to us] *f. 137, H.*   5–6 becum(að into heofonan rice) *H.*   6 -nyss *H.*
7 ætfor(an minum fæ)der *H.*   9 (gehyrdon) *H.*   beboda *H.*   10 (moy)ses
H.   11 him *H.* Ne] *no cap. in MSS.*

SOURCES. 5–24 [*Matth. v. 20*] Dico enim vobis, quia nisi abundaverit iustitia
vestra plus quam scribarum et Pharisæorum, non intrabitis in regnum cælorum.
     [*21*] Audistis quia dictum est antiquis: Non occides: qui autem occiderit, reus
erit iudicio.
     [*22*] Ego autem dico vobis: quia omnis, qui irascitur fratri suo, reus erit
iudicio. Qui autem dixerit fratri suo, raca, reus erit concilio. Qui autem dixerit,
fatue, reus erit gehennæ ignis.
     [*23*] Si ergo offers munus tuum ad altare, et ibi recordatus fueris quia frater
tuus habet aliquid adversum te:
     [*24*] relinque ibi munus tuum ante altare, et vade prius reconciliari fratri tuo:
et tunc veniens offeres munus tuum.

and se ðe man ofslihð, se bið domes scyldig.
Ic secge eow to soðan þæt se bið domes scyldig,
se ðe nu yrsað wið his agen[n]e broðor.
Se ðe him hosp gecwyð, se bið þeahtes scyldig,   15
and se ðe [hine hæt] stuntne, se bið wites scyldig
on þam witnigendlican fyre þære toweardan worulde,
buton he ðone gylt gebete on his life.
Gif ðu geoffrast Gode ænige lác æt his weofode,
and þu þonne geþencst þæt þin broðor hæfð   20
sum *þing ongean þe, gesete þine lac   *p. 365
ætforan þam weofode, and fær ðe ærest hraðe
to þinum a'g'num breðer, and hine geglada;
and þonne þu eft cymst, geoffra þine lác.

þis godspel is nu gesæd sceortlice eow þus;   25
and we secgað eow þæt sume men wendon
þæt seo ealde æ on Moyses timan
wære miccle stiðre mannum to gehealdenne
þonne Cristes boboda, þe he gecwæð him sylf
on ðære niwan lage æfter his tocyme,   30
under Godes gife, on ðæs godspelles timan,
swa swa we healdan sceolon gif we hyrað Gode;
ac hy magon gehyran her on ðisum godspelle
þæt Cristes beboda, þe he bebead mannum,
syndon miccle maran þonne Moyses lagu;   35
and we sceolon liðian and ure lif awendan
to ðæs Hælendes bebodum, gif we habban wyllað
þa micclan myrhðe mid him, swa swa he us behet.
We ne magon *libban on ðisum life nateshwon,   *p. 366
þæt we ne agylton wið God and wið men   40
on worde and on weorce; ac we sceolon symble

12 (of)slihð H.   13 (scyl)dig H.   14 agenne] sic H; agene U.
15 gecwið H.   16 hine hæt H; wat hine U (wat on erasure, perhaps originally hwæt; cf. infra, 150).   scy(ldig) H.   22 fær] far H.   23 agenum H.
24 (eft) H.   25 godspell H.   28 gehealdenne] healdenne H.
30 tokyme H.   31 gyfe H.   35 micclan. H.   36 And (first) H.
37 wyllað] willan H.   38 mycclan H.   40 agilton H.   41 word(e)
H.   symle H.

26-35 [*Haymo, Hom. CXVIII*] Qui putant præcepta Veteris Testamenti
districtiora esse quam Novi, discant ex præsenti lectione suam ignorantiam
confiteri, audiantque ipsum Salvatorem discipulis dicentem: *Amen dico vobis,
nisi abundaverit*, etc.

to Gode gecyrran and his mildsunge biddan;
for ðon þe he is gearu, gif we hine biddað
mid inneweardre heortan, þæt he us mildsige;
and him is miccle leofre ures lifes rihtin[g]   45
þonne ænig oðer sceat, gif we geswicað yfeles.
Ælce dæg we syngiað, and ælce dæg we sceolon
urne Hælend gladian mid sumre gódnysse,
se ðe æfre [wile] us mannum milds(i)an;
and he nyle naht eaðe þæs synfullan deað,   50
ac he swyðor wyle þæt he gecyrre and lybbe;
and se ðe bote underfehð, and he beo syððan
hræðe þæs of life, he sceal to reste gewiss,
for þon þe he gecyrde fram his synnum to Gode.
Se Hælend us sæde, swa swa ge gehyrdon ær,   55
'Soð ic eow secge, þæt ge sylfe ne becumað
into heofonan rice, buton eower rihtwisnys
beo eallunga mare ætfo*ran minum Fæder   *p. 367
þonne þæra bocera is and ðæra Sunderhalgena.'
þa boceras syndon and þa Sundorhalgan   60
þa ealdan witan, þe wæron gefyrn,
under Moyses lage, swa micclum gelærede
þæt hy ða ealdan áé on heora wisan cuðon;
ac hy ne heoldon swaþeah þa halgan Godes áé
swa wel swa hy sceoldon. þa cidde hym se Hælend   65
swiðe oftrǽdlice, for ðan þe hy ne heoldon
þa halgan beboda swa swa God sylf hym bebead;

42 miltsun(ge) *H*.   43 ðon] þan *H*.   44 innewerdr(e) *H*. miltsige *H*.
45 rightinge *U*; rih(: : : : :) *H*.   46 sceatt *H*.   47 (syngiað) *H*.
48 sumere g(odnysse) *H*.   49 wile] *sic H; om. U.* miltsian *H*; *the* i *erased in U, perhaps to make two words,* milds an.   50 nele *H*. (þæs synful)lan *H*.
51 swiþor wile *H*.   52 A(nd se ðe bote) *H*.   53 hraðe *H*. (he sceal to reste) *H*.   54 þon] þan *H*.   54–55 s(ynnum to gode. Se hælend) *H*.
55 gehirdon *H*.   56 S(oð ic eow secge, þæt ge sylfe ne be)cumað *H*.
57–58 (buton eower rihtwisnys beo eallunga mare ætforan minum fæder) *H*.
59 þonne] *first word visible f. 137*^v, *H*.   59–60 sun(derhalgena. Þa) *H*.
60 sundor-] synder- *H*.   61 wi(tan þe wæ)ron *H*.   63 (þæt hy ða) *H*.
64 (hal)gan *H*.   65 Þa] *no cap. U*; Ða *H*. him *H*.   66 (swi)þe *H*. -hrædlice *H*.   67 (s)wa swa *H*. hym *om. H*. bebead] bead *H*.

50–51 [*Ez. xxxiii. 11*] Vivo ego, dicit Dominus Deus, nolo mortem impii, sed ut convertatur impius a via sua, et vivat.

60–69 [*These freely developed introductory remarks rest on such passages in the gospels as the following: 63–67, Matth. xxiii. 2–3, xv. 3–20, Marc. vii. 6–23; 68–69, Luc. xi. 39, Matth. xxiii. 28.*]

ac hy woldon hym sylfe þæt hy halige wæron,
and wæron swaþeah misworohte wiðinnan.

þa sæde se Hælend, þe geseah heora heortan,   70
swiðe egeslice word, hym þus cidende:
Uos iustificatis uos coram hominibus;
Deus, autem, nouit corda uestra:
Ge tellað eow rihtwise on manna gesihþum,
ac God soðlice cann swaðeah eowere heortan;   75
ge synd swa swa byrgenu þe beoð wiðutan agrafene
mid ofergeweorcum, swiðe *wel amette,   *p. 368
and syndon afyllede mid forrotodnysse,
and ge swaþeah lufiað hlisan and herunge.

Hym wæs beboden, on heora gehealdsumnyssum   80
on Moyses lage, þæt hy moston lufian
heora agene frynd, and hatian heora fynd;
ac us bead se Hælend, her on ðysum life,
þæt we lufian sceolon symble, butan hiwunge,
ure agene freond, and ælcne Cristene man,   85
and eac for Godes lufan lufian ure fynd,
þæt ure rihtwisnys beo mare þonne heora,
we ðe habban sceolon þæt heofonlice líf,
gif we gehyrsume beoð Godes hæsum mid weorcum.

Hym wæs beboden þæt hy ne hæmdon unrihtlice   90

68 hym] hi *H.*   69 misworhte *H.*   71 hym] heom *H.*   72 (Uos)
H. Second uos *originally in both MSS*; *erased in U, then restored in margin.*
74 rihwise *H.*   75 swaðeah *om. H.*   76 Ge sind *H.*   birgena *H.*
80 Hym] Heom *H.*   gehealtsumnesse *H.*   82 agenne frind *H.*   find *H.*
83 þisum *H.*   84 symle *H.*   85 frind *H.*   86 lufon *H.*   find *H.*
87 -ness *H.*   90 Heom *H.*

72–75 [*Luc. xvi. 15*] Vos estis, qui iustificatis vos, etc.

76–78 [*Matth. xxiii. 27*] Similes estis sepulcris dealbatis, quæ aforis parent
hominibus speciosa, intus vero plena sunt ossibus mortuorum, et omni spurcitia.

79 [*Matth. xxiii. 6, 7*] Amant autem primos recubitus in coenis, et primas
cathedras in synagogis, et salutationes in foro, et vocari ab hominibus rabbi.

80–89 [*Haymo*] Iustitia scribarum et Pharisæorum erat, diligere amicum et
odio habere inimicum: iustitia autem eorum, qui intraturi sunt in regnum
cælorum, maior esse debet, ut non solum amicum in Deum, sed etiam inimicum
diligant propter Deum, dicente Domino: *Diligite inimicos vestros, benefacite his
qui oderunt vos, . . . ut sitis filii Patris vestri qui in cælis est (Matth. v. 44–45).*

90–98 [*Haymo*] Iustitia scribarum et Pharisæorum erat, non moechari cum
uxore proximi sui; iustitia eorum qui regnum cælorum intrare desiderant
maior esse debet, ut non solum adulterium non perpetrent in corpore, sed etiam
nec delectent in corde, propter illud quod Dominus ait: *Qui viderit mulierem,* etc.
(*Matth. v. 28*).

wið oþra manna wíf; ac us sæde Crist þus:
Omnis qui uiderit mulierem ad concupiscendum eam
iam mechatus est eam in corde suo.

þæt is on Englisc,
Ælc man þe sceawað wífman mid luste, 95
þæt he hy habban wolde, þæt him witodlice bið
þæt forliger *gefremod on his agenre heortan
þurh þone unlust, þæt he hire gewilnode. *p. 369
We secgað swaðeah þæt si eaðre to betenne
þa yfelan [geþohtas þonne þa yfelan dæda, 100
gyf man þone yfelan] willan [a]went to beteran.
Hy teoðodon heora wyrta, and wolice forleton
þa maran beboda þe Moyses bebead
on þære halgan Godes æ hym to gehealdenne.
Nu sceole we healdan swa þa læssan beboda, 105
þæt we ða maran eac mid weorcum gefyllan.
Hy tæhton mid wordum, swa swa hit awriten is,
Godes lare mannum, and forleton þa weorc;
ac se biþ mære lareow, swa swa se Hælend sæde,
se þe him sylf gedeð, and he syððan swa tæcð, 110
and onginneð þa bysne on him sylfum ærest.

93 *eam*] *underdotted for deletion in* U. 95 Ælc] *cap.* H, *not* U. man]
þæra H. wifmann H. 97 forligr H. 98 (þæt) he H. 100 *first*
yfelan] yfe(lan) H. 100–1 geþohtas ... þone yfelan] *sic* H; *om.* U.
101 awent] þe awent U; (awent) H. 102 teoðedon H. wirta H.
103 (maran) H. 104 hym] heom H. (to gehealden)ne H. 105 Nu]
no cap. in MSS. sceolon H. 106 (ða maran eac) H. gefyllon H.
107 (swa swa hit awriten) H. 108 lare] lage H (*rightly?*). 109 (se
biþ mære lareow, swa) H. 110 gedeð] wel (gedeð) H. 110–11 (gedeð,
and he syððan swa tæcð, and onginne)ð H. 111–12 (ærest. Hym wæs behaten, gif hy heoldon) H.

99–101 [*Not in Haymo.*]
102–6 [*Haymo*] Iustitia scribarum et Pharisæorum esse cernebatur, quod
decimabant mentam et anethum et cyminum et omne olus horti, maiora autem
legis prætermittebant (*Matth. xxiii.* 23). Iustitia eorum qui regnum Dei intraturi
sunt magis abundare debet, ut sic minima præcepta Dei custodiant, quatenus
maiora non prætermittant (*ibid.*).
107–8 [*Matth. xxiii. 2–3*] Super cathedram Moysi sederunt scribæ et Pharisæi.
Omnia ergo quæcumque dixerint vobis, servate, et facite: secundum opera vero
eorum nolite facere: dicunt enim, et non faciunt.
109–11 [*Matth. v. 19*] Qui ... fecerit et docuerit [mandata legis], hic magnus
vocabitur in regno cælorum. [*Haymo, building on Matth. xxiii. 4:*] Iustitia eorum
qui regnum cælorum intrare volunt maior esse debet, ut mandatum Dei primi
custodiant, nec prætermittant quæ alios custodienda docent vel docuerunt.

Hym wæs behaten, gif hy heoldon Godes ǽ,
eorðlice wæstmas, and Crist witodlice
behet þæt ece lif þam þe his word healdað,
þæt þe mannes eage ne mihte geseon,   115
ne eare gehyran, *ne heorte asmeagan,   *p. 370
þa micclan mærðe þe se mildheorta Crist
þam eallum behet þe hine lufiað;
and þærtoeacan he forgifð us ure neode.

Nu mote we habban maran rihtwisnysse,   120
nu us synd behatene þa heofonlican speda,
þæt we moton sona siþian to Criste
on urum forðsiþe, gif we ær mid wærscipe
ure synna gebetað sylfwilles on life.

'Ge gehyrdon þa bebodu þe God bebead gefyrn   125
þam ealdan Israhele under Moyses lage,
and hym þus sæde: Ne ofslih ðu mannan;
and se ðe m[a]n ofslihð, se bið domes scyldig.
Ic secge eow to soþan þæt se bið domes scyldig,
se ðe nu yrsað wið his agenne broðor.'   130
On ðam dome man toscæt hwilc his scyld wære,
and oft he bið unscyldig on ðam dome getæht,
se ðe ær wæs geteald þæt he scyldig wære;
and man mæg gegladian mid gódum *willan   *p. 371

---

113 -mas] f. *138*, H.   114–15 li(f þam þe his word healdað, þæt) H.
116 ea(re) ge(hyran, ne heorte a)smeagan H.   117 mærða H.   117–18 cri(st
þam eallum) H.   119 forgyfð H.   119–20 ne(ode. Nu) H.
120 -nesse H.   121 behaten(e þa) H.   122 sona siþian] siþian sona H.
123 (forð)siþe H.   124 (on life) H.   125 beboda H.   126 isr(a)-
hele H.   127 hym] him H.   Ne] *no cap. in MSS.*   ofsleh H.   128 mann
H; men U.   130 irsað H.   broþer H.   131 d(ome) H.   hwilc]
hwæt H.   134 and] And H.

112–19 [*Haymo*] [*Veteris Testamenti*] temporali iustitia temporale præmium
exspectabatur, dicente Domino: *Observa et audi præcepta Domini Dei tui, ut
bene sit tibi et longo vivas tempore, et ingressus possideas terram lacte et melle
manantem* (*Deut. vi. 3, with substitutions from v. 16 and vi. 17, 18*). Perfectio Novi
Testamenti vitam pollicetur æternam, quam *nec oculus vidit, nec auris audivit,
nec in cor hominis ascendit, quæ præparavit Deus diligentibus se* (*I Cor. ii. 9*).
120–4 [*Haymo*] Quibus ergo maius præmium promittitur, maior debet esse
iustitia.
131–3 [*Haymo, restating Augustine, De Sermone Domini in Monte*] In iudicio
. . . causa discutitur, et is qui reus esse putabatur, nonnunquam innocens in-
venitur.
134–42 [*Ælfric develops this distinction independently of Haymo or Augustine,
though Augustine concedes that it is more serious to kill than to insult, and Haymo*

þa færlican yrsunge, and forfón mid wisdome,   135
eað þonne he gebete gif he bið ofslagen.
To ægþer þæra þinga, þæt is yrre and mansliht,
gæð se rihta dóm; ac hit bið swaþeah
leohtre on bote on ðam lybbendan men,
þeah þe he yrsige, and hit eft gehæle,   140
swa swa þis godspell on æfteweardan sægð,
þæt we magon gegladian þone þe we ær abulgon.
  'Se þe his breþer hosp gecwyð, se bið þeahtes scyldig.'
Her syndon nu twa þing, þæt yrre and se hosp,
and þær gæð geþeaht to þam twam þingum,   145
þæt man mid geþeahte secge him his wite,
hwæt he sylf þrowige for ðam twam þingum;
ac swaþeah hwilon swa scyldig man ætwint,
be ðam þe se trahtnere us sægð on Leden.
  'And se ðe hine hæt stuntne, se bið wites scyldig   150
on ðam witnigendlican fyre þære toweardan worulde.'
H'e'r syndon nu þreo *þing, and forþig mare wite: *p. 372
þæt yrre and se hosp, and eac teonræden;
and þas þing sceolon, swa swa us sægð seo bóc,
on ðam toweardan wite beon afeormode,   155
buton se man hy sylfwilles gebete.
  Micele maran gyltas man mæg gebetan
her on þisum life, and þone Hælend gegladian,

137 (þæ)ra H.   139 libbendan H.   140 e(ft) H.   141 segð H.
142 þone] þonne H.   ær om. H.   143 gecwið H.   145 (gæð) H.
149 segð H.   151 witniendlican fire H.   152 þr(eo) H.   forþi H.
154 segð H.   156 silf- H.   157 mara(n) giltas H.   158 geg(la)dian H.

---

eventually points to the remedium reconciliationis *which the Lord himself sets forth
in verses 23–24.*]
144–9, 152–5 [*Haymo, restating Augustine*] Notandum autem in hoc loco, quia
gradatim de minimis ad maiora ascenditur, quoniam pro qualitate peccati vin-
dictam comminatur. In primo enim loco unum solummodo posuit, id est iram;
secundo, duo, id est iram, et vocem iræ commotionem significant[em]; in tertio,
tria, iram, vocem, et contumeliam. Sicut ergo maius peccatum est dicere fatue,
quam solummodo irasci, vel dicere racha: sic gravius est reum esse gehennæ
ignis, quam reum iudicio, vel concilio. In iudicio enim causa discutitur, *etc.* (*ut
supra*, 131–3); in concilio si quis reus convictus est, qua poena puniatur ab aliis
tractatur, et adhuc evadere solet; in gehenna autem ignis, nulla est liberatio. . . .
Gehennæ nomen . . . inferni poena designatur.
156 [*Haymo*] Sed ne asperam videretur Salvator protulisse sententiam, cum
dixerit reum esse gehennæ ignis eum qui dixerit fratri suo fatue, statim remedium reconciliationis subiunxit.

þæt he ne þurfe þrowian on ðam toweardan life.

God cwæð þurh his witegan þæt he wolde mildsian   160
ælcum men þe gecyrð fram his synnum to him,
þam þe mid geomerunge gewyrcð dædbote,
and his synna [ne beoð syþþan] on gemynde.
Lareowas sceolon læran and styran,
and witan sceolon þreagan þa ðwyran and þa stuntan,   165
ægþer ge mid wordum ge mid weorcum hwilon,
swa swa Crist sylf dyde, þe cidde þam Iudeiscum
for heora gedwyldum and dyrstigan anginne.
Paulus se Apostol on his pistole cwæð þus:
Argue, obsecr[a], *increpa, in omni patientia et doctrina: *p. 373
Þrea ðu and bide, cíd mid geðylde,   171
on ealre lare to lifes bebodum.
Gif hwa nu þurh steore sum styrne word gecwyð
to his underþeoddum for heora stuntnysse,
ne bið na þæt gelic þam unþeawfæstan men,   175
þe for his receleaste misræceð oðerne,
for nanre steore, ac for stuntnesse.

160 (cwæð þurh) H, cw̄ partly visible.   miltsian H.   161 (fram his) H.
162 gewircð H.   162–3 dæd(bote and his synna) H.   163 ne beoð syþ-
þan] sic H; syððan ne beoð U (inferior allit.)   164–5 l(æran and styran,
and wi)tan H.   165 þwiran H.   165–6 stunta(n, ægþer ge mid
wordum) H.   167 c(rist sylf dyde, þe cidde þam iudeiscum) H.
168 gedwildum H.   168–170 (dyrstigan . . . obsec)ra H.   170 (obsec)ra
H(first letters visible f. 138ᵛ); obsecro U.   171 (þrea ðu and bide) H.
cid] 7 cid H.   173 (Gif hwa nu) H.   gecwiþ H.   174 underþeod-
(dum f)or H.   stuntnesse H.   175 na þæt] þæt na H.   -fæstum (men)
H.   176 misræcð H.   177 (ac) H.   -nysse H.

160 [Act. x. 43] Huic omnes prophetæ testimonium perhibent, remissionem
peccatorum accipere per nomen eius omnes qui credunt in eum.
    161–3 [Is. xliii. 25] Ego sum, ego sum ipse qui deleo iniquitates tuas
propter me, et peccatorum tuorum non recordabor. [xliv. 22] Delevi ut nubem
iniquitates tuas, et quasi nebulam peccata tua; revertere ad me, quoniam
redemi te. [Ier. xxxi. 34] Propitiabor iniquitati eorum, et peccati eorum non
memorabor amplius.
    164–77 [Augustine makes a similar reservation, reading sine causa after
irascitur in Matt. v. 22 and treating it as implicit in the parallel clauses that
follow] Hoc est unde defenditur, quod Apostolus Galatos vocat stultos (Galat.
iii. 1, 3), quos etiam fratres nominat: non enim id facit sine causa. [Haymo,
following Jerome, explicitly rejects sine causa and does not meet the problem raised
by Augustine and Ælfric.]
    170–2 [II Tim. iv. 2. Quoted by Cæsarius, Sermo CXLVIII, commenting on
Matth. vii. 1–2: Propter apertam . . . iniquitatem dictum est: Argue, etc. Cf.
supra, XIII. 88–97 and 183–8.]

We sceolon us gebletsian and abiddan æt Gode
þat he us gehealde, and urne muð þurh-[hlyn]ne,
swa swa se witega bæd, þysum wordum cweðende: 180
*Pone, Domine, custodiam ori meo, et hostium circumstantie labiis
   meis:*
Sete þu, leof Drihten, minum muðe hyrdrædene,
[and] duru minum welerum, þinre wearde abútan.
Duru he abæd, þæt he fordyttan mihte
þa idelan spræca, and undon his muð   185
to wisdomes spræcum, and to wurðianne God,
swa 'swa' man belycð and geopenað *þa duru.   *p. 374
   Vton nu gehyran þæs Hælendes læcedom,
hu we magon gehælan her on ðisum life
ure yfelan word wið ðone þe 'we ge'gremodon.   190
'Gif ðu geoffrast Gode ænige lác æt his weofode,
and þu þonne geðencst þæt þin broðor hæfð
sum ðing ongean þe, gesete þine lac
ætforan þam weofode, and far þe ærest raðe
to þinum agenum breðer, and hine geglada;   195
and þonne þu eft cymst, geoffra þine lác.'
Se Hælend cwæð eft on sumere oðre stowe,
þonne ge sylfe standað on eowrum gebedum,
forgifað þonne on eowrum heortum
eallum oðrum mannum þe wið eow agyltað   200
þæt se Heofonlica Fæder eowre synna forgife;
and butan ge forgifon, ne forgifð he na eow.

---

178 gebletsian] bletsian *H.*   abiddan] biddan *H.*   179 (us g)ehealde *H.*
þurh-hlynne] þurhine *U,* þurh hine *H (see note).*   180 þisum *H.*   cwe-
ðende] *sic H;* (ge)cweðende *U.*   181 hostium] ostium *H.*   circumstantiæ *H.*
183 and] *sic H; om. U.*   (mi)num *H.*   184 abæd] bæd *H.*   fordittan
(mihte) *H.*   186 wurðienne *H.*   187 belicð *H.*   190 gegremedon *H.*
193 gesete] gesete þærrihtes *H.*   194 hraðe *H*   196 geoffra] geoffra
þonne *H.*   199 forgyfað *H.*   200 agyltað] agilton *H (rightly?).*   201 forgyfe *H.*   202 And buton *H.*   forgifon] heom forgifon *H.*   forgyfð *H.*

178–87 [*Not in Haymo or Augustine.*]
181–3 [*Psal. cxl. 3.*]
188–90 [*Haymo, in sentence quoted above,* 156, *introduces the next verse of the
text as* remedium reconciliationis.]
197–202 [*Marc. xi.* 25, 26] Et cum stabitis ad orandum, dimittite si quid
habetis adversus aliquem, ut et Pater vester qui in cælis est, dimittat vobis
peccata vestra. Quod si vos non dimiseritis, nec Pater vester, qui in cælis est,
dimittet vobis peccata vestra. [*For Haymo's divergent use of this passage see note
on* 197–213.]

þonne hæfð ure broðor sum þing ongean us,
gif we him deredon oððe gedydon unðanc;
þonne sceole we don be ures Drihtnes lare,   205
gegladian urne broðor mid góódum ingehýde,
*þone Cristenan 'man', butan ælcere hiwunge,   *p. 375
þæt God sylf underfó glædlice ure lác,
se ðe nele underfón nan þing ǽr æt ús,
ær we habban sibbe on soðfæstum mode.   210
Gif us ænig man derað oððe gedeð unþanc,
þæt we sceolon forgifan, swa swa se Hælend sæde,
þæt us ure synna syððan beo[n] forgifene.
    Vre lac syndon þe we offriað Gode
ure halgan gebedu, and þæt we gehelpon   215
þam earmum mid urum ælmessum,
and ælc þing þe we doð urum Drihtne to lofe;
þa beoð ealle Godes lác, and we mid gódum willan
þa sceolon geoffrian, þæt hy andfenge beon,
and Gode licwyrðe, þe lufiað æfre sibbe,   220
and he mid smyltnysse symble demð eallum.

203 Ðænne H.   204 gedidon H.   205 drihtenes H.   206 godum
inngehide H.   209 (n)ele H.   210 habbon H.   (mo)de H.   212 sceo-
(lon for)gyfan H.   213 beon] beoð U; no reading in H.   (for)gyfene H.
215 (gebedu, and þæt we g)ehelpon H.   216 ælmyssan H.   217 and]
And H.   (ælc þing þe we doð) H.   218 (and we mid godum willan) H.
219 andfencge H.   220 (and gode licwyrðe, þe lufiað æfre s)ibbe H.
221 symle H.   221–2 (demð eallum. Be ðam sang se sealmwyrhta) H.

203–13 [Augustine, De Sermone Domini in Monte, Lib. I, cap. x. 27] Si in mentem venerit quod aliquid habeat adversus nos frater, id est, si nos eum in aliquo
læsimus; tunc enim ipse habet adversus nos: nam nos adversus illum habemus,
si ille nos læsit: ubi non opus est pergere ad reconciliationem; non enim veniam
postulabis ab eo qui tibi fecit iniuriam, sed tantum dimittes, sicut tibi dimitti a
Domino cupis, quod ipse commiseris. [Ælfric passes over Augustine's insistence
that one is to go to one's brother in spirit rather than in body, but takes the warning
against hypocrisy from the following sentence] Ita enim etiam si præsens sit,
poteris eum non simulato animo lenire, atque in gratiam revocare veniam
postulando, si hoc prius coram Deo feceris. [For Ælfric's 203 sq. Haymo says
exactly the opposite] Tunc . . . frater noster adversum nos habet aliquid, quando
nos lædit.
    214–21 [Haymo, modifying Augustine] Nec putandum est quod ei tantummodo
munera offerimus, cum manibus oblationem ante altare deportamus; sed quando
orationi insistimus, . . . cum eleemosynas tribuimus, hospitem suscipimus, nudum
cooperimus, et cætera his similia pietatis opera implemus, tunc munera Deo
offerimus. Cavendum ergo summopere est, ne malum discordiæ contra aliquem
in corde teneamus, et propter hoc nostra munera in conspectu Dei accepta non
sint, quomodo Deo placabilem hostiam . . . offerre non possumus quamdiu
proximis implacabiles sumus.

Be ðam sang se sealmwyrhta, þus secgende him to:
Adiutor meus, tibi sallam, et cetera.

þæt is on Engliscre spræce, þu eart min gefylsta;
þe sylfum ic singe; þu eart min onfónd,   225
min agen soð God, and min mildheortnys.
*He het hine mildheortnys, for ðan þe he milde is,   *p. 376
and he on manega wisan þam mannum gehylpð
þe mid anrædnysse to him æfre 'h'opiað.
þam is wuldor and wurðmynt a to worulde, AMEN.   230

223 Adiutor] *f. 139, H.*   psallam *H.*   224 (on engliscre spræce, þu eart
min ge)fylsta *H.*   226 so(ð god, and) *H.*   -nyss *H.*   227 -nyss *H.*
(he milde is) *H.*   229 anrednesse *H.*   (to him) *H.*   230 wyrðmynt *H.*

222–30 [*Not in Haymo or Augustine.*]
223–6 [*Psal. lviii. 18*] Adiutor meus, tibi psallam, quia Deus susceptor meus
es; Deus meus, misericordia mea.

NOTES

30. *lage.* The word stands in both manuscripts, but *æ*, which is to be
expected after 27, would provide alliteration now lacking unless we count
the weak *on*. Because of the theme both *æ* and *lagu* are frequently used
in this homily, but *lagu* may have been introduced here once too often.

35. *lagu.* Correct here, and probably plural. See note on xx. 34.

50 sq. The quotation from Ezekiel appears as ordinary prose in *CH* II.
602 (*De Penitentia*), and this is repeated in *LS* XII. 152.

52. *and he beo syððan hræðe þæs of life,* almost 'even if he die very
soon afterwards'. The conditional idea is indicated by the subjunctive,
but we are at least very close to the familiar Middle English use of *and* as
'if' or 'even if'. At 140 below *and* somewhat similarly approaches 'if', but
the sequence can perhaps better be regarded as elliptical, for in strict
logic the *and* presupposes *gif* rather than *þeah þe* in the preceding clause.
See Glossary, *and.*

68. *woldon,* 'would have it', 'maintained'. See Glossary, *willan.*

71–78. These two quotations about the scribes and Pharisees, one from
Luke, the other from *Matthew*, occur in the same order in Ælfric's early
homily for the ninth Sunday after Pentecost, *CH* II. xxx, p. 404. They
are not included in Haymo's comment on verse 20.

94. *Þæt is on Englisc.* Possibly a scribal addition, and in any case extrametric.

97 sq. Ælfric's effort to spell out the implications of the Latin has produced a cumbersome sentence with weak alliteration, but its structure, with

respect to which both manuscripts agree, can be understood if we take the two clauses, *þæt he hy habban wolde* and *þæt he hire gewilnode*, as parenthetical elaborations of *mid luste* and *þurh þone unlust* respectively. For somewhat similar use of *þæt*, see IV. 290 and VI. 340.

100 sq. The reading of H is clearly right. U's error is probably a simple case of eye-skip, with an unsuccessful effort to restore the sense by addition of *þe* before *awent*.

133. *se ðe ær wæs geteald þæt he scyldig wære.* Evidently a mixed construction, in which the clause is substituted for the usual adjective: 'who earlier was considered guilty.'

136 sqq. This passage is confusing, but I suppose that in 136 the first *he* refers to the angry man, the second to the object of his anger, and that the phrase *on ðam lybbendan men* is short for 'in the case of the living man'; that is, the penance for anger is lighter if the object of one's anger is still living.

140. *and.* See note on 52 above.

155. *on ðam toweardan wite beon afeormode.* The words *afeormode* here and *witnigendlican*, 151 (repeated from 17) suggest the purgatorial fire, which Ælfric probably intended. See the references to purgatory in XI. 187 sqq., and esp. 226, where *afeormode* is combined with *ðæt witniendlice fyr*. Also, *CH* II. 592/8–10. Augustine's comment (*PL* XXXIV. 1241) seems to open the door to Ælfric's inference when, after granting that killing a man seems much worse than insulting him, he says: 'Quisquis autem dixerit quod graviore supplicio in maiore iustitia punitur homicidium, si gehennæ igne punitur convicium, cogit intellegi esse differentias gehennarum.' Here in 155 should we not read *fyre* for *wite*, thus supplying alliteration and making the statement more specific?

171 sq. In the *Letter to Wulfgeat*, Assman I. 307 sq., the same text is more literally translated:

> þrea and bide, cid eac mid wordum,
> on eallum geðylde, and on ealre lare.

179. *þurh[hlyn]ne*: *þurh hine* H, *þurhine*, U. There is a vague plausibility in the reading of H and if it is right we need only suppose that the scribe of U failed to repeat the letter *h*. But Ælfric does not often write so negligently as this, and I think it probable that a verb of some weight, parallel to *gehealde*, has been lost. With some trepidation I have altered the text to *þurh-hlynne*. There is no record of the verb *hlynnan* with this prefix, but *þurh* is used freely to make compounds, especially by writers who are familiar with Latin verbs with the prefix *per-*. The simple verb *hlynnan* is used to mean *sound* or *resound* in various senses. In the *Regius Psalter* (ed. F. Roeder, Halle, 1904) it occurs in a translation of *Ps.* xvii. 14: 'intonuit de celo Dominus', *hlynde of heofone* (*Dryhten*). If Ælfric indeed used the word here with the prefix *þurh*, his sentence means that we should pray to the Lord that he will guard us (from uttering calumnies)

and himself sound out or thunder through our mouths (when it is our duty to administer correction). Ælfric goes on to quote the psalmist, who emphasizes rather the idea of putting an armed guard about the mouth, as if to prevent the passage of anything unseemly; but it will be noticed that Ælfric, in his comment on the verse, puts equal emphasis on opening the mouth for the passage of wisdom. The etymologically correct spelling *hlynne* has been chosen rather than some intermediate spelling such as *hlinne* or *hline*, for there is no telling by what route the unsatisfactory *þurh hine* was reached.

183. *þinre wearde abutan*. I think this phrase can best be taken as a kind of dative absolute, 'with thy protection round about'. Admittedly the Latin suggests rather that *þinre wearde* is a genitive depending on *duru*; but if so, what is one to do with *abutan*?

184. *fordyttan*. This rather unusual word is used in Ælfric's translation of *Genesis* viii. 2, to translate *clausi*, where, after the flood, the waters are shut off.

197–213. Haymo's interpretation of *Matth.* v. 23, 24 seems to have resulted from the conviction that *Marc.* xi. 25 sq. (quoted by Ælfric 198–202) must be just another way of saying the same thing. Hence he wrenches the meaning of *habet aliquid adversum te* in spite of the fact that both Augustine and Jerome (in his commentary on *Matthew*, PL xxvi. 37) had taken it as one would expect, to mean that the brother has been the injured party. Augustine also, however, as the source-quotation shows, had *Marc.* xi. 25 sq. in mind, and treated it as complementary rather than the same. Ælfric's careful presentation of the passage in *Mark* before he begins his interpretation of *Matthew* may be momentarily confusing, but it is soon clear that he has rejected Haymo in favour of Augustine and is bent on showing that the two texts apply to alternative situations.

213. *beon*. The *beoð* of U is probably a mere slip. Though H has no reading, the subjunctive is surely required. Cf. 201.

XVI[1]

DOMINICA X POST PENTECOSTEN

Luc. xvi. 1–9

An influential interpretation of the parable of the unjust steward was set forth by Augustine in two closely related writings. One was chapter xxxiv of the *Quæstiones in evangelium secundum Lucam* (*PL* xxxv. 1348–9), which was quoted in its entirety by Bede in his commentary on *Luke* and reappears, sometimes a little modified, in Haymo's Homily cxxi for the tenth Sunday after Pentecost. The other was the more expansive *Sermo* cxiii, dealing particularly with the last verse (*Luc.* xvi. 9), the injunction to make friends by means of the mammon of iniquity. This sermon is not quoted by Bede and reappears only partially in Haymo. Augustine was concerned in both these writings to extract the obviously intended lesson about the practical advantages of almsgiving, and at the same time to reject the fraudulence of the steward. The commentators who followed him, including Ælfric, have these same two purposes in view and work them out with varying degrees of elaboration and emphasis.

Ælfric reveals clearly his acquaintance with the passage in the *Quæstiones*, which, however, he need not have known except as a part of Bede's exposition. Whether he knew *Sermo* cxiii beyond the little he would have absorbed from Haymo is a question. The main reason for thinking that he had read it is a cluster of resemblances at lines 157–82, including the use of the same quotation at 159–62. Elsewhere it corresponds less closely to Ælfric than Bede or Haymo does.

In the main, then, Ælfric relies on Bede's commentary and Haymo's homily, both of which are more elaborate than Augustine and have non-Augustinian passages of which Ælfric avails himself. As in Homily xv, he takes full advantage of the introductory matter supplied by Haymo. When he takes up the verses of the gospel

On the group xiii–xvi, see xiii, introduction, pp. 493–4.

one by one he makes as much use of Bede (and of Augustine as quoted by Bede) as of Haymo.

What is most interesting, however, is Ælfric's independent development of the Augustinian attack on the steward's fraudulence. He finds an excellent means of distinguishing between the good and bad aspects of worldly wisdom by introducing the famous injunction of *Matth.* x. 16: 'Be ye wise as serpents and harmless as doves.' None of the other expositors makes use of this text, though it is Augustine who has expounded it for Ælfric in another place: in *Sermo* LXIV, which explores the two symbols elaborately with particular reference to martyrs. Under Augustine's guidance the wisdom of the serpent becomes as saintly as the innocence of the dove, and the lesson of expediency so disconcertingly conveyed by the unjust steward is balanced by a vision of selfless love and purity. By means of this passage, which complements the introductory praise (inspired by Haymo) of God's loving care of man, Ælfric does fuller justice than his predecessors to the two aspects of Augustine's interpretation of the parable.

One other influential interpretation of the parable should be set beside Augustine's, though I am not sure that Ælfric made direct use of it. This is contained in Jerome's *Epistula* CXXI, *Ad Algasiam Liber Quæstionum Undecim*, cap. 6 (*CSEL* 56, pp. 21–27). It is mainly an attempt to relate the parable, with its theme of thanksgiving, to the orderly progression of Jesus's teaching in this section of *Luke*, and to show how it applies to the scribes and Pharisees on the one hand and the disciples on the other. Bede reflects Jerome's interpretation in his introductory remarks and at one or two points elsewhere. Haymo makes much heavier use of it, going so far as to include the alternative interpretation reported noncommittally by Jerome at the end, according to which the unjust steward typifies St. Paul. Among the ways by which Jerome's interpretation could have reached Ælfric must be mentioned the homiliary of Paulus Diaconus as originally constituted. In this the sixth chapter of Jerome's letter was assigned as a homily to the fifth Sunday after the nativity of Peter and Paul, whereas in the Migne edition (*PL* XCV), which has a different system of counting for the summer months, its place has been taken by an anonymous homily for the tenth Sunday after Pentecost. This homily has some similarity to Ælfric's at a few points, but it was probably composed nearly a hundred years after his time, for it reappears in a later volume of the patrology (*PL* CLX. 1121–8), where it is attributed to Odo, bishop of Cambrai, who died in 1113. The specific attribution is doubtful, but it is probably safe to assume that the homily was written about 1100, and did not find a place in Paul's homiliary before the twelfth century. Thus Ælfric's copy (or copies) of the homiliary may well have retained Jerome's piece.[1] I have quoted a bit of it for lines 269–92, where it may have supplemented Bede and Haymo (as it certainly lies behind their comments), but at most it cannot have contributed more than a few minor elaborations of the basic ideas. The truly pervasive influence in this homily is Augustine's.

[1] According to the list of the original homiliary given by Leclercq and again by Smetana, Jerome's piece is numbered 11. 62. On the homiliary and its importance for Ælfric see the Introduction, p. 156. Ælfric had certainly read another chapter of Jerome's letter. See XXVIII.

DOMINICA X POST PENTECOSTEN

Homo quidam erat diues, qui habebat uillicum, et reliqua

Se Hælend sæde þus to his halgum apostolum,
her on þisum life libbende mid mannum,
*for ðon þe he oft gespræc wið hy on bigspellum: *p. 399
Sum welig man wæs iú, se hæfde tungerefan;
þa wea'r'ð se gerefa forsæd wið his hlaford,   5
þæt he his gód sceolde swiðe him fram aspendan;

Text based on U (Trinity B. 15. 34), pp. 398–414. Collated with H (Cotton Vitellius C. v), ff. 142ᵛ–5. In the list of variants round brackets enclose portions of the text as witnessed by U (including the modern punctuation) for which there is approximately the right space but no longer any reading in the damaged H.

For homilies XIII–XVI, where the manuscripts are the same, the following variants are excluded: H regularly has *byð, gyf, hi, mann, menn, þiss, þuss* where U has *bið, gif, hy, man, men, þis, þus*. But H usually has *man* for the indefinite pronoun 'one'. U's *hy* and *hym* were often written *hi* and *him* at first. A substitute scribe has written f. 145 (beginning at line 256) in H, but without noticeable change in spelling.

In H, the pointing is normally by half-lines; in U, intermittently so. Capitalization of sentences has been regularized. It more nearly accords with H than with U.

Sup.: DOMINICA IX. POST OCTAVAS PENTECOSTEN H.   uilicum H.
1 (S)e H.   Wanley, Catalogus, p. 210, confirms as far as line 2, life. 3 for þan þe H.   (o)n H.   5 Ða H.   6 aspendan] aspenan H.

SOURCES. 1, 4–38 [*Luc. xvi. 1*] Dicebat autem et ad discipulos suos: Homo quidam erat dives, qui habebat villicum: et hic diffamatus est apud illum quasi dissipasset bona ipsius.

[*2*] Et vocavit illum, et ait illi: Quid hoc audio de te? redde rationem villicationis tuæ: iam enim non poteris villicare.

[*3*] Ait autem villicus intra se: Quid faciam quia dominus meus aufert a me villicationem? fodere non valeo, mendicare erubesco.

[*4*] Scio quid faciam, ut, cum amotus fuero a villicatione, recipiant me in domos suas.

[*5*] Convocatis itaque singulis debitoribus domini sui, dicebat primo: Quantum debes domino meo?

[*6*] At ille dixit: Centum cados olei. Dixitque illi: Accipe cautionem tuam: et sede cito, scribe quinquaginta.

[*7*] Deinde alii dixit: Tu vero quantum debes? Qui ait: Centum coros tritici. Ait illi: Accipe litteras tuas, et scribe octaginta.

[*8*] Et laudavit dominus villicum iniquitatis, quia prudenter fecisset: quia filii huius sæculi prudentiores filiis lucis in generatione sua sunt.

[*9*] Et ego vobis dico: facite vobis amicos de mammona iniquitatis: ut, cum defeceritis, recipiant vos in æterna tabernacula.

and se hlaford sona gelangode hine,
and befran hine þa, Hwæt gehyre ic be ðe?
Betǽc þine wícan; ne miht þu beon leng
on minum folgoþe. And se gerefa þa cwæð   10
on his agenum mode, Hwæt mæg ic la nu don?
nu ic beo bescíred, and ic sylf ne mæg
mid minum fotum delfan, ne ic ne mæg for sceame
ahwær bedician. And he eft þa cwæð,
Ic wylle nu betwyx þisum tilian me freonda   15
on þam þe aht sceolon minum hlaforde nu,
þæt hy me underfón into heora husum,
þonne ic betæht hæbbe þas wican me fram.
He gelaðode þa sona his underþeod`d'an him tó,
þa þe aht sceoldon his hlaforde on feo,   20
and cwæð to heora anum, Hwæt ahst þu to gyldenne?
*He cwæð þæt he sceolde syllan his hlaforde   *p. 400
hundteontig óman mid ele ametene.
þa het se gerefa him awritan fiftig.
He cwæð þa to oðrum, Hwæt scealt þu þinum hlaforde?   25
He cwæð þæt he sceolde him hundteontig mit`t'an hwætes.
And se gerefa het him on gewrite settan
þæt he hundeahtatig him agifan sceolde.
Hwæt þa heora hlaford herode eft syððan
þone gerefan on his unrihtwisnysse,   30
for ðan þe he snotorlice wið hine sylfne gedyde;
for ðan þe woroldmen, þyssere worlde bearn,
syndon micel[e] snoteran on heora cynrene
þonne þæs leohtes bearn, þæt synd þa geleaffullan.
þa sæde se Hælend eft syððan him þus to: 35
Wyrcað eow freonda of ðam unrihtan welan,
þæt hy underfón eow on eowrum forðsiþe
to him on ðam ecum eardungstowum eft.

12 bescyred H.   14 bedecian H.   17 (i)nnto H.   20 (his) H.
21 gylden(ne) H.   23 (mid) H.   ametene] afyllede H.   25 (þa to o)ðrum
H.   26 (him hundteon)tig H.   27 And] An (!) H.   27–28 (settan þæt he
hund)eahtatig H.   29 hla(ford herode eft syð)þan H.   31 (ðan þe he
snotorlice wið hine s)ylfne H.   32 woruldmenn H.   32–33 (þyssere
worlde bearn, syndon micele) H.   33 micelre U (cf. 216).   snoterran H.
cy(n)r(ene) H.   34 þonne] f. 143, H.   35 s(e hæ)le(n)d H.   hiom H.
36 Wyrceað H.   unriht(an) welum H.   37 eow] eow eft H.   38 hiom
H; both MSS. have point after this word.   eft] om. H, which has ðær ge æfre
ma wunien over line in hand resembling main scribe's.

Se welega man þe hæfde *þone túngerefan   *p. 401
is se ælmihtiga God, þe ah ealle þing,   40
and he betæhte mannum his micclan welan
her on þisum andwerdan life, þæt he geuðe us
andgites and gesceades, swa swa þam englum,
toforan oþrum gesceaftum, and þærtoeacan
us forgifð ure neode on life,   45
þurh his micclan cyste; for ðan þe he mancynn lufað,
þa ðe hine oncnawað and him cyððe to habbað
þurh soðne geleafan and singalre lufe.
We synd his gerefan, þe his welan habbað,
and we yfele aspendað his æhta him fram,   50
þonne we ure andgit to yfele awendað,
and ure mennisce gescead to mánfullum leahtrum;
and we nyllað mid gesceade us sylfum gewissian,
ne wyrcan his willan þe wyle us habban;
and him nane æhta ne synd swa inmede   55
swa him synd to agenne ure sawle clæne.
Be þam sang se sealmwyrhta, þus secgende us:
*Homo, cum in honore esset, non intellexit, *et cetera:*   *p. 402
Se mann witodlice, þa ða he on wurðmynte wæs,
he hit ne understod; ac þam stuntum nytenum   60
he wearð wiðmeten, and wæs hym þa gelíc.
Ælc þara manna þe his andgit awent
to yfelum weorcum fram rihtwisnysse,
and nele understandan his agenne wurðmynt,

---

42 andweardan *H.*   45 forgyfð *H.*   neoda *H.*   46 manncynn *H.*
50 aspendað] aspenað *H.*   53 nellað *H.*   gewisian *H.*   54 wyrcean *H.*
55 innmede *H.*   56 sawla *H.*   57 -wyrchta *H.*   59 wyrðmynte
H.   61 heom *H.*   62 þæra *H.*   63 -nesse *H.*   64 wyrðmynt *H.*

39–49 [*Haymo, Hom. CXXI*] Spiritualiter, homo iste Deus omnipotens est....
Qui bene dives esse dicitur, quia apud illum sunt *omnes thesauri sapientiæ et
scientiæ absconditi* (*Col. ii.* 3). . . . Illius villici nos sumus quos ad imaginem et
similitudinem suam creavit, quibus etiam sensum et intellectum præbuit. . . .
Et revera magnas suas divitias Deus omnipotens nobis commisit, quando ratio-
nalem sensum et intellectum communem cum angelis præ ceteris creaturis tribuit.
    50–56 [*Haymo*] Male autem divitias Domini nostri dispensamus, quando
sensum discretionis, quem ad usum boni accepimus, in usum convertimus
vitiorum.
    57–61 [*Psal. xlviii.* 13] Et homo, cum in honore esset, non intellexit: com-
paratus est iumentis insipientibus, et similis factus est illis.
    62–83 [*Free elaboration of the preceding themes.*]

þæt he is sylf geworht to Godes anlicnysse,   65
and mid gewitleaste unwurðað hine sylfne
fram þam micclan wurðmynte, þæt he on meoxe licge
on þam fúlum leahtrum, fúlre þonne nyten,
he aspent yfele his hlafordes æhta,
þonne he his agen gescead on synnum eall aspent,   70
and hine wácne gedeþ and unwurðne symble.
þas synd'an þa' leahtras þe misliciað Gode:
eawbryce and forliger, and ælces cynnes reaflac,
morðdæda and manslihtas and ealle manaðas,
wiccecræft and wiglung and þa wógan domas,   75
stala and leasunga and þa micclan druncennyssa,
untíma-ǽt and oferfyll *and þæt man wyrce unlybban,   *p. 403
and þæt man nylle freolsian mid nanum wurðmynte
þone halgan Sunnandæg, þam Hælende to lofe,
þe on ðam Sunnandæge him sylf aras of deaðe—   80
and he manega wundra geworhte on ðam dæge—
ne his halgena mæssedagas, þe man healdan sceolde,
and gán to cyrcan, Godes lof to gehyrenne.
Vton nu geedlæcan, þæt is, eft eow nu secgan,
þisses godspelles anginn, swa swa we ǽr sædon,   85
þæt ge magon þe eað þæt andgit understandan:
'Sum welig man wæs iú, se hæfde tungerefan;
þa wearð se gerefa forsæd wið his hlaford,
þæt he his gód sceolde swiðe him fram aspendan;
and se hlaford sona gelangode hine,   90
and befran hine þa, Hwæt gehyre ic be ðe?
Betǽc þine wícan; ne miht þu beon leng
on minum folgoðe.'

---

67 wyrðmynte H.   meoxe] meoxe galnesse H.   68 on] 7 on H.
69, 70 aspenð H.   71 symle H.   72 synd H.   73 eaw-
brice H.   forligr H.   78 nele H.   wyrðmynte H.   81 þ(am) H.
84 þæt is] 7 H.   (secgan) H.   85 þises H.   86 þ(e eað þæt) H.
87 Sum] Se hælend cwæð, Sum H.   ma(n wæs iu, se hæf)de H.   88 þa]
Ða H.   88–89 (wið his hlaford, þæt) H.   89–90 a(s)p(endan; and se
hlaford sona gela)ngode H (ngode first letters visible f. 143ᵛ).   92 (wica)n H.

67, 68 [Cf. II Petr. ii. 22] Contigit enim eis illud veri proverbii: Canis reversus
ad suum vomitum; et Sus lota in volutabro luti.
72–83 [Somewhat similar lists are at I Cor. vi. 9–10; Gal. v. 19–21.]

On twa wisan us gelangað and him to clypað se Hælend,
oððe on andweardum *life ærest to dædbote,   *p. 404
oððe on ðam oðrum life eft to þam dome.   96
Nu sceole we beðencan us sylfe her on life,
þæt we to yfele ne beon eft on ðam dome.
'And se gerefa þa cwæð on his agenum mode,
Hwæt mæg ic la nu dón, nu ic beo bescíred,   100
and ic sylf ne mæg mid minum fotum delfan,
ne ic ne mæg for sceame ahwær bedician?'
We ne magon delfan, ne we ne moton wyrcan
nane góde wæstmas ænigre drohtnunge
æfter þisum life, gif we ærðan noldon;   105
ne þær ne bið nán earnung, ac bið edlean gewiss
ealra ure dæda, be ðam þe we dydon ǽr;
ne we ne magon bedecian for bysmore þær,
gif we æmtige beoð ælces gódes þonne—
swa swa þa stuntan mædenu, þe mid heom sylfon næfdon   110
on heora leohtfatum nan leoht þam brydguman,
Hælende Criste, swa swa he him sylf sæde,
*and woldon þa biddan oððe gebicgan hym leoht;   *p. 405
ac hy wurdon belocene wiðutan fram Criste,
for ðon þe hy næfdon him nane lihtinge ætforan.   115
Be ðam ylcan gecwæð eft Godes wisdom:
For þæs wintres cyle nolde se asolcena erian;

94 ge(langað and h)im *H.*   clypað] clypiað (!) *H.*   95 andweardan *H.*
98 yfel(e) *H.*   100 bescyred *H.*   102 bedekian *H.*   103 wircean *H.*
107 ura *H.*   dydon] gedidon *H.*   108 bismore *H.*   110 sylfum *H.*
113 heom *H.*   115 for þan þe *H.*   116 gecwæð] he cwæð *H.*

94–98 [*Haymo*] Dupliciter nos vocat Deus, in præsenti ad pænitentiam, et
in futuro ad iudicium. Vocamur ergo ad reddendum rationem villicationis
nostræ, cum de præsenti vita ad eius iudicium ducimur. . . . Et posthæc non
poterimus villicare. . . . Imitetur villicum, qui in futuro sibi prudenter præ-
vidit.
103–20 [*Bede, In Lucam*] Ablata quippe villicatione fodere non valemus, quia
finita hac vita, in qua tantum licet operari, nequaquam ultra bonæ conversationis
fructum, ligone devotæ compunctionis licet inquirere. Mendicare, confusionis
est. Illo scilicet pessimo genere mendicandi, quo virgines illæ fatuæ mendicasse
referuntur, quæ ingruente tempore nuptiarum oleo virtutum deficiente, sapienti-
bus dixerunt: *Date nobis de oleo vestro, quia lampades nostræ exstinguuntur* (*Matth.*
xxv. 8). Et de quo Salomon ait: *Propter frigus piger arare noluit; mendicabit ergo*
æstate, et non dabitur ei (*Prov. xx. 4*).

he bedecað eft on sumera, and him ne bið na getiðad.
þæt is, þæt he on life lytel swanc for Criste,
and he ða ecan myrhþe ne mæg þonne abiddan.   120
'He eft þa syððan gecwæð on his agenum geðance,
Ic wylle nu betwyx þisum tilian me freonda
on ðam [þ]e aht sceolan mínum hlaforde nú,
þæt hy me underfón into heora husum,
þonne ic betæht hæbbe þas wícan me fram.   125
He gelaðode þa sona his underþeoddan him to,
þa ðe aht sceoldon his hlaforde on feo,
and cwæð to heora anum, Hwæt ahst þu to gyldenne?
He cwæð þæt he sceolde syllan his hlaforde
hundteontig óman mid ele ametene.   130
þa het se gerefa *him awritan fiftig.'   *p. 406
Ele wyxt on tre'o'wum, eall swa wín deð;
ac þa elebeamas beoð maran on wæstme,
and þa berian grytran, and hy man gaderað and wringð,
and man et þone ele, swa swa we etað buteran,   135
on manegum estmettum, and he is mett[a] fyrmest.
Man deð hine to leohte eac on ðam lande
on fægerum leohtfatum, for ðan þe he fæt is,
and wynsumlice byrnð binnan Godes cyrcan;
he is swiðe deorweorðe, and hine man deð to fulluhte,   140
and to Godes þen'u'n'g'um, þonne he gehalgod bið.
'He cwæð þa to oðrum, Hwæt scealt þu þinum hlaforde?
He cwæð þæt he sceolde him hundteontig mittan hwætes;
and se gerefa het him on gewrite settan
þæt he hundeahtatig him agifan sceolde.'   145
He lissode þam mannum þæt he mihte hopian
to heora freondrædene, þæt hy underfengon

---

118 getiðod H.   122 betweox H.   123 þe] sic H; þæte (!) U.   sceolon H.
127 sceoldon] sceolon H.   128 gildenne H.   130 ametene] afyllede H.
132 swa] swa swa H.   134 gryttran H.   135 et] ytt H.   136 (and) H.
metta] sic H; mette U.   138 (f)ægerum H.   fætt H.   139 bin(na)n H.
140 deorwyrþe H.   141 (to god)es H.   142 (scealt þu þinum) H.
143 mittan] mittana H.   143–4 (hwætes; and se geref)a H.   145–6 (him
agifan sceolde. He liss)ode H.   147 (freondrædene, þæt hy under)fengon
H. (Space for four or five more letters even if H had -rædenne and spelled out
þæt.)

132–41 [Not in Bede or Haymo.]
146–58 [Bede, quoting Augustine, Quæst. in ev. Luc., cap. 34] In villico hoc

hine eft syððan into heora husum;
ac ðas *dæde we sceolon swiðor understandan   *p. 407
on gastlicum andgite, and us tilian freonda,   150
ge on Godes þenum ge on Godes þearfum,
mid urum weldædum, þæt we wunian moton
on ðam ecum eardungstowum æfter urum forðsiþe
mid ðam Godes mannum þe we ure gód doð nu.
Ne sceole we na mid fácne us freond gewyrcan,   155
ac þis is soð bysen hu we sceolon dón
of rihtum gestreonum, swa swa we rædað on bocum:
dælan nu ælmyssan, and don beforan us,
þæt we habban hy eft be hundfealdum us sylfum,
þær þær nán þeof ne mæg ne ne mot hy forstelan,   160
ne nán moððe ne mæg ne nán óm hym derian,
ac hy andsunde þær us beoð gehealdenne.
Ælc man sceal don her be his agenre mæðe;
se þe mare hæbbe, do be his mæðe;
se ðe læsse hæbbe, dó of his lytlan,   165

---

148 innto H.   husum] f. 144, H.   154 nu] nu for godes naman 'on
ðys scortan timan' H (the words over line probably in same hand as those at line
38).   155 sceolon H.   freond] frind altered to frynd H.   gewyrcean H.
159 habbon H.   161 heom H.   162 ansunde H.   gehealdene H.
165 litlan H.

---

quem dominus eiciebat de villicatu, et laudavit eum quod in futurum sibi
prospexerit, non omnia debemus ad imitandum sumere. Non enim aut domino
nostro facienda est in aliquo fraus, ut de ipsa fraude eleemosynas faciamus, aut
eos a quibus recipi volumus in tabernacula æterna tamquam debitores Dei et
Domini nostri fas est intellegi; cum iusti et sancti significentur hoc loco, qui
eos introducant in tabernacula æterna qui necessitatibus suis terrena bona com-
municaverint.
155–8 [Haymo, modifying Augustine, loc. cit.] Ista per similitudinem dicuntur,
ut intellegamus quia si laudari potuit is qui fraudem fecit, eo quod in futurum
sibi prudenter præviderit, multo magis nos laudabiliores erimus, si de propriis
substantiis largas eleemosynas fecerimus: et dum in præsenti vivimus, in futurum
nobis prospexerimus.
157 [Augustine, Sermo CXIII] De iustis laboribus facite eleemosynas: ex eo
quod recte habetis date. [Similarly in later passages Haymo.]
159–62 [Matth. vi. 20] Thesaurizate autem vobis thesauros in cælo: ubi neque
ærugo, neque tinea demolitur, et ubi fures non effodiunt, nec furantur. [Cf.
Augustine, ibid.] Illæ sunt veræ divitiæ, quæ cum habuerimus, perdere non
possumus. . . . Audi Dominum tuum: Thesaurizate, etc. [inexactly quoted].
163–72 [This elaboration not in Bede or Haymo, though Haymo later refers to the
passage from Luke given below.]

þæt nán man ne beo butan *ælmyssan.   *p. 408
Be ðam cwæð se Hælend on oþrum godspelle,
Gelaða to þínum gódum þearfan and wannhale,
blinde and healte, and þu bist eadig;
for ðan þe hy nabbað hwæt hy þe forgeldon;   170
þe 'bið' forgolden witodlice on ðara rihtwisra æriste.
þæt is on Domes-dæge, þonne we of deaðe arisað.
   Zachéus se ríca wæs unrihtwis æt fruman,
ac syððan he underfeng þone fyrmestan cuman,
þone Hælend sylfne. þa sæde Zachéus,   175
Drihten leof, ic wylle dælan mine æhta,
þone healfan dæl þearfum, and þærtoeacan ic wylle
be feowerfealdum forgyldan swa hwæt swa ic reafode.
   And se Hælend þa sǽde sona him to andsware,
Nu todæg is geworden hæl þisum hirede;   180
for þan þe Zachéus swa wæs gerihtwisod
þurh þæs Hælendes tocyme, þe com to his huse.
   Cristes apostolas, swa 'swa' us [cyþ]að béc,
forleton heora æhta ealle *for Criste,   *p. 409
and him swa folgodon swa hwider swa he ferde;   185
and hy hæfdon mid him þa heofonlican speda.
   Sum earm wudewe wearp ænne feorðling

166 man] mann huru H.   169 byst H.   170 forgyldon H.
171 þæra H.   178 forgylda(n) H.   179 andsw(a)re H.   183 cyþað]
sic H; secgað U.   187 wydewe H.   fe(orð)ling H.

167–72 [Luc. xiv. 13] Sed cum facis convivium, voca pauperes, debiles, clau-
dos, et cæcos:
[14] et beatus eris, quia non habent retribuere tibi: retribuetur enim tibi in
resurrectione iustorum.
~~173–82 [Augustine, Sermo CXIII]~~ Sed iam si ... de malo est quod habetis, iam
nolite malum addere, et facite vobis amicos de mammona iniquitatis. Numquid
Zacchæus de bono habebat? ... Maior erat publicanorum. ... Multos presserat,
multis abstulerat, multa congesserat. Intravit domum eius Christus, et venit
salus super domum eius: sic enim ait ipse Dominus, Hodie salus domui huic facta
est. [Augustine now tells the rest of the story with quotations. Bede and Haymo
mention Zacchæus as an example of liberality but say nothing of his earlier unrighteousness.]
   175–80 [Luc. xix. 8] Stans autem Zachæus, dixit ad Dominum: Ecce,
dimidium bonorum meorum, Domine, do pauperibus; et si quid aliquem de-
fraudavi, reddo quadruplum.
   [9] Ait Iesus ad eum: Quia hodie salus domui huic facta est.
   183–203 [Freely elaborated.]
   183–6 [Cf. Matth. xix. 27–29.]
   187–93 [Marc. xii. 42] Cum venisset autem vidua una pauper, misit duo
minuta, quod est quadrans.

betwux oðrum mannum þe wurpon heora ælmyssan
to ðam halgan weofode binnan Hierusalem,
and se Hælend sæde sona be hyre 190
þæt heo mare brohte þonne ænig oðer man,
for þan þe heo brohte ealne hire bigleofan
mid cystigum mode, and Crist hy þa herode.
Se Hælend cwæð eac, Gif hwa sylð drincan
anum þurstigum men huru ceald wæter, 195
þæt he hæfð his mede þære lytlan weldæde;
and se góóda willa, þe wel wyle symble,
is Gode andfenge, swylce he offrige him lác.
þus we sceolon geearnian þa upplican wunu'n'ge
mid þyllicum dædum, urum Drihtne to lofe, 200
mid nanum andsætum facne, ne mid ænigum swicdome,
þæt we gastlice gefyllon þas godspellican word,
be ðam þe ge gehyrdon *her on þissere rædinge. *p. 410
'Hwæt þa heora hlaford herode eft syððan
þone gerefan on his unrihtwisnysse, 205
for ðan þe he snotorlice wið hine sylfne gedyde.'
Vre drihten herað mid beteran herunge
his getreowan wicnere, þe his willan gefremode
on ðam gastlicum tilungum, and him þus to cwið:
Euge serue bone et fidelis, et reliqua: 210

---

188 betwyx *H.*   ælmessan *H.*   189 hierusale*m altered to* ierusale*m H.*
192 hyre *H.*   193 herede *H.*   194 S(e) *H.*   195 h(uru) *H.*
197 (and se gooda) *H.*   symle *H.*   198 (he offrige him lac) *H.*   200 (mid
þyllicum dædum) *H.*   drihtene *H.*   201 and(sætum facne, ne mid ænigum)
H.   202–3 (þas godspellican word, be ðam þe ge) *H.*   203 gehyrdon]
f. 144ᵛ, H.   204 herede *H.*   205 -nesse *H.*   206 snoterlice *H.*
209 to cwið] cwið to *H.*

[*43*] Et convocans discipulos suos, ait illis: Amen dico vobis, quoniam vidua
hæc pauper plus omnibus misit, qui miserunt in gazophylacium.
[*44*] Omnes enim ex eo, quod abundabat illis, miserunt; haec vero de penuria
sua omnia quæ habuit misit totum victum suum.
194–6 [*Matth. x. 42*] Et quicumque potum dederit uni ex minimis istis calicem
aquæ frigidæ tantum in nomine discipuli: amen dico vobis, non perdet mercedem
suam. [*Quoted by Bede, following Augustine.*]
207–9 [*Bede, quoting Augustine*] Si laudari potuit ille a domino cui fraudem
faciebat, quanto amplius placeant Domino Deo, qui secundum eius præceptum
illa opera faciunt.
210–14 [*Matth. xxv. 21, 23*] Ait illi dominus eius: Euge serve bone, et fidelis,
quia super pauca fuisti fidelis, super multa te constituam, intra in gaudium
domini tui.

Eala þu góda þeowa, and me wel getrywe,
þu wære getrywe on lytlum þingum me;
nu ic þe gesette ofer manegum þingum;
gang nu on blisse on þines hlafordes gódum.

'þa worldmen soðlice, þissere worlde bearn,   215
syndon micele snoteran on heora cynryne
þonne þæs leohtes bearn, þæt synd þa geleaffullan.'
þa worldmen cunnon þa worldcundan snoternysse,
and þa yfelan hocas þe se Hælend onscunað,
be ðam is awriten þisum wordum on bocum: 220
Sapientia enim huius mundi *stultitia est apud Deum: *p. 411
þissere worlde wisdom is stuntnyss ætforan Gode.
þu telest to wisdome þæt þu þin gewill hæbbe,
and þu mæge oferdrifan oþerne man mid wó;
ac Crist wile habban unsceððinysse on ús,   225
and þa bilehwitnysse, swa swa he us bebead:
Estote prudentes sicut serpentes, et simplices sicut columbe:
Beoð swa snotere swa swa neddran syndon,
and swa bylehwite swa swa culfran beoð.

Seo næddre is eallra nytena snoterost,   230
and se deofol þurh hy beswac þa frumsceapenan men;
nu sceole we beon snotere wið ðæs deofles swicdomas,
swa swa se Hælend sæde, and besceawian gleawlice
þæs deofles lotwrencas, þæt he us ne forlære.

Seo næddre awurpð ælce geare hire ealdan haman,   235

211 getreowe H.   212 ge(t)riwe H.   214 (ga)ng H.   215 woruldmenn H.   worulde H.   216 mycele H.   cynnrene H.   218 woruldmenn H.   woruldcundan H.   222 worulde H.   223 telst H.   gewill]
will H.   224 mage H.   225 wyle H.   -nesse H.   226 bilewitnesse H.   227 columbæ H.   228 næddran H.   229 bilewite H.
230 ealra H.   232 sceolon H.   235 awyrpð H.

218–26 [Haymo] Filii sæculi prudentiores filiis lucis in generatione sua sunt, quia
cum illi sint callidi, astuti et ingeniosi, deceptores, duplices animo, isti e contrario simplices, humiles, puri, benigni, nescientes malum pro malo reddere. . . .
Qui recte in generatione sua prudentes dicuntur, quia tales non in generatione
Dei, sed in sua computantur, quia prudentia huius sæculi stultitia est apud Deum
(I Cor. iii. 19: Sapientia enim huius mundi, etc.).
227 [Matth. x. 16, as given.]
230–57 [Neither the preceding text nor this exposition of it is in Bede or Haymo.
Ælfric follows in part the exposition cited below.]
235–9 [Augustine, Sermo LXIV on Matth. x. 16] Serpens enim cum fuerit
senectute prægravatus, et senserit pondus vetustatis, coarctat se per cavernam,
et deponit tunicam veterem, ut novus exultet. Imitare illum, christiane. . . .

and bið þonne befangen mid eall-níwum felle;
uton wé swa dón, awurpan ure synna,
and þa yfelan þeawas, and leornian þa gódan,
*þæt we mid Godes gife beon ymbscrydde wiðinnan.   *p. 412
Seo næddre wyle eac bewerian hire heafod,   240
and hy ealle bewindan on em[b]hwyrfte þæs heafdes,
þæt man huru þæs heafdes hentan ne mæge.
Swa we sceolon eac dón, gif we snotere beoð,
ne lætan us nan þing swa leof swa urne Hælend,
þe is ure heafod; and we for his lufan   245
urne lichaman sceolon syllan to deaðe,
gif hit swa micel neod bið, ær we hine wiðsacon
and ure sawle forleoson, þe is selost æhta.
Culfre is swiðe bylewit, and eall butan geallan,
and lufað annysse betwyx hyre geferum,   250
and swiðe unhearmgeorn and unhetol oðrum.
Healdan we þas þeawas, þæt we unhearmgeorne beon,
and butan byternysse betwux gebroðrum symble,
þæt we mannum ne derian mid unrihtum dædum,
ac habban us annysse on ealre rihtwisnysse,   255

---

239 gyfe *H.*   240 hyre *H.*   241 emn- *U*; ymb- *H.*   244 (ne) læton
H.   245 (for) *H.*   247 hyt *H.*   mycel (neod) *H.*   249 (Culfre is) *H.*
bilewite *H*; byle(h)wit(e) *U.*   250–1 (hyre geferum, and) *H.*   251 oðrum]
aðru*m* *H.*   252 Healdon *H.*   (þeawas þæt we unhea)rmgeorne *H.*
253 biternysse betwyx *H.*   253–4 gebroð(rum symble, þæt we mannum) *H.*
254 derion *H.*   255–6 habbon (us annysse on ealre rihtwisnysse, and
læ)ton *H.*

Paulus apostolus tibi dicit: *Exuite vos veterem hominem cum actibus suis, et induite
novum* (*Col. iii. 9, 10; Ephes. iv. 22, 24*).
240–8 [*Augustine*] Imitare illum et in hoc: serva caput tuum. Quid est, serva
caput tuum? Tene apud te Christum. Si forte aliquis vestrum advertit aliquando,
cum voluerit colubrum occidere, quomodo pro capite suo totum corpus obiicit
ictibus ferientis. Illud in se feriri non vult, ubi se novit vitam habere. Et Christus
vita nostra est. . . . Audi et Apostolum: *Caput viri Christus est* (*I Cor. xi. 3*). Qui
ergo Christum servat in se, caput suum servat pro se. [*Ælfric's application in
246–8 is not verbally dependent on Augustine, but the latter treats the text with
reference to martyrs.*]
249–57 [*Augustine*] Amo in columba quod fel non habet. . . . Iam vero quid
opus est commendare multis verbis simplicitatem columbarum? . . . Attende
columbas in societate gaudere: ubique simul volant, simul pascuntur, nolunt
esse solæ, communione gaudent, charitatem servant, gemitibus amoris mur-
murant; osculis filios generant. Nam quando columbæ, quod plerumque adver-
timus, inter se rixantur de cellulis suis, quodam modo pacata contentio est. . . .
Columba amat et quando rixatur; lupus odit et quando blanditur.

and lætan gehwæne habban þæt þe his is mid rihte;
þonne hæbbe we *þa bylewitnysse þe se Hælend sylf tæhte.

*p. 413

'þa sæde se Hælend 'eft' syððan hym þus to:
Wyrcað eow freonda of ðam unrihtan welan,
þæt hy underfón eow on eowrum forðsiðe   260
to him on ðam ecum eardungstowum eft.'
þa unrihtan welan syndon witodlice
þæt weoruldlice feoh, on ðam þa unrihtwisan menn
[besettað heora hiht, and on þam hopiað;
ac þa rihtwisan menn] awændað heora feoh   265
to heora lifes neodum, and lybbað be ðam feo,
and habbað heora hyht to þam heofonlicum spedum,
to þam ecum þingum on eornost swaðeah.
Se þe ælmyssan dæleð of ðam eorðlicum feo,
and of [þam] sceortum welum þissere worulde,   270
Godes þeowum and his þearfum, God sylf him forgylt eft,
swa þæt he wunu'n'ge hæfð on heofonan rice
mid þam þe he dælde and gedyde his gód.
Ealswa þa lareowas þe lærað Godes folc,
and manega gebetað mid heora gebysnungum,   275
magon witan gewis þæt hy wunian moton
on þære ecan *myrhðe mid ðam ælmihtigan Gode,   *p. 414

256 (m)id, f. 145, H, where another scribe takes over from the first for two folios.
257 bilewitnesse H.   258 heom H.   260 eow] eow eft H.   261 eft]
om. H; cf. 37–38 supra.   263 woruldlice H.   þa] om. H.   menn] om. H.
264–5 besettað . . . menn] sic H; om. U.   265 awendað H.   267 hiht H.
heofonlican H.   269 dælð H.   eorðlicum] heofonlican (!) H.   270 þam]
sic H; om. U.   272 heofenan H.   274 Eall swa H.   275 geby-
senungum H.   276 gewiss H.

262–8 [Bede, quoting Augustine, Quæst. in ev. Luc.] Mammonam iniquitatis
ob hoc appellat istam pecuniam quam possidemus ad tempus, quia mammona
divitiæ interpretantur. Nec sunt istæ divitiæ nisi iniquis, qui in eis constituunt
spem atque copiam beatitudinis suæ. A iustis vero cum hæc possidentur, est
quidem ista pecunia, sed non sunt illis divitiæ, nisi cælestes et spiritales, quibus
indigentiam suam spiritaliter supplentes, exclusa egestate miseriæ, beatitudinis
copia ditabuntur.
269–78 [Bede] Si autem hi qui præbent eleemosynam de iniquo mammona
faciunt sibi amicos a quibus in æterna tabernacula recipiantur, quanto magis hi
qui spiritales largiuntur epulas, qui dant conservis cibaria in tempore suo,
certissima debent spe summæ retributionis erigi? [Cf. Jerome, Epist. CXXI. 6]
Si ergo iniquitas bene dispensata vertitur in iustitiam, quanto magis sermo
divinus, in quo nulla est iniquitas, qui et apostolis creditus est, si bene fuerit
dispensatus, dispensatores suos levabit in cælum!

for þan þe hy getreowlice tilodon heora hlaforde.

Se Hælend sylf sǽde on sumere oðre stowe,
Se ðe on lytlum þinge bið his hlaforde getrywe,   280
se bið him getrywe on ðam maran þingum;
and se ðe ungetrywe bið on þam læssan þinge,
se bið ungetrywe on ðam maran þinge.
Lytel þing is geteald þises lifes ryne
wið ða ecan worulde, þe ne wurð na geendod.   285
þa woruldcundan þing syndon witodlice læssan
þonne þa gastlican, þe is Godes sylfes lár,
þæt is se halga wísdóm, þe us simble tiht
up to urum Scyppende, þe us gesceop to mannum.
Se ðe on woruldþingum wurð ungetrywe,   290
ne wurð he on þam gastlicum Gode 'getrywe',
þæt he ða heofonlican pund holdlice dæle.
Getrywsige us se Hælend þurh þone Halgan Gast,
þæt we his willan gewyrcan moton;
þam sy á wuldor on écnysse, amen.   295

278 getrywlice tiledon *H.*   280 byd (*sic*) *H.*   281 marum *H.*
285 wyrð *H.*   287 þa] *om. H.*   288 halga] *om. H.*   symble tyhð *H.*
290 wyrð *H.*   291 wurð] wyrcð (*!*) *H.*   294 gewyrcean *H.*   295 si
H.   wuldor] wuldor and wyrðmynt *H.*

279–92 [*Luc. xvi. 10: i.e. the verse following Ælfric's pericope*] Qui fidelis est in
minimo, et in maiori fidelis est; et qui in modico iniquus est, et in maiori iniquus
est. [*Haymo*] Audiat ergo hoc dives, audiat Christianus, discat tribuere minima,
ut possit accipere magna. Quia *qui in minimo fidelis est*, ut Dominus ait, *et in
magno fidelis erit*. Discat dare transitoria, ut mereatur accipere æterna. [*Bede*]
Ipso iudice attestante, *qui fidelis est in minimo*, id est, in pecunia cum paupere
participanda, *et in maiore fidelis est*, illo videlicet actu, quo specialiter adhærere
Creatori, et unus cum eo spiritus effici desiderat. [*Jerome, directly after the passage quoted above*] Quam ob rem sequitur: *qui fidelis est in minimo*, hoc est in
carnalibus, *et in multis fidelis erit*, id est in spiritalibus. *Qui autem in parvo iniquus
est*, ut non det fratribus ad utendum, quod a Deo pro omnibus est creatum, iste
et in spiritali pecunia [*cf.* 292] dividenda iniquus erit. . . . 'Sin autem,' inquit,
'carnales divitias, quæ labuntur, non bene dispensetis, veras æternasque
divitias doctrinæ Dei [*cf.* 287] quis credet vobis?'

NOTES

6, 89. By using *sceolde* Ælfric emphasizes the fact that in this parable
Jesus does not say whether the charges against the steward are true or
false. See Glossary, *sceolan*, b.

23, 130. *oman.* This word was cited by Napier, *COEL*, from MS. U.
He recognized its derivation from Lat. *ama (hama)* 'a water-bucket', and

its relation to mod. German *Ohm*, Dutch *aam*, which came to be applied to a liquid measure for wine of about forty gallons. See *OED*, *aam*, and Glossary, *ōme*.

44 sq. *and þærtoeacan us forgifð ure neode on life.* Cf. xv. 119. There, as here, Ælfric adds this benefit to the list given in his source.

55. *inmede.* Cited by Napier from MS. U, as above. Evidently a compound of *in* and a mutated derivative of *mod.* For other occurrences see Glossary.

73–83. This is perhaps Ælfric's most elaborate alliterative list of offences. There are earlier prose lists, taken directly from St. Paul (*Gal.* v. 19–21 and *I Cor.* vi. 9 sq.), in *De Auguriis*, *LS* xvii. 24–27 and 34–44, and an alliterative list, also based on St. Paul but less strictly, in *Letania Maiore*, *CH* II. xxi, pp. 330, 332. This ends with a full comment on eating at improper times, though the compound *untima-æt* is recorded only here (see Glossary). Still another list, containing in the middle four half-lines with alliterating pairs of nouns, occurs at the end of Ælfric's addition to *CH* I. xvii for the second Sunday after Easter, which is to be published by Dr. Clemoes; and an alliterative list of offenders is in our xi. 375 sqq. Wulfstan made frequent use of such lists and was apparently never tired of contriving ways to vary their form and expression. See Bethurum's *Wulfstan*, vii. 128 sqq.; viiic. 158 sqq.; xa. 11 sqq.; xc. 79 sqq.; xiii. 92 sqq. Ælfric's simple reminder about keeping Sundays and mass-days and going to church may be contrasted with the crude violence of the 'Sunday letter', versions of which are in Napier's *Wulfstan*, nos. xliii–xlv and lvii. (See Jost, *Wulfstanstudien*, pp. 221 sqq.) In xix. 119–30 Ælfric deals with the related question, how often the laity may and should partake of the eucharist.

117 sq. Ælfric translates this proverb in exactly the same words in his *Letter to Wulfgeat*, Assmann i. 229 sq. (p. 9). This was noted by Napier in his transcription of the homily from MS. U. Cf. note on xv. 171 sq.

163–98. With this whole passage on almsgiving compare *CH* I. 580 sqq. (part of the homily for St. Andrew on *Matth.* iv. 18–22), where Ælfric treats fully all the examples given here: first the apostles, then Zacchæus, the poor widow, and the hypothetical giver of a cup of cold water. Only two of these examples were in Ælfric's immediate sources for the present homily, and these sources do not bring out, as does his own earlier homily, that each man is to give according to his means (163). This principle and the four examples are from Gregory, *Hom. in Evang.* v, *PL* lxxvi. 1093 sq. The two examples in lines 187–98 (the widow and the giver of water) occur also at *CH* II. 106/8 sqq. (which reappears as part of Napier lv, a compilation, p. 287/12 sqq.).

174. *he underfeng þone fyrmestan cuman.* This characterization of Jesus as the foremost stranger, which is not in Ælfric's immediate sources, has interesting connexions. It depends for part of its effect on one of the acts of mercy enumerated in the speech at the Last Judgement: in Ælfric's translation, 'Eac ic wæs cuma, and ge me underfengon' (*Matth.* xxv. 35, as at xi. 414). The excitement naturally attending the idea of entertaining God in the guise of a stranger is likely to emerge whenever, in the gospels, Jesus visits anyone. Ælfric had earlier paraphrased from Augustine (*Sermo* ciii, as recognized by Förster, *Anglia* XVI. 34) a passage on the entertainment of Jesus by Mary and Martha, in which the idea of receiving God as a stranger is already put into relation with *Matthew* xxv. The passage occurs in the homily on the Assumption of the Virgin, *CH* II. 438:

> Nu ðencað sume men þæt ða wif wæron gesælige þæt hi swilcne cuman underfengon. Soð þæt is, gesælige hi wæron, ac swaþeah ne ðurfe we ceorian . . .; forðan ðe he cwæð, 'Swa hwæt swa ge doð on minum naman anum ðam læstum, þæt ge doð me sylfum.'

Now this very passage is adapted to Zacchæus in Brotanek I, Ælfric's extra homily for the dedication of a church, which ought by its largely non-rhythmical style to have been composed very soon after the *Catholic Homilies*. The passage begins (Brotanek, p. 13):

> Nu cwið sum man on his geþance, þæt þes Zacheus gesælig wære þurh swylcne cuman, þæt he moste þam Ælmihtigan mid his mettum þenian. Soð þæt is, gesælig he wæs; ac swaþeah ne þurfe we forþi ceorian. . . .

The resemblance of the two passages as a whole is so great that it was one of Brotanek's strongest arguments on behalf of Ælfric's authorship of the dedication homily, especially since the main source of the latter (Bede's commentary on *Luke* xix. 1–10) contains only an oblique hint of the idea. Another facet of this idea, namely the reception of God as a spiritual guest in the heart, is set forth in *John* xiv. 23, on which Ælfric had commented at some length in *Letania Maiore* (*CH* II. 316). He came back to it in our x. 38 sqq., where the opening words again echo the passage on Mary and Martha: 'Gesælig bið se mann þe swilce cuman underfehð.'

176–80. With these lines compare the following passages from Ælfric's earlier treatments of the story of Zacchæus:

> (*a*) Drihten, efne ic todæle healfne dæl minra goda ðearfum, and swa hwæt swa ic mid facne berypte, þæt ic wylle be feowerfealdum forgyldan. Drihten him to cwæð, Nu to-dæg is ðisum hirede hæl gefremmed. [*CH* I. 582.]

> (*b*) Ic wille nu, min Drihten, wædlum and þearfum
> dælan healfe mine æhta, ealles þæs þe ic hæbbe,
> and gif ic hwæne bereafode unrihtlice oð ðis,
> ic wylle þæt be feowerfealdum mid freondrædene forgildan.
> þa cwæþ se Hælend sona to Zachee þus:
> Nu to-dæg is gefremmed þisum hirede hæl. [Brotanek, p. 5.]

The first of these passages is non-rhythmical; the second, unlike the greater part of the homily in which it occurs, is rhythmical. Curiously, the alliterative pattern of the last line, in Brotanek and here, is less regular than in the early, non-rhythmical version; but Ælfric achieves much greater rhythmic force by putting the alliterating nouns in the second half of the line, most of all by the full periodic suspension of the Brotanek version.

219. *hocas*. This metaphorical use is not clearly recognized in the dictionaries until a much later period. See Glossary.

235. *haman*. This somewhat specialized use of *hama* for the slough of a snake was cited by Napier, *COEL*, from MS. U.

251. *unhearmgeorn and unhetol*. These words also were cited by Napier from MS. U, as above.

273. *mid þam þe*, 'with those to whom'. Cf. 154.

279. *on sumere oðre stowe*. This may seem an odd way of referring to the verse that immediately follows the pericope Ælfric is expounding. Was he led by Haymo's way of introducing it into momentary forgetfulness of where it occurs? He could hardly have forgotten for long if he had consulted either Jerome or Bede, as I am quite sure he did. Probably, then, he only felt that a more specific reference was needless, or might even be distracting.

XVII

DOMINICA XII POST OCTAVAS PENTECOSTEN

Marc. vii. 31–37

THIS composite homily celebrates four of Christ's miracles. More than half of it is devoted to an exposition of the miracle described in the pericope for the day, but this is followed by accounts of three other miracles, two of them supplied with a few sentences of exposition, the third restricted to the gospel narrative. The two miracles in the middle are presented in a text that was once an independent composition of Ælfric's and a look at its earlier history may be enlightening.

In Thorpe's MS. (ULC Gg. 3. 28, our K), which alone has preserved Ælfric's Second Series as a separate entity, the homily for the third Sunday after Pentecost is followed by a short piece entitled *Alia Narratio de Evangelii Textu*, evidently intended to be read on the same occasion, though Thorpe gave it a separate number (II. xxvii). It also follows the third Sunday in MSS. C, D, E, and F. This piece contains a fairly close translation of two gospel passages (*Matth.* viii. 23–27 and *Marc.* v. 1–15, 18–20) describing Christ's stilling of the tempest on the Sea of Galilee and his subsequent healing of the man possessed by a legion of devils, each passage being followed by a very brief comment on its significance. Ælfric introduces these accounts with the following explanation:

> Mine gebroðru, we wyllað eow gereccan sume Cristes wundra, to getrymmincge eoweres geleafan. We sind gecnæwe þæt we hit forgymeleasodon on ðam dæge þe mann þæt godspel rædde, ac hit mæg eow nu fremian swa micclum swa hit ða mihte.

Now the only reasons I can discover why these miracles are treated as a pendant to the third Sunday are, first, that the main homily for that day (on the feast to which the invited guests would not come, *Luc.* xiv. 16–24) is rather short, and secondly, that near the end of it miracles are mentioned as one of the ways by which God invites us to his feast (Thorpe II. 376/29 sq.). Hence Ælfric might well have considered finding another resting-place for the *Alia Narratio*, though not, I think, the one chosen in MS. M, where it is assigned to the fourth Sunday after Epiphany, the day on which its first gospel-text, *Matth*. viii. 23–27, was to be read. Doubtless that is the day to which Ælfric refers in the prefatory remarks quoted above; but the *Alia Narratio* is too short for a full homily and too even-handed in its treatment of the successive miracles to be appropriate for the day.

It is probable, then, that Ælfric left the *Alia Narratio* alone until he incorporated it in the present homily. In doing so he very properly omitted the apologetic second sentence quoted above (as M had done also), for here, instead of being a somewhat arbitrarily attached pendant, it is part of an intelligible design. The pericope for the thirteenth Sunday is itself an account of a miracle, and Ælfric gives it a full enough exposition to meet the requirements of the day. But now, by adding the *Alia Narratio*, he gives preeminence to the general theme of Christ's miracles above the particular themes appropriate to the one miracle of the day. That he does this with full awareness is indicated by the introductory passage on the miracles (8–17), which was hardly needed as a prologue to the first miracle alone, and by the extra, fourth miracle (*Luc*. iv. 31–37) he has added at the very end. This final passage, incidentally, is so clearly Ælfric's and so closely linked with the *Alia Narratio* that there can be little doubt of his responsibility for the entire compilation.[1]

Our only surviving witness, unfortunately, for the later portions of the homily is H, into which it was inserted by the interpolator; and H is not only damaged by fire but not wholly reliable as an authority for Ælfric's compositions. There is reason, however, to believe that U, which supports H for homilies XIII–XVI, once supported it for XVII also. U is still intact from Easter to the tenth Sunday after Pentecost, but it breaks off abruptly in the midst of the homily for the eleventh Sunday (*CH* I. XXVIII). Within these limits it gives at least one homily for every Sunday, including the

---

[1] We may deduce further that when Ælfric thus disposed of the *Alia Narratio* he had no intention of composing a homily for the fourth Sunday after Epiphany —at least not a homily on *Matth*. viii. 23–27. No Ælfrician homily for this day has in fact been found.

homily for the third Sunday after Pentecost to which the *Alia Narratio* was formerly appended. But the *Alia Narratio* is not there. The chances are that in U's exemplar, and in U itself when it was complete, the *Alia Narratio* had become a part of the homily for the thirteenth Sunday after Pentecost.

There is little to be gained by fixing a date for the homily, since it does not allude to contemporary matters. Presumably it belongs with homilies XIII–XVI as a partial fulfilment of Ælfric's effort, during the latter part of his career, to round out his series of homilies for the Sundays after Pentecost.[1]

Ælfric's sources for the exposition of his main text, *Marc.* vii. 31–37, are of course to be distinguished from his sources for the brief passages of exposition in the *Alia Narratio*. For the main text he relies chiefly on Bede's Homily II. 6 (ed. Hurst). Bede himself had apparently assigned this homily to Holy Saturday, but in the homiliary of Paulus Diaconus it was assigned first to mid-August (*I Post Laurentii*) and later to the thirteenth Sunday after Pentecost, as likewise in the collection of Smaragdus.[2] The only readily available rival to Bede's homily was Haymo's Homily CXXIV, for the same Sunday on the same text. This Ælfric certainly used, but less frequently than might be expected from his practice in some other homilies. I have found reason to quote Haymo only parenthetically, as it were, for the passages beginning at 106, 113, and 187.

At one point (78–81) Ælfric apparently consulted Bede's commentary on *Mark* for geographical information about Decapolis. The substance of Bede's statement comes, indeed, from Jerome's *Liber de Situ et Nominibus Locorum Hebræorum*, and is repeated in Haymo's homily, but the phrase *ad orientem* appears only in Bede's commentary, and Ælfric's *on eastdæle* (78) seems to depend on it. If Ælfric did in fact turn to Bede's commentary he found, and apparently rejected, the curious contention about the scene of the action to which I have alluded under Sources at line 78.

It is uncertain which of several authorities Ælfric turned to for his interpretation of *Matth.* viii. 23–27 in the *Alia Narratio* section. Four authorities were readily available to him: Jerome's commentary on *Matthew*, which nevertheless cannot have contributed more than one detail (*reðran*, 213), and most probably contributed even this indirectly; a homily for the fourth Sunday after Epiphany

---

[1] See XIII, introduction, pp. 493–4.
[2] On the homiliary of Paulus see the Introduction, pp. 156–7.

ascribed to Origen[1] in the homiliary of Paulus Diaconus (original version and Migne's as well); a homily for the same Sunday by Haymo (no. xx); and Bede's commentary on the parallel text, *Marc.* iv. 35–40. Origen's homily supplies all the details that are essential to Ælfric's interpretation, but it resembles Bede's commentary in a few points and Haymo's homily, for which it was enthusiastically quarried, in many. For the sequence of thought and the expression I have found Bede and Haymo alternately a little closer to Ælfric than Origen is, but I am not sure that a certain overplus of enthusiasm in Ælfric for the display of divine power was not generated by the eloquence of Origen. It is inherently probable that Ælfric had read this sermon.

For *Marc.* v. 1–15, 18–20 Ælfric depended mainly on Bede's commentary. A brief bit of information about the size of a legion (*eorod*) at 249 sqq. is probably recollected, as Max Förster surmised, from a passage in Smaragdus that had been consulted for another homily. (See Sources, 249.)

The final miracle (*Luc.* iv. 31–37), being treated simply as a narrative, has only the Bible for authority.

It may seem strange that Ælfric should insert an old composition, mainly in ordinary prose, into the midst of a homily written in his fully matured rhythmical style; but comparable juxtapositions are in fact very common: witness *LS* xii and xvii; our xix and xxx; and the rhythmic additions, numbered xxvi–xxviii, to homilies in ordinary prose. It should be observed, however, that the *Alia Narratio* is partly rhythmical at several points where I have maintained the prose way of printing it, and so regularly rhythmical at the end that I have arranged it in metrical lines.

---

[1] Falsely attributed to Bede by Martène and printed as his by Giles, but now included in *Origenes Werke*, ed. E. Benz and K. Klostermann (Leipzig, 1941), XII. 256–62.

DOMINICA XII POST OCTAVAS PENTECOSTEN

Ðæs Hælendes eard wæs on Iudea lande,
Galileiscre scire, þa þa he her on life wæs,
on þære byrig Nazareth; ac he wæs geboren
on þære byrig Bethleem, swa swa bec secgað.
Ða ferde he geond eall þære foresædan scire,   5
to eallum samnungum, symle lærende þæt folc,
⁊ bodigende godspell ⁊ Godes rice mannum,
⁊ ealle gehælde þe untrume wæron,
⁊ he ælce adle ⁊ ælce untrumnysse adræfde
of eallum þam mannum þe him mihton to cuma(n).   10
His hlisa þa asprang to Sirian lande,
ofer eall þæt rice, þæt is swiþ(e) rum land;
⁊ him man gebrohte þa to fela bedridan menn,
⁊ (þa) monaðseocan, ⁊ þa sylfan wodan,
⁊ on manegum adlum misli(ce ge)swencte;   15
⁊ se soþa Hælend gehælde hi ealle,
⁊ him þa (: : : : : : : : : : : :) folc gehwanon.
   Nu segð us se godspellere þe þi(ss godspell ge)sette
þe nu gebirað to þissere mæssan,
MARC(VS : : : : : : :, se þe) wæs martyr for Criste,   20

Text based on H (Cotton Vitellius C. v), ff. 172–5. For lines 1–202, 277–314 this copy is unique. Lines 203–76 have been interpolated from the *Catholic Homilies* and are collated with the six manuscripts listed at line 203. The numerous lacunæ in H which have resulted from the fire of 1731 are indicated by round brackets. When what is missing seems reasonably certain the necessary letters are supplied within the brackets. Otherwise the approximate number of letters is indicated by colons, and conjectural readings, if any, are put at the bottom of the page.

1 *MS. has first three words in capitals.*   17 (fyligde micel)?   20 MARC . .]
sic MS. (VS gehaten, se þe)?

SOURCES. 5–17 [*Matth. iv. 23*] Et circuibat Iesus totam Galilæam, docens in synagogis eorum, et prædicans evangelium regni, et sanans omnem languorem et omnem infirmitatem in populo.
   [*24*] Et abiit opinio eius in totam Syriam, et obtulerunt ei omnes male habentes, variis languoribus et tormentis comprehensos, et qui dæmonia habebant, et lunaticos, et paralyticos, et curavit eos.
   [*25*] Et secutæ sunt eum turbæ multæ de Galilæa, et Decapoli, et de Ierosolymis, et de Iudæa, et de trans Iordanem.

þæt ure Hælend be(: : : : : : : : : : : : : : : : :) sæ,
farende fram gemærum (: : : : : : : : : : : : : : : :
: : : : : : : : :)*eiscan, on þam sælande   *f. 172ᵛ
swa o(: : : : : : : : : : : :te)ne tyn (burhsci)ra.

Ða gebrohte man him to, tomiddes þam folce,   25
ænne dumne mann, 7 se wæs eac swilce deaf,
7 bædon þone Hælend þæt he hine hrepode
mid (: : : : : : : : : : : : : : :)um; 7 se Hælend sona
gelædde þone mannan ut of þære (meniu).

He dyde þa his fingras innto his earan,   30
7 mid his halwendan spatle hys tungan hrepode,
7 beseah to heofenum, 7 sæde mid geomerunge
to þam duman menn þis an dyrne word,
Effeta: þæt is on Englisc, to geopenigenne;
þæt his earan wurdon 7 his muð geopenode.   35

Hwæt þa, sona wurdon his earan geopenode,
7 his tungan bend wearð unbunden eac,
7 he rihtlice spræc mid his agenum gereorde.

Ða bebead se Hælend þam þe hine brohton
þæt hi hit ne sædon nanum menn nateshwon;   40
ac hi þæs þe swiþor hit sædon mid wundrunge,
7 cyddon his mærþa mannum, þuss secgende:
Wel he gedyde ealle þing þurh his wundorlican mihte:
he gedyde þæt þa deafan mihton wel gehyran,
7 he gedyde þam dumban þæt hi mihton sprecan.   45

Ðiss godspell is nu gesæd þuss sceortlice on Englisc;

21–24 *See note.*   24 swa o(n bocum synd gehate)ne? *Cf. line* 80.   28 mid (his halwendum fingr)um? (*Cf. line* 121.)   29 (meniu) *partially visible; cf. line* 114.   42 *MS has half-line point after* mærþa *instead of grammatical point after* mannum.

21–45 [*Marc. vii. 31*] Et iterum exiens de finibus Tyri, venit per Sidonem ad Mare Galilææ inter medios fines Decapoleos.

[*32*] Et adducunt ei surdum, et mutum, et deprecabantur eum, ut imponat illi manum.

[*33*] Et apprehendens eum de turba seorsum, misit digitos suos in auriculas eius: et expuens, tetigit linguam eius:

[*34*] et suspiciens in cælum, ingemuit, et ait illi: Ephphetha, quod est adaperire.

[*35*] Et statim apertæ sunt aures eius, et solutum est vinculum linguæ eius, et loquebatur recte.

[*36*] Et præcepit illis ne cui dicerent. Quanto autem eis præcipiebat, tanto magis plus prædicabant:

[*37*] et eo amplius admirabantur, dicentes: Bene omnia fecit: et surdos fecit audire, et mutos loqui.

nu wylle we geedlæcan eft þa ylcan word
þæs halgan godspelles, 7 eow geopenian
þæt gastlice andgit be endebyrdnesse
þære haligan lare, mid hyre getacnungum.   50
Tirus 7 Sidon syndon twa burga,
be þam spræc se Hælend on sumere stowe hwilon,
þa þa he cidde swiþe þam burgum
þe he on geworhte his wundra 7 tacna,
(þæt) hi noldon gelyfan for his liflicum tacnum,   55
ne hi sylfe gerihtlæcan for his soþum wundrum.
He cwæð to þære byrig þe hatte Corozaim,
7 to anre oðre byrig, Bethsaida gehaten,
Wa þe, Corozaim; wa þe, Bethsaida:
gyf swylce wundra wurdon gefremode   60
on Tyro 7 Sidone swa swa syndon
on eow gefremode, gefyrn hi gedydon
mycele dædbote on hæran 7 on axon.
Nu secge ic to soþan þæt sumera þinga
byþ læsse wite on Domes-dæg Tyro 7 Sidone   65
þonne eow sylfum beo, þe gesawon mi(ne) wundra.
  Se Hælend genealæhte to þam sælande
to þam worigendum (yþ)um, ðe hæfdon getacnunge
þ[ære] unstæððignesse þæs stuntan men(nisce)s
þe butan geleafan leofedon oð þæt,   70
of þam he wolde habban (: : : : : :)e to his gyfe,
to þære miltsunge his micclan cystignesse,
for (þan þe : : : : : : : : : :), swa swa þæt godspell us segð,

---

69 þære] þa *MS.*   71 (gehwæn)e?

53–65 [*Matth. xi. 20*] Tunc coepit exprobare civitatibus, in quibus factæ
sunt plurimæ virtutes eius, quia non egissent pænitentiam.
  [*21*] Væ tibi Corozain, væ tibi Bethsaida: quia, si in Tyro et Sidone factæ essent
virtutes quæ factæ sunt in vobis, olim in cilicio et cinere pænitentiam egissent.
  [*22*] Verumtamen dico vobis: Tyro et Sidoni remissius erit in die iudicii,
quam vobis.
  67–72 [*Bede, Hom. II. 6*] Veniente in carne Domino, exceptis paucis de Iudæa
fidelibus, totus pene mundus ab agnitione et confessione veritatis surdus erraret
et mutus. Sed *ubi abundavit peccatum, superabundavit gratia (Rom. v. 20)*. Venit
namque Dominus ad mare Galilææ, ubi noverat ægrotare quem sanaret. Venit
suæ gratia pietatis ad tumentia, turbida, et instabilia gentium corda, in quibus
noverat esse qui ad suam gratiam pertinerent.]*Ælfric develops the idea independently.*]
  73–75a [*Bede*] Et bene inter medios fines Decapoleos ad mare Galilææ,
ubi ægrotum sanaret, venisse perhibetur, quia relicto ob perfidiam populo qui

þæt he gegaderode þa Go(des bearn : : : : : : :)
þe wæron tostencte, to his staðolfæstnesse 75
(: : : : : : : : : : : : : : :), þæt hi lif hæfdon on him,
se þe ure lif is 7 eac þæra (: : : : : : : : : :).
(: : : : : : : : : : ge)haten þa on eastdæle,
begeondan þære (: : : : : : : : : : : : :),
(: : : : : : : : : : :) bocum, þæt is Tyn Burhscira, 80
to *(þam) com se Hælend, sw(a swa se)gð þiss (godspell), *f. 173
7 he þær ge(hælde) þurh his halgan hrepung(e
þ)one deafan 7 þone dumban, 7 ge(dyde) hine halne,
swa swa he ælcne dyde þe him to genealæhte.
Ð(es deafa) mann getacnode 7 þes dumba witodlice 85
eall Adames cynn, þe ad(ea)fode swiþe
þurh þære næddran word, þe wæron us deadl(ice)
on þære forgægednysse ongean Godes bebod,
þæt mancynn n(olde) mid geleafan gehiran
þa halgan Godes word to his wissunge (þonne). 90
Mancynn adumbode eac fram his Drihtenes herungum
syþþan (he) æne gespræc his agen bepæcend,
7 wið hine motode mid mycelre dyrstignysse,
for þan þe hit is yfel, 7 mid attre gemenged,
þæt se mann motige wið þone manfullan deofol, 95
swa swa git doð foroft dryme(n) 7 wiccan
on heora scincræfte, to beswicenne swa
þa ungesælige [sic] me(n) þe to him secað.

74 Go(des bearn on anum)? 78 An eard wæs ge)haten? 79 (ea
Iordanen : : : :)? 80 (Decapolis on)? 81 þam, godspell *partially
visible.* 89 n(olde) *seems likelier than* n(e mihte). 90 (þonne) *or* (þa)?
Right-hand margin uneven.

decalogi mandata acceperat, exteras venit ad gentes, ut sicut Ioannes ait, *Filios
Dei qui erant dispersi, congregaret in unum (Ioan. xi. 52).*
78–81 [*Bede, In Marc. vii. 31*] Decapolis est (ut ipso nomine probatur) regio
decem urbium trans Iordanen ad orientem. [*Haymo, Hom. CXXIV, repeats
this in substance but omits* ad orientem, *according to the text in Migne. Ælfric
seems to ignore or avoid the ensuing contention in Bede's commentary that the action
takes place in Galilee across the water from Decapolis. Bede's homily has only the
allegorical interpretation in the preceding quotation, but it implies that the action
is in Decapolis.*]
85–90 [*Bede, Hom. II. 6*] Surdus ille et mutus . . . genus designat humanum,
in his qui ab errore diabolicæ deceptionis divina merentur gratia liberari.
Obsurduit namque homo ab audiendo vitæ verbo, postquam mortifera serpentis
verba contra Deum tumidus audivit.
91–93 [*Bede*] Mutus a laude Conditoris effectus est, ex quo cum seductore
colloquium habere præsumpsit.

Ne mihte na se deafa ne se dumba abiddan
þone halgan Hælend his agene hæle;　　　　　　　　100
ac his magas bædon, þe hine gebrohton to Criste,
þæt he hine gehælde þurh his halgan mihte;
7 he mildelice þam mannum getyþode,
for þan þe he eall-god is, 7 æfre wel wille
eallum rihtgeþancodum þe on hine truwiað.　　　　105
Swa we sceolon eac dón, gif sum ure freonda
ne mæg þurh hine sylfne secan æt his Drihten(e)
his sawle læcedom mid soðre andetnysse;
we sceolon him fulstan 7 him fore gebiddan,
7 mid Godes lare gelome hine tyhtan,　　　　　　110
þæt he hi(s) sawle hæle gesece æt his Drihtene,
þæt he gehyran mage 7 herian his Scyppend.
Ðiss halige godspell segð þæt 'se Hælend sona
gelædde þone mann ut of þære meniu,'
for þan þe he hine alædde of þæs folces gehlide,　　115
þæt he hine awende fram his ærran gewunan
to hi(s) halgum bebodum mid gehyrsumnesse,
þæt he on godum þeawum Gode gelicode,
7 to Godes wegum awende hine sylfne.
'He dyde þa his fingras innto his earan.'　　　　　120

99–102 [*Bede*] Quia ipse surdus Salvatorem agnoscere, mutus rogare nequibat, adducunt eum amici, et pro eius salute Domino supplicant.

106–12 [*Bede, partially*] Sic nimirum, sic in spiritali necesse est curatione geratur, ut si quis humana industria ad auditum confessionemque veritatis converti non potest, divinæ pietatis offeratur aspectibus, atque ad sanandum eum supernæ manus flagitetur auxilium. [*Perhaps also Haymo*] Tales ut auditum et loquelam spiritalem recipere possint, a magistris et doctoribus Ecclesiæ Domino adducuntur.

113–19 [*Ælfric simplifies suggestions from Bede and Haymo: Bede*] Prima namque salutis spes est, quemlibet assuetos vitiorum tumultus turbasque deserere, et sic ad suscipienda sanitatis munera humiliter caput inclinare. . . . At qui miserante et adiuvante Domino turbidam priscæ conversationis vitam mutavit, qui inspirationem divinæ gratiæ corde concepit, qui verbo doctrinæ cælestis confessionem veræ didicit fidei, restat ut confestim optata sanitatis gaudia consequatur. [*Haymo*] Sed prius ipsum a turba separat, et postea sanat, ut intelligat genus humanum se aliter sanitatem animæ non posse recipere, nisi prius pristinos errores relinquens, a turba immundorum spirituum, et tumultu vitiorum sese redderet alienum.

120–9 [*Bede*] Digitos quippe surdo in auriculas ut audiat mittit, cum per dona gratiæ spiritalis diu non credentes ad auditum sui verbi convertit. . . . Per digitos namque Domini Spiritus Sancti dona significari et ipse docet dicens, *Si ego in digito Dei eiicio dæmonia* (*Luc. xi. 20*): quod alius evangelista manifestius ponit, *Si ego in spiritu Dei eiicio dæmonia* (*Matth. xii. 28*). [*Bede's quotations seem to*

Ðæs Hælendes fingras, þe halwende syndo(n),
getacniað soðlice þa seofonfealdan gyfa
þæs Halgan Gastes, þe ure heortan onlihtað;
7 þurh þa ylcan gyfe he onlihte his mod,
þæt he mih(te) gehyran þa halwendan lare,   125
7 andgit swa habban þurh þone Ha(l)gan Gast;
7 se Hælend adræfde, þurh þone ylcan Gast,
þa egesl(ican) deofla of þam gedrehton mannu*m*,
7 he him gewitt forgeaf him (syl)fum to wyrðmynte.
   'Mid his halwendan spatle he hrep(ode his) tungan,'   130
þæt he sprecan mihte, 7 mannu*m* eac cyþan
(: : : : : : : : : : : : :) him mid menniscum gesceade,
þæt ælc mann sceol(de, : : : : : : : : : : : :) onliht,
his geleafan andettan oþrum me(: : : : : : : : : : : : : : : : :).
   '(He be*sea)h to heofonu*m*, 7 sæde mid geom(erunge *f. 173ᵛ
to) þam dum(ba)n menn þis (an dyrne word):   136
Effeta: þæt (is) on Englisc, (to) geopenigenn(e).'
To heofonum (he) beseah mid swiþlicere geomerunge,
for þan þe he gesceop him sylf (: : : : : : : : : : :)
to heofonlicu*m* þingu*m*, 7 him hearde ofhreow   140
þæt we swa (: : : : : : : :) þa befeollon þanon
(on) þa eorðlican þing ealles to utlice.
(He ge)swutelode eac mid his sylfes geomerunge
þæt we sceolon gewilnian (þære h)eofonlican wununge,
to þære þe we wæron geworhte æt fruman,   145
(mid) modes geomerunge 7 mid manegu*m* tearu*m*,
for þan þe swa mycel þing (m)ot beon geearnod
mid mycelre gewilnunge 7 þæs modes godnesse.

---

132 (Godes mærða on)? (*First two letters either* go *or* to.)   133 sceol(de,
þa God his mod)?   134 me(nn : : : : : : : : : : : : : :)? (*The concluding word
may have been an adverb ending in* -lice.)   135–7 *Cf. lines* 32–34.   139
(us æt fruman)?   141 (feorran)? (*Last letter either* r *or* n; *cf. Bede's* longe.)

---

have prompted Ælfric's elaboration in 127–9, though the ground has been prepared
for it in the introductory paragraph, line 14.]
   131–4 [*Bede*] Expuens, linguam muti, ut loqui valeat, tangit, cum per ministerium prædicationis rationem fidei, quam confiteri debeat, præstat.
   138–42 [*Bede*] Suspiciens in cælum ingemuit, quia nos quos ad cælestia
possidenda creavit, longe in terrestria deiectos esse doluit.
   143–8 [*Bede*] Suspiciens in cælum ingemuit, ut nobis qui a cælestibus gaudiis
per terrena oblectamenta discessimus, ad hæc per gemitus et suspiria insinuaret
esse redeundum.

He cwæð þa *effeta*, þæt ys to geopenigenne,
for þære deafnysse þe him derode oð þæt;   150
ac his halwende hrepung his earan undyde.

Be þære ylcan dæde doð git Godes þenas
þonne hi cild fulliað, þæt hi settað heora fingras
innan þæs cildes earan mid heora spatle,
7 on þæs cildes nosu, secgende *effeta*.   155
Ðæt spatl getacnað, swa swa þes traht segð,
þone upplican wisdom þe hit gewilnian sccal,
7 þære nosa stenc getacnað þone stenc
be þam þe se apostol Paulus þuss awrat:
Christ*i bonus odor sum*us *Deo in omni loco*:   160
We syndon us sylfe soðlice Cristes bræð,
Gode sylfum god bræð on ælcere stowe.

Be þam ilcan gecwæð se eadiga Iob:
Swa lange swa [s]eo oreðung is on us wunigende,
7 Godes Gast on urum nosu*m*, ne sceolon we sprecan   165
unrihtwisnysse on urum welerum,
ne leasunga smeagan mid ure tungan ahwar.

'Hwæt, þa sona wurdon his earan geopenode,
7 his tungan bend wearð unbunden eac,
7 he rihtlice spræc mid his agenum gereorde.'   170
We sprecað rihtlice on rihtu*m* geleafan,

164 seo] þeo *MS*.

149–51 [*Bede*] Quod autem ait Effeta, id est, adaperire, propter aures dicit sanandas, quas surditas diutina clauserat, sed ad audiendum iam tactus patefecit ipsius.

152–67 [*Bede*] Unde credo mos increbuerit Ecclesiæ, ut sacerdotes illius his, quos percipiendis baptismi sacramentis præparant, prius inter cætera consecrationis exordia de saliva oris sui nares tangant et aures, dicentes *Effeta*: per salivam quidem oris sui, gustum quo initiandi sunt supernæ sapientiæ designantes: per tactum vero narium, ut abiectis delectationibus noxiis, solum Christi semper amplectantur odorem, de quo dicit Apostolus: *Christi bonus odor sumus Deo in omni loco* (*II Cor. ii. 14, 15*), et ut meminerint se iuxta exemplum beati Iob, donec superest halitus in eis, et spiritus Dei in naribus eorum, non loqui iniquitatem labiis, nec lingua mendacium meditari debere (*adaptation of Iob xxvii. 3–4*).

171–9 [*Bede*] Qui ergo recte loqui baptismatis nostri tempore didicimus, corde credendo ad iustitiam, ore autem confessionem faciendo ad salutem, curandum summopere est, ne post baptisma ad iniusta et noxia verba declinemus. . . . Non solum a malis aures linguamque satis est castigare loquelis, si non etiam iuxta Psalmistam inclinemus aurem nostram in verba oris Dei (*Psal. lxxvii. 1*), si non os nostrum loquatur sapientiam, et meditatio cordis nostri prudentiam (*Psal. xlviii. 4*). Sed et cunctos simul interioris exteriorisque hominis nostri sensus, quia cuncti in baptismo abluti sunt, oportet mundos ac bonis operibus

þæt we rihtlice gelyfon on þone lyfigendan God,
⁊ we hine andettan, us sylfum to hæle.

Nu sceole we hogian þæt we hine ne gremion
æfter urum fulluhte ealles to swiþe,   175
þurh unrihtwise word ⁊ þa yfelan dæda;
ac we sceolon swiþor hine symle gladian
on mode ⁊ on muþe, ⁊ eac mid þam (dæd)um,
þæt ure andetness us idel ne beo.

'Ða bebead se Hælend þam þe hine brohton   180
þæt hi hit ne sædon nanum menn nateshwon;
ac hi þæs (þ)e swiþor hit sædon mid wundrunge,
⁊ cyddan his mærða mannum, (þu)ss cweðende:
Wel he gedyde ealle þing þurh his wundorlican mih(te:
h)e gedyde þæt þa deafan mihton wel gehyran,   185
⁊ he gedyde þ[am] dum(ban þæt hi) mihton sprecan.'
Se Hælend, þe mihte swylce wundra gefrem(man,
mihte) eac don þæt hi digle wæron;
ac he bebead þam mannum (: : : : : : : : : : : : : : : : : : :)
for þan þe he sealde him sylf us swa bysne   190
(: : : : : : : : : : : : : : : : þe w)e for Gode gedoþ
þæne idelan gylp æfre for*b(ugon   *f. 174
: :).
Se idela gylp (: : : : : : : :) h(: : : : : : : : : : : :

178 dæd-] *The lower half of each letter is visible.*   186 þam] þæt þa *MS,*
but cf. line 45.   hi] *The top of the* i *is visible.*   189 (þæt hi hit nanum ne
sædon)?   191 (þæt we on þam godum dædum þe w)e?   194–5 (huru
is an) h(eafodleahter, Gode swiðe and)sæte? (*The* eafo *of* heafod- *almost intact
though out of position.*)

servemus insuper ornatos semper. [*Ælfric's treatment of the sentiment retains only
a few of Bede's details.*]
187–202 [*Bede*] Quare, fratres carissimi, hæc acta credamus? Numquid
æstimandum est, quod unigenitus Dei Filius signum faciens, et abscondi hoc
voluerit, et contra voluntatem illius sit patefactum in turbas, nec potuerit
silentio signum tegere si vellet, quod potuit facere cum voluit? An forte nobis
exemplum dare voluit, ut virtutum opera facientes, vitium iactantiæ per omnia
gloriamque vitemus humanam, ne bona nostra actio, per inanem vulgi favorem
supernæ retributionis munere privetur? [*Haymo: cf. esp.* 198–202] Bonis
exemplum ostendit, ut etiam in bono opere inanem gloriam et iactantiam cave-
amus, iuxta quod alibi ipse præcipit, ut intremus in cubiculum, et clauso ostio
oremus Patrem nostrum. Et Pater noster, qui videt in abscondito, reddet nobis
(*Matth. vi.* 6). [*At* 200 *Ælfric includes a reminder of Matth. vi.* 4] Sit eleemosyna
tua in abscondito. [*Bede continues with a subtler discussion of the problem in which
he refers to texts in Matth.* v *and* vi, *but does not mention directly those which appear
in Haymo and Ælfric.*]

: : : : : : : : : : : : :)sæte, 7 we (eac) sceolon   195
þone yfelan unþeaw us fram ascy(r)ian,
gyf we habban wyllað þa heofonlican (m)ede,
for þan þe [se] Hælend swiþe oft forbead
on (his halgum) godspellum þysne heafodleahter,
7 het us on digelnysse don ure ælmyssan,   200
7 ure gebedu binnan urum locum,
þæt God sylf hit us forgilde, þe gesihð úre digelnysse.
We wyllað eow gereccan sume Cristes wundra, to getrymminge
eowres geleafan. Vre Drihten stah on scyp, 7 him fyligdon his
leorningcnihtas. Efne þa færlice aras mycel styrung 7 hreohness 205
on þære sǽ, swa þæt þæt scyp wearð mid yþum oferþeht. Se wind
witodlice heom stod ongean mid ormætum blæde. And se Hælend
wearð on slæpe on þam steor-setle. Ða genealæhton his leorningcnihtas 7 hine awrehton, þuss cweðende: Drihten, gehelp ure; we
losiað! He andwyrde, Eala ge lytles geleafan, to hwi synd ge afyrhte? 210
He aras þa, 7 þywde þone wind 7 þa sǽ, 7 het hi stille beon. Hwæt
þa sona wearð geworden mycel smyltnyss on þære sae, swa þæt þa

---

198 se] *not in MS.*   199 his halgum *partially visible.*   203–76 *From Catholic Homilies, 'Alia Narratio de Evangelii Textu', incompletely printed by Thorpe, II. 378–80. Here collated with Thorpe's MS, K (ULC Gg. 3. 28), f. 209ʳ⁻ᵛ, and with five others: C (CCCC 303), pp. 255–6: D (Bodley 342), ff. 71ᵛ–73; E (CCCC 198), ff. 266–7ᵛ: F (CCCC 162), pp. 468–72; and M (ULC Ii. 4. 6), ff. 18ᵛ–21ᵛ. Variants in spelling and E's Latin glosses are omitted.* 203 before We] *Title as above DEFK;* Ewangelium *C; space without title M; followed by* Mine gebroðru, -a, *CDEFKM.*   eow . . . wundra] sume cristes rinda (sic) eow gereccan *E.*   204 after geleafan] We sind gecnæwe þæt we hit forgymeleasodon on ðam dæge þe mann þæt godspel rædde, ac hit mæg eow nu fremian swa micclum swa hit ða mihte. *CDEK.*   stah] astah *CDEFKM.* 207 witodlice] *not in CDEFKM.*   208–14 Ða . . . gehyrsumiað] *om. Thorpe, present in all MSS.*   209 awehton *EM.*

203–14 [*Matth. viii. 23*] Et ascendente eo in naviculam, secuti sunt eum discipuli eius.
[*24*] Et ecce motus magnus factus est in mari, ita ut navicula operiretur fluctibus; ipse vero dormiebat [in puppe, *Marc. iv. 38*].
[*25*] Et accesserunt ad eum discipuli eius, et suscitaverunt eum, dicentes: Domine, salva nos, perimus.
[*26*] Et dicit eis Iesus: Quid timidi estis, modicæ fidei? Tunc surgens, imperavit ventis et mari [Et exsurgens comminatus est vento, et dixit mari: Tace, obmutesce. *Marc. iv. 39*], et facta est tranquillitas magna.
[*27*] Porro homines mirati sunt, dicentes: Qualis est hic, quia venti et mare obediunt ei? [*With Ælfric's* reðran, 213, *cf. Jerome, In Matth.*] Non discipuli, sed nautæ, et cæteri qui in navi erant, mirabantur. [*Quoted by Bede, In Marc. iv. 40; Haymo, Hom. XX. Same idea in Origen, PL XCV. 1199.*]

reðran, micclum wundriende, cwædon: Hwæt la, hwylc is þes,
þæt ægðer ge windas ge sæ him gehyrsumiað?

Se Hælend geswutelode mid þam slǽpe þa soþan menniscnysse, 215
7 mid þam wundre his godcundan mægenþrymnysse. He slep swa
swa soð mann, 7 he þa yþiendan sǽ mid anre hæse gestilde swa
swa ælmihtig Scyppend, þe ǽr g(e)sette þære sǽ gemæru, þæt heo
nateshwón ne mot middaneard oferga(n).

Hi þa oferreowon þone brym 7 gelendon on þam lande þe is 220

213 wundriende] wundredon 7 *E.*   214 þæt] þe *F.*   215 þa] his
KM.   216 7 . . . mægenþrymnysse] *om. E.*   217 yðiende *CDEF.*

215–19 [*Bede, In Marc. iv. 35*] In hac navigatione Dominus utramque unius
eiusdemque suæ personæ naturam dignatur ostendere dum ipse qui ut homo
dormit in navi furorem maris verbo compescit ut Deus. [*Haymo, Hom. XX*]
Ipse enim erat in navi, qui in principio terminum constituit maris, dicens:
Hucusque venies, et non procedes amplius, et hic confringes tumentes fluctus tuos
(*Iob xxxviii*). [*Origen has same ideas. For* 218–19 *cf. Psal. ciii. 9*] Terminum
posuisti quem [aquæ] non transgredientur; neque convertentur operire terram.

220–48 [*Marc. v. 1*] Et venerunt trans fretum maris in regionem Gerasenorum.

[*2*] Et exeunti ei de navi, statim occurrit de monumentis homo in spiritu
immundo,

[*3*] qui domicilium habebat in monumentis, et neque catenis iam quisquam
poterat eum ligare,

[*4*] quoniam sæpe compedibus et catenis vinctus, dirupisset catenas, et com-
pedes comminuisset, et nemo poterat eum domare.

[*5*] Et semper die ac nocte in monumentis et in montibus erat, clamans, et concidens se lapidibus, [ita ut nemo posset transire per viam illam, *Matth. viii. 28*].

[*6*] Videns autem Iesum a longe, cucurrit et adoravit eum;

[*7*] et clamans voce magna dixit: Quid mihi et tibi, Iesu Fili Dei Altissimi?
adiuro te per Deum, ne me torqueas.

[*8*] Dicebat enim illi: Exi spiritus immunde ab homine.

[*9*] Et interrogabat eum: Quod tibi nomen est? Et dicit ei: Legio mihi nomen
est, quia multi sumus.

[*10*] Et deprecabatur eum multum, ne se expelleret extra regionem.

[*11*] Erat autem ibi circa montem grex porcorum magnus, pascens.

[*12*] Et deprecabantur eum spiritus, dicentes: Mitte nos in porcos ut in eos
introeamus.

[*13*] Et concessit eis statim Iesus. Et exeuntes spiritus immundi introierunt
in porcos; et magno impetu grex præcipitatus est in mare ad duo millia, et
suffocati sunt in mari.

[*14*] Qui autem pascebant eos, fugerunt, et nuntiaverunt in civitatem . . .

[*16*] qualiter factum esset ei qui dæmonium habuerat, et de porcis.

[*14*] Et egressi sunt videre quid esset factum:

[*15*] et veniunt ad Iesum, et vident illum qui a dæmonio vexabatur, sedentem,
vestitum, et sanæ mentis. . . .

[*18*] Cumque ascenderet navim, coepit illum deprecari qui a dæmonio vexatus
fuerat, ut esset cum illo.

[*19*] Et non admisit eum, sed ait illi: Vade in domum tuam ad tuos et annuntia
illis quanta tibi Dominus fecerit, et misertus sit tui.

gehat(en) Gerasenoru*m*. Efne þa þa hi upp eodon, arn þær an wod
mann togeanes þam Hælende, se hæfde wununge on hæþenu*m*
byrgenu*m*, 7 hi(ne) ne mihte nan mann mid racenteagum gehealdan,
ne mid fótcopsu(m) gehæftan, for þan þe he eaþelice tobræc þa
isenan racenteaga, 7 þa fotcopsas eall tocwysde. He wunode on 225
dunu*m* dæges 7 nihtes, 7 on byrgenu*m*, hrym*en*de, 7 beatende hine
sylfne mid stanu*m*, 7 nan mann ne mihte þæs weges faran. He arn
þa to þam Hælende, þa þa he hine g(e)seah, 7 feoll to his fotum,
mid mycelre stemne clypiende, Eala þ(u) Hælend, þæs Hehstan
Godes Sunu, ic halsige þe þæt þu me ne tintr(egie). Se Hælend 230
him cwæ*ð* to, Ðu unclæna gast, gewit of þam menn. A(nd he) hine
þa befran hwæt his nama wære. Ða *and*wyrde se uncl(æna gast)
þurh þæs wodan mu*ð*, 7 cwæ*ð*, Min nama is eorod, for þ(an þe we
her ma)nega synd. And bæd hine þa micclu*m* þæt he hine of 234
þ*(am earde ne adræfde. Ða stod þær onemm ða dune micel heord *Last letter
swyna,)*7 þa deofla bædon þæt hi mosto(n into ðam swynu*m*. visible f. 174.
[þa geðafode se Hælend þæt ðam deoflum. And hí gewiton of ðam *f. 174ᵛ,
men into ðam swynu*m*.] þa swyn ða e)alle endemes scuton into line 2.
þære s(æ, sume twa) þusend(:), 7 þær adruncon þurh þone
(deofel)lican scy(f)e. Ða swanas flugon afyrhte to þære byrig, 7 240
cyddon (be þa)m swynu*m*, 7 be þam witseocan menn. Ða comon
þa ceastergewaran sona to þam Hælende, 7 gesáwon þone wodan
mann wel gescrydne, 7 gewittiges modes, se þe ær awedde. Ða
gewende Crist to scype, 7 se gewitseoca hine bæd þæt he moste
mid him. Drih(t)*en* him *and*wyrde, Far þe ham to þinu*m* hiwu*m*, 245
7 cyþ heom hu mycele mihte Drih(t)*en* on þe geworhte, 7 hu he þe
gemiltsode. He þa ferde, swiþe bodigende Dri(h)tenes wundra,
and menn þæs wundredon.

221 hierasenoru*m* CD. arn þær] arn CDKM; þa arn EF. 223 gehealdan]
not in CDEFKM. 224–48 for þan þe . . . wundredon] *om. Thorpe; present in
all MSS.* 225 racenteaga] racenteagan CKM. þa] *om. CDEF.* eall]
ealle CDEFKM. 230 halsige þe] ðe halsige KM; þe nu halsige CDEF.
getintregie M. 232 þa] *not in CDEFKM.* 235 þær] þær ða M. heord]
eorod M. 237–8 þa . . . swynum] *sic CDEFKM (exc. of ðam men om.
CDEF); om. H.* 239 þusend((:)] ðusend CDEFKM, *but H has traces of
another letter, probably o, a, or e.* þær] hi þær EF. 240 swanas] *glossed*
swinherdes E. 241 -seocum CDEF. 243 mann] *not in CDEFKM.*
245 hiwum] *not in CDEFKM.* 246 heom] *not in CDEFKM.* 247 þa
ferde] ferde þa F.

[20] Et abiit, et coepit prædicare in Decapoli quanta sibi fecisset Iesus; et
omnes mirabantur.

An eorod is on bocum geteald to syx þusendum, 7 swa fela
awyrgedra gasta wæron þam anum menn getenge, oðþæt se mild- 250
heorta Hælend to þam lande reow, 7 hine ahredde.

Ða deoflu oncneowon urne Hælend Crist,
7 þæt Iudeisce folc hine dwollice wiðsoc,
7 syndon forþi wyrsan þonne þa awyrgedan deoflu,
þe feollon to his fotum mid fyrhte fornumene.   255
Ne dorston þa deoflu, þa þa hi adr(æf)de wæron,
into þam swynum, gyf he heom ne sealde leafe,
ne into nanum menn, for þan þe se ælmihtiga Drihten
ure gecynd hæfde on him sylfum genumen.

Ða swyn hi gecuron for heora sweartum hiwe,   260
7 for þære fulnesse fenlices adelan.

Se mann þe hæfð swynes þeawas,
7 wyle hine aþwean mid wope fram synnum,
7 eft hine befylan fullice mid leahtrum,
swa swa swin deð, þe cyrð to meoxe   265
æfter his þweale, þeawleas nyten,
þonne byð he betæht þam atelicum deoflum
for his fulum dædum, þe he fyrnlice geedlæcð.

---

251 hælend] drihten *EFKM*; *om. CD.*   hreow *CDE.*   252 hælend]
drihten *KM.*   253 hine] *om. M.*   wiðsoc] wiðsocon *CDEF.*   254 syndon]
sind K; synd *CDEM.*   255 þe] þa *M.*   257 he heom] him god *CD* (god
over line D).   258 nanum] anum *M.*   ælmihtiga] metoda *CDEFKM.*
260 heora] ðam *CDEFKM.*   sweartan *M.*

---

249 [*Smaragdus, Migne, PL CII. 182*] Una legio apud veteres sex millibus
complebatur hominum. [*Originally used by Ælfric at CH II. 246 and here apparently recalled: see Max Förster, Anglia XVI. 42.*]

252–5 [*Bede, In Marc. v. 6–7*] Quanta Arrii vesania Iesum creaturam et non
Deum credere, quem Filium Dei altissimi dæmones credunt et contremescunt!
Quæ impietas Iudæorum, eum dicere in principe dæmoniorum eiecisse dæmonia,
quem ipsa dæmonia fatentur nihil secum habere commune!

256–7 [*Bede, In Marc. v. 13*] Et notandum quod spiritus immundi nec in
porcos irent, nisi hoc illis benignus ipse Salvator petentibus, quos certe in
abyssum posset religare, concederet.

260–71 [*Cf. Bede, In Marc. v. 11–12*] In quorum tamen interitu figuraliter
homines immundi, vocis et rationis expertes, iudicantur, qui in monte superbiæ
pascentes, lutulentis oblectantur in actibus. Talibus enim per cultus idolorum
possunt dæmonia dominari. Nam nisi quis porci more vixerit, non in eum
diabolus accipiet potestatem, aut ad probandum tantum, non autem et ad per-
dendum accipiet.

262–6 [*Cf. II Petr. ii. 21–22*] Melius enim erat illis non cognoscere viam
iustitiæ, quam post agnitionem retrorsum converti ab eo. . . . Contigit enim eis
illud veri proverbii: . . . Sus lota in volutabro luti.

Se þe oft gegremað God þurh leahtras,
7 æfre geedlæcð his yfelan dæda,   270
he byþ swyne gelic, 7 forscyldegod wið God.
  Uton we herian urne Drihten symle
on his micclum wundrum, 7 us miltsunge biddan,
7 yfel forlætan, 7 eft ne geedlæcan,
þæt we moton ætwindan þam wælhreowan deoflum   275
7 Gode geþeon þurh gode gehealtsumnesse.
  We wyllað eow gyt secgan sum wundor be Criste,
(7) þas geendunge eallswa geglengan,
a[n]fealdum andgite, swa swa (Luc)as hit awrat
on þære Cristes bec, þuss cweðende be him: 280
  Se (Hæle)nd ferde iv́ [sic] to Capharnon-byrig
on Galileiscum earde, þær (þær his eð)el wæs,
and he hi þær lærde on heora restendagum,
and hi ealle (: : : : : : : : : his) wundorlican lare,
for þan þe his spræc wæs on swiðli(c : : : : : : : : : :   285
: : : þ)ær wæs þa an wod mann on þære gesamnunge
mid þam (: : : : : : : : : : : : : : : : : : :) afylled,
7 se awyrgeda gast þas word þa clypode
*swiðe ge(: :) Crist,   *f. 175
(: : : : : : : : : : : : : : : : : : :), hwæt is u(s) gemæ(n)e?   290
þu (co)me to fordo(n)ne 7 to amyrr(enne us)!

---

269 þurh leahtras] þurh leahtrum CDK.   274 ne] om. M.   275 wæl-
hreowan] -um FKM.   276 þurh gode] þurh godre CDEFKM.   after
gehealtsumnesse] þam sy wuldor and wurðmynt á to worulde. Amen. CDEFKM
(Amen om. M). End of extract from Catholic Homilies.   279 andfealdum
MS.   284 (wundredon his)? (his partially visible; see note on wundredon).
285–6 swiðli(cere mihte. And þ)ær? (Spacing favours -ere and unabbreviated
And.)   287 (fulan gaste deoflice)?

281–305 [Luc. iv. 31] Et descendit in Capharnaum civitatem Galilææ, ibique
docebat illos sabbatis.

[32] Et stupebant in doctrina eius, quia in potestate erat sermo ipsius.

[33] Et in synagoga erat homo habens dæmonium immundum, et exclamavit
voce magna, dicens:

[34] Sine, quid nobis et tibi, Iesu Nazarene? venisti perdere nos? scio te quis
sis, Sanctus Dei.

[35] Et increpavit illum Iesus, dicens: Obmutesce, et exi ab eo. Et cum
proiecisset illum dæmonium in medium, exiit ab illo, nihilque illum nocuit.

[36] Et factus est pavor in omnibus, et colloquebantur ad invicem, dicentes:
Quod est hoc verbum, quia in potestate et virtute imperat immundis spiritibus,
et exeunt?

[37] Et divulgabatur fama de illo in omnem locum regionis.

Eala (ic) wat ge(are) þæt þu eart God(es) Halg(a).
Se Hæ(le)nd þa s(ona) þreade þone deofol,
þuss him secgende: Swi(ga) þu hrað(e),
7 gewi(t aw)eg of þisum wodan menn;   295
7 he swa sona þone sceoccan adræ(fde)
of þam earm(an) menn, heom eallum tomiddes,
7 se deofol ne miht(e) naht derian þam menn.
Ða wearð mycel óga on eallum þam mannum,
7 hi swiþe (spræ)con, secgende heom betwynan,   300
Hwæt is la þiss word, þuss wundorlic on him,
þæt he on anwealde 7 on mihte bebytt
þam unclænum gast(um) þæt hi ut gewitað?
Ða wearð gewidmærsod wide his hlisa
on æ(lcere) stowe ealles þæs eardes.   305
  Swylce wundra worhte se [wel]willenda H(æ)lend
her on þisum life, to geleafan t(r)ymminge,
þæt þa mihton sec(gan) þe gesawon his wundra,
7 we magon witan þe þa word gehyrað,
swa swa his godspelleras be him sylfum awriton,   310
þæt he is Godes Suna þe gesceop ealle þing,
7 ús þa alysde mid his agenum lífe
of deofles a(n)wealde; þæs we him á secgað
wuldor 7 wyrðmynt mid wordum 7 dædum. AMEN.

---

293 *After* deofol *an extra space, probably a letter erased.*   294 Swiga] *no
cap. MS.*   295 *Bracketed letters partially visible.*   301 wundorlic *at
end of line, followed by traces which are not certainly those of another letter. Adverb
seems less likely than adjective.*   306 wel-] *not in MS. See note.*

NOTES

Title. As will be seen from XIII–XVI, MS. H, which is here the only
authority, numbers the Sundays after the octave instead of after Pentecost
itself. According to the system in U, this is the thirteenth Sunday after
Pentecost.

5–17. Cf. XIa. 102–27 and note. An earlier version of the same passage
in *Matthew* is in *LS* XVI. 134–41. Unfortunately it does not include the
beginning of verse 25, represented here by the imperfectly preserved
line 17.

21–24. A troublesome passage. One might expect the first line to
include the adjective *Galileisc* and the next two to include both Tyre and
Sidon, since they are not only in the Latin but are expressly named in

Ælfric's exposition at line 51. The -*eiscan* of line 23 is not proper to *Sidon*; it suggests rather *Galileiscan* or *Iudeiscan*. But some sense can be achieved by reading *Sidoneiscan* and attributing the *e* to an inaccuracy in the formation of the adjective or, more probably, to a scribal deviation encouraged by leaving -*iscan* for the top of a new page. Again, line 24, if I have guessed its content correctly by comparison with 80 and by the presence of a nominative plural ending -*e* on the past participle, ought to be preceded by the Latin form *Decapolis*, for which there is no room in the manuscript. If this name is supplied, and if the blank spaces in the first three lines are stretched slightly beyond what I have estimated, we can read as follows:

> þæt ure Hælend be(com to þære Galileiscan) sæ,
> farende fram gemærum (þæs Tyriscan folces
> geond þæt Sidon)eiscan, on þam sælande [Decapolis],
> swa o(n bocum synd gehate)ne tyn (burhsci)ra.

This squares with the Latin and with what Ælfric says later (51, 67, 78–80), but I do not think Ælfric would have approved of my treatment of Tyre and Sidon, and if Decapolis is indeed missing, we may have lost a whole line. Ælfric generally uses *swa swa* as a subordinating conjunction rather than *swa*. I have put *tyn* (*burhsci*)*ra* here in lower case, in contrast to 80, where we undoubtedly have a place-name.

73. Did the missing words express the idea that Christ died or that he came into the world? Bede has partially quoted the passage in which Caiaphas is said to have prophesied *quod Iesus moriturus erat pro gente; et non tantum pro gente, sed ut filios Dei, qui erant dispersi, congregaret in unum* (*Ioan.* xi. 51 sq.). But Ælfric may rather have been guided by Bede's repeated use of the verb *venire*.

92. *agen bepæcend*. Probably we should read *agenne*, accusative singular masculine. Cf. 99 sq., note.

94. *mid attre gemenged*. In *De Auguriis*, *LS* XVII. 127, Ælfric says of the devil, *eall hit bið ættrig þæt him of cymð*.

96. With this attack on *drymen and wiccan* compare not only the original *De Auguriis* but the addition to it, our XXIX.

98. *þe to him secað*, 'who resort to them (for help)'. This idiom has not been recognized in BT and is dated too late by the *OED*, *seek* 13, which begins the list of illustrations with a quotation from a Trinity College homily of about 1200. Actually one of the quotations in BT, I. 2, '*to try to get* (the source from which a thing is sought marked by *tó*)', lacks an accusative object and may be the earliest surviving instance of the idiom. It is in *Andreas*, 907 sqq.:

> þær is help gearu,
> milts æt mærum, manna gehwylcum,
> sigorsped geseald, þam þe seceð to him.

Neither G. P. Krapp nor the latest editor of the poem, K. R. Brooks (Oxford, 1961), has anything to say about *seceð* here. Very likely they agree with BT that it is an elliptical variant of the transitive use. But the ellipsis is vague, since the reference must be to all three of the previous nouns, *help, milts,* and *sigorsped.* I prefer to think that we are dealing with the intransitive idiom, 'to anyone who resorts to him'. It seems probable indeed that the intransitive *secan to,* in which *to* may govern either the place where or the person from whom some unnamed benefit is sought, has developed from the corresponding transitive idiom in which the benefit sought is clearly specified. BT has another quotation, this time from Ælfric, under II. 2, '*to seek* a place, *to visit, resort to*', where instead of the usual accusative we find the adverb *ðider*: *Hi syððan gewunelice ðider sohton,* 'they afterwards resorted thither', *CH* I. 504/6, where what is actually sought is the help of God and St. Michael. Surely this also should be considered an example of intransitive *secan to.*

99 sq. *abiddan þone . . . Hælend his agene hæle.* The double accusative here is probably incorrect. Other examples of *abiddan* in these homilies have the accusative or a clause for the thing asked for and *æt* with the dative for the person from whom it is to be obtained. (So, with acc. object, I. 231; VIII. 73; XXII. 90; and with clause, VIII. 126; XV. 178; XXVII. 19). But the unprefixed *biddan* sometimes takes the accusative of the person addressed and the genitive of the thing (V. 14; VI. 54), or the genitive of the thing without mention of the person addressed (see the Glossary); and BTS cites an example of *æt Gode abiddan* with genitive of the thing, from *CH* I. 170/29 sq. I suspect we should read *agenre hæle* as a genitive. For another probable error in the inflection of *agen,* see the note on 92.

142. *utlice.* This adverb has not been recorded in the dictionaries of Old English, though the adjective *utlic* 'external, foreign' appears in BT with two citations from the Old English Bede (ed. Miller, EETS, O.S. 95, pp. 308/30 and 360/16), and Hall-Meritt adds a passage from the *Rule of Chrodegang* (ed. Napier, EETS, O.S. 150, p. 61/21), where the meaning is 'remote' (*an utlicre stowe*). Ælfric's rueful *ealles to utlice* can be taken as 'all too remotely', adding further emphasis to the conjectured *swa feorran* 'so far away' in line 141. But it can also be taken as 'all too completely', with emphasis on the completeness of our preoccupation with the earthly things into which we have fallen. The OED has *outly,* adv., in the sense 'out and out, utterly, completely', the first quotation dated 1290 from the *South English Legendary,* and it may well be that this sense was already available to Ælfric. If so, it was very likely the dominant sense in his mind; but both senses may have been present, for both are relevant, and in this passage they support each other.

172 sq. *gelyfon, andettan.* Do these subjunctives represent only a conventional doubt after a verb of saying, or does Ælfric mean to emphasize the possibility that these are idle words, in anticipation of line 179?

176. *þurh unrihtwise word and þa yfelan dæda.* Is the shift from indefinite to definite merely a variation or a climactic device? In the corrupted

passage at II. 196 sq. there may have been comparable variation, but it looks as if *dæda* had preceded *word*.

187. *gefrem(man)*. This form and *gefremian* are both represented in Ælfric manuscripts. See the Glossary, *fremian* and *gefremian*.

203–76. The gospel-passages partially omitted by Thorpe from his edition of the homilies were printed in full by A. S. Napier, *Archiv für das Studium der neueren Sprachen und Literaturen*, CI and CII (1898–9), from several manuscripts other than Thorpe's. The two passages here (*Matth.* viii. 23–27 and *Marc.* v. 1–15, 18–20 are in CII. 36 sq., taken from MS. Bodley 342 (D), ff. 71ᵛ, 72. My report of D's readings, from photostats, corresponds with Napier's, except that I have not recorded variations of spelling.

262–66. With this adaptation of *II Petr.* ii. 21 sq. compare XIII. 230–4, and the glancing allusion in XVI. 67 sq.

284. The conjectured *wundredon* 'wondered at' would normally govern the genitive, and *his wundorlican lare* can be so construed. The play on words is of a sort not unusual in Ælfric. For *wundrian* with the genitive, see line 248 in the present homily and the Glossary.

306. [*wel*]*willenda*. The emendation seems necessary, especially in view of the other occurrences of *se welwillenda Hælend*, with various inflectional endings, at VII. 156; XI. 144; XVIII. 157.

XVIII

SERMO DE DIE IUDICII

(1) *Luc.* xvii. 20, 21, 24, 26–31, 34–37

(2) *Matth,* xxiv. 15–25, 29–31, with substitutions from
Marc. xiii. 14–27

THIS and the three following homilies belong to the *quando volueris* category, not being assigned to specific occasions in any of the manuscripts. They have no direct connexion with one another and no attempt has been made to put them in chronological order. Indeed the present homily may be the latest of them and xxi is pretty certainly the earliest, though the prose part of xix may antedate it. I have put xviii first because it is mainly exegetical, like all the preceding homilies except xi and xia.

Ælfric here takes up a long familiar theme, that of the Last Days. The title, *De Die Iudicii,* is proper enough but may be somewhat misleading, in that there is no full description of the fateful day such as Ælfric has provided in xi. The passage from *Luke* on which the first half is based describes the unpredictable suddenness of the day and its instantaneous, irrevocable consequences, but there is no judgement scene, such as *Matthew* xxv provides, to give focus to the action. And the *Matthew–Mark* passage in the second half concentrates on the terrible persecution that is to precede the Judgement, leaving the arrival of the day itself until the very end of the account. The main emphasis in the first half falls on the three estates of the Christian world, each with its mixed company of good and bad, soon to be sundered for ever. That of the second half falls on Antichrist's reign of terror and the extraordinary fortitude demanded of those who hope to be saved. This part takes us back to Aelfric's preface to the First Series of the *Catholic Homilies,* and to his brief references to Antichrist in the homily for martyrs (*CH* II. 540, 542). It reminds us also of one of Wulfstan's basic themes, and has in fact served as a source for his most elaborate treatment of the Last Days, the homily *Secundum Marcum*.[1]

Such indications as we have from the manuscripts point to a fairly late date for *De Die Iudicii*. It was once, probably, at the very end of Q, following the homily for a confessor, Assmann IV, which was written no earlier than 1006 for Æthelwold II of Winchester; and the two manuscripts that actually contain it, P and R, had access to the texts of late compositions, including the homily just mentioned.[2] We cannot be sure, however, that *De Die Iudicii* did not owe its position in Q to its unassigned, *quando volueris* character rather than to its having been composed after the other homilies in that volume. Because it had no proper day it could not well have been included in M (which, though it exhibits a number of homilies composed in the middle years, is restricted to one part of the Temporale), nor in U (which admits several later homilies but is similarly restricted), nor even among the interpolated homilies of H (where the interpolator, though he drew on late texts, was governed in his selection by the complex annual cycle of the First Series). Thus the evidence is not very clear. The most we can say with any assurance, perhaps, is that the homily should have been composed after 1000.

It is hardly safe to suppose that the passage of the millennium brought about a change in Ælfric's attitude toward the imminence of the Judgement. Wulfstan's *Secundum Marcum* cannot be precisely dated either, but it was certainly composed later than 1000, for in it Wulfstan says: 'þusend geara and eac ma is nu agan syððan Crist wæs mid mannum' (Bethurum v. 44 sq.). For Wulfstan the years that elapsed beyond the prophesied millennium, even as late as 1014, the date of the *Sermo ad Anglos*, did not greatly lessen the conviction that the time of Antichrist was close at hand. Ælfric does not commit himself in *De Die Iudicii*, but it was pretty certainly after 1000 when he reissued the admonitory section of his preface to the First Series in the archetype of MS. Q, and there he repeats what he had said earlier: 'Menn behofiað godre lare swiðost on þisum timan þe is geendung þyssere worulde, and beoð fela frecednyssa on mancynne ærðan þe se ende becume.' For both men the end of the world is imminent, though the moment

---

[1] Bethurum v. See the notes on 227, 330, and 347 sqq.

[2] Only the Kansas leaf now survives of the copy of Assmann IV once in P. See the description of P in the Introduction pp. 53–54 and 58.

of its arrival is unpredictable and the prophecies have not all been fulfilled. But Ælfric, in the course of his many homilies, before and after the millennium, dwells less on the days of Antichrist than on the general doom itself, and less on the sensational aspects of the doom than on *godre lare*.

I have not been able to discover any earlier sermon on precisely the verses that Ælfric has translated from *Luc.* xvii,[1] or from *Matth.* xxiv and *Marc.* xiii, let alone any sermon on the two texts together. Sources he certainly had, probably more than I have come upon, but the selection and combination of the gospel passages and the careful limitation of his exposition to the topic of the Last Days and the Judgement must be regarded as his own until some model turns up. We may notice both the careful exclusion from *Luc.* xvii. 20–37 of verses that do not advance the prediction (including the notable close of verse 21, *Ecce enim regnum Dei intra vos est*), and the use of *Marc.* xiii. 14–27 as a guide to what shall be chosen from *Matth.* xxiv, which would otherwise have repeated some of *Luc.* xvii. And we may notice also the careful adaptation (line 227) of the first sentence of *Luc.* xvii. 20 as a means of introducing the passage from *Matth.* xxiv. Ælfric thus brings out the parallel and the contrast between the answer given to the Pharisees and the answer given to the disciples.[2]

For the interpretation of the passage from *Luke* Ælfric probably relied chiefly on Bede's commentary; but he found Bede only vaguely helpful for his comparatively simple purposes except at one point, the passage on the two men in one bed, the two women at the mill, the two men in the field (*Luc.* xvii. 34, 35). Here Bede is heavily indebted to Augustine's *Quæstiones in Evangelium secundum Lucam*, cap. xliv (*PL* xxxv. 1357), which takes up these verses by themselves. Augustine's interpretation contains everything essential to Ælfric's and may have been familiar to him in its original form;[3] but since Bede incorporates all that is needed and

___

[1] A sermon on the whole of *Luc.* xvii. 20–37, for Friday in the twelfth week after Pentecost, is in the Rabanus Maurus collection (*PL* cx. 423 sqq.), but it is simply a section of Bede's commentary on *Luke*.

[2] The *amen* at 216 suggests that the first part might once have stood alone, though it may have been induced simply by the doxology, here appropriate enough. Certainly all that follows is carefully related to what has gone before.

[3] It appears as a homily for the fifth Sunday before Christmas in the original homiliary of Paulus Diaconus and for the third Sunday in Advent in the Migne version, *PL* xcv, hom. vi. It was originally attributed correctly to Augustine;

adds an elaboration about the figure of the mill that Ælfric probably took into account, it has seemed unnecessary to quote Augustine also. The same may be said of Ælfric's treatment of verse 37, for which Bede has been quoted. Bede is here indebted to Augustine's *Quæstiones in Evangelicum secundum Matthæum* (*PL* xxxv. 1331). Here, however, Ælfric takes only the kernel of the interpretation, giving no heed to details in either expositor.

For the passage from *Matthew* and *Mark* the problem of sources is more complicated. The two commentaries most readily available to Ælfric, Jerome's on *Matthew* and Bede's on *Mark*, contain a good many interpretations that do not pertain to the Last Days. Yet Ælfric seems to have consulted Bede's at least and probably Jerome's as well, gleaning what he could for his purposes.[1] At line 281 Jerome supplies a reminder of St. Paul's description of Antichrist in *II Thessalonians* ii—a description already familiar to Ælfric as to everyone who has investigated the subject of Antichrist, but perhaps welcome because of the hint it gave for the development of his comment. Bede, repeating some of Jerome's comment, leaves out all mention of St. Paul's description. Here, and here alone, there is reason to think that Jerome was directly consulted, though his influence is more importantly manifested a little later, in the passage beginning at 328. Here Ælfric is clearly following Jerome's interpretation, but he may have taken it at second hand, for Bede quotes Jerome verbatim. I am not sure that Bede had anything to do with the comment at 369, for the three years and a half that Bede and Ælfric (but not Jerome) assign to Antichrist's reign was a figure already established in Ælfric's mind. At one other point, however, I think Bede may have been more influential than would appear from my quotations. This is the passage (347 sqq.) where Ælfric compares the days of the martyrs with those of Antichrist, pointing out that the martyrs could at least work miracles, whereas the elect in the time of Antichrist will be obliged to see the miracles wrought by their tormentors. Now Bede has this idea at the appropriate place—that is, as a

---

but Migne refers it to Maximus, amongst whose works it is indeed printed (*Sermo 2*, *PL* LVII. 533 sqq.), though its interpretation is wholly different from that of Maximus's *Hom.* 2 on the same text (*PL* LVII. 225 sqq.).

[1] I do not cite the pseudo-Bede commentary on *Matthew* (*PL* xCII), though it could have supplied what Ælfric needed at 281, 328, and 369, because it is a mere abridgement of Jerome with a few sentences added from Bede, and there is no very good evidence that Ælfric ever consulted it.

comment on *Marc.* xiii. 19 (*Matth.* xxiv. 21), just where Ælfric
introduces it. Furthermore, this is the one place in Bede's commentary where he gives full attention to Antichrist. Hence I feel sure
that Ælfric's own comment was stimulated in the first place by Bede.
But the original idea was Gregory's, in a comment on *Job* xl. 12
(*Moralia*, xxxii. 24), where he refers to *Matth.* xxiv. 24 and develops the comparison I have mentioned with great force. Now
Gregory's comment seems to me a good deal closer to Ælfric than
Bede's, except at the very end, where Bede may have contributed
something too. I believe, therefore, that Bede's comment reminded
Ælfric of the passage in Gregory—evidently a passage he already
knew—and that Gregory's presentation, being simpler and clearer
than Bede's, became his principal guide.

Except for this distinctive passage from Gregory (or Gregory
and Bede combined), what Ælfric says about Antichrist is hard to
document. The chances are that most of the details, including the
the three and a half years of Antichrist's sway, are supplied from
memory. Some details correspond to what Ælfric had said in
his Preface; a few, relating to Antichrist's ministers, are new. I
have attributed them at 303 and partially at 388 to the influence
of Adso's *De Ortu et Tempore Antichristi*, a letter written about
954 to the Frankish Queen Gerberga. The best edition is by
Ernst Sackur in *Sibyllinische Texte und Forschungen*, Halle, 1898,
pp. 104–13.[1]

One other source must be mentioned, though it served only for
Ælfric's comment on *Matth.* xxiv. 19 at lines 320–5. This was a
sermon by Cæsarius of Arles, no. CLIV in Morin's edition. The
passage quoted as Ælfric's source (Morin, II. 630) is apparently
original with Cæsarius, though much else is taken verbatim from
Augustine's *Enarratio in Ps. xxxix.* 28.

What will be evident, however, to anyone who observes the
intervals between source-quotations at the foot of the page, is that
the greater part of this homily is a free and relatively simple

---

[1] Among the writings dealing with Antichrist that Ælfric seems certainly to
have been familiar with are, besides Adso's letter, the concluding chapters of
Gregory's *Moralia*, and Jerome's commentary on *II Thess.* ii in *Epist.* CXXI. 11,
ad Algasiam. The latter is positively referred to in our XXVIII. Whether Ælfric
had consulted Haymo on *II Thess.* ii in his commentary on St. Paul's Epistles
is a question. Adso repeats a good deal that is in Haymo and has added details.
Some of the elaborations in Ælfric's Preface are not in any of these writings.
On the subject of Antichrist in general see Bethurum, *Homilies of Wulfstan*,
pp. 278 sqq.

exposition of the gospels, taken solely as predictions of what is to happen at the end of the world. Ordinarily Ælfric's gaze is focused on the future, but once, after he has stated the ideal for those who cultivate God's acre, he bursts forth in an eloquent complaint (169–88) against the priests of his own time.

SERMO DE DIE IUDICII

*Interrogatus autem I*esus *a Pharisaeis quando uenit regnum Dei,*
et *reliq*ua

Seo halige Cristes bóc þe ymbe Cristes wundra sprycð
segð þæt ða Sunderhalgan on sumne sǽl
ahsodan urne Hælend Crist ymbe hys tocyme,
and ymbe Godes ríce on þam mycclan dæge
þe we Domes-dæg hatað; and he hym andwyrde þuss: 5
Ne cymð na Godes rice be nanre cepinge,
ne menn ne cweþað ná, efne he cymð nu;
for þam þe he cymð fǽrlice, swa swa fǽrlic liget,
þe scýt fram eastdæle scinende oð westdæl.
An[d] swa swa gefyrn gelámp on Noeys flode,   10

Text based on R (CCCC 178), pp. 101–14. Collated with P (Hatton 115),
ff. 23–30ᵛ. Once apparently also in Q (CCCC 188), but now only the rubric,
followed by an erasure of two and a half lines, survives on the last remaining
page, 460.

Excluded variants: (1) Where R has *mann, mann-, menn, þuss,* P has *man,
man-, men, þus.* (2) For R's *i* in *bið, hwider, þider, þissere,* P has *y.* (3) For R's *y*
in *hy, hym, hyne, hys, hyt,* P has *i.* (4) Where R has *-an* in the preterite plural and
in the present plural of preterite present verbs, P almost always has *-on.* (The
slightly less consistent variants in the present subjunctive are recorded.)
(5) Where *R* has *fela, good-, ymbe,* P has *feala, god-, embe.*

Sup.: phariseis *P.*   1 halie *P.*   sprecð *P.*   3 acxodon *P.*   hælend]
hælend drihten *P.*   7 na] naut *P.*   cimð *P.*   8 þam] þan *P.*
10 And] 7 *P*; An *R.*   noes *P.*

Glosses in R and P, Latin: 2 sunderhalgan: farisei *R.*   on sumne sæl:
aliquando *R.*   3 ahsodan: *inter*rogaba*nt R.*   7 efne: ecce *R.*   8 liget:
fulgur *RP.*   10 gefyrn: dudu*m R.*
ME: 2 sæl: time *R.*

Sources. 2–9 [*Luc. xvii. 20*] Interrogatus autem a Pharisæis: Quando venit regnum Dei? respondens eis, dixit: Non venit regnum Dei cum observatione:
[*21*] neque dicent: Ecce hic, aut ecce illic. . . .
[*24*] Nam, sicut fulgur coruscans de sub cælo in ea, quæ sub cælo sunt, fulget:
ita erit Filius hominis in die sua. [*Matth. xxiv. 27*] Sicut enim fulgur exit ab
oriente, et paret usque in occidentem.
10–15*a* [*26*] Et sicut factum est in diebus Noe, ita erit in diebus Filii hominis.
[*27*] Edebant, et bibebant: uxores ducebant, et dabantur ad nuptias, usque
in diem, qua intravit Noe in arcam: et venit diluvium, et perdidit omnes.

menn æton and druncon and dwollice leofodan,
cnihtas wifodon and wif ceorlodan,
oðþæt Noe eode into þam arce.
þæt flód þa becóm færlice ofer hi ealle,
and eall mancynn adrencte, buton eahta mannum, 15
þe innan þam arce wæron, swa swa hym wissode G[o]d.
And swa swa on Loðes dagum eft syððan gelamp,
menn æton and druncon, bohtan and sealdan,
byttlodan and plantodan, and beeodan heora tilunga;
þa sende God færlice, sona swa Lóð wæs 20
of þære byrig alæd, ofer þam fif burhscirum
fýr and swefel, swylce hit rénscúr wære,
and mid ealle forbærnde þa fif burhscira.
Eall swa bið on þam dæge þe ure Drihten bið æteowed,
and he cymð to demenne on þam micclan dome 25
*eallum manncynne, ælcum be hys weorcum. *p. 102
Gif hwa bið on þære tide ymbe hys tilunge,
[oððe on his húse,] oððe on hys æcere,
ne mæg he geefstan þæt he aht ahredde
oððe aweg gebringe, gewæda oððe fáta. 30

---

14 ealle] om. P (rightly?) 15 eal P. 16 wissode G[o]d] wissode gód R;
god gewissode P. 17 Loðes] both MSS. have lotes in later hands over loðes.
19 bytlodon P. tylunga P. 21 burhscyrum P. 23 -scire altered to -scira
R; -scyra P. 28 oððe on his húse] sic P; om. R. 30 gewædu P. fatu P.

Glosses, Latin: 15 buton: preter R. 16 innan: intra R. 19 byttlodan:
fundabant R. beeodan: excercebant R. 21 alæd: ductus R.
22 swefel: sulfur R (gloss erased P). renscur: pluuia P. 24 æteowed:
ostensum, apertum R. 28 æcere: agro P. 29 geefstan: properare,
festinare RP. ahredde: liberet P. 30 gewæda: veste R, vestes P. fata:
vasa RP.
ME: 24 æteowed: ischawed P.

17–24[28] Similiter sicut factum est in diebus Lot: Edebant, et bibebant: eme-
bant, et vendebant: plantabant, et ædificabant:
[29] qua die autem exiit Lot a Sodomis, pluit ignem, et sulphur de cælo, et
omnes perdidit:
[30] secundum hæc erit qua die Filius hominis revelabitur.
27–39[31] In illa hora qui fuerit in tecto, et vasa eius in domo, ne descendat
tollere illa: et qui in agro, similiter non redeat retro. [Cf. Matth. xxiv. 17, 18,
p. 600 below.]
[34] In illa nocte erunt duo in lecto uno: unus assumetur, et alter relinquetur:
[35] duæ erunt molentes in unum: una assumetur, et altera relinquetur: duo
in agro: unus assumetur, et alter relinquetur.
[36] Respondentes dicunt illi: Ubi Domine?
[37] Qui dixit illis: Ubicumque fuerit corpus, illuc congregabuntur et aquilæ.

On þære nihte beoð twegen on ánum bcddc;
an þæra bið genumen, and oðer bið forlæten.
And twa grindað þonne on anre cwyrne ætgædere;
seo an bið genumen, and seo oðer bið forlæten.
Twegen beoð on æcere erigende ætgædere;   35
se án bið genumen, and se oðer bið forlæten.
Hi andwyrdan þá and hyne ahsodan þuss:
Hwider beoð hy genumene? And he hym cwæð to,
Swa hwær swa þæt hold bið, þider gadriað þa earnas.

We willað eow nu secgan sceortlice, gif we magon,   40
þa diglostan word on þisum Drihtenlican godspelle,
for þon þe ge eaðe ne magon hyt eall understandan.
We habbað nu gehyred on þisum halgan godspelle
þæt we ne magon na cepan, ne ˈnaˈnum menn nis cuð,
hwænne ure Drihten cymð to demenne mancynne   45
on þam endenyhstan dæge þysse worulde;
ac we gelyfað swaþeah þæt us alogen ne bið
þæt he cymð soðlice mid hys scínendum englum
on þisseˈreˈ worulde geendunge
us to demanne, ælcum be hys geearnungum;   50
and he þonne forgifð þam þe hym gehyrsumedan,
and þam þe hine gegladodan mid góódum weorcum æfre,
þa écan myrhðe and þa écan (mid)wununge
mid eallum his halgum on heofonan rice.

þa earman synfullan, þe hyne forsawan on life,   55
and mid yfelum dædum hyne æfre gremodan,
þa beoð besencte on þære sweartan helle,

---

32 þara P.   33 gryndað P.   37 acsodon P.   39 gaderiað P.
40 wyllað P.   41 ðysum P.   42 þon] þam P.   43 þysum P.
46 endenextan P.   þyssere P (preferable).   47 ac] a P (with k or h over
line).   50 demenne P.   51 gehyrsumodon P.   53 mid-] sic P, erased R.
56 gremedon P.

Glosses, Latin: 32 bið forlæten: relinquitur R.   37 andwyrdan: responderunt RP.   41 diglostan word: secretiora uerba R.
42 ge: vos RP (and frequently, unnoted, hereafter).   47 a[c] we gelyfað: sed
nos credimus P.   alogen: falsum R, mentitus RP. P has m̄tu in margin in another
hand, perhaps for mentitu(s).   51 þam: quibus R.   52 gegladodan:
placuerunt R   55 earman: miseras R   forsawan: spreuerunt R.
ME: 37 andwyrdan: answereden P (? erased).   44 forsawon: forsoken P
(? erased).

47–59 [Cf. Bede, In Luc. xvii. 21–30. Ælfric here avoids all specific interpretation
and develops the basic assumptions independently.]

mid þam awyrgedum deoflum, æfre to worulde;
and se ðe þyses *ne gelyfeð, nys hys geleafa naht.   *p. 103

Se Hælend us sæde soðlice gelicnysse   60
be Noeys flode and Loðes alysednysse;
nu wite ge sume hu hit wæs be Nóe
and be hys flóde, ac eower fela nát
hu hyt wæs be Loðe; ac we wyllað eow secgan.
Loð wæs iu geháten sum halig Godes þeʻgʼn,   65
Abrahames broðor sunu, ǽr Moyses æ;
se eardode þá on þam yfelan leodscipe
Sodomitiscre burhware, þa wæron synfulle menn,
and bysmorlice forscyldgode on sceamlicum dædum.
þa forbærnde hi God mid heora fif burhscirum   70
mid heofonlicum fyre and hellicum swefle;
ac he sende on ǽr twegen scinende englas
to þam geleaffullan Loðe, and alædde hyne út
of þam fulan mancynne, þæt he mid him ne forwurde.

Eall swa bið on Dome[s]-dæge on ures Drihtnes tocyme: 75
þæt fýr cymð swa færlice þæt menn foresceawian ne magon,
and mid egeslicum bryne ealne middaneard ofergæð;
and menn þonne ne gymað, for þam micclan ógan,

58 awyrigedum *P.*   59 gelyfð *P.*   nis *P.*   61 noeis *P.*   65 þegen *P.*
67 -scype *P.*   68 buruh- *P.*   69 forscyldegode *P.*   70 -scyrum *P.*
75 Eal *P.*   domes *P*; dome *R.*   dryhtnes *P.*   76 forsceawian *P.*

Glosses, Latin: 60 gelicnysse: similitudine*m R.*   65 iu: quonda*m R.*
68 burh-: ciuis *R.*   69 bysmorlice: ridiculose *R.*   forscyldgode: delin-
quentes *RP*, peccaue*runt in margin R.*   70 hi: illos *R.*   71 swefle: sulfure
RP.   72 on ær: ante *R.*   73 alædde: duxit *R.*   74 ne: no*n R.*   forwurde: *in*teriret *R*, *p*eriret *P.*   76 foresceawian: *p*reuide*re R.*   77 egeslicum: terribili *R.*   78 gymað: cura*nt R*, capiu*nt* cura*m RP.*   ogan: timore *R,*
metu *P.*
ME: 66 æ: lawe *R*; *gloss erased P.*   71 swefle: *gloss erased P.*

60–61 [*Bede, on verse 26*] Subitum adventus sui diem plurimis affirmat
exemplis. Nam quem fulgori cito omnia transvolanti comparaverat, eundem
diebus Noe vel Loth, quando repentinus mortalibus supervenit interitus,
æquiperat.
65–74 [*Free summary of the story in Gen. xviii, xix.*]
71 [*Bede may have suggested the epithet 'hellicum' by his partially disagreeing
comment on verse 29*] Notandum quod ignis et sulphur quæ de cælo pluisse com-
memorat non ipsam perennis supplicii flammam sed subitaneum diei illius
significat adventum. Neque enim ignis ille perpetuus superveniens impios puniet
sed ipsi potius a conspectu iudicis eiecti in ignem mittentur æternum, quamvis
et eidem igni sulphur non dubitemus inesse, testante Ioanne (*Apoc. xx. 9, 10*).

æniges oðres þ[i]nges butan þæs anes brógan,
ne nan mann ne mæg ætberstan þam bradan fyre ahwider;   80
and þæt fyr þonne afeormað þas eorðan,
and hi geedniwað to ænlicum híwe,
and heo ne bið na forburnen, ac bið geclænsod
from eallum þam fylþum þe hyre fram frymðe becomon,
and heo swa on ecnysse eall scinende þurhwunað.   85
'On þære nihte beoð twegen on ánum bedde;
án þara bið genumen, and oðer bið forlæten.'
Niht is her gecweden for ðære nytennysse,
and for þære mycelan ehtnysse on Antecristes tíman;
þonne beoð twegen menn on ánum bedde ætgædere;   90
án þæra bið genumen, and oðer *bið forlæten.   *p. 104
Ða beoð þonne on bedde þe beoð on stillnysse,
and fram eallum woruldcarum æmtige þonne beoð,
and Godes þeowdóm begað mid góódum inngehyde;
ac hi ne beoð na twegen, ac on twá todælede.   95
Oþre beoð gecorene and Gode gecwéme,
oðre beoð mid híwunge on his þeowdóme afundene.

---

79 þinges] sic P; þnges R.   buton P.   84 from] fram P.   85 eal P.
87 ðæra P.   92 stil- P.   93 æmtige þonne] þonne æmtige P.
94 in- P.

Glosses, Latin: 79 brogan: terror R, terrorem P.   80 ætberstan: euadere R.
ahwider: alicubi R.   81 afeormað: purgat R.   þas: illam P.   82 hi:
eam P.   geedniwað: renouat R, renouatur P.   ænlicum: ameno, iocundo R.
87 byð forlæten: relinquitur P.   88 nytennysse: ingnorantiam R.
89 ehtnysse: persecutionem R.   90 bedde: lecto P.   92 Ða: illi R.
stillnysse: tranquillitate R.   94 þeowdom: officium R.   begað: excercent
R.   inngehyde: sciencia R, scientia P.   95 twegen: duo R.   96 gode:
deo P.   97 hiwunge: simulatione R, ficticia P.   þeowdome: officio R.
afundene: probati P.

---

88 [*See note.*]
89–94 [*Bede, on verse 34*] In illa ergo nocte, dixit, in illa tribulatione tam tene-
brosa, *ut in errorem inducantur, si fieri potest, etiam electi* (*Matth. xxiv. 24; cf.
line 258 below*), duo erunt in lecto, illi videlicet qui otium et quietem eligunt,
neque negotiis sæcularibus, neque negotiis ecclesiasticis occupati, quæ illorum
quies lecti nomine significata est.
95–109 [*Partly from Bede, on end of verse 34*] Non quasi de duobus hominibus
dictum est sed de duobus generibus affectionum. Qui enim propter Deum
continentiæ studuerit, ut sine sollicitudine vivens cogitet quæ Dei sunt (*cf.
I Cor. vii. 32, 34*), assumetur a Deo; qui vero vel humanæ laudis amore, vel alia
qualibet vitiorum corruptione statum monasticæ vitæ, quo imbutus est, læserit,
hic ubi relinquendus sit Ieremiæ lamentationes insinuant (*Lam. i. 7*).

þonne genimð se Hælend to hys heofonlican ríce
þa þe æmtige wæron fram eallum woruldcárum,
æfre on his þeowdóme oð ðone endenyhstan dæg;   100
and sume eac of þam, ðe ungesælige wæron,
and mid leasre hiwunge and lyffetunge ferdon,
he forlæt bæftan hym, and hi beoð þonne
belocene wiðutan þære écan myrhðe.

Swa bið se án genumen and se oðer forlǽten   105
þe on þam bedde beoð þonne gemette—
þæt is, on þære stilnysse heora staþolfæstan modes;
na twegen menn ána, ac on twa wisan gemodode,
oðre mid soðfæstnysse, oðre mid hiwunge.

'Twa grindað þonne on anre cwyrne ætgædere;   110
se[o] án bið genumen, and seo oðer bið forlæten.'
Ær he cwæð twegen, nu he cwæð twá,
on anre cwyrne emlice grindende.

þæt synd þa woruldmenn þe woruldþing begað;
and seo woruldcaru is þære cwyrne wiðmeten,   115
þe æfre gæð abutan ymbe fela geþohtas
and mislicum dædum þe menn behofiað,
and hefegum geswincum, swa swa ge sylfe wíton.

Be þysum he cwæð twá, and nolde cweðan twegen,
for þam þe hi soðlice ne beoð on swylcere fullfremednysse   120
þæt hi sylfe magon hy[m] sylfum wissian,

100 -nextan P.   106 beoð þonne] þonne beoð P.   108 gemodude P.
111 seo an] sic P; se an R.   120 þam] þan P.   ful- P.   121 hy sylfum R;
him sylfum P.

Glosses, Latin: 100 oð: usque RP.   101 þam: illis R.   102 hiwunge:
simulatione P.   lyffetunge: adulatione RP.   108 gemodode: animati R.
109 hiwunge: dissimulatio R.   110 þonne: tunc P.   112 Ær: prius P.
113 emlice: equanimiter R, equaliter P.   114 begað: excercent R.
115 woruldcaru: studia R.   is . . . wiðmeten: comparatur (twice) R.
117 behofiað: indigent R.   120 fullfremednysse: perfectione R.

112–25 [Partly from Bede, on verse 35] Molentes appellat eos qui in plebibus
constituti reguntur a doctoribus, agentes ea quæ sunt huius sæculi, quos et
feminarum nomine significavit, quia consiliis, ut dixi, peritorum regi eis expedit.
Et molentes, dixit, propter temporalium negotiorum orbem atque circuitum.
Quas tamen in unum molentes dixit, in quantum de ipsis rebus et negotiis suis
præbent usibus Ecclesiæ. Unaquæque enim huius mundi actio mola est, quæ
dum multas curas congerit, humanas mentes quasi per gyrum vertit, atque ex
se velut farinas proiicit, quia inquieto cordi semper minutissimas cogitationes
gignit.

ac hy sceolan lybban be heora lareowa wissunge,
bisceopa and mæssepreosta, and heora misdæda betan
be heora scrifta tæcinge, *and of heora tilunge   *p. 105
dón symle ælmyssan; ac hi ne magon swaþeah   125
þam beon geefenlæhte þe ealle þing forleton
for þæs Hælendes lufon, and hym æfre þeowodon.
Forði synd twá gecwedene, and na twegen weras,
for þam woruldcarum þe hi on wuniað.
Of þam woruldmannum witodlice beoð   130
on twá wisan gemodode and mislice gelogode;
sume beoð gecorene, sume wiðercorene;
sume hi libbað heora líf rihtlice,
sume wólice and on synnum geendiað;
þonne genimð se Hælend to hys heofonlican rice   135
on þam micclan dæge of þam woruldmannum
þa ðe mid góódum willan and weorcum æfre
hym ær gecwemdan oð heora lifes ende,
and þa wiðercorenan beoð wiðútan belocene;
þonne bið seo án genumen, and seo oðer forlæten.   140
'Twegen beoð on æcere, erigende ætgædere;
se an bið genumen, and se oðer bið forlæten.'
Hér he cwæð twegen, and nolde cweþan twá,
for þære fullfremednysse and fægerum geþingþum
þe þa habban sceolan þe on Godes æcere swincað.   145
Godes æcer is Godes gelaþung,
þæt is, eall Cristen folc þe on Crist gelyfð,
swa swa Paulus cwæð on sumum his pistole

122 heora] *om. P.*   124 scriftes *P.*   131 gemodade *P.*   144 ful-
P.   geðincðum *P.*

Glosses, Latin: 126 beon geefenlæhte: *com*parari, coe*qu*ari, imitant*ur R*;
assimiliati *P.*   127 þeowodon: ministrabant *R.*   129 woruldcarum:
studio *R.*   130 witodlice: *certe R.*   131 gelogode: dispositi *R.*
132 wiðercorene: rep*robi R.*   134 wolice: indirecte *R.*   137 þa: eos *P.*
138 oð: us*qu*e *R.*   139 wiðercorenan: rep*robi R.*   144 fullfremednysse:
perfectione*m R.*   fægerum: pulcra *R.*   geþingþum: apice *R.*

126–7 [*Cf. Matth. xix. 27–29; Luc. xviii. 28–30; but the immediate reference
is to the monastic clergy of the first category, lines 92 sqq.*]
130–40 [*Ælfric substitutes a simpler and more general distinction for Bede's.*]
146–52 [*Bede, on verse 35, second part*] Significat autem eos qui operantur
Ecclesiæ ministerio, tanquam in agro Dei, cui suus agricola dicebat: *Dei
agricultura estis* (*I Cor. iii. 9*).

to þam geleaffullum mannum þe he to geleafan gebigde:
Dei agricultura estis, Dei edificatio estis.   150
þæt is on Englisc,
Ge synd Godes tilung and Godes getimbrung.
Witað nu þis:
Biscopas and mæssepreostas syndon manna lareowas;
hi sceolan hogian ymbe þæs Hælendes tilunge,   155
þæt hi manega sawla of manncynne *gestrynan   *p. 106
þam welwillendan Hælende, þe wile us habban.
Hi sceolon þone Cristendóm dón Cristes folce,
and mid heora lare symle to geleafan weman,
and æfre mid weorcum hym wel bysnian,   160
and on heora þeowdome þe hi Gode þeowiað
hym foreþingian; þonne beoð hi rihtlice
Godes tilian on þam gastlican ǽcere,
and hi swa miclum beoð on maran geþingðe,
swa hi ma sawla of manncynne begytað   165
to heofonan rice; and hi habbað ealdordom
on þam ecan life ofer eallum þam sawlum
þe hy Gode gestryndon mid þære gastlican teolunge.
    Is swaþeah to lyt þæra lareowa nú
þe þus don wille, and is manncynn forþi   170
miclum geyrmed, for þam þe þæra is
feawa folces lareowa þe geornlice hógie
hu man yfel alegce and únrihtwisnysse,
and riht arǽre, swa swa we rædað on bócum:
Canes muti non possunt latrare: 175

---

152 syndon, beoð *over line P.*   tilung] eorðteolung *P* (*see note*).   154 Bisceopas *P.*   manna *R.*   155 hi] his *P.*   156 manega] managa *altered*
to maga *P.*   gestrynon *P.*   157 wyle *P.*   159 symble *P.*   to geleafan
weman] weman to geleafan *P.*   weman] *sic both MSS. originally but perhaps*
altered to wenian *R.*   160 bysnian] gebysnian *P.*   164 geþincðe *P*
168 tilunge *P.*   170 wylle *P.*   mancyn *P.*   173 alecge *P.*

Glosses, Latin: 149 gebigde: *conuertit R.*   153 Witað: *custodite R.*
156 maga (*from* managa): *possint P.*   gestrynan: *lucrentur R.*   159 symle:
semper R.   weman: *suadere RP,* [h]ortare *R.*   161 þeowdome: *offitio R.*
163 tilian: *acricole R.*   164 geþingþe: *apice R.*   166 ealdordom:
principatum P.   168 gestryndon: *lucrati sunt R.*   171 geyrmed: *miser R.*

153–88 [*Ælfric expands independently of Bede.*]
175 [*Is. lvi. 10*] Canes muti non valentes latrare.

Hi synd þa dumban hunda[s], and hy ne magon beorcan.
þis cwæð se witega be Godes lareowum,
þe noldan bodian and gebigan manncynn
to Godes willan þá on þam timan þe hi wæron.
Nu is hit gyt wyrse on urum tíman,   180
þæt we ealle suwiað, and unriht gæð forð
ópenlice and digollice, and we embe ne hógiað.
Witodlice þa lareowas þe ús lár of cóm,
hi bododan þam hæðenum and þam hetelum ehterum,
and heora lif sealdon for Godes geleafan;   185
ac we ne durran nú to þam gedyrstlæcan,
þæt we Cristenum cyninge oððe Cristenum folce
Godes beboda and Godes willan secgan.
Nu synd twegen gecwedene þe Gode tilian sceolan
on þære gastlican tilunge *on Godes gelaðunge,   *p. 107
for þam ðe hi ne beoð ealle on áne wisan geworhte.   191
Sume hi beoð geor'n'fulle, sume gymelease,
sume ánræde, sume asolcene,
sume nyttwyrðe, [sume unnyttwyrðe,]
sume swiðe fremfulle, sume swiðe derigende.   195
þonne bið se án genumen, and se oðor forlæten,
þonne se Hælend genimð to his halgum englum
ða góódan lareowas into Godes rice,
and þa yfelan beoð wiðútan belocene.
On þisum þrim endebyrdnyssum bið eall mancynn belocen: 200

176 hundas] sic P; hundan R.   177 lareowam P.   178 gebygan P.
182 digellice P.   188 secgon P.   191 þam] þan P   194 nytwurðe P.
sume unnytwurðe P; om. R.   195 swyðe P (twice).   196 oðer P.
200 þysum þrym P.

Glosses, Latin: 178 bodian: predicare R.   gebigan: conuertere R.   179 þa:
tunc RP.   181 suwiað: scilemus, tacemus R; silemus P.   182 digollice: clam R.   embe: circa R.   183 Witodlice: certe R.   184 bododan: predicauerunt R.   hetelum: exosis R.   ehterum: persecutoribus R.
186 gedyrstlæcan: audaciam habere, presumere R.   188 beboda: pre-
cepta R.   193 anræde: instantes R, constantes P.   asolcene: pigri RP.
195 fremfulle: beningni RP.   197 genimð: capit R.   200 endebyrdnyssum: ordinibus R.

ME: 176 synd: beoð P (erased).

189-99 [Ælfric's distinction between the good and the bad is independent of
Bede's.]
200 [Bede, on verse 35, end of second part] Nec puto alia genera esse hominum
quibus constat ecclesia quam ista tria habentia binas diĩerentias propter assum-
ptionem et relictionem.

twegen on þam bedde, and twa æt þære cwyrne,
twegen on þam æcere, swa swa ge gehyrdon nú.
'Hi andwyrdan þa and hyne ahsodon þuss:
Hwider beoð hi genumene? And he hym cwæð tó,
Swa hwær swa þæt hold bið, þider gaderiað þa earnas.'   205
þa Sundorhalgan ahsodan þone Hælend þa þus:
hwíder þa góódan sceoldan gegripene beon,
oððe hwider þa yfelan beon forlætene.
Ða andwyrde he be þam góódum, and nolde be þam yfelum.
þa earnas getacniað þa geþungenan halgan;   210
and swa swa earnas hi gegaderiað þær þær þæt hold bið,
swa beoð þa halgan weras to þam Hælende gegadorade,
þær þær he on menniscnysse mihtiglice rihsað,
soð mann and soð god, án Godes Sunu
þæs ælmihtigan Fæder, mid þam he æfre ricsað,   215
and mid þam Halgan Gaste, on ánre godcundnysse, amen.
þa þe beoð forlætene and belocene wiðútan
of þam þrim werodum, þa gewendað to helle,
mid eallum deoflum fordemede on ecnysse;
and hi næfre syððan nane miltsunge ne begitað,   220
for þam ðe hi æfre ǽr on synnum wunedon.
*We habbað nu gesæd hu ða Sundorhalgan   *p. 108
ahsodon þone Hælend be ende þissere worulde;
nu wille we eow secgan sceortlice, gif we magon,
hu hys agene leorningcnihtas hyne ahsodon be þam,   225
swa swa seo [Cristes] bóc us cyð be þam ylcan:

203 axodon P.   205 gaderiað] gegaderiað P.   206 sunder- P.
axodon P.   211 þar ðar P.   212 gegaderode P.   213 þar ðar P.
mihtilice rixað P.   215 rixað P.   218 þrym weredum P.   219 fordemde P.   220 begytað P.   221 þam] þan P.   wunodon P.   223 acxodon P.   224 wylle P.   225 acxodon P.   226 cristes] sic P; om. R.

Glosses, Latin: 205 hold: cadauer R.   206 sundorhalgan: farisei RP.
208 forlætene: relicti R.   210 geþungenan: perfecti R.   213 rihsað:
rengnat R.   217 þa: illi R.   forlætene: relicti R.   222 sundorhalgan:
farisei R.   223 ahsodon: interrogabant R.   226 cyð: dicit R.
ME: 218 werodum: folc R.

206-21 [Partly from Bede, on verses 36, 37] Duo Salvator interrogatus, ubi
scilicet boni assumendi, et ubi sint mali relinquendi, unum dixit, aliud sub-
intellegendum reliquit. Sanctos enim secum futuros asseuerando, reprobos
nimirum a sua visione secernendos et ideo non alibi quam cum diabolo damnan-
dos insinuat. Ubicumque ergo fuerit Dominus corpore, illo congregabuntur
electi, . . . quorum per resurrectionem renovabitur ut aquilæ iuventus (Ps. cii. 5).

*Interrogatus Ie*sus *a discipulis de consu*mm*atione se*culi,
*dix*it *eis*, *Cum aute*m *uideritis abhominatione*m *desol*[*a*]*tionis*, et
*reliq*ua.

Ða halgan apostolas þe mid þam Hælende ferdon,
þa þa he her on worulde wunode mid mannum,   230
ahsodan hyne endemys be þissere worulde geendunge;
he hym þa andwyrde, and hym þus to cwæð:
þonne ge geseoð standan on þære halgan stowe
onscuniendlic deofolgild, swa swa Danihel awrát,
se ðe þæt ræde oððe rædan gehyre,   235

227 consumatione seculi *P*.   228 abominatione*m P*.   desolationis]
sic P; desolutionis *R*.   231 acxodon *P*.   234 onscunigendlic *P*.   -gyld *P*.
daniel *P*.

Glosses, Latin: 231 ahsodan: *inqu*irebant *R*.   endemys: *per* ordine*m*, similit*er*,
parit*er R*; parit*er* omn*es P*.   234 onscuniendlic: abominatione*m R*,
abhominabil*is P*.   deofolgild: idolu*m R*.   235 ræde: legat *R*, legit *P*.

227–8 [*Matth. xxiv.* The beginning of the Latin, Interrogatus . . . dixit eis, *is
a freely composed introduction, based on verse 3, to verses 15 sqq., starting with*
Cum. *Cf. the beginning of Luc. xvii. 20, above. In what follows Ælfric gives only
the verses from Matth. xxiv that correspond to Marc. xiii. 14–27, and sometimes
prefers the readings of the latter.*]

233–69 [*Matth. xxiv. 15*] Cum ergo videritis abominationem desolationis,
quæ dicta est a Daniele propheta, stantem in loco sancto, qui legit, intelligat:
[*16*] tunc qui in Iudæa sunt, fugiant ad montes:
[*17*] et qui in tecto, non descendat tollere aliquid de domo sua:
[*18*] et qui in agro, non revertatur tollere tunicam suam.
[*19*] Væ autem prægnantibus, et nutrientibus in illis diebus.
[*20*] Orate autem ut non fiat fuga vestra in hieme, vel sabbato.
[*21*] Erit enim tunc tribulatio magna, qualis non fuit ab initio mundi usque
modo, neque fiet. [*Marc. xiii. 19*] Erunt enim dies illi tribulationes tales, quales
non fuerunt . . . neque fient.
[*22*] Et nisi breviati fuissent dies illi, non fieret salva omnis caro: sed propter
electos breviabuntur dies illi. [*Marc. xiii. 20*] Et nisi breviasset Dominus dies,
non fuisset salva omnis caro: sed propter electos quos elegit, breviavit dies.
[*23*] Tunc si quis vobis dixerit: Ecce hic est Christus, aut illic: nolite credere.
[*24*] Surgent enim pseudochristi, et pseudoprophetæ: et dabunt signa magna,
et prodigia, ita ut in errorem inducantur (si fieri potest) etiam electi. [*Marc.
xiii. 22*] . . . dabunt signa et portenta, ad seducendos (si fieri potest) etiam electos.
[*25*] Ecce prædixi vobis. . . . [*Marc. xiii. 23*] Vos ergo videte: ecce prædixi vobis
omnia.
[*29*] Statim autem post tribulationem dierum illorum sol obscurabitur et
luna non dabit lumen suum et stellæ cadent de cælo et virtutes cælorum com-
movebuntur: [*Marc. xiii. 24*] . . . sol contenebrabitur. . . .
[*30*] et tunc . . . videbunt Filium hominis venientem in nubibus cæli cum
virtute multa et maiestate. [*Marc. xiii. 26*] . . . in nubibus cum virtute multa et
gloria.
[*31*] Et mittet angelos suos, . . . et congregabunt electos eius a quattuor ventis,
a summis cælorum usque ad terminos eorum. [*Marc. xiii. 27*] . . . a summo
terræ usque ad summum cæli.

undergyte he þonne þæs witegan word.
Ða þe on Iudea lande þonne lybbende beoð,
þa fleoð þonne to muntum and to micclum dunum;
and se ðe on his huse bið on þam healicum hrófe,
ne astige he þonne of þam sticolan hrofe,   240
þæt he hys yddisce ahredde þe on þam huse bið.
And se þe on æcere beo ymbe hys tilunge,
ne cyrre [he] underbǽc to genimenne hys reaf.
Wá þam eacniendum on þam yfelum dagum,
and þam fedendum on þære frecednysse.   245
Biddað eornostlice þæt hyt ne beo on wintra,
oððe on reste[n]dæge, þonne ge æmtige beoð.
þonne beoð witodlice swylce gedrefednyssa
swylce næfre ær næran, ne eft ne gewurþað.
Butan God gescyrte þa sorhfullan dagas,   250
eall manncynn forwurde witodlice ætgædere.
Ac for hys gecorenum he gescyrte þa dagas.
Gif hwá þonne eow sægð þæt Crist sylf *beo   *p. 109
þonne on worulde wuniende mid mannum,
ne gelyfe ge þæs, for þam þe [lease Cristas   255
on þam timan] arisað and fela tacna wyrcað,
menn to beswicenne mid heora scincræftum,
and eac þa gecorenan menn, gif hit gewurðan mæg.
Warniað eow [eornost]lice; ic hyt hæbbe eow gesæd.
Sona æfter þære gedrefednysse adeorcað seo sunne,   260

236 -gite P.   238 þonne] om. P (rightly?)   mycclum P.   240 sticelan P.
243 he] sic P; om. R.   hreaf P.   245 fedyndum P.   247 resten-] sic P;
reste- R.   250 Buton P.   252 gecorenum] gecorenum halgum P.
253 segð P.   253–4 beo þonne] þonne beo P.   255 þam] þan P.
255–6 lease . . . timan] sic P; on þam timan lease cristas R (spoils alliteration).
259 Warniað] cap. P, not R.   eornost-] sic P; georn- R.

Glosses, Latin: 237 Ða þe: qui R.   240 ne astige he: non ascendet R (!).
241 yddisce: familiam RP.   243 genimenne: capere P.   reaf: vestem R.
244 Wa: ve R.   eacniendum: preingnantibus R, prengnantibus P.   245 fedyndum: nutrientibus P.   frecednysse: periculum R; tribulatione, periculo P.
246 eornostlice: igitur R.   247 oððe: vel R.   restedæge: sabato RP.
248 witodlice: certe R.   gedrefednyssa: persecutio R, tribulatio P.
251 forwurde: periret RP.   witodlice: certe R.   252 gescyrte: abreuiauit R.
255 lease: seoudo R, pseoudo P.   257 scincræftum: magicis artibus RP.
259 warniað: cauete RP, muniamini R.   260 gedrefednysse: persecutione R, tribulatione RP.   adeorcað: obscurabitur R.
ME: 256 feala tacna: gloss erased P.   257 scincræftum: wicchecreft P
(? erased).

and mid ealle aþeostraŏ, and eac se móna,
and steorran feallaŏ færlice of heofonum,
and heofonan mihta beoŏ þonne astyrode.
Menn geseoŏ þonne mannes Sunu cumende
on þam healicum wolcnum mid micclum wuldre;   265
he asent þonne soŏlice hys englas,
and hy gegaderiaŏ Godes gecorenan menn
fram þam feowor windum þissere worulde,
and of þære eorŏan up oŏ þa heofonan.
We habbaŏ nu gesæd þis halige godspell   270
ánfealdum andgyte, and we eac willaŏ
þæt gastlice andgyt þurh God eow secgan.
'þa halgan apostolas þe mid þam Hælende ferdon,
þa þa he her on worulde wunode mid mannum,
ahsodan hyne endemes be þissere worulde geendunge;   275
he hym þa andwyrde, and hym þus to cwæŏ:
þonne ge geseoŏ standan on þære halgan stowe
onscunigendlic deofolgyld, swa swa Danihel awrat,
se ŏe þæt ræde, oŏŏe [r]ǽdan gehyre,
undergyte he þonne þæs witegan word.'   280
Iú on ealdum dagum, ær ŏam þe Cristendom wære,
menn worhton deofolgyld wide geond þas woruld,

263 (beoŏ) beoŏ *R* (*first erased*).   265 mycclum *P*.   267 gegaderiaŏ]
gegaderaŏ þonne *P*.   268 feower *P*.   271 wyllaŏ *P*.   272 secgan]
gescegan *P*.   275 acxodon *P*.   endemys *P*.   276 þa] *om. P*.   278 daniel
P.   279 rædan] *sic P*; þæt rædan *R*.   280 undergite *P*.   282 -gild *P*.

Glosses, Latin: 263 mihta: *virtutes RP*.   astyrode: moti *R*.   265 wolcnum: nube *RP*.   wuldre: *gloriam R*.   269 oŏ: usq*ue R*.   271 anfeal-
dum andgyte: simplici *intellectu RP*.   272 andgyt: sensu*m R*.
275 ahsodan: *interrogabant R*.   endemes: similite*r R*, *pariter RP*.
278 onscunigendlic deofolgyld: abhominabil*is* [*sic*] idolu*m R*, abominati*ones P*.
279 ræde: legat *R*.   281 Iu: q*uondam R*, olim *P*.
ME: 265 wuldre: glore *P* (*? erased*).

281–306 [*Cf. Jerome, In Matth. xxiv. 15*] Quando ad intellegentiam provo-
camur mysticum monstratur esse quod dictum est. Legimus autem in Daniele
hoc modo [*quotes Dan. ix. 27*]. . . . De hoc et apostolus loquitur: quod homo
iniquitatis et adversarius elevandus sit contra omne quod dicitur Deus, et
colitur; ita ut audeat stare in templo Dei, et ostendere quod ipse sit Deus, cuius
adventus secundum operationem Satanæ destruat eos, et ad Dei solitudinem
redigat, qui se susceperint (*inexactly II Thess. ii. 4, 5, 9, 10*). Potest autem
simpliciter aut de Antichristo accipi, aut de imagine Cæsaris. . . . Abominatio
quoque, secundum veterem Scripturam, idolum nuncupatur. [*Bede, In Marc.
xiii. 14, repeats first sentence and last two, omitting references to Daniel and Thess.*]

and hi þærto gebædon; ac ure Drihten adwæscte
þone hæðenscype mid hys halgan tocyme,
and þone Cristendóm arærde þurh hyne sylfne ærest,   285
and þurh hys leorningcnihtas, and þurh hys lareowas
*syððan.   *p. 110
Nu ne wyrcð nan mann nu on þysum timan,
gif he geleafan hæfð, hæþengyld openlice;
ac se arleasa Antecrist on [ende] þissere worulde
wyrcð fela wundra þurh hys fcondlican mihte,   290
and þurh Godes geþafunge, and segð þæt he God si;
and þurh hys mycclan wundra menn bugað to hym
and on hine gelyfað, hym sylfum to forwyrde;
ac þa gecorenan halgan hym wiðcweðað æfre,
þeah ðæ þa gedwolan hys gedwyldum gelyfan.   295
Hwæt bið mare deofolgyld þonne se deofollica Antecrist
hym Godes wurðmynt geahnige, and hyne God talige,
and men hym to gebiddan þurh hys leasan tácna,
and þone Hælend forseon, þe is eall soðfæstnyss?
On þære halgan stowe stent þonne þæt deofolgyld,   300
swa swa se apostol awrát on sumum hys pistole:
Ita ut in templo Dei sedeat, ostendens se tamquam sit Deus:
Swa þæt he sitt on Godes temple, and segð þæt he God sy.
Him farað mid æfre ungesewenlice deoflu,

---

286 *second* hys] *om. P.*   289 ende] *sic P; om. R.*   291 sy *P.*   292 mice-
lan *P.*   295 ðæ] ðe *P.*   gedwolan] dwolan *P.*   gelyfon *P.*   298 men
hym] him men *P.*   gebiddon *P.*   299 -nys *P.*   303 sit *P.*   304 deofla *P.*

Glosses, Latin: 283 adwæscte: destruxit *R.*   287 wyrcð: operatur *R.*
289 arleasa: impius *R.*   290 wyrcð: operatur *R.*   291 geþafunge:
permissione *R.*   292 bugað: conuertunt *R.*   293 forwyrde: damnatione *R.*   295 gedwolan: heretici *R.*   gedwyldum: heresim, errorem *R.*
297 geahnige: apropriat *R*, appropriat *P*, possideat *RP.*   talige: predicet *R*,
iudicet *P*, dicat *RP.*   298 gebiddan: adorent *R.*   299 forseon: contemp-
nent *R*, spurciant *P* (*as if from* spurcio *rather than* spurco, *but perhaps a miswriting of* spernant).
ME: 291, 303 sy: beo *P.*   295 gedwolan: vnbileued *P* (? *erased*).

---

302 [*II Thess. ii. 4, as given.*]
303–5 [*Cf. Adso, De Ortu et Tempore Antichristi, ed. Sackur, pp. 107–8*] Et
maligni spiritus erunt duces eius et socii semper et comites indivisi [*v.l.* invisi].
. . . Deinde per universum orbem nuntios mittet et prædicatores suos. Prædicatio
autem eius et potestas tenebit a mari usque ad mare. . . . Faciet quoque signa
multa, miracula magna et inaudita.

þurh ða he wyrcð wundra wide geond þas eorðan,   305
and ofer eallum manncynne becymð seo ehtnyss.
'þa ðe on Iudea lande þonne libbende beoð,
þa fleoð to muntum and to micclum dunum;
and se ðe on his huse bið on þam healicum hrofe,
ne astige he þonne of þam sticolan hrófe,   310
þæt he hys yddisce ahredde þe on ðam [huse] bið.
And se ðe on æcere beo ymbe hys tilunge,
ne cyrre he underbæc to genimene hys reaf.'—
We moton eow secgan swa swa ge magon understandan,
hwilum anfealdlice be eowrum andgite,   315
hwilum eow geopenian þa inran digolnysse,
for þam þe ge eaðe ne magon hyt eall understandan.
'Wa þam eacniendum on þam yfelum dagum,
and þam fedendum *on þære frecednysse.'   *p. 111
Hwæt agyltað þa wif, þe be Godes hæse tymað   320
and heora cild fedað on þære frecednysse?'
Ac þis is gecweden be þam leasum Cristenum,
þe beoð mid leahtrum afyllede, swa swa gefearhsugu,
and mid unwrencum þa unwaran fordoð,
and heora yfel geea[c]niað swylce mid fo[str]e.   325

307 lybbende P.   310 sticelan P.   311 huse] sic P; om. R.
313 genimenne P.   315 hwilum altered from hwilcum R; hwilon P.   andgyte P.   316 hwilon P.   digel- P.   317 ðam] ðan P.   322 Ac] no cap.
RP.   325 geeacniað] geearniað R; getacniað P.   fostre] sic P; forste R.

Glosses, Latin: 305 ða: illos R, ea P.   wyrcð: operatur R.   geond: per R.
306 seo ehtnyss: ipsa (?) persecutio R.   307 þa: illi R.   310 ne astige
he: non ascendet R.   311 yddisce: familiam RP.   313 underbæc:
retro R.   reaf: vestem R.   315 hwilum: aliquando R.   andgite: sensu R.
316 geopenian: aperire R.   inran: interiora R.   digolnysse: secreta R.
318 Wa: ve R.   eacniendum: prengnantibus RP.   319 fedendum: nutrientibus RP.   frecednysse: periculum R, tribulatione P.   320 agyltað:
delinquunt R.   hæse: precepto R.   321 frecednysse: periculo R, tribulatione P.   323 leahtrum: crimine R.   gefearhsugu: prengnans porcus R,
prengnans sus P.   324 unwaran: incautos RP.   325 swylce: quasi R.
forste: gelu (repeated in margin!) R; fostre: nutritione P.

320–5 [Cæsarius, Sermo CLIV. 3 on Matth. xxiv. 19] Quid enim mali fecit
mulier, quæ de proprio marito concepit? Quare illi in die iudicii male erit, quæ
hoc fecit quod Deus iussit? Non ergo de mulieribus quæ iuste concipiunt et
pariunt hoc credendum est, sed de illis quos supra diximus, qui iniuste con-
cupiscendo rem alienam imprægnati esse videntur. [In the preceding section of
the sermon Cæsarius quotes from Augustine an imaginary instance of someone who
covets his neighbour's property and is tempted to take unfair advantage of him.
Hence perhaps Ælfric's 'unwrencum'.]

'Biddað eornostlice þæt hyt ne beo on wintra,
oððe on restendæge, þonne ge æmtige beoð.'
Ne mænde he þone winter þe gewunelice cymð
on þæs geares ymbryne, ac swa swa he on oðre stowe cwæð,
Quia abundabit iniquitas, refrigescet caritas multorum.   330
þæt is, on Engliscum gereorde, þæt on þam yfelan timan
arist seo unrihtwisnyss, and swiðe gemenigfylt,
and seo soðe lufu swiðe acolað,
na ealra manna, ac swiðe manegra,
þæt hy nateshwón ne lufiað þone lifigendan God,   335
ne hyra nyhstan, ne furðan hy sylfe;
for ðon se ðe God ne lufað, ne lufað he hyne sylfne.
Se restendæg is, swa swa we rædað on bócum,
halig freolsdæg on Iudea folce,
swa swa we healdað þone halgan Sunnandæg   340
fram woroldlicum weorcum; and we sceolan wilnian æfre,
and æt Gode biddan, þæt we ne beon æmtige
fram góódum weorcum, and on Godes lufan acolode,
þonne us se endenyhsta dæg onsigende bið.
'þonne beoð witodlice swylce gedrefednyssa   345
swylce næfre ær [næron, ne eft] ne gewurðað.'
Micel ehtnys wæs on anginne Cristendomes,

---

329 ymbrene *P.*   330 abundabið *P.*   refriescet *P.*   332 -nys *P.*
332, 333, 334 swyðe *P.*   335 lyfigendan *P.*   336 heora nextan *P.*
337 for ðam *P.*   341 woruld- *P.*   342 and] *erased* P.   biddan] *om. P.*
343 lufe *P.*   344 -nexta *P.*   346 næron ne eft] *sic* P; *om. R.*   347 Mycel
P.   ehtnyss *P.*

Glosses, Latin: 326 eornostlice: igit*ur R.*   327 restendæge: sabato *RP.*
æmtige: vacui *R.*   331 gereorde: lingua *R.*   332 gemenigfylt: m*ul*ti-
plicat *R.*   333 acolað: ref*ri*gescit *R.*   335 nateshwon: nulaten*us R.*
336 furðan: ecia*m R.*   337 for ðon: quia *R.*   338 restendæg: sabat*us*
(for -um) *R.*   344 onsigende: *imminens RP.*   345 witodlice: *certe R.*
swylce: talia *R.*   gedrefednyssa: p*er*secut*io*, p*ertur*batio, t*ri*bulati*ones R*;
t*ri*bulat*io* P.   346 gewurðað: er*unt R.*   347 ehtnys: p*er*secut*io R.* wæs: fuit *R.*

328–44 [*Jerome, In Matth. xxiv. 20; Bede, In Marc. xiii. 18*] Si autem de consummatione mundi intellegitur, hoc præcipit ut non refrigescat fides nostra, et
in Christum charitas, neque ut otiosi in opere Dei torpeamus virtutum Sabbato.
330 [*Matth. xxiv. 12, Vulg. 'Et quoniam' for 'Quia'.*]
347–65 [*Gregory, Moralia, xxxii. 24*] Sed considerandum valde est, cum
Behemoth iste caudam suam sicut cedrum sublevat (*Iob xl. 12*), in quo tunc
atrocior quam nunc se exerit surgat. Quæ enim poenarum genera novimus, quæ
non iam vires martyrum exercuisse gaudemus? Alios namque improviso ictu
immersus iugulo gladius stravit, alios. . . . Cum igitur Behemoth iste caudam

and eac lange syððan for Cristes geleafan,
ær ðam þe man mihte þysne middaneard gebígan
fram þam hæþenscype þe hy on afedde wæron   350
to þam soðan geleafan þæs lyfigendan Godes.
Man acwealde þa Cristenan mid mislicum cwylmingum,
and mid menigfealdum tintregum hi ge*martyrode;   *p. 112
ac hym geuðe se Hælend þæt hy mihton þa wyrcan
þa ilcan wundra þe he sylf geworhte.   355
Nú ne bið hit na swa on Antecristes timan;
he tintregað þa halgan, and eac tácna wyrcð,
and þa halgan ne magon on þam timan gewyrcan
ænige tácna, ac hi yfele beoð
forþam gedrefede, þonne se deofol wyrcð   360
menigfealde wundra, and hi sylfe ne magon
nane mihte gefremman on manna gesihðe.
þonne wet se deofol, and gewitnað þa halgan
mid swylcum [tintregum] swa we secgan ne magon,
and mid deof'l'es mihte macað fela wundra.   365
    'Butan God gescyrtte þa sorhfullan dagas,
eall manncynn forwurde witodlice ætgædere;

349 gebygan P.   350 -scipe P.   353 gemartirode P.   355 ylcan P.
359–60 beoð forþam] forðam beoð P.   362 mihta P.   gesyhðe P.
364 tintregum] sic P; wundrum, vel tintregum over line (early correction) R.
366 Buton P.   gescyrte P.   367 mancyn P.

    Glosses, Latin: 349 gebigan: conuertere R.   352 cwylmingum: cruciatibus
R.   353 tintregum: tormentis R.   354 geuðe: concessit R, consescet
(sic, for concessit?) P.   þa: tunc R.   357 tintregað: tormentat R.
358 gewyrcan: operare R.   360 gedrefede: turbati RP.   362 mihte:
virtutem R.   gefremman: facere R.   363 wet: furit RP.   gewitnað:
punit RP, lanit R.   366 gescyrtte: abreuiasset R.   sorhfullan: dolores R.
367 forwurde: periret R.   witodlice: certe R.   ætgædere: pariter R.
    ME: 357 tintregað: pineð P (? erased).

suam in fine mundi nequius dilatat, quid est quod in his tormentis tunc atrocius
crescat, nisi hoc quod in Evangelio Veritas per semetipsam dicit: Surgent
pseudochristi et pseudoprophetæ, etc. (Matth. xxiv. 24)? Nunc enim fideles nostri
mira faciunt, cum perversa patiuntur; tunc autem Behemoth huius satellites,
etiam cum perversa inferunt, mira facturi sunt. Pensemus ergo quæ erit humanæ
mentis illa tentatio, quando pius martyr et corpus tormentis subiicit, et tamen
ante eius oculos tortor miracula facit. Cuius tunc virtus non ab ipso cogitationum
fundo quatiatur, quando is qui flagris cruciat signis coruscat? [Bede, In Marc.
xiii. 19, developing the latter part of Gregory's comment, concludes] Quis ergo
ad fidem convertitur incredulus, cuius iam credentis non pavet et concutitur
fides, quando persecutor pietatis fit etiam operator virtutis, idemque ipse qui
tormentis sævit [cf. 363] ut Christus negetur provocat miraculis ut Antichristo
credatur?

ac for his gecorenum halgum he gescyrte þa dagas.'
Ðreo gear he ricsað and syx monðas on mancynne,
on eallre modignysse, eall mid deofle afylled,   370
and on eallum unþeawum and egeslicum fylðum
hys lif bið gelogod on þam lytlan fyrste;
and ælcne mannan he tiht to hys fulum þeawum,
and on ælce wisan he wile mancynn fordón.
Ac for Godes gecorenum God 'ge'hradað hys timan.   375
'Gif hwa þonne eow segð þæt Crist sylf beo
þonne wunigende on weorolde mid mannum,
ne gelyfe ge þæs, for þam ðe lease Cristas
on þam timan arisað, and fela tacna wyrcað,
menn to beswicanne mid heora scincræftum,   380
and eac þa gecorenan menn, gif hit gewurðan mæg;
warniað eow eornostlice; ic hit hæbbe eow gesæd.'
Ure Hælend Crist ne cymð na to mancynne
openlice æteowed on þissere weorolde
ær þam micclan dæge þonne he mancynne demð;   385
ac þa leasan Cristas and þa leasan witegan
þonne cumað on Antecristes timan;
hi syndon hys lima and hys leasan geferan,
and geond þas woruld farað mid feondlicum cræfte,   389
and to fela beswicað mid *heora scincræfte;   *p. 113

369 rixað P.   six P.   370 ealre P.   ealle *corrected to* eall R.   374 wyle
P.   377 wunigende on weorolde] on worulde wunigende P.   378 ge]
om. P.   þam] þan P.   380 geswicenne P.   384 worulde P.   387 þonne]
þe þonne P.

Glosses, *Latin*: 368 gescyrte: abreuiabit R.   369 ricsað: renxnet (? *for*
rengnat) R.   372 gelogod: dispositum R.   373 tiht: [h]ortatur R.
375 gehradað: preoccupat, preuenit, festinat R; accelerat P.   378 þæs:
hoc R.   lease: seudo P.   lease cristas: pseudo profethe R.   380 scincræftum: magicis artibus R.   382 warniað: cauete RP.   383 ne cymð:
non venit R.   384 æteowed: ostensus R.
ME: 380 scincræftum: wicchecreft P (? *erased*).   384 æteowed: ischawed
P (? *erased*).

369 [*Cf.* Bede, In Marc. xiii. 20] Hæc tribulatio . . . tribus annis ac dimidio,
quantum de prophetia Danielis (*Dan. xii. 11*) et apocalypsi sancti Ioannis (*Apoc.
xiii. 5*) conici potest, ecclesiam per orbem impugnatura esse creditur. [*Cf. also
Adso, op. cit. p. 109*] Hæc autem tam terribilis et timenda tribulatio tribus annis
manebit in toto mundo et dimidio. [*This standard calculation of the time is already
in Ælfric's Preface. CH I. 4.*]
388 [*Cf. quotations from Adso at 303 and Gregory, 'satellites', at 347; for* lima
see note.]

ac þa beoð gehealdene þe þurhwuniað oð ende
on Cristes geleafan, swa swa he sylf gecwæð.

He gewarnode þa, swa swa þis gewrit us segð,
hys halgan apostolas, and eac us þurh hi,
þæt we georne healdan hys geleafan æfre,   395
and ure líf syllan ær we hyne wiðsacon;
and hyt soðlice gewyrð swa swa he sylf sæde,
swa swa we nu ræddon on þissere rædinge.

'Sona æfter þære gedrefednysse adeorcað seo sunne,
and mid ealle aþeostrað, and eac se mona,   400
and steorran fcallað færlicc of hcofonum,
and heofonan mihta beoð þonne astyrode.'
Sona æfter þære ehtnysse bið Antecrist ofslagen
þurh Cristes mihte on hys tocyme,
and engla werodu beoð astyrede,   405
and mid þam Hælende cumað of þam heofonlican þrymme
swutollice æteowde, swa swa us segð þis godspell.

'Menn geseoð þonne mannes Sunu cumende
on þam healicum wolcnum mid micclum wuldre.'
Crist sylf is mannes Sunu, swa swa he sæde foroft;   410
he is anes mannes sunu swa swa nan oðer man nis;
he cymð þonne on þam wolcnum mid micclum wuldre
to þam micclan dóme, swa swa hit awriten is.

'He asent þonne soðlice hys englas,
and hi gegaderiað Godes gecorenan menn   415

393 He] cap. P, not R.   395 healdon P.   396 syllon P.   wiðsacan (sic) P.
401 heofonan P.   406 and transposed to follow hælende P.   407 swutellice
P.   413 micclum P.   415 gegaderiað] gegaderiað þonne P.

Glosses, Latin: 391 gehealdene: salui R.   oð: usque R.   393 gewarnode:
premuniuit RP.   þa: tunc R.   394 hi: eos RP.   395 georne: bene R.
397 gewyrð: erit R.   399 gedrefednysse: perturbatione, tribulatione R.
401 feallað: cadunt R.   402 mihta: virtutes R.   beoð ... astyrode:
mouentur R.   403 ehtnysse: persecutione R.   405 werodu: chorus R.
astyrede: moti R.   407 æteowde: ostensi R.   409 wolcnum: nube R.
415 hi: illi R.
ME: 405 werodu: ferede P (? erased).   407 æteowde: ischawed P (? erased).
409 wuldre: glore P (? erased).

391 sq. [Matth. xxiv. 13] Qui autem perseveraverit usque in finem, hic
salvus erit.
403 sq. [II Thess. ii. 8] Et tunc revelabitur ille iniquus, quem Dominus Iesus
interficiet spiritu oris sui, et destruet illustratione adventus sui eum. [Adso, op.
cit. p. 113, quotes this verse and adds that Antichrist will be killed either by Christ
himself or by the archangel Michael, per virtutem . . . Christi.]

fram þam feower windum þissere worulde,
and of þære eorðan up oð þa heofonan.'
Ða englas þonne bláwað heora byman hlúde,
and eall manncyn arist þe æfre cucu wæs
of heora byrgenum, and þa englas gebringaþ   420
þa gecorenan menn to Criste sylfum,
þæt hi mid him ricsian on heofonan rice
on lichaman and on sawle, gesæliglice æfre.
Crist cwæð on oðre stowe be þam árleasum þuss:
Exibunt angeli et separabunt malos de medio iustorum,   425
et mittent eos in caminum ignis,
ibi erit fletus et stridor dentium.
þæt [is] on Englisc, Englas farað *þonne   *p. 114
and asyndriað þa yfelan and þa synnfullan menn
fram þam rihtwisum, þe ricsiað mid Gode,   430
and awurpað hi ealle innto ðam widgillan fyre
þære bradan helle, on þære hy byrnað æfre,
þær bið wóp and wanung, and tóða gristbitung;
and hi nahwar ne wuniað butan on þam wítum æfre.
Soðlice þa halgan siðiað mid Criste   435
to heofonan rice mid hys halgum englum,
ge weras ge wifmenn, swa swa hi on worulde lyfodon,
and siððan wuniað gesælige mid him
on unasecgendlicre blisse á butan ende, Amen.

417 and] *erased* P.   heofenan P.   419 mancinn P.   422 rixian P.
428 is] *sic* P; *om.* R.   þonne] *om.* P.   429 syn- P.   430 rixiað P.
431 into P.   widgyllan P.   434 buton P.   437 wifmenn] winmen P.
438 siððan] hi syððan P.   439 -licere P.

Glosses, Latin: 419 cucu: uiuus R.   429 asyndriað: sep*arabunt* R.
431 awurpað: mitte*nt* R.   widgillan: (. . .)to *vel* spatioso R (*the first gloss cut
off by binder*).   433 gristbitung: stridor R.   434 witum: penis R.
435 siðiað: (. . .)u*nt* R (*cut off by binder*).
ME: 419 cucu: quike P (? *erased, usually* cwike).   434 witum: pine P
(? *erased*).   437 weras: *gloss erased* P.

425-7 [*Matth. xiii. 49, 50, as given.*]

NOTES

88. *Niht is her gecweden for ðære nytennysse.* This statement seems to
reflect a long-established association. Compare the homily on Virgins,
where Ælfric is commenting on *Matth.* xxv. 6, *Media autem nocte clamor
factus est (CH* II. 568/4–6): 'Hwæt getacnað seo midniht buton seo deope
nytennys? for ðan ðe seo geendung þyssere worulde cymð þonne men
læst wenað.'

117. *and mislicum dædum.* The *and* appears (as an ampersand) in both manuscripts, but this gives us a mixed construction, the normal accusative *geþohtas* after *ymbe*, then the datives *dædum* and *geswincum.* By substituting *on* for *and* we can improve both the grammar and the sense. Not that Ælfric's elaboration of the figure is altogether clear even so, but at least 'thoughts' are put into a different category from 'deeds' and 'labours'.

144. *and.* Once again, perhaps, we should read *on.* At *CH* II. 450/2, Ælfric says that Job, after the devil's persecution, was *fulfremedre on geþincðum,* 'more perfect in honours,' and this looks like the same idiom.

152. *tilung* R, *eorðteolung* P. The hitherto unrecorded compound in P translates *agricultura* more explicitly than the simple *tilung* in R, but *tilung* more obviously satisfies the alliterative and rhythmic pattern, and it gains further support by its repetition in 155, 168, 190, 242, and 312. Karl Jost, in 'Unechte Ælfrictexte', *Anglia* LI. 185, pointed out that Ælfric normally uses *yrþling* or *tilia* for a cultivator of the soil, not the comparatively rare *eorðtilia.*

169–88. This complaint against the bishops and priests of the time is strongly reminiscent of the *Letter for Wulfsige,* where Ælfric had already made use of the quotation from *Isaiah, Canes muti non possunt latrare* (175), both allusively in his Latin preface to Wulfsige and then directly in the body of the letter (Fehr, *Hirtenbriefe,* pp. 1 and 15). There, however, his basic concern is the laxity of the secular priesthood: their refusal to remain celibate and their ignorance quite as much as their failure to admonish the laity; and the burden of the preface is to urge Bishop Wulfsige to scold the priests. Here, ignorance and lax behaviour are less clearly in view than torpor and sheer cowardice in the face of unbridled wrong in the community at large. Ælfric says *we ealle suwiað* and *we ne durran,* though he himself was not altogether silent even when it came to admonishing his Christian king, as may be seen in IX and XXII.

227. *Interrogatus Iesus a discipulis de consummatione seculi, dixit eis.* This introduction to *Matth.* xxiv. 15 was presumably composed in order to bring out the parallel to *Luc.* xvii. 20 sqq., where its counterpart is actually in the gospel. Hence the composer ought to have been either Ælfric himself or some earlier author I have failed to discover who treated the two texts together. When we find Wulfstan using the same introduction to the sermon entitled *Secundum Marcum* (Bethurum v), we may be sure he took it from Ælfric. And in fact there are other clear echoes of the second half of *De Die Iudicii* in *Secundum Marcum,* as I have pointed out below in the notes on 330 and especially 347 sqq.

241, 311. *yddisce,* 'household goods, possessions', regarded by Holthausen and Hall–Meritt as a derivative of *ēad.* See the Glossary for the form. The gloss *familiam* in both manuscripts is misleading.

247. *þonne ge æmtige beoð.* This is Ælfric's gloss on the text, derived from the commentary on which he elaborates at 328–44.

291. *Godes geþafunge*. This may be inferred from *Matth.* xxiv. 22 and *Marc.* xiii. 20; it is explicit in *II Thess.* ii. 11, where St. Paul thinks that God will permit men to believe in a lie in order that they may be judged for not having believed in the truth. Ælfric does not give reasons here, but in his Preface, *CH* I. 4, he had explained God's permission as induced partly by the increasing sinfulness of mankind and partly for the purification of the elect. Later, in an additional passage that appears at the conclusion of the Antichrist section of the Preface (p. 6/18) in manuscripts Q, R, and T (Junius 121), he summarized St. Paul's statements in *II Thess.* ii. 9–11, as interpreted by Jerome, *Epist.* cxxi. 11—that is, with specific reference to the unbelieving Jews. Wulfstan restates Ælfric's first explanation in Bethurum v. 77 sqq.

297. *hyne God talige*, 'claim to be God'. The emphasis is on Antichrist's pretensions rather than on self-deception, which would be suggested by the usual definition of *talian* as 'account, consider'. He appropriates God's honours and, according to line 291, says that he is God. The basis for all this is *II Thess.* ii. 4, quoted by Ælfric at 302. Hence in the earlier Preface, *CH* I. 4, we find it said that Antichrist *cwyð þæt he sylf God beo*, and Wulfstan has a similar statement, Bethurum v. 76. An approach to the meaning of *talian* here recommended is suggested by Klaeber's discussion of *soð ic talige* at *Beowulf* 532 (*Modern Philology*, III. 261). This expression, he says, 'does not mean "I say (tell) the truth", as nearly everybody has translated it, but primarily "I consider it true (a fact)" . . . and then (putting theory into practice) "I stand up for that opinion of mine . . .", or "I claim it to be a fact." (Earle: "rightly I claim").' The reflexive use here makes it desirable to distinguish a little more sharply between considering and claiming, but Klaeber's concluding definition holds very well.

330. Ælfric's quotation of *Matth.* xxiv. 12 may have prompted Wulfstan to quote it in *Secundum Marcum*, Bethurum v. 26.

340. Is something missing before this line? The comparison between the Jewish and the Christian days of rest seems incompletely expressed, and the *æmtige fram* of 342 sq. has no adequate antecedent in the mere *fram* of 341. We might supply, *swa þæt on þære ealdan æ hi heoldon hine æmtigne*.

347–65. This passage, with Gregory behind it, is evidently the basis for the contrast between the days of the martyrs and those of Antichrist in Wulfstan's *Secundum Marcum*, Bethurum v. 53–66. Wulfstan has also made use of Ælfric's Preface, *CH* I. 4, which is echoed in subsequent lines (Bethurum, p. 291, notes on 68 sqq.). Perhaps Wulfstan's use of *scincræft*, 71, owes something to Ælfric's use of it at 257, 380, and 390.

363. *wet*. The mad fury of Antichrist conveyed by this word may have been suggested by Bede's *sævit* or by some other Latin passage that has escaped my attention, but no such expression occurs in the text of Adso as edited by Sackur. It does occur in the anonymous (and decidedly free) translation of Adso, Napier XLII (pp. 198/5; 200/1, 8) which seems to echo

Ælfric's preface at the beginning but is otherwise not close to him. Ælfric himself does not refer to Antichrist's madness in the Preface, nor in the brief references to him in *CH* II. 540, 542, and our XXVIII. Wulfstan, on the other hand, is full of the idea. He refers to Antichrist's *wodscinn* (Bethurum 1b. 34) and to the time when he *wedeð* (Bethurum II. 52; III. 13, 44)—thus far in pieces that do not stem from Ælfric. Then, in the very passage of *Secundum Marcum* in which he is developing his own version of the present passage in Ælfric, Wulfstan says that God will let *þone deofol Antecrist rabbian and wedan* (Bethurum v. 66). On the whole the chances are that the idea of Antichrist's madness came naturally to all these writers (though here and there with an additional prompting from another, perhaps) because of the widespread notion in the gospels and elsewhere that madmen are possessed by the devil. See, for example, homily IV.

388. *lima*. The limbs of Antichrist, like those of Satan, are the more or less inevitable counterpart of the limbs of Christ in *Ephes*. iv. 16 and elsewhere. Hence it is probably unnecessary to inquire where Ælfric encountered the figure. It is not in Adso, but it can be found in Gregory (*Moralia* xxix. 15) and in Haymo's commentary on *II Thess*. ii (*PL* CXVII. 780), from which a good many of the details in Adso's letter are borrowed. In both Gregory and Haymo the *membra* of Antichrist are introduced as precursors (Cain, Judas, Simon Magus, Nero, etc.) rather than as his associates in the last days, but once the figure is established its application to the latter becomes obvious.

XIX

DE DOCTRINA APOSTOLICA

THE title of this homily calls attention to the heavy emphasis given in the middle to St. Paul's teaching concerning chastity and marriage. Lines 71 to 106 contain fairly close translations from *I Corinthians* vii in an irregular order. There is Pauline doctrine at the beginning also, where Ælfric likens the sterner precepts of the faith to the strong meat required by adults and urges the putting away in due course of childish things. Indeed the counsels of perfection for the celibate and the married are only the leading topic in a sermon that urges men to set higher standards of conduct for themselves in other ways also. Both clergy and laity are included, but the laity especially are in view, and after they have been instructed with respect to marriage they are urged to avail themselves of the none too frequent opportunities granted them for partaking of the eucharist. This passage brings the prose part of the homily and the direct admonitions to an end. A rhythmic, largely narrative section, nearly as long as the other, is added, in which two *exempla* from Bede are used to forestall a not unfamiliar response to the earlier precepts. They enforce the doctrine that no matter how great a sinner a man is he must not despair; for those who despair are surely lost.

Evidently, therefore, although the homily is unassigned in both the manuscripts where it occurs in full, it is especially suitable for Lent or Rogationtide. We may associate it particularly with the Ash-Wednesday homily in the *Lives of Saints* (XII), which embodies a good deal of the *De Penitentia* (*CH* II. 602 sqq.); with the beginning of *De Auguriis* (*LS* XVII), assigned in some manuscripts to Rogationtide, and with *Letania Maiore* (*CH* II. XXI). The *exempla* from Bede may remind us also of the various visions that Ælfric recounts as exemplary warnings for Rogationtide immediately after the piece just mentioned (*CH* II. XXII–XXIV). In MS. P, where nothing is assigned to a specific occasion, we nevertheless find *De Doctrina Apostolica* in the midst of the Rogationtide pieces named above. It stands between *De Auguriis* and *Letania Maiore*, which is followed in turn, as in *CH* II, by the visions. In MS. C, on the other hand, it stands with other homilies on general topics from the *Lives of Saints*, including the appendix. *De Duodecim Abusivis* comes just before, *De Falsis Diis* and the *Interrogationes* just after, with *De Memoria Sanctorum* (*LS* XVI) and the Ash-Wednesday homily (*LS* XII) not far away. Its place in P is the more appropriate, but perhaps, as Dr. Clemoes has suggested,[1] C can give us a hint as to the company in which Ælfric first issued it. Series I and II were amply supplied with homilies for Lent and Rogationtide; the *Lives* set, on the other hand, could have absorbed another piece of this type, with or without specific assignment. *De Doctrina Apostolica* did not belong to the original set of the *Lives*, if we can trust Skeat's MS. (our W) for this negative evidence; but perhaps Ælfric added it, either internally or more probably to the appendix, in some later issue.

As a whole, the homily would naturally be dated after the *Lives*, but the fact that the first part is in ordinary prose and the second (131–254) in rhythmic prose suggests very strongly that the two parts were not composed at the same time. So far as we can tell, Ælfric did not write extended pieces, whether discursive or narrative, in ordinary prose after the transitional period marked by certain pieces in the *Lives of Saints*. I am inclined, therefore, to associate the first 130 lines with the beginning of *De Auguriis*, where certain other teachings of St. Paul's are summarized in ordinary prose, and to suppose that both these passages are leftovers from the period of the *Catholic Homilies*. Dr. Clemoes has suggested that they were first issued as parts of letters before being converted into homilies.[2] It may be so, but I am unable to point to anything distinctively epistolary about them, and both passages seem to me appropriate for a congregation.

Besides the two manuscripts that contain the complete homily there are two others that have excerpts from it in association with other Ælfrician matter. The excerpts are reasonably good witnesses for the portions of the text they include, but whether Ælfric was responsible for the compilations may be doubted. The longer excerpt occurs in MS. N (Faustina A. ix), in a homily that should

---

[1] *Chronology*, p. 226.

[2] *Chronology*, pp. 221, 225. The argument that the list of the capital sins in *De Doctrina Apostolica* is later than that in IV seems to me insecure. See the notes on 127–9 below and on IV. 249–51.

have been assigned to the third Sunday after Easter but begins imperfectly because of a missing leaf. What is left contains (ff. 160–2ᵛ) a combination of the latter part of Ælfric's *De Septiformi Spiritu*, beginning 'utan biδ gesewen' (Napier VIII, p. 58/1), and the first of the two *exempla* from Bede in *De Doctrina Apostolica*, with a conclusion adapted from that which follows the second *exemplum*. Dr. Clemoes has suggested that this combination was made by Ælfric himself as a stop-gap for his Temporale until he produced Assmann VI, a normal homily on the pericope for the third Sunday after Easter, which appears only in MS. U.[1] Against this suggestion, however, there are a number of objections. (1) There is no apparent reason why the sevenfold gifts should be treated on this occasion, and the combination of the little treatise with the *exemplum* produces a very odd homily. (2) The *exemplum* has a carefully designed position in *De Doctrina Apostolica*, prefaced as it is by lines 131–5 on the danger of falling into despair, and followed by another *exemplum* to the same effect and a conclusion in which the theme of despair is reasserted. The compilation in N lifts the *exemplum* out of this context, treating it as an illustration of presumption, then tacks on enough of the original conclusion to introduce the theme of despair, now a mere afterthought. (3) The rearrangement of the conclusion involves an expansion of the last line that lacks all pretence of rhythmic order. (4) The fact that this compilation does not occur in the closely related but selective O may be accidental, but its absence from the more distantly related M is likely to be significant. Certainly the unsupported testimony of N cannot be taken seriously where Ælfric's authorship is in question. At several points N is filled out by sermons that are not Ælfric's at all. (5) Dr. Clemoes's chief reason for holding Ælfric responsible is his belief that the compilation is referred to at IX. 144 and XI. 69; but as I have said in the note on IX. 144, these references are probably to *CH* I. XXII. (6) Apart from N, there is no evidence that Ælfric had composed *De Septiformi Spiritu* before the early years of the eleventh century, when he began to write pieces for Wulfstan. A compilation containing it is likely to have been put together too late for inclusion in the Ælfrician Temporale represented jointly by M–N–O. On this ground also, then, the compilation is likely to have entered N or an ancestor of N by interpolation.

---

[1] *Chronology*, pp. 228 sqq., esp. p. 232.

I do not feel quite so certain that the other compilation in which *De Doctrina Apostolica* figures cannot be charged to Ælfric. It is the unique *De Virginitate* of V (CCCC 419), consisting of a portion of the *Letter to Sigefyrth* on chastity (Assmann II) in the expanded homiletic form of MS. H, followed by lines 34–43, 53–60 of *De Doctrina*, followed in turn by the two passages printed in this edition as no. xxx, the first of which is unique. It is just possible that Ælfric was responsible for putting these pieces together, though I prefer to think not. On this matter see the introduction to xxx.

For textual purposes V is too short to be of much use; N is occasionally useful for the first *exemplum*. Neither reveals any clear relationship to the other two manuscripts. In the main we must take our choice between P, which is remarkably conservative in spelling for the second half of the eleventh century and plainly the heir of a good tradition, and the considerably later C, full of twelfth-century levellings and not without pure blunders. But P has its lapses too, and some of these C can correct.

There is little that needs to be said about the sources. In the first part of the homily the Bible supplies a good deal, and I have rarely gone beyond it. At 102–4 a sermon on chastity by Cæsarius of Arles (ed. Morin, *Sermo* XLIII, *CCSL* CIII. 189 sqq.), and at 106–8 *De Bono Coniugali* by Augustine are quoted for passages that seem directly or indirectly responsible for what Ælfric has added to St. Paul's teachings, and at 62–65 there is clear reference to a story in the *Vitæ Patrum*. No doubt further sources could be found for some of the more or less proverbial sentences near the beginning. The second part, after the introductory lines (131–5) is a fairly close paraphrase of two stories from the fifth book of Bede's *Ecclesiastical History*.

After the preceding paragraphs had been sent to the press there appeared a separate edition of the homily by W. Braekman.[1] In many respects this is an admirable performance. It partly supplements what I have done, and my study of it has enabled me to remedy some faults in my own edition which might otherwise have escaped attention in the proofs. Nevertheless, there are some weaknesses to which I must call attention lest there be doubt at points where the two editions disagree.

---

[1] 'Ælfric's Old English Homily "De Doctrina Apostolica": An Edition', in *Studia Germanica Gandensia*, V (1963), 141–73.

Dr. Braekman has provided an elaborate introduction followed by a text in which the readings of the three principal manuscripts are presented in great detail (the fourth, my V, being treated separately in the introduction) and the numerous Worcester corrections and glosses of the basic manuscript, my P, are fully reported. By including all variants, even variant accents, and the Worcester corrections, he goes beyond the limits of this edition. On the other hand, he does not include a glossary, and does not annotate particular expressions. His introduction partly duplicates my work, especially in the account of Ælfric's sources, where he has correctly identified nearly all those that are presented below and has printed some in full. Valuable supplements are his discussion (pp. 152–3) of the reception of the eucharist by the laity, on which Ælfric touches in lines 119–30, and the comparisons (pp. 159–62) between Ælfric and the anonymous translator of the Old English Bede (who should not, of course, have been called Alfred) in their renderings of the *exempla*.

There are two weak spots in the introduction, of which the more important is his analysis of the relationship of the manuscripts. This is based on an uncritical treatment of identical readings. Thus, to show that N (his C) is more closely related to C (his B) than to P (his A), he gives five examples of agreement between N and C against P; but these are all instances in which N and C may well have inherited the correct reading. In fact the first and fourth examples are illusions due to his own misreading of P, which agrees with the others. In my judgement there is little likelihood of a close relationship between N and C. The genuine instances of agreement against P are all very plausible readings, and I have admitted them to my text because they seem to me superior, though sometimes very slightly so. There is not enough evidence either way to justify a firm decision about the relationship, and I have preferred to leave the question open. Dr. Braekman then suggests much more tentatively that V is more closely related to C than to P. Once again the instances of agreement that he cites may well be instances of *correct* readings. It would not be surprising, however, in view of the south-eastern associations of C and the relevant part of V (as described in my Introduction, pp. 82–83), if there were a fairly close textual link between them. An instance of agreement that Dr. Braekman does not mention, the reading with *eac* in line 40, may be an instance of scribal alteration, for although it actually makes the sense of the passage clearer, P's reading, which lacks the word, is closer to the Latin that Ælfric is translating. By retaining P's reading in my text I have given some support to the notion that C and V are closely related, but one uncertain instance will hardly justify a conclusion.

A slighter weakness is to be found in Dr. Braekman's comments on the style of the homily. Although he prints the whole text as prose, he points out correctly that the last part, containing the *exempla*, is in Ælfric's alliterative (or rhythmical) style, and illustrates this briefly by a metrical arrangement. But he wrongly attributes the same style to the beginning of the homily (lines 1–20 in his edition, 1–19 in mine). These opening lines do of course contain some alliteration and some neatly balanced phrases, but they belong to the intermediate style that appears frequently in Ælfric's earliest prose, as I have explained in my Introduction, pp. 109–12.

Instead of adding to the textual apparatus the variant readings of the two little extracts in V, Dr. Braekman prints these extracts in full in his introduction, pp. 143–4. These are correct except for *hære* in the first extract, line 3 (where V has the correct *þære*) and *beheat* in the second extract, line 1 (where V has *behat* corrected to *behet* by a point under the *a* and a superscript *e*). The passage in V that precedes these extracts, which Dr. Braekman quotes on p. 143, is indeed an echo, as he says, of *De Doctrina Apostolica*, 66–70 (his 70–74), and it has not previously been printed from this particular manuscript, but it corresponds to Ælfric's *Letter to Sigefyrth*, Assmann II, 183–8. The reading *þeniende* (not *þeniendne*), instead of *þeowigende* as in several manuscripts, supports Joscelin's transcript of the lost text of Cotton Vespasian D. xiv.

Dr. Braekman's discussion of the date and nature of the homily (pp. 145–7) follows the lead of Dr. Clemoes, and accordingly makes much of the order in which the deadly sins are listed (pp. 154–5). Here he may of course be right, but I am not convinced, as I have already said in the earlier part of this introduction.

I turn now to Dr. Braekman's text and apparatus. The latter, as I have said, is admirably detailed and includes matter of interest that is beyond the scope of my edition. Both text and apparatus, however, contain some flaws that may be misleading unless they are pointed out. In the following comment the line numbers of my text are given first; then, in parenthesis, those of Dr. Braekman's text.

His text is based, like mine, on P (Hatton 115), to which he adheres even when the reading of another manuscript is superior, though he does allow himself to correct one obvious blunder (*hlare* for *mid hlafe* in the first paragraph). His readings of P, however, are not quite accurate. He omits two words: *soðe* in 136 (141) and *word* in 156 (156), supposing that they are present in the other two manuscripts only. In 246 (224), having overlooked the *h* of *hangode*, which has been added above the line in P in a contemporary hand, he prints the remainder as two words, *an gode*. More trifling errors are *gerihtwisad* for *gerihtwisod* at 96 (101), where indeed the form of the *o* is not very clear, and *wylle* for *wyle* at 103 (109).

His division of words differs from mine on several occasions, sometimes perhaps justifiably, but it seems definitely wrong to print the following compounds as two words: 113 (118) *bearn-eacnigendum*, 138 (142) *forð-mann*, 158 (158) *a-eode*, 228 (210) *sylf-willes*, 230 (212) *to-dal*. I have already mentioned his *an gode* for '*h'angode*, 246 (224). The very next word, *forscyldegod*, is printed *forscylde god*, a mistake for which the scribe was partly responsible, since he divided the word in that way at the end of a line. Conversely, it is hardly proper to print *læwedum hade*, 115 (120) as one word.

More serious, perhaps, is a procedural fault. Dr. Braekman has observed that P has been marked for correction of its spelling at a great many places, nearly always by simply putting substitute letters over the line, but sometimes by using in addition a point directly below the letter to be changed, and sometimes, to indicate deletion rather than substitution, by using a point only, without superscription. He has properly recognized that most of these editorial marks were inserted by much later correctors at Worcester, and most of them, accordingly, he reports in a separate section of his apparatus at the foot of the page. But whenever he observes that a corrector has 'expunged' a letter (in the medieval Latin sense, by a subscript point) he treats the correction as if it were authoritative and prints the corrected reading in his text. Thus he prints *eldre* for *yldre* at 5 (5), *seal* for *sceal* at 24 (26), though it is really the *sceal* in the next line that has an expunged *c*, *lystan* for *hlystan* at 25 (27), *moder* for *meder* at 60 (64), *forkeorfan* for *forceorfan* at 61 (65), *swylke* for the second *swylce* in 77 (82), *gesikelon* for *gesicelon*, properly *gesicelod*, at 148 (150), *swelte* for *swulte* (probably indicating a weak preterite instead of the traditional strong one) at 151 (153), *spræke* for *spræce* at 156 (156), *irenum* for *isenum* at 191 (182). He also prints *wurðon* for *wurdon* at 64 (69) and *cwæðon* for *cwædon* at 186 (178), where the original *d* has been changed to *ð* directly by addition of a stroke of the type used for *ð* by the Worcester scribe with the tremulous hand.

Since all these editorial marks appear to express a corrector's usage rather than Ælfric's and to widen the gap between P and its exemplar, it is surely improper to incorporate them in the text. Nearly all of them, moreover, indicate the same pronunciations as those that have superscript letters without subscript points. They are typical of the Worcester corrections of the twelfth and thirteenth centuries and have been classified by S. J. Crawford in *Anglia* LII (1928), 1–25, on the basis of P itself and other manuscripts in the Bodleian library. In my Introduction, p. 187, I have referred to Crawford's study and explained why I have not reported any corrections of this sort in the Worcester manuscripts. Since the corrections are not all in the same hand nor entirely consistent phonologically, a study more complete than Crawford's and more elaborate in its analysis would be welcome; but it is not pertinent to an edition of Ælfric. To report the corrections is of course allowable, but Dr. Braekman's special treatment of those distinguished by expunction leads to serious confusion.

An exception may be noted. The Worcester scribe with the tremulous hand makes, at one point, a different sort of correction. In line 4 he adds the word *mid* in the margin. This is not a modernization but an effort, obviously successful, to recover the authentic reading. Whether it was guided by consultation of another copy or, as is probable, by simple apprehension of the demands of the context, it must certainly be reported.

I will not attempt a complete list of errata, most of which are very minor, in Dr. Braekman's apparatus. The majority of the variants are correctly reported. It is difficult, however, to deal with C (CCCC 303), because the scribe often corrects himself in the middle of a word, writing the wrong letter and then immediately, without erasure, writing the correct letter on top of it. This leads to odd appearances, like the *unamasisumode* reported by Dr. Braekman as C's reading at 64 (68–69). I have decided not to report a variant here, because it is evident that the scribe of C wrote *unamas*, then, noticing that he had left out the *n*, wrote an *n* on top of the high *s* so that the combination looks like *si*. What he intended, in spite of appearances, was simply *unamansumode*. At one or two points C's reading, though unambiguous, has been misread by Dr. Braekman, who has trouble with the high *s* and the ligature *st*. Thus he misreads C's *unwislic*, 128 (134), and *unwislice*, 163 (162), as *unwillic, unwillice*, and reports that C's *astealde*, 49 (53) and *gast*, 196 (185), which are correctly written with the normal ligature of high *s* and *t*, have undergone correction to *st* from *sl* and *h* respectively. At 202 (190) he misreads C's correct *Ne* as *He*, not noticing the consistent though at first glance confusing forms of C's capitals. Another slip of the eye occurs at 246 (224), where he reports that the *e* in C's *gode* has been corrected from *g*. Here he has mistaken a curved mark of abbreviation in the line below for the tail of a *g*. C had *gode* originally.

One of the stronger features of Dr. Braekman's edition is his decipherment of the glosses. Here he has made remarkably few mistakes if one considers that the Latin glosses are shakily written and much abbreviated and most of the vernacular glosses have been partially erased. Among the few mistakes are *euacuam* for *euacuaui* at 18 (20), *acursed* for what I think is *akursed*, 22 (24), and *þeos* for *þeof*, 246 (224). Two or three other slight misreadings at points where I had originally given up have suggested what I think are the right readings: *neode* rather than *nede* at 117 (122), *vorbisne* rather than *vos bisne* at 136 (141), *þen* rather than *þæt* at 249 (226). I had originally passed over, as too faint, *bilimede* at 45 (49), *holie* and *amerseden* at 63 (67), *anon* at 63 (68), where he gives conservatively only *a . . n*, *riule* at 112 (118), and *riht hand* at 234 (215); and I had misread *flures* at 113 (119) and *glore* at 249 (226). Here and there my renewed attention to the glosses has led me to make additional conjectures where neither of us had been able to discern a plausible reading.

DE DOCTRINA APOSTOLICA

On manega wisan lærð Godes lar þa Cristenan. On þære lare is ægðer ge liðnys ge stiðnyss, for þan ðe ealle men ne magon anes modes beon. Ærest man fet þæt cild mid meolce, and syððan mid hlafe. Gif ðu hit fetst ærest 'mid' hla[f]e, hit ne leofað sona. Eft, þonne hit yldre byð, hit behofað þæs hlafes, and stiðran metes. 5 Swa is eac on Godes lare liðnyss and stiðnys, þæt se ðe gyt ne mæg þa mæstan beboda healdan, þæt [he] huru leornige on ðam liðran bebodum hu he on sumne sæl hine sylfne gewylde to maran stiðnysse mid his modes gecnyrdnysse. An eorðlic cyning hæfð meniges cynnes menn, sume geþungenran, sume ungeþungenran. Swa 10

Text based on P (Hatton 115), ff. 35ᵛ–40ᵛ. Collated with C (CCCC 303), pp. 301–6; V (CCCC 419), pp. 352–4 (two excerpts, lines 34–43, 53–60, written consecutively); and N (Cotton Faustina A. ix), ff. 160ᵛ–2ᵛ (containing the first of the two *exempla* from Bede and a modified conclusion: lines 136–207, 242–5, 250–4).

Excluded variants: (1) For P's short *y* in *byð, hyre, hwylc, gehwylc, swylc, þyses, þysum, wyle, wylle, ylca*, and its long *y* in *swyðe*, the other manuscripts, especially C, often have *i*, none being entirely consistent. (2) The prevailing -*nyss(e)* of P is occasionally -*niss(e)* in C, more often -*ness(e)* in all three of the other manuscripts, and the uninflected form often has single *s*. (3) Variations of *mann, man; menn, men; buton, butan* occur inconsistently in all the manuscripts. (4) C usually has *ðan* for *ðam* in both singular and plural.

Capitalization of sentences has been regularized.

The Latin glosses of P are mostly the work of the famous Worcester scribe with the trembling hand. The Middle English words, whether meant for glosses or corrections, are sometimes in a bolder hand of perhaps almost the same period (1225?), but the character of the script and even the reading are often hard to determine because most of these words have been partially erased. A few are almost entirely obliterated.

3 æræst C. siððan C. 4 mid] *sic C; added in tremulous hand, margin*, P. *second* hlafe] *sic C;* hlare P. 5 behofeð C. hlafæs C. 7 mæstan] maran C (*rightly?*). he] *sic C; om.* P. 9 eordlic C. menges C.

Glosses in P, *Latin*: 9 gecnyrdnysse: studio. 10 geþungenran: boni.
Glosses in P, *Middle English* (*including respellings of older words*): 1 manega: monie. 4 *first* hlafe: bread (? *erased*). 9 cyning: king (*erased*).

SOURCES. 3–9 [*Cf. I Cor. iii. 2*] Lac vobis potum dedi, non escam; . . . adhuc enim carnales estis. [*Heb. v. 12*] Facti estis quibus lacte opus sit, non solido cibo. [*13*] Omnis enim qui lactis est particeps, expers est sermonis iustitiæ; parvulus enim est. [*14*] Perfectorum autem est solidus cibus; eorum qui pro consuetudine exercitatos habent sensus ad discretionem boni ac mali.

gedafenað eac Gode þæt he gode men hæbbe and geþungene
þenas to his ðenungum, and him nateshwon ne licað þæt hi ealle þa
liðnysse lufian, ac he wyle þæt hi sume ða softnysse forhogion, and
heardnysse niman to healicum geþincðum. Paulus, þeoda lareow,
cwæð, swylce be him sylfum—ac he mænde mid þam eac oðre 15
menn—, Ða ða ic wæs lytel and iung, ic spræc swa swa iungling,
ic cuðe swa swa lytlingc, ic þohte swa swa lytlingc. Eft, þa þa ic to
werlicere ylde becom, ic awearp and aidlode *þa idelnyssa þe ic *f. 36
on cildlicre ylde beeode. Eft cwæð sum witega, *Puer centum
annorum maledictus erit*: Hundteontig-wintre cild byð awyrged. 20
Ðæt is on andgite, Se mann ðe hæfð ylde on gearum, and hæfð
cildes þeawas on dysige, þæt se byð awyrged. Ælc treow blewð
ær þan þe hit wæstmas bere, and ælc corn bið ærest gærs. Swa eac
ælc godes cinnes mann sceal hine sylfne to godnysse awendan, and
wisdom lufian, and forlætan idelnysse. He sceal hlystan wisdomes 25
æt wisum mannum, for þan swa he oftor Godes lare gehyrð, swa
he gehendor byð þam wisdome. Ne sceal nan mann forhogian þæt
he gehyre Godes lare, for þan ðe hit byð swyðe pleolic þam men
þæt he his Scyppendes beboda gehyran nelle, swylce he Godes
hæse forseo. Wæteres gecynd is hnesce, and stanes gecynd is 30
heard, ac swaþeah þæt wæter foroft dropmælum þyrlað þone
heardan stan. Swa eac Godes word þurhgæð þæs mannes heortan,
and ahnexað to Godes bebodum, gif he gelome þa lare gehyrð.
    God cwæð æt fruman to mancynne, on middaneardes anginne,

11 geðafnað *C*.   12 ðegenas *C*.   13 forhogian *C*.   14 nimon *C*.
17 *first* swa swa] swa *C*.   lytling . . . litling *C*.   18 wærlicre *C*.   idelnesse *C*.
19–22 Eft . . . awyrged] *transposed in C to follow* idelnysse, 25.   20 awyrgað *C*.
22 Alc *C*.   blowð *C*.   23 ærest gærs] *tr. C*.   24 cynnes *C*.   awændan *C*.
27 byð] beoð *C*.   29 sceppendes *C*.   30 Wætere *C*.   hnesse *C*.
34 God]   *Here begins the excerpt in V, p. 352, line 17*.   middar- *C*.

    Glosses in *P*, *Latin*: 11 gedafenað: dec*et*.   14 geþincðum: bono.   17 cuðe:
sapiebam.   18 aidlode: euacuaui.   21 andgite: i*n*tellectu.   22 blewð:
floret.   28 pleolic: periculosu*m*.
    ME: 18 aidlode: *illeg. gloss*.   22 awyrged: akursed (*? erased*).   27 gehen-
dor: ner (*? erased*).

    16–19 [*I Cor. xiii. 11*] Cum essem parvulus, loquebar ut parvulus, sapiebam
ut parvulus, cogitabam ut parvulus; quando autem factus sum vir, evacuavi
quæ erant parvuli.
    19–20 [*Elliptical version of Is. lxv. 20*] Puer centum annorum morietur, et
peccator centum annorum maledictus erit.

Weaxað and beoð gemenigfylde, and gefyllað þas eorðan. Eft on 35
þære niwan gecyðnysse, þæt is on godspel-bodunge, cwæð Crist
to ðam Iudeiscum, Ic secge eow to soðan, [þæt] swa hwa swa his
wif forlæt, buton heo dyrne-ceorl hæbbe, and gif he oðer wif
nimð, þonne byð he *forliger, and se ðe þæt forlæte[ne] wif *f. 36
genimð byð forliger. Ða cwædon Cristes leorningcnihtas him to, 40
Gif ðam w[e]re is þus mid wife, selre him byð þæt he ne wifige.
Ða cwæð Crist, Ne underfoð ealle men þis word, ac þam þe hit
forgifen byð. Sume eunuchi synd þe beoð swa acennede, and sume
eunuchi synd þe synd fram mannum swa gemacode, and sume
eunuchi synd ðe hi sylfe forhabbað fram hæmede for heofonan 45
rices myrhðe. Healde ðis se þe hit healdan mæge. Gif Crist hete
ealle men healdan mægðhád, þonne wurde mancyn raðe geendod.

Nu is Criste leofre þæt se man be his [agenre] gecorennysse þa
clænnysse geceose þe he sylf astealde, þonne he ealle menn
bebunde mid þam anum bebode. And seo cláne lác, þæt is 50
mægðhád, sceal beon Gode mid [glæd]nysse geoffrod, na mid
neadunge ænigre hæse.

Wite gehwa, se ðe þa clænnysse Gode æne behæt, þæt he hit eft
ne awæge. Fæder and moder moton heora bearn to swa hwylcum

35 Wexað *CV*.   gemænigfylde *C*.   36 gecyðnesse *V*.   cwæd *C*.
37 sæcge *V*.   þæt] þæt *CV*; *om. P*.   39–40 þonne . . . genimð] *om. C*.
39 forlætene] *sic V*; forlæte *P*.   40 genimð] nimð *V*.   byð] bið eac
CV.   forligr *C*.   leornig- *V*.   41 were] *sic CV*; wære *P*.   wifie *C*.
42 hit] *om. C*.   43–52 Sume eunuchi . . . hæse] *om. V*.   43 Sume]
ume, *space for capital blank C*.   44 þe synd] *om. C*.   46 mæge] wile
marked for deletion, followed by mage *C*.   47 þonne] þonum *C*.   hraðe *C*.
48 agenre] *sic C*; *om. P*.   50 bebunde] gebunde *C*.   51 glædnesse *C*;
clænnysse *P*.   53 Wite] *V resumes after omission*.   clænnesse *CV*.   behæt]
behated *C*; behat, *corrected over line to* behet *V*.   eft] *om. V*.   54 awege *C*.
modor *C*.   motan *V*.

Glosses in P, Latin: 39 forlæte: dimissam.   43 acennede: nati.
54 awæge: mutet.
ME: 39 forliger: eaubriche (*? erased*).   41 wære: *illeg. gloss.*   43 eunuchi:
igeldede.   synd: beoð.   44 fram: of.   45 ðe hi sylfe forhabbað fram
hæmede: bilimede (*over* hæmede; *erased*; *cf.* 62).   52 hæse: heste (*? erased*).

35 [*Gen. i. 28*] Crescite et multiplicamini, et replete terram.
37–46 [*Matth. xix. 9*] Dico autem vobis, quia quicumque dimiserit uxorem
suam, nisi ob fornicationem, et aliam duxerit, moechatur: et qui dimissam
duxerit, moechatur. [*10*] Dicunt ei discipuli eius: Si ita est causa hominis cum
uxore, non expedit nubere. [*11*] Qui dixit illis: Non omnes capiunt verbum istud,
sed ðquibus datum est. [*12*] Sunt enim eunuchi, qui de matris utero sic nati sunt;
et sunt eunuchi, qui facti sunt ab hominibus; et sunt eunuchi, qui seipsos
castraverunt propter regnum cælorum. Qui potest capere, capiat.

cræfte gedon swa him leofost byð, and God bead þæt ealle bearn 55
beon gehyrsume fæder and meder. Gif hi þonne heora bearn Gode
betæcað, to his clænum ðeowdome, and þæt bearn byð him ungehyrsum, þonne getimað him swa swa hit awriten is: *Nemo in-
obediens parentibus saluus erit*: Ne byð nan man gehealden þe
byð ungehyrsum fæder and meder. 60
Ne mot nan man his lima *ne his gesceapu forceorfan. We rædað *f. 37
on þære béc, Uita Patrum, þæt twegen munecas gehældon hi sylfe;
ac ealle ða halgan lareowas hi amansumodon sona, and hi mid
mycel[r]e earfoðnysse eft begeaton þæt hi unamansumode wurdon,
for þan ðe béc hit forbeodað. 65
God behet þurh þone witegan Isaiam þam mannum þe on
mægðhade wuniað, and þa clænnysse gecuron þe him gecweme is,
þæt he wolde him forgifan þa selestan wununge on his huse, þæt
is on heofonan rice, and þone selran naman him gesettan, toforan
sunum and dohtrum, se þe ne byð næfre adilegod. Se apostol 70
Paulus, ealra þeoda lareow, awrat on his pistole ðus: Ic secge
wydewum, and þam ðe butan hæmede wuniað, þæt him is swyðe
gód þæt hi swa þurhwunian, swa swa ic sylf. Eft cwæð se ylca

55 hym *V.*   byð] beoð *C*; bið *V.*   bead] bebead *CV.*   56 geher-
sume *C.*   moder *CV.*   hy *V.*   57 betæceð *C.*   hym *V.*   ungehersum *C.*
59 parentibus] parentibus suis *V.*   60 meder *corrected to* moder *over line*
P; modor *C*; moder *V.*   *End of excerpt in V.*   61 forceorffan *C.*
62 uita *corrected to* uitas *over line P*; uitas *C.* (*See note.*)   twege *C.*   silfe *C.*
64 mycelre] *sic C*; mycele *P.*   66 þone] his *C.*   68 se(o)loston, -on
altered to -an *C.*   69 heofonū *altered to* heofonā *C.*   70 adylegod *C.*
73 -wunion *C.*

Glosses in *P*, Latin: 63 hi: eos (*twice, second time wrongly*).   69 þone:
illum.   70 byð . . . adilegod: preteribit.
ME: 62 gehældon: bilimeden.   63 halgan: holie (*erased*).   amansumodon: amerseden (*erased*).   sona: anon (? *erased*).

58–59 [*Apparently not Biblical; but cf. Ex. xx. 12; Deut. xxvii. 16; Eph. vi.
1–2, etc.*]
62–65 [*Vitæ Patrum, V. xv. 88, Migne, PL LXXIII. 968 sq. Ælfric summarizes
freely. In the Latin the two monks are excommunicated successively by three arch-
bishops and the pope before they are brought to repentance by the bishop of Cyprus.*]
66–70 [*Is. lvi. 4, 5*] Quia hæc dicit Dominus eunuchis: Qui custodierint
sabbata mea, et elegerint quæ ego volui, et tenuerint foedus meum, dabo eis in
domo mea et in muris meis locum, et nomen melius a filiis et filiabus: nomen
sempiternum dabo eis, quod non peribit.
71–73 [*I Cor. vii. 8*] Dico autem non nuptis, et viduis: Bonum est illis si sic
permaneant, sicut et ego.
73–89 [*I Cor. vii. 28*] Si autem acceperis uxorem, non peccasti; et si nupserit
virgo, non peccavit. . . .

apostol, Gif ðu wif nimst, þu ne syngast; and gif mæden ceorlað,
heo ne syngað. Ic secge swaþeah þæt þes tima is swiðe sceort. 5
Beon forði þa ðe wif habbað swylce hi nan nabbon; and þa ðe
blissiað swylce hi na ne blission; and þa ðe bicgað swylce hi hit
nagon; and þa ðe brucað þyses middaneardes, beon hi swylce hi
his ne brucon. Ðises middaneardes hiw gewit. Se man þe butan
wife wunað hogað hu he Gode gecweme; and se þe mid wife 80
wunað hogað embe woruldþing, and hu he his wife gecweme.
And clæne mæden cepð Godes willan, þæt heo halig sy ægðer ge
on lichaman ge on sawle; and seo ðe ceorlode smeað embe
woruldþing, and hu heo hyre were licige. *Ðæt wif byð under *f. 37
hyre weres iuce þa hwile þe he leofað; and gif heo hyre wer oferbit, 85
þonne byð heo frig, swa heo on wydewan hade wunige, swa heo
ceorlige, gif heo iung byð and ungehealtsum; ac heo byð gesælig
gif heo on wudewan hade wunað, be minum ræde. Ic wene þæt
ic hæbbe Godes Gast on me.

Se ylca ðeoda lareow, Paulus, cwæð: God byð þam men þæt 90

74 nymst C.	80 hogað] hogeð C.	82 clene meden C.
hi C æðer C.	83 ceorlode] ceorlað C.	84 licige] gelicige C.
86 *first* heo] hio C.	wudewan C.	87 ungehaltsum C. ac] and C.
88 gef *corr. to* gif C.		

Glosses in P, Latin: 74 wif nimst: nubseris.   77 blissiað: Gaudent.
bicgað: emunt.   79 hiw: figura.   gewit: preterit.   86 *first* swa: siue.
ME: 85 iuce: ioke.

[29] Hoc itaque dico, fratres: Tempus breve est; reliquium est, ut et qui
habent uxores, tamquam non habentes sint;
[30] ... et qui gaudent, tamquam non gaudentes; et qui emunt, tamquam non
possidentes;
[31] et qui utuntur hoc mundo, tamquam non utantur, præterit enim figura
huius mundi.
[32] ... Qui sine uxore est, sollicitus est quæ Domini sunt, quomodo placeat
Deo.
[33] Qui autem cum uxore est, sollicitus est quæ sunt mundi, quomodo
placeat uxori. . . .
[34] Et mulier innupta, et virgo cogitat quæ Domini sunt, ut sit sancta corpore et spiritu; quæ autem nupta est, cogitat quæ sunt mundi, quomodo placeat
viro. . . .
[39] Mulier alligata est legi quanto tempore vir eius vivit; quod si dormierit
vir eius, liberata est. Cui vult nubat, tantum in Domino.
[40] Beatior autem erit si sic permanserit, secundum meum consilium; puto
autem quod et ego Spiritum Dei habeam.
90-94 [I Cor. vii. 1] Bonum est homini mulierem non tangere;
[2] propter fornicationem autem unusquisque suam uxorem habeat, et
unaquæque suum virum habeat. . . .
[5] Nolite fraudare invicem, nisi forte ex consensu ad tempus, ut vacetis
orationi. . . .

he wif ne hreppe; swaþeah, þe læs þe hi on forliger befeallon,
wifige se ðe wille, and ceorlige seo ðe wille; and heora naðor
oðerne ne bepæce; cepan hi huru þæt hi magon on gewissum timan
hi clænlice to Gode gebiddan. Gif hwylc gelyfed man hæfð
ungeleafful wif, and heo wylle wunian mid him, ne forlæte he hi; 95
þæt ungeleaffulle wif byð gerihtwisod þurh þone geleaffullan wer.
And gif hwylc geleafful wif hæfð ungeleaffulne wer, and he wylle
wunian mid hyre, ne forlæte heo hine; se ungeleaffulla wer byð
gerihtwisod þurh þæt [ge]leaffulle wíf. Ic bebeode—swaðeah na
ic ac God sylf bebyt—þæt wer and wif hi ne totwæman. Gif hi 100
þonne þæt doð, wunian hi butan hæmede, oððe hi eft hi gegaderian.
—Eac hit wære rihtlic, æfter boca tæcinge, þæt se cniht ungewemmed wære oððæt he wifode, swa swa he wyle þæt his mæden
ungewemmed him to cume.
  Se ylca apostol cwæð, Ælc man hæfð synderlice gife fram Gode, 105
sum swa, sum elles. [Swa] mycel is se sinscipe, þæt þeah hwa hæbbe

91 þy læs ðe *C.*   forligr *C.*   92 hiore *C.*   93 cepon *C.*   94 gelyf-
ed] geleafful *C.*   95 ungeleafful] ungelifed *C.*   wunian mid him] mid
him wunian *C.*   96 geleaffullan] geleaffulle *C.*   97 ungeleaffull'n´e *C.*
98 wunian mid hyre] mid hire wunian *C.*   99 geleaffulle] *sic C*; leaffulle *P.*
100 totwæmon *C.*   101 wunian *altered to* wunion *C.*   hemede *C.*   oððe]
oððæt *C (but cf. Latin).*   102, 104 ungewæmmed *C.*   106 Swa] *sic C*;
su*m erased P.*

  Glosses in P, Latin: 94 gelyfed: fidelis.   100 totwæman: diuida*n*t.
101 butan: sine.   105 synderlice: propria*m.*   106 sinscipe: *coniugium.*
  ME: 106 sinscipe: wicchekreft (*in marg., erased; see note*).

94–101 [*I Cor. vii. 12*] Si quis frater uxorem habet infidelem, et hæc consentit
habitare cum illo, non dimittat illam.
  [*13*] Et si qua mulier fidelis habet virum infidelem, et hic consentit habitare
cum illa, non dimittat virum:
  [*14*] sanctificatus est enim vir infidelis per mulierem fidelem, et sanctificata
est mulier infidelis per virum fidelem.
  [*10*] Iis autem qui matrimonio iuncti sunt, præcipio non ego, sed Dominus,
uxorem a viro non discedere;
  [*11*] quod si discesserit, manere innuptam, aut viro suo reconciliari. Et vir
uxorem non dimittat.
  102–4 [*Cæsarius, Sermo XLIII, CCSL CIII. 190*] Velim tamen scire, si
illi qui uxores non habent, et, priusquam coniugiis copulentur, adulteria com-
mittere nec metuunt nec erubescunt, utrum velint sponsas suas, antequam ad
nuptias veniant, ab aliquibus adulteriis violari. . . . Quare unusquisque sponsæ
suæ non servat fidem, quam sibi ab ipsa servari desiderat?
  105–6 [*I Cor. vii. 7*] Unusquisque proprium donum habet ex Deo, alius
quidem sic, alius vero sic.
  106–8 [*Augustine, De Bono Coniugali, cap. vii, PL XL. 378*] Tantum valet illud
sociale vinculum coniugum, ut cum causa procreandi colligetur, nec ipsa causa

untymende wíf, and heo ne mage bearn *habban, þæt se wer ne *f. 38 mot swaþeah hi forlætan, and oðer tymende geniman, for þan ðe God Ælmihtig mæg eaðe gedon, gif his willa swa byð, þæt þæt untymende wif byð tymende, swa swa he dyde Abrahames wife, and 110 Isaaces, and gehwylce oðre. Nis swaþeah hæmed geset for nanum þinge buton for bearnes gestreone, and æfter þam boclican regole, ne sceolde nan man bearneacnigendum wife genealæcan, ne monoð-seocum, ne þam ðe for ylde untymende byð. Se ðe þis healdan mæg, he byð fulfremed on læwedum hade, swa swa we be mane- 115 gum mannum rædað. Se ðe hine sylfne to þyssere forhæfednysse gewyldan ne mæg, he ah þearfe þæt he mid ælmyssan and mid sumere dædbote hine sylfne geclænsie.

Is eac to witenne þæt Cristene men sceoldon gán to husle oftor þonne hi doð, swa swa man deð þær ðær man þone Cristendom wel 120 hylt. Eawfæste men magon gan to husle be Godes leafe Sunnan-dagum on Lenctenfæstene, and on ðam þrim Swigdagum, and on Easterdæge, and on þam þunresdæge on þære Gangwucan, on ðam dæge þe Crist to heofonum lichamlice astah, and on Pente-costen, and on ðam feower Sunnandagum þe beoð æfter þam 125 feower Ymbrenfæstenum. Ðus mæg don se ðe rihtlice leofað, gif he ne byð underþeod þam eahta heafodleahtrum: þæt is, modignyss and gifernyss, unrihthæmed and gitsung, un[wis]lic weamodnyss *and þyssere worulde unrotnys, asolcennyss and idelgylp. Se þe *f. 38 swa oft gán nelle to husle, gange huru þriwa on geare.   130

---

107 and] þæt C (rightly?)   hi C.   hæbben C.   108 forlæton C. 110 swa swa] swa C.   wife] wif C (rightly?).   111 heemed (probably an imperfect correction of he- to hæ-) C.   116 rædað] on bocum rædað C (rightly?).   ðisre C.   117 þeaffe C.   ælmessan C.   118 silfne C.   ge-clænsige C.   120 þonne] þonum C.   121 Eawfeste C.   122 læncten-C.   123 Easter-] æstær- C.   on þam þunresdæge] on þone þunres-dæg C.   127 heofod- C.   128 unwislic] sic C; unrihtlic P.   129 ðisre C.   130 nele C.   geara C.

Glosses in P, Latin: 113 bearneacnigendum: prengnantem.   123 gang-wucan: rogationum.   127 eahta heafodleahtrum: vii. (sic) mortalia pecata.   128 gifernyss: Gula.   unrihthæmed: luxuria.   weamod-nyss: ira.   129 asolcennyss: accidia, pigricia.   130 þriwa: ter. ME: 112 regole: riule (erased).   113 bearneacnigendum: mid childe (?erased).   113–14 monoðseocum: flures.   117 þearfe: neode (?erased). 130 þriwa: þrie.

---

procreandi solvatur. Possit enim homo dimittere sterilem uxorem, et ducere de qua filios habeat: et tamen non licet.

Gif man seocne mann huslað, he sceal his synna geandettan,
and he ne sceal na ortruwian, ne on orwennysse befeallan,
ac hihtan on þone Hælend, and hopian to his miltsunge,
for ðan se þe ortruwað be Godes arfæstnysse,
and hihtleas geendað, se losað on ecnysse.   135
Be ðam we magon secgan sume soðe bysne,
swa swa Beda awrat, ðysum wordum secgende:
He cwæð þæt sum forðmann wære on Myrcena lande,

132 na *om. C.*   135 se] he *C.*   136 Be ðam] *Here begins excerpt in N,*
f. 160ᵛ, last line. bisne *C.*   137 Beda] se halga beda *C.*   138 myrcna *C.*

Glosses in P, Latin: 132 ortruwian: desperare, diffidere.   133 hihtan:
confidere.   135 hihtleas: non confidens.   138 forðmann: prediues.
ME: 136 bysne: vorbisne (*? erased*).   138 forð-: hei-.

138–207 [*Bede, Eccl. Hist., Lib. V. cap. xiii*] Fuit quidam in provincia Mer-
ciorum cuius visiones ac verba, non autem et conversatio, plurimis, sed non
sibimet ipsi, profuit. Fuit autem temporibus Coenredi . . . vir in laico habitu
atque officio militari positus; sed quantum pro industria exteriori regi placens,
tantum pro interna suimet neglegentia displicens. Ammonebat ergo illum sedulo,
ut confiteretur, et emendaret, ac relinqueret scelera sua, priusquam subito mortis
superventu tempus omne pænitendi et emendandi perderet. Verum ille, fre-
quenter licet admonitus, spernebat verba salutis, seseque tempore sequente
pænitentiam acturum esse promittebat. Hæc inter tactus infirmitate, decidit in
lectum, atque acri coepit dolore torqueri. Ad quem ingressus rex, diligebat enim
eum multum, hortabatur, ut vel tunc, antequam moreretur, pænitentiam ageret
commissorum. At ille respondit, non se tunc velle confiteri peccata sua, sed cum
ab infirmitate resurgeret; ne exprobarent sibi sodales, quod timore mortis
faceret ea, quæ sospes facere noluerat; fortiter quidem, ut sibi videbatur, locutus,
sed miserabiliter, ut post patuit, dæmonica fraude seductus.
   Cumque morbo ingravescente, denuo ad eum visitandum ac docendum rex
intraret, clamabat statim miserabili voce: 'Quid vis modo? quid huc venisti?
non enim mihi aliquid utilitatis aut salutis potes ultra conferre.' At ille: 'Noli,'
inquit, 'ita loqui, vide ut sanum sapias.' 'Non,' inquit, 'insanio, sed pessimam
mihi scientiam certus præ oculis habeo. . . . Paulo ante . . . intraverunt domum
hanc duo pulcherrimi iuvenes; . . . protulitque unus libellum perpulchrum, sed
vehementer modicum, ac mihi ad legendum dedit; in quo omnia, quæ umquam
bona feceram, intuens scripta repperi, et hæc erant nimium pauca et modica.
Receperunt codicem, neque aliquid mihi dicebant. Tum subito supervenit
exercitus malignorum et horridum vultu spirituum domumque hanc et exterius
obsedit, et intus maxima ex parte residens implevit. Tunc ille, qui . . . primatu
sedis maior esse videbatur eorum, proferens codicem horrendæ visionis, et
magnitudinis enormis, et ponderis pene inportabilis, iussit uni ex satellitibus
suis mihi ad legendum deferre. Quem cum legissem, inveni omnia scelera, non
solum quæ opere vel verbo, sed etiam quæ tenuissima cogitatione peccavi, mani-
festissime in eo tetricis esse descripta litteris. Dicebatque ad illos, qui mihi
adsederant, viros albatos et præclaros: "Quid hic sedetis, scientes certissime,
quia noster est iste?" Responderunt: "Verum dicitis: accipite et in cumulum
damnationis vestræ ducite." Quo dicto statim disparuerunt; surgentesque duo

swyðe leof þam cyninge þe Kenred wæs gehaten.
Se þegen wæs gymeleas on his þeawum and dædum,   140
and dyslice leofode, and fordyde hine sylfne.
Ða manode hine se cyning þæt he his mandæda geswice,
and his synna geandette mid soðre behreowsunge,
þylæste he færlice forðferde mid his synnum.
Se cyning hine lufode, and gelome [hine] swa tihte,   145
ac he forseah his láre, and let him eaðe embe þæt,
cwæð [þæt] he wolde on fyrste fon to dædbote.
He wearð ða gesicelo[d] sarlice æt nextan,
and se cyning Kenred com to him licgendum,
and bæd þæt he sceolde his synna geandettan   150
mid soðre behreowsunge huru ær he swulte.
He cwæð þæt he nolde cyðan þa his synna,
ac syððan he gewyrpte he wolde hi geandettan,
þy læs ðe hine man tælde, swylce he for yrhðe hi geandette
þa on his untrumnysse, þa ða hé ansund nolde.   155
*Him þuhte þæt he spræce þegenlice word,   *f. 39
ac he wæs beswicen þurh þone swicolan deofol,
swa swa hit him aeode earmlice syððan.
His wise wæs ða wyrsigende, and him weox seo untrumnys,

139 cenred CN.   143 geandgedte (sic) C.   144 þylæste] þy læs þe N,
þe læs þe C.   færlice forðferde] tr. C.   145 second hine] sic CN; om. P.
147 þæt] sic CN; om. P.   148 gesicelod] sic C; gesicclod N; gesicelon P.
149 cenred CN.   150 geanddettan C.   151 soðre] soðe C.   behreo-
sunge C.   152 þa] om. C.   153 hi] hy N.   154 þy] þe C.   hi]
hy N.   geanðette C.   156 Hym N.   158 hyt N.   159 wyrsiende N.

Glosses in P, Latin: 141 fordyde: p_erdidit._   146 eaðe: facile.
148 gesicelon: _infirmus._   152 cyðan: dicere.   153 gewyrpte: con_ualuit._
154 yrhðe: pusillanimitate.   155 ansund: sospes.

_ME_: 140 þegen: þein (_erased_).   146 forseah: forhowede (? _divided,_ forho
wede, _and erased_).

nequissimi spiritus, habentes in manibus vomeres, percusserunt me, unus in
capite et alius in pede: qui videlicet modo cum magno tormento inrepunt in
interiora corporis mei, moxque ut ad se invicem perveniunt, moriar, et paratis ad
rapiendum me dæmonibus in inferni claustra pertrahar.'
     Sic loquebatur miser desperans, et non multo post defunctus, pænitentiam,
quam ad breve tempus cum fructu veniæ facere supersedit, in æternum sine
fructu poenis subditus facit. De quo constat, quia . . . non pro se ista, cui non
profuere, sed pro aliis viderit. . . . Quod autem codices diversos per bonos sive
malos spiritus sibi vidit offerri, ob id superna dispensatione factum est, ut
meminerimus facta et cogitationes nostras non in ventum diffluere, sed ad examen
summi Iudicis cuncta servari. . . . Hanc historiam . . . simpliciter ob salutem
legentium sive audientium narrandum esse putavi.

and se cyning eode eft in to ðam seocan.   160
He clypode ða earmlice, and cwæð to þam cyninge,
Hwæt woldest þu nu æt me? Ne miht þu me nanum góde.
Ða cwæð se cyning him to, Ne clypa þu swa unwislice;
wite þin gewit. He andwyrde and cwæð,
Ne eom ic na gewitleas, ac min gewit is yfel.   165
Me comon lytle ær to twegen Godes englas,
and brohton me ane boc, seo wæs beorhte scinende,
ac heo wæs swyðe gehwæde, and heton me ræd[a]n.
Ic ða sceawode þa boc and þæron geseah
þa feawa godan dæda þe ic [dyde seldon,]   170
þa wæron swyðe feawa; and hi færlice genamon eft
þa bóc æt me, and me nan þing ne sædon.
Efne þa færlice comon þa cwealmbæran deoflu,
swyðe anþræc werod, and eall ðis hus afyldon,
and manega wiðutan on ælce healfe sæton.   175
Hwæt ða se fyrmesta forðteah ane bóc
mycele and ormæte, swylce mannes byrðen.
He het þa ræcan me to rædenne þa bóc,
and ic þæron geseah mid sweartum stafum awritene
ealle mine synna þe ic sið and ǽr gefremode,   180
and mine yfelan geþohtas on þære atelican béc,
swyðe swutelice, swa swa ic sylf oncneow.
Ða cwædon þa deoflu to þam Drihtnes englum
ðe ða lytlan boc me brohton, Hwæs abide ge her?
Ge sylfe *witon þæt þeos sawul is ure.   *f. 39ᵛ
Ða englas þa cwædon to þam atelicum deoflum,   186
Soð ge secgað; nimað his sawle
to ðam ecum witum on [e]owrum forwyrde.

---

162 woldost C.   163 clypa] clypode C.   166 lytle ær] nu lytle ær C.
ænglas C.   168 rædan] sic CN; rædon P.   170 feawan N.   dyde
seldon] sic CN; seldon dyde P.   171 hy N.   173 deofla CN.
174 anþræc] anðræclic C; angrislic N.   eal N.   hus] ós C.   176 formesta
C.   177 micele N.   byrðæn C.   179 þæron] ðær C.   181 atelice C.
183 deofla CN.   184 abide ge] anbidige N.   185 sawl N.   188 eowrum]
sic CN; heowrum P.

Glosses in P, Latin: 168 gehwæde: parua.   174 anþræc: orribilis.
178 ræcan: porrigere.   184 Hwæs abide ge her: quid expectas hic.   185 Ge:
vos.   187 ge: vos.   188 on forwyrde: in interitu.
ME: 173 Efne: lo.   179 stafum: lettres.

And þa englas sona of minre syhðe gewiton.

Ða arison sona of þam sweartan flocce   190
twegen egeslice deoflu mid isenum tolum,
swylce twa scearu, and slogon me hetelice,
an on þæt heafod and oðer on þone fot,
and gað nu þa dyntas þæs deofollican sleges
to minum innoðe mid ormætum sarum,   195
and þonne hi togædere cumað, min gast sceal gewitan
of þam earman lichaman mid þam atelicum deoflum
to hellicum clysingum, on ðam hatan fyre.

Ðus clypode se earming mid orwennysse,
and he hraðe þæs gewát to ðam ecum witum   200
butan dædbote, mid ðam deoflum genyðerod.

Ne fremode his gesyhð him sylfum nan þing,
ac for oðrum mannum him wearð æteowed þæt,
þæt þa beon gerihtlæhte þe ðas rædinge gehyrað,
for ðan ðe ure dæda beoð ealle awritene,   205
swa yfele, swa gode, on ecum gemynde,
and us [eft beoð] æteowde on ðam endenextan dæge.

Us sæde eac Beda be sumum gelæredum smyðe,

---

189 syhðe] gesihðe *CN* (*rightly?*).   190 arisan *C*.   191 deofla *CN*.
isenum] egeslicum *N*.   192 scaru *C*.   193 þæt heafod, þone fot] *tr. N*.
194 deoflican *CN* (*rightly?*).   196 hy *N*.   197 earmam *C*.   201 dæd-
bode *C*.   geniðerod *C*.   202 gesihðe *C*.   203 æteowod *C*.   207 eft
beoð] *sic CN*; beoð eft *P*.   208-41 *om. N*.   208 Beda] se halga beda *C*.
gelaredan *C*.   smiðe *C*.

Glosses in P, Latin: 189 gewiton: euanuer*unt*.   193 an: un*us*.   *first* on: *in*.
194 sleges: ictus.   198 clysingum: claustro.   199 orwennysse: despera-
tione.   201 genyðerod: da*m*natus.   208 smyðe: Fabro, *final* o *like* u
(*in margin, perhaps pointing to subject of exemplum*).
ME: 192 scearu: scherren.   200 witum: pine (*erased*).   207 æteowde:
ischawede (*? erased*).

208-41 [*Bede, ibid., cap. xiv*] Novi autem ipse fratrem . . . positum in monasterio nobili, sed ipsum ignobiliter viventem. Corripiebatur quidem sedulo a
fratribus ac maioribus loci. . . . Et quamvis eos audire noluisset, tolerabatur
tamen ab eis longanimiter; . . . erat enim fabrili arte singularis. Serviebat autem
multum ebrietati, et ceteris vitæ remissioris inlecebris; magisque in officina sua
die noctuque residere, quam ad . . . orandum in ecclesia . . . consuerat. . . . Percussus . . . languore, atque ad extrema perductus, vocavit fratres, et . . . coepit
narrare, quia videret inferos apertos, et Satanan demersum in profundis tartari,
Caiphanque cum ceteris, qui occiderunt Dominum, iuxta eum flammis ultri-
cibus contraditum: 'in quorum vicinia,' inquit, 'heu misero mihi locum de-
spicio æternæ perditionis esse præparatum.' Audientes hæc fratres coeperunt

se wæs mynsterman, and gemearcod Gode.
Se lufode druncennysse, and dyslice leofode, 210
and læg on his smiððan, and forlet his tidsangas,
and þa gebroðra ne mihton gebetag his unþeawas.
He wearð ða æt nextan geuntrumod to deaðe,
and geseah helle gata him sylfum geopenode,
and eac þone *deofol on þam deopum witum, *f. 40
and þa arleasan Iudeiscan, þe urne Drihten ofslogon, 216
ealle fordemede on þam ecan fyre;
and geseah him sylf eac, hwær his setl wæs gegearcod
on ðam hellican fyre, and wanode him sylfum,
and sæde þam gebroðrum hwæt him geswutelod wæs. 220
Ða bædon þa gebroðra þæt he gebuge to Gode
mid soðre behreowsunge, ær þan ðe he sáwlode.
He andwyrde mid orwennysse, Hu mæg ic nu gecyrran,
þonne ic sylf geseah min setl on helle?
And he gewat þa swa mid þam wordum of life, 225
butan huslunge, and hi ne dorston him fore gebiddan.
Him getimode þa [swa], swa swa us secgað béc:
þæt se ðe sylfwilles nele his cyrican gesecan,
þæt he sceal unþances into helle gan.

211 tidsangas] tit sances C.   212 unðæawas C.   214 gesah C.
216 iudeiscum C.   217 fordemde C.   218 silf C.   settel C.
223 andwyrde] andwyrde and cwæð C.   gecyrran] cyrran C.   227 first
swa] sic C; om. P.   228 sylfwilles nele] tr. C.   circan C.   gesecean C.

Glosses in P, Latin: 223 orwennysse: desperatione.
ME: 215 deopum witum: (. .) pine (? erased).   216 arleasan: illeg. gloss.
218 setl: stol (? erased).   219 wanode: Gronode.   228 cyrican: chirchen
(erased).

---

diligenter exhortari, ut vel tunc positus adhuc in corpore, pænitentiam faceret.
Respondebat ille desperans: 'Non est mihi modo tempus vitam mutandi, cum
ipse viderim iudicium meum iam esse completum.'
Talia dicens, sine viatico salutis obiit, . . . neque aliquis pro eo vel missas
facere, vel psalmos cantare, vel saltim orare præsumebat. [From preceding para-
graph] Unde accidit illi, quod solent dicere quidam, quia, qui non vult ecclesiæ
ianuam sponte humiliatus ingredi, necesse habet in ianuam inferni non sponte
damnatus introduci. [Return to original order] O quam grandi distantia divisit
Deus inter lucem et tenebras! Beatus protomartyr Stephanus passurus mortem
pro veritate, vidit cælos apertos, vidit gloriam Dei et Iesum stantem a dextris
Dei; et ubi erat futurus ipse post mortem, ibi oculos mentis ante mortem . . .
misit. At contra, faber iste tenebrosæ mentis et actionis, imminente morte, vidit
aperta tartara, vidit damnationem diaboli et sequacium eius; vidit etiam suum
infelix inter tales carcerem, quo miserabilius ipse desperata salute periret.

Eala, hu mycel todal is on Godes domum!   230
Se eadiga Stephanus, þa ða he ehtnysse þolode,
and to deaðe wæs gebroht for Drihtnes geleafan,
ða geseah he swutelice þone soðfæstan Hælend
æt his Fæder swyðran, þurh ða scinendan heofonan,
þyder þe he to sceolde for his soðan geleafan.   235
And þes earma smið openlice geseah
þa hellican wita and þa hetelan deofla,
þyder þe he, ungesælig, him sylf toweard wæs,
æfre to wunigenne on witum mid him
for his yfelnysse and orwennysse,   240
for þan ðe he nolde furðon on his ende gecyrran.
Us secgað béc foroft þæt manega gebugon on ende,
on heora forðsiðe, to Gode mid fæstum geleafan,
*and mid soðre behreowsunge, and heora synna geandettan,
*f. 40ᵛ
and God him þa gemiltsode for his micclan godnysse.   245
Se sceaða þe 'h'angode forscyldegod on rode
mid andetnysse 'bæd Cristes arfæstnysse',
and Crist him sona behet þæt he cuman moste
ðæs ylcan dæges mid him to ðam ecan wuldre.
Ælc þæra þe geortruwað and geendað butan hihte,   250
se losað openlice on ðam ecan forwyrde;

---

230 micel *C.*   233 þone] þonne *corr. to* þone *C.*   soðfestan *C.*   234 scine-
nendan *C.*   235 þider *C.*   scolde *C.*   238 ðider *C.*   towærd *C.*
241 furðon] wurðon *C.*   his] *om. C.*   242–54 *N selects from and rearranges
these lines in the order* 250–3, 242–5, 254, *with changes as noted.*   242 Us
... manega] Swa us secgað bec *þæt* manega foroft *N.*   243 Gode] þam soðan
hælende *N.*   fæstum] anrædum *N.*   244 geandetton *CN.*   245 gemilt-
sode] mildsode *N.*   micclum (*!*) *C.*   246–9 *om. N.*   246 angode *C.*
247 bæt *C.*   249 ecean *C.*   wuldre] wurdre *C.*   251 eacean *corr. to*
ecean *C.*

Glosses in P, Latin: 230 todal: differentia.   236 þes: iste.   242 gebugon: *conuerterunt.*   246 sceaða: fur.   forscyldegod: reus.   250 geortruwað: despe*rat.*   hihte: co*n*fidentia.   251 forwyrde: da*m*natione.
ME: 231 ehtnysse: (martir)dom (*? erased*).   234 swyðran: riht hand
(*? erased*).   246 sceaða: þeof (*erased*).   249 ðam: þen (*? erased*).
wuldre: glore (*erased*).

246–9 [*Luc. xxiii. 40–43, esp. 42–43*] Et dicebat ad Iesum: Domine, me-
mento mei, cum veneris in regnum tuum. Et dixit illi Iesus: Amen dico tibi,
hodie mecum eris in paradiso.

XIX DE DOCTRINA APOSTOLICA 635

and se þe hopað to Criste becymð to miltsunge
huru on Domes-dæg, for þæs Hælendes godnysse.
Se us gelæde to ðam ecan life. AMEN.

252 becumð *C.*   mildsunge *N.*   253 -dæge *C.*   254 *N adapts this
line to an expanded conclusion*: Se éca drihte*n* us ah'r'edde fram eallum freced-
nyssu*m*, and to ðam écan life gelǽde. Se þe leofað and rixað mid fǽder and
halgum gaste, a butan énde wé cweþaþ. AMEN.

NOTES

20. *hundteontig-wintre.* Cited by Napier, *COEL*, from this passage in P.
There are many similar adjectives ending in *-wintre* with other numerals,
an-, twi-, þri-, feower-, etc. Between one and twenty the only numerals
not represented in Hall–Meritt are six, eleven, thirteen, and nineteen.

38. *dyrne-ceorl.* This compound has not been recorded in the dictionaries, but in the context we cannot well take the two words separately. As
an adverb, *dyrne* would impose a foolish limitation; as a separate adjective
it ought to be inflected, *dyrnne*, and would not adequately restrict the
meaning of *ceorl.* There are several recorded compounds beginning with
dyrne that refer to fornication and adultery: *dyrneforlegernes, dyrnegeligre,*
etc.

45. *hi sylfe forhabbað fram hæmede.* This seems to be a deliberate
substitution for the Vulgate, *seipsos castraverunt,* which the West Saxon
gospels translate directly as 'hig sylfe belistnodon'. The gloss *bilimede*
ignores or rejects Ælfric's distinction, reverting to the Vulgate. At line 61
below castration is expressly forbidden.

62. *Uita Patrum.* The singular *vita* was used regularly by Ælfric for the
title of this work, in harmony with the explanation given by Gregory of
Tours with reference to his use of the title for his own similar work on
the Gaulish–Frankish saints: 'Unde manifestum est, melius dici *vitam
patrum* quam *vitas*, quia, cum sit diversitas meritorum virtutumque, una
tamen omnes vita corporis alit in mundo.' (*Gregorii Eps. Turonensis Liber
Vitæ Patrum*, Monumenta Germaniae Historica, Scriptores Rerum
Merovingicarum I. 662. Quoted by C. W. Jones, *Saints' Lives and
Chronicles*, p. 214, note 21.) Editors have sometimes undertaken to correct
the manuscripts: e.g. *CH* II. 272, where Thorpe emends to *Uitae*; Assmann III. 229, where Assmann accepts an earlier emendation from abl.
uita to ap. *Vitas.*

102–4. Cf. Assmann II. 147–52:

Hit wære swyþe rihtlic æfter rihtum life,
þæt se cniht heolde hine sylfne clæne,
oðþæt he wifode, swa swa he wyle habban
clæne mæden, þonne hi cumað togæderes.

And æfter Godes gesetnysse eall swa scyldig byð geteald
se forlegena cniht swa þæt forlegene mæden.

These six lines are only in the expanded version of Assmann II that appears in MS. H and, as an excerpt, in the *De Virginitate* of MS.
V, for which see the introduction to XXX. All six correspond in sentiment to the
sermon by Cæsarius of which a small part is quoted as a source for 102–4.
In the *Institutes of Polity* (ed. Jost, p. 130) we find a directive in Wulfstan's manner that is probably derived from Ælfric:

> Ðæt bið rihtlic lif, þæt cniht þurhwunige on hys cnihthade oððæt he
> on rihtre mædenæwe gewifige, and habbe þa siððan and nænige oðre,
> þa hwile seo libbe.

Jost has noted the resemblance to Assmann II, and this (perhaps by way
of *De Virginitate*) is probably the source, for the preceding sentence in
Polity echoes Assmann II. 132–4.

106. The gloss *wicchekreft*, partially erased but still legible in the margin
of P, seems to have been intended, though wrongly, for *sinscipe*. Perhaps
the glossator hastily confused *sin* with *scin* and thought of *scincræft*,
which he had glossed *wicchecreft* at XVIII. 257 and (less clearly) 380.
Other letters seem to have been erased in the margins at this point, but
I cannot make out what they were.

119–30. Dr. Braekman (edition, pp. 152–3) points out that this is
Ælfric's most explicit recommendation on the frequency with which the
holy sacrament should be received by the laity. He cites earlier recom-
mendations, beginning with Bede's letter to Egbert of York.

127–9. The order of the sins in this list corresponds to pseudo-Alcuin,
Liber de Virtutibus et Vitiis, cap. xxvii sqq. (*PL* CI. 632 sqq.), except that
unrotnys (*tristitia*) and *asolcennyss* (*accidia*) have changed places. In this
respect the order here is the same as in *CH* II. 218 and *LS* XVI. 267 sqq.,
whereas in IV. 251 and the second Old English letter for Wulfstan (Fehr,
Brief III, sec. 147 sqq.) the order is the same as pseudo-Alcuin's. But
pride comes first instead of last only in the present list and the letter. On
an attempt to use the position of pride in Ælfric's lists to determine the
order of composition of IV and XIX see the note on IV. 249–51.

128. *unwislic* C, *unrihtlic* P. My choice of *unwislic*, in some such sense
as 'irrational', depends partly on Ælfric's comment on *weamodnyss* in the
second Old English letter for Wulfstan (Fehr, *Brief* III. 162): 'þæt se
mann ne mæge his mod gewildan, ac butan ælcum wisdome waclice (*v.l.*
wodlice) irsað.' A similar comment occurs in *CH* II. 220/12 sqq., but
without use of the word *wisdom*. P's *unrihtlic* might be used to distinguish
lawful from unlawful *yrsung*, but surely *weamodnyss* is always *unrihtlic*,
and so are all the other sins; whereas *unwislic*, though redundant, helps
to emphasize the difference between ungoverned rage and legitimate anger.
Probably *unriht* has been carelessly repeated by a scribe from *unrihthæmed*.

138. *forðmann*, 'man of rank'. Napier, *COEL*, cited the word from this passage in MS. P. It is Ælfric's substitute for Bede's *vir in laico habitu atque officio militari positus*.

174. *anþræc* P. See the Glossary for this form and the evidence of Ælfric's use of the word. The other manuscripts seem to have reached out for something more familiar.

192. *scearu*. Ælfric was probably translating *vomeres* as in Plummer's text of Bede, or possibly *cultra* as in some manuscripts. Both the Moore and the Leningrad MSS. (the two earliest) suffer from a scribal omission at this point. The Moore MS. has *vomeres* in another hand in the lower margin; the Leningrad has the final *-es* on the side, the rest having been cut off by a binder. See Plummer's footnote and the facsimile of the Leningrad Bede (ed. O. Arngart, Copenhagen, 1952), f. 136*b*.

194. *dyntas*. The context here seems to demand that the word mean 'impressions' rather than 'blows'. See Glossary.

209. *gemearcod Gode*. Does Ælfric mean that he was tonsured? See Glossary.

227. *swa, swa swa*. This reading of C supplies alliteration between half-lines and improves the sense: 'Then it so befell him as books tell us (it must befall): that . . .'.

XX

DE POPULO ISRAHEL

Exod. xxxii, *Num.* xi, xiii, xiv, xvi, xxi

THIS homily, taking up the story of the Israelites in the wilderness at nearly the point where Ælfric had left it in his homily on the Egyptian captivity, the passage of the Red Sea, and the ten commandments (*CH* II. XII, the first half), concentrates on seven occasions when the people murmured or actively rebelled against God and Moses and incurred God's wrath. Though it has survived in only two manuscripts, one of which is imperfect, it deserves a place of distinction among Ælfric's numerous treatments of Old Testament materials. It is designed as a homily, not a simple translation, since it not only selects passages in accordance with a theme but introduces comments, at certain points extensive. Thus it belongs in the same company as the two homilies (the one already mentioned on *Exod.* i–xx and the *Secunda Sententia* on *Joshua*) assigned to Mid-lent Sunday in *CH* II (188 and 212 respectively). Not so full of Biblical narrative but very similar in its leading themes and at one point overlapping in matter is *De Oratione Moysi*, *LS* XIII. All four of these have to do with aspects and episodes of the journey from Egypt to the promised land, and all but *De Populo Israhel* are assigned to Mid-lent. They form a group distinct from the homilies that deal with the Creation and from those that deal with other parts of the Old Testament, even the overtly homiletic *Job* and *Judges*, and certainly the more exclusively narrative *Kings, Esther, Judith* (with homiletic conclusion), and *Maccabees*. And they are likewise to be distinguished from Ælfric's translations of parts of the Pentateuch,[1] including the latter half of *Numbers*, which overlaps *De Populo Israhel*, giving less freely composed versions of chapters xiii, xiv, xvi, and xxi, besides much else that is not in the homily.

[1] I limit the list provisionally, with Clemoes, *Chronology*, 218, to *Genesis* i–iii, vi–ix, xii–xxiv. 22 (the version in our MS. L); *Numbers* xiii–xxxi; *Joshua* (except i. 1–10 and xii). All these translations are selective, omitting chiefly non-narrative material.

De Populo Israhel was apparently composed too late to be included in the *Lives of Saints* as originally issued. In MS. P it is followed directly by *Judges*, *De Duodecim Abusivis*, the *Interrogationes*, and the sermon excerpted from *Kings*, the last three being members of the *Lives* set and its appendix as represented by MS. W. Possibly both *De Populo Israhel* and *Judges* were appended to the *Lives* in a later issue; but in any event the association of these two is intelligible enough. In the other manuscript, X^d (Cotton Otho C. i, vol. 2), *De Populo Israhel* follows upon the unpublished *De Creatore et Creatura* and *De Sex Ætatibus Mundi*, which may have been consecutive parts of a letter somewhat like that to Sigeweard on the Old and New Testaments. The association here is again intelligible but on the whole less close, and only these three consecutive pieces, imperfect at beginning and end, survive in X^d as witnesses to some otherwise lost volume.

Ælfric's references to earlier writings here in xx. 335 and in xii. 224 show that *De Populo Israhel* is later than the first half of the Mid-lent homily, *CH* II. xii, as indeed we do not need to be told, and earlier than xii, a matter less obvious. If we assume further, as already suggested above, that it is later than the *Lives of Saints*, we shall narrow the range considerably and date it fairly close to the turn of the century, for the *Lives* set was probably issued in the late nineties and xii is a part of the ordered Temporale in M and was probably issued before 1005 when Ælfric became abbot.[1] Thus *De Populo Israhel* would have been produced near the end of the period, beginning with the *Catholic Homilies* and continuing beyond the completion of the *Lives*, when Ælfric was most active in translating and commenting on portions of the Old Testament.

So far as I have been able to discover, *De Populo Israhel* had no model among Latin homilies and very little of the comment that Ælfric supplies has any direct precedent, or depends on any interpretation not furnished at one place or another in the Bible itself. It is somewhat surprising to find that virtually nothing of value has been contributed by Bede's or Rabanus's commentary on the Pentateuch (the latter an omnium gatherum), or by Augustine's or Isidore's *Quæstiones*, which include comments on some of the passages Ælfric treats. Isidore is possibly an exception for the

---

[1] On the chronological problem see the Introduction, pp. 146–8, and the discussions relating to MS. M, pp. 9–10 and 39 sqq.; also Clemoes, *Chronology*, pp. 243 sq.

passage at 128–39, but if so he is only elaborating an interpretation of manna given by Jesus himself. At one later point, the interpretation of the episode of the fiery serpents and the exaltation of the serpent of brass (333–52), Ælfric was indeed dependent on both Bede and Augustine, as the note explains, by way of his own previous digest of their interpretation; but once again it is a speech by Jesus that supplies the basic idea. The magical property attributed to the manna in lines 16–21 and again in 124–5 depends on an interpretation in the book of *Wisdom*, not on the partial echoes of it in the commentators. And the basic interpretation of the whole io stated by St. Paul in *I Corinthians* x, a chapter to which Ælfric refers directly in his conclusion (390 sqq.). As often when he makes use of Old Testament material, Ælfric allows some of the stories to speak for themselves; but in the middle and at the end there are extended comments, and these seem to spring mainly from his own thorough acquaintance with the Bible and his own reflections on it. At the beginning and at a few other points his own earlier writing is partially recalled. For all these matters the notes should be consulted.

DE POPULO ISRAHEL. QUANDO UOLUERIS

We habbað nu gesæd, swa we sceortlicost mihton,
on þam ærran cwyde, hu se ælmihtiga God
his agen folc ahredde fram Faraoes þeowte,
and hu hi siðodon ofer ða Readan Sæ,
and hu he hi afedde feowertig geara   5
mid heofonlicum mete, and þær nan man næs
on eallum þam fyrste furðon geuntrumod,
ne heora reaf næs tobrocen binnon þam fyrste.
Nu wylle we git secgan sum ðing be ðam folce.

Syx hund þusend manna, swa swa Moyses awrat,   10
wæron on þære fyrde, wigendra manna,
buton þam ceorlfolce, and cildum and wifum,
and God hi ealle afedde swyðe eaðelice,
swa þæt him ælce dæg com edniwe mete to
mid þam upplicum deawe æt heora geteldum,   15
swa hwær swa hi wicodon, and se wæs on swæcce

Text based on P (Hatton 115), ff. 101ᵛ-8. Collated with Xᵈ (Cotton Otho C. i, vol. 2), ff. 154ᵛ, 153ʳ⁻ᵛ, 155ʳ⁻ᵛ, which is incomplete (lines 1–268 only) and considerably damaged by fire. Nearly every line has lost at least a few letters, and the losses at tops and bottoms of pages are more severe. The limits of these pages have been noted among the variants, but the lacunae are noted only where a reading in P seems doubtful. In general it appears that the two manuscripts differed only in minor details. Several sentence-capitals, lacking in both manuscripts, have been supplied.

Sup.: *Line for title left blank Xᵈ*: *at top of f. 155* DE POPULO ISRAHEL QUAND. . . .
1 scortlicost *Xᵈ*.   3 aredde *Xᵈ*.   pharao'e's: *later hand adds* þes ifeles kinges *Xᵈ*.   4 sæ] *later hand adds* mid druge fotum *Xᵈ*.   9 secgean *Xᵈ*. folke *Xᵈ*.   12 cildum and wifum] wifum *and* cildum *Xᵈ*.   13 swiþe *Xᵈ*. 14 dæge *Xᵈ*.

Glosses in P and Xᵈ, Latin: 2 ærran cwyde: *p*rimo testame*n*to P.   3 þeowte: seruitute P.   4 siðodon: *p*errexer*unt* P.   7 furðon: eciam P; *glosses in Xᵈ above* furþon *and* geuntrumod *obscure*.   8 binnon: infra (*for* intra) P. 11 wigend*ra* manna: *p*relianciu*m* P, bellator*um* Xᵈ.   12 buton: *p*reter P, excepto Xᵈ.   14 edniwe: renouatu*m* P.   16 wicodon: manser*unt* P. swæcce: Gustu PXᵈ.

Sᴏᴜʀᴄᴇs. 2–40 [*Summary of Exod. xii–xx, mainly as in CH II. 194–8. See notes.*]
16–21 [*Sap. xvi. 20, 21*] Pro quibus angelorum esca nutrivisti populum tuum; et paratum panem de cælo præstitisti illis sine labore, omne delectamentum in

ælces cynnes werednysse þæs þe þam menn gelyste.
Ðæt is swutellice to secgenne þæt se mete awende,
on þæs mannes muðe þe þone mete æt,
to þæs metes swæcce ðe him sylfum gelicode,   20
swa hú swa he wolde habban to gereorde.
And of heardum stane him arn wæteres stream
him eallum genoh, and eac heora orue,
for þan ðe se ælmihtiga God, þeah ðe he eaðe mihte,
nolde him win sendan on þam westene þa,   25
ne furðan ealu, flowende of ðam stane.
   God sylf *com ða sume dæg him to   *f. 102
on anum mycclum munte þe menn hata ð Sinai,
swa þæt eall þæt folc mihte geseon swyðe mycel fýr
ofer ealne þone munt mid egeslicum lige,   30
for þan ðe God sylf com mid ðam fyre ðyder,
and mid bymena dreame, and mid micclum þunore.
He gesette þa æ eallum þam folce,
þæt synd rihte lagu, hu men lybban sceoldon,
and ænne God wurðian æfre mid geleafan,   35
for þan ðe nan god nys þe ænige godcundnysse hæbbe
buton se ána þe ealle þing 'ge'sceop.
He worhte feala wundra on ðam westene þa,
ac þæt folc wæs wiðerræde witodlice to oft,
and to swyðe gegremedon þone soðan God.   40
   Moyses wunode on þam munte mid Gode

---

17 men X^d.   21 gereorde] reorde X^d.   23 orfe X^d.   24 eaða X^d.
25 sendean *corr. to* sendan X^d.   27 dæge X^d.   28 men X^d.   hateð X^d.
29 swiðe X^d.   32 mycclum X^d.   34 (sy)nt X^d.   lagu] *f. 153*, X^d,
which follows 154ᵛ because of misbinding.   sceoldan X^d.   36 nys] nyss X^d
(*as if* godnyss).   38 fela X^d.   39 ac] eac X^d.

Glosses, *Latin*: 17 (we)rednysse: *glossed illegibly* X^d.   20 swæcce: Gustu
P, sapore (*last letter doubtful*) X^d.   25 win: vinum P.   26 ne furðan:
nec eciam PX^d.   ealu: servisiam(*for* cervisiam) P.   30 lige: flamma P.
36 god: deus P.   39 wiðerræde: contrarius P.
   ME: 22 arn: orn P.   25 westene: *gloss erased* P (westelond?).   34 lagu:
la'we' P.

---

se habentem, et omnis saporis suavitatem. Substantia enim tua dulcedinem tuam
quam in filios habes ostendebat, et deserviens uniuscuiusque voluntati, ad quod
quisque volebat convertebatur.
   41–42 [*Exod. xxiv. 18*] Ingressusque Moyses medium nebulæ, ascendit in
montem: et fuit ibi quadraginta diebus, et quadraginta noctibus.

feowertig daga on án, and þæt folc þa hwile
worhton him god of golde agotenne,
and him lac offrodon, and swyðe þæs fægnodon
on heora gebeorscype, and begunnon to plegenne   45
ætforan þam gode þe hi of golde geworhton.
Ða cwæð God to Moyse on þam munte Sinai,
Astih adune hraðe of ðysum steapum munte;
þis folc hæfð gesyngod, and hi sylfe worhton him
agotenne god of golde nu iu,   50
and him lac offriað, and to him gebiddað.
Moyses þa astah of þam sticolan munte,
and com to ðam folce ætforan þam gode,
and cwæð to him eallum mid [an]rædum mode,
Gif her æni man sy of eallum þysum folce   55
þe on God gelyfe, gange se to me.
Hwæt þa sona eode eall seo mægð him to
of Leuies cynne, and he cwæð him þa to,
Gað nu hraðe ealle unforhte mid wæpnum
þurh ealle þas fyrde fram ende oð oðrum,   60

---

43 agotene X^d.   44 fagenodon X^d.   45 -scipe X^d.   48 þissum
X^d.   54 anrædum] *sic* X^d; rædum *P*.   55 ænig X^d.   mann X^d.
si X^d.   59 hræðe X^d.   60 oð] to X^d.

Glosses, Latin: 43 god: deos *or* deus (*for* deum) *P*.   48 hraðe] cito *P*.
50 nu iu: eciam *nunc P*.   54 rædum: crudeli (*understanding* reðum?) *P*.
57 mægð: gen*eratio P*.

42–46 [*Exod. xxxii. 1–6*] Videns autem populus quod moram faceret descen-
dendi de monte Moyses, congregatus adversus Aaron, dixit: Surge, fac nobis
deos, qui nos præcedant. . . . Dixitque ad eos Aaron: Tollite inaures aureas de
uxorum, filiorumque et filiarum vestrarum auribus. . . . Quas cum ille accepisset,
formavit opere fusorio, et fecit ex eis vitulum conflatilem. . . . Surgentesque
mane, obtulerunt holocausta, et hostias pacificas; et sedit populus manducare,
et bibere, et surrexerunt ludere.
47–51 [*Ibid. 7–8*] Locutus est autem Dominus ad Moysen, dicens: Vade,
descende; peccavit populus tuus, . . . feceruntque sibi vitulum conflatilem, et
adoraverunt; atque immolantes ei hostias, dixerunt: Isti sunt dii tui, Israel, qui
te eduxerunt de terra Ægypti.
52–56 [*Ibid. 15, 19, 26*] Et reversus est Moyses de monte. . . . Cumque
appropinquasset ad castra, vidit vitulum, et choros. . . . Et stans in porta
castrorum, ait: Si quis est Domini, iungatur mihi.
57–62 [*Ibid. 26, 27*] Congregatique sunt ad eum omnes filii Levi, quibus ait:
Hæc dicit Dominus Deus Israel: Ponat vir gladium super femur suum. Ite, et
redite de porta usque ad portam per medium castrorum, et occidat unusquisque
fratrem, et amicum, et proximum suum.

and ofsleað *ealle tomiddes þam folce   *f. 102ᵛ
þa ðe ge gemetað for þyssere mandæde.
Ða eode seo mægð be Moyses hæse
þurh ealne þone here æfre ofsleande,
and hi ofslogon on þam dæge þreo and twentig þusenda,   65
and Moyses tobræc and tobrytte þone god
eall to duste þa, and þæt gedwyld alede.
Eft æfter þysum hi begunnon ceorian
mid mycelre murcnunge ongean God Ælmihtigne,
for heora geswince þe hi swuncon on þære fare;   70
ac Gode ne licode na heora geleafleast,
ne heora ceorung, ac asende him to
fýr of heofonum, and forbærnde sona
sumne dæl þæs werodes for heora wodnysse.
Ða clypodon hi ealle endemes to Moysen,   75
and Moyses gebæd þone ælmihtigan God
for ðam dyrstigan folce, and þæt fyr wearð adwæsced.
Ðas race we secgað eow nu to rihtinge,
þæt nan mann ne sceole ceorian ongean God
mid dyrstigum anginne, ne his Drihten gremian,   80
se þe æfre wyle wel þam ðe hit geearniað,
and he ða gefrefrað þe his fultumes biddað.
Hi ongunnon eft ceorian and swyðe murcnian,

---

62 þyssere] þisse Xᵈ.   mandæda Xᵈ.   71 na] om. Xᵈ.   72 asende]
sende Xᵈ.   74 weoredes Xᵈ.   76 ælmihtigne Xᵈ.   77 adwædsced
alt. to adwæssced Xᵈ.   78 eow nu] nu eow Xᵈ.   80 dyrstigum alt. to
ðyrstigum (!) Xᵈ.   81 se þe] þe Xᵈ.

Glosses, Latin: 62 þa: eos P.   mandæde: iniquitate P.   63 mægð:
tribus P.   66 tobrytte: contriuit P.   69 murcnunge: murmure P.
74 werodes: populi P.   75 endemes: pariter P.   77 dyrstigan: audaci,
temere P.   78 race: narrationem P.   rihtinge: correctionem P.   80 mid
dyrstigum anginne: initio presumtuoso P.   82 ða: illos P.
ME: 83 ceorian: gru : : : (erased: gruche?) P.

63–65 [Ibid. 28] Feceruntque filii Levi iuxta sermonem Moysi, cecideruntque
in die illa quasi viginti tria millia hominum.
66–67 [Ibid. 20] Arripiensque vitulum quem fecerant, combussit, et contrivit
usque ad pulverem.
68–77 [Num. xi. 1–2] Interea ortum est murmur populi, quasi dolentium pro
labore, contra Dominum. Quod cum audisset Dominus, iratus est; et accensus in
eos ignis Domini devoravit extremam castrorum partem. Cumque clamasset
populus ad Moysen, oravit Moyses ad Dominum, et absorptus est ignis.
83–88 [Num. xi. 4–6] Vulgus quippe promiscuum, quod ascenderat cum eis,
flagravit desiderio, sedens et flens, iunctis sibi pariter filiis Israel, et ait: Quis

æfter flæscmettum swyðe oflyste,
and sædon him betwynan, Hwa sylð us flæscmete? 85
Witodlice we wæron wel on Egipta lande
on fisce and on fugele, and on feala estmettum;
nu we naht ne geseoð buton þysne ænne mete.
Ða wearð Moyses micclum astyred,
ac God him cwæð tó þæt him cuman sceolde, 90
eallum þam folce, na to anum dæge,
ac to anum monðe, flæscmættas genoge,
oððæt him wlatode þære gewilnunge.
God sende him ða *sona, mid swyðlicum winde, *f. 103
micel fleogende fugelcyn feorran ofer sæ; 95
þa flugon endemes into þære fyrde,
swa þæt ælc man gefeng on eallum þam folce
swa micel swa he wolde and he gewyldan mihte;
and æton swa swyðe of þære sande ealle.
Ne ateorode him se mete ðe hi swa micclum gewilnodon, 100
ac þæt flæsc cleofode þa gyt on heora toðum,
and þa ða hi fulle wæron, þa feollon hi deade,
feala þæs folces, for þan [þe] hi fandodon Godes.
Hwi woldon hi gremian God swa unðearfes,

84 swiðe X^d.　　85 us] us nú X^d.　　87 fela X^d.　　89 mycclum X^d.
94 sen(de), *last letters visible f. 153*, X^d.　　95 (m)icel, *first letters visible f. 153^v*,
X^d.　　fugellcynn X^d.　　97 mann X^d.　　98 mycell X^d.　　99 ætan X^d.
swa] þa X^d.　　swiðe X^d.　　100 ateorodo X^d.　　101 clifode X^d.
103 þe] *sic* X^d; *om. P.*　　fandodan X^d.

Glosses, *Latin*: 87 estmettum: deliciis *P.*　　89 astyred: motus (?) *P.*
94 swyðlicum: vehem*en*ti, valido *P.*　　96 þa: q*u*i *P.*　　endemes: p*a*riter *P.*
100 ateorode: defecit *P.*　　102 *first* þa: tunc *P.*　　104 unðearfes: sine
necessitate *P.*
ME: 96 endemes: *gloss erased* (isome?) *P.*　　100 ateorode: wonede (*erased*) *P.*

dabit nobis ad vescendum carnes? Recordamur piscium quos comedebamus in
Ægypto gratis; in mentem nobis veniunt cucumeres, et pepones, porrique et
cepe, et allia. Anima nostra arida est, nihil aliud respiciunt oculi nostri nisi man.
89 [*Ibid. 10*] Moysi intoleranda res visa est.
90–93 [*Ibid. 16, 18–20*] Et dixit Dominus ad Moysen: ... Ut det vobis Dominus carnes, et comedatis, non uno die ... sed usque ad mensem dierum, donec
exeat per nares vestras, et vertatur in nauseam.
94–103 [*Ibid. 31–34*] Ventus autem egrediens a Domino, arreptas trans mare
coturnices detulit, et dimisit in castra. ... Surgens ergo populus toto die illo, et
nocte, ac die altero, congregavit coturnicum, qui parum, decem coros. ...
Adhuc carnes erant in dentibus eorum, nec defecerat huiuscemodi cibus, et ecce
furor Domini concitatus in populum, percussit eum plaga magna nimis. Voca-
tusque est ille locus: Sepulcra concupiscentiæ.
104–27 [*Largely from first part of Exod. See note.*]

þæt hi mid ceorunge forsawon þone mete   105
þe him ælce dæg edniwe becom,
and woldon habban wyrta and þa gewunelican mettas
þe hi ær hæfdon æt ham on Egipta [lande],
þa ða hi worhton Pharaoes weallas,
and his burga getimbrodon on bysmorlicum þeowte,   110
and man ælcne beswang mid gescyndnysse ða,
buton he þæt weallweorc wel ða gefyrþrode.
And heora hyse-cild eac man het acwellan
of þam twelf mægðum, þa ða hi to mannum comon.
Nu alysde hi God of ðam laðum þeowte,   115
and heora fynd acwealde, and Pharaó þone cyning,
þe hi swa geswencte, on þære sǽ middan,
þæt þær nan man ne becom cucu ða to lande
buton Israhela folc, ðe ferdon of ðam lande
gangende mid fotum, þurh Godes mihte ealle,   120
ofer ða Readan Sǽ, swa swa we rædað on bocum.
Nu wæron hi oflyste þurh heora unlustas
flæsclicra metta, unmægðlice swaþeah,
for þam ðe se heofonlica mete hæfde ælcne swæc
ælcere werodnysse *þe ænig mete hæfð,   * f. 103ᵛ
and wæs eac wurðlicor þonne ða wyrta wæron   126
þe hi æt ham sudon on heora croccum mid flæsce.
Se heofonlica mete hæfde þa getacnunge

106 dæge X^d.   107 (w)oldan X^d.   haban X^d.   108 (ham on egipta)
lánde X^d; lande om. P.   110 burhga X^d.   111 mann X^d.   gescynd-
nysse] scyndnysse X^d.   112 wel ða] (ða) well (?) X^d.   113 hyse-] om.
X^d.   mann X^d.   acwellann X^d.   118 ða to lande] to þam lande X^d.
123 unmægðlice] unmæðe(lice) X^d? 124 mete] P has mark of abbrev. or
accent over first e, probably a slip of the pen.   125 wered- X^d.   126 weorð-
licor X^d.   127 sudon] ge(sudon) X^d.   128 þa] om. X^d (rightly?).

Glosses, Latin: 105 ceorunge: murmure P.   106 edniwe: renouatum P.
107 wyrta: herbas P.   þa: illos P.   109 weallas: menia X^d.   110 þeowte:
seruitute P.   112 buton: nisi P.   gefyrþrode: promoueret P.   113 heora
hyse-cild: eorum masculos P.   114 mægðum: tribu P.   115 hi: eos P.
þeowte: seruitute P.   118 cucu: uiuus P.   119 buton: preter P.
123 unmægðlice: immoderate P.   124 swæc: Gustum P; saporem X^d.
126 wurðlicor: dingnior P; dulcius (?) X^d.   wyrta: herbe P.
ME: 118 cucu: cwic P.

128–39 [Ps. lxxvii. 24–25] Panem cæli dedit eis. Panem angelorum mandu-
cavit homo.
[Ioan. vi. 32] Amen, amen dico vobis, non Moyses dedit vobis panem de
cælo, sed Pater meus dat vobis panem de cælo verum. [33] Panis enim Dei est

ures Hælendes Cristes, þe com of heofonum to us,
þe is engla bigleofa and ealra manna líf   130
þe on hine gelyfað, and hine nu lufiað.

þone acwealdon syððan þæt ylce Iudeisce cynn,
and noldon hine habban heora sawlum to bigleofan;
ac we gelyfað on hine, and lif habbað þurh hine,
and he is us inmeddre þonne ða `est´mettas,   135
for þan ðe we æfre habbað ealle þing þurh hine,
ge on ðyssere worulde ge on ðære toweardan,
and us nanre werednysse ne byð wana mid him,
gif we hine ænne habbað on urum geleafan.

Se ælmihtiga God æfter þysum gespræc   140
to Moyse þam heretogan, and het hine sendan
of ðæs folces meniu menn to ðam lande,
þær þær hi to sceoldon, and sceawian þæt land,
for þan ðe God wolde his agen word gefyllan,
and þæt folc gelædan to ðam behatenan lande,   145
swa swa he gefyrn behet þam heahfædere Abrahame.
Moyses þa genamode of ðam twelf mægðum
twelf heafodmenn, and het faran to þam lande,
and sceawian þa wæstmas on wuda and on felda,

129 heofenan (?) X^d.   132 acwealdan X^d.   ylce] om. X^d.   140 þyssum
X^d.   141 moysen X^d.   hertogan X^d.

Glosses, Latin: 132 þone: illum P.   135 inmeddre: sapidius (written
twice) P.   þonne: quam P.   143 sceawian: videre P.   146 gefyrn:
olim P.   147 genamode: assumsit P.   mægðum: tribu P.   149 sceawian:
videre P.

ME: 135 inmeddre: uel imundre (OE gemyndre) X^d.

---

qui de cælo descendit, et dat vitam mundo. . . . [35] Ego sum panis vitæ; qui
venit ad me, non esuriet; et qui credit in me, non sitiet umquam.
[Isidore, Quæst. in Exod., PL LXXXIII. 298] Manna utique, quod est
Christus, qui tamquam panis vivus de cælo descendit, . . . non iam murmuranti
populo, et tentanti Synagogæ, sed credenti et in illo spem ponenti datur
Ecclesiæ. . . . Hic est panis cæli, et verus cibus angelorum.
  140–3 [Num. xiii. 2, 3] Locutus est Dominus ad Moysen, dicens: Mitte viros
qui considerent terram Chanaan, quam daturus sum filiis Israel, singulos de
singulis tribubus, ex principibus.
  147–52 [Ibid. 4, 18–21] Fecit Moyses quod Dominus imperaverat, de deserto
Pharan mittens principes viros, quorum ista sunt nomina. [In 5–17 the twelve,
with their tribes, are named.] Misit ergo eos Moyses ad considerandam terram
Chanaan, et dixit ad eos: . . . considerate terram, qualis sit, . . . humus, pinguis
an sterilis, nemorosa an absque arboribus. . . . Et afferte nobis de fructibus
terræ.

and het h[i] eac bringan him to sceawienne   150
of þæs landes wæstmum, þæt hi witan mihton
hwæðer þæt land wære wæstmbære and god.
Hi ferdon þa sona to ðam foresædan lande,
and sceawedon þone eard, and eac swylce brohton
sume winbogas mid berion afyllode   155
and oðre ofætan *him eallum to sceawienne,   *f. 104
and cwædon to Moyse and to ealre þære meniu,
Ðæt land we sceawedon þe ðu us to sendest;
þær is swyðe gód eard, ac he is earfoðe
us to begytenne þurh urne fultum swaðeah;   160
þær synd mycele burga and mærlice geweallode,
and þær we gesawon eac swylce entas,
Enaches cynnes þæs ealdan entes;
we synd wið hi geðuhte swylce oðre gærstapan.
Ða wurdon hi ealle wundorlice astyrode   165
mid mycelre ceorunge, and sædon him betwynan,
Uton eft gecyrran to Egipta lande,
þæt we on ðam lande ne licgan ofslagene,
ne ure wíf and cild ne wurðon gehergode.

150 hi eac] heac P; *no reading* X^d. (sceawi)genne X^d.   152 wære] *end*
f. 153^v, X^d; skip to 155. (wæst)mbære, *f. 155, X^d.*   153 foresædon X^d.
155 afyllede X^d.   156 sceawigenne X^d.   158 land] *om.* X^d.   160 begitenne X^d.   161 mycclæ X^d.   burhga X^d.   gewealleda X^d.   163 entes]
entas *alt. to* entes X^d.   165 astyrede X^d.   166 mycelere X^d.   betweonan
X^d.   167 egypta X^d.

Glosses, Latin: 151 hi: illi P.   152 wæstmbære: fructuosus P.   156 oðre
ofætan: alium fructum P.   163 enaches cynnes: de genere enoc P.   þæs
ealdan] illi vete[r]is (!) P.   169 ne wurðon: non sint P.   gehergode: vastati P.

153–64 [*Ibid. 22, 24, 26–29, 32, 34*] Cumque ascendissent, exploraverunt
terram. . . . Absciderunt palmitem cum uva sua, quem portaverunt in vecte
duo viri. De malis quoque granatis et de ficis loci illius tulerunt. . . . Reversique
exploratores terræ . . . venerunt ad Moysen et Aaron; . . . locutique eis et omni
multitudini, ostenderunt fructus terræ, et narraverunt, dicentes: Venimus in
terram, ad quam misisti nos, quæ re vera fluit lacte et melle, ut ex his fructibus
cognosci potest; sed cultores fortissimos habet, et urbes grandes atque muratas.
. . . Nequaquam ad hunc populum valemus ascendere, quia fortior nobis est.
. . . Ibi vidimus monstra quædam filiorum Enac de genere giganteo, quibus
comparati, quasi locustæ videbamur.
165–9 [*Num., xiv. 1–4*] Igitur vociferans omnis turba flevit nocte illa; et murmurati sunt contra Moysen et Aaron cuncti filii Israel, dicentes: . . . non inducat
nos Dominus in terram istam, ne cadamus gladio, et uxores ac liberi nostri
ducantur captivi! . . . Constituamus nobis ducem, et revertamur in Ægyptum.

Iosue, swaþeah, and se snotera Chaleph,   170
þe þær asende wæron mid þam foresædum ærendracan
to sceawigenne þæt land, sædon ða him eallum,
Se eard þe we sceawedon is swyðe ænlic and gŏd,
and God sylf us gelæt and to ðam earde gebringð.
Ne beo ge na wiðerræde ongean Godes ræde;   175
eaðelice we magon þæt mancynn ofercuman;
ne beo ge na afyrhte, for þan ðe God is mid us.
Ða wurdon hi ealle wundorlice him grame,
and woldon hine oftorfian wodlice mid stanum;
ac Godes wuldor ætywde, þæt hi ealle gesawon,   180
and God sylf gespræc sona to Moysen:
Hu lange wyle þys folc me to tale habban,
and humeta nellað hi me gyt gelyfan
on eallum þam wundrum þe ic worhte ætforan him?
Ælc þæra manna þe is of ealre þyssere menigu   185
nu þritigwintre, þe ðus ceorod[e]
soðlice ongean me, ne sceal he becuman
to ðam æðelan *earde þe eow behaten wæs,   *f. 104ᵛ
buton Iosue ana and his gefera Chaleph.

171 foresædon X^d.   -racum X^d.   173 sceawodon X^d.   swiðe X^d.
174 gebringeð X^d.   176 manncynn X^d.   ofercumann X^d.   177 God]
(god) sylf X^d.   179 wo'd'lice X^d.   180 ateowde X^d.   182 þis X^d.
habban] þus habban X^d (*rightly?*).   183 hig X^d.   185 þara X^d.   eallre X^d.
186 ðus ceorode] *sic* X^d; ðu sceorodest (*!*) P.

Glosses, Latin: 171 ærendracan: nuncii P.   173 ænlic: solitari*us* P, amenu*m*
X^d.   174 gelæt: duc*et* P.   175 ge: vos P.   wiðerræde: discordantes, dis-
sentientes P.   177 ge: vos P   178 him: ei P.   179 wodlice: exose
(*erased*) P.   182 tale: schandalu*m* P.   183 humeta: q*ua*liter P.
188 æðelan (earde): pat*ria* P.

170–7 [*Ibid. 6–9*] At vero Iosue . . . et Caleb, . . . qui et ipsi lustraverant
terram, . . . ad omnem multitudinem filiorum Israel locuti sunt: Terra, quam
circuivimus, valde bona est. Si propitius fuerit Dominus, inducet nos in eam. . . .
Nolite rebelles esse contra Dominum; neque timeatis populum terræ huius,
quia sicut panem, ita eos possumus devorare. . . . Dominus nobiscum est,
nolite metuere.
   178–81 [*Ibid. 10, 11*] Cumque clamaret omnis multitudo, et lapidibus eos
vellet opprimere, apparuit gloria Domini super tectum foederis cunctis filiis
Israel. Et dixit Dominus ad Moysen:
   182–93 [*Ibid. 11, 29–32*] Usquequo detrahet mihi populus iste? Quousque non
credent mihi, in omnibus signis quæ feci coram eis? . . . Omnes qui numerati
estis a viginti annis et supra, et murmurastis contra me, non intrabitis terram,
super quam levavi manum meam ut habitare vos facerem, præter Caleb, filium
Iephone, et Iosue, filium Nun. Parvulos autem vestros . . . introducam, ut videant
terram quæ vobis displicuit. Vestra cadavera iacebunt in solitudine.

Eowre cildra sceolon, ðe nu synd unwittige,   190
habban þone eard þe eow swa mislicað,
and eowre lic sceolon licgan bæftan him
on ðysum westene for eower unrihtwisnysse.
Æfter þysum wordum wearð Godes yrre
egeslice geswutelod on ðam ærendracan   195
þe þæt land sceawedon, and hit syððan tældon,
and ealles þæs folces mód swa mistihton ongean God,
swa þæt hi ealle feollon on þæs folces gesyhðe,
mid Godes yrre ofslagene, buton se snotera Chaleph,
and se æðela Iosue, hi ane twegen leofodon,   200
for þan ðe God cwæð be him þæt hi becuman sceoldon
to þam foresædon lande for heora geleafan.
Ðæt folc þa þæs on merigen macodon hi gearwe,
astigon ða endemys up to anre dúne,
sædon þæt hi woldon siðian to þam earde;   205
ac Moyses him forbead micclum þus cweðende:
Ne fare ge, ic eow bidde, swa fuse to þam lande,
for þan ðe God nis nu nateshwon mid eow,
þylæste ge feallon ætforan eowrum feondum.
Hi swaþeah ablende mid gebeote ferdon   210
butan Godes dihte mid dyslicum anginne;

192 sceolan X^d.   193 ðissum X^d.   eowre X^d.   195 -racum X^d.
197, 198 folkes X^d.   201 becuman] cuman (be- *erased*) X^d.   203 mergen
X^d 209 -læste] læs þe X^d.   f(eal)lan X^d.   211 bu(tan), *last letters visible*
f. 155, X^d.   mid, *first word visible f. 155ᵛ*, X^d.

Glosses, Latin: 196 tældon: schandalizabant *P*.   199 buton: nisi *P*.
205 siðian: ire *P*.   207, 209 ge: vos *P*.   210 mid gebeote: cum com-
minatione *P*, minandu (*sic*) X^d.   211 butan: sine *P*.
~~ME: 194 yrre: (gro)me (? erased) P.~~   ~~204 endemys: alle some (erased) P.~~
208 nateshwon: nout (? *erased*) *P*.

194–200 [*Ibid. 36–38*] Igitur omnes viri, quos miserat Moyses ad contem-
plandam terram, et qui reversi murmurare fecerant contra eum omnem multitudinem, detrahentes terræ quod esset mala, mortui sunt, atque percussi in
conspectu Domini: Iosue autem . . . et Caleb . . . vixerunt ex omnibus qui
perrexerant ad considerandam terram.

203–9 [*Ibid. 40–42*] Et ecce mane primo surgentes ascenderunt verticem
montis, atque dixerunt: Parati sumus ascendere ad locum de quo Dominus
locutus est; quia peccavimus. Quibus Moyses: Cur, inquit, transgredimini
verbum Domini, quod vobis non cedet in prosperum? Nolite ascendere, non
enim est Dominus vobiscum, ne corruatis coram inimicis vestris.

210–13 [*Ibid. 44, 45*] At illi contenebrati ascenderunt in verticem montis.
. . . Descenditque Amalecites et Chananæus, qui habitabatin monte;et percutiens
eos atque concidens [gladio, *43*], persecutus est eos usque Horma.

ac him com togeanes þæt Chananeisce folc,
and hi swyðe ofslogon mid swurdes ecge,
and on fleame gebrohton þ[a] fyrdlafe,
þæt hi mihton geseon þæt hi swuncon on ydel,   215
swá swá ælc þæra manna deð þe ongean his Drihten winð.
Æfter þysum arison eft ongean Moysen
þridde healf *hund manna mid mycelre ceorunge,   *f. 105
þære heafodmenn wæron þus gehatene:
Chore and Dathan, Abiron and Hón.   220
Hi axodon ða mid gráman þa Godes þegnas,
Moysen and Ááron, Hwi wylle ge swa mycclum
eow sylfe ahebban ofer ðysum folce?
And þrafodon hi swyðe hwi hi sceoldon habban
anweald ofer hi. Ða cwæð Moyses him to,   225
Nimað nu tomerigen eower ælc his storcyllan,
þæt ge steran magon ealle ætforan Gode,
and God þonne geswutelað hwæne he gecyst to his þenungum.
Ða þæs on merigen wolde Moyses gestillan
and mid wisdome alecgan heora wodnysse;   230

214 þa] þære P; *no reading* X^d; *see note.*   215 idel X^d.   216 *Probably
transposed*, (winð ongean his) drihten X^d.   217 þissum X^d.   218 myc-
lere X^d.   219 þære] *sic both MSS.*, *for* þæra.   220 Abiron] *and* abiron X^d.
221 gramann X^d.   þa] þæs X^d.   223 þissum X^d.   224 And þrafodon
hi swyðe] *no reading* X^d *but lacuna followed by* mid mycclum céaste, *evidently
added to or replacing* swyðe.   *second* hi] hig X^d.   226 -mergen X^d.
229 gestillan] hi gestillan X^d.   230 wodnysse] *no reading* X^d.

Glosses, Latin: 215 on ydel: *in* vano P.   216 winð: *p*reliatu*r* P.
219 þære: q*u*or*u*m P.   heafodmenn: capitales P.   221 þa: illos P.   222 ge:
vos P.   223 ahebban: extoll*ere* P.   224 *In margin beside* þrafodon:
argum*entum* P.   *first* hi: illos P.   225 hi: eos P.   226 storcyllan:
t*u*rribul*um* (thuribulum) P.   227 ge: vos P.   228 hwæne: que*m* P.
229 gestillan: mitigare P.

217–20 [*Num. xvi. 1, 2*] Ecce autem Core, . . . et Dathan atque Abiron, . . .
Hon quoque . . . surrexerunt contra Moysen, aliique filiorum Israel ducenti
quinquaginta viri proceres synagogæ.
221–5a [*Ibid. 3*] Cumque stetissent adversum Moysen et Aaron, dixerunt:
Sufficiat vobis, quia omnis multitudo sanctorum est, et in ipsis est Dominus.
Cur elevamini super populum Domini?
225b–8 [*Ibid. 4–7*] Quod cum audisset Moyses, . . . locutus . . . ad Core et
ad omnem multitudinem, Mane, inquit, notum faciet Dominus qui ad se
pertineant. . . . Tollat unusquisque thuribula sua, tu Core, et omne concilium
tuum; et hausto cras igne, ponite desuper thymiama coram Domino; et quem-
cumque elegerit, ipse erit sanctus.
229–30 [*The motive attributed to Moses is not explicit in the Bible.*]

sende þa to Dathan and to his ge[fer]um,
þæt hi comon him to, and cuðlice to spræcon;
ac hi forsawon endemes his hæse,
and mid maran wodnysse hine micclum tyrigdon,
and þone ælmihtigan God gremedon to swyðe,   235
þe hine gesette him to heretogan.
Se Chore þa genam, þe we ær foresædon,
and ealle his gegadan, Gode to forsewennysse,
ælc his recelsfæt ætforan Godes getelde,
and ontendon þone stor, swa swa man steran sceal,   240
swylce hi mihton hi sylfe gewyrcan
Gode to sacerdon, bu[t]on he sylf hi gecure,
swa swa Áaron wæs, se arwurða bisceop,
þone þe God sylf geceas, and gesette him to bisceope
on þa ealdan wisan æfter Moyses æ.   245
Mid þam þe [hi] ðus dydon mid dyrstigon anginne,
þa ætiwde þær sona gesewenlice Godes wuldor,
and [God] cwæð to Moysén, Gað him fram hraðe.
*And seo eorðe tobærst under heora fotum,   *f. 105ᵛ

---

231 geferum] *sic Xᵈ*; gerefum *P.*   233 endemæs *Xᵈ.*   234 wodnysse]
sic both MSS.   235 swiðe *Xᵈ.*   240 mann *Xᵈ.*   sceall *Xᵈ.*   241 hig
(twice) Xᵈ.   gewyrcean *Xᵈ.*   242 buton] *sic Xᵈ*; bunton *P.*   244 bysceope
Xᵈ.   246 hi] *sic Xᵈ; om. P.*   dyrstigum *Xᵈ.*   247 æteowde *Xᵈ.*
248 God] *conj.; om. both MSS.*   raðe *Xᵈ.*   249 tobærst] bærst *Xᵈ.*

Glosses, Latin: 233 endemes: om*nes P.*   234 tyrigdon: exasp*er*aba*nt P.*
238 gegadan: socii *P.*   239 recelsfæt: t*urri*bu*lum P.*   getelde: taber-
nac*ulum P.*   242 gode: deo *P.*   bunton (*i.e.* buton): n*isi P.*   246 dyrstigon: tem*er*e, audaci *P.*   249 tobærst: cr*epuit P.*
ME: 247 ætiwde: (s)cheiwe(d)e (*? erased*) *P.*   wuldor: glore (*? erased*) *P.*

231-4 [*Ibid. 12–15*] Misit ergo Moyses ut vocaret Dathan et Abiron. . . .
Qui responderunt: non venimus. Numquid parum est tibi quod eduxisti nos de
terra, quæ lacte et melle manabat, ut occideres in deserto, nisi et dominatus
fueris nostri? Revera induxisti nos in terram, quæ fluit rivis lactis et mellis, et
dedisti nobis possessiones agrorum et vinearum; an et oculos nostros vis eruere?
Non venimus. Iratusque Moyses valde, ait ad Dominum: Ne respicias sacrificia
eorum.
237-40 [*Ibid. 16–18*] Dixitque ad Core: Tu, et omnis congregatio tua, state
seorsum coram Domino. . . . Tollite singuli thuribula vestra, et ponite super ea
incensum, offerentes Domino ducenta quinquaginta thuribula; Aaron quoque
teneat thuribulum suum.
246-8 [*Ibid. 18–21*] Quod cum fecissent, . . . apparuit cunctis gloria Domini.
Locutusque Dominus ad Moysen et Aaron, ait: Separamini de medio congrega-
tionis huius.
249-54 [*Ibid. 31–34*] Dirupta est terra sub pedibus eorum, et aperiens os suum,
devoravit illos cum tabernaculis suis et universa substantia eorum. [*27,* Dathan

and forswealh Dathan for his dyrstignysse,   250
and þone Abíron, mid eallum heora hiwum,
mid wifum and mid cildum, þær þær hi wicodon;
and hi swa cuce ferdon fordóne to helle,
and ælc man fleag aweg, for heora hreame afyrht.
Ðær com eac swylce fyr færlice fram Gode,   255
and forbærnde þone Chore þær þær he bær þone stor,
and þridde healf hund manna mid him forburnon,
mid heora recelsfˋa῾tum, for heora dyrstignysse,
þæt hi ongean Godes willan worhton hi to sacerdum,
and þone forsawon þe he him geset hæfde.   260
On þam æftran dæge þe ðis gedon wæs,
ongan eall þæt folc flitan wið Moysen,
and wið þone Ááron þe we ær embe spræcon,
mid mycelre ceorunge, sædon [þæt] hi hæfdon
Godes folc ofslagen, and gremedon hi swyðe,   265
and mid micclum gehlyde macodon þa ceaste,
oððæt hi begen flugon binnan Godes getelde;
and þær æteowde sona gesewenlice Godes wuldor,
and fyr com fram Gode, and forbærnde þæs folces

---

250 dyrsti- X^d.   254 fleah X^d.   255 fyr] (fyr) fyr P.   260 gesett X^d.   264 þæt] sic X^d; and P.   266 mycclum X^d.   macedon X^d. 268 æt-] Here X^d breaks off with end of f. 155^v.

Glosses, Latin: 251 þone: illum P.   hiwum: familia P.   252 wicodon: manserunt P.   253 fordone: damnati P.   258 recelsfatum: turribulis P. 260 þone: illum P.   262 ongan: incepit P.   264 and (mistake for þæt): si (unsuccessful effort to account for it) P.   266 gehlyde: tumultu P.   267 binnan: infra (for intra) P.
ME: 251 hiwum: hinen P.   268 æteowde: sch(ei)wede (? erased) P.

---

et Abiron . . . stabant in introitu papilionum suorum, cum uxoribus et liberis, omnique frequentia.] Descenderuntque vivi in infernum operti humo, et perierunt de medio multitudinis. At vero omnis Israel, qui stabat per gyrum, fugit ad clamorem pereuntium, dicens: Ne forte et nos terra deglutiat.
255–8 [Ibid. 35] Sed et ignis egressus a Domino interfecit ducentos quinquaginta viros qui offerebant incensum.
261–8 [Ibid. 41–43] Murmuravit autem omnis multitudo filiorum Israel sequenti die contra Moysen et Aaron, dicens: Vos interfecistis populum Domini. Cumque oriretur seditio, et tumultus incresceret, Moyses et Aaron fugerunt ad tabernaculum foederis. Quod, postquam ingressi sunt, operuit nubes, et apparuit gloria Domini.
269–73 [Ibid. 44–49, but Ælfric abridges and rearranges] Dixitque Dominus ad Moysen: Recedite de medio huius multitudinis, etiam nunc delebo eos. Cumque iacerent in terra, dixit Moyses ad Aaron: Tolle thuribulum, et hausto

feowertyne þusenda mid færlicum bryne,   270
oððæt Ááron eode ut of ðam getelde
mid his storcyllan, and stod him tomiddes,
gebæd ða for hi, and se grama geswác.
   On ðysum mæg gehyran se ðe hæfð ænig andgyt
þæt hit byð swyðe hearmlic þam ðe huxlice tælð   275
bisceopas and sacerdas, þe syndon Godes bydelas,
and to lareowum gesette to lærenne Godes folc,
þonne se lareow *him segð Godes gesetnyssa   *f. 106
and his beboda, him sylfum to þearfe,
and he þonne forsyhð, and to forsewennysse hæfð   280
ge þone Godes bydel ge þa Godes beboda,
be þam cwæð se Hælend to his discipulum:
Qui uos audit me audit, et qui uos spernit me spernit.
Ðæt is [on] urum gereorde, Se þe eow gehyrð,
he gehyrð me þurh ða gehyrsumnysse,   285
and se þe eow forsihð, he forsyhð me.
Hi forsawon Moysen and þone mæron bisceop,
Ááron his broðor, mid bysmorlicum hospe,
ac God sylf gewræc heora forsewennysse,
for þan ðe hi God tældon þa ða hi tældon hi.   290
Swa deð ælc þæra manna þe his ealdor forsyhð,
þe byð Godes speligend on gastlicere lare,
on þam ealdorscype þe him God geuðe;
gif he hine forsyhð, his sawul sceal þrowian
þæt ylce wite, buton he hit ær gebete,   295
þe hi ða þrowodon on heora lichaman.

284 on] *not in MS.*

Glosses in P, Latin: 274 andgyt: *intellectum.*   275 huxlice tælð: dedecore
scandalizat.   278 gesetnyssa: *institutionem.*   280 þonne: *tunc.*
288 hospe: obprobrio.   289 gewræc: vindicauit.   290 tældon: scandali-
zabant.   292 speligend: vicarius, vices (*see note*).   293 geuðe: *concessit.*
296 ða: *tunc.*
     ME: 271 getelde: pauilun.

---

igne de altari, mitte incensum desuper, pergens cito ad populum ut roges pro
eis; iam enim egressa est ira a Domino, et plaga desævit. Quod cum fecisset
Aaron, et cucurrisset ad mediam multitudinem, quam iam vastabat incendium,
obtulit thymiama, et stans inter mortuos ac viventes, pro populo deprecatus
est, et plaga cessavit. Fuerunt autem qui percussi sunt, quatuordecim millia
hominum, et septingenti.
     283–6 [*Luc. x. 16, as given.*]

Hi wæron flæsclice menn, and underfencgon heora wite
on ðyssere worulde, æfter Moyses æ;
we syndon gastlice menn under Godes gife nu,
and ure sawul sceal, gif we forseoð God,   300
þæt wite underfon on þære toweardan worulde,
buton we swa gesælige beon þæt we hit sylfe gebeton
ær ure geendunge wið ðone ælmihtigan God.
Eft on oðrum timan þæt Israhela folc,
þa ða hi ferdon mid þam foresædan Moyse, 305
and becomon to ðam lande þe is gecweden Edom,
þa begunnon hi to cidenne mid micelre ceorunge
ongean þone ælmihtigan God for heora geswince,
and ongean *Moysen, and mid graman cwædon, *f. 106ᵛ
Hwi læddest þu la us of Egipta lande, 310
þæt we her swulton on ðysum westene?
We nabbað þone hlaf þe us lyste etan,
and us nu wlatað wið þysne leohtan mete.
Ða for þære ceorunge sende him God tó
byrnende næddran, swa swa us bec secgað, 315
and þa fyrenan næddran þæs folces feala
to deaðe geætrodon mid egeslicum geslite.
Hi comon þa to Moyse, and cwædon him þus to:
We habbað gesyngod þæt we swa spræcon
ongean þone ælmihtigan God and ongean þe, leof; 320
gebide nu for us, þæt God afyrsige
þas næddran fram us. And Moyses þa sona
gebæd for þam folce, swá swá hi hine bædon.
Ða spræc se ælmihtiga God to þam arwurðan Moysen,

Glosses in P, Latin: 303 wið: *contra.* 313 wið: *contra.* leohtan: leuis.
316 fyrenan: ignei. 317 geslite: morsu. 321 afyrsige: auferat.
ME: 311 swulton: deide (*? erased*). 314 ceorunge: grucunge (*? erased*).

304–13 [*Num. xxi. 4, 5*] Profecti sunt autem . . . ut circumirent terram Edom.
Et tædere coepit populum itineris ac laboris, locutusque contra Deum et Moysen, ait: Cur eduxisti nos de Ægypto, ut moreremur in solitudine? Deest panis,
non sunt aquæ; anima nostra iam nauseat super cibo isto levissimo.

314–23 [*Ibid. 6, 7*] Quamobrem misit Dominus in populum ignitos serpentes,
ad quorum plagas et mortes plurimorum, venerunt ad Moysen, atque dixerunt:
Peccavimus, quia locuti sumus contra Dominum et te; ora ut tollat a nobis serpentes. Oravitque Moyses pro populo.

324–32 [*Ibid. 8, 9*] Et locutus est Dominus ad eum: Fac serpentem æneum,
et pone eum pro signo; qui percussus aspexerit eum, vivet. Fecit ergo Moyses

Hat nu gewyrcan ane ærene næddran,   325
and gesete þa upp, swylce to tacne,
and se þe beo tosliten, beseo to þære næddran
þe of ðam are bið gemacod, and he leofað gesund.
Hwæt þa Moyses het macian þa næddran,
and gesettan to tacne, swa swa God sylf hine het,   330
and þa toslitenan menn besawon to þære næddran,
and wurdon swa gehælede fram þæra wyrma geslite.
  Se Hælend sylf sæde on sumum his godspelle
hwæt þeos dæd getacnode on ðam diglan andgyte,
and we hit gesetton on Englisc on sumum oðrum spelle.   335
We wyllað swaðeah secgan sceortlice her nu
þæt seo ærene næddre, þe butan attre wæs,
hæfde getacnunge ures Hælendes deaðes,
þe butan ælcere synne sylf þrowode for ús,
'and mid his unscyldigum deaðe us fram deaðe ahredde,   340
fram þam ecan deaðe þe us' *þurh Adam becom   *f. 107
of ðære næddran lare þe hine forlærde.
Ða terendan næddran, þe totæron þæt folc,
syndon ure synna, þe us tosliton wyllað;
ac we sceolon behealdan ðæs Hælendes þrowunge   345
mid soðum geleafan, and we beoð sona hale.
Ðæt folc on ðam westene wæs þa gehæled
þurh ða ærenan næddran fram þam andweardan deaðe;
ac se Hælend sæde þæt þa sceolon habban
þæt éce líf mid him þe on hine gelyfað.   350
Seo gehiwode anlicnys gehælde ða hwilwendlice,
and þæt soðe þing nu sylð us þæt ece lif.

340–1 and . . . us] *inserted by regular scribe at bottom of page.*

Glosses in P, Latin: 325 ærene: enea*m*.   326 þa: illa*m*.   327 beseo: respiciat.   328 gesund: sospes.   332 gehælede: salui.   geslite: morsu. 337, 339 butan: sine.   343 terendan: mordentes.   344 tosliton: morde*re*. 347 gehæled: salu*us*.   349 þa: illi.   351 gehiwode: simulata, ficta. anlicnys: imago.   gehælde: sanau*it*.   ða: *tunc*.   hwilwendlice: te*mp*ora*liter* (*repeated faintly in margin*).   *ME*: 331 toslitenan: ibitene.

---

serpentem æneum, et posuit eum pro signo; quem cum percussi aspicerent, sanabantur.
  333 sqq. [*Ioan. iii. 14, 15*] Et sicut Moyses exaltavit serpentem in deserto, ita exaltari oportet Filium hominis; ut omnis, qui credit in ipsum, non pereat, sed habeat vitam æternam. [*For Ælfric's elaboration, 333–52, see notes.*]

God afandode þa þæs folces anrædnysse
on ðam langsumum færelde feowertig geara;
he wolde þæt hi wæron mid weorcum gehyrsume   355
his halwendum bebodum, him to ecere hæle.
Ða wurdon hi wiðerræde wolice foroft,
and þone ælmihtigan God swa egeslice gegremedon
þæt eall seo yld wearð on þam westene ofslagen,
buton twam mannum anum, Iosue and Chaleph.   360
Hi wæron gehyrsume Godes hæsum æfre,
and hi forþi hæfdon þone behatenan eard,
and þæt þæt micele mare is, Godes mildse þærtoeacan.
Feowertig wintra hi wæron on þam westene farende,
and Moyses geendode eac on þam færelde,   365
þa þa he on ylde wæs hundtwelftig geara;
and his broðor Ááron eac þær geendode,
and Moyses gesette þone foresædan Iosue
þam folce to heretogan, swa swa him bebead God.
Seo geoguð þe wæs on þam *westene afedd   *f. 107ᵛ
wæs þa geweaxen, and to wíge ful strang,   371
and Iosue hi lædde to ðam behatenan lande;
and hi gefyldon swa, þeah ðe heora fæderas noldon,

Glosses in P, Latin: 353 anrædnysse: *constanciam.*   354 færelde: Gressu.
357 wiðerræde: dissencientes.   wolice: tortuose.   359 yld: etas.
365 geendode: obiit.   368 gesette: posuit.   370 geoguð: iuuent*us.*
371 wige: pr*e*lio.   373 gefyldon: impleue*runt.*

353–75 [*This concluding summary of the narrative is very freely composed, but
now and then recalls specific passages.*]
353–6 [*Cf. Deut. viii. 2*] Et recordaberis cuncti itineris, per quod adduxit te
Dominus Deus tuus quadraginta annis per desertum, ut affligeret te, atque
tentaret, et nota fierent quæ in tuo animo versabantur, utrum custodires mandata illius, an non.
359–60 [*Num. xxvi. 63–65*] Hic est numerus filiorum Israel, qui descripti
sunt a Moyse et Eleazaro sacerdote, in campestribus Moab . . .; inter quos
nullus fuit eorum qui ante numerati sunt a Moyse et Aaron in deserto Sinai;
prædixerat enim Dominus (*Num. xiv. 29, 30*), quod omnes morerentur in solitudine. Nullusque remansit ex eis, nisi Caleb, filius Iephone, et Iosue, filius Nun.
365–6 [*Deut. xxxiv. 5, 7*] Mortuusque est ibi Moyses . . . in terra Moab. . . .
Moyses centum et viginti annorum erat quando mortuus est.
367 [*Num. xx. 29*] Illo [Aaron] mortuo in montis [Hor] supercilio, [Moyses]
descendit cum Eleazaro.
368–9 [*Num. xxvii. 22, 23*] Fecit Moyses ut præceperat Dominus. Cumque
tulisset Iosue, statuit eum coram Eleazaro sacerdote et omni frequentia populi;
et impositis capiti eius manibus, cuncta replicavit quæ mandaverat Dominus.

Godes willan mid weorcum, and gewunnon þone eard
mid wundorlicum sige, swa swa hit awriten is.   375
Ðam folce wæs behaten þurh þone heofonlican God
þæt hi sceoldon habban soðlice renscuras
and eorðlice wæstmas on wuda and on felda,
ofæt[an] and ele, and éac swylce wín,
and heora fynd oferwinnan, gif hi wurðodon hine,   380
and mid ealre heortan hine æfre lufodon.

Ac Crist sylf behet us on his halgan godspelle
þæt we sceolon habban, þær þær he sylf wunað,
þæt ece lif mid him and mid eallum his halgum,
gif we hine wurðiað on ðysum andweardan life,   385
and mid soðum geleafan hine lufiað æfre.

He het us swyðost cepan þæs soþan lifes æfre,
and cwæð þæt we sceoldon symle eac habban
ure eorðlican neode þærtoeacan soðlice.

Paulus se apostol, ealra þeoda lareow,   390
manode þone leodscipe þe he to geleafan gebigde,
and ealle Cristene menn, and cwæð þæt we sceoldon
geornlice us warnian wið ða yfelan ceorunge,
þæt we swa ne gegremion God Ælmihtigne nu
mid urum yfelum þeawum, swa swa þæt ealde folc dyde   395
on þam westene þa, wiðerrædlice to swyðe.

374 þone] *written a second time and crossed out in MS.*   379 ofætum *MS.*
See note.

Glosses in P, Latin: 375 sige: tri*umpho.*   379 ofætum: fructu*m.*
380 oferwinnan: vince*re.*   wurðodon: adorare*nt.*   391 gebigde: co*n*ue*r*tit.
393 warnian: cau*e*re.   396 þa: tu*n*c.

376–81 [*Cf. Deut. xi. 13, 14, 23*] Si ergo obedieritis mandatis meis, quæ ego
hodie præcipio vobis, ut diligatis Dominum Deum vestrum, et serviatis ei in
toto corde vestro, et in tota anima vestra, dabit pluviam terræ vestræ tempora-
neam et serotinam, ut colligatis frumentum, et vinum, et oleum.... Disperdet
Dominus omnes gentes istas ante faciem vestram, et possidebitis eas, quæ
maiores et fortiores vobis sunt.

382–6 [*Among many partly relevant texts, cf. Ioan. vi. 40 and xiv. 2; Matth.
xix. 28, 29.*

387–9 [*Matth. vi. 33*] Quærite ergo primum regnum Dei, et iustitiam eius,
et hæc omnia adiicientur vobis.

392–8 [*I Cor. x. 10, 11*] Neque murmuraveritis, sicut quidam eorum mur-
muraverunt, et perierunt ab exterminatore. Hæc autem omnia in figura con-
tingebant illis; scripta sunt autem ad correptionem nostram, in quos fines
sæculorum devenerunt.

Hit stent on bocum awriten for ure beterunge,
and to mycelre bysne us endenextum mannum,
þæt we geearnian sceolon æfre þæt betere,
and þa [e]can myrhðe mid Gode Ælmihtigum.   400
Nu syndon manega *menn þe secgað þæt hi nellað   *f. 108
Godes lare gehyran, þelæste hi sceolon
habban maran wit[a] gif hi witon þa lare,
and gif hi nellað don swá swá Drihten bebyt,
hi sylfe gerihtlæcan þurh þa soðan lare.   405
Nu cweðe we þærtogeanes, þæt gif se cyning asent gewrit
to sumon his þegena, and he hit forsyhð swa swyðe
þæt he hit nele gehyran, ne his aseon,
þæt se cyning ne byð na swyðe bliðe him,
þonne he geaxað hu he hine forseah.   410
Seo halige lár nis na on eallum leodscypum
swa swyðe swa on sumon, ac us secgað béc
þæt hi mihton tocnawan þone ælmihtigan God
þurh þa gesceafta þe he gesceop on worulde,
þæt he is ana to wurðigenne þe geworhte ealle þing. 415
Se man þe hæfð lare on his leodscype genoge,
and mæg ða gehyran butan micclum geswince,
and nele hi gehyran, ne Gode gehyrsumian,
næfð he nane beladunge wið ðone leofan Drihten.
Se þe lare næfð, ne lare ne gehyrð,   420
se mihte habban sume beladunge;
ac Paulus se apostol cwæð on his pistole þus:
Qui sine lege peccabunt, sine lege peribunt.
Ðæt is, on Engliscere spræce,

---

400 ecan] eacan *MS.*   403 wita] wite *MS. See note.*   408 ne his
aseon] *sic MS. See note.*

Glosses in P, Latin: 403 wite: pena*m*.   witon: sciu*n*t.   408 aseon:
videre(*perhaps for* seon *only as the* a *is marked for separation*).   409 him: ei.
413 tocnawan: discer*n*ere, co*n*noscere.   417 ða: ea (*sic*).   butan: sine.
419 beladunge; excusatione*m*.   wið: *contra.*

412–15 [*Rom. i. 18–21*] Revelatur enim ira Dei de cælo, super omnem im-
pietatem et iniustitiam hominum eorum qui veritatem Dei in iniustitia detinent.
. . . Invisibilia enim ipsius, a creatura mundi, per ea quæ facta sunt, intellecta,
conspiciuntur; sempiterna quoque eius virtus, et divinitas: ita ut sint inexcusa-
biles, quia, cum cognovissent Deum, non sicut Deum glorificaverunt, aut gratias
egerunt.
423–6 [*Rom. ii. 12*] Quicumque enim sine lege peccaverunt, *&c.*

Ða þe buton Godes ǽ synna gewyrcað,   425
þa eac butan Godes ǽ on ende forwurðað.
Gerihtlǽce ús se leofa Drihten Crist,
and us gewenie to his willan ǽfre,
þam is wuldor and lof a to worulde, AMEN.

Gloss in P, Latin: 426 forwurðað: peribunt.

NOTES

1–8. This paragraph alludes in line 2 to the first part of *Dominica in Media Quadragosimœ*, *CH* II. xii, and sums up several of the features of the story as told there (Thorpe, pp. 194, 196). The preservation of the people's health and clothing (here mentioned at 6–8, in Thorpe at p. 196/12–14) is spoken of in *Deut.* viii. 4; xxix. 5, 6; *Neh.* ix. 21.

10–12. Cf. *CH* II. 194/14, *six hund þusenda wigendra manna, buton wifum and cildum*. The exact figure, according to *Numbers* i. 46 and ii. 32, was 603,550, the count being limited to the fighting men over twenty. Ælfric is guided mainly by the generalization made earlier, *Exod.* xii. 37, 38: 'Profecti sunt filii Israel de Ramesse in Socoth, sexcenta fere millia peditum virorum absque parvulis. Sed et vulgus promiscuum innumerabile ascendit cum eis.' Ælfric had not mentioned the *vulgus promiscuum* earlier, but now he applies to this body the rare compound *ceorlfolc* (see Glossary).

13–21. This passage on the manna is more elaborate than that in *CH* II. 194/32 sqq. Added is the descriptive detail of line 15, *mid þam upplicum deawe æt heora geteldum* (*Exod.* xvi. 13 and *Num.* xi. 9), and also the interpretation derived from the *Liber Sapientiæ* as quoted under Sources. This is much closer to what Ælfric says than the inexact reflections of it in Bede's commentary on the Pentateuch (on *Num.* xi, *PL* xci. 363) or a pseudo-Augustinian sermon excerpted from Origen (*PL* xxxix. 1793–5; see *Origenes Werke*, VI, ed. Baehrens, Die griech. christ. Schriftsteller, Leipzig, 1920, p. 216/3 sqq.: 'Nunc ergo festinemus cæleste manna suscipere, istud enim manna, prout vult quisque, talem saporem reddit in ore eius.'). The passage in Bede is quoted below in the note on 104–39.

22–26. The miracle of the water flowing from the rock (*Exod.* xvii. 1–7) is described in *CH* II. 196/2–6, but nothing is said there about wine or ale. This comment is suggested by *Deut.* xxix. 6: 'Panem non comedistis, vinum et ciseram non bibistis, ut sciretis quia ego sum Dominus Deus vester.'

27–37. This passage, summarizing *Exod.* xix, xx, sets the stage for the first main episode of the homily, the worship of the golden calf. The same material is treated at greater length in *CH* II. 196, 198, where the ten commandments are enumerated.

34. *lagu*. Both manuscripts have this spelling for the nominative plural, and there is probably another instance at xv. 35, where two different manuscripts are the witnesses. An accusative plural *lagu* has already been observed in the D version of the Chronicle for 1052 (*fulle lagu beheton*), and Plummer's Glossary (*Two Saxon Chronicles*, I) treats it as an old neuter plural: that is, as a representative of the ON neuter plural, pre-historically **lagu*, historically *lǫg*, with the collective sense 'law', from which the OE word was borrowed. This solitary instance is still cited in Hall–Meritt. The OE word is regularly treated by Ælfric and others as a strong feminine like *gifu* in the singular, and except in rare instances (perhaps only the three cited above) its plural is the analogically correct *laga*. That Ælfric should have used a plural reflecting the ON form is, however, understandable, since he was one of the first English authors to adopt the word in writing. The *OED, law*, sb.[1], holds that the written use of the word is to be dated from about 1000, a date that falls in the middle of Ælfric's literary career. A little earlier than 1000 is Ælfric's introduction of *lagu* into his Grammar as a definition of Latin *ius* (Zupitza, p. 59/15: whether *lagu* here is singular or plural is uncertain: the *laga* of two manu-scripts suggests the plural); but most instances of it in his work seem to belong to the homilies and letters written after the *Lives of Saints*. (See the Glossary for instances in this edition.) An instance of the eventually normal plural *laga* occurs at xiii. 208 in MS. U, but MS. H has the singu-lar *lage*, which better conforms to the context. Hence the *laga* of U is probably a scribal substitution and not a witness for Ælfric's form in the plural. On grounds of date alone, Ælfric is more likely to have used a half-Scandinavian plural than the author of the D version of the Chronicle for 1052; but this author was probably writing in the strongly Scandi-navian north. (For early instances of the word, see BT, BTS, Dodd's Glossary to Napier's *Wulfstan*, and Liebermann's Glossary, *Gesetze der Angelsachsen*, II.)

38–40. No doubt Ælfric's generalization applies to the entire sojourn in the wilderness, but the miracles described in *Exod.* xv–xvii are perhaps chiefly in view.

41–67. The first main episode of the homily, presented without com-ment. Note the postponement of Moses' destruction of the idol until the end.

50. *nu iu*. The gloss *eciam nunc* in P, suggesting 'even now', perhaps comes a little closer to the emotional force here than 'already', the defini-tion in BTS, under *geó*.

61. *and ofsleað ealle tomiddes þam folce*. Has an alliterating word dropped out? An anticipatory *þa* after *ealle*, correlative with *þa ðe* in the next line, would perhaps be enough, for Ælfric is not averse to these minor links.

66. *tobræc and tobrytte*. Ælfric perhaps found the two verbs in the Latin, *combussit et contrivit*, hard to reconcile with each other; and in any case he was selecting only a few details from the Biblical account. The

translation in the *Old English Heptateuch*, Crawford, p. 278 (probably not Ælfric's), gives both verbs: *forbærnde and forbrytte*.

68–82. The second episode, with five lines of obvious comment.

68. *Eft æfter þysum hi begunnon ceorian*. Alliteration could readily be achieved by putting *eft* before or after *ceorian*.

74, 230, 234. *wodnysse*. Especially at 74 there may be some temptation to read *wohnysse*, 'perversity'; but P has *wodnysse* in all three places, and X^d agrees at the two places, 74 and 234, where it has a reading. Besides, Ælfric's use of *wisdom* in 230 confirms *wodnysse* there. Evidently he means to emphasize the sheer insanity of rebellion against God, whether it takes the form of murmuring or of challenging the authority of his chosen representative.

79. Here alliteration could be achieved by substituting Ælfric's other verb, *murcnian*, for *ceorian*.

83–103. The third episode, to be followed by a long comment, 104–39.

83. The rhymed endings of *ceorian* and *murcnian* may be accepted as a substitute for alliteration.

103. *hi fandodon Godes*. So *Ps.* lxxvii. 18: *Et tentaverunt Deum in cordibus suis, ut peterent escas animabus suis*. Cf. *Exod.* xvii. 2, where the people demand water and Moses asks, *Cur tentatis Dominum?* Also *Num.* xiv. 22: *Et tentaverunt me iam per decem vices*; *Deut.* vi. 16: *Non tentabis Dominum Deum tuum, sicut tentasti in loco tentationis*; *Ps.* xciv. 9; cv. 14; and especially, perhaps, *I Cor.* x. 9: *Neque tentemus Christum, sicut quidam eorum tentaverunt, et a serpentibus perierunt*.

104–39. This is the first long comment, built mainly on the story in *Exodus*, but completed at the end (128–39) by an interpretation given by Jesus himself. The reminder of hard times during the period of servitude in Egypt (109–14) depends on *Exod.* i. 11–22 and repeats with some amplification what was said in the earlier homily, *CH* II. 190/34–192/2. Then follow seven lines, again resumptive, on the drowning of the Egyptians and the Israelites' passage of the Red Sea. Now Ælfric returns to the original cause of complaint and uses the magically adaptable taste of manna, which he had introduced in accordance with the *Liber Sapientiæ* at 16–21 above, to put the trouble-makers completely in the wrong. In this he is more extreme than Bede, who had thought there must be *some* reason for complaining against the manna, and decided that it could assume the taste of every kind of food except flesh: 'Sed tamen historialiter sciendum est cur filii Israel carnem desideraverunt, habentes manna: quod ita solvitur, quia manna omnis cibi similitudinem habuit, præter carnis. Sic et sancta Scriptura omnem satietatem quæ proficit habet, præter voluntatem peccatricem.' (*In Pentateuchum: Num.* xi, *PL* xci. 363). And finally Ælfric reveals (128–39) that the manna thus scorned typifies Christ himself, according to his own declaration in *John* vi. This had been mentioned in the earlier homily (*CH* II. 202) but is here elaborated as the climax of the whole passage. I am not at all sure that Isidore's comment on the manna, though closer to Ælfric's than any other I have seen, was responsible for the contrast between the unbelieving Jews and the preacher's faithful congregation, for it is almost inevitable and Ælfric has worked it out beyond anything in Isidore, with full attention to the contrast between manna and the *estmettas* of the world.

114. *þa ða hi to mannum comon*, 'when they were born'. A particularly clear instance of the idiom. Cf. note on 1. 43.

140–216. The fourth episode, subdivided at 203, presented with only incidental comment. Here begins the partial correspondence with Ælfric's translation of *Numbers* xiii sqq. in the *Old English Heptateuch*.

156. *ofætan*. See note on 379 below.

164. *we synd wið hi geðuhte swylce oðre gærstapan*. There are two interesting idioms here: (1) The passive expression, *beon geþuht*, 'to seem', is well attested. With the active, impersonal *þyncan*, accompanied by a dative of person, the seeming is said to occur in the mind of one or more specified observers. With the passive form the seeming is attributed to whatever is named as the subject, regardless of who does the observing. Here the seeming is contingent on the comparison introduced by *wið hi*. (2) The word *oðre*, 'other', has the force of such modern substitutes as 'so many', 'veritable'. The purpose of such expressions is to insist upon a likeness between obviously, even grotesquely dissimilar members of a comparison. Translate, 'we seem, in comparison with them, like so many grasshoppers'. The same idiom in the singular is a little less unfamiliar: cf. *CH* II. 194, 21 sq., *þæt wæter stod him on twa healfa swilce oðer stanweall*, 'the water stood on both sides of them like another (a veritable) stone wall'. At the corresponding place in the translation of *Numbers* Ælfric has, *ðam we ne synd ðe gelicran ðe lytle gærstapan* (Crawford, p. 317).

186. *þritigwintre*. I do not understand why this is not *twentigwintre*, but the alliteration with *þe* and *ðus* seems to confirm it. At the corresponding place in Ælfric's translation of *Numbers* the clause specifying the age is altogether omitted.

214. *þ[a] fyrdlafe*, MS. *þære*. Since *gebringan* regularly takes the accusative the emendation seems necessary. Perhaps the scribe started to treat *fyrd* as a separate word, *þære fyrde lafe*, 'the remnant (acc.) of the army (gen.)'; but Ælfric himself is unlikely to have chosen this alternative, which produces an awkward likeness in the three endings. He uses *fyrdlaf* as a compound at *LS* xxv. 377, and the similar *herelaf* in the same composition at line 592. In his translation of *Numbers* Ælfric follows the Latin more closely and does not refer to a *fyrdlaf*.

217–60. The fifth episode, again without comment except at 241–5 and 258–60.

240. *stor*. The vowel of this word is usually considered long and is so marked in the Glossary, although Professor Campbell in his *Old English Grammar*, § 524 n., suggests that it may as well be short and so prints it. He is influenced, perhaps, by certain implications in Max Förster's article, *Englische Studien*, LXX (1935), 49–54, to which he refers for the derivation from Vulgar Latin *stōrax* by way of Old Irish *stōr*. But Förster himself treats the Old English word as *stōr*, and this seems proper in view of the derivative weak verb *stēran*. If the vowel had been short, the umlauting suffix *-jan* would have given *sterian*.

241–5. The term *bisceop* is applied to the priests of the old law in the *Letter for Wulfsige* (Fehr, *Brief I*. 18), and Aaron is called the first bishop at xxi. 218. Application to pagan as well as Jewish priests is as old as the Old English Bede and Orosius. See BT and BTS.

261–73. The sixth episode, a sequel to the preceding but the subject of an extended comment in its own right, 274–303.

274–303. This application to the Christian priesthood is so much of a piece with Ælfric's ideas as expressed elsewhere, especially in the *Letter for Wulfsige*, that it is easy to believe he developed the passage independently. I do not know of a source.

292. *speligend*, glossed *vicarius* and *vices* in P. Is the form *vices* a mere blunder, or some odd vernacular form? If it is an early example of *vice*, sb. 7, in the *OED*, how is the final *s* to be explained?

304–32. The seventh and last episode, to be followed by a comment, 333–52. The narrative corresponds at several points to Ælfric's translation of *Numbers*, but is much freer and thus achieves greater ease in carrying out the rhythmic pattern.

333–52. This interpretation, based on *John* iii. 14, 15, was first set forth by Ælfric at the end of *Dominica V Quadragesimæ*, *CH* II. 238, 240, the sermon to which he refers in the phrase, *on sumum oðrum spelle*, 335. There he had begun with the quotation from *John* and told the story in *Numbers* as a part of his interpretation. The interpretation as a whole, as Max Förster has partially indicated (*Anglia* XVI. 14 sq.), is very skilfully put together from two sources. One is Augustine's commentary on *John*, Tractate XII. 11; the other is Bede's Homily II. 18, on *John* iii. 1–16. (Förster quotes from this as it is incorporated in the pseudo-Bede commentary on *John*, which in this section is really Alcuin's.) Ælfric's summary of the interpretation here is drawn, I think, rather from his own homily than from these sources, although in the course of shortening he has left out most of the sharp little sentences of antithesis and paradox from Augustine and thus tipped the balance on Bede's side. A selection and rearrangement of the sentences in the earlier homily will show how close is the relationship to lines 337–52 here:

Hwæt wæs seo up-ahafene næddre buton Cristes deað on rode? Seo ærene næddre hæfde næddran gelicnysse, ac heo wæs buton ælcum attre; swa eac Crist hæfde ure gelicnysse, ac he næfde nane synne on his leomum, ac ðurh his up-ahafennysse on ðære rode he gehælde ure synna. . . . We behealdað Cristes deað, þæt us se deað ne derige, þe of ðære næddran asprang, seo ðe Adam forspeon. [*Earlier*] Hwæt getacnodon þa terendan næddran buton synna on urum deadlicum flæsce? [*Later*] Uton behealdan [*later*, mid geleafan] þone ahangenan Crist, þæt we beon fram ðam ættrigum synnum gehælede. . . . Hi wæron gehælede fram deaðe to hwilwendlicum life, and her is gecweden þæt we sceolon habban þæt ece lif. . . . Seo gehiwode anlicnys getiðode þam toslitenum mannum hwilwendlic lif; þæt soðe ðing, þe ðurh ða ærenan næddran getacnod wæs, þæt is Cristes deað, getiðað us þæt ece lif.

Ælfric returned to the theme of the serpents for the third time, with allusion to his two earlier treatments of it, in our homily XII. 227–38. There he is expounding the whole pericope for the octave of Pentecost, *John* iii. 1–15, and comes to Jesus's reference to the brazen serpent at the very end. For the exposition of the sermon as a whole he depends mainly on Bede's Homily II. 18, the same that he had used for the serpents the first time in *Dominica V Quadragesimæ*, and at one point there is a trace of Augustine's twelfth tractate; but the exposition of verses 14 and 15 is there confined to six lines of review of the story in *Numbers* and six lines of interpretation. I have quoted Bede for this at the foot of the page because Ælfric had certainly been rereading Bede and was ultimately indebted to him; but his summary might just as well have been made from the present homily or simply from memory of everything he had read and written on the subject.

353–75. Ælfric brings the story of the forty years in the wilderness to an end with the death of Moses and a glance ahead at Joshua's entry into the promised land, a theme he had already treated in the second part of his Mid-lent homily, *Secunda Sententia de Hoc Ipso*, *CH* II. 212 sqq.

376–89. Comment on the theme of the promised land: the difference between God's promises to the Israelites and Christ's promises to us.

379. *ofæt*[*an*], MS. *ofætum*. Since an accusative is called for, the dative form in the manuscript is clearly wrong. The question is whether it should be taken as an error for the accusative plural *ofætu*, from the strong neuter *ofet*, *ofæt*, 'fruit', or for the accusative singular (less probably plural) of the inadequately attested *ofæte*, wk. fem., meaning, perhaps, 'edible produce, food', and so also, in a more general way than the other word, 'fruit'. This word appears with a question mark in BTS and Hall–Meritt, since its existence has been conjectured from the appearance, at line 194 of Ælfric's *Hexameron* as edited by Crawford, of the phrase *to ofætan*, apparently 'for food'. Crawford's three oldest manuscripts (which are Q, R, and P in the present edition) concur in this reading, whereas two later ones (our O and S) have *ofetum* as if from *ofet*. In the passage a dative singular meaning 'food' makes better sense than a dative plural meaning 'fruits', for it is said that God created many kinds of trees with their fruits (*wæstmum*),

mannum to ofætan and to oðrum neodum.

It is reasonable, therefore, to infer a weak feminine *ofǽte*, possibly, as Toller suggests, meaning literally 'what one eats of'. Indeed it may be that popular etymology was responsible for the invention of the word. The strong neuter *ofet* is common Germanic and its true etymology is unknown; but the frequent spelling *ofæt* suggests that there was a tendency to regard the second syllable as a derivative of *etan* 'to eat'. Ælfric seems, at any rate, to have used both *ofet*, *ofæt* (as BTS attests) and *ofǽte*. For the present homily has a clear example of *ofætan* as an accusative (either singular or plural) at line 156. The phrase *oðre ofætan*, if singular, confirms the feminine gender, but it may well be plural, meaning something like 'other things to eat' rather than, in a strict sense, 'other fruits'. But there is no need to exclude altogether the sense 'fruit', and the glossator is within his rights when he gives *fructum*. Here at line 379, where some distinction from *ele* and *win* is desirable, it may be permissible to take *ofætan* as a singular implying 'solid food'. At any rate, in view of line 156, *ofætan* seems a little more probable than *ofætu* 'fruits'.

403. *maran wit[a]*. Since *wīte* 'punishment' is consistently neuter in Old English and in lines 295 and 301 of this very homily, the reading of the manuscript here, *maran wite*, can hardly be accepted. The choice is between the accusative singular, *mare wite*, and the accusative plural, *maran wita* (cf. xix. 237). On the whole it seems better to choose the plural, since the emendation required is less radical. Indeed the scribe may have considered the final *-e* of *wite* an acceptable plural form, though in these manuscripts generally the dissyllabic neuters end in *-a*, less frequently *-u*, and in this particular word a difference from the singular is desirable.

408. *ne his aseon*. A later scribe was evidently enough troubled by this reading to mark *aseon* for separation into *a* and *seon*, but this will hardly improve matters. A partitive genitive *his* depending on either *aseon* or *seon* does not seem probable, and I cannot find any precedent for it. More likely a word has been left out. I tentatively suggest that we read, *ne his aht aseon*, 'nor look upon any of it'.

XXI

DE FALSIS DIIS

By a combination of accidents and deliberate choices, this homily has become as familiar by title and by a small part of its text as, perhaps, anything in Ælfric, and yet it has not until now been edited in its entirety. Of the seven manuscripts that contain some portion of the text only one, R, approaches completeness, and only two others, C and L, could lead one to a fair estimate of the original length and range of the homily. But C and L are of the twelfth century, unreliable witnesses for Ælfric's forms, and R, though earlier and only slightly at variance with the formal standards of Ælfric's day, is not as a whole one of the foremost Ælfric manuscripts and has not often caught the attention of editors. The chief authority, certainly, seemed to be W, the one manuscript that had preserved Ælfric's preface to the *Lives of Saints* and had approximated (though with several interpolations by other writers) the original order and content of the series. According to its table of contents, *De Falsis Diis* was the second of three general homilies that had followed the saints' lives and brought the volume to a close, but enough leaves have been lost at the end to deprive us of the third piece altogether and of almost three quarters of the second, *De Falsis Diis*. Hence the careful edition of the text of W made by C. R. Unger in 1846 gave no adequate notion of the content of the original homily. Still less did Kemble's selection from W in his *Salomon and Saturn* or Müllenhoff's edition of the page of modified excerpts in X^k. All three of these partial editions focused attention on Ælfric's treatment of the Græco-Roman gods and his incidental attack on their Danish counterparts. It is easy to understand the interest aroused by these passages, tantalizingly brief and imperfectly informative though they are. Nearly the same emphasis was produced by two other edited texts. One of these, the version contained in S, edited by Kluge in his *Lesebuch*, has lost approximately the same number of lines as W at a slightly different spot (151–644) through some mechanical defect in an ancestral copy. What remains deals in generous proportion though incompletely with the classical and Scandinavian gods. The other text is the adaptation of Ælfric's homily by Wulfstan. This adaptation, preserved in T (Hatton 113), has been edited in Napier's *Wulfstan* and again in Bethurum's *Homilies of Wulfstan*. It is built on a very small part of Ælfric's text (lines 72–161 only) and deals almost exclusively with the topic already mentioned.

Except to the few who have explored the manuscripts it has not been evident that the long account of Daniel's exposure of false gods in the days of Darius and of Cyrus, as printed in Warner's *Early English Homilies* from the twelfth-century MS. G, is an extract from *De Falsis Diis*.[1] Now, however, the whole extent of this massive homily is on view and it is evident how small a place in it has been given to Saturn and his progeny. Ælfric has indeed captured attention by his defamation of these gods, but the real force of his attack is carried by the stories from the Old Testament, which include the overthrow of Dagon by the ark of the covenant, the discomfiture of the priests of Bel by Daniel, his destruction of the dragon, and his two escapes from the lions by the miracles of the living God. The ancient record is continued into the period of grace by the exposure of the fraudulent idol Serapis in Alexandria under Theodosius and the defeat of Apollo administered by Gregory the Thaumaturgist. With Apollo, who had not been mentioned earlier, we return nevertheless to the group of pagan gods first enumerated. The claim of their worshippers that they were in being long before Christ and ought therefore to be preferred is now quickly set aside: the Son of God, though he assumed flesh in the sixth age, is co-eternal with the Father; Saturn and the other gods were once mere men, who were not even born until after the Flood.

Ælfric's contemptuous dismissal of Danish paganism may be variously interpreted. Undoubtedly the paganism of the fresh armies of pillagers during the 'nineties constituted not only a fundamental source of antagonism but a threat, and made comparisons with the Philistines and the Babylonians especially apt. The homily would hardly have come into being without the sense that the

---

[1] EETS 1917. The first episode, corresponding to 300–51 below, had been edited from the same manuscript by Max Förster in his *Altenglisches Lesebuch für Anfänger*, Heidelberg, 1913; fifth ed., rev., 1949. In G the excerpt is added to Ælfric's *Dom. XII Post Pent.*, *CH* II. xxxiii, which contains other matter from *Daniel*; but the addition was not, I think, authorized by Ælfric, for it is not really appropriate. For an authorized addition see xxvi.

age-old struggle between the true God and the pretenders was being renewed. A certain partisan zeal, as well as discretion, may be detected in the fact that when the days of the week are introduced, though *Sunnandæg* and *Monandæg* are mentioned and must have caught attention, the attack is directed entirely against the ancient heathen and the Danes. The identity of Óðon and Woden, þór and þunor, Fricg and Frig (let alone Saturn), though it could hardly be missed, is left without comment. It does not appear, however, that Ælfric was greatly worried about the outcome, or aware of any serious defection amongst the English. His references to the Danish gods—to þór as the counterpart of Jove at 124–5, to Óðon as the counterpart of Mercury at 140, to Fricg as the counterpart of Venus at 177, and to the Danish error in making þór the son of Óðon in 141–9—are dispassionately expressed and reveal neither intimate knowledge of the forms of worship nor much fear of their being adopted. Even his reference to high mountains as the scene of sacrifices to Mercury, though it probably shows some knowledge of the worship of Mercury's counterpart, Odin, is verbally close to a generalizing passage in his principal Latin source.[1] He seems to keep the Danish error at an academic distance while he entrenches the Christian stronghold against an attack that has not yet reached dangerous proportions. What he has written is much more a reassuring celebration of God's triumph over a series of foolish pretenders than a frontal assault on contemporary evils.

There is evidence, however, that Ælfric's casual references to the Danes carried weight with at least one Scandinavian preacher. In a group of homiletic pieces that have survived in the Old Icelandic codex called the *Hauksbók* there is one that has long since been recognized as related to Ælfric's.[2] The only question has been whether it is taken directly from Ælfric's homily or from an antecedent common source.[3] So long as comparisons were limited to

---

[1] See line 138 and note.

[2] *Hauksbók, udgiven* [by E. and F. Jónsson] . . . *af det kongelige nordiske Oldskrift-Selskab* (Copenhagen, 1892–6), I. 156–64. Also in *Nokkur Blöð úr Hauksbók . . . gefin út af Jóni Þorkelssyni* (Reykjavík, 1865), pp. 13–23.

[3] C. P. Caspari pointed out the similarity and concluded that the ON homily was derived from Ælfric: see *Martin von Bracaras Schrift De Correctione Rusticorum*, p. cxxii. Max Förster, commenting on the manuscripts of *De Falsis Diis* and its source, held that both homilies were derived from an undiscovered Latin source intermediate between the known one, *De Correctione Rusticorum*, and Ælfric. See *Arch. für das Studium der neueren Sprachen*, CXXII. 261–2.

the early part of the Norse homily there was perhaps some room for doubt. Now that the whole homily can be put beside Ælfric's there can hardly be further question. The Norse writer is very free, but he follows Ælfric's order exactly aside from certain understandable omissions, and he moves through the same sequence of Biblical examples to the conclusion of the Daniel story. It is hardly credible that anyone before Ælfric put the materials together in this fashion, because the Latin writers had no need to repeat large sections of Biblical narrative, and there is no evidence for a vernacular homily on this subject before Ælfric. One odd detail seems to associate the Norse homily with the version in MS. R, namely the blunder by which the name Venus is regarded as a masculine form and replaced by Vena.[1] R makes this mistake at lines 150 and 177. The *Hauksbók* introduces it at the first mention of the goddess, line 115 in Ælfric,[2] where it also has Iuna for Iuno. It repeats Vena at the passage corresponding to line 150 and has Venu, apparently, at the passage corresponding to 177.[3] There are no other signs of kinship with R, however, and two persons of little Latin might have arrived at the same error. At one point the *Hauksbók* recognizes the force of Ælfric's reference to the Danes by adding to Ælfric's mention of Jove in his list of the days of the week a clause in the first person plural: 'whom we call Oðenn'.[4]

In considering the sources of Ælfric's homily it is convenient to distinguish the early part (1–209), in which most of the themes are developed, and the rest (210–676), in which most of the space is taken up with a series of exemplary stories. The sources of these stories are fairly easily established and will be mentioned first. We start with one from *I Samuel* and this is followed by several from *Daniel*, all these following the Vulgate fairly closely. The overthrow of the idol Serapis in Alexandria offers a slight complication, in that Ælfric has conflated material from two accounts, one in the *Historia Ecclesiastica* of Rufinus, the other in the *Historia Tripartita* attributed to Cassiodorus. The story of Gregory the

---

[1] Wilhelm Levison, in *England and the Continent in the Eighth Century*, App. X, pp. 302–14, presents part of a text containing a garbled version of some of the sentences from *De Correctione Rusticorum* on the classical deities, in which Venus is regarded as a man.

[2] The scribe of R wavered between the two forms at 115.

[3] *Hauksbók*, I. 158/17, 18; 159/1, 14.

[4] Ibid., 159/13: 'þann er ver kollum Oðenn.' Ælfric had made the identification at 140, but here, at 175, he does not repeat it.

Thaumaturgist, bishop of Neocaesarea, and his victory over Apollo comes straight from another passage in Rufinus, the same that Ælfric turned to later for two *exempla* in Homily VIII. It is clear that Ælfric is dependent on the version given by Rufinus and not on the Latin *Vita* attributed to Gregory of Nyssa,[1] because in Rufinus and Ælfric the first episode, in which the Thaumaturgist seeks shelter in a temple of Apollo, takes place during a snowstorm while he is crossing the Alps, whereas in the *Vita*, somewhat more plausibly for a bishop of Neocaesarea, it takes place during a rainstorm on the outskirts of a city in Asia Minor.

The sources of the discursive part of the homily (chiefly 1–209) are not so easily determined and can be only partially set forth here. One source, however, has long been recognized as paramount: namely, certain paragraphs in a sermon entitled *De Correctione Rusticorum* by Martinus Bracarensis or Martin, bishop of Braga (in Galicia), who died in 579.[2] The sermon was first elaborately edited by C. P. Caspari,[3] who pointed out in some detail its relation to the attack on the classical gods in *De Falsis Diis*. The influence of *De Correctione Rusticorum*, as shown by the quotations from it under Sources, is intermittently discernible in lines 28–196, and especially strong in 72–180, where the supposed beginnings of idolatry are set forth and the classical gods are singled out for attack. What is not so clear is that Martin's sermon sets the pattern for the entire homily by putting the attack on false gods in the perspective of man's relation to the true God from Adam to the present. This historical perspective was congenial to Ælfric, as we know from several of his writings, including *De Initio Creaturæ*, in which, incidentally, he first describes the beginning of idolatry after the flood. The long series of historically ordered *exempla* in 210–648 are not dependent on Martin's sermon; but the basic similarity of design is brought out when we notice that lines 494–510, the transitional passage in which, after the last of the stories about Daniel, Ælfric ushers in the sixth age with the coming of Christ and the apostolic beginnings of the Christian campaign

---

[1] *Bibliotheca Casinensis*, III (1877), *Florilegium Casinense*, 168–79.

[2] See Claude W. Barlow, ed., *Martini Episcopi Bracarensis Opera Omnia* (New Haven, Yale Univ. Press, 1950), p. 6. Barlow seems to be mistaken in believing (pp. 7, 175) that Pirmin's *Scarapsus* was an intermediary between Martin's sermon and Ælfric's.

[3] *Martin von Bracaras Schrift De Correctione Rusticorum*, Christiania, 1883. My references are to this edition, which is especially pertinent to *De Falsis Diis*

against idolatry, is paralleled in its general purport, though not in its language, by one of the later paragraphs (the thirteenth in Caspari's edition) of *De Correctione Rusticorum.*

Nevertheless, there is much in the opening part of *De Falsis Diis* for which Martin of Braga was not responsible. Two passages in particular have been elaborated from only the barest suggestion in Martin. One passage, on Adam's life before and after the fall (33–71), seems by its easy movement, its pathos, and its lyrical touches to be written very freely, perhaps by distant recollection of more than one unidentified source, but certainly at a great remove from Martin. The other passage, 181–209, falls into two parts. The opening lines (181–9), on the assignment of the seven planets to the gods, were suggested, I think, by Ælfric's recollections of Bede; but the rest, making a vigorous attack on images, has a good deal in it that I can account for in only the most general way. Image-worship in itself is of course mentioned by Martin, and what is said about the devils depends in part, I think, on the passage I have quoted from Isidore; but much else seems, as I have explained in the notes, reminiscent of *Isaiah* and the book of *Wisdom* without being close enough to warrant quotation of particular passages as direct sources.

Again, even in the section closest to Martin there are many details that Ælfric has added and some modifications he has introduced, presumably from what he has read or learned elsewhere. In addition to what is suggested on these matters in the notes, it is well to remember that Ælfric had already composed an outline of the subject in *De Initio Creaturæ.* Some of the ideas there expressed persist, as may be seen from the following sentences (*CH* I. 22/27 sqq.):

Ða siððan [*after Babel*] wearð mancynn þurh deofol beswicen, and gebiged fram Godes geleafan, swa þæt hi worhton him anlicnyssa, sume of golde, sume of seolfre, sume eac of stanum, sume of treowe, and sceopon him naman; þæra manna naman þe wæron entas and yfeldæde. Eft ðonne hi deade wæron þonne cwædon þa cucan þæt hi wæron godas, and wurðodon hi, and him lac offrodon; and comon þa deoflu to heora anlicnyssum, and þæron wunodon, and to mannum spræcon swilce hi godas wæron.

I am not sure of Ælfric's source for this brief passage. He may already have known Martin and have used his ideas with virtually the same modifying influences that appear in *De Falsis*

Diis—a Biblical way of speaking about image-making, and especially the direct connexion of devils with idols that we find in the passage quoted from Isidore for lines 197 sqq.

The whole of Isidore's long essay on the gods of the gentiles (*Etymologiarum lib.* VIII, *cap.* xi) may, in fact, have been vaguely influential. Its possible relevance was first suggested by Professor Bethurum in her notes on Wulfstan's revision of Ælfric.[1] Besides the moderating influence discussed in the note on 99 sqq. and the suggestion in the passage quoted for 197 sqq., Ælfric may have owed to the essay a good deal of general information about the gods with which to confirm, or qualify, what he found in Martin. If so it is not surprising that it does not appear directly; for Martin's purpose was similar to his own, whereas Isidore's was not.

Although eight manuscripts, including the Wulfstan revision, figure in this edition, only three of them (R, C, and L) contain anything approaching the whole extent of the text, and there is little decisive evidence of relationship among them. One piece of evidence alone outweighs all the rest and establishes a basic division into two groups. The passage in lines 141–9 occurs completely only in R and S, not at all in C, L, W, and X^k. The first six lines of it occur also, with very slight changes, in Wulfstan's revision in T. These lines are a parenthetical answer, in a style thoroughly characteristic of Ælfric, to an objection that might be brought from the Danish quarter to what has previously been said about the parentage of Jove. It is conceivable that, if Ælfric had included the parenthesis in his first version, certain scribes would have omitted it as an unnecessary interruption; but such editing in these homilies is rare. It is much more probable that the passage is one of Ælfric's afterthoughts, inserted into the first version of the homily at a later time and thus constituting a second version. Such an explanation is strongly supported by the fact that, in general, L and W, less reliably C, represent early texts of the *Lives of Saints*, R and S late texts of Ælfric's work as a whole. It is also supported by the presence of the greater part of the passage (characteristically without Ælfric's fussy reference to authorities) in Wulfstan's revision, which would hardly have been written before the days of Ælfric's

---

[1] *Homilies of Wulfstan*, 335. Miss Bethurum cites the essay as it reappears, verbatim, in Rabanus Maurus, *De Universo lib.* xv, *cap.* vi (*PL* cxi. 426–36), where indeed Ælfric might have come upon it; but he would probably have known it as Isidore's. Miss Bethurum's notes should also be consulted for much general information on the topic that I have not attempted to repeat here.

abbacy and would have been drawn from a late, not an early, state of Ælfric's text.[1]

The distinction between RS (for whose derivation from a common ancestor at some remove from Ælfric there is evidence in other homilies) and CLW is thus of primary significance. The excerpts in X^k are probably taken from a manuscript containing an early state of the text also, though their failure to include lines 141–9 might be otherwise explained. For the relationship of G there is no evidence, since it does not contain the relevant part of the homily; but what we know of it in general suggests that it should be classed with CLW.

I can find no other evidence of revision in the homily. C's omission of a long passage at 515–64 is probably a deliberate editorial cut, but cannot have been authorized, for it falsifies the historical sequence. For the same reason the passage cannot be a later addition. Some small verbal variations occur here and there, but the manuscript grouping with respect to them is inconsistent and they are all just as likely to be due to scribal modifications as to revision by the author.

Among the small indications of manuscript groups the following may be mentioned. The group RS (partly, no doubt, because so large a part of the text is omitted in S) is very slightly indicated except at 141–9. The two manuscripts share a small error, the omission of an essential *ne*, at 72. (Here Wulfstan's revision has *ne* like the other manuscripts, but he would surely have inserted it if it had been missing in his copy of Ælfric's homily.) Other points of agreement (RS and L against CW at 19, RS and C against LWX^k at 117) cannot be regarded as significant because, since either reading is acceptable, we cannot tell which is original. We cannot even be sure that one of the two groups is closely related, for deliberate scribal choices may have coincided in such a way as to interfere with the lines of inheritance.

More interesting are three instances of agreement between R and Wulfstan's revision (T) against the other manuscripts:

    95   an *CLW and S*; ana *RT*.
   111   afligde *CLWX^k and S*; aflymde *RT*.
   154   halige *CLW*; healice *RT*. (*S lacks this passage.*)

---

[1] This conclusion was first put forward by Dr. Clemoes in his review of Bethurum's *Homilies of Wulfstan*, *MLR*, LIV (1959), 81–82.

I am at a loss to explain this phenomenon, because there is every reason to believe that Wulfstan's copy of Ælfric's homily came straight from the author, whereas R and S shared an ancestor that had deliberately introduced unauthorized additions. If the three variants above belonged to a second edition sent out by Ælfric, why do they not appear in S as well as R? Their heritage from Ælfric should have been identical apart from what was lost in the two lines after they had separated. It looks as if the three variants had been Wulfstan's substitutions, and R had somehow inherited them by some later borrowing. If Wulfstan had entered his changes in his copy of Ælfric, this copy might have been consulted by some scribe in the line of R after its separation from the line of S.

At several points where R, C, and L are the only witnesses, R and CL disagree as we should expect, but I cannot tell for sure which is correct. Hence there is no proof that C and L are related to one another more closely than to other descendants of the first version of the homily. The chief instances are these:

225 eodan *R*; eodon (eoden *C*) to þam temple *CL*.
226 licgende *R*; licgan *CL*.
243 þa *R*; heora *CL* (*accepted in the text but not certain*).
455 *second* he *R*; *om. CL*.
497 fylðe *R*; fulnesse *CL*.

It is therefore somewhat disconcerting to find R and C united in the erroneous reading *þone* at 512, where L has the ambiguously abbreviated *þoñ* for what should be *þonne*; but here the temptation to err is so great that it is easy to believe that R and C have produced the wrong reading independently.

At 49, 324, 463, 481 there are still other groupings where either reading can be accepted. I think we must reckon here with minor bits of editorializing indulged in by some of the scribes. It would certainly be rash to establish minor groups on the strength of any of these instances.

DE FALSIS DIIS

O fratres dilectissimi, diuina s[c]riptura cultum unius ueri Dei

Text based on R (CCCC 178), pp. 142–63 (lines 1–313, 318–676). Collated with W (Cotton Julius E. vii), ff. 238–40ᵛ (1–140, 150–91); C (CCCC 303), pp. 306–17 (1–140, 150–296, 299–301, 304–514, 565–676); L (ULC Ii. 1. 33), ff. 175ᵛ–84ᵛ (1–140, 150–508, 510–44); S (Hatton 116), pp. 365–73 (1–150, 645–76); G (Cotton Vespasian D. xiv), ff. 44ᵛ–48ᵛ (excerpt on Daniel, lines 300–496); and Xᵏ (Paris, Bibl. Nat. Lat. 7585), f. 238ᵛ (a paragraph of excerpts, 104–17, 122–4*a*, 126–7, 134–5*a*, 140*a*, 150–2: facsimile in Dubois, *Ælfric*, facing p. 84). For the select variants from T (Hatton 113), containing Wulfstan's revision of lines 72–161, see apparatus at line 72.

Printed editions of W, S, G, and Xᵏ are cited as follows when they differ from their respective manuscripts: Un (Unger, the text of W, *Annaler for nordisk Oldkyndighed og Historie*, Copenhagen, 1846, pp. 67–81); Ke (Kemble, the text of W from line 99 on, *Solomon and Saturn*, pp. 120 sqq.); Kl (Kluge, the text of S, omitting all Latin, *Angelsächsisches Lesebuch*, 3. Aufl., Halle, 1902, pp. 87–90: cited here from 4. Aufl., 1915, pp. 86–89; Wa (Warner, the text of G, *Early English Homilies*, pp. 38–41); and Mf (Müllenhoff, the text of Xᵏ, *Zeitschrift für deutsches Altertum*, XII [1865], 407–9). Secondary editions based on the printed texts cited above are disregarded. On Förster's edition of 300–51 from G see above, p. 668, n. 1.

Excluded variants: 1. Interchange of short *i* and *y* in *bliss, gif, him, hine, hire, his, hwider, hwilc, micel, siððan, six, swilc, þider, þisne, þisum*. R and L tend to use *hym* for the plural. 2. Interchange of long *i* and *y* in *git, hi, si, swiðe*. 3. Interchange of *i* (rare) and *e* (frequent in S, occasional in C) with the commoner *y* in the suffix *-nyss*. 4. Substitution of *þan* for the demonstrative adjective *þam* or *þæm*, very frequent in C and G. 5. Interchange of *þan* (the commonest) with *þon* and *þam* in *for þan þe, be þan þe*. 6. Substitution of single for double consonants at the end of *eall, full, mann, menn, -nyss*, etc. 7. Variations of *micl-, miccl-, micel-* in inflected forms of *micel*. 8. Interchange of *-an* and *-on* in *butan, seofan*, and the plural endings of verbs, present and past. Verbs in R have *-an* with exceptional frequency. (Substitution of *-on* for *-an* in the infinitive is recorded.) 9. Interchange of the pret. plural *-odon* with *-edon* (fairly common), *-adon* (infrequent), *-oden* (rare); and of sing. *-ode*, the usual form, with *-ade*. 10. Interchange of *good* (usual in R) and *god* (usual elsewhere) for 'good', with or without accent. 11. Interchange of *þar, hwar* (frequent in R) and *þær, hwær* (usual elsewhere). 12. Substitution of *þe, þeo* for *se, seo*, which occurs nearly always in L and nowhere else. 13. A curious blunder peculiar to C, *þonum* for *þonne* at lines 27, 385, 652 and elsewhere, apparently by misinterpretation of the abbreviation *þonñ*. Once also *þone* at 396. 14. Most of the levelled endings in G, since they are on display in Warner's edition. 15. G's frequent *heo* for *hi*. 16. The spelling *cyng* (frequent in L and G) for *cyning* is reported only when R has an odd form. 17. Variations of proper names: *Danihel* (regular in R) appears occasionally elsewhere, but *Daniel* is more frequent; *Darig-* and *Dari-* vary in the name *Darius*; *Bel* is replaced by *Bæl* frequently in L and occasionally, as at 355, in C.

Seven or eight sentence-capitals have been supplied without notice.

Title: FALSI *S*.   1–5 *om*. *Kl*.   1 O] F (*anticipating* fratres) *C*. scriptura] *sic CLSW*; sriptura *R*.

nos docuit, his uerbis dicendo: Unus est Dominus, una fides, unum baptisma, unus Deus et Pater omnium, qui est super omnes, et per omnia, et in omnibus nobis. Ex quo omnia, per quem omnia, in quo omnia; ipsi gloria in secula. 5

Eala ge gebroðra ða leofostan, þæt godcunde gewrit us tæhte þone biggeng anes soðes Godes, þisum wordum cweþende: An Drihten ís, and án geleafa, and án fulluht; án God and Fæder ealra þinga, se ðe is ofer ealle þing, and þurh ealle þing, and on us eallum. Of þam synd ealle þing, and þurh þone synd ealle þing, 10 and on þam synd ealle þing; sy him wuldor á to worulde, amen.

Se æl*mihtiga Fæder gestrynde ænne Sunu of him sylfum, *p. 143 butan wifes gemánan, and þurh þone Sunu he geworhte ealle gesceafta, gesewenlice and ungesewenlice. Se Sunu is eall swa eald swa se Fæder, for þæm þe se Fæder wæs æfre butan anginne, 15 and se Sunu wæs æfre butan anginne of him acen[n]ed, eall swa mihtig swa se Fæder. Se Halga Gast nis na acenned, ac he is þæs Fæder and þæs Suna willa and lufu, of him bam gelíce, and þurh þone Gast syndon ealle gesceafta geliffæste þe se Fæder gesceop þurh his Sunu, se ðe is his wisdom. þeos halige þrynnyss is án ælmihtig 20 God æfre unbegunnen and ungeendod. Hi synd þry on naman, Fæder, and Sunu, and [Halig] Gast; and hy ne synd na þry Godas, ac hy þry syndon án ælmihtig God untodæledlic, for þam þe hym þrym is án gecynd, and án ræd, and án weorc on eallum þingum.

3 baptima *C.*   unus] unus est *Un.*   4 in quo omnia] *om. L.*   5 saecula *W.* *after* secula] amen *L.*   6 *preceded by rubric,* SERMO ANGLICE *S.*   Eale *L.* leofestan *SW.*   godcundæ *C.*   7 bigeng *LS*; bigæncg *C.*   soðas *C.* 8 *first* an] *om. W.*   *third* an] *cap. RC.*   Fæder] an fæder *C.*   9 þur|c'h *C.* 10–11 þincg (*thrice*) *W.*   10 þurh þone] on þam *S.*   11 on þam] þurh þone *S.*   elle *L.*   14 gesceafte *L.*   -segen- (*twice*) *S.*   15 þæm] þan *CLSW.* 16 and se sunu... anginne] *om. S.*   acenned] *sic CLSW*; acened *R.*   18 sunu *L.*   heom *C.*   19 gast] halgan gast *CW.*   gesceafta] gesceafte *LW.*   geliffeste *C.*   20 ðrymnyss *L.*   21 þreo *S.*   namum *L.*   22 halig *CLSW*; se halga *R.*   godas] godes *C.*   22–23 þreo (*twice*) *S.*   23 ac] *and C.* syndon] synd *C.*   heom *C.*

Glosses in *R and S, Latin*: 6 ge: vos *R.*   ða leofostan: dilectissimi *R.*   7 biggeng anes soðes godes: cultum vnius veri dei *RS.*   þisum: his *RS.*   wordum cweþende: uerbis dicendo *S.*   8 drihten: deus *R.*   geleafa: fides *S.*   9 on: in *S.*   10 Of þam: ex quo *R.*   Of: ex *S.*   þurh þone (on þam *S*): per quem *S* (!).   11 a: semper *R.*   12 gestrynde: Genuit *RS.*   13 butan: absque *R.* 16, 17 acenned: Genitus *RS.*   19 þone: illum *RS.*   geliffæste: uiuificata *R.*

Sources. 2–4 [*Ephes. iv. 5, 6*: Unus . . . nobis, *as given.*] 4–5 [*Rom. xi. 36, as quoted by Augustine, De Vera Religione, PL XXXIV. 172. See note.*]

And selre us is soðlice to gelyfanne 25
on þa[s] halgan þrynnysse, and hi geandettan,
þonne us sy to smeagenne to swiðe embe þæt.
Ðeos þrynnyss gesceop þa scinændan englas,
and Adam and Éuan eft syððan to mannum,
and sealde hym anweald ofer eorðlice gesceafta; 30
and hi mihtan wunian [symle] butan deaðe,
gif hi þæt an Godes bebod næfre ne tobræcan.
Ða wunode Adam swa orsorh on blisse,
and him [n]an gesceaft sceð[ð]an ne mihte,
þa hwile þe he gehcold þæt heofonlicc bebod. 35
Him [ne derode nan fýr,] þeah þe [he] mid fotum on stópe,
ne nan wæter ne mihte þone mann[an] adrencan,
þeah þe he on yðum urne færlice.
Ne nán wildeor ne mihte, ne nan wurmcynn ne dorste
[derian þam menn] mid hys muðes slite. 40
Ne hungor ne þurst, ne hefigtyme cyle,
ne nán *swiðlic hæte, ne seocnyss ne mihton   *p. 144

25 gelyfenne *LSW*; gelefenne *C*.   26 þas] *sic CLSW*, þa *R*.   þrym-
nysse *L*.   geandyttan *S*.   27 ymbe *W*.   28 ðrymnyss *L*.   scinendan
CLSW.   29 efan *S*.   30 heom *C*.   31 wunigean *L*.   symle *CW*;
symble *S*; *om. R*; æfre *L*.   32 an] *om. S*.   nefre *S*.   34 nan] *sic
CLSW*; nan þing ne nan *R*.   sceððan *C*; scæððan *W*; sceððian *R*; sceaþan
S; sceaðigean *L*.   35 geheold] heold *C*.   heonfolice *Kl* (*mispr.*).   36 ne
derode nan fyr *CLSW*; nan fýr ne derode *R*.   he] *sic CLSW*; *om. R*.
37 mannan] *sic SW*; mann *RL*; man *C*.   adræncan *CL*.   39 wyrm-
CLSW.   40 derian þam menn] *the order of CLSW*; þam menn derian *R*.
derigean *L*.   41 hunger *CLSW*.   -tima *W*; -time *C*.   42 hæto *W*.
-nys *W*; -ness *C*; -nessa *S*.

Glosses in R and S, Latin: 26 geandettan: *confiteri R*.   27 þonne:
quam RS.   embe þæt: *circa hoc S*.   32 bebod: *preceptum RS*.
33 orsorh: *se securus* (*sic*) *R*.   34 sceððian: *nocere vel ledere R*.   sceaþan:
furare (*!*) *S*.   37 þone: *illum S*.   38 yþum: *vndis S*.   40 muðes
slite: *morsu RS*.   41 hefigtyme: *graue RS*.   cyle: *frigus R*.   42 swiðlic:
uehemens RS.
    ME: 27 smeagenne: *þenchene R*.

28–71 [*Greatly elaborated from Martin of Braga's De Correctione Rusticorum*, § 4] Post istam vero ruinam angelicam placuit Deo de limo terræ hominem
plasmare, quem posuit in paradiso; et dixit ei, ut, si præceptum Domini ser-
vasset, in loco illo cælesti sine morte succederet. . . .; si autem præterisset Dei
præceptum, morte moreretur. . . . Diabolus . . ., invidia ductus, suasit homini,
ut mandata Dei transcenderet. Pro qua offensa iactatus est homo de paradiso in
exilio mundi istius, ubi multos labores et dolores pateretur.

Adam geswencan on þam earde,
þa hwile þe he þæt lytle bebod mid geleafan geheold.
Eft, þa þa he agylt hæfde, and Godes bebod tobræc,   45
þa forleas he þa gesælþa, and on geswincum leofode,
swa þæt hine [biton lys] bealdlice and flean,
þone þe ær ne dorste se draca furþon hreppan.
He moste þa warnian wið wæter and wið fýr,
and behealdan wærlice þæt he hearde ne feolle,   50
and mid agenum geswince him ætes tilian;
and þa gecyndelican good þe him God on gesceop,
he moste þa healdan, gif he hi habban wolde,
mid mycelre gymene, swa swa gyt doð þa góódan,
þe mid geswince healdað hi sylfe wið leahtras.   55
Eac swylce seo sunne, and soðlice se móna
wurdon benæmde heora wynsuman beorhtnysse
æfter Adames gylte, na be agenum gewyrhtum.
Be seofonfealdan wæs seo sunne þa beorhtre
ærþam se mann agylte, and se mona hæfde   60
þære sunnan beorhtnysse, swa swa heo scinð nu ús.
Hi sceolan eft swaþeah æfter Domes-dæge habban
be fullan heora beorhtnysse, be þam þe hy gesceapene wæran;
and se mona ne ealdað æfter þam dæge,

---

43 geswæncan *CL*; gesvincan *Un* (*wrongly*).   45 agylt] *sic CLSW*;
agylt(e) *R*.   46 geswicum *C*.   47 biton lys *CLSW*; lys biton *R*.
48 forþon *LS*.   reppan *S*; hrepan *L*.   49 warnian] hine warnian *S*; hine
warnigean *L*.   50 he] *om. Un* (*wrongly*).   51 agenum] his agenum *L*.
geswynce *C*.   ætas *W*.   52 -lice *L*.   53 healden *W*.   53–54 gif
he hi habban wolde *after* gymene *S*.   54 mycelre] mycele *W*.   56 soðlice]
om. L.   57 benæmede *CLSW*.   winsuman *C*.   59 -fealdum *CLSW*.
60 ærðan *CLS*.   61 þere *S*.   scynð *W*.   62–63 *Un wrongly prints*
habban be fullan *after* beorhtnysse.   63 beoht- *W*.   -nessa *S*.

Glosses in R and S, Latin: 43 geswencan: fatigari *R*.   44 bebod: preceptum *R*.   geheold: seruauit *R*.   45 þa þa: tunc (*!*) *S*.   bebod: imperium *R*.   47 bealdlice: audacter *RS*.   48 þone: illum *R*   þone þe:
quem *S*.   furþon (forþon): eciam (etiam) *RS*.   hreppan: tangere *RS*.
49 warnian: cauere *RS*.   50 behealdan: videre *RS*.   wærlice: caute *R*.
51 agenum: propria *S*.   ætes: cibos *R*.   52 good: bona *RS*.   53 healdan:
custodire *R*.   54 gymene: cura *RS*.   doð (?): obseruant *R*.   goodan:
boni *R*.   55 healdað: custodiunt *R*.   leahtras: crimina *R*.   56 Eac
swylce: similiter *S*.   57 benæmde: ablati *R*; subtracti *S*.   wynsuman:
iocundo *R*.   58 gewyrhtum: meritis *S*.   59 þa: tunc *S*.   63 be
fullan: plene *S*   64 ne: Non *S*.   ealdað: decrescit *RS*.

ME: 57 wurdon: weren *R*.   64 ealdað: woneð *R*.

ac bið ansund scinende, swa swa seo [sunne] deð nú.   65
Menn magon eac geearnian mid micelre earfoðnysse
þæt hi wunian mid Gode on wynsumnysse æfre
æfter Domes-dæge, a butan deaðe,
þa þe nu gehyrsumiað his hæsum mid weorce;
and þa þe God forseoð beoð besencte on helle   70
on þam ecum witum and endeleasum cwylmingum.
Nu [ne] ræde we on bocum þæt man arærde hæþengyld
on eallum þam fyrste ǽr Noes *flode,   *p. 145
oðþæt þa entas worhtan þone [wundorlican] stýpel
æfter Noés flóde, and hym swa feala gereorda   75
God þar forgeaf swa þæra wyrhtena wæs.
Ða þa hi toferdon to fyrlenum landum,
and mancynn þa weox, þa wurdon hi bepæhte
þurh þone ealdan deofol þe Adam ǽr beswác,
swa þæt hi worhton wolice him godas,   80
and þone Scyppend forsawon þe hy gesceop to mannum.
Hi namon þa [to] wisdome þæt hi wurþodon him for godas

65 sunne *CLSW*; *om. R.*   66 geearnigean *L.*   earðfoðnesse *C.*
67 (wunian) wunian *R.*   69 weorce] weorcum *S.*   71 on] to *L.*   ecum
witum and] *om. S.*   72 *Here begins Wulfstan's revision of Ælfric in T (Hatton
113), ff. 58ᵛ–61, after an introductory sentence. Select variants, marked (T), include only the few that may have a bearing on the Ælfrician archetype.*   ne] *sic
CLW(T); om. RS.*   rædde *W.*   -gild *CW.*   74 oððet *C.*   wundorlican
CLSW(T); om. R.   75 fela *CLW(T);* fæla *S.*   gereorda] gereord *LSW (em. to
gereorda Kl.).*   78 þa weox] weox ða *L.*   79 deofoll *S.*   80 wohlice *S;
om. L.*   81 sceppend *C;* scippend *L.*   forsægon *S;* forsawon *alt. to* forsæwon
R.   82 þa] *misprinted* þä (*i.e.* þæ) *Un.*   to] *sic CLSW(T); om.,* ham to *inserted
over line by trembling hand R.*

Glosses in R and S, Latin: 65 ansund: *integer RS.*   67 wynsumnysse:
iocunditate *R.*   68 a: semper *R.*   69 þa: illi *S.*   70 þa (þe): illi
R; qui S.   forseoð: spernunt *R.*   besencte: submersi *R.*   71 cwylmingum: cruciatu *R.*   72 hæþengyld: idolum *RS.*   74 oðþæt: vsque *R;*
donec *S.*   entas: Gigantes *RS.*   75 gereord(a): lingua *RS.*   77 þa þa:
quando *S.*   toferdon: diuerterunt *R;* dispersi *S.*   fyrlenum: longinquis *RS.*
80 wolice: iniuste *R;* inique *S.*   81 forsawon: despecxerunt *R.*   82 wurþodon: adorabant *R;* adorarent *S.*
ME: 71 witum: pine *R.*   78 wurdon: weren *R.*

72–81 [*Partially suggested by De Correctione Rusticorum, § 6*] Post diluvium
iterum recuperatum est genus humanum per tres filios Noe, reservatos cum
uxoribus suis. Et cum coepisset multitudo subcrescens mundum implere,
obliviscentes iterum homines Creatorem mundi, Deum, coeperunt, dimisso
Creatore, colere creaturas.
82–98 [*Ibid.*] Alii adorabant solem, alii lunam vel stellas, alii ignem, alii aquam

þa sunnan and þone monan, for heora scinendan beorhtnysse,
and him lac offrodan, and forletan heora Scyppend.

Sume menn eac sædon be þam scínendum steorrum 85
þæt hi godas wæron, and wurþodan hy [georne].

Sume hi gelyfdon on fýr for his færlicum bryne,
sume eac on wæter, and wurðodan hi [for godas];
sume on þa eorþan, for þon þe heo ealle þing afet.

Ac hi mihton tocnawan, gif hi cuðan þæt gescéad, 90
þæt se is ána God þe hi ealle gesceop,
us mannum to bryce, for his micclan gódnysse.

þas gesceafta doð swa swa hym gedihte heora Scyppend,
and ne magon naht don butan Drihtnes willan,
for þan þe nan scyppend nis butan se á[n] soða God, 95
and we hine wurðiað mid gewissum geleafan,
cweþende mid muðe and mid modes incundnysse
þæt se is ana God þe ealle þing ges[c]eop.

Git þa, þa hæþenan noldan beon gehealdene
on swa feawum godum, ac fengon to wurðianne 100
mislice éntas and men him to godum,

---

83 -nyssæ *L.*   84 ofrodon *L.*   forlætan *S.*   85 scynendu*m W;*
scinendan *C.*   steorran *CS.*   86 godes *C.*   georne] *sic CLSW(T);* for
godas *R.*   87 gelefdon *C.*   færlican *C.*   88 for godas] *sic LSW;* for
godes *C;* georne *R; second half of line om.* (*T*).   89 sume] *cap. R;* suma *C.*
90 tocnawon *L.*   92 brice *CLSW(T).*   93 hyra *W.*   sceppend *C.*
95 þon *S.*   buto *C.*   an] *sic CLSW;* ana *R(T).*   96 geleafon *S.*
97 cwæþende *W;* cweðenne *C.*   98 se] he *L.*   þincg *W.*   gesceop] *sic*
CLSW; geseop *R;* gescop (*T*).   99 *Ke(mble) begins here, printing from W.*
þa, þa] þa *Un* (*wrongly*), (*T*).   100 wurðigenne *CLSW;* wurðienne (*T*).

Glosses in R and S, Latin: 86, 88 wurþodan, wurðodan: adorabant *R.*   89 afet:
pascit *R.*   90 gescead: ratione*m S.*   92 bryce: usui *R;* vsum *S.*
95 scyppend: creator *R.*   96 wurðiað: adoramu*s R.*   gewissum: certa *RS.*
97 modes: *m*entis *S.*   (mid) incundnysse: intencione *R;* intime *S.*   99 þa
þa: *quando* (!) *S.*   gehealdene: pacati *RS;* contenti *R;* obseruati (!) *S.*
100 fengon: incepe*runt R.*   wurðianne: adorare *R.*   101 mislice: diuersos,
varios *R.*   entas: Gigantes *S.*   men: ho*m*ines *S.*   godum: diis *R.*

---

profundam vel fontes aquarum, credentes hæc omnia non a Deo esse facta ad
usum hominum, sed ipsa, ex se orta, deos esse. [*Ælfric adds the earth in line* 89
and greatly modifies the expression of the idea in 90–98.]

101–3 [*In De Corr. Rust.* § 7 *the devil and his subordinates deceive men into
worshipping them by assuming the names of criminals:* imponentes sibi vocabula
sceleratorum hominum, qui in omnibus criminibus et sceleribus suam egerant
vitam, ut alius Iovem, etc.]

þa þe mihtige wæron on woruldlicum geþincðum,
and egefulle on life, þeah þe hy [leofodon] fúllice.
Án man wæs eardiende on þam ílande Creta,
Saturnus geháten, swiðlic and wælhreow,   105
swa þæt he abát hys suna, þa þa hí geborene wæron,
*and unfæderlice macode heora flæsc him to mete.   *p. 146
He læfde swaþeah ænne to l[i]fe,
þeah þe he abite his gebroðra on ǽr;
se wæs Iouis geháten, hetol and þrymlic.   110
He [afligde] his fæder of þam foresædan iglande,
and wolde hine acwellan, gif he him come tó.
Se Iouis wæs swa swiðe gál, þæt he on hys swustor gewífode;
seo wæs geháten Iuno, swiðe healic gyden.

102 þa þe] þa þa L.   worold- L.   geþingðum LS.   103 leofodon] sic
CSW; lifodon L; gelyfdon R.   104 Here begins the passage excerpted in X^k,
f. 238^v.   eardigende LSW; eardigenne C; eardgynde X^k.   iglande CLW(T);
eglande S; iglonde X^k.   cretæ X^k.   105 wælreow S.   106 suna] sunus CL;
sunan S.   þa þa] sona swa X^k.   geborena L.   107 mæte W.   108 swaþeah
ænne] anne swaþeah X^k.   enne C.   to] him to S.   life] sic CLSWX^k(T);
lafe R.   109 om. X^k.   gebroðra] broðre L; broðra (T).   110 þrymlic]
grimlic and eac þrymlic X^k; þwyrlic S; for half-line, se wæs hetol feond (T). See
note.   111 afligde] sic CLSWX^k; aflymde R(T).   þam foresædan iglande]
cretan X^k.   eglande S.   112 acwelle L.   come to] to come X^k.   113 Se]
om. X^k.   swa swiðe gal] ormæte gal ésne swa X^k.   swiðe] om. W.   hys] his
agenre X^k(T).   swuster CLX^k; swyster (T).   gewifede W; tallice gewifode
X^k.   114 seo] se W (em. to seo UnKe).   gehaten Iuno] Iuno gehaten X^k.

Glosses in R and S, Latin: 102 þa þe: illos quos (!) R; illos qui S.   geþingðum: bono, elatione S.   103 egefulle: terribiles RS.   gelyfdon: viuebant
R.   leofodon: vixerunt S.   104 eglande: insula S.   105 swiðlic:
uehemens RS.   wælhreow (wælreow S): atrox R; valde crudelis S.
106 abat: comedit R.   suna: filios R.   hi: illi S.   107 unfæderlice:
orphanos (!) R.   110 hetol: odiosus, prauus R; exosus S.   þrymlic (?):
prauus (uncertainly placed in margin) R.   þwyrlic: prauus S.   111 aflymde
(afligde): fugauit RS.   113 gal: libidinosus RS; lasciuus S.   114 gyden:
dea RS.
ME: 102 geþincðum: gode R.

105-12 [This introductory account of Saturn and Jove has no counterpart in
De Corr. Rust., in which § 7 describes Jove first as below, and Saturn later, between
Mercury and Venus] Alius quoque dæmon Saturni sibi nomen adscriptit, qui,
in omni crudelitate vivens, etiam nascentes suos filios devorabat.
113-17 [De Corr. Rust. § 7] Ut alius Iovem se esse diceret, qui fuerat magus
et in tantis adulteriis incestus, ut sororem suam haberet uxorem, quæ dicta est
Iuno, Minervam vero et Venerem, filias suas, corruperit, neptes quoque et
omnem parentelam suam turpiter incestaverit.

Heora (ge)dohtra wæron Minerua and Uénus.   115
þa forlæg se fæder fu(l)lice buta,
and manega his magan ma[n]lice gewemde.
þas mánfullan menn wæron þa mæroston godas
þe þa hæþenan wurðodan, and worhton him to godum;
ac se sunu wæs swaþeah swiðor gewurðod   120
þonne se fæder wære on heora fulan bigeng[e].
þes Iouis is arwurðust ealra þæra goda
þe þa hæþenan hæfdon on heora gedwylde;
and he hatte þór betwux sumum þeodum,
þone þa Deniscan leoda lufiað swiðost.   125
His sunu hatte Mars, se macede æfre saca,
and wrohte and wáwan he wolde æfre styria[n].
þisne wurðodan þa hæðenan for healicne god,
and swa oft swa hi fyrdadon, oððe to gefeohte woldan,
þonne offrodon hi heora lac on ær þisum god[e].   130

115 gedohtra] *sic SW*; ge- *erased R*; dohtra *CLX^k*; twa dohtra (*T*). wæron]
wæron gehaten *S*. Minerua] *Ke em. to* Diana. *See note.* Uenus] uena
altered to uenus (*or conversely*) *R*. 116–17 *om.* (*T*.) 116 fullice] *sic*
CLWX^k; *first* l *erased R*; fulice *S* (fullice *em. Kl*). butu *Ke.* 117 magon *S*.
manlice *LW*; manlice and drædlice *X^k*; manfullice *RCS*. gewæmde *CX^k* (*Mf*
gevæde, *overlooking abbrev.*); forwemde *Ke.* 118–21 *om. X^k*. 118 mærostan *CLW*(*T*); merestan *S*. 119 heþenan *S*. heom *C*. 120 swidor *C*.
121 on ... bigenge] *om.* (*T*) fule *C*. biggencge *W*; bigæncge *C*; biggænge *S*;
bigenge *L*; bigengum *R*. 122 is] wæs *X^k*. ærwurðost *C*; arwurþost
LW(*T*); awurðost *S* (ar- *Kl*); se arweorðesta *X^k*. eallra *S*. 122–3 ealra
... hæfdon] god *X^k*. 123 gedwilde *S*. 124–5 betwux ... swiðost] *om.*
X^k. 125 þane *Ke* (*wrongly*). leoda] *om. S.*; leode *Ke.* 126 suna *X^k*.
macode *CLSW*(*T*); makode *X^k*. saca]sace and wrace *X^k*; gewinn (*T*) (*but cf.*
T at 127). 127 wrohte] worhte *S*. and wawan] *om. X^k*; and saca and wraca
(*T*). he wolde æfre styrian] astyrode *X^k*; he styrede gelome (*T*). styrian] *sic*
CSW; styrigan *L*; styrian gefeoht *R*. 128–32 *om. X^k* 129 hi] he *Ke*
(*wrongly*). 130 offrode *L*. gode] *sic CLSW*; gedwolgode (*T*); godum *R*.

Glosses in R and S, Latin: 116 buta: *ambas S*. 117 magan: *parentes RS*.
manfullice: *nequiter R; inique S*. gewemde: *violauit, maculauit, suadebat*
(*i.e. gewēmde*) *R; contaminauit, inficiebat S*. 118 manfullan: *iniqui R*.
121 bigengum, biggænge: *cultu RS*. 122 þes: *iste RS*. arwurðust: *venera-*
bilior RS. 123 gedwylde: *errore RS*. 124 hatte: *vocatur S*. þeodum: *Gente RS*. 125 þone: *illum S*. 126 saca: *contentiones S*.
127 wrohte (worhte): *iurgia RS; scandala R*. wawan: *ve (as if for* wa *or*
walawa) *R*. styrian gefeoht: *mouere prelium R*. 128 healicne god:
summo deo S. 129 fyrdedon: *itinerauerunt S*. (oððe) to gefeohte woldan: *vel preliabant R; pungnauerunt S*. 130 on ær: *ante R*.
ME: 129 fyrdadon: wolden faren, *and in margin* ferdeden *R*.

126–7 [*De Corr. Rust.* § 7] Alius autem dæmon Martem se nominauit, qui fuit
litigiorum et discordiæ commissor.

Hi gelyfdon þæt he mihte micclum him [f]ultumian
on þam gefeohte, for þam þe he gefeoht lufode.
Sum man wæs gehaten Mercurius on lífe,
se wæs swiðe facenfull and swicol on dædum,
and lufode eac stala and leasbregdnyssa.   135
þone macodan þa hæþenan him to mæran gode,
and æt wega gelætum him lac offrodan,
and to heagum *beorgum him brohtan onsæg[ed]nysse.   *p. 147
Ðes god wæs [a]rwyrðe betwyx eallum hæþenum,
and he is Óðon geháten oðrum naman on Denisc.   140
Nu secgað þa Deniscan on heora gedwylde
þæt se Iouis wære, þe hi þór hátað,
Mercuries sunu, þe hi Oðon hatað;
ac hi nabbað na riht, for þam þe we rædað on bocum,
ge on hæþenum ge on Cristenum, þæt se hetola Iouis   145
to soðan wære Saturnes sunu,

131 gelifdon *C*.   fultumian] *sic CLSW*(*T*); gefultumian *R*.   133 Sum
. . . life] Mercurius hatte heora an god X^k.   mærcurius *C*.   134 faken-
X^k.   135 eac] *om. X^k*.   135–9 and leasbregdnyssa . . . hæþenum] *om. X^k*.
135 -bregdnyssa] -bred- *CSW*; -bræd- *L*; -nysse *CLW*; -nesse *S*.   137 wega
gelætum] wegelætu*m C*; wega gelætan *L*.   geoffrodon *L*.   138 beorh-
gum *L*.   onsæged-] *sic W* (onsægd- *Ke*), *L*; onsægd- *S*; onseged- *C*; onsæg- *R*;
(*T*) *substitutes* oft mistlice loflac.   139 arwurða *W* (arwurðe *em. Un*); arwurðe
CLS(*T*); ærwyrðe *R*.   betwux *CLSW*(*T*).   hædenu*m L*.   140 and he]
þes X^k.   is] *om. S*.   oðen X^k.   oðrum . . . denisc] *om. X^k*.   naman] *followed
by* gehat, *marked for deletion C*; mannu*m L*.   dænisc *C*.   141–9 *om. CLWX^k*;
complete only in RS; first six lines in T, for which all variants are given.   141 þa
deniscan] sume þa denisce men *T*.   gedwilde *S*.   142 hy *T*.   143 hatað]
namiað *T*.   144 ðan *T*.   145 hetula *T*.   146 wære] is *T*.

Glosses in R and S, Latin: 132 gefeoht: prelium *R*.   134 facenfull:
dolosus, fraudulent*us RS*.   135 leasbregdnyssa: lasciuia*m vel* petulantiam
R; the same uninflected S.   136 þone: illu*m RS*.   137 wega gelætum:
exit*us* viaru*m R*.   138 beorgum: montibu*s RS*, collibu*s S*.   onsæg(d)nysse:
sacrificiu*m RS*, victima*m R*.   139 Ðes: iste *RS*.   ærwyrðe (arwurðe):
uener*abilis RS*.   140 gehaten: vocat*ur S*.   oðrum: alio *S*.   141 gedwylde: errore *R*.   142 hi: illi *R*.   145 *first* ge: eciam *RS*.   hetola:
exosus *R*.   146 to soðan: vere *R*.

133–7 [*De Corr. Rust.* § 7] Alius deinde dæmon Mercurium se appellare voluit,
qui fuit omnis furti et fraudis dolosus inventor; cui homines cupidi quasi deo
lucri, in quadriviis transeuntes, iactatis lapidibus acervos petrarum pro sacrificio
reddunt.
138 [*Earlier in same paragraph, but not with reference to Mercury, there is mention of* sacrificia in excelsis montibus. *See note.*]

and þa béc ne magon beon awægede
þe þa ealdan hæðenan be him awriton þuss;
and eac on martira þrowungum we gemetað swa awriten.

Sum wif hatte Uen[us], seo wæs Ioues dohter,   150
swa fracod on galnysse þæt hire fæder hi hæfde,
and eac hire broðor, and oðre gehwylce,
on myltestrena wísan; ac hi wurðiað þa hæþenan
for [halige] gydenan, swa swa heora godes dohter.

Manega oþre god[a]s wæron mislice afundene,   155
and eac swilce gydenan, on swiðlicum wurðmynte
geond ealne middaneard, manncynne to forwyrde;
ac þas synd þa fyrmestan, þeah ðe hi fú(l)lice leofodan.
Se syrwienda deofol, þe swicað embe mancyn,

147–9 *om. T.* 147 awægde *S.* 148 heþænan *S.* 150 Sum ...
dohter] Seo uenus þe wæs Iouis dohtor wæs X^k. Sum] Sum man *S*,
followed directly by mid godre gebysnunge, *line* 645b, *probably because of lost
leaves in an ancestral MS.* uenus $CLWX^k(T)$; uena on leden, þæt is on denisc
fricga *R* (*cf.* 177). seo] ðe *L.* iouis *C.* dohtor $CWX^k(T)$; dohͭ *L.*
151 fraced *L*; wracod *C.* 152 broðor] *End of excerpts in* X^k, *which adds*: Nu
mæg her manna gehwilc gehyran hwet þas swæmas wæron þe hæþene weorþodon
and ure yldran him to gebædon: gode lof þæt we þas ne kunnan and þæt heora
gemýnd is adilegod. 153 myltustrena *L.* 154 halige] *sic CLW*;
healice *R(T). See note.* dohtor *CW*; dohͭ *L.* 155 Monega *Ke.* godas] *sic
CLW(T)*; godes *R.* afundenæ *C.* 156 -licum] -lice *C.* wurðmunte *L.*
157 -eard] -geard *Ke.* 158 formestan *C.* fullice *CLW; first* l *erased and
accent added R;* fúlice (*T*). 159 syrwigenda *CLW.*

Glosses in R and S, Latin: 147 awægede: mutati *R; commoti RS.* 148 þe:
qui (*for* quos) *S.* 149 þrowungum: passione *S. Hereafter until* 645b *S
has nothing; all glosses* 150–645a *from R.* 150 on leden (*added in R*): latino.
150 marg. vena, frica. (*Both MSS. have names of gods and other topics in margin;
ordinarily of no interest and not reported.*) 151 fracod: fragilis. 153 myltestrena: meretrici. 154, 156 gydenan: dee. 156 swilce: tales.
swiðlicum: vehementi. 157 forwyrde: damnatione. 159 syrwienda:
insidiator. swicað: decipit, fraudatur.

150–3 [*De Corr. Rust.* § 7] Alius etiam dæmon Venerem se esse confinxit,
quæ fuit mulier meretrix. Non solum cum innumerabilibus adulteris, sed etiam
cum patre suo, Iove, et cum fratre suo, Marte, meretricata est.

155–8 [*Not directly stated in De Corr. Rust.*]

159 65 [*In the Latin it has been stated at the beginning that the devil and his
subordinate demons have taken the names of wicked men and women in order to
mislead mankind. Ælfric has omitted this, but recalls it partially in producing his
own version of the opening of* § 8] Ecce tales fuerunt illo tempore isti perditi
homines, quos ignorantes rustici per adinventiones suas pessimas honorabant,
quorum vocabula ideo sibi dæmones adposuerunt, ut ipsos quasi deos colerent
et sacrificia illis offerrent et ipsorum facta imitarentur, quorum nomina invoca-
bant.

C 2710.2   O

gebrohte þa hæþenan on þæt healice gedwyld,   160
þæt hi swa fúle menn him fundon to godum,
þe þa leahtras lufodan, þe liciað þam deofle,
þæt eac heora biggengan heora bysmor lufodan,
and ælfremede wurdan fram þam ælmihtigan Gode,
se ðe leahtras onscunað, and lufað þa clænnysse.   165
Hi gesettan eac þa þære sunnan and þam monan,
and þam oðrum godum, ælcum his dæg:
ærest þære sunnan þone Sunnandæg,
and syððan þam monan þone Monandæg;
and þone þriddan dæg *hi þeowdan Marte,   *p, 148
heora feoht[e]-gode, him to fultume.   171
þone feorþan dæg hi sealdan, him to frofre,
þam foresædan Mercurie, heora mæran gode.
þone fiftan dæg hi freolsodan mærlice,
Ioue to wyrðmynte, þam mærestan gode.   175
Ðone sixtan dæg hi gesetton þære sceamleasan gydenan
Uen[us] gehaten, and Fric[g] on Denisc.
þone seofoðan dæg hi sealdan Saturne þam ealdan,
þæra goda fæder, him sylfum to frofre,
endenexð swaþeah, þeah he yldost wære.   180

161 fundon to godum] to godum gecuran (*T*). *End of Wulfstan's revision of Ælfric, His brief conclusion is independent.*   163 bigencgan *C*; biggencgan *Ke*. bismær *C*.   164 ælfre'mæ'de *L*.   wurdor (*!*) *C*   165 leahtres *C*. 166 þæra *W* (þære *em. Un*; ðære *Ke*), *L*.   þam] þa *W*, *Ke* (þam *em. Un*). 168 þonæ *C*.   sunandæg *C*.   170 ðridan *L*.   þeodon *L*.   171 feohte] *sic CLW* (feohtegode *as one word Un*); feohta *R*. *See note.*   172 feorðan] feorðe *C*.   173 mercuriæ *W* (Mercurie *Ke*); mærcurie *C*; mercurige *L*. 175 wurð- *CW*.   -mente *C*.   mærostan *W*.   176 syxtan *Ke*.   scam- *W* (sceam- *Ke*), *C*.   177 uenus *CLW*; uena *R*.   fricg *CL*; frycg *W*; fricge *R*. 178 seofanðan *L*.   180 endenext *L*.   þeah] þeah þe *W*.   yldest *W*.

Glosses in R, Latin: 160 healice: precipuo, summo.   gedwyld: errore. 162 leahtras: crimina.   163 biggengan: cultores.   164 ælfremede: alieni. 165 leahtras: crimina.   onscunað: abominatur.   166 *Marginal heading*: De institutione dierum.   167 godum: deos.   170 þeowdan: seruierunt. 171 feohta gode: preliatore.   174 freolsodan: celebrabant.   176 sceam- leasan: impudica (*sic*).   gydenan: dee.   180 endenexð: vltimus.
ME: 164 wurdan: weren.

166–80 [*Partly from De Corr. Rust.* § *8*] Homines infideles . . . Deum habent iratum et non ex toto corde in fide Christi credunt, sed sunt dubii in tantum ut nomina ipsa dæmoniorum in singulos dies nominent, et appellent diem Martis et Mercurii et Iovis et Veneris et Saturni, qui nullum diem fecerunt, sed fuerunt homines pessimi et scelerati in gente Græcorum.

Hi woldan [g]it wurðian arwurðlicor þa godas,
and forgeafon him steorran, swilce hi ahton heora geweald:
þa syfan tunglan, sunnan and monan,
and þa oðre fíf, þe farað æfre
ongean þone róder to eastdæle werd,   185
ac hi gebigð seo heofon underbæc æfre.
Ac þa steorran swaþeah scinon on heofonum
on frymþe middaneardes, ær þa mánfullan godas
wurdon acennede, oððe gecorene to godum.
Hi worhtan eac anlicnyssa þam arwurþum godum,   190
sume of smætum golde, and þa asmeadan mid cræfte,
sume of hwitum seolfre, sume eac of stanum,
sume of mislicum antimbre, be þam þe heora mihta wæron;
and him hús arærdon, þæt hi heton tempel,
and þarinne gelogodan heora leofan godas   195
mid leade gebundene, and [gebædon hi] þarto.
þa gesawon þa deoflu, þe hi beswicon on ǽr,

181 git] sic CW; gyt L; þagit R.   183 seofon CW; seofan L.   184 þe]
þa W.   185 rodor LW; roðer C.   wærd C; weard L.   186 seo] sic
RCLW; se em. Un. See note.   undær- C.   189 wurdon acennede] acennede
wurdon C.   190 onlicnissa C.   arwurðan C.   191 smætum] last word
f. 240ᵛ in W, cet. desunt (Ke supplies golde to complete the phrase).   193 sume]
sume eac C.   194 templ CL.   195 godas] godes C.   196 gebædon hi] sic CL; hi gebædon R.   197 deofla L.

Glosses in R, Latin: 181 git: adhuc.   182 swilce: quasi.   183 syfan
tunglan: vii. planete (marg.)   185 roder: firmamentum.   187 scinon:
lucebant.   188 manfullan: iniqui.   189 acennede: nati.   gecorene:
electi.   190 anlicnyssa: simulacra.   arwurþum: pio (sic).   191 þa: illa.
193 antimbre: materia; in marg., metallo, matera (sic).   be þam þe: pro ut.
194 heton: vocabant.   195 gelogodan: posuerunt, composuerunt.
196 leade: plumbo.   197 þa: tunc.
ME: 186 gebigð: turnð, drauh (?).   189 wurdon: weren.

181–6 [Cf. Bede, De Temporum Ratione, VIII] Verum gentiles cum observa-
tionem a populo Israhel hebdomadis ediscerent, mox hanc in laudem suorum
deflexere deorum, . . . eisdem utique monstris suos dies, quibus et errantia sidera
consecrantes. [Bede, De Natura Rerum, XII] Inter cælum terramque septem
sidera pendent . . . quæ vocantur errantia, contrarium mundo agentia cursum, id
est, lævum, illo semper in dextram præcipiti. [See note.]
190–6 [De Corr. Rust. § 8] Suaserunt etiam illis dæmones, ut templa illis
facerent et imagines vel statuas sceleratorum hominum ibi ponerent et aras illis
constituerent.
197–201 [Isidore, Etym. VIII, cap. xi] Simulacrorum usus exortus est, cum ex
desiderio mortuorum constituerentur imagines vel effigies, tanquam in cælum
receptis: pro quibus se in terris dæmones colendos supposuerunt, et sibi sacri-
ficari a deceptis et perditis persuaserunt.

þa fægran anlicnyss[a], and flugon þarto,
and þurh þa anlicnyssa spræcon to þam earmum mannum,
and hi swa forlæddon mid heora leasungum,   200
and to hellicum suslum heora sawla gebrohtan.
Smiðas hi worhtan sm[e]alice mid cræfte,
and oft gesealdon *þa sylfrenan godas,   *p. 149
sumne to maran wurðe, be þam þe he gemacod wæs,
sumne eac waclicor, be þam þe his wurð wæs.   205
And swa lange swa he slóh þone samworhtan god,
and mid his græfseaxe holode hetelice þa eagan,
ne stód him nan ege for þære anlicnysse;
ac þonne heo geworht wæs, he wurðode hi for god.

We rædað on þære béc þe is *Liber Regum* geháten   210
þæt þa hæðenan Philistei fuhton gelome
wið þæt Israhela folc, þe ana þa gelyfde
on þone ælmihtigan God, on Abrahames wisan.
þa on sumne sæl gelamp hit for heora synnum, swaþeah,
þæt þa hæþenan fuhton on þam folce sige,   215
and *arcam Domini* gelæhtan—þæt is Drihtnes scrín,
on þam scrine [wæs] gehealden se heofonlica mete,
and Áárones gyrd, þæs æreston bisceopes,
and Moyses tabulan, þe on þam munte wæron

---

198 fægeran *CL.*   -nyssa] *sic CL*; -nysse *R.*   200 hi swa] swa hi *L.*
leasungam (*or* -an?) *C.*   201 suslum] pine *L.*   sawle *L.*   202 Smiðos *C.*
smealice] *sic CL*; smalice *R.*   207 -sexe *CL.*   hetelice þa eagan] his eagan
hetelice *C.*   208 for] of *C.*   210 rædeð *C.*   bec] boc *L.*   212 þe] þa *C.*
gelefdon *C*   213 abrames *L.*   214 synnan *C.*   215 hæþenan] *om. L.*
fuhton] gefuhton *C* (*rightly?*).   sigæ *C.*   216 gelahton *C.*   217 on]
On *L.*   wæs] *sic CL*; *om. R.*   gehealdon *C.*   heofenlice *L.*   218 ærestan
CL.   bisceopas *C.*

Glosses in R, Latin: 200 forlæddon: deceperunt.   201 suslum: supplicio.
202 smalice: subtiliter.   204 wurðe: precio.   205 waclicor: vilius.
wurð: precium.   209 wurðode: adorabat.   212 þe: que.   214 on
sumne sæl: aliqua vice.   215 sige: victoriam.   217 gehealden: seruatur,
but in marg., custodiebant.   218 gyrd: virga.

ME: 200 forlæddon: bicherden.   206 samworhtan: halfmak[ede], *ending
cut off by binder.*

214-16 [*I Reg.* (*I Sam.*) *iv. 10, 11*] Pugnaverunt ergo Philisthiim, et cæsus est
Israel, ... et ceciderunt de Israel triginta millia peditum. Et arca Dei capta est.

217-20 [*Heb. ix. 4*] ... et arcam testamenti circumtectam ex omni parte auro,
in qua urna aurea habens manna (*Ex. xvi. 33*) et virga Aaron quæ fronduerat
(*Num. xvii. 10*), et tabulæ testamenti (*II Par. vi. 11; Deut. x. 2; Ex. xxv. 16,
xl. 18*).

mid Godes fingre awritene, his folce to láre. 220
þa ferodon þa hæþenan þæt foresæde scrín
mid þam heofonlican haligdome ham to heora temple,
and settan hit þa arwurðlice up to heora gode,
se god hatte Dagón, þam hæþenum swyðe dyre.
Eft þa on ærnemergen, þa þa hy inn eodan, 225
þa fundon hi heora god on þære flore licgende
ætforan þam Godes scríne, swylce he friðes bæde.
Hi hofan eft þa Dagón to þam Drihtnes scríne,
þær þær he ær stód, and stopan him þanon.
Coman þa eft on mergen, and cunnodan hu hit wære; 230
þa wæs Dagones heafod æt þære dura forcorfen,
and his twa handbreda ahéawene æt þam þerrscwalde,
and Dagón læg heafodleas ætforan þam [halgan] scrine,
for þam *þe hit ne gedafenode þære deofollican anlicnysse *p. 150
þæt heo wið þæt halige scrín swa healice stode. 235
þa sende God sona mid graman to þære leode

---

220 fringre L.   folce] folc C.   222 heofen- C.   223 þa] om. L.   godæ
C.   224 se] and þe L.   heðenum C.   dyre] leof C.   225 -morgæn C;
-morgen L.   eodan] eodon (eoden C) to þam temple CL.   226 flore] flora C.
licgende] licgan CL.   228 eft] om. L.   eft þa] ða eft C.   230 morgen C.
231 wæs] þæs C.   232 aheawene] aheawen CL.   þrexwolde CL.   233 hal-
gan] sic CL; om. R.   234 gedafnode L; geðafnode C.   deoflican CL
(rightly?).   235 halige] halig C.   236 sænde C.

Glosses in R, Latin: 222 haligdome: sanctuario.   223 arwurðlice:
honorifice.   224 dyre: carus.   228 þa: tunc.   229 stopan: ibant.
230 cunnodan: probauerunt.   232 handbreda: palme.   þerrscwalde: limite.
234 gedafnode: decuit.   235 wið: iuxta.   236 leode: Gente.
ME: 221 ferodon: berren, beren.   227 friðes: treoucas.

221–33 [I Reg. v. 1–5] Philisthiim autem tulerunt arcam Dei, et asportaverunt
eam . . . in Azotum . . . et intulerunt eam in templum Dagon, et statuerunt
eam iuxta Dagon. Cumque surrexissent diluculo Azotii altera die, ecce Dagon
iacebat pronus in terra ante arcam Domini; et tulerunt Dagon, et restituerunt
eum in locum suum. Rursumque mane die altera consurgentes, invenerunt
Dagon iacentem super faciem suam in terra coram arca Domini; caput autem
Dagon, et duæ palmæ manuum eius abscissæ erant super limen; porro Dagon
solus truncus remanserat in loco suo. . . .
236–48 [Ibid. 6–9, 12] Aggravata est autem manus Domini super Azotios, et
demolitus est eos. . . . Et ebullierunt villæ et agri in medio regionis illius, et nati
sunt mures, et facta est confusio mortis magnæ in civitate. Videntes autem viri
Azotii huiuscemodi plagam, dixerunt: Non maneat arca Dei Israel apud nos.
. . . Et mittentes congregaverunt omnes satrapas Philisthinorum ad se, et dixerunt: Quid faciemus de arca Dei Israel? Responderuntque Gethæi: Circum-
ducatur arca Dei Israel. [Their five cities (line 243) are enumerated at vii. 17.]

færlicne manncwealm, and þa Philisteos acwealde,
for þam þe hi hæfdon þæt halige scrín
þær on heora hæþenscipe, swylce hy hit habban woldon.
Him comon eac mýs tó, manega geond þæt land,   240
and heora æceras aweston, and þone eard fordydon.
Ða gecwædon þa landleodan þæt hi lædan woldan
þæt Godes scrin him fram, geond [heora] fíf burga,
fram scíre to scíre, þæt se cwealm geswice.
Hi ferodan þa þæt scrín geond þa fíf burga,   245
and swa hwar swa hit becóm, swa [com] se cwealm sóna
and mid færlicum deaðe þa Philistheos acwealde,
and hi earmlice hrymdon for þam reþan deaþe.
Hi axodan þa heora witan hwæt him wislicost þuhte,
hu him to donne wære embe þæt halige scrín,   250
hwæðer hi hit hám asendon, oððe hi hit hæfdon þar leng.
Ða andwyrdon þa witan þam axiendan þuss:
Gif ge þæt halige scrín hám sendan wyllað,
ne sende ge hit na æmtig, ac arwurðlice mid lacum.
Foð nu togædere of eower fíf burgum,   255
and wyrcað Gode to lace fíf gyldene hringas

---

237 þa] *om. L.*   239 heore *C.*   heðen- *C.*   240 Heom *C.*   eac
mys to] to eac mys *C.*   242 gecwe'a'don *C.*   -leodan] -leoda *CL.*
243 heora] *sic CL*; þa *R.*   246 com] *sic CL*; *om. R.*   247 færlicum]
þam færlicum *L.*   philisteos *CL.*   249 witan] wysan witan *L.*
250 donna *L.*   251 asendon] sendon *CL.*   læng *C.*   252 *and*werdon *L.*
axiendu*m C*; axigendu*m L.*   253 sændan *C*; sendon *L.*   255 togadere *L.*
eower] eowru*m CL.*   256 gildene *L.*

Glosses in R, Latin: 239 þær: ibi.   240 mys: mures.   geond: p*er.*
241 aweston: exterminaba*nt.*   fordydon: damnaba*nt.*   242 landleodan:
incoli.   243 geond: p*er.*   244 geswice: cessar*et.*   245 geond: p*er.*
248 reþan: cr*u*deli.   249 witan: sapientes.   252 witan: sapientes.
253, 254 ge: vos.   254 æmtig: vacuus.   arwurðlice: honorifice.

Et circumduxerunt arcam Dei Israel. Illis autem circumducentibus eam, fiebat
manus Domini per singulas civitates interfectionis magnæ nimis. . . . Fiebat
. . . pavor mortis in singulis urbibus, . . . et ascendebat ululatus uniuscuiusque
civitatis in cælum.
    249–58 [*I Reg. vi. 2–5*] Et vocaverunt Philisthiim sacerdotes et divinos,
dicentes: Quid faciemus de arca Domini? Indicate nobis quomodo remittamus
eam in locum suum. Qui dixerunt: Si remittitis arcam Dei Israel, nolite dimittere
eam vacuam, sed quod debetis reddite ei pro peccato. . . . Iuxta numerum
provinciarum Philisthinorum quinque anos aureos facietis, et quinque mures
aureos, quia plaga una fuit omnibus vobis, et satrapis vestris. . . .

and fif gyldene mys, þæt se grama geswíce,
for þam þe eow eallum wæs an wite gemæne.
Wyrcað eac ænne wæn wurðlice to þam scríne,
and ane níwe cæpsan eowrum lacum to fætelse,   260
and nimað twá geonge cý, þe under iuce ne cómon,
þæt hi þæt halige scrín ham ferian magon
mid þam gyldenum lacum þe ge Gode geoffriað,
and healdað þa cealfas æt hám getígede;
þonne mage ge tocnawan, gyf þa cy willað   265
gán forð on *þone weg fram heora cealfum,   *p. 151
þæt hit Godes yrre wæs þe éow swa geswencte.
Gif hi þonne gan nellað mid þæs Godes scríne heonon,
þonne mage ge tocnawan þæt se cwealm næs forþi,
þurh Godes yrre, ac gelamp elles.   270
Hwæt, þa Philistei þa fengon to þam ræde,
and geworhton fif hringas of heora fif burhgum,
and fif gyldene mýs, and macodan þone wæn
mid ealre þære fare, and geforþodan þæt scrín.
þa eodan þa iungan cý, geiucode to þam wæne,   275

---

258 eallon *C.*   260 niwæ *C.*   261 iunge *CL.*   iuce] *sic CL*; guce *altered to* iuce *R.*   262 ferigan *L.*   264 getigede] *sic CL*; i *altered to* e *R.*   265 maga *L.*   267 geswæncte *C.*   268 heonon *C*; henon *L.*   269 magon *C.*   271 fiengon (*!*) *C.*   272 burgum *CL.*   273 guldene *C.*   274 þæra *C.*   275 geongan *C.*

Glosses in R, Latin: 257 mys: mures.   258 wite: pena.   259 wæn: currum.   260 cæpsan: hespetecam.   fætelse: vase.   261 cy: vaccas. iuce: iugo.   263, 265 ge: vos.   265 cy: vacce.   267 wæs: fuit. geswencte: fatigauit.   268 heonon: inde.   269 ge: vos.   270 elles: alia de causa.   273 wæn: currum.   275 wæne: curru.

ME: 259 wæn: wein.   273 wæn: wein.   275 geiucode: iʒeokede, iʒokede.

259–70 [*Ibid.* 7–9] Et facite plaustrum novum unum; et duas vaccas fetas, quibus non est impositum iugum, iungite in plaustro, et recludite vitulos earum domi. Tolletisque arcam Domini, et ponetis in plaustro, et vasa aurea, quæ exsolvistis ei pro delicto, ponetis in capsellam ad latus eius, et dimittite eam ut vadat. Et aspicietis: et siquidem per viam finium suorum ascenderit contra Bethsames, ipse fecit nobis hoc malum grande; sin autem minime, sciemus quia nequaquam manus eius tetigit nos, sed casu accidit.

271–81 [*Ibid.* 10–12] Fecerunt ergo illi hoc modo; et tollentes duas vaccas, quæ lactabant vitulos, iunxerunt ad plaustrum, vitulosque earum concluserunt domi, et posuerunt arcam Dei super plaustrum, et capsellam, quæ habebat mures aureos et similitudines anorum. Ibant autem in directum vaccæ per viam quæ ducit Bethsames, et itinere uno gradiebantur, pergentes et mugientes, et non declinabant neque ad dexteram neque ad sinistram; sed et satrapæ Philisthiim sequebantur usque ad terminos Bethsames.

to Israhela lande, hlowende swiðe
æfter heora cealfum, and ne gecyrdon swaþeah
of þan rihtan wege, swilce hi gewittige wæron.
And þa Philistei folgodan þam wæne
to Israhela lande, and forleton hit þar;   280
and se manncwealm geswác þa, and þæra músa gedrecednyss.
Israhel eac þa beah anmodlice to Gode,
and God hi þa geheold wið ða hæþenan leoda,
and him sige forgeaf, þæt hi slogon heora fynd,
and on sibbe wunodan on Samuheles dæge.   285
Hér we magon tocnáwan be þam hæðenum godum,
hwilce mihte hi hæfdon ongean þone ælmihtigan God.
Hi ne synd na godas, ac synd gramlice deofla,
sawla bepæcendras and synna ordfruman,
þe heora biggengan gebringað into þam bradan fýre   290
hellicre cwylminge, þanon hi ne cumað næfre.
    Us is eac fulcuð be þam þrim cnihtum
on Chaldea rice, þe se cyning awearp
into byrnendum ófne, for þam þe hi ne bugon to his godum
fram þam ælmihtigan Gode, þe ealle þing gescéop.   295
God hi eac ahredde wið ðone gramlican cyning,
swa þæt heora fex furþon on þam fyre næs forswæled,
ac eodan him singende on þam swegendan líge,
hergende heora Drihten, and ungederode þurhwunodan.

278 þan] þam L.   281 gedrecced- L.   283 leode C.   284 him]
hým (!) L.   285 samueles L.   286 tocnawon L.   288 godes C.
deofle C.   290 bigængas C; bigengas L.   292 þrym L.   293 cyning]
cyning nabugodonosor L.   294 bugon] gebugon L.   297 heora fex
furþon] furðon heora feox C.   feax L.   297–8 on þam fyre næs . . . on
þam] næs on þam, cet. om. (homœoteleuton) C.   299 herigende L.

Glosses in R, Latin: 278 gewittige: sensati.   281 musa gedrecednyss:
murium tribulatio.   282 beah: conuertit.   anmodlice: vnanimiter.
283 geheold: custodiebat.   leoda: Gente.   284 sige: victoriam.
285 sibbe: pace.   289 bepæcendras: deceptores.   290 biggengan:
cultores.   291 cwylminge: supplicio.   294 ofne: clibano, camino.
bugon: conuerterunt.   297 furþon: eciam.   299 ungederode: illesi.
    ME: 284 fynd: feond.

282–5 [I Reg. vii. 4, 13, 14] Abstulerunt ergo filii Israel Baalim et Astaroth,
et servierunt Domino soli. . . . Et humiliati sunt Philisthiim; . . . facta est
itaque manus Domini super Philisthæos, cunctis diebus Samuelis. . . . Libera-
vitque Israel de manu Philisthinorum, eratque pax inter Israel et Amorrhæum.
    292–9 [A free epitome of Dan. iii, including the Prayer of Azarias and the
Song of the Three Children, Vulgate verses 24–90.]

*On þam ilcan lande wæs þa se witega Danihel,   *p. 152
Godes heahþegen, haliges lifes mann.   301
þa on Daries dagum gedemdon his witan
þæt binnan þrittigum dagum ne bæde nan mann
nane bene æt Gode, butan æt þam cyninge,
and woldan swa besyrwan þone unscyldigan Danihel,   305
for þon þe he wæs swyðe dyre Darige þam cinge.
Ða dyde se witega swa swa his gewuna wæs,
eode into his upflore, and feoll þær on cneowum,
and gebæd hyne to Gode, gebigedum [limum],
oðþæt þa hæþenan coman, þe his cepton georne.   310
Hi wregdon þa Danihel to Darige þam cinge,

300 *Here begins excerpt in* G, *ff. 44ᵛ–48ᵛ, Wa(rner) pp. 38/4–41/22.*   þam
ilcan lande] þære ilcan burh Babilonie þe we embe specað G.   ylcan CL.
þa] on daries dagen G.   wytege G.   daniel CGL (*a very frequent spelling in*
CGL; *not noted hereafter*).   301 hehðeign G.   302 þa] þa eft L.
on Daries dagum] *om.* G.   his] þa G.   wyten G.   302–3 gedemdon ...
dagum] *om.* C.   303 þrittigum dagum] þrittig dagen G.   nan mann] *om.* L.
305 besyrwian C.   306 dúre L; dere C.   cyninge CL; cynge G.
308 -flora L.   fel C.   þær] þære G.   309 gebegedum C; 'on' gebeg-
den G.   limum] *sic* CL; lymen G; cneowum 'vel limum' (*original scribe*) R.
310 his cepton] *sic* RCGL; hiscewton Wa.   311 wreigdon G.   cyninge
CL; cynge G.

Glosses in R, Latin: 302 witan: sapientes.   305 besyrwan: insidiare.
306 dyre: carus.   308 upflore: solio.   309 gebigedum: flexis.
310 oðþæt: donec.   cepton: id est expectabant.   311 wregdon: accusabant.
ME: 305 unscyldigan: ungulti.

302–6 [*Dan. v. 31, vi. 4–7*] Et Darius Medus successit in regnum. . . . Porro
rex cogitabat constituere [Danielem] super omne regnum; unde principes et
satrapæ quærebant occasionem ut invenirent Danieli ex latere regis; nullamque
causam et suspicionem reperire potuerunt, eo quod fidelis esset. . . . Tunc . . . locuti
sunt [regi]: Dari rex, . . . consilium inierunt omnes principes . . . ut decretum
imperatorium exeat. . .: Ut omnis qui petierit aliquam petitionem a quocumque
deo et homine, usque ad triginta dies, nisi a te, rex, mittatur in lacum leonum.
307–10 [*Ibid. 10, 11*] Quod cum Daniel comperisset, id est, constitutam
legem, ingressus est domum suam; et . . . in coenaculo suo . . . flectebat genua
sua, et adorabat, confitebaturque coram Deo suo, sicut et ante facere consue-
verat. Viri ergo illi curiosius inquirentes, invenerunt Danielem orantem et
obsecrantem Deum suum.
311–22 [*Ibid. 12–18*] Et accedentes locuti sunt regi super edicto: Rex, numquid non constituisti ut omnis homo qui rogaret quemquam de diis et hominibus . . . nisi te, rex, mitteretur in lacum leonum? . . . Daniel . . . non curavit de
lege tua et de edicto quod constituisti, sed tribus temporibus per diem orat
obsecratione sua. Quod verbum cum audisset rex, satis contristatus est; et pro
Daniele posuit cor ut liberaret eum, et usque ad occasum solis laborabat ut
erueret illum. Viri autem illi . . . dixerunt ei: Scito, rex, . . . quia . . . omne

sædon þæt he forsáwe heora ealra gesetnysse,
and woldon hine besceofan into þæra leona seaþe.
[Ða swanc se cyning swiðe oð æfen,
wolde ðone witegan bewerian wið hi. 315
Ac ða ða he ne mihte na leng, ða let he hine niman
and wurpan þam leonum þe lagon on þam seaðe.]
þa cwæð Darius se cyning to Danihele þam witegan,
Ðin God þe þu wurðast wile þe aḥreddan.
And he þa geinseglade wiðutan þone seað, 320
and wearð swa sárig þæt he slapon ne mihte
on ealræ þære nihte, ne he ætes ne gymde.
Darius þa se cining on dægred arás,
eode to þam seaðe, and sarlice clypode,
Danihel, þu Godes mann, mihte la þin God 325
wið ða leon þe gehealdan? And he andwyrde sona,
þu leofa cining, leofa þu on écnysse;
min God me asende to sona his engel,
and he þæra leona muð beleac mid his bendum,

312 forsawe] forsege *G.*   ea'l're *L*; eallre *G.*   -nyssa *L.*   313 besceo-
fan] bescufen *G.*   314–17 *om. R; text from C, emended from L.*   314 cyng
GL.   oð æfen] *sic GL*; ofhæfen *C. See note.*   315 bewerigan *L.*   hi] heom
G.   316 læng *G.*   317 leonum] *sic L*; leonan *C.*   þe] þa *L.*   on] inne *G.*
second þam] *sic L*; ðan *CG.*   319 wyle *GL.*   320 -seglode *CL*, -segelode *G.*
321 slæpan *C*; slapan *L*; slæpen *G.*   322 ealre *CGL.*   ðæræ *C.*   gemde *G.*
323 cyning *C*; cyng *GL.*   dæigred *G.*   324 eode] and eode *GL.*
325 mihte] *om. L.*   326 andwyrde] andwerde *L*; andswarede þa *G.*
327 cyning *CL*; cyng *G.*   *second* leofa] lifa *L.*   328 asænde *C*; sænde *G.*
329 ðære *CGL.*   leone *CG.*

Glosses in R, Latin: 312 forsawe: *contem*sit.   gesetnysse: statuta, institu-
tio*nem.*   313 seaþe: lacu; *in margin,* lacu*m.*   320 geinseglade: sing-
nau*it.*   seað: lacu*m.*   322 gymde: gustauit.   323 dægred: aurora.
324 seaðe: lacu*m.*   325 mihte: potuit.   326 gehealdan: saluare.
327 *second* leofa: viue.

decretum quod constituerit rex, non liceat immutari. Tunc rex præcepit, et
adduxerunt Danielem, et miserunt eum in lacum leonum. Dixitque rex Danieli:
Deus tuus, quem colis semper, ipse liberabit te. Allatusque est lapis unus, et
positus est super os laci, quem obsignavit rex annulo suo. . . . Et abiit rex in
domum suam, et dormivit incoenatus; cibique non sunt allati coram eo,
insuper et somnus recessit ab eo.
323–32 [*Dan. vi. 19–22*] Tunc rex primo diluculo consurgens, festinus ad lacum
leonum perrexit; appropinquansque lacui, Danielem voce lacrymabili inclamavit,
et affatus est eum: Daniel, serve Dei viventis, Deus tuus, . . . putasne valuit te
liberare a leonibus? Et Daniel regi respondens, ait: Rex, in æternum vive! Deus
meus misit angelum suum, et conclusit ora leonum, et non nocuerunt mihi, quia
coram eo iustitia inventa est in me; sed et coram te, rex, delictum non feci.

[þæt] heora nan ne mihte minum limum derian,   330
for þan þe on me is afunden ætforan Gode rihtwisnyss,
and ic wið ðe, cyning, ne worhte nanne gylt.
Se cyning þa sóna swiðe þæs fægnode,
and het up atéon ardlice Danihel,
and þa in [a]wurpan þe hine wregdon ǽr.   335
Hi wurdan þa gebrohte mid bearnum and wifum,
and into þam seaðe sona aworpene,
and þa leon hi gelæhton, and heora lima totǽron,
ær þam þe hi furðan moston feallan adúne.
Ða sende se cyning sona ænne pistol   340
geond *ealle his leoda, and hi luflice grette,   *p. 153
þisum wordum awritene: Ic wille þæt min folc
on eallum minum ríce anmodlice buge
to Daniheles Gode, and hine ondrædon.
He is se lifigenda God, and éce on weorulde,   345
and his ríce ne bið towórpen on ecnysse.

---

330 þæt] sic CGL; 7 R.   minum limum] mine leome G.   331 ætforan
gode rihtwisnyss] rihtwisnyss ætforan gode L.   ætforen CG.   -nysse G.
332 nænne CGL.   335 awurpan] sic CL; awurpen G; wurpan R.   wrægdon
C; wreigdon G.   336 Hi] and hi C.   338 lima] lymen G.   339 Entire
line replaced by: mid grimme toðen ær heo on grund feollan G.   furðon C;
forðon L.   341 leode CG.   342 awritenne C.   343 eallum] altered
from ealle R; ealle G.   minum] mine L; minre G.   344 ondrædon]
ondræde L (grammatically correct).   345 is] his C.   lyfigenda C.   worulde
CL.   346 on ecnysse] næfre G.

Glosses in R, Latin: 333 fægnode: exultauit.   334 ardlice: mox.   335 þa:
illos.   336 bearnum: filiis.   337 seaðe: lacum.   338 gelæhton:
apprehenderunt.   339 furðan: eciam.   feallan: cadere.   adune: deorsum.
343 buge: conuertat.   344 ondrædon: metuant.   346 toworpen: de-
structum.
ME: 336 wurdan: weren.   346 toworpen: destrut (or meant for destruc-
tum, as in marg.?).

333–9 [Ibid. 23, 24] Tunc vehementer rex gavisus est super eo et Danielem
præcepit educi de lacu. . . . Iubente rege, adducti sunt viri illi, qui accusaverant
Danielem, et in lacum leonum missi sunt, ipsi, et filii, et uxores eorum; et non
pervenerunt usque ad pavimentum laci, donec arriperent eos leones, et omnia
ossa eorum comminuerunt.
340–9 [Ibid. 25–27] Tunc Darius rex scripsit universis populis . . .: Pax vobis
multiplicetur! A me constitutum est decretum ut in universo imperio et regno
meo, tremiscant et paveant Deum Danielis; ipse est enim Deus vivens, et
æternus in sæcula; et regnum eius non dissipabitur, et potestas eius usque in
æternum. Ipse liberator, atque salvator, faciens signa, et mirabilia in cælo et in
terra, qui liberavit Danielem de lacu leonum.

He is soð Alysend, and tacna Wyrcend
on heofonum and on eorðan, se ðe heold Danihel
wið þa reþan déor, þæt hi him derian ne mihton.

Danihel leofode þa swiðe leof þam cyninge,   350
oðþæt Cyrus cyning to þam cynedóme feng,
and Danihel wearð þa þæs cyninges gedrinca,
and he hine arwurðode ofer ealle his þegnas.

Þa wæs on Babilone, þære micclan byrig,
þæra hæþenra god, se wæs geháten Bél,   355
and hine man dæghwamlice fedde mid feowertigum sceapum,
and him man wín sealde, six sestras to þam dæge,
and twelf sestras melues to his metsunge.

Se cyning hine wurðode, and cóm ælce dæge
hine to gebiddanne to Bél þam gode;   360
and Danihel se snotra forseah þone Bél,
and gebæd hyne æfre to þam ælmihtigan Gode.

Ða axode se cyning on anum dæge Danihel,
Hwi nelt þu þe gebiddan to Béle þam gode?
þa andwerde Danihel anrædlice þam cyninge,   365

347 alesend G.   wyrcenda L; wyrecende G.   348 heold] geheold G.
349 ræðan C.   350 leofode . . . leof þam cyninge] lufode . . . þone cyng L.
353 arwurðode C.   his þegnas] þegnas his C.   354 þæra C.   355 þære
CG.   356 feowertig G.   after sceapum] and mid feower hryðerum L.
358 melues] melwæs C; meluwes L; melewes G.   359 dæge] dæg CL
(rightly?).   360 to] to 'to' (false correction in margin) G.   gebiddenne CL.
bel RCL; bele G; cf. 364.   361 snotera C; snotere GL.   forseh G.
363 point after dæge G; see note.   365 andwyrde C; andswarode G.

Glosses in R, Latin: 347 tacna wyrcend: singna faciens.   348 heold:
saluauit.   349 reþan: crudelis.   351 oðþæt: donec.   352 gedrinca:
pincerna (repeated in margin).   353 arwurðode: honorauit.   355 þæra:
eorum.   358 melues: farine.   361 snotra: prudens.   forseah: despicit
(for despexit?).   362 gebæd: adorauit.   365 anrædlice: constanter.

350–1 [Dan. vi. 28] Porro Daniel perseveravit usque ad regnum Darii, regnum-
que Cyri Persæ.

352–3 [Dan. xiv. 1] Erat autem Daniel conviva regis, et honoratus super
omnes amicos eius.

354–62 [Ibid. 2, 3] Erat quoque idolum apud Babylonios nomine Bel; et im-
pendebantur in eo per dies singulos similæ artabæ duodecim, et oves quadraginta,
vinique amphoræ sex. Rex quoque colebat eum, et ibat per singulos dies adorare
eum. Porro Daniel adorabat Deum suum.

363–9 [Ibid. 3, 4] Dixitque ei rex: Quare non adoras Bel? Qui respondens ait
ei: Quia non colo idola manufacta, sed viventem Deum, qui creavit cælum et
terram, et habet potestatem omnis carnis.

Ic nelle wurðian þa geworhtan godas,
ac ic gelyfe on þone lyfigendan God,
se þe heofonas and eorþan and ealle þing gesceop,
and hæfð þone anwald ealles flæsces.

Ða andwyrde se cyning eft þam witegan,   370
Ne þinc[ð] þe, la, Danihel, þæt þes deorwyrða Bél
sy lifiende g[o]d, nu he lyfað be mettum,
and dæghwamlice drincð þæt we him dóð to láce?

Ða [cwæð] Danihel, Ne dwela þu, cyning;
þes god is æren wiðútan agóten,   375
and læmen wiðinnan, and ne lyfað be mettum,
ne he næfre ne [æ]t oð ðisne and*wyrdan dæg.   *p. 154

þa geswearc se cyning sona on móde,
and hét þa biggengan þe Béle þeowdan
cuman to his spræce, and cwæð him þuss tó: 380
Buton ge me secgan þæt þæt soð is be þisum,
hwa þas mettas þicge þe we maciað Béle,
ealle ge sceolan sweltan, gif ic gesund beo.

---

366 wurðigean *L.*   367 geleue *C*; gelefe *G.*   368 þing] gesceaften *G.*
369 anweald *CL.*   370 andwyrde] andswerede *G.*   371 Ne] Hwu *G.*
þincð] *sic GL*; þinc *RC.*   -wurða *CL*; -wurðe *G.*   372 sy] ne sy *G.*
lyfigende *C*; lifigenda *L*; leofigende *G.*   god] *sic CGL*, gód *R.*   nu he lyfað]
Ne lyfeð he *G.*   leofað *C*; lifað *L.*   metum *L*; mete *G.*   373 dæghwom- *L.*
laca *G.*   374 cwæð] *sic CGL*; andwyrde *R.*   þu] þu la *G.*   375 wiðutan]
and wiðutan *C.*   376 lamen (*altered from* læmen?) *C.*   leofað *C*; lifað *L.*
metum *CL*; mete *G.*   377 æt] *sic CGL*; yt *R.*   -werdan *C*; -weardan *L.*
379 biggengan] bigencgas *CL*; biggengas *G.*   þeowdon *CL*; þeowwedon *G.*
381 þæt þæt] þæt *G.*   ðyssum *L*; þyssen *G.*   382 metas *L.*   machi-
geð *G.*   383 swyltan *L.*

Glosses in R, Latin: 369 flæsces: carnis.   372, 376 lyfað: viuit.   mettum:
cibis.   374 ne dwela: ne erres.   375 þes: iste.   æren: æeneus (*sic*).
376 læmen: lamineus.   377 yt: comedit.   oð: donec.   andwyrdan: pre-
senti.   378 geswearc: suspirauit (*!*).   379 biggengan: cultores.   þeowdan: ministrabant.   381, 383 ge: vos.   382 þicge: sumit.   383 gesund: incolumis, sospes.

370–7 [*Ibid.* 5, 6] Et dixit rex ad eum: Non videtur tibi esse Bel vivens deus?
An non vides quanta comedat et bibat quotidie? Et ait Daniel arridens: Ne
erres, rex; iste enim intrinsecus luteus est, et forinsecus æreus, neque comedit
aliquando.
378–88a [*Ibid.* 7, 8] Et iratus rex vocavit sacerdotes eius, et ait eis: Nisi
dixeritis mihi quis est qui comedat impensas has, moriemini. Si autem osten-
deritis quoniam Bel comedat hæc, morietur Daniel, quia blasphemavit in Bel.
Et dixit Daniel regi: Fiat iuxta verbum tuum.

Gif ge þonne æteowiað þæt he ytt þas mettas,
þonne sceal Daniel sweltan deaðe,   385
se þe tǽlde Bél and to bysmore hæfde.
Ða cwæð Danihel to þam cyninge þus:
Stande þin word, cyning. And hi stopon to þam temple.
þær wæron hundseofantig þara sacerda ealra,
þe þeowdon Bele on his biggengum simle.   390
þa cwædon hi ealle anmodlice to þam cinge,
We gað nu ealle út ætforan þe, cyning,
and sete þu sylf þa sanda him beforan,
and beluc þa duru, gyf þu us ne gelyfst,
and geinsegla þa locu mid þinum agenum hringe,   395
and þonne þu on ærnemergen in gæst and sceawast,
gif þás lac ne beoð bebrocene þurh Bél,
beo hit ure lifleast; and gif Bel hi geytt,
swelte þonne Danihel, þe swa hyne hyrwde.
Hi eodan þa ealle út ætforan þam cyninge,   400
and he sylf gelogode þa lác ætforan Bél;
and Danihel het syftan on þæs cyninges gesihthe

384 ytt] ett *G.*   metas *L.*   385 swyltan *L.*   386 bismore *C*; bise-
mære *G.*   388 cyning] *followed by incomplete* e *R.*   389 þæra *CL.*
390 bigencgum *L*; bigencge *C*; bigengen *G.*   391 cyninge *CL*; cynge *G.*
393 þu] þe *G.*   sande *GL.*   394 gelefst *G.*   395 locu] dure *G.*   age-
num] *om. G.*   hrincge *C*; ringe *G.*   396 þone *C.*   -morgen *CL*; -morgan *G.*
sceawast] gesceawast *L.*   397 þas] þa *G.*   bebrocene] gebrucene *G.*
398 lifleast] lifleaste *G.*   geyt *C.*   399 swylte *L.*   hyrwde] hyrewede *G.*
400 ealla *C.*   401 béle *L.*   402 gesihðe *CGL.*

Glosses in R, Latin: 384 ge: vos   æteowiað: ostendatis.   mettas: cibos.
386 tælde: vitup*er*auit.   389 þara: eor*um* (*over* ealra *by mistake*).   390 biggengum: cultus.   392 We gað: im*us.*   395 locu: claustra.   399 hyrwde:
blasfemauit, vitup*er*auit; *with marginal* hirwde: irritau*it.*   401 gelogode:
posuit.
ME: 402 syftan: siften.

388*b*–99 [*Dan. xiv. 9–11*] Erant autem sacerdotes Bel septuaginta.... Et venit
rex cum Daniele in templum Bel. Et dixerunt sacerdotes Bel: Ecce nos egredimur
foras; et tu, rex, pone escas, et vinum misce; et claude ostium, et signa annulo
tuo; et cum ingressus fueris mane, nisi inveneris omnia comesta a Bel, morte
moriemur, vel Daniel qui mentitus est adversum nos. . . .
400–10 [*Ibid. 13, 14*] Factum est igitur postquam egressi sunt illi, rex posuit
cibos ante Bel; præcepit Daniel pueris suis, et attulerunt cinerem, et cribravit
per totum templum coram rege; et ingressi clauserunt ostium et signantes annulo
regis abierunt. Sacerdotes autem egressi sunt nocte iuxta consuetudinem suam,
[*12* . . . quia fecerant sub mensa absconditum introitum,] et uxores et filii eorum,
et comederunt omnia, et biberunt.

axon geond þa flore, þæt he eft mihte tocnáwan
hwá on þa flor stópe þe onfenge þæs metes;
and se cyning þa [ge]inseglode ardlice þa dúru.   405
Hwæt, þa sacerdas þa, mid cildum and wifum,
eodan into ðam temple under þære eorðan,
ealle on þære nihte, and æton þone mete,
swa swa heora gewuna wæs, and þæt wín eal druncon,
and Bél heora god ne abát þær[a] lác[a].   410
*Eft þa on ærnemergen eode se cyning   *p. 155
mid Danihele to þam temple, and þa duru sceawode;
þa stód heo swa geinseglod swa swa hi hi on æfen forleton.
Hi geopenodan þa duru and in besáwon.
þa clypode se cyning, and cwæð to þære anlicnysse,   415
Mære eart þu, Bél, and mid þe nis nan facn.
Ða hloh Danihel, and gel[et]te þone cyning,
þæt he in ne eode, and axode hine þuss:
Hwæt þincð þe, la cyning? hwæþer þú mage tocnáwan
hwæs fotlæsta þu geseo on þissere flore astapene?   420
þa beheold se cyning, and cwæð to Danihele,

403 axan CL; axen G.   þa flore] þa flor C; da flor L; þone flor G.
403–4 þæt . . . stope] added by original scribe of C, who first skipped þæt . . . flor
and wrote stowe for stope.   404 þa] þone CG.   405 ge-] sic CGL;
om. R.   406 cildum and wifum] wifen and cilden G.   cildrum L.
407 under þære eorðan] om. L.   under] urder C.   409 druncen L;
druncan G.   410 Bel] be C.   þæra laca] þære lac R; þære lace CL; þære
lacan G. See note.   411 þa] om. G.   -morgen L; -moregan G.   after cyning]
to L.   413 hi hi] hi hig C.   414 besawon] besegan G.   416 þu] þu la G.
facn] facne G.   417 gelette] sic CGL; gelæhte R.   419 þincð] þinc L.
mage] muge G.   tocnawan] gecnawen G.   420 hwæs] hwæ't' G.   þissere]
ðysre L; þyssen G.   flora C.   astapene] gestapone G.

Glosses in R, Latin: 403 axon: cineres.   404 þe onfenge: qui acceperunt.
405 ardlice: mox.   410 ne abat: non comedit.   412 sceawode: vidit.
413 geinseglod: singnata.   hi hi: illi eam.   on æfen: vespere.   414 in
besawon: introspexerunt.   415 anlicnysse: simulacro.   416 facn: dolus,
fraus.   417 hloh: risit.   420 fotlæsta: vestigium.

411–20 [Ibid. 15–18] Surrexit autem rex primo diluculo, et Daniel cum eo.
Et ait rex: Salvane sunt signacula, Daniel? Qui respondit: Salva, rex. Statimque
cum aperuisset ostium, intuitus rex mensam, exclamavit voce magna: Magnus
es, Bel, et non apud te dolus quisquam. Et risit Daniel, et tenuit regem ne in-
grederetur intro, et dixit: Ecce pavimentum; animadverte cuius vestigia sint
hæc.
421–31 [Ibid. 19–21] Et dixit rex: Video vestigia virorum, et mulierum et
infantium. Et iratus est rex. Tunc apprehendit sacerdotes, . . . et ostenderunt
ei abscondita ostiola per quæ ingrediebantur, et consumebant quæ erant super

Ic geseo on þisum axum ealdra manna stapas,
wífa and cilda. And he wearþ ða yrre.
He het þa gelæccan þa leasan sacerdos,
and hi þa unþances æteowdon him þa duru   425
under þære flore, þar hi inn eodan,
and þone mete þigdon þe wæs gemynt þam gode.
Ða het se cynin[g] sóna ofslean hi ealle,
and betæhte þone god to Daniheles dóme.
þa tobræc Danihel Bél þone g[o]d,   430
and towearp his tempel unwurðlice eall.
þa wæs on þære byrig gcwunod an draca,
and þa Babiloniscan bæron him mete,
and hine for god wurðodan, þeah þe he wyrm wære.
Ða cwæð se cyning sume dæg to Danihele þuss: 435
Ne miht þu nu cweþan þæt þes ne sy cucu god;
gebide þe to him, þeah þe þu to Bele noldest.
þa andwyrde Danihel [ðus eaðelice þam cyninge]:
Ic gebidde me æfre to þam ælmihtigon Gode,
se þe is lyfigende God; and gif þu me leafe sylst,   440
ic ofslea þisne dracan buton swurde and stafe.

422 axum] axe L.   423 cildra CL; cildre G.   wearþ] gewearð G.   yrre]
urre L; eorre G.   424 sacerdas CL; sacerdes G.   426 þære] ðæra L; þan
G.   flore] flora CL.   þar] þær C; þære G.   427 þigdon] þycgden G.   goden
G.   428 cyning] sic CL; cynin R; cyng G.   430 god] sic GL; gód RC.
431 templ C.   433 babyloniscan C.   bæron him mete] him mete
bæron G.   434 þeah þe] þeh G.   wurm CL; wyrem G.   435 dæg]
dæige G.   436 cweðen C.   cucu] cwice G.   437 þeah þe] þeh G.
438 andwyrde] andwerde L; andswarode G.   ðus eaðelice þam cyninge L,
C (þan), G (þuss eðelice þan cynge); þam cininge þus eaðelice R.   439 ælmihtigan CL; ælmihtigen G.   440 leafe] geleafe G.

Glosses in R, Latin: 422 ealdra: senior*um.*   424 leasan: falsos.
425 æteowdon: ostendeba*nt.*   427 þigdon: su*m*seru*nt.*   429 þone:
illu*m.*   431 towearp: destruxit.   432 draca: Draco (*margin as heading*).
434 wurðodan: adoraba*nt.*   436 cucu god: uiuus d*e*us.   437 gebide þe
to him: adora eu*m.*   439 gebidde: adoro.
ME: 427 þigdon: eten.

mensam. Occidit ergo illos rex, et tradidit Bel in potestatem Danielis, qui subvertit eum et templum eius.
432–41 [*Dan. xiv. 22–25*] Et erat draco magnus in loco illo, et colebant eum
Babylonii. Et dixit rex Danieli: Ecce nunc non potes dicere quia iste non sit Deus
vivens; adora ergo eum. Dixitque Daniel: Dominum Deum meum adoro, quia
ipse est Deus vivens; iste autem non est Deus vivens. Tu autem, rex, da mihi
potestatem, et interficiam draconem absque gladio et fuste.

Ða cwæð Cyrus se cyning þæt he cunnian moste
gif he butan wæpnum *mihte þone wurm acwellan.   *p. 156
Danihel þa worhte þam dracan þas lác:
he nam pic and rysel, and punode togædere,   445
and mid byrstum gemengde, and berode to welerum,
and seað hi swiðe, and sealde þam dracan.
Ða tobærst he sóna swa he abát þæs metes,
and Danihel cwæð þa to þæs dracan biggengum,
Nu ge magon geseon hwæne ge swa wurðodan.   450
þa wurdon geæbyligde þa Babiloniscan þearle,
and cómon to þam cyninge, and cwædon mid graman,
þes ælþeodega Danihel hæfð þinne anwald genumen;
he is cyning geworden; he acwealde þone dracan,
and urne Bél he towéarp, and his biggengan he ofsloh;   455
betæce hine nú us, elles we þe ofsleað.
Ða ne mihte se cyning wiðcweðan him eallum,
ac betæhte þone witegan þam witle[a]sum folce,

---

442 cunnian moste] moste cunnian *L.*   443 wyrm *G.*   445 pich *G.*
rysl *CL*; hrysel *G.*   togadere *L.*   446 byrston *L*; byrsten *G.*   gemængde
G.   berede *CG.*   welru*m L*; weleren *G.*   449 cwæd *C.*   bigencgu*m*
C; bige*n*gum *L*; boggengan *G.*   450 magon] mugen *G.*   hwæne] hwan *G.*
451 wurðen *G.*   geæbyligde] gebolgene *G.*   452 cwæðen *CG.*   453 ælðe-
odiga *CL*; ælðeodige *G.*   danihiel *L.*   andweald *C*; anweald *GL.*   455 bigencgas *C*; bigengas *L*; biggenges *G.*   *second* he] *om. CL.*   456 betæce]
Betæh *G.*   457 wiðcweðen *C.*   heo*m CG.*   458 witleasum] *sic CL*; wit-
lease *G*; witlesum *R.*

Glosses in R, Latin: 442 cunnian: probare.   445 rysel: adipe*m vel* pingue-
dine*m.*   449 biggengum: cultorib*us.*   450 ge: vos (*twice*).   hwæne:
que*m.*   451 geæbyligde: in*di*ngnati.   þearle: valde.   453 þes: iste.
ælþeodega: alienigena.   455 towearp: destruxit.   biggengan: cultores.
456 betæce: tradite.   elles: sin aute*m.*   458 witlesum: furioso, i*n*sensato.
ME: 446 byrstum: burstles.   welerum: balles.

442–50 [*Ibid. 25, 26*] Et ait rex: Do tibi. Tulit ergo Daniel picem, et adipem, et
pilos; et coxit pariter, fecitque massas, et dedit in os draconis; et diruptus est
draco. Et dixit: Ecce quem colebatis.
451–63 [*Ibid. 27–31*] Quod cum audissent Babylonii, indignati sunt vehementer; et congregati adversum regem, dixerunt: Iudæus factus est rex; Bel
destruxit, draconem interfecit, et sacerdotes occidit. Et dixerunt, cum venissent
ad regem: Trade nobis Danielem, alioquin interficiemus te et domum tuam.
Vidit ergo rex quod irruerent in eum vehementer, et necessitate compulsus,
tradidit eis Danielem. Qui miserunt eum in lacum leonum; et erat ibi diebus
sex. Porro in lacu erant leones septem, et dabantur eis duo corpora quotidie, et
duæ oves; et tunc non data sunt eis, ut devorarent Danielem.

and hi hine wurpan in to þam wilderon,
þar wæron syfon leon, and he þar six dagas wunode.　　460
Ælce dæge man sealde ærþan þam leonum
twa sceap to bigleofan and twegen leapas oð ðæt;
ac him næs þa nan geseald, þæt hi tosliton Danihel.
þa wæs on Iudea lande an geleafful witega,
Abbacuc gehaten, se hæfde rifteras　　465
abedene to his corne, and bær him heora mete.
Him cóm þa fleogende tó færlice Godes engel,
and hét beran þone mete to Babilonian hraþe,
and syllan Danihele, þe sæt on þam pytte.
Ða cwæð se Abbacúc to þam engle þuss:　　470
La, léof, ic ne geseah þa burh þe þu segst
ne ic nát þone seað, ne embe secgan ne gehyrde.
þa gelæhte se engel Abbacúc be þam feaxe,
and bær hine swiftlice to þære foresædan byrig
and to þær[a] leona seaðe, swiðe swiftum flyhte.　　475
Ða clypode Abbacúc to þam oþrum witegan,

459 wurpon *C*; worpon *L*; wurepan *G*.　　wildeorum *CL*; wildeoran *G*.
460 syfan *C*; seofan *L*; seofon *G*.　　syx *L*.　　six dagas wunode] wunede six
dages *G*.　　461 dæge] dæg *CL*; dæig *G*.　　462 twa . . . oð ðæt] twa
hryþera and twa seap *L*.　　sceap] scæp *C*; scep *G*.　　463 heom *G*.　　næs]
wæs *L*.　　nan] *om. CG*.　　nan . . . danihel] oftogen ælces fodan syx dagas, þæt
hí þone godes mann abitan sceoldan *L*.　　465 Abacuc *C*; abachuc *G* (*not
noted hereafter*).　　rifteras] riperes *G*.　　466 heom *G*.　　467 fleohgende *L*;
fligende *G*.　　470 se] *om. L*.　　471 geseh *G*.　　þe þu segst] næfre *L*.
segst] 'emb' sæigst *G*.　　474 swyft- *C*.　　475 þæra] *sic L*; þære *RCG*.
swiðe] *om. L*.　　swyftum *C*.　　flihte *CGL*.

Glosses in R, Latin: 462 bigleofan: victui.　　463 tosliton: deuorarent.
464 an: unus.　　465 rifteras: messores.　　468 hraþe: cito.　　469 pytte:
lacu.　　472 seað: lacum.　　embe: circa.　　473 gelæhte: apprehendit.
475 seaðe: lacum.

464–72 [*Dan. xiv. 32–34*] Erat autem Habacuc propheta in Iudæa; et ipse coxerat
pulmentum, et intriverat panes in alveolo, et ibat in campum ut ferret messori-
bus. Dixitque angelus Domini ad Habacuc: Fer prandium quod habes in Baby-
lonem Danieli, qui est in lacu leonum. Et dixit Habacuc: Domine, Babilonem
non vidi, et lacum nescio.
473–83 [*Ibid. 35–38*] Et apprehendit eum angelus Domini in vertice eius, et
portavit eum capillo capitis sui, posuitque eum in Babilone, supra lacum, in
impetu spiritus sui. Et clamavit Habacuc, dicens: Daniel, serve Dei, tolle prandium quod misit tibi Deus. Et ait Daniel: Recordatus es mei, Deus, et non
dereliquisti diligentes te. Surgensque Daniel comedit. Porro angelus Domini
restituit Habacuc confestim in loco suo.

Ðu Godes mann Danihel, nim þisne mete þe to
þe *þe God sende. And he sona andwyrde,   *p. 157
Eala þu min G[o]d, þu wære mín gemyndig,
and þu ne forlætst þa þe lufiað þe.   480
And he [æ]t sona of þære Godes sande,
and se engel ardlice eft Abbacúc ferode
to his lande ongean ofer swiðe langne weg.
Eft þa on þone seofoðan dæg eode se cyning
sarig to þam seaðe, and beseah into.   485
þa efne sæt Danihel ansund betwux þam deorum.
þa clypode se cyning, and cwæð þuss to Gode:
Eala þu Drihten God þe Danihel on belyfð,
mycel eart þu and mihtig. And he het his menn sona
upp ateon Danihel of þæra deora seaðe.   490
He het þa in [a]wurpan þe hine ær forwregdon,
and hi wurdon abitene on anre beorhthwile
ætforan þam cyninge fram þam frecum deorum.

Feala we mihton secgan be swilcum leasum godum,
hu bysmorfulle hi wæron and heora biggengon tihton   495
to eallum fracodnyssum, and to endeleasum morðdædum;
and se wæs þam godum dyrost þe dyde mæste fylðe.

478 sænde G.   andwyrde] andswarode G.   479 god sic CGL; gód R.
480 forlæst L.   481 æt] sic L, e(a)t (?) R; æt þa CG.   482 ængel CG.
hardlice C.   485 beseh G.   487 clypod L.   þuss to Gode] to gode
þuss G.   488 belefð G.   490 þæra] ðære CG.   deora] leona L.
491 awurpan] sic CL; awurepen G; wurpan R.   þe] þa þe G (rightly?).
492 beorhthwile] bearhtmhwíle L.   493 fran C.   494 Fela CL;
Feale G.   495 hu] and hwu G.   bismer- C; bisemær- G.   bigengas CL;
biggengas G.   496 fracod-] fraced- L; frac- C.   morðdædum] morð-
dæden G.   End of excerpt in G, which adds an independent close: mancyn
dwylden, oððæt se hælend crist to þyssen life becom (cf. 498).   497 mæste]
mæst L.   fylðe] fulnesse CL.

    Glosses in R, Latin: 477 nim: tolle.   þe to: tibi.   480 þa: eos.
481 et: comedit.   482 ardlice: mox.   ferode: ferebat.   485, 490 seaðe:
lacum.   486 efne: ecce.   ansund: incolumis.   491 þe (instead of þa):
eos.   492 beorhthwile: momento.   493 frecum: auidos (sic).   495 biggengon: cultores.   tihton: ortabant, suadebant.   496 fracodnyssum: fragi-
litate, periculo.   morðdædum: morticino.
ME: 492 wurdon: weren.

484–93 [Ibid. 39–41] Venit ergo rex die septimo ut lugeret Danielem; et venit
ad lacum, et introspexit, et ecce Daniel sedens in medio leonum. Et exclamavit
voce magna rex, dicens: Magnus es, Domine Deus Danielis. Et extraxit eum de
lacu leonum. Porro illos qui perditionis eius causa fuerant, intromisit in lacum;
et devorati sunt in momento coram eo.

Hwæt þa ure Hælend Crist com to þisse weorulde
on þære sixtan ylde, and he soðfæstnysse tæhte,
and mid manegum wundrum manna heortan onlihte,   500
and geswutolade mid tacnum þæt he soð God is,
þonne he of deaðe arás þurh his drihtenlican mihte,
and to heofonum astáh ætforan hundtwelftigum mannum,
wera and wifa, þe his gewitan wæron
on eallum þam wundrum þe he ætforan him geworhte.   505
Ge habbað oft gehyred be þæs Hælendes wundrum,
and be his halgan lare, and hu hold he is mancynne,
þam þe leahtras forseoð and lufiað heora Scyppend;
for þan þe him [synd] swiðe laðe þa leahterfullan biggengan,
for þan þe his gecynd *is þæt he clænnysse lufige.   *p. 158
Is eac nu for langsum to secganne hu his geleaffullan apostolas
towurpon þon[n]e hæþengyld æfter þ[æs H]ælendes upstige,
and þa fracodan godas afligdon mid mihte
of heora anlicnyssum þar men on locodan.
Ða apostoli hi tobræcon, and heora biggengas towurpan;   515
and þa gódan cyningas þe to Gode gebugon
heton mid ealle þa anlicnyssa tocwysan;
and man worhte of þam godum góde cytelas and hweras,

---

498 ðissere C; ðysre L.   worulde C; worolde L.   500 manna] mannum (!) C.   501 geswutelode CL.   505 heom C.   geworhte] worhte
CL (rightly?).   508 scypend L.   509 Entire line om. L.   synd] synd
altered to send C; om. R, beoð inserted over line in the trembling hand.   biggengas
C.   510 clen- C.   511 for] om. CL (rightly?).   secgenne C; secgænne L.
-fullen C.   512 þonne] þone RC; þoñ L; see note.   -gild C.   ðæs hælendes
CL; þælendes R.   515–64 Entire passage om. C.   515 Ða apostoli]
þapostoli L.   bigengas L.   517 -nysse L.

Glosses in R, Latin: 501 tacnum: signis.   504 gewitan: testes.   506 Ge:
vos.   508 þe leahtras forseoð: qui crimina contempnunt.   509 leahterfullan: criminosos (sic).   biggengan: cultores.   510 gecynd: natura.
511 for langsum: diuturnum.   512 towurpon: destruxerunt.   hæþengyld:
idolorum cultores.   513 fracodan: fragiles.   afligdon: fugabant.   514 anlicnyssum: simulacris.   515 biggengas: cultores (but see note).   towurpan:
destruxerunt.   516 gebugon: conuerterunt.   517 tocwysan: conterere.
ME: 518 cytelas: cheteles.   hweras: hweres.

516–20 [Cf. Hist. Eccl. Trip. ix. 27] Præceperat imperator [Theodosius] ut
studio Theophili in Alexandria paganorum templa destruerentur. ... Idola
siquidem deorum conflabantur ad faciendas ollas et Alexandrinæ ecclesiæ
diversas utilitates.

and mislice andluman of þam gemyltum [a]nlicnyssum,
and notodan þæs áres, þe ær ynnytt wæs.   520
On Egypta lande on Alexandria-byrig,
þe wæs heafodburh þa Egyptiscre þeode,
wæs se fyrmesta god [þ]e þæt folc wurþode
Seraphis gehaten, swiþe namcuð þa.
Him wæs fram ealdum dagum aræred micel tempel   525
mid wundorlicum cræfte, wurðlice gefadod,
and þæs anlicnyss wæs ænlice geworht
of ælcum antimbre þe of eorþan cymð—
of ælcum treowcynne, and of ælcum wecge,
mid golde beworht and mid hwitum seolfre.   530
Seo anlicnyss wæs swiðe heah on lenge,
manegra fæðma, of micclum antimbre geworht,
and heo wæs swa brád betwux þam bigelsum gefæstnod
þæt heo mid twam handum þa twegen weallas geræhte,
and [þæt] hús wæs swaþeah swiðe heah and wíd.   535
Heo wæs swiðe egeslic on to beseonne,

---

519 andluman] andlaman *L.*   anlicnyssum *L*; godu*m* and anlicnyssu*m R.*
520 notodan] notudon *L.*   522 heafodburh þa] þa heafodburh *L (rightly ?).*
523 þe] *sic L*; þæte *R.*   524 serapis *L.*   524–5 þa. Him] · þa him *R*; ða ·
him *L.*   525 arær/red *(because of new line) L.*   templ *L.*   526 gefadud
L.   527 þæs anlicnyss] godes anlicnysse *(!) L.*   529 wecge] wecgu*m L.*
531 længe *L.*   532 antimbre] ti*m*bre *L.*   533 betwyx *L.*   535 þæt] *sic
L*; *om. R.*

Glosses in *R*, *Latin*: 519 mislice: varias.   andluman: utensilia.   godum
(added in R): diis.   520 ares *(marg.* æres): eris.   524 þa: tunc.
525 aræred: erectu*m.*   526 wurðlice: honorifice.   gefadod: dispositu*m.*
527 þæs: ei*us.*   ænlice: sing*ulariter,* iocunde, amene, delectabili*ter.*   528 antimbre: metallo, materia.   529 wecge: la*m*mina.   532 antimbre:
matera *(sic).*   536 egeslic: te*rr*ibilis.
ME: 522 þeode: folke.

521–35 [*Rufinus, Hist. Eccl. XI. 23*] Serapis apud Alexandriam templum
auditum quidem omnibus puto, plerisque vero etiam notum. . . . Ædes erat
pretiosis edita columnis et marmoris saxo extrinsecus ample magnificeque constructa. In hac simulacrum Serapis ita erat vastum, ut dextera unum parietem,
alterum læva perstringeret, quod monstrum ex omnibus generibus metallorum
lignorumque compositum ferebatur. . . . [*Gold and silver are explicitly mentioned
in the description of the inner walls of the temple, and the arched construction
assumed in line 533 is attributed to the whole group of buildings of which the temple
is the centre*: cuncta . . . opere forniceo constructa.]
   536–41 [*Partly from Rufinus, ibid.*] Persuasio . . . quædam ab ipsis gentilibus
fuerat dispersa, quod, si humana manus simulacrum illud contigisset, terra
dehiscens ilico solveretur in chaos cælumque repente rueret in præceps. [*Partly
from Hist. Eccl. Trip. IX. 28*] . . . simulacrum, quod magnitudine sua terrebat

for hire micelnysse on menigfealdum cræfte,
and þa Egy[p]tiscan leoda gelyfdon on þone god,
and his biggengon sædon, gif him hwa abulge,
þæt seo heofon sona sceolde afe[a]llan,   540
and seo eorðe nyþan mid ealle toberstan.
Eft þa þa se tíma cóm on Theodosiges dagum
þæs æþelan caseres, þe ealle hét *tobrecan   *p. 159
þa leasan godas mid micclum geleafan,
þa wearð eac tobrytt se arwyrða Seraphis.   545
Hine mann sloh þa swiðe mid scearpre æxe,
ac he hit ne gefredde, for þam þe he wæs treowen,
ne he nan word ne cwæð, for þam þe he cucu næs,
ne seo heofon ne feoll, ne seo eorðe ne tobærst;
ac man cearf ardlice him of þæt heafod.   550
þar wearð þa micel gamen þæt feala músa scutan
of þære anlicnysse, þa hire o[f] wæs þæt heafod,
floccmælum yrnende geond þa widgillan flór,
þæt men mihton tocnawan þæt þar wæs músa wunung,
and nan godcundnyss, [ne] godes geleafa.   555

---

537 cræfte] cræftum L.   538 egiptiscan L; egyrptiscan R.   539 bigen-
gan L.   sædun L.   him hwa] hwa him L.   540 afeallan] sic L; afellan R.
542 theodosies L.   544 þa] last word on f. 184ᵛ, L; cet. desunt (a quire gone).
From 544 leasan to 564 incl., R is the sole authority.   552 of] ofe (of in
margin, trembling hand) R.   555 ne] supplied by conj.; om. R.

Glosses in R, Latin: 538 leoda: gentes. þone: illo.   539 biggengon:
cultores.   him: ei.   hwa: quis.   abulge: offenderet.   540 afellan:
cadere.   541 nyþan: deorsum.   543 æþelan: nobilis.   545 tobrytt: con-
fractum.   arwyrða: venerabilis.   550 ardlice: mox.   551 þa: tunc.
gamen: ludus.   musa: mures.   553 widgillan: latam.

---

inspicientes. Ferebatur etiam sermo fallax, quia, si quis iuxta eum accederet,
mox terra commoveretur et pestis cunctos invaderet.

542–5 [Ælfric's own transition, but cf. Hist. Eccl. Trip. IX. 27] Præceperat
imperator [Theodosius] ut studio Theophili in Alexandria paganorum templa
destruerentur. Theophilus . . . templum . . . Serapis . . . subvertit.

546–50 [Partly from Hist. Eccl. Trip. IX. 28] Iussit [Theophilus] alicui
habenti securem, ut Serapem forti percussione concideret. . . . Porro Serapis
neque doluit, nempe ligneus, neque vocem emisit sicut exanimis. Cum vero
eius abstulissent caput. . . . [Partly from Rufinus, loc. cit.] Unus ex militibus . . .
correptam bipennem . . . maxillæ veteratoris inlidit. Clamor adtollitur utro-
rumque populorum, neque tamen aut cælum ruit aut terra descendit. Inde
iterum atque iterum repetens . . . [he cuts off the head and the pieces are burnt].

551–5 [Hist. Eccl. Trip., loc. cit.] Cum vero eius abstulissent caput, greges
soricum exinde cucurrerunt; erat enim habitatio soricum Ægyptiorum deus.

Man toheow þa sticmælum þone sceoccenan god,
and mid langum rapum his lima toferode;
his heafod hi drogon mid hospe geond þa burh,
and his lima forbærndon, and þone búc æt nextan,
to micelre wæfersyne tomiddes þam folce;   560
and þa Cristenan tobræcon, swa swa se casere hét,
ealle þa ánlicnyssa þæra ærenra goda
on Alexandria and on eallum burgum,
and þæt ealde gedwyld wearð þa adwæsced.

Man funde éác syððan under þam fulum weofodum   565
cnapena heafda, þe man acwealde þær
þam godum to offrunge, and oðre fracodnyssa,
swa þæt heora biggengan þa bysmorlican fylþa
sceawian ne mihton, ofsceamode forþearle
þæt hi swa lange folgodon swa fulum hlafordum,   570
and gebugon þa to Gode, to his clænum biggengum.

    Git we willað secgan be sumum leasum gode,

---

565 Man funde] *Here C resumes.* weofodon *C.* 566 acwealde] acwealda
C. 567 fracednysse *C.* 568 hyra *C.* biggengas *C.* bismor- *C.*
571 *first* to] *om. C.* biggencge *C (rightly ?).* 572 Get *C.* leasa *C.*

Glosses in R, Latin: 556 þa: *tunc* sticmælu*m:* paulati*m.* sceoccenan god:
lingneu*m* de*um* demonior*um.* 557 toferode: digereba*nt.* 558 hospe:
obprobro (*sic*). 559 æt nextan: v*l*timo. 560 wæfersyne: spe*ctaculum.*
562 anlicnyssa: simulac*ra.* ærenra: aeneu*m* (*sic*). goda: deor*um.* 564 gedwyld: heresis. adwæsced: destructa. 567 þam godum to offrunge:
illis diis sacrificio. fracodnyssa: *pericula.* 568 biggengan: cultores.
569 sceawian: vid*ere.* forþearle: valde. 571 gebugon: *conuerterunt.*
þa: *tunc.* biggengum: cultui. 572 leasum: falso.

556–60 [*Partly ibid.*] Tunc eum partibus incidentes igne concremaverunt,
caput autem per totam traxerunt urbem. [*Partly Rufinus, loc. cit.*] Post hoc
revulsum cervicibus et depresso modio trahitur caput, tum pedes aliaque
membra cæsa securibus et rapta funibus distrahuntur, ac per singula loca
membratim in conspectu cultricis Alexandriæ senex veternosus exuritur. Ad
ultimum truncus qui superfuerat in amphitheatro concrematur.

    561–4 [*Ælfric sums up a number of implications in both sources, neither of which
provides a clear model for this.*]

    565–71 [*Rufinus, XI. 24*] Horret animus dicere ... quæ funera, quæ scelera in
illis, quæ dicebant adyta, tegebantur, quot ibi infantum capita desecta inauratis
labris inventa sunt, quot miserorum cruciabiles mortes depictæ, quæ cum
proderentur in lucem ac sub auras prolata ferrentur, licet confusione ipsa gentiles et pudore diffugerent, tamen si qui adesse potuit, mirabatur tot sæculis se
illis tam nefariis et tam pudendis fraudibus inretitum. Unde et plurimi ex his
... fidem Christi et cultum veræ religionis amplexi sunt.

þe æfter Cristes menniscnysse þurh Cristes geleafan
eaðelice wearð of his anlicnysse adræfed.
Gregorius wæs geháten [sum] *swiðe halig biscop,   *p. 160
se worhte miccle wundra and mihta þurh G[o]d.   576
Se rád on wintres dæge embe sume neode
ofer þa micclan muntas þe man Mundiú hǽt,
and ne mihte for snáwe nahwider gecyrran
þær he wícstowe hæfde; ac þar wæs gehende   580
án hæþen tempel, gehalgod þam gode
þe wæs geháten Apollo, and he þyder gecyrde
and wunode on þam temple, for þæs wintres cyle.
þær stod seo anlicnyss þæs ærenan godes
bin[n]an þam temple, and his biggenga   585
axode æt þære anlicnysse [o]ftrædlice gehwæt,
and se deofol sylf andwyrde of þære anlicnysse,
and sæde þam sacerde þe hine synderlice wurðode
menigfealde gedwimor, and he hi þam mannum sæde
þe hwæs befrunon æt þære feondlican anlicnysse;   590
and se sacerd lyfode be þam lácum symble
þe þa hæðenan brohton to þam healican gedwylde.

575 sum] *sic* C; *erasure* (susum?) R.   bisceop C.   576 god C; gód R.
579 ne] ne ne C.   581 templ C.   585 binnan] *sic* C; binan R.
586 þære] ðæra C.   oftrædlice] *sic* C; and 'heo' sæde þam sacerde oftrædlice R
(*anticipating* 588a *because of homœoteleuton; error discovered but extra phrase not
deleted*).   587 sylf] *om.* C.   589 manig- C.   591 leofode C.   symle C.
592 gedwilde C.

Glosses in R, Latin: 574 anlicnysse: sumulacro (*sic*).   adræfed: expulsus.
580 wicstowe: mansionem.   gehende: prope.   582 gecyrde: diuertit.
~~584 ærenan: enee (*sic*).~~   ~~585 biggenga: cultores (*sic*).~~   ~~586 gehwæt:~~
quodlibet.   588 synderlice: specialiter.   589 gedwimor: fantasma.   hi:
ea.   þam: illis.   590 hwæs: quid, quicquid.   befrunon: interrogabant.
591 lyfode: vixit.   lacum: oblationibus.   symble: semper.   592 gedwylde:
herrore.
ME: 580 wicstowe: herboruwe.

577–83 [*Rufinus, addition to Eusebius, Eccl. Hist. VII, after 28. 2; ed. Momm-
sen p. 954 sq.*] Unum de [Gregorii] gestis adiciam: iter ei fuisse quondam per
Alpes dicitur hiemis tempore, et cum pervenisset ad summum Alpium iugum,
nivibus repleta erant omnia, nullum usquam diversorium, fanum ibi tantum
Apollinis erat, cui succedens, transacta nocte discessit.
584–92 Sacerdos vero erat quidam fani eius, cui consulere simulacrum
Apollinis mos erat et reddere responsa poscentibus, ex quo ei etiam alimoniæ
quæstus esse videbatur.

Ða wearð se god afliged of þære fúlan anlicnysse
þurh þone halgan wer þe þær wicode on niht,
and ne mihte andwyrdan þurh þa anlicnyssæ   595
þam earman sacerde, swa swa he ǽr dyde.
He offrode þa lác gelóme þam gode,
and seo anlicnyss ne mihte geandwyrdan þam biggengan.
He wearð þa geancsumod earmlice on mode,
ac him sæde se deofol þas word on slæpe: 600
Hwi clypast þu to me þar þar ic cuman ne mæg?
Se oðer hine axode, hwæt se intinga wære
hwi he þar cuman ne mihte; and þa cwæð se deofol
þæt he adræfed wære of þære dyrnan wununge
þurh Gregories tócyme; and þa cwæð se sacerd,   605
Hwæt tæcst þu nu to ræde? And he him hraþe andwyrde,
Ne mot ic nateshwón into þære stówe faran
buton *ic hæbbe leafe þæs halgan Gregories.   *p. 161
þa macode se sacerd his fare on mergen
ofer langne weg to þam geleaffullan biscope,   610
and his fét gesohte, his sið bemænende,
þæt his bigleofa moste mid ealle him losian,
for þam þe he afligde færlice mid his tocyme

595 anwyrdan C. -nisse C.   596 sacerde] mannan ne þa sacerde C.
597 offrude C.   598 -nyss] -nesse C.   geanwyrdan C.   biggencgan C.
599 wearð] weard C.   geangsumod C.   600 þas word on slæpe] on slæpe
þas word C (rightly?).   609 his fare on mergen] on morgen his fara C (right
order?).   610 bisceope C.

Glosses in R, Latin: 593 afliged: fugatus.   594 wicode: mansit.
597 þa: *tunc*.   598 biggengan: colenti.   602 intinga: causa.
604 adræfed: eiec*tus*.   606 tæcst: doces.   hraþe: cito.   607 nateshwon: nullate*nus*.   609 fare: iter.   612 bigleofa: victus.   losian:
perire.   613 afligde: fugau*it*.
ME: 611 sið: mesauent*ure*.

593-8 Igitur post digressum Gregorii offerre consulta et responsa poscere
sacerdos accessit ex more, nihil inde responsi veniebat. Repetit victimas, silen-
tium permanet. Iterum atque iterum litat, surdis ingerit fabulam.
599-608 Cumque stupore novi silentii æstuaret sacerdos, noctu ei adsistens
dæmonium dicit in somnis: 'Quid me illic invocas, quo iam venire non possum?'
Percontanti causam adventu se Gregorii dicebat expulsum. Quid nunc remedii
daretur, cum perquireret, ait non aliter sibi licere ingredi locum illum, nisi
Gregorius permisisset.
609-14 Quibus auditis sacerdos occupat viam. . . . Pervenit ad Gregorium
adortusque [*v.l.* adoratusque] eum rem pandit ex ordine, . . . querelam depulsi
numinis ponit, ademptam facultatem sui quæstus deplorat. . . .

þone god þe he wurðode of his gewunelican stowe.
Ða awrat Gregorius þis gewrit to þam gode: 615
Ic grete þe, Apollo, and ic þe leafe sylle
eft to farenne ínto þinre stowe,
and þa þing to donne þe þu ær dydest.
Se sacerd genam þa [sona] þæt gewrit,
and ham swiðe efste, and wið ða anlicnysse   620
léde þæt gewrít; þa gewearð se deofol sona
oninnan þa anlicnysse, and eft to him spræc,
swa swa he ær dyde, þæs þe he hine axode.
þa begann se sacerd swiðe to smeagenne,
and cwæð on his mode, Nú þes min god þus færð: 625
Gregorius hine afligde, and he fleah sona awég,
and eft cuman ne mihte into his anlicnysse,
butan Gregorius him lyfde. La hú ne is [forðy]
Gregorius betera þonne þes mín god sy?
He beléac þa his tempel, mid geleafan onbryrd,   630
and ferde eft ongean mid þam ilcan gewrite
to þam arwurðan biscope, and him ealle asæde
be his godes geancyme, and be his modes smeaunge,
and feoll to his fotum, fulluhtes biddende,
and þæt he hine betæhte þam heofonlican Gode,   635

---

616 selle *C*.   619 sona] *sic C*; *om. R*.   621 legde *C*.   sona] *om. C*
(*rightly?*).   622 þa anlicnysse] þære anlicnesse *C*.   625 cwæt *C*.
628 lifde *C*.   forðy] forði *C*; *om. R*.   629 Gregorius] *om. C*.   632 bisceope *C*.   ealle] eal *C*.   asæde] sæde *C*.

Glosses in R, Latin: 620 efste: *properauit*.   wið: *iuxta*.   623 þæs: ea.
625 þes: iste.   626 afligde: fugau*it*.   628 lyfde: *con*sessit(*for* concessit).
630 onbryrd: *contritus* (*!*).   632 asæde: narrau*it*.   633 geancyme: reditu.
modes: *mentis*.
ME: 624 smeagenne: þenchen.   633 smeaunge: þouhte.

615–23 At ille nihil moratus scribit epistulam in hæc verba: 'Gregorius
Apollini. Permitto tibi redire ad locum tuum et agere quæ consuesti.' Hanc
epistulam sacerdos accipit et ad fanum defert, positaque ea iuxta simulacrum
adfuit dæmon ac dedit responsa poscenti.
     624–9 Tum ille in semet ipsum conversus ait: 'Si Gregorius iussit et deus iste
discessit nec potuit redire nisi iussus et rursum iubente Gregorio restitutus est,
quomodo non multo melior isto Gregorius, cuius hic obtemperat iussis?'
     630–6 Clausis igitur ianuis fani descendit ad Gregorium epistulam secum,
quam acceperat, referens omnemque apud eum rei gestæ ordinem pandens,
simulque ad pedes eius prosternens rogat, ut illi se deo offerat, cuius virtute diis
gentium Gregorius imperabat.

þurh þæs mihte þe he afligde þæra hæþenra godas.

He bæd þa swa lange mid geleafan þone bisceop
þæt he hine cristnode; and he clænlice lyfode
syððan of þam dæge on swiðlicre forhæfdnysse,
and ealle woruldþing forlét, and wunode mid þam bisceope. 640
He wearð þa gefullod, *and swa fullfremedlice þeah   *p. 162
on halgum mægnum, mid micclum geleafan,
and on Godes láre, þæt he æfter Gregorie
to biscope wearð gehalgod, and geheold wislice
þone biscophád mid godre [ge]bysnunge,   645
Gode to gecwemednysse, swa swa us [cyðað] béc;
and ures Drihtnes geleafa adwæscte þæt hæþengild,
for þan þe se Cristendóm cóm gehwær and þær.

Oft sædon þa hæþenan þæt ure Hælend [Crist]
cóme æfter heora godum, and hi yldran wæron,   650
and cwædon þæt þa yldran godas arwurðran wæron
and swiðor to wurðianne þonne se ðe sið cóme.
Ac þa dysgan nyston þæt ure Drihten wæs æfre

636 þe] *om.* C (*rightly?*) godes *altered to* godas R; godes C.   637 þone]
ðane C.   638 þæt] oð ðæt C.   leofode C.   644 bisceope C.   645 bis-
ceop- C.   mid] *here S resumes, having skipped from the beginning of line* 150 *with
no sign of omission; the sentence thus produced is nonsense.*   gebysnunge] *sic* S;
gebisnunge C; bysnunge R.   646 cyðað] *sic* CS; secgað R (*no allit.*)
647 and] and 'mid' (*added in trembling hand*) R.   -gyld S.   648 gehwer S.
þer S.   649 crist CS; *om.* R.   651 cwædon C; cwedon S.   652 wurðigenne CS.   sið] siððan S.   come] *sic all three MSS. originally;* 'i' come R.
653 dysegan S.

Glosses in R *and* S, Latin: 636 þæs: illius R.   639 swiðlicre forhæfdnysse:
uehementi continencia R.   641 fullfremedlice þeah: perfectus proficiebat R.
642 mægnum: virtutibus R.   644 geheold: custodiuit R.   647 adwæscte:
destruxit R.   hæþengild: idolum R.   648 gehwær: vbique RS.
650 æfter heora godum: post eorum deos S.   hi yldran: illi seniores RS.
wæron: fuerunt S.   *Margin opp.* 650 *in* R: Iudei dixerunt quod dii eorum
venerunt post deum nostrum.   651 yldran godas: seniores dii S.   arwurðran:
honorabiliores R; uenerabiliores S.   652 swiþor: magis S.   to wurðianne:
adorandi R; adorare S.   þonne se þe: quam illi qui (!) S.   sið: post R.
653 dysgan: stulti R.

637–44a Cumque enixius et pertinacius persisteret, catechumenus ab eo factus
est. Et cum se vitæ castissimæ et abstinentissimæ derelictis omnibus non solum
erroribus dæmonum, sed et sæculi actibus mancipasset, etiam baptisma con-
secutus est, et in tantum vitæ merito ac fidei virtute profecit, ut ipse beato
Gregorio in episcopatu successor extiterit.
644b–8 [*Not in Rufinus.*]

mid his heofonlican Fæder on fullfremedre mihte,
æfre ælmihtig God of þam ælmihtigan Fæder,   655
and cóm syððan to mannum, þa þa he sylf wolde,
on soðre menniscnysse, mancynn to alysenne.
And þa godas þe þa hæþenan heoldon mid gedwylde,
þa gescop úre Hælend mid his heofonlican Fæder—
ac he ne gesceop hi na to godum, ac to oðrum gesceaftum—
for þam þe nan gesceaft nis þe se án God ne gesceope,   661
þeah þe hi sume wurdan awende to deoflum,
and sume man wurðode wolice for godas.
Nis nan oðer god, ne nan oðer scyppend,
buton seo halige þrynnyss, þe is þrymwealdend God,   665
se ðe ána gewylt ealra gesceafta,
and ælcum men forgylt eft be his weorcum
on þissere weorolde geendunge, and eac hwilon ær.
Ure Hælend cwæð swaþeah be his halgum þegnum,
Ego dixi, dii estis, et filii Excelsi omnes: 670
Ic cwæð þæt ge synd godas, and ealle suna þæs Hehstan.
Swa micelne wurðmynt forgeaf se mildheorta *Drihten   *p. 163
his halgum þegnum, þæt he hét hi godas;
ac nan mann næfð swaþeah nane mihte þurh hine sylfne,
buton of þam ánum Gode þe ealle þing gesceóp,   675
þam sy wuldor and lof a to worulde. AMEN.

654 heofen- *S.*   658 godes *C.*   gedwilde *S.*   659 gesceop *CS.*
660 godu*m*] gode, s *added over line by trembling hand, S.*   661 gesceaft]
om. S.   662 awænde *C.*   663 wohlice *S.*   godes *C.*   664 sceppend *C.*   668 þissere] ðisre *C*; þyssere *S.*   worulde *CS.*   ær] her *S.*
670 *Latin om. Kl.*   671 synd] sin *C.*   godes *C.*   suna] suna*n S.*   þæs]
þas *C.*   hextan *C.*   672 mycelne *S.*   673 þegenu*m S.*   675 ðincg *C.*

Glosses in R and S, Latin: 654 fullfremedre: pr*e*fecta (*for* perfecta) *R.*   658 godas: dii *S.*   heoldon: obs*er*uaba*nt S.*   gedwylde: errore *R.*   659 þa: eos *R*;
illos *S.*   660 gode's': deos *S.*   662 awende: co*n*uersi *R.*   663 wurðode:
adoraba*nt R.*   wolice: i*n*[i]uste *R*; iniuste *S.*   665 buton: n*i*si *S.*
668 hwilon: aliquando *RS.*   her (*for* ær): hic *S.*   669 þegnum: seruis *R.*
671 ge: vos *RS.*   sunan: filii *S.*   hehstan: excelsi *R.*   673 þegnum:
seruis *R.*
ME: 662 wurdan: weren *R.*

670 [*Ps. lxxxi. 6, as given.*]

NOTES

1–5. This Latin beginning is unusual for Ælfric; but after the first sentence it is entirely from St. Paul, and we must remember that Ælfric's expositions of gospel-texts were to be preceded each time by the reading of the entire text in Latin. (See CH I. 152/2–3; 166/2–3; etc.) Somewhat surprisingly, the verse from *Romans* in lines 4–5 is quoted in a form used by Augustine in *De Vera Religione*, as noted under Sources, and also in *De Doctrina Christiana*, v (*PL* XXXIV. 21). Since Ælfric normally quotes the Vulgate (which here reads, for the first part, *Ex ipso, et per ipso, et in ipso sunt omnia*), I cannot help suspecting that he lifted the entire beginning from some Latin sermon of the Augustinian era; but I have not been able to find such a one.

31. Unger suggested *sittan* for *wunian* to alliterate with *symle*; but this use of *sittan* is hardly Ælfrician; and though *beon*, alliterating with *butan*, would be more plausible, the manuscripts offer no encouragement to emendation. Even *symle*, about which they disagree, is supported by representatives of both textual branches, C–W and S. Did Ælfric feel that the three endings in *-an* (two of which might have been spelled *-on*) were an acceptable substitute for alliteration? All we can be sure of is that his rhythmic lines as reported by the manuscripts do not invariably alliterate.

33–55. The theme of prelapsarian bliss and the ills that followed is somewhat more elaborately treated in the *Hexameron*, 413–48, 454–78. Compare especially lines 47 sq. here with *Hex.* 460–4:

> and hine biton lys and lyftene gnættas
> and eac swylce flean and oðre gehwylce wyrmas,
> and him wæron deregendlice dracan and næddran
> and ða reðan deor mihton derian his cinne,
> ðe hine ealle ær arwurðodon swyðe.

99–103. Here Ælfric modifies Martin of Braga's account, as if by recollection of one or more other authorities. Not only does he defer until later all mention of the part played by devils, but his description of the men who came to be worshipped as gods is less completely unfavourable, at least in this opening generalization. One of several places where he might have found precedent for his description is the beginning of Isidore's long account of the gods of the gentiles, *Etymologiarum lib.* VIII, *cap.* xi (*PL* LXXXII. 314 sqq.): 'Quos pagani deos asserunt, homines olim fuisse produntur, et pro uniuscuiusque vita vel meritis coli apud suos post mortem coeperunt. . . . Fuerunt. . . quidam viri fortes aut urbium conditores.' Isidore then blames the devils for causing these men to be worshipped as gods instead of merely honoured. Even more dignity is assigned to the men in Lactantius, who calls them *reges maximi et potentissimi* (*Divin. Inst.* I. 8; *CSEL* XIX. 30). Ælfric's mention of giants, *mislice entas*, owes nothing to Martin and probably little to Isidore's *viri fortes*. The idea was already in his head (along with Martin and Isidore, perhaps) when he wrote *De Initio Creaturæ*, where the men for whom idols were named are described as *entas and yfel-dæde* (*CH* I. 22/31). In the present sermon at line 74 he has mentioned the *entas* who built the wondrous steeple. Very likely the giants associated with Babel (and therefore with Babylon and Bel, whom Isidore equates with Saturn) had something to do with Ælfric's notion. He may also have had in mind Hercules (referred to as *þam ormætan ente* at *LS* xxxv. 113) and the Titans.

108–12. Neither Martin nor Isidore (in the passage cited above) mentions Jove's relationship to Saturn, his escape from being eaten, or his expulsion of Saturn from Crete, though Isidore has a long account of Saturn himself and says the pagans regarded him as *origo deorum et totius posteritatis*. The story as Ælfric tells it could have been derived from Ovid or Lactantius, but its features are too commonly known to be traced. Servius, commenting on *Æneid* VIII. 319 sq. (*Primus ab ætherio venit Saturnus Olympo, arma Iovis fugiens et regnis exul ademptis*), says: 'Hoc dicit secundum poeticum morem; nam Saturnus rex fuit Cretæ, quem Iuppiter filius bello pepulit.' In *LS* v. 172 sqq. Ælfric shows a similar awareness of the story where his source, the *Acta S. Sebastiani* (*ASS.*, Jan. II. 635, § 41), deals with it somewhat allusively.

110. *þrymlic.* I have refrained from adopting the tempting *þwyrlic* of MS. S. In spite of its obvious applicability to Jove as portrayed here and its familiarity as a word in Ælfric's writings, I think it must be classified as an unauthorized emendation, almost certainly incorrect. The evidence of the manuscripts is flatly against its being a direct inheritance from Ælfric's original, for R and S stand together as the inheritors of a revised text by way of a common ancestor at some remove from Ælfric. If *þwyrlic* had been inherited by S from Ælfric, it would have been in an ancestor of R also, and R's agreement with C, L, and W in the reading *þrymlic* would have to be attributed to contamination or sheer coincidence. And in spite of the apparent superiority of *þwyrlic* to *þrymlic* in the context, I think there are signs that Ælfric had *þrymlic* in mind. First, as already remarked, he has conceded in line 102 that the men who came to be worshipped as gods were *mihtige on woruldlicum geþincðum and egefulle*. Secondly, he has described Saturn, in line 105, as *swiðlic and wælhreow*. When he now, at 110, describes Jove as *hetol and þrymlic*, I think he is reversing the order, choosing *hetol* as a parallel to *wælhreow* and *þrymlic* as a parallel to *swiðlic*. Both *swiðlic* and *þrymlic*, which we may take, perhaps, as 'mighty' or 'majestic' in a morally neutral way rather than as 'glorious', serve as partial explanations for the honour accorded to these men by the world, and carry out also the idea of the awe they inspired. Nevertheless it should be said that the only recorded instance of the adjective *þrymlic* in Ælfric's work is taken by BTS from Kemble's edition of this very passage as it stands in MS. W. The adverb *þrymlice* is cited from Ælfric once only, and there its full meaning is called on to convey admiration for the glorious reign of King Josiah (*LS* xviii. 470). Moreover, the manuscripts show that *þrymlic* troubled several readers. Besides the tempting substitution in S we have *grimlic and þrymlic* in X^k

and, on the part of Wulfstan (in T), a deliberate rewriting: *se wearð hetol feond*. A minor puzzle is the presence of the gloss *pravus* not only in S, where it is rightly attached to *þwyrlic*, but also in R, where it is written twice, once as if glossing *hetol*, again not far removed from *þrymlic*. I think the glossator transferred the gloss from S or another manuscript now lost without fully realizing its impropriety.

115. Kemble's emendation of *Minerua* to *Diana* was made without knowledge of the unanimity of the manuscripts or the clear confirmation of their reading in the Latin source. I am not sure whether Ælfric would have regarded *Uenus* as capable of alliterating with *wæron*. At 150 the name need not alliterate with *wif* and *wæs*, and at 177 it may be called upon to alliterate with *Fricg*.

117. *magan*, 'kinswomen'. Although by its form this word could be the accusative plural of either *māga*, wk. m., or *māge*, wk. f., the context strongly favours the feminine word. The presumptive source has *neptes* 'granddaughters' or 'nieces', not the indeterminate *parentes* chosen by the glossator. Indeed, it is doubtful whether Ælfric would have used the wk. masculine *māga* except in the obviously inappropriate sense 'son' or 'male descendant'. His usual term for 'kinsman' is the strong masculine *mæg*, nap. *māgas*, with which *māgan*, taken as apf., forms a satisfactory contrast. Cf. *LS* x. 215: *Menn hæfdon on frymðe heora magan to wife*. The same distinction is found in Middle English. See *OED, mowe*.

124. The identification of Jove with Thor, Mercury with Odin (line 140), and Venus with Fricg (line 177) is the same, even to the spellings, as that which occurs in Ælfric's life of St. Martin, *LS* XXXI. 714 sqq. In both places he has added these identifications to the names of the classical deities provided by his Latin sources.

138. *and to heagum beorgum him brohtan onsæg[ed]nysse*. According to E. A. Philippson, *Germanisches Heidentum bei den Angelsachsen*, p. 161, this line points to a characteristic feature of the worship of Woden–Oþinn rather than of Mercury, for whose customary places of worship Martin of Braga has properly mentioned only the crossroads. So also Bethurum, *Homilies of Wulfstan*, 338, where the considerable evidence, much of it from place-names, for the worship of Odin on mountains is conveniently summed up. In all probability Ælfric had heard enough about the religious ceremonies of the Danes to know of this feature, and it was natural for him to attribute it to Mercury, since he was considering Mercury and Odin as the same deity. It seems possible that he was also aware, if only from place-names, that the same god, called Woden, had been worshipped on high places by his ancestors; but whatever he may have known about the English Woden he kept to himself: a deliberate reticence appears, I think, when he discusses the days of the week, 166 sqq. As to the present passage, it should be observed that Martin of Braga had put the idea of sacrifices on high mountains into Ælfric's head, though not with reference to Mercury. At the beginning of the paragraph introducing the classical gods (*De Corr. Rust.*, § 7) Martin speaks of the demons, ministers of the

devil, who began to appear to men in various forms, 'et loqui cum eis et expetere ab eis, ut *in excelsis montibus* et in silvis frondosis *sacrificia sibi offerrent* et ipsos colerent pro deo'. With this generalization to support him and the knowledge that Mercury was one of the Olympian gods, Ælfric would have needed no more than a vague notion of Odin-worship to bring forth his assertion. We need not reject Philippson's inference, but we should certainly hesitate to suppose that Ælfric's words reflect precise knowledge or any vivid personal experience. I wish to thank Mrs. Ursula Dronke, who is concerned with the annotation of *Sigtýs bergi* in the *Atlakviða*, for calling my attention to this problem afresh.

141–9. On the textual importance of this passage, which is shown to be a later addition by its appearance only in R, S, and, partially, Wulfstan's revision (T), see the introductory comment, pp. 673–4.

145–9. It is characteristic of Ælfric's scholarly training that he should appeal to the authority of the heathen as well as the Christian writers, and should accord such particular respect to the *ealdan hæðenan* as witnesses to Jove's true parentage, a question that, with his euhemeristic assumptions, he regards as one of ordinary human genealogy. I cannot say which of the heathen authorities he had in mind; but the passions of the martyrs to which he refers in 149 probably included two with which he deals in the *Lives of Saints*. In the Latin source behind *LS* v. 166–81 (the *Acta S. Sebastiani* attributed to Ambrose, *ASS*, Jan. II. 635, § 41) Jove is explicitly said to be the son of Saturn, and in the source behind *LS* xxxv. 104–18 (*Passio SS. Martyrum Chrysanthi et Dariæ*, Mombritius, *Sanctuarium* (Paris, 1910), I. 274) the same relationship is implicit.

150. On R's *Uena* see the introductory comment, p. 670.

154. *halige*, CLW; *healice*, R(T). The alignment here might indicate a minor revision by Ælfric, though the absence of the passage from S deprives us of a useful witness. I prefer to think that *healice* is a scribal substitution, because *halige* provides a sharper contrast to the lust attributed to the goddess.

166–80. In this passage on the days of the week Ælfric seems deliberately to avoid the obvious identifications. He names *Sunnandæg* and *Monandæg* without acknowledging the fact that the names have persisted, as indeed is all too obvious; but when he comes to the other days he keeps back the English names and points the finger of scorn only at the Danes. He must have been aware of what some at least of the English names stood for. Evidently he had no wish, as did some churchmen, to abandon the names, and to remind the English of their ancient heathenism would have introduced an unnecessary complication at best; yet his silence attracts attention.

171. *feoht[e]-gode*. Unger was probably right in assuming a compound *feohte-god* 'war-god', of which the first member is the uninflected *feohte*, corresponding to the weak feminine *feohte*. MS. R alone insists on

two words and therefore has *feohta*, genitive plural of the strong neuter
feoht. Admittedly C and L are unreliable witnesses, since they are so late
that their *feohte* might be a mere levelling of *feohta*; but W's *feohte* has
weight, and the compound itself yields a superior meaning.

181–6. Under Sources, it is suggested that Ælfric's transition from the
days of the week to the planets was influenced by a passage in Bede's *De
Temporum Ratione*, and his comment on the planetary motion by a passage
in Bede's *De Natura Rerum*. Ælfric's familiarity with both works is
attested by his *De Temporibus Anni*, where (at IX. 5) he refrains from trying
to explain the planetary motion. Later, in the *Interrogationes* (ed. MacLean,
lines 114 sqq.), he departs from Alcuin to insert an explanation from *De
Natura Rerum*, beginning: 'Witodlice seo tunglene heofon tyrnð æfre
onbutan þas eorþan easten westwerd, and hire winnað ongean þa seofon
dweligendan tunglan.' Later (MacLean 135 sqq.) he elaborates: 'Ðas
seofon tunglan gað æfre eas[t]werd ongean þa heofonan, ac seo heofon is
strengra, and abret hi ealle underbæc westward mid hire ryne, and is fo[r]ði
mannum geþuht swylce seo sunne and þa foresædan tunglan gangon
westweard. Soð þæt is: westwerd hi gað unþances; ac hi gað swaþeah
ealle be heora mihte æfre eastwerd.' Presumably the *Interrogationes* and
De Falsis Diis were written at about the same time.

186. *seo heofon.* This form occurs also at 540 and 549 in the present
homily, in the quotation from the *Interrogationes* in the preceding note,
and several times elsewhere in Ælfric, including *De Temporibus Anni*, v.
3, and *CH* I. 262/6, 11. It is apparently Ælfric's substitute for the weak
seo heofone in the nominative singular, since he uses *heofonan* for the singular in the other cases, as the Glossary shows; and in all probability he
uses the strong masculine word only in the plural, *heofonas*, etc. An
instance of *heofone* in *Hexameron* 34 is supported only by our MS. P and
an untrustworthy Parkerian copy in Q, against *heof-on*, *-an*, *-en* in O, R,
and S; yet the preceding line has stated that God created *heofonan*.
Ælfric appears to use the singular primarily to describe the heaven of the
fixed stars, the firmament, for which his other term is *se rodor*. Hence,
at *Hexameron* 149 we read, *Ðone rodor God gehet heofon.* (The gender
here is not indicated, but in view of what has been said above the chances
are it should be classified as feminine.) When he uses the plural it is
probably with some thought of invisible regions beyond the firmament
rather than simply the Ptolemaic heavens, for in *Hexameron* 118 he speaks
of *ða upplican heofonas ða englas on wuniað*.

187–9. Ælfric returns to this type of argument more elaborately in
649–63. Martin of Braga has used it with a slightly different turn in the
passage quoted for lines 166–80.

190–209. Although the first ten lines or so have some foundation in
De Correctione Rusticorum and the *Etymologiæ*, the passage as a whole,
with its emphasis on the precious materials of the images, their beauty,
the skill of the craftsmen who made them, and above all the scornful contrast between the craftsman's superiority to his artifact while he is making

it and his stupid veneration for it when it is finished, suggests some quite different source. Behind it, I am sure, are certain Biblical passages, among them *Is.* xlvi. 5–7 and especially *Sap.* xiii. 10–19, where the whole process of making an image, fixing it in place, and then treating it as a god is elaborately ridiculed in very much the same spirit. But the details here are different enough to suggest that Ælfric was using his own inventive powers more freely than usual, or that there was an intermediary whose work I have not found.

191. *asmeadan.* We might expect *asmiðedon*, as in *LS* ii. 113 sq., 'and het asmiðigen of smætum golde hyre anlycnysse'. But the manuscripts agree on *asmeadan.* Apparently we must take it in the unrecorded sense 'designed', for which there is some oblique support in the compound, *smeawyrhta* 'a skilled worker', and also in *smealice*, on which see the next note.

202. *smealice.* The examples of this word in BT and BTS show its connexion with subtlety, depth, and mental acuteness, notions that are easily associated with the verb *smeagan* also; but the examples have to do with situations in which a process of thought rather than the craftsmanship of a sculptor is under consideration. Here the meaning is probably 'subtly' or 'cunningly', unless 'exquisitely' be admitted as a possibility. See BT, 'sméalic, adj., III. *exquisite, choice* (?)', based on a gloss of the comparative, 'smealicran *exquisitiores*'.

226. *licgende.* Since Ælfric regularly treats *god* as masculine even when he is referring to a pagan deity, the strict grammatical form of the participle would be *licgendne*. Ælfric may have preferred to leave it uninflected in this position; but there is a fairly strong possibility that the participle is a scribal modification of the infinitive *licgan* to which the other two manuscripts testify. For a few examples (all from poetry) of *findan* with an infinitive see BTS, s.v., I. 5*a* and 6.

242. *landleodan*, R. The weak form is attested beside the strong *-leoda* of C and L, and also *-leode*. See Glossary. I am uncertain of Ælfric's preference.

255. *eower*, R; *eowrum* CL. Once again the choice is clouded, but the uninflected *eower* is permissible and easier in this combination.

256. *hringas.* By translating *anus* as if it were *anulus* Ælfric perhaps deliberately misses the point. Was there some precedent for this?

260. *cæpsan.* Napier (in *COEL*) cited the word from this passage in R, its only occurrence. It is a wk. fem. *cæpse* 'box', from Lat. *capsa.*

The gloss *hespetecam* for *cæpsan* in MS. R. Apparently this gloss is a hybrid composed of Germanic *hespe* 'hasp' (OE *hæpse*, ME *haspe*, *hespe*, ON *hespa*, etc.—see *OED*) and Latin *t(h)eca* from Greek θήκη 'box, case, chest', as in *bibliotheca*. DuCange lists these two elements separately under *haspa* (also *aspa*) and *theca*, defining the latter as 'capsa' and citing a Latin life of St. Egidius, so that the combination, meaning 'box with a hasp', seems within reach of a glossator of the early thirteenth century. For the suggestion that *hespe* is to be taken as a form of *hasp* I am indebted to Dr. Roger Lass, to whom I presented the problem as one I could not solve. I find the suggestion irresistible. The glossator here is probably the man with the tremulous hand, though the letters are somewhat firmer than usual.

274. *geforþodan*, 'sent forth'. This meaning is not adequately represented by 'further, advance' in Hall–Meritt, and does not appear under *geforþian* in BT; but *forþian* is once so defined in BTS.

292–9. Ælfric had told this story at greater length in the second Christmas homily, *CH* II. 18/19 sqq.; and before that, briefly, in the homily on St. Clement, *CH* I. 570/9–20.

300–51. The passage corresponding to these lines in MS. G has been printed in metrical lines by Förster in his *Altenglisches Lesebuch für Anfänger* (Heidelberg, 1913; fünfte Aufl., 1949, pp. 35–38). There G's revision of the opening lines can be more clearly apprehended than in Warner's text of G.

314. *oð æfen* GL; *ofhæfen* C. The Latin text shows plainly, if there were a doubt, that the reading of G and L is correct. C's error was probably brought about by the expectation that *swiðe* would be followed by a participial adjective, as indeed it often is. Since *ofhebban* is unrecorded, the supposed meaning of *ofhæfen* need not concern us.

346. R's gloss *destrut* for *toworpen* is an early and hitherto unregistered form of *destroyed* close to OF *destruit*. The nearest parallel cited by the *MED* under *destroien* is *destruet* (*c.* 1225, *Ancrene Wisse*, MS. CCCC 402, f. 105; ed. Tolkien, EETS 249, p. 198).

352. *gedrinca*. Cited from this passage in R by Napier in *COEL*, but incorrectly defined as 'cupbearer' on the strength of the gloss *pincerna*, whereas the Latin *Daniel* has *conviva* 'a table companion'. BTS gives the right meaning, but Hall–Meritt, citing Warner's text of this passage from G, has 'cupbearer'. The ON version of Ælfric's homily in the *Hauksbók* (see above, p. 669 and n. 2) has it right also, for it reads (I. 162. 13): 'þa var Daniel en motu nautur hans.' Cleasby–Vigfusson defines *mötu-nautr*, m., as 'a messmate'.

363. *Danihel*. In Warner's edition this is taken as vocative at the start of the question, as suggested by the punctuation of her manuscript, G. But the other manuscripts punctuate after the name, and it seems better to take it as object of *axode*. The Latin accords with this pattern, and the lines balance better also.

380. *cuman to his spræce*, 'come to speak with him'. See note on XII. 55.

383. *gif ic gesund beo*. On the idiom, see Glossary, *gesund*.

403. *flore*; 404, *flor*; both acc. sing. On the inconsistent forms of this word see the Glossary.

410. *þær[a] lac[a]*. I have thus ventured to correct all the manuscripts, which differ among themselves but seem never to have it right. A partitive genitive after *abat* is to be expected, and *þære lace* in CL can be so interpreted (whereas R's *þære lac* is simply ungrammatical and G's *þære lacan* confuses declensions). But although Ælfric himself on rare occasions seems to have used *lac* as a feminine singular (see Glossary), his ordinary practice is to treat it as a neuter plural, except in the phrase *to lace* (lines 256, 373), where it is a dative singular and may be either neuter or feminine. In the immediate context, with reference to the gifts offered to Bel, *lac* is clearly established as a nominative plural neuter at 397, and may be presumed to be the corresponding accusative at 401. Hence the genitive plural neuter is to be expected here. Actually C and L (like G) have enough levelled endings to make it seem possible that their reading is a mere levelling of *þæra laca*. Indeed all the Ælfric manuscripts have a tendency to substitute *þære* for *þæra*.

417. *gelette*, CGL; *gelæhte*, R. Either of these words could be justified as an approximation of *tenuit*, but *gelette* seems a little more appropriate. I hardly think we can take *gelæhte* as the author's substitution in a second edition, though it may have been a variant in a copy made for the author.

420. *fotlæsta*. Napier noted this instance of *fotlæst* in the feminine plural, citing it from R in the addenda to *COEL*.

445–7. This passage is simplified in the *Hauksbók*, p. 163/16 sq., as follows: 'Hann toc bic oc bustír oc istr oc veldi alt saman oc gaf honum at eta.' Consequently it does not help us to solve the riddle described in the next note.

446. *welerum*. Though all four manuscripts are in substantial agreement about this word (*welerum* RC, *welrum* L, *weleren* G), which looks like the dative plural of the familiar *weler* 'lip', it can hardly mean 'lip' here. Ælfric's phrase *berode to welerum* corresponds to *fecit massas* in the Vulgate *Daniel*. Even if we try to get around the difficulty by taking *to* as 'for', we hardly succeed: 'kneaded for the lips' is both an odd and a vague way of conveying the idea of *fecit massas*. Moreover, the thirteenth-century glossator (the Worcester scribe with the tremulous hand) wrote *balles* over *welerum*, and one must reckon with the possibility that his gloss was accurate. Accordingly I have long tried to discover evidence for attaching to *weler*, or to some word of closely similar form with which it might have been confused, such a meaning as 'rounded mass', 'cake', or 'ball'. No evidence has emerged, but I shall mention the avenues I have explored thus vainly before proposing a solution less directly related to the gloss.

Old English *weler* 'lip' is held to be the result of metathesis of **werel-*, corresponding to Gothic *wairilō*, and without the suffix, Old Norse *vǫrr*. These words are referred to the Indo-European root **u̯er-* 'a raised place (on the surface of the earth or on the skin)'. (Walde–Pokorny, *Vergleichendes Wörterbuch der indogermanischen Sprachen*, I. 266.) Such a root might conceivably give rise to a word meaning a lump or rounded mass, but apart from this passage there is not the slightest indication in any of the Germanic languages that it did so.

Equally without substantiating evidence and phonologically questionable is the possibility of a connexion with OE *wealwian*, LWS *wilwan* 'to roll' (spelled *wylian* at *LS* VIII. 204), which has cognates in Latin, Gothic, and Old Norse, and is referred to the Indo-European root **uel-* 'turn, twist, roll' (Walde–Pokorny, I. 302). But the Germanic derivatives, like the Latin *volvere*, have a -*u*- after the root. If the word in question were likewise a derivative, one would expect, for Late West Saxon, a spelling *weal(w)-* or *wil(w)-* or *wyl(w)-* rather than the four times attested *wel-* of the manuscripts. Nor is there any recorded Old English word of appropriate meaning that might have been spelled *wilerum* or *wylerum* by Ælfric and miswritten *welerum* by the scribes.

It appears barely possible that a scribe close to Ælfric had substituted *welerum* for *pelerum*, for although there is no doubt of the reading of the four extant manuscripts, *wynn* (the runic *w*) and *þ* are easily confused. In spite of the fact that no such word as *peler* has been recorded for Old English or for any Germanic language, I have explored the possibility of a connexion with Latin *pila* 'ball' by way of some Vulgar Latin derivative, or by way of Old British *pêl* 'ball' or its diminutive *pelen*. But the ordinary Old English gloss for Latin *pila* is *þoðer* 'ball, sphere', and the whole notion of a lonely *peler* disguised as *weler* appears hopelessly far-fetched.

In short, I have not found adequate grounds for interpreting *welerum* as a close rendering of *massas* with a meaning approximating 'balls', or as a deceptive miswriting of such a word. I turn, therefore, to what seems a more promising interpretation.

Under the word *weler* in Bosworth-Toller, among illustrations of the one meaning 'lip', is cited the gloss 'welrum *buccis, buccellis*', which is printed in the Wright–Wülcker *Vocabularies* (I. 195/32) from MS. Harley 3376, a tenth-century glossary described in Ker's *Catalogue*, no. 240. Now *bucca*, though in post-classical times it could mean 'lip' as well as the puffed-out 'cheek' or 'mouth', on rare occasions meant 'mouthful' or 'morsel' (the Lewis and Short *Latin Dictionary* cites Petronius and Martial for this meaning); and the diminutive *buccella* regularly means, not 'lip', but a small 'morsel' or 'portion'. Since I have not traced the gloss to its source, I cannot be sure what the glossator meant, but it seems possible that *weler* 'lip' had undergone a semantic development comparable to that of *bucca* and *buccella*, so that it could refer to a portion of food small enough to be received by the lips all at once—hence a 'mouthful' or 'morsel'. If we take *berode to welerum* as 'kneaded to morsels' we have the essential meaning of *fecit massas*, and can regard the gloss *balles* as merely a reasonable guess or a deliberately inexact substitute.

This hypothesis is strengthened, I believe, by what looks like a comparable though hitherto unregarded semantic development of the Germanic alternative to *weler*, OE *lippa*, modern *lip*, as suggested by certain passages in *Piers Plowman* to which Professor E. T. Donaldson has directed my attention. Skeat's glossary of that poem lists *lippe* 'morsel, portion, part, bit' and *lyppe* 'a portion, part', with reference to three passages that are essentially only two. In one, Avarice confesses to lending money to people who are willing to lose part of every coin, 'a lippe in eche noble' (C-text, VII. 245), or 'a lyppe at euery noble' (B-text, V. 250). In the other, Recklessness says he would rather have 'a lippe of godes grace' than all the wit and learning of Clergy and Scripture (C-text, XII. 226). Relevant also, I think, is *lipet* 'a small piece or bit', cited by the *OED* from Lydgate (*A Ballade of Jak Hare*, 18: 'Of euery dyssh a lypet out to take', *Minor Poems*, ed. MacCracken, Part II, EETS, O.S. 192, p. 446; also in J. Norton-Smith's annotated edition, *John Lydgate, Poems*, Oxford, 1966, p. 12).

Now it is true that the *OED* classifies the *lippe* of *Piers Plowman* as a separate word, *lipe*, sb. 1, surviving in the Cumberland dialect with the pronunciation [lɔip], and meaning either 'a portion, a slip' or 'a pleat or fold'; and it classifies Lydgate's *lipet* as a diminutive of this word rather than of *lip*. Under the first meaning of *lipe* we find, besides the two passages from *Piers Plowman*, two quotations from glossaries of the Cumberland dialect dated 1851 ('*Lipe*, a fragment') and 1878 ('*Lipe*, a large portion. Usually applied to land'). But for etymology the *OED* says merely, 'Cf. OF. *lipee* (F. *lippée*)', a suggestion that leads us back indirectly to the ordinary word *lip*.

Old French *lipee* is cited by Godefroy, *Dictionnaire de l'ancien langue française* (IV. 794b), from a text of the fourteenth century, where it refers to a draught of wine: 'Lors trait une grande *lipee*'; and again (X. 86a) as *lippee* 'bon morceau' from a text of the sixteenth century: 'Le roy d'Angleterre emportait tousjours quelque lippée'. The word survives as *lippée* in modern French, and is defined in E. Littré's dictionary as 'ce qu'on peut prendre avec la lippe, bouchée', a definition that points to the generally assumed derivation from OF *lippe* 'a protruding lower lip', a word still in use which has been found as early as the thirteenth century and is regarded as a borrowing from a Low German dialect. (See, for example, E. Gamillscheg, *Etymologisches Wörterbuch der französischen Sprache*, p. 564; W. v. Wartburg, *Französisches etymologisches Wörterbuch*, XVI. 467–8.)

I am inclined to suspect that, though the Cumberland *lipe*, with its pronunciation [lɔip], may well be derived from an Anglo-French *lipee*, the *lippe* of *Piers Plowman* and the *lipet* of Lydgate are directly related to the ordinary English *lip*, itself spelled *lippe* or *lyppe* in the fourteenth century. In any event, my conjecture that Ælfric was using *weler* in the sense of a mouthful or morsel may seem less improbable in the light of the comparable sense-development of *bucca*, *buccella*, and certain members at least of the *lip* family.

451–93. This story had been told somewhat more briefly by Ælfric in his homily on St. Clement, *CH* I. 570/21–572/22.

472. *embe secgan*. It is tempting to take these words as a compound, but the ellipsis of the object of *embe* (*þone seað*) may be better conveyed by

giving *embe* the slightly greater emphasis and deliberateness of utterance that it can sustain as a separate word. For a few similar examples of near-compounds of *embe* and a verb, see Glossary, *ymbe*; and note also the clear separation at XII. 71, *þe Crist embe þa spræc*.

483. *ofer swiðe langne weg*. The *Hauksbók* here (I. 164/11) has 'um mioc langan veg' where the Vulgate has nothing to correspond—a clear sign that Ælfric's homily has been used.

492. *beorhthwile*. The form *bearhtmhwile* of L shows the derivation more clearly, but the shortened form of the other manuscripts may be Ælfric's. See Glossary.

494–510. There is a comparable passage in *De Correctione Rusticorum*, § 13, but it is altogether different in detail.

497. *fylðe*, R; *fulnesse*, CL. Ælfric uses both words, the context would allow either, and in the absence of any certainty about the relationship of C and L I have allowed R's reading to stand.

512. *towurpon þon[n]e hæþengyld*. The emendation *þon[n]e*, which is at least countenanced by the ambiguous *þoñ* (regularly for *þonne*, rarely for *þone*) in L, seems almost certain on grounds of sense as well as grammar. The scribes who wrote *þone* (as did those of R and C) were following the normal expectation of the word-order but violating the traditional gender of -*gyld*. There is no other instance, to judge by the dictionaries, of masculine instead of neuter gender for this word, and the neuter *þæt* is duly given at line 647 below. Furthermore, there is no clear antecedent for a demonstrative *þone* at this point in the homily, whereas *þonne* makes good sense. Ælfric has alluded vaguely to such false gods as have appeared in the stories of Daniel, and has intimated that many of them were worshipped before the coming of Christ (lines 494–7). He then ushers in the revolutionary sixth age, touching lightly on Christ's manifest divinity, displayed at his ascension as well as by his miracles, and proceeds to the period immediately following the ascension, saying: 'It is also a very long story to say how his faithful apostles *then overthrew idolatry*, after the Saviour's ascension, and powerfully put to flight those abominable gods from their images, while men looked on.' The odd word-order is partially justified, I think, by the rhythmical balance of the line.

515. *biggengas*. The gloss *cultores* in R must be wrong, for it is plain that the meaning here, as normally in Ælfric, is 'religious practices', 'rites'. Ælfric's usual word for 'worshippers' is *biggengan*. See Glossary.

537. *on menigfealdum cræfte*. The relation of this phrase to *micelnysse* is not clear to me, and I suspect we should read *and* for *on*. What Ælfric is referring to is probably a number of subtle contrivances which had been devised, according to Rufinus, *ad stuporem admirationemque videntium*. Thus a narrow window placed with great accuracy allowed the sun to seem to kiss the lips of Serapis at the very moment when an iron image of the sun was being 'magically' elevated by a magnet hidden in the ceiling.

Rufinus makes much of these devices and then says there were *multa alia* that he has no time to describe. (*Hist. Eccl.* XI. 23, in *Eusebius Werke*, II[ii]. 1027 sq.)

556. *sceoccenan.* The gloss in R, *deum demoniorum*, suggests that this might be a miswriting of *sceoccena*, gen. pl. of *sceocca*, but though *sceoccen* is found here only, Napier was probably correct in accepting it and defining it as 'devilish' in *COEL*. It is formed like *treowen* 'wooden', which may also have been in the glossator's mind, since he adds *lingneum*.

559. *buc*, here obviously 'trunk' of the body, a meaning not recorded for OE. The *OED* gives it for ME *bouk*, q.v., but suggests it may have been borrowed from the cognate ON *búkr*. A further use of the word in nearly the same sense by Ælfric seems to have escaped attention because of the unreliability of the late MS. B (Bodley 343) in which it is contained. It occurs in Belfour IX (the revision of *LS* 1), p. 86/5, as the lodging of the soul while on earth, and is aptly translated 'frame' by Belfour. This is cited by the *MED*, *bouk*, 1. (c), but only as 'c 1175 (? OE)'.

577. *embe sume neode*, virtually 'on some business'. Cf. XXVII. 85.

633. *geancyme*, 'return', as properly glossed, *reditu*, in R. On this unrecorded meaning see Glossary.

669. *Ure Hælend cwæð swaþeah be his halgum þegnum, Ego dixi*, etc. Ælfric's statement that these words of the psalm were spoken by the Saviour to his servants is consistent enough with the traditional interpretation of the psalms, but seems slightly at odds with Jesus's own treatment of the verse when he quotes it at *John* x. 34. One can see better the train of associations in Ælfric's mind by turning to I. 350 sqq., where the verse is quoted in support of *John* i. 12. Homily I was undoubtedly composed later than XXI, and may show some added complications in Ælfric's understanding of the verse, but no doubt the basic connexions were established long before.

XXII[1]

'WYRDWRITERAS US SECGAÐ ÐA ÐE AWRITAN BE CYNINGUM'

(Part of a lost composition pertaining to the defence of the kingdom)

THE segment of discourse here edited appears without title and without formal conclusion in MS. P alone. Evidently excerpted from some larger composition, it stands in the company of other short, sometimes excerpted, pieces of Ælfric, several of which occur also in R and S. Perhaps the short pieces in all these manuscripts are derived from a single collection that has since disappeared.

This particular excerpt has to do with the government of the kingdom and its defence against the invader, but it needs careful reading to be rightly assessed, because it has been so delimited as to lack unity. The first eighty-six lines are designed to show by the example of history that some of the most successful rulers have delegated their military power to carefully chosen generals, thus lightening their own burdens and greatly extending the range of their defence against enemies (lines 3–5), while they have avoided the risk of depriving the people of leadership by an untimely death (47–49), and gained time to attend at home to other business for the people's need (86). The greatest need of all in Ælfric's mind was God's support and protection, and this is partially indicated in the description of the emperor Theodosius II, who sent his generals against the enemy and stayed at home to ensure their success by prayer (73–77); but Ælfric has saved the greatest example of this until the end. In lines 87–94 he tells how Moses sent Joshua against Amalek and controlled the outcome of the battle by his prayer (a story he had told at length in *De Oratione Moysi, LS* XIII), and adds, to show God's commitment to the cause of Moses, how in after years the Amalekites were utterly crushed by Saul.

---

[1] In editing these lines I have profited by a trial edition undertaken as a class exercise by a former pupil, Mr. R. K. Diebold.

This final example serves as a transition to a new topic, which is boldly opened but left unfinished in lines 95–103, where the excerpt ends. The primary theme is that the well-being of the realm depends on God. All guidance and all defence must come ultimately from him, and we must seek his counsel with constancy of mind and complete sincerity, so that the promises we make to him will be *fæste and getreowe, trumran þonne stanweall.* For God is truth, and loves truth, and will destroy all those that utter falsehoods. We have thus entered upon a new phase of the discussion, aimed, it would seem, at all those in authority rather than the king alone, and needing further development and due subordination to the master-theme of the national welfare, which remains latent in the excerpt.

Taken as a whole the excerpt sounds more like a letter than a sermon.[1] Like other letters of Ælfric's it is homiletic in manner, a formal admonitory discourse that might suitably be addressed to a group rather than a single correspondent; but the advice contained in the greater part of it would hardly have been offered to an ordinary congregation. The heavy insistence on authorities in the part about kings and their need of generals shows how much Ælfric is concerned lest his advice should not be heeded. I think he must be addressing some nobleman of influence, hoping to reach the king himself and his chief ministers. He was probably acquainted with other noblemen besides his patrons, Æthelweard (now presumably dead) and Æthelmær, and the three correspondents, Wulfgeat, Sigefyrth, and Sigeweard, whose names have come down to us. It is even possible that his advice was solicited.

We have some indication of the date of Ælfric's composition in his allusion, within the excerpt, to two earlier writings, the second part of *LS* VII, on Gallicanus, and the epilogue to the homily on *Judges.* Of these the second is the later, having been written, we may assume, after the publication of the *Lives of Saints* as a set. Since he speaks of *Judges* as having been written *hwilon* (not, for example, *hwene ær*), it is possible that several years had elapsed since then, and I am inclined on general grounds to suspect that the excerpt belongs to the period of Ælfric's abbacy; but of this there is no proof.

The ideals that lie behind the excerpt and are partly stated

[1] This opinion has already been expressed by Dr. Clemoes, *Chronology,* 241.

within it may be found elsewhere in Ælfric, with particular clarity perhaps in homily IX. 48–54, where both the king's responsibility for the defence of the realm and his dependence on God for all authority and all victory are set forth. In the introduction to IX (pp. 373 sqq.) I have given reasons for supposing that Ælfric's views, though grounded in the Old Testament and in Augustinian doctrine, were somewhat affected by such later writings as *De Duodecim Abusivis* and Sedulius Scottus's *De Rectoribus Christianis*. On God as the source of victory and the need for prayer Sedulius is both explicit and copious, and it is hard not to believe that Ælfric was affected by him at several points in his writings, especially those mentioned in the note on IX. 52–54. One of the most memorable passages is the list of kings who triumphed by their faith in God in the epilogue to *Judges*, to which Ælfric here refers us for the victories of Theodosius II.

What distinguishes the present passage is the elaborate plea for a delegation of the king's authority to generals. This is made nowhere else in Ælfric's surviving works, so far as I can remember, and it seems to be a matter that he has thought out for himself under the guidance of the *wyrdwriteras*, both in and out of the Bible. His examples are confined to the Old Testament and the *Historia Ecclesiastica Tripartita* ascribed to Cassiodorus, but he may be speaking truly when he refers to a larger company, heathen as well as Christian, as witnesses he could summon. In the tedious quotations about David one may detect something of the discoverer's anxiety for formal proof of his statements. Underlying the whole passage, however, is the much deeper anxiety that crops up in many places in Ælfric as a counterpoise to his otherworldly serenity. There is such a thing as *iustum bellum*, as he says in his account of the Maccabees (*LS* xxv. 708), 'wið ða reðan flot-menn, oþþe wið oðre þeoda þe eard willað fordon', and there is now a great need that it be waged successfully. In the injunction to seek from God himself *urne ræd mid anrædum mode* (96 sq.) it is hard not to detect an allusion to the *unræd* so unhappily associated with Ethelred.[1]

---

[1] Some interesting speculations concerning the occasion for Ælfric's argument have very recently appeared in a separate edition of this piece by W. Braekman. See the additional note, p. 733 below.

THE TEXT

Wyrdwriteras us secgað, ða ðe awritan be cyningum,
þæt þa ealdan cyningas on ðam ærran timan
hogodon hu hi mihton heora byrðena alihtan,
for þan ðe an man ne mæg æghwar beon, and ætsomne
ealle þing aberan, þeah ðe he anweald hæbbe.   5
Ða gesetton þa cyningas, him sylfum to fultume,
ealdormen under him, and hi oft asendon
to manegum gewinnum, swa swa hit awriten is
ge on hæþenum bocum ge on Bibliothecan;
and þa ealdormen gewyldon þa onwinnendan fynd,   10
swa swa we wyllað secgan sume bysne be þam
of þam Leden-bocum, þæt man us ne lihnige.

Dauid se mæra cyning, þeah ðe he cene wære,
he asende his heretogan, swa swa hit segð on Leden
on þæra Cyninga Bocum, swa swa we cyðað her   15
on Ledenum gereorde, þæt man us gelyfe:
Misit Dauid Ioab ducem, et omnem exercitum bellatorum,
    et cetera:
*Dauid se cyning asende his heretogan,   *f. 63ᵛ
Íoáb gehaten, and [he] gefeaht wið Amón,
and his fynd afligde mid ealre his fyrde.   20
Factum est ergo, uertente anno,
eo tempore quo solent reges procedere ad bella,
misit Dauid Íoáb, et cetera.

This piece is found only in P (Hatton 115), ff. 63–64ᵛ, where it stands as a
separate item but without title and without formal conclusion.

---

1 Wyrd- . . . awritan] *in capitals across first line of MS.*   19 he] *not in
MS.*   22 sol(u)ent *MS.*

Glosses, Latin: 7 hi: illos.   8 gewinnum: prelio.   10 gewyldon:
vice*runt*.   12 lihnige: mentia*tur*.
ME: 1 *Respelled above the line*: wurðwritares us seggeð þeo þe awriten [be]
(kinges), *the last word partially erased.*   13 mæra: *gloss erased.*

Sources. 17 [*II Reg. (II Sam.) x. 7*] Quod cum audisset David, misit Ioab et
omnem exercitum bellatorum.
18–20 [*Summarizes the rest of the story, verses 8–14.*]
21–23 [*II Reg. xi. 1, as given except* autem *for* ergo, *and* ad bella procedere.]

can ðeofler:·

þuuð   þrttturef   uf fcɣɣcð'   þco þc aþrttcıı
ꟼYRÐ ꟼRITEKAS ꟾSSEEGAÐ ÐAÐEAꟼKITAꟾ
becyrtınɣum, þ þa ealdan cynınɣaf; onðam
appan tı man hoꝼoðn huhꟾ milrcon heoþa
byꝥðena alıhrcan, foꝛꝥanðe anman, nemæɣ
iɣ hꝛaꝛ beon. ꟾ ætꝛomneꞽ ealleꝥınɣ abꝗꞽan, þeah
ðe he anꝥealb habbe; Ðaɣeꝛecꞇon þacynınɣaf
him ꝼylꝼum coꝼulꞇume ealdoꝛ men unoeꝛ hꞽ
ꟾ hꞽoꝼꞇ aꝛenꞇon ꞇomaneɣum ɣeꝥınnum, ꝛpa
ꝛpahꞇc aꝛꝛꞇcenꞽıꝛ, ɣeon hæꝥenum boaꞽ, ɣeon
bıblıꞇhecan· ꟾ þaealdoꝛ men ɣeꝼylðon þa on
ꝛınnonðan ꝛynð, ꝛꝛaꝛꝛa peꝛyllað ꝛecɣan
ꝛume byꝼne, beꝥam oꝛꝥam leðen bocum, þ man
uꝛ nelıhrıꝥɣe; Ðauꞇo ꝛemæꝥıa cynınɣ þealıðe
he cene pæꝥe, he aꝼcꞇðe hıꝛheꝛe ꞇoɣan ꝛpaꝛꝛa
hıꞇ ꝛeꝥð onleðenꞽonꝥæꝛıa cynınɣa bocum, ꝛpa
ꝛꝛape cyðað heꝛ onleðenum ɣeꝛeoꝛꞇðe; þæꞇ
man uꝛɣelyꝛe; ꙩ ıꝛꞇ ðauꞇo ıoabðucem eꞇ
omñe exeꝛꞇcꞇum bellaꞇoꝛum eꞇ ceꞇæꝛıa;

Bodleian MS. Hatton 115, f. 63. The beginning of XXII following *De Septiformi Spiritu*, Napier VIII. In the main hand, with the characteristic Worcester marks and glosses.

Dauid se cyning asende eft Íoáb
on ðam oðran geare to ðam Ammoniscum,   25
and he oferwann hi mid þæs cyninges werode,
and sige ðær geferde, swa swa us segð seo racu.
Dixit ergo Dauid, nunc magis aflicturus est nos
Sibá filius Bochri, et cetera.
Siba wæs gehaten sum Dauides þegena,   30
se astyrode þæt folc mid feondlicre spræce
ongean þone cyning Dauid, and cwæð þæt hi ne sceoldan
Dauide fylian, ne be his ræde faran.
Ða fleah se Sibá mid fleamdome aweg;
ac Íoáb se heretoga his heafod begeat   35
æt þære burhware þe he to geboren wæs.
Factum est autem rursum prelium
aduersus Israhel Philistinorum, et cetera.
Eft wæs geworden wið Israhel gefeo[h]t;
on ðam gefeo[h]te wæs sum wundorlic ent   40
se wolde ofslean þone cyning Dauid,
ac him gehe[a]lp sona Abisai his ðegen,
Ioabes broðor, and he þone ent ofsloh,
for þon ðe he geseah hu he syrwde embe Dauid,
wolde hine forstelan betwux his þegenum.   45
Ða sworon sona ðæs cyninges ðegenas ealle,
and sædon him þus to: Ne scealt ðu næfre heonon forð
mid us to gefeohte, þinum feore to plyhte,

34 Ða] *no capital in MS.*   39, 40 gefeoft, gefeofte *MS.*   40 ðam *altered*
to ðæm *MS.*   42 geheolp *MS.*   47 Ne] *no capital in MS.*

Glosses, Latin: 26 oferwann: victit.   27 sige: victoriam.   40 ent:
gigans.   44 syrwde: ins[id]iabatur.

24–27 [*Loosely summarized from the remainder of II Reg. xi. 1 and xii. 26,*
passing over the story of Bathsheba and Uriah, and David's part in the victory over
the Ammonites.]
28, 29 [*II Reg. xx. 6*] Ait autem David ad Abisai: Nunc magis afflicturus
est nos Seba, filius Bochri, quam Absalom . . . .
30–36 [*Summarizes II Reg. xx. 1–22.*]
37, 38 [*II Reg. xxi. 15*] Factum est autem rursum prælium Philisthinorum
adversum Israel. . . .
40–49 [*II Reg. xxi. 16, 17*] Iesbibenob, qui fuit de genere Arapha, cuius
ferrum hastæ trecentas uncias appendebat, et accinctus erat ense novo, nisus est
percutere David. Præsidioque ei fuit Abisai, filius Sarviæ, et percussum Philis-
thæum interfecit. Tunc iuraverunt viri David, dicentes: Iam non egredieris
nobiscum in bellum, ne extinguas lucernam Israel.

*þelæste þu adwæsce Israhe[l]a leohtfæt:— *f. 64

þæt wæs Dauid him sylf be ðam ðe hi sædon swa. 50

Constantinus, se casere ðe ærest beah to Cristendome,
hæfde ænne heretogan se hatte Gallicanus,
þone he asende oft mid swiðlicere fyrdincge
ongean ða onwinnendan leoda þe wunnon ongean þone casere,
and he hi æfre gewilde to ðæs caseres willan. 55

And se Gallicanus wearð syððan swa halig
þæt he wundra worhte and wearð gemartirod for Criste,
swa swa ic awrat on Englisc on sumum spelle íu.

Gratianus wæs gehaten sum healic casere,
swyðe on God gelyfed, swa swa us segð seo bóc 60
Tripartita Istoria, þæt is, Þryfeald Gereccednyss.
Ða wunnon wið hine þa wildan hæþenan,
ac se casere asende him sona togeanes
Theodosium his heretogan, and he feaht wið ða hæþenan,
and he feala ðusenda afylde þæra hæþenra, 65
and he for þam micclan sige syððan wearð casere,
swa swa seo boc us segð, sece se þe wylle.

Ða caseras woldon ða cenan men ofaxian,
and him fultum findan and hi eac fyrðrian
to ealles folces ðearfe, and hi forð tihtan, 70
and wurðodon hi syððan hi sige hæfdon,
swa swa we nu sædon be Theodosige.

Theodosius se gingra and se wurðfulla casere

49 israhera MS.

Glosses, Latin: 49 leohtfæt: lucernam.   53 swiðlicere fyrdincge: valido
populo.   58 iu: olim.   64 heretogan: Ducem (?) partially erased.
66 sige: victoria.   69 fyrðrian: promouere.   71 sige: victoriam.

51–58 [Ælfric merely refers back to his own account, LS vii. 296 sqq. See note.]
59–60 [Hist. Eccl. Tripartita, IX. 2] Gratianus . . . pietatem . . . operibus
demonstrabat initiaque sui regni rerum omnium Domino dedicavit.
62–67 [IX. 4] Porro Gratianus Thraciam barbaros vastare cognoscens Italia
relicta Pæoniam venit. . . . Cum barbari elevati victoria inexpugnabiles esse
viderentur . . . [Theodosium] ab Hispaniis evocans et magistrum militum esse
denuntians cum expeditu ad barbaros destinavit. . . . Immensaque cædes tunc
facta est barbarorum. . . . Cumque pauci omnino transissent dies, qui pro
victoriæ inspectione missi fuerant, remearunt peremptaque hostium multa milia
narraverunt. Quamobrem lætatus princeps Theodosium fecit imperatorem.
73–78 [Ælfric's generalization is confirmed by several passages in the Hist. Eccl.
Trip.: e.g. XI. 9; XI. 15; and XI. 18. Cf. also the following statement at the end
of XI. 17] Si quando bella moverentur, secundum David confugiebat ad Deum,

sende oft his heretogan, swa swa us segð seo racu,
to gehwylcum gefeohtum for his leode ware,   75
and he him sylf wolde singan his gebedu,
and Gode betæcan symle his fyrde,
*and God him eac fylste and his folc bewerode,   *f. 64ᵛ
swa swa we awriton on sumon spelle hwilon.

Langsume tale we magon macian be ðysum   80
gif we wyllað secgan be þam ðe us secgað béc,
of þam ðe us becymð se wisdom and seo wissung,
hu oft wurdon asende þa sigefæstan heretogan
to manegum gewinnum heora leodum to ware;
and ða cyningas sæton him sylfe swaðeah   85
æt ham ymbe oðre bysga h[eora] leod[um] to þearfe.

Moyses se mæra, þe mihte wið God sprecan,
he asende Iosue, swa swa us segð *Exodus*, togeanes Amalech;
and Moyses þa hwyle motode wið God
and abæd him sige æt þam soðfæstan Gode.   90
Ðis gewræc Saul eft syððan on Amalech,
swa þæt he be Godes hæse gehergode þone eard,
and þa hæðenan acwealde, and heora cynn adylegode,
for þan ðe hi wunnon wolice wið Moysen.

Ure wissung and ure waru sceal beon of Gode,   95
and we sceolon secan æt Gode sylfum urne ræd
mid anrædum mode, and on eornost sprecan,
þæt ure behat beon þe we behatað Gode

86 his leode *MS*.

Glosses, Latin: 83 sigefæstan: *vi*ctoriosi.   to: *contra* (*misplaced over* to *in*
heretogan).   84 gewinnum: *p*relio.   to ware: cauendu*m* (*!*).   89 motode:
loqu*e*batur.   90 sige: *vi*ctoria*m*.   91 gewræc: vindicauit.   93 adylegode: deleu*it*.   94 wolice: i*n*iuste.
ME: 89 motode: spac (*? erased*).

---

sciens eum proeliorum auctorem, [et] inimicos orationibus superabat. [*All these*
passages in Book XI are drawn from the Ecclesiastical History of Socrates.]
87–90 [*Free summary of Ex. xvii. 8–16.*]
91–94 [*I Reg.* (*I Sam.*) *xv*, *esp. 1–9, 32, 33*] Et dixit Samuel ad Saul...: Hæc
dicit Dominus exercituum: Recensui quæcumque fecit Amalec Israeli, quomodo
restitit ei in via cum ascenderet de Ægypto. Nunc ergo vade, et percute Amalec,
et demolire universa eius; ... interfice a viro usque ad mulierem, et parvulum
atque lactentem, bovem et ovem, camelum et asinum. ... Percussitque Saul
Amalec, ab Hevila donec venias ad Sur. ... Et apprehendit Agag, regem
Amalec, vivum; omne autem vulgus interfecit in ore gladii. ... Et in frusta con-
cidit eum [Agag] Samuel coram Domino, in Galgalis.

fæste and getreowe, trumran þonne stanweall;
for þan ðe God is soðfæstnyss, and he soðfæstnysse lufað, 100
and he ealle ða fordeð þe leasunga sprecað,
swa swa hit on Leden stent ðysum wordum awriten:
Perdes omnes qui loquuntur mendacium.

99 fæste] *the* e *underdotted as if for deletion MS.*   103 Perdes] *no capital in MS.*

Glosses, Latin: 99 trumran: firmior; *another gloss, probably ME, erased.*

103 [*Psal. v. 7, in part, as given.*]

NOTES

1. Cf. the opening sentence of the homily on St. Bartholomew, *CH* I. 454: 'Wyrdwriteras secgað þæt ðry leodscipas sind gehatene India.'

9. *on hæþenum bocum.* I do not know what heathen histories he had read. Cf. xxi. 148.

12. *þæt man us ne lihnige*; 16. *þæt man us gelyfe.* Ælfric's concern for authority and his fondness for Latin quotations are everywhere apparent, but here he insists more than usual on the validity of his testimony.

20. *fynd.* Evidently accusative plural, as the form regularly indicates. The phrase *mid ealre his fyrd* applies to Joab's army (referred to as *omnem exercitum bellatorum* in the Latin), not to Ammon's. Cf. 26, *mid þæs cyninges werode.*

34. *fleamdome.* This is the only record of the word, which was cited from P by Napier in *COEL.*

42. *geheolp*, MS. It is conceivable that the scribe wrote this form intentionally instead of the normal *gehealp*, but it is more likely as careless an error as *gefeoft* in 39 and 40 or *israhera* in 49.

51–58. Ælfric's full account of Gallicanus, to which he here refers, is in *LS* vii. 296–429, the *Alia Sententia quam scripsit Terrentianus* appended to the *Natale Sancte Agnetis.* The approximate source has been identified as the *Passio Gallicani* in Mombritius, *Sanctuarium* (Paris, 1910), I. 569–71. See J. H. Ott, *Über die Quellen der Heiligenleben in Aelfrics Lives of Saints I* (Halle, 1892), pp. 26 sqq.

64. Theodosius I is mentioned as the destroyer of idols in xxi. 542, and his victory achieved by the aid of a miraculous storm is briefly described in the epilogue to *Judges*, lines 40–44 (*O.E. Hept.*, p. 415). The story of his encounter with Ambrose is told at length in xxvi.

79. *swa swa we awriton on sumum spelle hwilon.* That is, in the homily on *Judges*, Epilogue, 45–77 (*O.E. Hept.*, pp. 415 sq.).

87–90. The story touched upon in these lines is told fully in *De Oratione Moysi*, *LS* XIII. 1–29.

88. *swa swa us segð Exodus*. This parenthesis may be an afterthought, since the line is complete without it; but it adjusts itself well to the alliterative scheme and produces an interesting variation.

ADDITIONAL NOTE

A separate edition of this piece by W. Braekman ('Wyrdwriteras: an Unpublished Ælfrician Text in Manuscript Hatton 115', *Revue belge de philologie et d'histoire*, XLIV [1966], 959–70) came to hand after this volume was already in page proof. In his introduction, p. 963, Dr. Braekman makes the interesting and plausible suggestion that Ælfric composed the principal part of this extract in response to criticism of Ethelred for not leading his troops in person on several important occasions, thus breaking the precedent set by Alfred and his successors in the first half of the tenth century. Even if this is so, however, lines 68–72 suggest the need for more careful selection of generals than had hitherto been made.

Dr. Braekman's edition is similar in scope and method to his slightly earlier edition of no. XIX above, but here his text is free from contamination by the Worcester corrections. Its only blemish is the interpretation of the manuscript *gode fæste* (i.e. *Gode fæste*, lines 98 and 99 above) as a compound, *gode-fæste*. We differ about a few of the glosses, which are often hard to decipher. Instead of *mentiatur* (somewhat inaccurately glossing *lihnige*, 12) he has *inficiatur* (certainly wrong, but I was differently wrong until the last minute). He may be right in reading a partially erased *dvc* above *heretogan*, 18; I can see only faint and uncertain traces in my photostat. I think he is wrong in guessing *ba* (*run*?) over *heretogan*, 64, where I have guessed *Ducem*, and he is certainly wrong in reading *victoriali* for *victoriosi* in the margin as a gloss for *sigefæstan*, 83. In the same line, I have reported the very clear but inappropriate or misplaced abbreviation for *contra* above the *to* of *heretogan*, whereas he reports *comes* (without indicating an abbreviation). Finally, what he reports as a partially erased *licere* above *motode*, 89, and attributes to confusion between the infinitives *motian* and *motan*, is probably the correct ME gloss *spæc* or *spac*. The only Latin gloss for *motode* is therefore the marginal *loquebatur*, on which we agree.

XXIII

SANCTORUM ALEXANDRI, EVENTII, ET THEODOLI: PARS PRIMA

(The preliminary phases of the story concluded in *CH* II. xx)

THIS narrative, composed in the same rhythmical prose as the short piece on the passion of the three saints in the *Catholic Homilies*,[1] can hardly be the work of anyone but Ælfric. The scribe who copied it in part of an extra gathering at the beginning of MS. T (Hatton 114) indicated clearly that it was to be joined to the earlier piece, replacing some introductory lines and giving an account of the events preceding Alexander's confrontation with the tyrannical Aurelianus. When the two pieces are joined together according to the instructions, we have a complete rendering (with some minor abridgements and variations) of the *Acta Alexandri Papæ* as given in the Bollandist *Acta Sanctorum* for the third of May. Of the printed texts of the *Acta* this is the closest to Ælfric, though at one point (line 65) the text given by Surius is closer.[2] It had been established by Max Förster that Ælfric had used the fourth and last chapter of the *Acta Alexandri* for his narrative in the *Catholic Homilies*.[3]

Evidently Ælfric was not content to leave the rest of the story untold in English, though indeed the wonder is that he should have omitted the early chapters at first. Perhaps he was troubled by the fact that he had composed a homily on the invention of the cross for the same day, and thought he would keep this one within bounds by limiting it to the passions of Alexander and his attendant priests. We know, too, from the Latin preface to the Second Series, that he was pressed for time because of the Danish raids and had to make some of the homilies shorter than usual. Under these circumstances he may have thought the preliminary chapters

[1] Contained in MSS. D, E, K (Thorpe's), T (Hatton 114 as originally written), and Cotton Vitellius D. xvii. No longer in Cotton Otho B. x.

[2] *Historiae seu Vitae Sanctorum*, V (Maius), Turin, 1876, pp. 73–81.

[3] *Über die Quellen von Ælfric's Homiliae Catholicae. I. Legenden*, Inaug. Diss., Berlin, 1892, p. 38.

of the *Acta* dispensable or even distracting, for while they exhibit the miracles performed by Alexander they make much of two remarkable converts, Hermes and Quirinus. The passion of Quirinus is related at some length, though his day comes earlier, at the end of March. On second thoughts, however, one is bound to recognize the value of these preliminaries. As sensational narratives go this is ably constructed. The debate of Quirinus with Hermes, conducted with forbearance and leading to Quirinus's conversion, stands in significant contrast to the violent altercation between Aurelianus and Alexander with its ensuing horrors; and the preliminary conflict between Aurelianus and Quirinus helps to prepare us for these excesses as well as to make the rage of the tyrant a little more intelligible.

Ælfric does not always make the most of the story as it stands in the Latin *Acta*. Some relatively subtle touches are lost in the process of abridgement, and his rearrangement of the narrative at the beginning is of doubtful propriety. By putting first, in its chronological order, Alexander's resuscitation of Hermes's dead son, Ælfric gains narrative simplicity and a powerful beginning, but weakens the organization of the whole. Perhaps he judged rightly, however, that a congregation would not easily follow the complications of the more sophisticated Latin narrative.

The Worcester scribe who added this piece to Hatton 114 was not, in Ker's opinion, the same as any of the scribes who were responsible for other additions, and is to be sharply distinguished from the main scribe of the volume. All one can say is that his hand resembles other Worcester hands of the last quarter of the eleventh century, and that his spellings deviate markedly from those of the main scribe, who follows the prevailing LWS conventions. This man's spellings show certain Anglian traits:

(a) *a* for *ea* before *l, r* plus consonant: *aldlic*, 7, *cwartern*, -*e*, 69, 72, 78, etc. (14 times); *all*, 115; *alle*, 140.

(b) *ē* for *ȳ* (from EWS *ie*), *gelefan*, 98.

(c) *in*, prep., for *on*, 171.[1]

They also show a number of other small deviations from the standard, some of which are probably merely to be classified as late:

---

[1] I had failed to notice this *in* when I said (I. 82/23 above) that MS. V had the only instance (at xxx. 114, not 111) of *in* for *on* in the homilies here edited. My oversight does not affect the argument.

(d) interchange of *i* and *ig* in *byri*, 12 (acc. s.!); *fifti*, 40; *hig*, 106 and 108 (asf.), 155 (ap.); *twenti*, 157; *hungria*, 182.

(e) *ig* for palatal *g* in -*dæig*, 19, 25; *þeigne*, 53; *aweig*, 153; *mæigð*-, 197.

(f) The infinitive ends in -*en* for -*an* at 82 (twice), 119, 162, 167 (first), 175, 190, 194 (first), 198.

(g) The past participle ends in -*an* for -*en* at 115.

(h) *a* for *æ* in *hafð*, 34; *ic habbe*, 102.

(i) miscellaneous: *Godd*, 31; *weorld*- (for *woruld*- or less often *weoruld*-), 58; *woldost* for *woldest*, 97; *sculdon* for the prevailing *sceoldon*, 177; *hatst* for *hætst*, 108; *wurpun* for *weorpun* or the prevailing *wurpan*, inf., 194; *ealla* for acc. pl. *ealle*, 201; *Ða þa* for the regular *Ða þe* 'those who', 176; perhaps *æfninge* for the regular *æfnunge*, 90; and perhaps the variant *swyre* for *swuran* (acc. sing.), 132 (see note).

Of course many of these spellings can be found sporadically in manuscripts of the eleventh century or earlier, and some are perhaps mere blunders; but the very large number of deviations is striking and sets this text apart from all others in this edition.

[V. NON. MAII
SANCTORUM ALEXANDRI, EVENTII,
ET THEODOLI]

On ðissum dæge we wurðiað mid lofsangum
þone halgan papan þe is gehaten Alexander,
se ðrowode martirdom mid twæm mæssepreostum
þa wæron gehatene Euentius and Theodolus;
hi ðrowodon on ðissum dæge for heora Drihtnes geleafan.   5
He wæs se fifta papa æfter Petres ðrowunge,
iunglic on gearum, and aldlic on geleafan,
halig on his weorcum; and he gewende þa hæðenan
ðurh his godnesse to Godes geleafan,
and feala ðara burhwitena he gebigde to Gode.   10
    Hermes wæs gehaten se yldesta burhwita
on Romana byrig, and he ða byri bewyste
under þam casere Traianus gehaten.
Ða gelamp hit swa þæt his sunu forðferde,

Contained only in T (Hatton 114), ff. 5–8ᵛ.

Title] Supplied from CH II. xx. No heading by original scribe. The Worcester
scribe with the trembling hand adds, Alexandri, Euencii et Theodoli.

Glosses, Latin: 8 gewende: *conuertit.*   10 burhwitena: ciues (*!*)

SOURCES. 6–10 [*ASS, Acta Alexandri Papæ, I. 1*] Quinto loco a beato Petro
Apostolo Romanæ urbis Ecclesiæ Cathedram sedit Alexander, sanctitate in-
comparabilis; iuvenis quidem ætate, sed fide senior. Totius autem populi verum
affectum gratia ei divina contulerat: ut et Senatorum maximam partem con-
verteret ad Dominum.
    11–13 [*Ælfric's transition. Hermes is called* Præfectum Urbis, *Acta, I. 1, and
Trajan is named in I. 2.*]
    14–36 [*Ælfric puts first, in chronological order, the story of Hermes's son. In
the Acta Alexandri it is told later, II. 7, in a speech by Hermes to Quirinus*]
Unicus mihi cum esset filius, in nimio languore positus, qui adhuc ad litterarum
studia ambulabat, iste in Capitolium ductus est a me et a matre sua; et cum
sacrificassemus omnibus Diis, . . . mortuus est. Tunc increpare me coepit nutrix
eius, dicens: Tu si ad sancti Petri limina eum adduxisses, et credidisses Christo,
hodie filium tuum haberes incolumem. Cui ego dixi: Dum tu ipsa cæca sis facta,
et non sis curata, quomodo filium meum mihi reddes incolumem? . . . Vade, et
crede: et si tibi oculos aperuerit Alexander, credam quod et mihi possit resti-
tuere unicum filium. Tunc abiit ad ipsum cæca, circa horam tertiam: et ecce
hora diei sexta, reversa est ad me sana, imponensque mortuum filium meum in

seofon wintra cnapa, and he ða sarig wearð.   15
Ða cwæð þæs cildes fostormodor to þam sarigan fæder,
Gif ðu gelyfdest on Crist, and gelæddest ðinne sunu
to ðæs halgan Peteres cyrcan, na to hæðengildum,
þu hæfdest þinne sunu ansundne nu todæig.
Hermes hire cwæð to, Ðu eart ðe sylf blind;   20
gelyf ðu on Crist, and gif ðin geleafa ðe gehælð,
þonne gelyfe ic syþþan þæt he minne sunu
mage mihtelice of deaðe aræran.
Ða eode þæt blinde *wif ymb underntíd   *f. 5ᵛ
to Alexandre ðam papan, and eft ymbe mid-dæig   25
com ham to hire hlaforde mid halum eagum bliðe.
Heo genam ða þæs cildes lic, and mid geleafan eode
to ðæm halgan papan, and hine bæd georne
þæt he hit arærde þurh ðæs Hælendes mihte.
Hwæt ða Alexander on his gebedum cneowode,   30
and þæt cild sona arás of deaðe þurh Godd,
and seo fostermodor hit bær bliðe to ðam fæder,
hal and gesund, and he sona gelyfde
on ðone ælmihtigan God þe swylce mihte hafð.
Hermes þa se fæder eode to ðæm papan   35
and feoll to his fotum, fulluhtes biddende.
He wearð ða gefullod æt ðam foresædan papan
mid wife and mid cildum and mid gesibbum mannum
and mid æhtemannum, ealles twelf hundred
manna and fifti, ða he gefreode ealle   40
and mid æhtum gegodode on ðæm halgan Eastordæge.

Glosses, Latin: 18 na: *non.*   19 ansundne: *incolumem.*   39 æhte-:
viii (*!*).   40 ða he gefreode: *illos liberos fecit.*   41 æhtum: *opibus.*

humeris suis currere coepit. . . . Quæ cum venisset [ad Alexandrum], iactavit
eum ante pedes eius dicens: Domine, redeat ad me cæcitas, tantummodo ut iste
resuscitetur ad vitam. Tunc sanctus Alexander dixit ei, Sic vero istum puerum
resuscitet Christus, ut tibi semel quos redonavit non auferat oculos. Cumque
oratione facta sanasset eum et ipse per se veniens ad me, reddidisset filium meum
viventem et sanum, statim me misi ad pedes eius, et rogavi eum ut me faceret
Christianum: et ex eo die credidi Christo. [*Ælfric not only abridges but has the
nurse, not the pope, bring the child home.*]

37–41 [*Acta I. 1, continuing sentence about Alexander quoted for* 6–10 *supra*]
. . . et Præfectum Urbis quoque, Hermen, cum uxore et sorore et filiis, baptizaret,
cum mille ducentis quinquaginta servis suis, uxoribus quoque et filiis eorum,
quos omnes in die sancto Paschæ prius fecit fieri ingenuos, et ita baptizari:
quibus postea etiam multa . . . dona concessit.

Ðis wearð gecydd þæm casere Traiane,
hu Hermes his gerefa hæfde forlæten
ðone hæþenscipe þe he on gelyfde
and wære gefullod æt þam foresædon papan;   45
and he asende sona sumne heretogan to Rome,
Aurelianus gehaten, to ofsleanne ða Cristenan;
ac Traianus gewat on þæm ilcan geare.

Aurelianus þa ferde mid my*celre fare to Rome,   *f. 6
and he hæfde ðone anwald þe se oðer ǽr hæfde;   50
and he gebrohte on cwartern þone halgan papan
and Ermen ðone heahgerefan he het healdan on bendum
mid anum his þeigne, se hatte Quirinus.

Ða axode Quirinus þone arwurðan Ermen,
Hwi dest ðu ðe swa wacne, swa æðelboren swa ðu eart,   55
þæt þu þinne wurðscipe forlætst and on bendum þuss ligst?
Hermes him andwyrde ardlice and cwæð:
Se weorldlica wurðscipe is awendedlic,
and se heofonlica wunað ecelice.

Quirinus him cwæð to, Cwist ðu þæt ænig lif sy   60
æfter þissum life, be ðan ðe ðu gelyfst?
Hermes him andwyrde, Nu for feawum gearum
ic tælde þa Cristenan þe cwædon þæt ænig

Glosses, Latin: 48 gewat: obiit.   50 anwald: potestate*m*.   55 wacne:
vile*m*.   57 ardlice: cito.   63 tælde: repr*e*hendi.

42–50 [*Acta I. 2*] Unde cum hæc opera eius ad Traianum Principem pervenissent, misit Aurelianum Comitem utriusque militiæ de Seleucia Isauriæ, ad
interfectionem omnium Christianorum: unde nutu Dei eodem anno defunctus
est Traianus. Et ingresso urbem Aureliano, omnis senatus ita famulatus est ei,
ut ipsum Principem crederent esse Traianum.

51–53 [*Acta I. 2*] Statim ergo ut ingressus est Romam, . . . templorum
Pontifices . . . ita animum Aureliani ad iracundiam concitaverunt, ut Hermen
Præfectum Urbis in vincula mitteret, sed et S. Alexandrum Papam carceri
manciparet. . . . [*I. 3*] Igitur dum Hermes . . . haberetur in vinculis apud
Quirinum Tribunum,

54–61 [*Acta I. 3 cont.*] dicit ei Quirinus: Quæ ratio est ut vir illustris . . .
Præfecturæ carens honore tamquam privatum vinculis te onerari æquanimiter
feras? Sanctus Hermes dixit: . . . Dignitas terrena . . . mutatur: dignitas vero
cælestis æterna sublimitate subsistit. Dicit ei Quirinus: Miror te prudentem
virum ad tantam stultitiam devenisse, ut credas te extra istam vitam aliquid
habiturum. . . .

62–67 [*Acta I. 3*] Hermes dixit: Et ego ante hos annos ista deridebam, et
istam carnalem utilem esse dicebam vitam. [*Surius*, et solam hanc . . . vitam . . .
in pretio habendam existimabam.] Dicit ei Quirinus: Fac et me probare, ut si
ita est, sicut tu credidisti, et ego credam.

oðer lif wære æfter þissum life,
and ic ðiss an lif to lufienne tealde.   65
Quirinus him cwæð to, Do þæt ic cunne ðæt lif,
and ic swa gelyfe swa swa ðu gelyfst.
Hermes cwæð him eft to, Alexander se papa,
þe nu on cwarterne is, þurh Crist me onlihte,
and me geleafan tæhte, and ic gelyfe nu on God.   70
Gewend nu to ðam cwearterne and cyþ him uncer word.
Quirinus him cwæð to, Ic gange nu to ðam cwarterne,
and ic cweðe to Alexandre, Gif ðu Cristes bydel eart,
gecum to Ermen, oððe Hermes to þe,
þæt ic inc gemete ðurh Godes mihte ætgædere,   75
*and ic syþþan gelyfe swa swa ðu me tæcst.   *f. 6ᵛ
Hermes him andwyrde, Do swa ardlice.

Quirinus þa eode to ðam cwarterne hraðe,
and gesette ma wearda ofer ðone halgan wer,
and mid þrimfealdum locum þa duru beleac,   80
and mid þrimfealdum hæftnydum gehæfte ðone papan,
and het hine cunnien gif he acumen mihte
of ðam hæftnydum to ðæm halgan Ermen.
Alexander ða clypode to Criste and cwæð,
Eala Hælend Crist, ðe me hete gesittan   85
on Peteres setle, asend me þinne engel,
þæt he me gelæde to Ermen ðinum þeowan,
and eft on ærnemergen hider ongean gelæde,

Glosses, Latin: 65 tealde: iudicau*it*.   69 onlihte: illuminau*it*.   70 geleafan: fide*m*.   73 bydel: *preco*.   74 gecum: veni.   77 ardlice: mox.
79 gesette: posuit.   wearda: custodes.   81 hæftnydum: funib*us*.
gehæfte: vincit.   82 acumen: exire.   85 ðe: q*ui*.

68–77 [*Acta I. 4*] Hermes dixit: Sanctus Alexander, qui habetur in vinculis,
hoc me docuit. . . . [*Ælfric skips Quirinus's initial distrust of Alexander and
supplies his own transition at line* 71.] Quirinus dixit: . . . Ego vado ad eum et dico
illi: Si vis ut credam te verum Dei esse præconem, . . . aut te apud Hermen
inveniam, aut Hermen apud te, et omnia quæ mihi dixeris credam. Hermes
dixit: Ita fiat.

78–83 [*Acta I. 4*] Dicit ei Quirinus: Vadam ergo modo, et super eum vincula
triplicabo et custodes, dicamque illi ut eum apud te inveniam cænandi hora. . . .
[*II. 5*] Cumque isset et hoc dixisset Tribunus Quirinus sancto Alexandro, et
triplicasset ei custodes et claustra;

84–89 [*Acta II. 5*] mittens se in orationem Alexander, dixit: Domine Iesu
Christe qui me in Cathedra Apostoli tui Petri sedere fecisti, præsta mihi ut . . .
mittas ad me Angelum tuum, qui me . . . perducat ad famulum tuum Hermen,
et iterum matutino huc revocet me, nemine sentiente usque dum ego hic redeam.

swa þæt nan mann nyte hwænne ic fare oððe cume.
Hwæt þa on æfninge com Godes engel   90
mid leohte to Alexandre, and gelædde hine to Ermen,
to Quirines huse, þær þær he gehæft wæs.
Eft on ærnemergen eode Quirinus
into his hordcleofan, and þa halgan gemette,
Alexandrum and Ermen, on heora gebedum samod,   95
and leoht ætforan heom, and he wearð afyrht.

Ða halgan him cwædon to, Ðu cwæde þæt þu woldost sona
on God gelefan gif ðu us gesawe ætgædere:
gelyf nu on God, nu ðu us ætgædere gesihst.
Hermes him sæde eac hu his sunu wearð aræred   100
of deaðe to life þurh *Alexandres geleafan.   *f. 7
Quirinus him andwyrde, Ic habbe ane dohtor
wlitige on ansyne, ac heo is forðearle awlætt,
for ðon ðe heo is hoferode; ac gehelpað hire, ic bidde,
and ic syþþan gelyfe on ðone Hælend mid eow.   105
Ða cwæð Alexander, Læd hig to ðam cwarterne to me.
Quirinus him andwyrde, Ðu eart on minum huse nu,
and humeta hatst ðu hig bringan to þam cwarterne?
Alexander him cwæð to, Gang ardlice and bring hi,
for ðan þe ðu me ðær gemetest þonne þu mid hire cymst.   110
He eode ða sona, and Godes engel gelædde

Glosses, Latin: 92 gehæft: ligat*us*.   99 gelyf: crede.   103 wlitige:
pulcra*m*.   ansyne: facie.   108 humeta: q*ualiter*.   hatst: iubes.
109 ardlice: *constanter*.

90–92 [*Acta II. 5*] Primo igitur nocturno silentio affuit puer, faculam ardentem
ferens in carcerem, . . . et perduxit eum ad Hermen in domum Quirini, intra
clausum cubiculum.

93–96 [*Acta II. 6*] Et veniens post, Quirinus aperuit ostium: et inveniens eos
simul extensis manibus orantes, et faculam ardentem videns, exterritus est. . . .

97–99 [*Acta II. 6*] Dixerunt ei: Quoniam ex fide hanc definitionem habuisti in
corde tuo, ut si nos . . . sociatos videres, crederes; ecce vidisti nos, crede.

100–1 [*Ælfric here passes over Hermes's story of his son, which he has already
used for lines* 14–36.]

102–10 [*Acta II. 8*] Audiens hæc Quirinus . . . coepit dicere: . . . Habeo filiam
adultam, . . . cuius aspectum quidem pulchritudo condecorat, sed collum eius
struma circumdat. Hanc vos salvam facite, . . . et vobiscum Christum confiteor.
Dicit ei sanctus Alexander: Vade et adduc eam ad carcerem ad me cito. . . .
Quirinus dixit ei: Et cum tu hic sis in domo mea, quomodo te inveniam in
carcere? Sanctus Alexander respondit ei: Festinanter vade, quoniam qui me
adduxit ad te priusquam tu venires, reduci me ibidem faciet.

111–13 [*Acta II. 8*] Hæc cum dixisset, egressus est Quirinus. . . . Et . . . ecce

þone halgan papan eft to ðam cwarterne,
and se engel syþþan gewat.

Quirinus com þa syþþan and þæt cwartern gemette
all swa fæste belocan swa he hit ær forlet.   115
He unleac ða duru, and Alexander se papa
sæt on þam cwarterne swa swa he ær gecwæð.
Ða feoll Quirinus afyrht to his fotum,
ofdrædd þæt him Godes yrre on becumen sceolde.
Se papa hine frefrode, þæt he unforht wære,   120
and he æteowde þæm halgan his unhalan dohtor.
Ða het Alexander hine axian hraðc
hwæðer on ðam cwarterne wæron ænige Cristene menn
for Godes geleafan belocene on ðam witum.
He fandode þa, and afunde ðærinne   125
twegen mæssepreostas, mæres lifes menn,
Euentium and Theodolum, of estdæle *cumene.   *f. 7ᵛ
Ða het Alexander þæt he mid arwurðnesse
sceolde hi gefeccan swyþe raðe him to.
Quirinus þa mid ofste adyde of ðæm papan   130
ealle þa hæftnedu þe he mid gehæft wæs.

129 *after* sceolde] *MS has point here instead of after* arwurðnesse.

Glosses, Latin: 113 gewat: disp*ar*uit.   125 fandode: q*ue*siu*it*.
128 arwurðnesse: ven*er*at*i*o*ne*.   131 hæftnedu: ligat*ur*as.

infantulus ille cum facula paratus . . . revocavit eum [Alexandrum] in carcerem,
eique vincula reposuit et abscessit.

114–21 [*Acta II. 9*] Post unam vero horam venit ad custodes . . . Quirinus,
. . . et cum invenisset eos vigilantes, et claustra omnia integerrima atque signata,
sicuti dimiserat, aperiens invenit S. Alexandrum Papam, ad cuius pedes pro-
cidens, coepit clamare dicens: Peto, Domine, ut ores pro me, ne veniat super me
ira Dei, cuius tu es Episcopus. Cui respondens S. Alexander ait: Deus meus non
vult perire quemquam, sed converti peccantes. . . . Tunc prosternens se Quirinus
dixit: Ut iussisti, ecce ancilla tua filia mea.

122–7 [*Acta III. 9. Ælfric skips Alexander's first question,* Quot sunt in isto
carcere clausæ personæ? *and the reply,* Prope viginti.] Sanctus Alexander dixit
ei: Require si sunt hic aliqui pro nomine Christi clausi. Et cum requisisset,
invenit ac renuntiavit ei dicens: Est ibi Eventius Presbyter senex, et Theodolus,
quem dicunt de Oriente venisse Presbyterum.

128–34 [*Acta III. 9*] Dicit ei Alexander Papa: Vade cursim, et cum honore
adduc eos ad me. Tamen, dum vadis et venis, tolle boiam de collo meo, et induc
eam filiæ tuæ. Statim tollens omnia vincula ab eo Quirinus, osculari coepit pedes
S. Alexandri, dicens: Tuis manibus impone eam illi. At ubi imposuit urgere coepit
Alexander Quirinum ut iret. Qui dum vadit, ecce puer ille subito cum facula
apparuit, et venit ad puellam dicens ei: Salva esto. . . . Hæc cum dixisset,
abscessit. [*Ælfric's abridgement of this passage blurs the story.*]

Ða dyde se halga wer on his dohter swyre
þæt ilce geoc þe wæs on his agenum swuran,
and se fæder þa eode æfter ðam preostum.

Eft ða se fæder com mid þam foresædum preostum,   135
þa wæs his dohtor hal, and he ofwundrod cwæð:
Eala ðu halga fæder, far heonon ic ðe bidde,
ðe læs þe heofonlic fýr me færlice forbærne.

Alexander him cwæð to, Gif ðu me ænigne ðanc don wylt,
gedo þæt alle þas hæftlingas þe on ðissum cwarterne synt   140
gebugon to Cristendome þurh þine tyhtinge.

Ða cwæð Quirinus him to, Ge Cristenan syndon halie,
and þas hæftlingas synt swyþe fordone menn,
sume morðslagan, sume manfulle forligras,
sume unlybwyrhtan, sume yfeldæde,   145
sume eac forscyldegode mid mislicum leahtrum.

Alexander cwæð, Crist ure alysend
com to middanearde for synfullum mannum,
and he synfullan clypað simle to mildse;
ne twynie ðe nan ðing, læt hi cuman ealle to me.   150
Quirinus þa clypode to ðam mannum and cwæð:
Swa hwa swa wyle Cristen beon, cume hider to me;

Glosses, Latin: 140 gedo: fac.   141 gebugon: *conuertant.*   143 þas:
isti.   144 manfulle: *iniqui.*   145 unlybwyrhtan: pestiferi.   146 forscyldegode: *criminosi.*   150 twynie: dubites.

135–50 [*Acta III. 10*] Veniens autem pater puellæ Quirinus cum Eventio et
Theodolo Presbyteris, invenit filiam suam sanam, et coepit clamare: Exi hinc
de ista custodia, Domine Alexander, ne forte, dum tu hic tardas, veniat ignis de
cælo et consumat me. Dicit ei S. Alexander: Si vis mihi præstare beneficium,
suade omnibus, qui sunt in carcere, baptizari, ut fiant Christiani. Quirinus respondit: Vos Christiani sancti estis, horum autem alii effractores sunt, alii
adulteri, alii malefici, alii diversorum criminum rei. Dicit ei S. Alexander: Pro
peccatoribus filius Dei Dominus noster Iesus Christus de cælo descendit, et de
Virgine natus omnes vocat ad indulgentiam. Noli ergo dubitare, sed omnes fac
ad me venire.

151–60 [*Acta III. 10*] Tunc Quirinus dixit omnibus clara voce: Quicumque
voluerit fieri Christianus, fiat: et qui baptizatus fuerit, vadat liber quocumque
voluerit. [*III. 11*] Cumque venissent omnes ad S. Alexandrum Papam, aperuit
Deus os eius, et coepit dicere: [*Ælfric omits the sermon*]. . . . [*III. 12*] Cumque
universi credidissent, præcepit Eventio et Theodolo, ut manus eis imponerent, et
catechumenos eos facerent. Post hæc autem Quirinus, simul cum filia sua Bal-
bina et omni domo sua, baptizatus est, omnesque qui simul erant in custodia.
Et omnibus baptizatis apertus est carcer, et coepit esse quasi ecclesia. [*The
number twenty in line 157 is given earlier in the Latin: see quotation at 122
supra.*]

and se ðe gefulled beo, fare him freo aweig.
Hi comon ða ealle to ðæm arwurðan papan,
and he hig þa lærde, *and heora geleafan heom tæhte   *f. 8
oðþæt hi ealle gelyfdon on þone lifigendan God,   156
and wurdon gefullode wel twenti manna;
and Quirinus syþþan sona wearð gefullod
mid eallum his hiwum on ðæs Hælendes naman,
and þæt cwartern wearð þa gelic geleaffulre cyrcean.   160
  Ðiss wearð þa gecydd þam cwellere Aureliane,
and he het him gelangien þone gelyfedan Quirinum,
and cwæð him sona to, Ic hæfde þe for sunu,
and þu me gebysmrodest, nu ðu gebogen eart
þurh Alexander to oðrum bigenge.   165
Ða cwæð Quirinus him to, Ic eom Cristen on eornest;
wylle ðu beswingen, wylle ðu ofslean,
wylle ðu adrencean, wylle ðu adydan,
wylle ðu forbærnan, ne beo ic nan oðer.
Witodlice ic dyde þæt þa gewurdon Cristene   170
ealle þe in ðam cwarterne beclysode wæron,
and ic hi ealle gescrydde mid eall-hwitum reafe,
and ic let hi frige faran gif hi woldon;
and Alexandrum ic bæd, and Ermen eac swylce,
þæt hi ut ferdon, ac hi faren noldon.   175
Ða þa scyldige wæron, þa secgað mid geleafan,
Gif we for urum synnum ofslagene beon sculdon,
and mid ealle amyrde, hu mycele swyþor

Glosses, Latin: 159 hiwum: familia.   160 gelic: similis.   161 gecydd:
notu*m*.   162 him gelangien: ad se duci, acc*er*siri.   164 gebysmrodest:
derides.   168 adydan: occid*ere*.   170 dyde: feci.   þa: illi.   173 frige:
lib*er*i.   176 Ða þa: q*ui*.   scyldige: rei.

161-5 [*Acta III. 13*] Tunc abiit Commentariensis ad Aurelianum, dixitque ei
universa quæ gesta sunt. Unde iratus iussit ad se adduci Quirinum, et dixit ei:
Ego te quasi filium dilexi, tu autem irrisisti me, deceptus ab Alexandro.
  166-83 [*Acta III. 13*] Dicit ei Quirinus: Ego Christianus factus sum. Vis
occidere, vis fustigare, vis incendere, aliud non ero. Nam et omnes qui erant in
carcere feci fieri Christianos, et dimisi eos, et noluerunt usquam ire. Sanctum
autem Alexandrum Papam, et virum illustrem Hermen rogavi, ut abscederent,
et noluerunt, ibique sunt omnes in carcere, dicentes: Si pro criminibus nostris
mori habuimus ac perire, quanto magis pro Christi nomine animas offerimus?
Ego vero rogavi eos ut exirent omnes qui baptizati sunt, et vestibus candidis
novisque vestiti, quia hoc exigit religio Christiana: sed ad martyrium omnes
usque nunc astant, parati ad necem suam, sicut esuriens paratus ad epulas. Iam
quod tibi placet, incipe facere.

sculon we ure sawla geoffrian for ures Hælendes naman.
Ealle hi gewilniað þe on ðam cwarterne wuniað   180
martirdom to þrowienne for Drihtnes geleafan,
swa swa se hungria mann his metes bið oflyst;
onginn nu to donne loc hwæt ðe geðynce.
Hwæt þa Aurelianus *mid yrre him cwæð to,   *f. 8ᵛ
Ic hate nu forceorfan þine scearpan tungan,   185
for ðon ðe ðu dorstest þus dyrstelice sprecan.
Quirinus him andwyrde, Eala ðu erming,
and þu ungesæliga, alys ðine sawle,
þæt þa ecan wita ðine sawle ne gelæccan.
Ða het Aurelianus on hengenne afæstnien   190
þone halgan wer, and aðenian his lima
swa swa man webb tyht; ac he nan word ne gecwæð.
He het þa forceorfan his handa and his fet,
and syþþan beheafdien, and swa hundum worpan.
His lic wearð þeah bebyrged fram þam geleaffullum Cristenum,
and his dohtor ðurhwunode for hire Drihtnes lufon   196
on clænum mæigðhade, Criste ðeowiende.
  Aurelianus het eac syþþan beheafdien
ðone arwurðan Ermen, and his agen swustor,
Theodora gehaten, bebyrgde his lic.   200
Ealla ða hæftlingas þe se halga papa
on ðæm cwarterne gefullode het se cwellere adrencan
on anum tobrocenan scipe on deoppre sæ,
and heora sawla swa siþodon to Criste.

Glosses, Latin: 186 dyrstelice: tem*ere*.   188 alys: redime.   190 hengenne: pati*b*ulo.   191 aðenian: extend*ere*.   192 tyht: extendit.
ME: 184 yrre: wreððe.

184–94 [*Acta III. 14*] Tunc fecit ei linguam abscindi, dicens: Linguam tuam
aufero, quia non timuisti sic audacter tua mihi pandere secreta, ut tacentem te
torqueri iubeam in eculeo [*Ælfric passes over the last clause, but cf. line* 192].
Quirinus dixit: Miser et infelix, libera animam tuam, ne æternæ te poenæ
suscipiant. Qui tortus in eculeo cum ab Aureliani non cessaret iniuriis, iussit ei
manus ac pedes abscindi, et sic eum decollari, et proiici canibus.
  195–7 [*Acta III. 14*] Tunc corpus eius rapientes Christiani in via Appia
sepelierunt. . . . Filia vero eius . . . in sacra virginitate permansit. . . .
  198–203 [*Acta III. 14*] Qui [Hermes] cum ab Aureliano decollatus fuisset,
corpus soror eius Theodora collegit. . . . Omnes in carcere baptizatos Aurelianus
cum navi vetusto in altum mare duci iussit, et illic ligatis ad colla lapidibus
mergi. [*Ælfric adds line* 204.]

Æfter sumum fyrste het se foresæda cwellere   205
þone halgan Alexandrum to him gelædan
mid þam twam mæssepreostum, and se manfulla him to cwæð,
Alexander papa, ic axie ærest ðe, *et reliqua.*

208] *Followed by the scribe's note:* þæt her to lafe is þu fintst æfter þam spelle *de inuentione sanctæ Crucis*, mid ðissum tacne: �†. *The reference is to MS. f. 153, where begins the piece, 'Sanctorum Alexandri, Eventii et Theodoli,' as in CH II. 308. The corresponding sign (a chrismon) directs us to line 8 in Thorpe's text,* 'Alexander papa, ic sece ærest æt þe, þæt þu me ardlice secge,' *etc.*

Glosses, Latin: 207 manfulla: iniquus.

205–8 [*Acta IV. 15*] Deinde Sanctum Alexandrum Papam iussit sibi exhiberi, dixitque ei: Exquiro a te prius. . . . [*Ælfric adds the masspriests in anticipation of later events.*]

NOTES

7. *iunglic on gearum and aldlic on geleafan.* Ælfric is following the Latin for this antithesis, but the turn of phrase is the same as in his description of St. Agnes: *cildlic on gearum and ealdlic on mode* (*LS* VII. 9).

10. *burhwitena*, Lat. *Senatorum.* BT and BTS cite *burhwita* from glosses and charters, but not as a way of describing a Roman senator.

15. *seofon wintra.* Probably for the adj. *seofonwintre.* Cf. *þritigwintre* in the Glossary and see note on *hundteontigwintre*, XIX. 20.

23. *mage mihtelice of deaðe aræran.* Any one of several transpositions would put the two alliterating words in different halves of the line: e.g. *mage of deaðe mihtelice aræran.*

26. Note the effective postponement of *bliðe*, best taken as an adjective. Cf. *þa eode heo eft to þam abbode sarig* (Ælfric's *exemplum*, Napier XXXI, p. 152/22 sq.) In 32 *bliðe* is probably an adverb.

39. *æhtemannum.* This word translates *servis* and seems to mean 'serfs', persons whose services were attached to the estates of their masters. BTS gives the meaning 'serf' from the Laws and from Ælfric's life of St. Sebastian, *LS* v. 308, where Skeat prints *æhta mannum* (v.l. *æhte*) as two words and translates, 'men on their estates'—for the sentence involves a distinction between these persons and an *inn-hyrede* (dat.), 'household servants'. One other passage from Ælfric is cited in BT with the assigned meaning 'husbandman, farmer, ploughman: *colonus*'; but this too may mean primarily 'serf'. The word occurs in *Old and New Testament*, 1208–9: '*Laboratores* sind þe us bigleofan tiliað, yrðlingas and æhte men to þam anum betæhte.' Clearly those who till the soil are described as *yrðlingas and æhte-men*, but Ælfric may have meant to distinguish between free farmers (*yrðlingas*) and serfs (*æhte-men*). The glossator of the present passage was inattentive enough to mistake *æhte* for the numeral *eahta*.

53. *mid anum his þeigne*, 'at the house of a thane of his'. Perhaps we should emend to *þeigna*, reading 'one of his thanes'. Cf. *an hys þegna*, XXVI. 85.

55. *Hwi dest ðu ðe swa wacne*, 'Why do you so degrade yourself?' For the idiom, see Glossary, *don*, I (*f*), and BTS, *don*, III. 3 and VI. The adjective *wac*, usually conveying moral weakness, is here used by the pagan Quirinus in contrast to *æðele* with implications of social disgrace.

65. *ic ðiss an lif to lufienne tealde*. There is perhaps a mild ellipsis to be recognized here, since *an* does duty for 'one' and 'alone'. The full statement might include the indeclinable *ana*, 'alone': *ðiss an lif ana to lufienne*. Cf. *hi wenað to soþum þæt þis lif ana sy*, *LS* v. 63, and for the various uses of *an* and *ana* see the Glossary.

80, 81. *þrimfealdum*. It is hard to be sure whether to regard this word as a full variant of *þryfeald* with a combining form, *þrim-*, derived from the dative of the numeral, or as a doubly-inflected compound presupposing the ordinary nominative form *þryfeald*. BT admits *þrimfeald* as a separate form, citing for comparison the compound *þrymnyss* or *þrimnyss* as a variant on *þry(n)nyss*, for which the present Glossary may be consulted. But it is noticeable that all the occurrences of *þrimfeald* cited by BT are datives with various prepositions, and though one of these datives is *þrimfealdre*, in which the second member agrees with a feminine noun in the dative singular, nevertheless it looks as if some writers, including Ælfric, regarded *þrim-* as an inflected dative corresponding to the nominative *þry-*.In Ælfric's *Grammar*, ed. Zupitza, pp. 286 sq., the nominative *þryfeald* is given next to the dative, *be þrimfealdum*. See also the dative plural, 'mid þrimfealdum lacum', *CH* I. 104/21; and in contrast the accusative plural, 'þryfealde lac', in the same homily, p. 161/4.

81, 83. *hæftnydum*; 131. *hæftnedu*. Here the abstract noun *hæftnyd*, 'captivity, confinement in bonds', is used concretely for that which binds, so that the plural means 'bonds' or 'shackles'. BTS under *hæftnid* cites two passages from Ælfric with plural forms (*LS* XXI. 167 and *CH* I. 338/4) and says they have the force of the singular ('custody' and 'thraldom' in the respective translations of Skeat and Thorpe). This seems possible, but both instances can be taken to mean 'shackles'. Indeed the passage in the *Lives of Saints* gains greatly by the concrete meaning, since presently the woman who has been put in *hæftnydum* is released by Swithun, so that the *fotcopsas* fall from her and she runs to the church, her hands still bound. Had she been kept in 'custody' in a locked chamber or under guard the miracle would have taken a different course. The other passage refers figuratively to the devil's *hæftnydum* from which we were released by the Saviour and can readily bear such a generalized sense as Thorpe's 'thraldom', but the plural form suggests something concrete such as 'bonds' or 'shackles'. These, of course, will ordinarily be interpreted as sins.

132. *on his dohtor swyre*. The form *swyre* for 'neck' is puzzling, especially

when followed by *swuran* in the next line. Ælfric's normal form is the ordinary LWS *swura*, wk. m., as at *LS* XII. 235 (nom. *swura*); VII. 32 (acc. *minne swuran*). Occasionally *y* appears for *u*, as at *CH* II. 326/7 (*foredum swyran*), and this is usually taken as a short *y*, a mere variant of short *u* after the *w*. (Cf. S–B 113, Anm. 4; Cpb, 241, 2, note 5.) What is troublesome about *swyre*, therefore, is the ending, which can most easily be taken as accusative after *on* with a verb signifying motion toward the object. The form is then probably enough contrasted with the dative *swuran* in the next line, which occurs after *on* and the motionless *wæs*. An accusative *swyre* would imply a weak neuter instead of a weak masculine, and there is some support for this (though it is not on record) in the established weak neuters for other parts of the body: e.g. *eage*, *eare*, *wange*. Very probably, however, the form *swyre* is not Ælfric's.

XXIV

'SE þE GELOME SWERAÐ'

(Addition to *CH* II. xxi: on False Swearing, Usury, and Manslaughter)

THIS disjointed little passage may be of some interest for what it says about usury, but we shall probably value it chiefly as a sign of Ælfric's continued attention to his most comprehensive treatment of Christian morals. The homily for Rogation Monday in the Second Series (*Letania Maiore*, *CH* II. xxi) is an omnium gatherum assembled from a number of sources, among which the precepts of Jesus and of St. Paul are the principal guides, supplemented here and there by the Mosaic law and the prophets.[1] Ælfric moves quickly from topic to topic, treating first the two basic Christian commandments and proceeding to a more or less bewildering array of particulars, in which the rules for married folk and for various ranks and conditions of men are included, and a great number of malefactors are reprehended. In spite of the casual organization of this compendium, it is evident that Ælfric devoted a good deal of care to its composition, since it is one of the few homilies of the Second Series to be written in his newly developed rhythmical style. Hence the fourteen added lines found in MSS. P and f[b] are stylistically similar to the rest.

The added lines occur as an extension of a passage on the rich, beginning at p. 326/34 in Thorpe's text and ending with a particular warning to dishonest merchants at p. 328/10. This passage is so relevant to most of the additional lines that I quote it here:[2]

> Eft, se ðeoda lareow lærde ða rican
> þæt hi hi ne onhebbon on healicere modignysse,
> ne heora hiht ne besetton on ðam swicelum welum,
> ac hihton on God, þæra goda Syllend.[3]
> Fela spræc se Hælend, and hefiglice be ricum;

---

[1] Certain incidental sources are mentioned in the note on x. 31.
[2] I have arranged Thorpe's text in rhythmical lines and omitted the accents.
[3] *I Tim.* vi. 17.

ac he hi eft gefrefrode, ðus fægre tihtende:
'Syllað ðone ofereacan eow to ælmes-dædum,
and efne ealle ðing eow beoð geclænsode.[1]
Hwæt fremað ænigum men, ðeah ðe he ealne middaneard
to his anwealdum gebige, gif he ana losað?'[2]
   Cypmannum gedafenað þæt hi soðfæstnysse healdon,
and heora sawla ne syllon ðurh swicole aðas,
ac lofian heora ðing buton laðre forsworennysse.
God soðlice fordeð ða swicolan and leasan.

This is the point at which the added lines are introduced, and it is evident that the first three continue the warning against false swearing, essentially what we should call fraudulent advertising. Both what Ælfric had originally said about the merchants and the second of the added lines refer back to the words of Jesus that have just been quoted, 'Hwæt fremað ænigum men', etc.

The same theme of unprofitable profits now leads to the attack on usury in the middle of the addition. It would seem that usury was as closely associated with merchants (*cypmen*) in Ælfric's time as in Shakespeare's. There is nothing surprising in Ælfric's reprehension of usury: as he says, it is forbidden in the law of Moses and in one of the prophets (Ezechiel), and it was forbidden by the medieval church. The Old English version of the penitential of pseudo-Ecgberht (II. 30) enjoins:

Ælcum geleaffullum men is forboden, þæt he his feoh ne his æhta to nanum unrihtum gafole ne læne: þæt is þæt he hine maran ne bidde to agifanne þonne he him ær lænde.[3]

But Ælfric rarely mentions the subject. Two passages only from his homilies are cited in Bosworth–Toller, and I recall no others. The first passage (*CH* I. 66/11) is a glancing allusion in a speech derived from a life of St. John the Evangelist. The other is a parenthetical though explicit reminder that usury is forbidden in the midst of an exposition of the parable of the talents (*CH* II. 554/9–11). The present heavily charged admonition is thus, it seems, Ælfric's major pronouncement.

The warning against manslaughter in the last three lines seems oddly placed. Did Ælfric simply remember that he had not been explicit enough about it elsewhere? Or did he mean to associate

---

[1] *Luc.* xi. 41.   [2] *Matth.* xvi. 26.
[3] Josef Raith, *Die altenglische Version des Halitgar'schen Bussbuches*, 2nd ed., Darmstadt, 1964 (*Bibl. der as. Prosa*, XIII), p. 35.

it with the misdeeds that might arise from the pursuit of riches?
Anyway it adds some weight to the generalization with which
Thorpe's next paragraph begins:

> Ealle we sceolon standan æfter ðisum life
> ætforan Cristes domsetle, þæt ælc ðær underfo
> swa hwæt he on lichaman adreah, oððe god oþþe yfel.

There is little to be learned about the date of this addition. Of
the five full copies of the homily, three are in MSS. D, F, and K,
and represent the textual tradition up to and including Thorpe's
text. M has only a few lines from the beginning in an unreliable
compilation and thus tells us nothing. Only the two manuscripts
that contain the addition, P and f^b, represent a textual tradition
later than Thorpe's K. On a further alteration of the homily in f^b,
for which Ælfric may or may not have been responsible, see the
description of f^b in the Introduction, pp. 89–90.

THE TEXT

Se þe gelome swerað, he byð forsworen untwylice;
he geeacnað his feoh mid his sawle lyre,
and his wite him wunað on ðære toweardan worulde.—
Godes æ us forbyt, and Godes witegan eac swa,
þæt nan man ne sylle nan feoh to gafole,   5
for ðan ðe se swicola mann ðe beswicð þa unwaran,
and se reða reafere þe bereafað þa Criatenan,
and se þe his feoh sylð to gafole ongean Godes bebod
beoð ealle gelice on heora arleasnysse.
Gif ðu ænigum menn gehylpst þe behofað þines feos   10
butan ælcum gafole, God ðe sylð þæs edlean.—
Manslyht is eac swyðe manfullic dǽd,
ealra synna mæst, buton þæt man wiðsace Gode:
for ðan ðe se mann is Godes anlicnyss.

Text based on P (Hatton 115), f. 46/3–16. Collated with f^b (Jesus College 15),
f. v/23–v^v/6. Round brackets indicate obscure or wholly illegible letters in f^b.
Where legible, f^b often but not invariably has *e* for long *æ*.

---

1 (he bi)þ *f^b*.   untwilice *f^b*.   3 ðere towe(ardan) *f^b*.   4 God(es
ǽ us forbytt) *f^b*.   *second* Godes] -s *cut off at margin f^b*.   5 s(y)lle *f^b*.
6 beswycð *f^b*.   8 (o)ng(ean) *f^b*.   9 arleasḷẹ(aṣ)ny(sse) *f^b*.   10 (æ)ni-
g(u)m *f^b*.   11 (ælcu)m *f^b*.   ðes *f^b*.   12 ded *f^b*.   13 eallra *f^b*.
mest *f^b*.   14 anlicn(ys) *f^b*.

Glosses in P, *Latin*: 1 untwylice: indubitant*er*.   10 þe behofað: q*ui* indiget.
11 butan: sine.
ME: 4 æ: lawe.   5 sylle: giue.

Sources. 4–5 [*Lev. xxv. 35–37*] Si attenuatus fuerit frater tuus . . . et vixerit
tecum, . . . pecuniam tuam non dabis ei ad usuram. [*Cf. Ex. xxii. 25; Deut. xxiii.
19; Ezech. xviii. 8–17; xxii. 12.*]
14 [*Gen. ix. 6*] Quicumque effuderit humanum sanguinem, fundetur sanguis
illius: ad imaginem quippe Dei factus est homo.

XXV

FOR ASCENSION EVE

(Three Additions to *CH* II. xxv,
In Letania Maiore, Feria IV)

THE Wednesday of Rogationtide is concurrently the Eve of the Lord's Ascension, and to this occasion Ælfric directs the homily mentioned in the title. It is an exposition of *John* xvii. 1–11, based mainly on Augustine's tractates CV–CVII.[1] Three extant manuscripts, C, D, and M, have the same version of the homily as that which Thorpe has printed from K, and it is probable that none of these represents a textual tradition later than K, for the section devoted to Rogationtide in M has apparently been derived from a textual tradition different from the rest, very probably earlier.[2] Hence the three additional passages that appear fully in R and were once perhaps complete in the codex represented by the fragmentary f^b (where now only a few words of the third passage can be easily made out) may actually have been composed almost immediately after the issue of the K-text, though we find it represented in manuscripts of a much later textual tradition. Whatever their date of composition, they are written in ordinary prose like the rest of the homily, not in the rhythmical prose that already appears in some of the homilies of the Second Series and soon becomes Ælfric's habitual style. It is true that one can put several of the sentences in the first passage into rhythmical lines with more or less satisfactory alliteration, but the passage as a whole, like the other two, resists such treatment, and I think a prose arrangement is better throughout.

The three passages, added to successive paragraphs on p. 368 of Thorpe's edition, represent what is probably a single intention, to expand the interpretation of the last three verses of the text,

---

[1] Max Förster, *Anglia* XVI. 35. A sermon for Ascension Eve in the collection of Paulus Diaconus was simply a copy of these tractates. Ælfric's version of the homiliary may have had tractate CIV also, which Förster thought had been slightly influential. See Smetana, *Traditio* XV. 198.

[2] See the description of M in the Introduction, pp. 42 and 43, note 1.

which had originally been treated rather hurriedly and without a sufficiently climactic effect. The first passage, adding two con-firmatory statements by Jesus to those already marshalled for verse 9, develops strongly the prospect of life in heaven for Christ's servants. The second, a mere couple of sentences, adds to the rather perfunctory statement about the Trinity that had been evoked by verse 10 ('Ealle mine ðing sindon ðine, and ðine ðing sindon mine'), showing cause for the glorification mentioned at the start of verse 11 ('Ic eom gemærsod on him'). The third, though attached to a paragraph on 'Ic cume to ðe' in verse 11, is partly a development of the seemingly opposite statement that had already been introduced as a qualification: 'Efne ic beo mid eow eallum dagum, oð gefyllednysse ðyssere worulde' (*Matth.* xxviii. 20). Ælfric brings several other passages to bear on the problem in order to show that both statements of Jesus, especially the second, are true, and to give full emphasis to the future life of the elect before his concluding comment on the great festival of the morrow.

Augustine's exposition of Ælfric's pericope in tractates CIV–CVII does not supply suggestions for the added passages. Part of the first passage, however, and part of the third seem to depend on other portions of Augustine's commentary on *John*,[1] and I suspect that a similar source could be found for the second passage.

---

[1] In the first passage Ælfric paraphrases passages from tractate LI. 11–13. According to Father Smetana, *Traditio* XV. 176, the thirteenth paragraph only was in Paul the Deacon's homiliary, original version, II. 68. Ælfric translated and interpreted *John* xii. 26 (the theme of the first passage and of Augustine's exposition) on another occasion, probably later, in the short homily for a martyr printed as Belfour VIII, of which the pericope is *John* xii. 24–26. A closely parallel passage is quoted in the notes below.

THE TEXTS

(a) Christ's Servants to be with Him in Heaven
(Thorpe II. 368, after first paragraph)

Be þyson cwæþ se Hælend on oðre stowe: Ðær þær ic sylf beo,
þær biþ mid me se þe me þenaþ. And swa hwa swa me þenað,
hyne arwurþað min Fæder se þe on heofonum is. Mid hwylcum
wurðmynte arwurþaþ se Fæder þone þén þe hys Suna þenað on
þysum lífe? Mid þam micclum wurþmynte þe Crist sylf cwæþ: 5
þæt he hæbbe wununge mid him þær þær he sylf biþ on þære ecan
myrhþe mid eallum hys halgum. Hwæt is se þen þe Criste þenað
*on ðysum lífe? Ælc þæra manna þe Cristes willan on ænige *p. 251
wisan gewyrcþ, he þenað Criste; and Crist þenað hym eft on
heofonan rice swa swa he sylf cwæþ: *Amen dico uobis, quod* 10
precinget sé, et faciet illos discumbere, et transiens ministrabit illis.
Ðæt is on urum gereorde, Soþ ic eow secge, þæt he begyrt hyne
sylfne, and deþ hi sittan, and he gæþ sylf and hym þenað.
Ðis sæde Crist be hym sylfum: þæt he wolde him sylf hys halgum
þenian on hys rice. To þyssere wynsuman þenunge becumaþ of 15

Text of all three passages based on the only well-preserved copy in R (CCCC
178), pp. 250/22–251/15, 251/26–30, and 252/8–30. Traces of the third passage
in fb (Jesus College 15), f. 4ᵛ, are recorded for (c) 8–10.

---

8 Ælc] *no capital in MS.*   12 Soþ] *no capital in MS.*

Latin glosses in R: 2 þenaþ *or* þenað: ministrat (*in margin*). 3 hyne: illu*m*.
4 þone . . . þe: illu*m* . . . q*ui; another hand,* quem.   7 þen: qui.   8 on
ænige: *in* aliq*uo.*   9 gewyrcþ: op*eratur.*   12 gereorde: lingua.
begyrt: precinget.   13 deþ: faciet.   15 wynsuman: iocund'
(*not clear what ending intended*).

SOURCES. 1–3 [*Ioan. xii. 26*] Ubi sum ego, illic et minister meus erit. Si quis mihi
ministraverit, honorificabit eum Pater meus.
3–9 [*Augustine, In Ioan. Ev. Tract. LI. 11, on preceding verse*] Quo honore,
nisi ut sit cum Filio eius? . . . Nam quem maiorem honorem accipere poterit
adoptatus, quam ut sit ubi est Unicus? . . . [*12*] Quid sit autem ministrare
Christo? . . . Ministrant ergo Iesu Christo, qui non sua quærunt, sed quæ Iesu
Christi.
10–12 [*Luc. xii. 37, as given.*]
15–16 [*Cf. Augustine, Tract. LI. 13, still on Ioan. xii. 26*] Nolite tantummodo
bonos episcopos et clericos cogitare. Etiam vos pro modo vestro ministrate

þyssere worulde ægþer ge þa gehadodan menn ge þa læwedan. Ærest þa gehadodan Godes þeowas þe nú Gode mid clænnysse þeowiaþ, and siþþan þa góódan læwedan menn þe heora lif rihtlice lybbað; ac to þam gereorde ne becymþ nan manhata ne nan swica, buton hi heora yfelnysse ær heora ende gebeton.   20

(b) As Great an Art to Preserve and Govern the World as to Create It

(Thorpe II. 368, after second paragraph)

Eall swa micel cræft is to gehealdenne þa gesceafta þe he gesceop, and him to gewissienne, eall swa micel swa swa wæs hi to gescyppenne þa þa hi næron. God us gesceop, and gif he us fedan nolde, we næron sona.

(c) Christ Feels with His Chosen on Earth and Promises Them Heaven

(Thorpe II. 368, after third paragraph)

Ure Hælend sitt on heofonum nú mid urum lichaman, and he gefrét swa hwæt swa ús gelimpþ þe hys lima syndon, swa swa he clypode to Saule þe nu is Paulus, þa þa he ehte þæra Cristenra manna, þus cweþende: *Saul`e', Saule, quid me persequeris?* Ðæt is

Latin glosses in R: (a) 17–19 *Summary in margin*: quod ordinati prius saluentur, *et* post laici.   19 gereorde: refect*ione*   manhata: hodiosus hominu*m*.

(b) 1 cræft; ars.   gehealdenne: custodire, saluare.   2 him: eos. gewissienne: regere.   2–3 gesceyppene: creare.

(c) 2 gefret: sentit.   3 ehte: p*ersequebatur*.

Christo, bene vivendo, eleemosynas faciendo, nomen doctrinamque eius quibus potueritis prædicando.

(c) 1–10 [*Augustine, In Ioan. Ev. Tract. XXI.* 7] Quia et nos membra sumus Filii; et nos membra tamquam quod discimus, ipse discit quodammodo in membris suis. Quomodo discit in nobis? Quomodo patitur in nobis? Unde probamus quia patitur in nobis? Ex illa voce de cælo: *Saule, Saule, quid me persequeris?* (*Act. ix.* 4.) Nonne ipse est qui iudex in fine sæculi residebit, et iustos ad dexteram ponens, iniquos autem ad sinistram, dicturus est: *Venite, benedicti Patris mei, percipite regnum: esurivi enim, et dedistis mihi manducare?* (*Matth. xxv.* 34, 35.) [*Also Tract. LVII.* 1] Sursum enim Christus est sedens ad dexteram Patris; sed profecto et hic est; propter quod et Saulo in terra sævienti dicit: *Quid me persequeris?*

on Englisc: Saule, Saule, hwi ehtst þu mín? Ne cwæþ he ná, hwi 5
ehtst þu mínra manna, ac hwi ehtst þu min, for þam þe he gefredde
hys halgena sarnyssa. Eft he cwæþ: *Esuriui enim, et dedistis mihi
manducare*: Me hingrode, and ge sealdon me etan. Him hingraþ
on hys þearfum, and swa hwæt swa we doþ Godes þearfum on
Godes naman, þæt we doð Gode sylfum. Eac þonne we ymbe God 10
smeagað, and to hym hopiað, we beoð mid him, swa swa Paulus
cwæþ: Ure drohtnung is on heofonum. Eft cwæþ ure Drihten be
hys gecorenum: *Gaudete, quia nomina uestra scripta sunt in caelo.*
Ðæt is on Englisc: Blissiað, for þam þe eowre naman synd awritene
on heofonum. Eft he cwæþ: *Non delebo nomina eorum de libro uitæ*: 15
ic ne adiligie heora naman of lifes béc. Ealra þæra manna naman þe
to Godes rice becumað synd awritene on þære líflican béc, and we
sceolon fundian mid geornfulnysse, and mid góódum weorcum,
þyder þær ure naman synd awritene.

5 *first* Saule *and* Ne] *no capitals in MS.*   8–10 *The following words can
still be made out in* f^b, *last two lines of f. 4^v*: me etan. . . . godes þearfum on
godes naman. ðæt we doð. . . . (*See above*, I. 90.)

Latin glosses in R: 5 ehtst: *persequeris.*   6 gefredde: *sensit.*
7 sarnyssa: *dolorem.*   8 ge: *vos.*   9 þearfum: *egenis.*   12 drohtnung: *conuersatio (repeated in margin).*   16 adiligie (*margin* adilie): *delebo.*
ME gloss: 11 smeagað: þenceð.

---

12 [*Philip. iii. 20*] Nostra autem conversatio in cælis est.
13 [*Luc. x. 20*] Gaudete autem quod nomina vestra scripta sunt in cælis.
15 [*Apoc. iii. 5*] Non delebo nomen eius de libro vitæ.

NOTES

(*a*) 1–3. Ælfric introduces the same quotation(*Ioan.*xii. 26) in two other
places. In Homily XI. 543–4 he abridges it slightly to make just two rhythmical lines:

þær ðær ic sylf beo, ðær bið min ðen,
and se ðe me ðenað, hine gearwurðað min Fæder.

In Belfour VIII, p. 74/15–17, where it is part of the pericope for a martyr
(applied to St. Vincent), he stretched it to three rhythmical lines, if one
can trust the late text:

ant þær ðær ic me sylf beo, þer bið eac min þeȝn,
7 þe ðe me ðenaþ, him þonne arwurðað
min Fæder Almihtiȝæ þe ðe is on heofenum.

(a) 3–7. Cf. Belfour VIII, p. 76/26–30:

Mid hwylce wurðmente arwyrðæð þe Fæder
þone mon þe þenæð on þisse life his Sunu,
butan mid þam wyrðmente þæt he wuniæn mote
on þam ecan life þær þær he sylf bið,
7 his wuldor iseon, 7 þare wynsumnesse
a butæn ende brucæn mid alle his halȝum?

Evidently, Ælfric either recalled the passage here edited or was using the same source. (There is always a chance of verbal substitution and transposition in Belfour's manuscript. I suspect that Ælfric originally put *brucan*, now in the last line as *brucæn*, at the end of the preceding line, leaving the alliteration of the last to the vowels.)

(b) On the implicit doctrine, see II. 220–31, the quotation from Alcuin there given, and the note on 212 sqq., where other occurrences of the same theme are mentioned. The turn of Ælfric's sentences here sounds to me Augustinian, but I have not found an exact source. (Cf. the passages quoted for II. 98–114 and VI. 119–28.)

(c) 8. *ge sealdon me etan*. Here is a clear instance of *syllan* with the infinitive *etan* with which to support the not so clear instances of *syllan* with the infinitive *drincan*. See the note on v. 13 and the Glossary, *drincan*.

XXVI

THEODOSIUS AND AMBROSE

(Addition to *CH* II. xxxiii, *Dominica XII Post Pentecosten*)

ÆLFRIC's homily for the twelfth Sunday after Pentecost contrasts the proud and the humble in an exposition of the parable of
the selfrighteous Pharisee and the contrite sinner at prayer, *Luke*
xviii. 9–14. The rather brief exposition, filling less than three
pages in Thorpe (II. 428/5–432/20), is followed by two pages of
examples showing how God humbled Nebuchadnezzar and his
son Belshazzar; after which the homily is speedily concluded
(Thorpe 436/19–27).[1]

Besides Thorpe's copy in K there are four other copies, in B, C,
D, and E, with the same version, and an unrevealing fragment in
fᵇ; but in three manuscripts we have various additions, all of them
undoubtedly written by Ælfric, but not all intended for this homily
and only one thoroughly appropriate to it. I shall mention the less
appropriate ones first.

The addition in G, which is on display in Warner's *Early English
Homilies*, pp. 38–41, is the passage on Daniel in *De Falsis Diis*, our
XXI. 300–493, with a concluding sentence that consists of the next
three lines of the original followed by an abridgement of three
more. The addition occurs after the next to the last paragraph in
Thorpe's text, replacing the benediction and doxology, for which
there is no substitute later. That Ælfric was not responsible for
this addition is shown clearly enough, I think, by the fact that the
theme of the overthrow of the false gods (which is proclaimed in the
conclusion of the added excerpt) has nothing to do with the theme
of the homily. The person who made the addition was thinking
only of adding more stories from the book of *Daniel*. Moreover,
it is unlike Ælfric to present so lame an abridgement of his own

---

[1] The expository portion is mainly from Bede's commentary on *Luke*, as
shown by Max Förster, *Anglia* XVI. 26. In addition, some resemblances to a
sermon by Augustine in the Migne edition of Paulus Diaconus are noted by
Father Smetana, *Traditio* XV. 200.

writing as what we find at the end (the refashioned beginning of the excerpt being less conspicuously inept), or to stop without a doxology.

In R we find no less than two additions, for both of which Ælfric was probably responsible; but they differ greatly from each other in character, style, and function. One, added at the very end, is the passage on first-fruits and tithes printed as the concluding part of our xxx. 75–114, but with an introductory sentence that ties it to the homily now under discussion:

Ge hyrdon nu þæt þiss godspell hrepode hwæthwega be þære teoðunge þe man Gode syllan sceal; be þam we willað eow sceortlice secgan.

This sentence, in ordinary prose like the original homily and like the passage on tithes, sounds very much like Ælfric, and what it says is true: the gospel has touched somewhat on tithes, for the Pharisee boasts that he has tithed all his possessions. Apparently, then, Ælfric at some time found it convenient to remind his congregation that tithes, though not to be boasted of, were still required. Since the twelfth Sunday after Pentecost will usually come in August, when the harvest is beginning, it might often be a good time for an admonition on tithes; but since the exact date varies from year to year, a preacher might sometimes find another Sunday more suitable. I think Ælfric must have attached the passage on tithes to this homily as a practical expedient for one or more particular occasions, without intending it as a permanent addition. That would explain why, though to judge by its style it should have been composed early, it is not to be found in the copy of the homily in H,[1] though this copy does have, true to type, the other stylistically more advanced addition in R that is yet to be described.

The one fully appropriate addition is the famous story here edited, that of the emperor Theodosius I and St. Ambrose, bishop of Milan. It is found in both R and H, a sentence or two ahead of the places where the other additions occur, just after the account of Belshazzar's feast has come to an end (Thorpe 436/18). Hence it serves as the climactic example of the humbling of a proud man, all the more valuable because of the rare virtue displayed on both

---

[1] The scribe of H did not leave it out on his own initiative, unless he had a second, unexpanded copy of the homily to guide him, because he gives the original doxology, which in R has been replaced by a different doxology at the end of the addition.

sides. Ælfric follows the account in the *Historia Ecclesiastica Tri-partita*, from Theodoritus, abridging it somewhat and sacrificing in the process some valuable details (especially the remarkably just and practical penance devised by Ambrose), but giving spirited expression to the whole in his most accomplished rhythmical style. Unlike the casually attached appendage on tithes, this addition has become an integral part of the homily and gives it a conclusion of great power.

THE TEXT

Gyt we wyllað eow secgan be sumon gesæligon cyninge
þe wearð eac geeadmet, ná únþances swaþeah,
ac for Godes ege for hys agenum gylte:
þæt wæs Theodosius, þe æfter ures Drihtnes tocyme
Cristendom underfeng and to fulluhte gebeah,   5
mid þam þe se Cristendóm þeonde wæs.
Constantinus se æþela wæs ærest Cristen
of eallum þam kaserum þe to Criste gebugon,
and he ana ahte ealles middaneardes geweald.
He awearp þone hæðenscipe, and awende his leode   10
to Cristes geleafan and to hys clænum biggengum.
He ne tobræc swaþeah þa deofolican tempel
þæra hæþenra goda for hys góódnysse,
ac forbead hys folce þa fulan bigengas
þære deofollican offrunge. Ac Theodosius   15
æfter feawum gearum feng to þam cynedóme,
ofer ealne middaneard geleaffull casere.
He het þa tobrecan þa deofollican biggengas,
and ealle þa anlicnyssa þæra ærenra goda,

Text based on R (CCCC 178), pp. 120–4. Collated with H (Cotton Vitellius
C. v), ff. 170ᵛ–2. Round brackets enclose portions of the text as given by R
for which H has approximately the right space but no longer any reading. The
addition follows line 18 in Thorpe, *CH* II. 436.

1 gesælige *H*.   2 (wearð eac geead)mett *H*.   3–4 his (agenum gylte:
þæt w)æs *H*.   4 drihtenes *H*.   5 (Cristendom underfeng 7) *H*.
6 se] *om. H*.   6–7 (þeonde wæs. Constantin)us *H*.   8 eallum]
f. 171 H.   (ka)seru*m* ð(e to Criste) *H*.   10 -scype *H*.   11 his *H*.
b(iggen)gu*m H*.   12 He] *sic H; no cap.* R.   deofollican *H*.   templa *H*.
13 þæra] *sic H; altered from* þære R.   his godnesse *H*.   14 his *H*.   biggengas *H*.   15 deofellican *H*.   Ac] *no capital in MSS.*   17 ea(lne) *H*.
18 deofolica(n big)gengas *H*.   19 -nessa *H*.

Glosses in R, Latin: 1 gesæligon: felice.   5 gebeah: *conuertit.*
6 þeonde: profiscen*s*.   7 þæela: nobilis.   8 gebugon: *conuerterunt.*
9 ahte: habuit.   10 awende: *conuertit.*   11 biggengum: cultu.
14 bigengas: cultu*m*.   17 geleaffull: fidelis.   18 biggengas: cultus.
19 anlicnyssa: simulacra.   ærenra: æenea (*sic*).

Sources. 4–27 [*See note.*]

and gyldene and seolfrene, for Godes geleafan,   20
and þa mæran tempel þe menn *macodon gefyrn   *p. 121
þam hæðenum godum to healicum wurðmyntum.
He wæs swiðe sigefæst for his soðum geleafan,
and æfre he oferwann his wiðerwinnan gehwær
þurh þæs Hælendes fultum þe he on gelyfde,   25
and he adwæscte gedwyld and þa gedwolan forseah,
and he þone soðan geleafan symle arærde.

Thesalonica wæs geháten sum heafodburh þa
on hys anwealde, swa swa ealle oðre wæron,
on þære gelamp þa for sumere ceaste   30
þæt man þæs caseres menn mistucode þær,
and sume hys gerefan oftorfodan mid stanum.
Þa wearð se casere þearle gegremod,
and asende his here to þære heafodbyrig,
het ealle ofslean þa ceastergewaran,   35
ge scyldige ge únscyldige for hys forsewennysse,
and man ofsloh þær þa seofon þusenda manna.
Ða wæs sum mære biscop, Ambrosius geháten,
on Mediolana-byrig, swiðe breme lareow
and swiðe ánræde mann. þa ofahsode he þiss,   40

---

20 sylf(r)e(ne) *H.*   21 templ *H.*   macedon *H.*   22 þa(m) *H.*
wyrðmynte *H.*   23 swyðe *H.*   28 T(he)salonica *H.*   29 his *H.*
32 his *H.*   oftorfodan] oftorfedon þær *H.*   34 asende] asende þa *H.*
her(e) *H.*   35 het] 7 het *H.*   'of'slean *H.*   36 ungescyldige *H.*
his *H.*   37 ofsloh þær] þær ofsloh *H.*   seof(on) *H.*   þusend *H.*
38 bisceop *H.*   40 mann] godes mann *H.*   þ(a) *H.*   ofaxode *H.*

Glosses in R, Latin: 20 geleafan: fide.   21 menn: multitudo.   gefyrn:
oli*m.*   22 healicum: *p*recipuo.   23 sigefæst: victoriosus.   24 oferwann: vicit.   wiðerwinnan: adu*er*sarios.   26 adwæscte gedwyld: destruxit
idola.   gedwolan: hereticos.   forseah: desp*e*cxit.   27 symle: se*m*per.
28 þa: *tun*c.   31 þæs: illius.   33 þearle: valde.   34 here: excercitu*m.*
35 ceastergewaran: ciues.   36 scyldige: rei.   for hys forsewennysse: *pro* sua
desp*e*cxione.   37 seofon þusenda: vii. m̄.   40 anræde: *cons*tans (*repeated
in margin*)   ofahsode: *inter*rogaui*t* (*first* t *oddly formed*).   þiss: hoc.

28–37 [*Hist. Eccl. Tripartita, IX. 30*] Thessalonica civitas est grandis et
populosa; in qua, dum fuisset orta seditio, quidam iudicum lapidati sunt atque
tracti. Hinc indignatus Theodosius iracundiæ non refrenavit infirmitatem; sed
iussit iniustos gladios super omnes evaginari et una cum nocentibus innocentes
interimi. Septem milia etenim hominum, sicut fertur, occisi sunt. . . .
38–48*a* Huiusmodi cladem plenam valde gemitibus audiens Ambrosius, cum
princeps Mediolani venisset et sollemniter in sacrum voluisset intrare templum,
occurrit foris ad ianuas et ingredientem his sermonibus a sacri liminis incessu
prohibuit:

and he swiðe bemænde þæt se mæra casere
swylce dæde gedyde ongean hys Drihten.
Hit gelamp þa siððan æfter lytlum fæce
þæt se casere cóm mid hys cempum farende
to Mediolana-byrig, wolde hyne gebiddan   45
æt þam biscopstóle, ac se biscop eode
út hym togeanes and forwyrnde hym ínnganges.
Ambrosius hym cwæð to: Eala þu casere,
nast þu þa micelnysse þæra manna slege[s]
þe ðu gefremodest þurh þine reðnysse,   50
ne þin mód ne oncnæwð þone micclan hefe
þinre dyrstignysse þe þu gedon hæfst;
oððe hwæþer þin miht þe mæge forwyrnan
þæt ðu þas synne ne sceole oncnawan?
Hyt gerist swaþeah þæt þæt gerád oferswiðe   55
þone woruldlican anweald, *and þu wite þæt ðu eart   *p. 122
mannes gecyndes þeah þu casere sý,

41 kasere H.   42 d(æde) H.   his H.   Drihten] drihtenes willan H.
43 syþþan H.   lyttlum H.   fæce] fyrste H.   44 his H.   45 medio-
la(na) H.   wolde] 7 wolde H.   hine H.   46 bisceop-, bisceop H.
H has point after eode.   47 him (twice) H.   48 him H.   49 mycel- H.
sleges] sic H; slege R.   50 þ(u) H.   53 hw(æ)þ(er) H.   54 oncnawan]
followed by another word at margin, H?   55 Hit H.   56 -li(can an)weald H.
57 (sy) H.

Glosses in R, Latin: 42 ongean: contra.   43 fæce: termino.   47 forwyrnde: prohibuit.   innganges: ingressum.   49 slege: occisione.
50 gefremodest: fecisti.   reðnysse: seueritate.   51 oncnæwð: connovit.
hefe: fletum, honus, grauedinem.   52 dyrstignysse: presumtionis.
55 gerist: decet.   gerad: sensus.   oferswiðe: vincat.   56 wite: scias.
ME: 43 fæce: first.

48b–73 'Nescis, imperator, perpetratæ a te necis quanta sit magnitudo, neque
post pausam tanti furoris mens tua molem præsumptionis agnoscit; sed forte
recognitionem peccati prohibet potestas imperii. Decet tamen ut vincat ratio
potestatem. Scienda quippe natura est eiusque mortalitas atque resolutio et
pulvis progenitorum, ex quo facti, ad quem redigendi sumus, et non flore
purpureo confidentem infirmitates operti corporis ignorare. Coæqualium hominum princeps es, o imperator, et conservorum; unus enim est omnium Dominus,
Rex omnium et Creator. (Quibus igitur oculis aspicies communis Domini templum? Quibus calcabis pedibus sanctum illius pavimentum? Quomodo manus
extendas, de quibus adhuc sanguis stillat iniustus? Quomodo huiusmodi manibus suscipies sanctum Domini corpus? Quo præsumptione ore tuo poculum
sanguinis pretiosi percipies, dum furore sermonum tantus iniuste sit sanguis
effusus? Recede igitur, recede, ne secundo peccato priorem nequitiam augere
contendas. Suscipe vinculum, quod omnium Dominus nunc ligavit; est enim
medicina maxima sanitatis.'

THEODOSIUS AND AMBROSE765

and hwanon þu cóme and to hwam þu gewendst.
þu eart mannum gelíc þeah þe þu mihte hæbbe,
untrum swa swa mann þeah ðe þu werige purpuran,   60
and án soðlice is ure ealra Drihte[n],
ealra þeoda Cyning, se ðe ana is Scyppend.
Mid hwylcum eagum besceawast þu þæs soðan Godes tempel,
mid hwylcum fotum gæst þu on Godes halgan flore,
hu miht ðu ahebban þine handa to Gode,   65
of ða[m þe] gyt dropað þæt unrihtwise blód
þe ðu þurh hatheortnysse nu hete ageotan?
Mid hwylcere dyrstignysse dearst þu underfon
þæt halige husel æfter swylcere dæde?
Gewit aweg, gewít, þe læs þe þe gewurðe   70
þin anwilnyss to deopran synne.
Underfoh þone bend þe ure Drihten geband:
he is se mæsta læcedóm þinre manfullan dæde.
    þa wiste se casere wel hwæt he mænde,
þæt he sylf wære gebunden þurh þæs biscopes hæse,   75
and fram Godes cyrcan ascyred swa wære
oðþæt se bisceop hyne [unbunde eft];
and he wæs þa gehyrsum hys hæsum sóna,

59 mann(um gelic) *H.*   60 (þu werige) *H.*   61 Drihten] drihte*n H*;
drihte *R.*   62 (þeoda Cyning, se) *H.*   Scyppend] ece scyppend *H.*
63 hwilcu*m H.*   (e)ag(um) besce(awast þu þæs) *H.*   soðan] (so)ðan *f. 171^v H.*
templ *H.*   64 Mid *H.*   hwilcu*m H.*   (fotum gæst þu) *H.*   go(de)s *H.*
flora *H.*   65 Hu *H.*   (t)o god(e) *H.*   66 (o)f *H.*   ðam þe] þam þe *H*;
ða *R.*   git *H.*   68 hwilcere *H.*   71 anwilnyss] anwille dyrstignyss *H.*
(de)opran *H.*   72 þone] þæne *H.*   73 (he i)s *H.*   74 (wel) *H.*
75 bisceopes *H.*   77 hine *H.*   unbunde eft] *sic H*; eft unbende *R.*
78 his *H.*

Glosses in R, Latin: 58 hwanon: *vnde.*   60 untrum: *infirmus.*   61 an:
vnus.   62 þeoda: *Gentium.*   ana: *solus.*   63 besceawast: *respicis.*
66 of ða[m] . . . dropað: *ex quibus distillunt (for distillat).*   67 hatheortnysse: *furore.*   hete ageotan: *iussisti fundere.*   68 dyrstignysse: *temeri-*
tate, presumptione.   70 Gewit: *discede.*   gewurðe: *fiat.*   71 anwilnyss:
opstinatio, obstinatio.   73 læcedom: *remedium.*   manfullan dæde: *ini-*
quitate.   76 ascyred: *priuatus, separatus.*   77 unbende: *solueret.*

74–84 His sermonibus imperator oboediens—erat enim divinis eruditionibus
enutritus et aperte sciens, quæ sunt propria sacerdotum, quæ regum—gemens
et deflens ad regalia remeavit. Cumque octo mensium continuorum transissent
tempora, propinquavit nativitatis Salvatoris nostri festivitas. Imperator autem
lamentationibus adsiduis in palatio residens continuas lacrimas incessabiliter
expendebat.

C 2710.2   T

gewende þa swa hám dreoriglice heofigende.

He sæt þa on hys bure biterlice wepende 80
eahta monðas fullice for hys misdæde,
þæt he næfre ne geswac þære sorhfullan geomrunge
oðþæt hit genealæhte þæs Hælendes gebyrdtide
to middanwintra þa he to mén wæs geboren.

þa wolde an hys þegna hyne frefrian, 85
Ruphínus geháten, and eode inn to him
þær se casere læg on þære flore wepende,
and ahsode hwi he wolde swa wundorlice heofian.
IIc cwæð þa mid wope, Me þincð þæt ðu plegast
and þu mine yrmðe naht ne gefredst. 90
Ic heofige and geomrie mine hefegan bendas,
for þam þe þeowum mannum *to þissere halgan tide *p. 123
and earmum mannum is inngang alyfed
innto Godes cyrican God to gebiddanne,
and ic ne mót nú gan innto Godes húse; 95
and eac þartoeacan me is heofon belocen.
þis he cwæð mid siccetunge and mid sarlicum wópe.
Ða cwæð Ruphinus þæt he yrnan wolde

---

79 gewende þa] 7 gewende H.   80 his H.   81 his H.   misdæda H.
84 menn H.   wæs geboren] geboren wæs H.   85 his H.   þegena H.
hine H.   frefrian] gefrefrian H.   86 rufinus H.   87 flora H.
88 axode H.   89 þingð H.   90 gefretst H.   91 geo-
me(r)ige H.   hefigan H.   92 þan H.   þisse(r)e H.   94 into H.
(g)odes H.   cyrcean H.   gebiddenne H.   95 (h)use H.   96 þær- H.
heofen H.   97 Ðiss H.   sicce(tu)nge H.

Glosses in R, Latin: 79 heofigende: lugens.   82 geomrunge: gemitu.
85 an: vnus.   90 yrmðe: miseriam.   gefredst: sentis.   91 heofige:
lugeo.   geomrie: fleo.   92 þeowum: seruis.   93 earmum: miseris.
inngang: ingressum.   alyfed: licitum.   96 heofon: celum.   97 siccetunge: suspiratione.   98 yrnan: currere.
ME: 79 heofigende: wepinde.   88 heofian: weopen.   90 gefredst:
felest.

85–97 Ingressus autem Rufinus tunc magister et singularem apud principem
fiduciam habens et videns principem in lamentatione prostratum accessit, ut
lacrimarum causas inquireret. At ille amarissime ingemescens et vehementius
lacrimas fundens: 'Tu,' inquit, 'Rufine, ludis et mea mala non sentis. Ego autem
lamentor et gemo calamitatem meam, quia servis quidem et mendicantibus
aperta sunt templa Dei, et proprium Dominum ingredientes licenter exorant,
mihi vero ingressus ad eum non est; insuper etiam cæli sunt clausi.' Hæc dicens
verba singula singultibus interrumpebat.
98–100 Rufinus: 'Curro,' inquit, 'si tibi placet, pontificique precibus per-
suadeo, ut solvatur vinculum quod ligavit.'

to þam halgan biscope, and hine georne biddan
þæt he únbunde þone bend þe he gewrað.   100
þa cwæð se casere, Ic cann hyne swa geare
þæt he nele awendan Godes rihtwisnysse
for minum cynedome to nanre wohnysse.

Hi eodan swaþeah begen to þam biscope sona,
and fundon hine sittende on cumena huse,   105
and se casere hyne bæd mid soðre eadmodnysse
þæt [he] hys bendas unbindan sceolde.
þa cwæð Ambrosius, Hwi come þu hider?
wilt þu forgægan Godes æ nú,
and mid þinum riccetere wéndan ongean God?   110
Se casere hym andwyrde, Ne eom ic na swa dyrstig
þæt ic durre tobrecan Drihtnes gesetnysse,
ne ic nelle ínn gan into Godes huse;
ac 'ic' bidde þe georne þæt ðu unbindan sceole
mine swaran bendas, and gebide for me   115

99 (to) H.   bisceope H.   georne biddan] biddan georne H.   100 (b)end
H.   101 geare] georne H.   102 awendon H.   104 eodon H.
bisceope H.   106 hine H.   (e)admodnesse H.   107 he] sic H; om. R.
his H.   108 (Hwi) H.   109 Wilt H.   110 ricce(tere) H.   111 kasere
H.   him H.   (swa d)yrstig H.   112 drihtenes H.   113 (inn gan)
H.   innto H.   115 (mine swaran) H.   me] me earminge H.

Glosses in R, Latin: 100 gewrað: strinxit.   101 cann: *con*nosco. geare:
bene.   102 awendan: mutare, au*ertere*.   104 begen: a*mbo*.   105 on
cumena huse: *in* domo hospitu*m*.   109 forgægan: *transgredere*, p*reuaricare.*
æ: lege*m*.   110 riccetere: nobilitate, tirannide (*second* n *seems written over
another letter*).   111 dyrstig: audax.   113 inn gan: *intra*re.   115 swaran:
gr*au*e. gebide: ora.
ME: 105 cumena huse: Gistenehuse.   115 swaran: heuie.

101–3 At imperator: 'Non', inquit, 'suadebis Ambrosio. Novi ego decretum
illius esse iustum, neque reverebitur imperialem potentiam, ut legem possit
prævaricari divinam.'

104–10 [*Ælfric omits complications*] Cumque Rufinus verbis plurimis uteretur
· . . imperator eum pergere cum festinatione præcepit; ipse vero spe data post
paululum est secutus. . . . Cumque ad sacra limina pervenisset, in sanctam quidem basilicam non præsumpsit intrare; sed veniens ad antistitem et inveniens
eum in salutatorio residentem supplicabat, ut eius vincula resolveret. At ille
tyrannicam dicebat eius esse præsentiam et contra Deum vesanire Theodosium
eiusque calcare leges.

111–17 Verum imperator: 'Non', inquit, 'insurgo adversus ecclesiasticas san-
ctiones nec inique ingredi limina sacra contendo; sed te solvere mea vincla
deposco et communis Domini pro me exorare clementiam nec mihi ianuam
claudi, quam cunctis pænitentiam agentibus Dominus noster aperuit.'

þæt God me geopenige hys huses inngang,
þone þe he geopenade eallum behreowsiendum.
Ða cwæð se biscop hym to, Hwær is þin dædbót
æfter swylcere unrihtwisnysse? oððe hu hæfst ðu gehæled
þa micclan wunda þinre manfullan dæde?   120
þa cwæð Theodosius, þu scealt me tǽcan
þone gastlican lǽcedóm, and to Gode me þingian,
and ic sceal underfón æt þe þa bóte.
Hwæt þa se biscop hym bóte þæs tæhte,
and het hyne warnian eft wið swylce dæde,   125
and hyne unband þa fram hys synna bendum
and lyfde him ingang into Godes huse;
and se casere gehyrsumode eallum hys hæsum
mid micelre eadmodnysse, and eode innto cyrcan,
læg on þære flore eallum *limum astreht,   *p. 124
and beot hys breost, biterlice wepende,   131
and bæd hym miltsunge hys misdæda æt Gode,
and gestod þa mæssan mid oðrum mannum.
We magon wundrian þæs mæran bisceopes,

116 (his huses inngan)g H.   117 geopenode H.   eallum] eallum
eallum H.   118 (Ða cwæð se biscop) hi(m to) H.   119 swilcere H.
-rihtwis(nysse) f. 172 H.   h(æ)fst H.   123 bote] dædbote H.   124 bisceop H.   him H.   125 hine H.   swylce] swilcere H.   126 hine H.
his H.   127 inngang H.   128 And H.   his H.   129 mycelre H.
-nesse H.   130 læg] 7 læg H.   flora H.   131 his H.   132 him
H.   his H.   133 gestod] gestod him H.

Glosses in R, Latin: 116 inngang: ingressum.   117 þone: illum.
behreowsiendum: penitentibus.   118 dædbot: penitencia.   119 hæfst
þu gehæled: sanasti.   120 manfullan: iniquo.   122 læcedom: remedium.
þingian: intercedere.   123 bote: emendationem.   125 warnian: cauere.
127 lyfde: concessit.   133 gestod: constitit.   134 margin for paragraph:
ingentia magnalia.   þæs: istius.

118–20 Tunc antistes: 'Quam', inquit, 'pænitentiam ostendisti post tantas
iniquitates? Quibus medicaminibus incurabilia vulnera plagasque curasti?'
    121–3 At imperator: 'Tuum', inquit, 'opus est et docere et medicamina tem-
perare, meum vero oblata suscipere.'
    124–33 [In the Latin Ambrosius requires that Theodosius make a new law to
prevent a recurrence of the injustice and Theodosius complies. Then follows] Quo
facto vinculum eius solvit Ambrosius. . . . Sic igitur sacratissimus imperator
ingredi limina præsumens . . . pronus in pavimento iacens, . . . frontemque percutiens et pavimento lacrimarum guttas aspargens veniam impetrare poscebat.
[In the Latin Theodosius is required by Ambrose to leave the chancel and stand with
the congregation during the celebration of the mass. Ælfric states only the result.]
    134–9 [Ælfric's conclusion, suggested by the Latin] Tali ergo tantaque et præsul

and hys anrædnyss is swyðe heriendlic,   135
and þæs caseres eadmodnyss eac þartogeanes
is swiðe micel, þæt he mihte swa forberan
on swylcum anwealde þæt he wære amansumod;
ac seo eadmodnyss hym becóm to écere hæle.

135 his *H.*   swiþe *H.*   136 þær- *H.*   137 is] wæs *H.*   mycel *H.*
138 swilcum *H.*   andwealde (*less probably* ond-) *H.*   139 Ac *H.*   him *H.*
hæle] *followed in both MSS. by the conclusion of the original homily, CH II.
436/19–27, except that R omits the last clause and the Amen in order to introduce another interpolation, for which see introduction, p.* 760.

Glosses in R, Latin: 135 anrædnyss: *constanciam* (*written twice in acc.*).
138 anwealde: *potestate.*

et imperator virtute clarebant. Ego namque utriusque opus ammiror, illius
fiduciam, huius autem oboedientiam, illius zeli fervorem, huius fidei puritatem.

NOTES

4–27. This historical summary depends ultimately, no doubt, on the
Tripartite History, from which the ensuing narrative is drawn, and on
Ælfric's other chief authority for the period, Rufinus. Ælfric touches upon
Constantine and Theodosius in the epilogue to *Judges* and in XXII. In
XXI. 542 sqq. he mentions the destruction of idols under Theodosius, one
example of which was the destruction of Serapis in Alexandria.

77. *unbunde eft* H, *eft unbende* R. Since the form *unbunde* of H is
clearly supported by *geband* in 72 and *gebunden* in 75 as well as by the
unbunde of both manuscripts at 100, I have accepted the word-order of H
also. BT has no example of the weak verb *unbendan*, though it records
bendan and *gebendan.*

115. *gebide.* Both manuscripts have the imperative here, with a con-
firmatory gloss in R, where the optative *gebidde* is rather to be expected.

133. *gestod þa mæssan mid oðrum mannum,* 'attended the mass, standing
with other men'. This use of *gestandan* with the accusative appears to be
normal in the sense 'to attend' a service at which one stands (BTS
gestandan, B. II). Ælfric is here leaving out a complication in his Latin
source, which tells how Theodosius, having made his offering at the mass,
stood (*stetit*) in the chancel as he had been accustomed to do in Constanti-
nople, until Ambrose explained that the chancel was reserved for priests
and told him his place was outside with the rest of the laity. Thus what
little distinction remains in Ælfric's abridgement is brought out, not by
gestod, but by *mid oðrum mannum.* It may seem a pity, however, to lose the
image in *gestod* by so general a definition as 'attend'.

XXVII

VISIONS OF DEPARTING SOULS

(Addition to *CH* II. xxxvi, *Dominica XVI Post Pentecosten*)

THE text here edited is not only imperfectly preserved but diverse in style. There is reason to believe that its opening and closing sections are the work of someone other than Ælfric, and therefore to doubt whether Ælfric ever added any part of it to the homily in which we now find it. Our witness is the third and last stratum of the copiously interpolated MS. H, a stratum that is otherwise limited to Ælfric's work but includes the probably unauthorized though ingenious compilation, XI*a*, and the possibly unauthorized combination of Assmann II and the close of Assmann III.[1] Ælfric's homily for the sixteenth Sunday after Pentecost (*CH* II. xxxvi) occurs in the version printed by Thorpe from K in four other manuscripts, B, C, D, and F, which represent for *CH* I and probably for *CH* II the textual tradition up to K. In H, the only other manuscript in which the homily has come down to us, it has been inserted in an expanded form. The character of the addition can be better understood if we look first at the original homily.

The homily as it stands in Thorpe is very brief, even allowing for Thorpe's omission of most of the gospel. The exposition fills only two and a half pages. The gospel-text is the passage from the Sermon on the Mount on the impossibility of serving two masters, including the injunction to consider the lilies of the field (*Matth.* vi. 24–34), and Ælfric has expounded it, as he says, according to Bede.[2] The exposition urges us to make use of transitory things without setting our heart's love on them, avoiding the snares of

---

[1] *De Sancta Virginitate.* See the description of H in the Introduction, pp. 30–31.

[2] He follows rather closely Bede's commentary on the parallel verses in *Luke* (xvi. 13 and xii. 22–31). This is a more probable source than the partially corresponding pseudo-Bede commentary on *Matthew* to which Max Förster refers, *Anglia* XVI. 26. Bede himself has drawn a good deal from Jerome's and Augustine's commentaries on the text in *Matthew*. The two passages from Haymo quoted by Father Smetana (*Traditio* XVII. 465) were probably influential also, for although they correspond roughly in sentiment to Bede on *Luke* xii, 22 and 30–31, they are closer to Ælfric in expression than Bede is.

avarice and recognizing that God's gift of physical sustenance and clothing is as nothing to his gift of eternal life. A final exhortation, not drawn from Bede, reminds us of the serious consequences of neglecting what may have seemed an over-refined distinction:

Dæghwomlice we sceolon gewilnian þæs ecan lifes, and ure synna symle wanian; for ðan ðe hi beoð gegaderode to micelre hypan, gif we hi weaxan lætað. Oft of ðinnum renscurum flewð seo eorðe.[1]

The proverb is apt, but Ælfric permitted himself a half-apologetic rejoinder to an anticipated protest before reaching the closing formulas:

þis godspel ðincð dysegum mannum sellic, ac we hit secgað swaðeah, weald ðeah hit sumum men licige.

In H this sentence is still present, but wisely transposed to precede the sentences quoted above. Hence Ælfric's central message comes just before the additional passage and leads into it as effectively as anything in the homily could. Nothing of the original version is left out. Even the two remaining sentences, containing Ælfric's formal conclusion, are preserved at the end of the addition.

It is easy to see why someone would have decided to expand the homily: it was both excessively short and lacking in force. The question is whether Ælfric himself had anything to do with the addition we find. It seems possible that he added the rhythmically composed *exempla* without the enclosing passages of ordinary prose. The *exempla* themselves are characteristic of him in choice of subject and diction as well as rhythmical form, so that we cannot well doubt their authorship; and he may have thought them sufficiently appropriate to the basic contrast in the homily between earthly and heavenly values. Yet their sensational extravagance seems better suited to a hard-hitting penitential sermon such as we find partially represented in the passages with which they are flanked in the manuscript, and when we look at these flanking passages we may begin to suspect that although they were written to enclose Ælfric's *exempla* they were not written for the sake of the homily but for some quite different piece. For one thing, they do not fully engage the theme of the homily. For another, in the second passage we find the expression *swa swa we nu hwene ær*

[1] Thorpe, II. 466/5–8.

sædon (109), but we look in vain for a clear antecedent in the first passage.[1] It seems probable that the reference is to a still earlier passage that the interpolator of Ælfric's homily did not include. Thus the following hypothetical sequence may come near the truth: (1) Ælfric composed the *exempla* for some undiscoverable occasion. (2) Another preacher incorporated these *exempla* into a homily of his own. (3) A third person, possibly the interpolator of MS. H, lifted out Ælfric's *exempla* and some of the surrounding matter to make the addition we find.

The most important question, however, is not the sequence of events but the authorship of the flanking passages, lines 1–14 and 107–23. There are a number of reasons for believing that Ælfric did not write them. Even without close study we may begin to doubt his authorship, for although the second of these passages refers to the *exempla*, showing that it was written later than they, yet both passages are non-rhythmical, a most extraordinary phenomenon if Ælfric was their author. And on close inspection we can see that the style differs noticeably, not only from his rhythmical but also from his ordinary prose. It is a loosely emotional style, lacking in concision and variety, stringing together phrases and clauses in simple series for cumulative emphasis.

In the second passage we can make a direct comparison with Ælfric's writing, because lines 109–14 are evidently an adaptation of a passage that occurs in his *De Penitentia* and again with very slight differences in the Ash Wednesday homily (*LS* XII. 167 sqq.). I quote from *De Penitentia*, Thorpe, II. 602:

Ne sceamige nanum men þæt he anum lareowe his gyltas cyðe, for ðan se þe nele his synna on ðissere worulde andettan mid soðre behreowsunge, him sceal sceamian ætforan Gode Ælmihtigum, and ætforan his engla werodum, and ætforan eallum mannum, and ætforan eallum deoflum, æt ðam micclan dome, þær we ealle gegaderode beoð. þær beoð cuðe ure ealra dædaeallum þam werodum, and se ðe nu ne mæg his gyltas for sceame anum men geandettan, him sceal sceamian ðonne ætforan heofenwarum, and eorðwarum, and helwarum, and seo sceamu him bið endeleas.

This passage represents perhaps the extreme to which Ælfric can sometimes go for the sake of emphasis. The heavy use of anaphora

---

[1] There is indeed talk of confession to a *scrift*, but not, as the second passage would lead one to suppose, of the shame involved, unless it is felt to be implicit in 11–14.

here is as conspicuous as the very slightly varied reiteration. At the same time it is a passage under full intellectual control. The adaptation in lines 109–14 below is by comparison lax. Why do we have in the same series *englum* and *heofonlicum werede*? Ælfric uses *eallum* with *mannum* and *deoflum* but not with *engla werodum*; the adapter insists on *eallum* every time and loses precision.[1]

But there is weightier evidence. Lines 1–11 and 114–21 echo passages in some of the non-Ælfrician portions of Napier's *Wulfstan*. The first six lines, now imperfectly preserved, were evidently a prolix expansion of two sentences in a homily by Wulfstan himself:

> An tima cymð ure æghwylcum þæt us wære leofre þonne eal þæt we on worulde wiðæftan us læfað, þær we a worhton, þa hwile þe we mihtan, georne þæt God licode. . . . Wa ðam þonne, þe ær geearnode helle wite.[2]

The next sentence, lines 6–11, apart from a few words inserted at the beginning, is an almost exact reproduction of the closing sentence of the same homily, not as it appears in the manuscripts considered most authoritative by Napier and Bethurum, but as it is modified in their M, Cotton Otho B. x:

> Utan andettan ure misdæda and synna ða hwyle þe we magon and moton, and betan georne swa ure scrift us wisige, and uton geswican æfre ælces yfeles, and don to gode þone dæl þe we magon; þonne gebeorge we us sylfum wiþ ece wite and geearnian [*MSS. BCE* geearniað] us heofona rice mid þam eall wealdendan Criste.[3]

Finally, lines 114–21 are almost identical with the following passage in an anonymous homily, Napier XLVI:

---

[1] The adapter, it will be noticed, uses *manna gehwylcum*, a formula that, according to Jost (*Wulfstanstudien*, 163, 174) never appears in Ælfric, and *beforan* (rare in Ælfric) for *ætforan* (habitual in Ælfric). Other suspicious words in the flanking passages are *swa* for *swa swa*, 8 (unusual but not unexampled), and *bewruge*, 119, *bewreo*, 120. BT does not cite Ælfric under *bewreon*, though it does under *oferwreon* and *onwreon*. The latter appears in our VII and XII.

[2] Napier XXII, pp. 113/14–114/3; Bethurum, *Homilies of Wulfstan*, XIII. 80–84. This passage reappears in the anonymous Napier XLIII, p. 209/9–14, with minor differences, including, as in our passage, omission of *georne* and dative *Gode*.

[3] Napier, p. 115/12–15, and Bethurum XIII. 103–6, according to MS. M. The relevant portion of this manuscript was totally destroyed by the fire of 1731, but these closing lines are in Wanley's *Catalogus*, p. 191. The last five words are part of a conclusion peculiar to M and reported only by Wanley and Napier.

We eow secgað to soðan, þæt se ðe nele her his synna nu andettan his scrifte, and betan swa he him tæcð, hine sceal on Domes-dæg gesceamian beforan Gode and eallum his halgum and eac eallum deoflum, swa þam men dyde, þe wurde færinga nacod beforan eallon folce, and he nyste þonne, mid hwam he þone sceamiendan lichaman bewruge: swa him bið on Domes-dæg, butan he his synna ær bewreo mid andetnesse and mid dædbote and mid ælmessan.[1]

Thus it appears that the author of the flanking passages was neither Ælfric nor Wulfstan but someone who made rather un-skilful use of both. It is conceivable that he was the same per-son as the author of Napier XLVI. The style of the last passage quoted above is far more in accord with the rest of Napier XLVI than with anything in Ælfric. It is also in accord with the style of Napier XXIX, in which some of the same ideas occur.[2] Both these pieces are intellectually simple but sometimes eloquent and not without imaginative touches. Napier XXIX includes an adaptation of the Old English version of Bede's poem, De Die Iudicii, and both homilies have exempla like Ælfric's in them, describing what happens to good and bad souls when they leave their bodies. It is difficult, however, to distinguish one of the anonymous authors in Napier's collection from another. Whoever the man we are here concerned with may have been, I think he originally incorporated Ælfric's exempla into another such homily as Napier XXIX and XLVI: a penitential piece with emphasis on the rewards and punishments to come and on the terrifying disclosures of the day of judgement. If so, then, as I have already suggested, an ingenious compiler such as the architect of the augmented MS. H may be credited with the rest. Wishing to extend Ælfric's Dominica XII Post Pentecosten, and quite probably recognizing Ælfric's hand in the exempla, this compiler then excerpted enough besides to construct a forceful if not entirely harmonious addition.

Lines 70–80, belonging to the portion of the text that is clearly by Ælfric, have already been printed as his in an article by Miss Winifred Temple which is described in the note on these lines.

---

[1] Napier, p. 238/10–18.

[2] See esp. p. 136/1–5, where the motif of confession before one man now appears with slightly varied expression. Jost, Wulfstanstudien, p. 205, has traced the motif here and in Ælfric to the Confessionale of pseudo-Ecgberht.

THE TEXT

[Lines 1–14 probably not by Ælfric]

(: *þæt we) on

worulde (wiðæ)f(t)an us læfað, 7 eall þæt (leofre) on þysum
m(idd)anearde is, þeah hit (huru w)ære eall on u(r)um anwealde
þa (hwi)le þ(e w)e her on life wæron, gyf (we a wor)hton, þ(a hwile
þe) we mihton, þæt Go(de licode). Wa þonne þam menn (þe he)r 5
on þisum life geearnað him hellewite. Uton nu (forþi,) leof(an
geb)roðra, andettan ure misdæda 7 synna þa hwile þe we magon (7
moton,) 7 betan (hi g)eorne, swa ure scrift us wisige; 7 uton geswican
(æ)fre ælces yfeles, 7 don to gode þone dæl þe we magon; þonne
gebeor(ge) we ús sylfum wið éce wíte, 7 geearniað us heofena 10
(rice) mid þam eall(we)aldendan Criste. Witodlice ne mot se deofol
ænigum menn þe hine (s)ylfne her on þisum life sylfwilles to his
scrifte for Godes ege wregð (na)n þæra gylta him ongean wyrpan
æfter his forðsiþe þe he ær be (h)is scriftes wissunge gebete.

We wyllað eow secgan sume bysne nu (b)e þysum, 15
þæt ge beon þe gewissran be eowre agenre þearfe.
On þære (h)algan bec þe hatte *Uita Patrum*
ús segð swutellice þæt sum munuc on (we)stene

first words visible, f. 176ᵛ

Contained in H (Cotton Vitellius C. v), ff. 176ᵛ–7ᵛ, only. On f. 176ʳ the scribe
concluded the sentence ending at line 8, p. 466 in Thorpe, having already transposed the following sentence and put it after line 4 in Thorpe. He probably
started the interpolation just before turning the page, but the last third of the
bottom line of f. 176ʳ and most of the top line of f. 176ᵛ have been destroyed.
As elsewhere, the gaps in H are indicated by round brackets. Sometimes enough
traces of letters remain to make a conjecture almost certain; sometimes the context or the Latin source points clearly to a particular word. In these instances the
missing letters are supplied within the brackets. Otherwise their approximate
number is indicated by colons.

1 þæt we] *partially visible though not unmistakable; similarly most other
bracketed letters in the first paragraph; but see notes.*

SOURCES. 18–24 [*Vitæ Patrum, VI, iii. 13, 14: Migne, PL, LXXIII. 1011 sq.*]
Subintravit . . . in animo [cuiusdam fratris] cogitatus, velle videre animam
peccatoris et iusti, quomodo abstrahitur a corpore. Et nolens Deus contristare
eum in desideriis eius, dum sederet in cella sua, ingressus est lupus ad eum.
. . . Lupus autem duxit eum usque ad aliquam civitatem, et dimittens fratrem
illum, recessit.

abæd æt his Drihtene *þæt* he moste geseon
hu se synnfulla mann (hi)s sawle ageafe,   20
7 hu se rihtwisa gewite of life.
Ða nolde se Hælend (hi)m þæs forwyrnan,
ac him wæs gewissod *þæt* he gewende to anre byrig (w)eard,
þæt he mihte geseon swutellice be þam.
Wiðutan þære byrig wæs (o)n sunderlicre wununge   25
sum namcuð wer sittende, swylce he ancer(se)tla wære,
ac his lif wæs eall on yfel gelogod,
Gode swiþe andsæte, swa (sw)a him aeode.
Se læg þa swiþe seoc ungesæliglice,
andbidigende (dea)þes mid eallu*m* his synna.   30
Ða geseah se munuc þe of þam westene (: : : : :)
þæt an egeslic deofol of þære deorcan helle co*m*
to *þam* seocan menn (on his) forðsiþe,
7 hæfde him on handa þryfyrclede force,
7 *þæt* wæs glo(wen)de isen, *þæt* he hine mid þære acwealde. 35
Ða co*m* stefen ufan fra*m* (þa)m ælmihtigan Gode
to þam sweartan deofle, þuss secgende him (to):
Swa swa ic moste on þisum menn habban
nane wununge næfre, (ne) minne willan on him,
swa þu eac ne arige ne (him ne miltsi)ge   40
(þon*ne* þu ut) atyhst his arleasan sawle.
Ða sette se deofol sona his (force)
swylce glowende isen into his heortan
7 hine lange drehte (mid : : :)licum witum;
7 æfter manegu*m* tidu*m* þone mann adydde,   45
(*þæt* he his sa)wle genam swa of þam lichaman,
7 hi lædde aweg mid (: : : : : : : : : : : : :) helle.

---

31 (stop)?   40–41 him . . . atyhst] *MS has traces of all letters except*
þon*ne* þ.

25–30 Cum vero sederet foras civitatem in monasterio, in quo erat quidam
habitans, qui habebat nomen quasi magni solitarii, ipse vero solitarius infirmus
erat, exspectans horam mortis suæ. . . . [*Ælfric supplies* 27 *and* 28, *and omits the
ironic account, which follows in the Latin, of the preparations for the funeral.*]
31–47 Facta autem exitus eius hora, vidit frater ille tartaricum inferni descen-
dentem super solitarium illum, habentem tridentem igneum, et audivit vocem
dicentem: Sicut anima ista non me fecit quiescere, neque una hora in se, sic
neque tu miserearis eius evellens eam. Deponens igitur tartaricus ille quem
tenebat tridentem igneum in cor solitarii illius, per multas horas torquens eum,
abstraxit animam eius.

Æfter þisum eode se ylca foresæda (munuc
oninnan þære) byrig, 7 he efne þa funde
ænne seocne mann (:   50
se) wæs ælþeodig mann, 7 he ana þær læg
*(:   *f. 177
: unge
: : : : : : : : : : : : : : : : :) Godes engla(s) him to,
Michael 7 Gabriel, swa swa God (: : : : : : : :),   55
þæt hi þæs mannes sawle sceoldon underfon,
7 sæton hi (: : : : : : : : :) healfa oðþæt he sawlade;
ac his sawul nolde swa ut, swylce (: : : : : : :) wære lað
út of þam lichaman.
Ða cwæþ Gabrihel to Michaele (: : : : :),   60
Genim þas sawle ardlice þe to,
7 uton siþian upp. Michael (him) andwyrde,
Us is beboden fram þam ælmihtigan Gode
þæt we (butan) sarnysse þas sawle genimon:
nu ne magon we forþig mid (nanre) earfoðnysse   65
þas sawle totwæman fram þam lichaman s(w : : : :).
Ða clypode Michael upp mid mycelre stefne 7 cwæþ:
Hu wylt þu, leof Drihten, embe þas sawle?
Heo nele us geþafian þæt heo ut g(e)wite.
Him com þa and`s´waru þuss secgende of heofonum: 70

48–49 (munuc oninnan þære)] cf. Latin and line 25 supra. Space favousr
oninnan rather than into.   55 (him bebead)?   57 hi(m ða on twa)?
58 (hit hire)?   60 (georne)?   66 s(wiðe)?

48–59 Posthæc autem ingressus frater ille in civitatem, invenit hominem pere-
grinum iacentem in platea ægrotum, non habentem qui ei curam adhiberet; et
mansit cum eo die una. Et cum venisset hora dormitionis eius, conspicit frater
ille Michaelem et Gabrielem descendentes propter animam eius. Et sedens unus
a dextris et alius a sinistris eius, rogabant animam eius, ut egrederetur foras; et
non exibat, quasi nolens relinquere corpus suum.
    60–69 Dixit autem Gabriel ad Michaelem: Assume iam animam istam ut
eamus. Cui Michael respondit: Iussi sumus a Domino, ut sine dolore eiiciatur,
ideoque non possumus cum vi evellere eam. Exclamavit ergo Michael voce
magna dicens: Domine, quid vis de anima hac, quia non acquiescet nobis, ut
egrediatur?
    70–82 Venit autem ei vox: Ecce, mitto David cum cithara, et omnes Deo
psallentes in Ierusalem, ut audiens psalmum ad vocem ipsorum egrediatur.
Cumque descendissent omnes in circuitu animæ illius cantantes hymnos, sic
exiens illa sedit in manibus Michael, et assumpta est cum gaudio. [Ælfric adds
the concluding details in 79–82.]

Ic asende nu rihtes þære sawle togeanes
Dauid mid his hearpan, 7 þone heofenlican dream,
ealle singende, þæt seo sawul gehyre
heora ealra stemna, 7 heo wyle swa ut.
Hi comon þa ealle to þære anre sawle   75
swyþe myrige singende, 7 heo 's'wa gewát
ut of þam lichaman mid þam lofsange
on Michaeles handum mid mycelre blisse,
7 heo wearð upp geferod mid eallum þam heape
to þam soðan Hælende, þe heo swa gelicode;   80
7 se munuc gewende to þam westene eft,
hæfde þa gesawen swa swa he sylf gewilnode.

  Vs segð seo ylce boc þæt sum oð(er) munuc hwilon,
swiþe geþogen mann on mihte 7 on gearum,
com (into) anre byrig embe his agene neode.   85
Ða gesæt he swa æt anes rice(s) mannes geate,
se læg þær on forðsiþe, 7 se munuc þa beheol(d,
for) þan þe he mihte geseon, for his micclum geearnungum,
hu se (mann) geendode on his forðsiþe.
Ða geseah se munuc mycelne (getru)man,   90
swylce ridendra manna mid swyþe reþum anginne,
(: : : : : : : : :) ansynes mid eall-sweartum lichaman,
7 þa hors wær(on : : : : : : : :) bæron þa deofla,
be þam þe he geseah þe hit eft ðu(: : : : : : : : :
: : : :) lihton þa ealle 7 inn stopon caflice,   95
7 (ælc) hæfde h(: : : : : : : : : : : : :) isenne sagol

71 nu rihtes] *Space for one or two letters at end of line after* nu *in MS. but
probably nothing missing. See note.*   92 (egeslices)? *Perhaps too many letters,
but margin uncertain.*   93 wær(on swearte þe)? wær(on blace þe)?
94 ðu(s gerehte)? *or* ðu(s asæde)?   95 (Hi a)lihton?   95 h(im on
handa ænne)?

83–89 Dixit iterum qui supra, de quodam sene, quia venit aliquando in
civitatem, ut venundaret vasa quæ operatus fuerat. Et cum explicuisset ea, contigit eum sedere ante ianuam cuiusdam divitis, qui iam moriebatur. [*Ælfric*
adds the explanation, 87b–89.]
  90–104 Sedens ergo senex ille, vidit equos nigros, et ascensores eorum nigros
et terribiles, habentes singulos baculum igneum in manu sua. Cum ergo iam
pervenissent ad ianuam illam, statuerunt equos suos foras, et intravit unusquisque cum festinatione. Infirmus autem ille videns eos, clamavit voce magna
dicens: Domine, adiuva me. At illi dixerunt ei: Nunc memor factus es Dei,
quando tibi sol obscuratus est? quare usque in hodiernum diem non exquisisti
eum, dum adhuc tibi splendor erat diei? Nunc autem in hac hora non est tibi
portio spei neque consolationis.

on fyres gelicnysse, 7 sto(don) be(: : : : : : : : :
þam ear)man seocan menn, 7 he geseah hi ealle.
He cl(ypode : : : : : : : : : : : : : : : :) mycelre angsumnesse,
Drihten, gehelp (min : : : : : : : : : : : : : : : :) deoflu: 100
Eart þu nu gemyndig þæs (ælmihtigan Godes
þonne þin sunne) þe is forsworcen mid ealle?
Hwi nold(est þu :)
þa hwile þe ðu hæfdest ænig(: : : : : : : : : : * : : : : : : : : : :

                                                        *f. 177ᵛ

: :
   : : : : : : : : : :   105
: : : : : :) þe he symle (: : : : : : : : : : : : : : : : : :) oð his
ende.

[The following lines probably not by Ælfric]

(: : : : : : : :)bað swylce forebysne gehyred ge be(: : : : : : : :)a
his agene (: : : : :) sece to scrifte, þæt him wyrðe God milde, for
þam swa swa we (nu hwe)ne ær sædon, betere is manna gehwylcum
þæt him her on worulde (befor)an anum menn for his gyltum 110
sceamige, þonne him sceamige (eft on) Domes-dæg beforan Gode
sylfum, 7 beforan eallum his englum, (7 be)foran eallum heofonlicum werede, 7 beforan eallum eorðlicum were(de), 7 beforan
eallum deoflum. Hit his eall soð þæt we gyt secgan wyllað: (Ðam)
þe nele her nu his synna andettan his scrifte, 7 betan swa he him 115
tæcð, him sceal on Domes-dæg sceamian beforan Gode sylfum,
7 eallum his halgum 7 eallum deoflum, swa þam menn dyde þe
wurde færinga nacod beforan eallum folce, 7 nyste þonne mid
hwam he his sceamigendlican bewruge: swa him byð on Domes-
dæge buton he his synna ær bewreo mid andetnesse, 7 mid dæd- 120
bote, 7 mid ælmyssum. Ealle þa synna þe we her wyrceað, ealle hi
beoð eft on us sylfum gesewene 7 geopenode, buton hi ær her on
worulde gebette beon.

100 gehelp (min! Ac him andwyrdon þa) deoflu?   104 ænig(ne hiht to
forgifennysse)?   106 (for ðan) þe he symle (wunode on his synnum)
oð his ende?   107 (*Leofan menn*, nu ge hab)bað?   be(ðoht, loc hw)a?
108 (þearfe)?   115 his] *sic MS. for* is.   123 beon] *followed by the original
conclusion of the homily:* God ús gerihtlæce, 7 to þam ecan life gelæde, swa swa
he behet þam þe hine lufiað. Si him wuldor 7 wyrðmynt on ealra worulda
woruld, AMEN.

NOTES

2–7. The left-hand margin of the manuscript near the top of the page has lost several letters. No recognizable traces remain for the first four letters of *wiðæftan* (2), any at all of *huru* (3), the first five of *we a worhton* (4), the first four of *þe her* (5), or the first three of *gebroðra* (7). Everything except *huru* (3), a pure guess to fill the space, is pretty well supported by the first Wulfstan passage quoted above, p. 773, or by the context. I am also doubtful about *leofre* (2) despite plausible traces, for the Wulfstan passage just mentioned makes me believe that another *leofre*, differently used, stood in the previous, now illegible line. As for the bracketed *hwi* of the first *þa hwile þe* (4), this cluster of letters seems to have been turned over when the damaged leaf was set in its paper frame, since there is no trace of it on the verso where it belongs, but it appears near the corresponding spot on the recto, somewhat askew, where it cannot have had any place originally. The repetition of *þa hwile þe* in lines 4 and 7 seems not uncharacteristic of this author.

15. The antecedent of *þysum* is by no means clear, whether we try to discover it in what has just been said or in the last sentences of the original homily. Cf. XIX. 136, where a comparable *ðam* refers to the statement immediately preceding. In all probability the original antecedent has been lost. With Ælfric's formula in this line compare the beginning of the unattached *exemplum* by him in Napier XXXI, p. 152/7: 'We willað nu secgan sume bysne to þisum.' Here more obviously the excerptor has sacrificed the antecedent of *þisum*.

44. *mid : : : licum witum*. Against *hellicum* is the lack of any trace of an ascender in the manuscript. Against *deoflicum* is the doubt whether there is enough space and the use of *deofol* two lines earlier. If *-licum* be allowed to carry the alliteration with *lange* we can supply a non-alliterating syllable such as *sar-*. But Ælfric may have had a better idea.

59. Apparently half a line containing *to* with a dative infinitive (as in VII. 40) has dropped out.

70–80. These lines have already been printed in an article by Winifred Temple, 'The Song of the Angelic Hosts', *Annuale Mediaevale* (Pittsburgh: Duquesne Univ. Press), II (1961), 5–14. Her text, on p. 7, is taken directly from the manuscript and is correctly printed, except that by some oversight the printer has omitted all the ampersands. (See also the next note, on line 71.) The article deals with the climax of the story as it appears in the *Vitæ Patrum*, in Ælfric, and in an Old Irish version, and touches on its Oriental antecedents. The main weight of the article, however, is on the word *dream*, as explained in the note on line 72.

71. *nu rihtes*. There is room for at least one more letter after *nu* at the end of a line in the manuscript and we might perhaps read *(ge)rihtes*, but certainly not *(þær)rihtes*, as Miss Temple suggests and I too once supposed. In the combination *þærrihte*, as in the modern 'thereupon', the *þær* points

to some time other than the present. Hence it cannot well be used in conjunction with *nu*. Ælfric uses *þærrihte* most often with the past tense, as at *LS* VII. 356; X. 94; XXI. 326; XXII. 131; XXXIV. 224. He uses it also, in our XI. 303, with reference to a quick succession of events in the distant future. But BT, under *rihte*, gives two examples of *nu rihte*, translating *iam nunc*, from the *O.E. Heptateuch* (*Exod.* ix. 19 and *Num.* xi. 23), and under *nu*, two more examples from Ælfric's *Grammar* (ed. Zupitza, pp. 94/14 and 123/17). The form *rihtes* here, instead of the usual *rihte*, may be scribal. As for *(ge)rihtes*, though the manuscript would admit such a reading it does not require it, and there is no record in the dictionaries of *gerihte(s)* as a temporal adverb.

72. *dream*. Miss Temple, in the article mentioned above, has shown that the word here must mean 'choir' rather than 'song' or 'music', and has pointed to several other passages in Old English where the same meaning, if not required, would be relevant. Though not recognized in the dictionaries, this meaning may be regarded as an extension (or parallel) of the concrete sense 'musical instrument' recorded in BT, *dream*, II. Elsewhere Ælfric uses the word with reference to heavenly singing, as at *CH* II. 342/10; 548/12; to the sound of trumpets, as at *CH* II. 86/35; and in one other passage, perhaps, to the heavenly choir: namely, at *LS* XXXI. 1389, 1395, though this meaning was not recognized by Skeat.

94. *þe hit eft ðu(s gerehte)*? The context requires some such clause, but since the beginning of the next sentence is also lost the number of letters missing here is hard to estimate. Ælfric need not have chosen an alliterating verb (such as *asæde*) since he had four minor words beginning with *þ* and two with *h*. Possible parallels are *LS* XXV. 513, *swa swa we her rehton*, and even *LS* XXVI. 247, *þa clypode he þone preost þe hit cydde eft þus*.

109–14. On the resemblance of these lines to a passage in *De Penitentia* see the introductory comment.

114–21. For the correspondence here with a passage in Napier XLVI see the introductory comment. The phrase, *þone sceamiendan lichaman*, in Napier's text looks like a euphemistic substitute for the hitherto unrecorded *his sceamigendlican* in line 119. The verb *bewreon* (119, *bewruge*, and 120, *bewreo*) is not recorded in BT as a verb used by Ælfric, though I hesitate to count its occurrence here among positive signs of a different author. Ælfric does use the negatively prefixed *onwreon* 'to reveal' (see Glossary); *awreon* 'to reveal' at *ONT* 879 (recorded in BTS); and *oferwreon* 'to cover' at *CH* II. 196/25. There may be unrecorded instances of *bewreon*, but, even if not, Ælfric tends to use prefixes so spontaneously that a rare use may crop up anywhere in his work.

XXVIII

'PAULUS SCRIPSIT AD THESALONICENSES'

(Lines on Antichrist added to *CH* II. xliv, *In Natale Sanctarum Virginum*)

ÆLFRIC'S homily for Virgins, the fifth and last in the group of homilies for the common of the saints at the end of his Second Series, expounds the parable of the wise and foolish virgins in *Matthew* xxv. 1–13. Under the joint guidance of Gregory and Augustine,[1] the coming of the bridegroom is taken as the coming of Christ to the great judgement, and at verse 6, *Media autem nocte clamor factus est*, the dread question of the time of the coming is opened up.[2] Ælfric first explains that the middle of the night represents profound ignorance, for the end of this world will come when men least expect it; and he quotes the passage in which St. Paul says the day of the Lord will come like a thief in the night (*I Thess.* v. 2). But now, following Augustine's lead for a sentence or two, he comments on the general anxiety:

> Oft cweðað men, 'Efne nu cymð domes dæg', forðan ðe ða witegunga sind agane, þe be ðam asette wæron. Ac gefeoht cymð ofer gefeohte, gedrefednys ofer gedrefednysse, eorðstyrung ofer eorðstyrunge, hungor ofer hungre, þeod ofer ðeode, and þonne gyt ne cymð se brydguma.

Thus far with Augustine, the end of the tenth century at one with the beginning of the fifth; but now Ælfric continues:

> Eac swilce þa six ðusend geara fram Adame beoð geendode, and ðonne gyt elcað se brydguma. Hu mage we þonne witan hwænne he cymð? Swa swa he sylf cwæð, 'on middre nihte'. Hwæt is 'on middre nihte' buton þonne ðu nast and þu his ne wenst, ðonne cymð he. Nis nan gesceaft þe cunne ðone timan þyssere worulde geendunge, buton Gode anum.[3]

---

[1] Max Förster, *Anglia* XVI. 15, lists the passages most directly indebted to Gregory (*Hom. XII in Evang.*) and Augustine (*Sermo* xciii).

[2] *CH* II. 568/1 sqq. The quotations below are from lines 8–13 and 13–19.

[3] *Matth.* xxiv. 36: *De die autem illa, et hora nemo scit, neque angeli cælorum, nisi solus Pater.*

Up to this point all the manuscripts agree. Four of them, B, D, E, and K (Thorpe's), represent the early textual tradition as it was established before the middle of the nineties. Two, P and V, represent traditions that originated some years after the turn of the century. In these two the passage just quoted is followed by a few lines that do not appear in the others.

The added lines form two small units that are related in theme but were obviously not to be treated equally as additions to the text of the homily. The first unit, in Latin, must have been originally a marginal note, a parenthetical reminder to the author and other learned readers of a relevant though perplexing prediction of St. Paul's (*II Thess.* ii. 7 sq.) in a well-known passage concerning Antichrist and the end of the world. The second unit alone, consisting of nine vernacular lines carefully composed in Ælfric's rhythmical style, can be accepted as an integral part of the homily. These lines allude generally to the same text without quoting it or implying that it has been quoted, and offer a free interpretation of it based on a comment by Jerome.

The Latin note has the same character as the notes that appear in Thorpe's text of the *Catholic Homilies* (from K) at I. 172/24, 186/25, 304/9, 374/25, 382/28, 478/32; II. 60/16, 92/34, 386/34, 390/3, 446/20. Unlike the short Latin texts that Ælfric quotes and translates, these notes cannot well have been intended for delivery from the pulpit as part of the homilies. They are asides to the learned.[1]

The interpolation proper testifies to Ælfric's effort to deal as responsibly as possible with the disturbing predictions of the last days. The general idea appears in Adso's popular account of Antichrist, which is discussed above, p. 588, as one of Ælfric's probable sources for xviii, but Adso does not document his statements. Ælfric characteristically goes here to the ultimate authorities, to St. Paul himself and to Jerome. Whether his addition belongs to the same period as his return to the subject of Antichrist in xviii is more than I can say. I have not found any allusion to this prediction elsewhere in Ælfric or Wulfstan, but Ælfric may have made use of another part of Jerome's *Epistula* cxxi in homily xvi. 269–92.

---

[1] A list of notes, Latin and English, in Ælfric's works is printed in Clemoes, *Chronology*, 219. It includes, for *CH* I and II, three similar Latin notes, marginal or interlinear, cited by Ker from MSS. A and K. To the Latin list should be added, for completeness, the notes cited above for *CH* I. 382 and II. 386, 390, and of course the passage here printed.

THE TEXT

Paulus scripsit ad Thesalonicenses,
nam ministerium iam operatur iniquitatis,
tantum ut qui nunc tenet, teneat donec de medio fiat,
et tunc reuelabitur ille iniquus, et cetera.—

Us gebycnode swaþeah se Godes bydel Paulus   5
sume swutelunge be ðysum on sumon his pistole,
and Hieronimus se snotera þa swutelunge trahtnode,
and cwæð þæt ne cymð na Antecristes tima
þa hwile þe se casere his cynedomes gewylt.
Ac syððan þæs caseres rice þe on Romana rixað   10
byð mid ealle toworpen, þonne cymð Antecrist,
and se byð ofslagen mid þæs Hælendes tocyme,
swa swa þeostru fordwinað on þære sunnan tocyme.

Text based on P (Hatton 115), f. 85/5–17. Collated with V (CCCC 421), pp.
86/19–87/17. These lines follow *buton Gode anum, CH* II. 568/19.

---

1 tesalonicens *V.*   5 gebicnode *V.*   6 swutulunge *V.*   þisum *V.*
11 bið *V.*   12 bið *V.*

Latin glosses in P: 5 gebycnode: i*n*nuit.   7 trahtnode: *gloss erased,*
perhaps ME.   11 toworpen: destru[c]tu*m.*   13 fordwinað: euanescu*nt;*
obscura*n*t*ur.*

SOURCES. 2–4 [*A slightly inaccurate reminder of II Thess. ii. 7, 8*] Nam
mysterium iam operatur iniquitatis; tantum ut qui tenet nunc, teneat, donec de
medio fiat. Et tunc revelabitur ille iniquus, quem Dominus Iesus interficiet
spiritu oris sui, et destruet illustratione adventus sui eum.
　8–14 [*Jerome, Epist. CXXI, ad Algasiam, cap. xi, on II Thess. ii. 3–8*] Si
enim aperte audacterque dixisset, non veniet Antichristus, nisi prius Romanum
deleatur imperium, iusta causa persecutionis in orientem tunc Ecclesiam con-
surgere videbatur. Quodque sequitur, *Iam enim mysterium operatur iniquitatis,*
tantum ut qui tenet nunc, teneat, donec de medio fiat, et tunc revelabitur ille iniquus,
hunc habet sensum: Multis malis atque peccatis, quibus Nero impurissimus
Cæsarum mundum premit, Antichristi parturitur adventus, et quod ille opera-
turus est postea, in isto ex parte completur, tantum ut Romanum imperium,
quod nunc universas gentes tenet, recedat, et de medio fiat, et tunc Antichristus
veniet, fons iniquitatis, *quem Dominus Iesus interficiet spiritu oris sui.* . . . Statim
ut ille advenerit, interficietur Antichristus. Et quomodo tenebræ solis fugantur
adventu, sic *illustratione adventus sui*, eum Dominus destruet atque delebit. . . .

NOTES

10. *Romana.* This genitive plural after *on* may be elliptical, but it seems more probable that some such word as *byrig* or *þeode* has dropped out.

13. *fordwinað,* 'vanish'. Ælfric uses the same verb with reference to smoke at *CH* I. 592/12 and to the devil at *CH* II. 504/4.

XXIX

MACARIUS AND THE MAGICIANS
SAUL AND THE WITCH OF ENDOR

(Addition to LS xvii, *De Auguriis)*

IN two manuscripts, R and S, the passage edited below has been
substituted for the last four lines of Ælfric's *De Auguriis* as it
appears in other manuscripts, and the substitution raises questions
which are partially but not fully answered by the author of the
colophon in R. According to this colophon, the homily 'be þam
wiglungum', which is obviously *De Auguriis*, is one of two that
have been 'geeacnode' from other homilies, and the clear implication is that the responsibility for the enlargement lies with the
author of the colophon or his supervisor, not with Ælfric.[1] The
very explicitness of the colophon invites belief. Moreover, the
testimony thus provided seems to accord with the distribution of
the unenlarged version of *De Auguriis* in the manuscripts, for this
survives not only in C, L, and W (Skeat's basic manuscript),
which can be expected to represent a relatively early state of the
text, but also in O, P, and V, the last especially a manuscript
that should be textually as late as R and S.

If we accept, provisionally at least, the colophon's testimony,
we must still ask where the compiler found his material and
whether he added anything of his own in order to adjust it to its
new position. The addition has three unequal parts: a bridge
passage of only three lines, establishing a link to *De Auguriis* and
introducing the topics to follow; then, in lines 4–35, the succinctly told story of Macarius and the magicians; and finally, in
lines 36–128, the much longer, carefully expounded story of Saul
and the witch of Endor. The first and third parts occur nowhere
else, but the second part, 4–35, concerning Macarius, is already
familiar to readers of Ælfric's *Lives of Saints*, for Skeat found it in

---

[1] See the description of R in the Introduction, I. 63–64. The conclusions set
forth below differ from those anticipated on p. 64. A fresh look at my argument
as it originally stood in proof has led me to modify it significantly.

MS. W immediately after his xxi, the account of St. Swithun's miracles. There it is headed 'Item Alia', and bears instructions, which Skeat followed, to insert it just ahead of the closing doxology of the preceding piece.

As it appears in lines 4–35 of the addition in R and S, the Macarius passage exhibits no substantive differences from its appearance in W, and we may deduce that the setting accorded to it in W is both prior and authoritative. The opening words, 'Mannum is eac to witenne', properly introduce a new topic at the point indicated for the insertion of the passage in W—that is, after Skeat xxi. 463; but after line 3 of the addition in R and S, the *eac* is clearly illogical. Whoever put the passage in this setting neglected to make the proper adjustment. Moreover, the attachment of the passage to Skeat xxi, though it may seem puzzling at first, is intelligible enough to be accepted as intentional on Ælfric's part. What is remarkable about St. Swithun, in view of the importance attached to him at Winchester, is that no details of his life were remembered there. Ælfric acknowledges this lack of information, and confines himself perforce to the saint's posthumous acts, recounting one miracle after another, including several dreams that are taken to be divinely authorized visions. Near the end (Skeat 403–13), Ælfric seems to fear that he may be encouraging a dangerous credulity, for he issues warning against taking for divine visions the false dreams inspired by the devil. The Macarius passage is a further warning of the same sort, this time against the false illusions created by the devil's agents, the magicians. It is a tribute to Ælfric's conscience rather than to his sense of literary design that he thus adds these notes of caution to his celebration of St. Swithun's miracles.

Now the final passage in R and S, on Saul and the witch, has precisely the same didactic purpose. Saul thought the witch had called up the spirit of the prophet Samuel to help him, but it was really the devil foretelling his doom. Beware lest the appetite for miracles lead to similar delusions! Is it not very possible, then, that at some later time Ælfric reinforced his appended warning by adding to the tale of Macarius the example of Saul? The transition from one to the other at line 36 is flawless; and if Ælfric had already put the pieces of his composition together in this fashion he had greatly simplified the task of the compiler.

There is no obstacle to this hypothesis in the manuscript record.

Of the two complete copies of the St. Swithun piece that survived into modern times (one in Cotton Otho B. x, now partially burnt, the other in W, Cotton Julius E. vii), only the one in W represents what may be called a second state by addition of the Macarius passage. We may readily imagine a third state with the further addition of the Saul passage. MS. W shares with several other manuscripts an early state of *De Falsis Diis* (xxi above), and MSS. R and S are witnesses to a later state.

If these conjectures are right, we have in lines 4–128 below an authentic composition of Ælfric's, produced in two instalments but intended to go together. In lines 1–3 we have a clever imitation of Ælfric's rhythmical style and diction, composed by the compiler in order to fit the rest to its new position at the end of *De Auguriis*.[1] So brief an imitation as this would have been relatively easy.

The compiler deserves credit for a remarkably apt collocation of texts, so apt indeed that I was for a long time tempted to believe that Ælfric himself had composed the Saul passage for *De Auguriis* (with perhaps lines 1 and 2 as introduction, and some suitable adverb in line 36 in place of *eac swylce*). There is certainly talk of witches in *De Auguriis* (Skeat XVII. 108–13 and 124–35), including in the first passage the question how it is that they can foretell what is going to happen. The discussion of Saul's delusion gives a fuller answer to this question, and the comment about contemporary witches (118–23 below) provides an effective reminder of the main theme of the homily. R's colophon would allow us to suppose that the compiler was responsible for adding no more than line 3 and the Macarius passage. But this hypothesis is not only more complicated than the other; it is rendered improbable by the absence of any addition in the other manuscripts of *De Auguriis*, by the fact that the addition, relevant though it is, has been placed inappropriately at the very end of the homily, where it forces cancellation of the now inapplicable conclusion, and by the fact that no fresh conclusion has been provided. It is not like Ælfric to let a homily end without a doxology and an Amen.

A few words must be added on the sources. The Macarius story

---

[1] If we accept these lines as Ælfric's, we make him solely responsible for the addition (as does Clemoes, *Chronology*, p. 239). But this is to reject the statement of the colophon, blame Ælfric for retaining *eac* in line 4, and disregard several bits of evidence mentioned below. The compiler probably composed introductory sentences for his other acknowledged enlargement (see above, I. 63–64).

seems clearly enough to have had a single source, the *Historia Monachorum* of Rufinus; but several sources may have contributed to the discussion of Saul and the witch. Ælfric refers to Augustine in line 50, and there is a genuine treatment of the subject by him, with Ælfric's main conclusions plainly indicated, in one of the chapters of *De Diversis Quæstionibus ad Simplicianum*.[1] But this chapter is strongly influenced, apparently, by an earlier work which passed for Augustine's also until comparatively recent times. This is the *Quæstiones Veteris et Novi Testamenti* in Migne, *PL* xxxv, edited more elaborately by A. Souter.[2] In *Quæstio* xxvii we find a discussion of Saul and the witch that is decidedly closer to Ælfric than the corresponding passage in Augustine. This is particularly evident at lines 77–85, where Augustine has nothing to correspond, and at line 111, where the pseudo-Augustine is responsible for the quotation Ælfric mistakenly attributes to St. Paul. Whether Ælfric had also read Augustine's version, which is virtually the same in substance at many points, is hard to tell. I have quoted a bit of it for line 101 because it is much closer to what Ælfric there says than the pseudo-Augustine, and a little closer than what I have quoted from Isidore. There is a very good chance that Ælfric was familiar with the passage in Isidore (which I think had something to do with the three lines 102–4, and possibly with 101), since it is a part of Isidore's treatment of the gods of the gentiles (*Etym.* VIII. xi), a treatment of which Ælfric seems to have made some slight use in *De Falsis Diis*.[3]

---

[1] *Lib.* II, *Quæst.* iii, 'Samuel per pythonissam evocari quomodo potuerit', *PL* XL. 142–4.

[2] *CSEL* L (1908). This work, which has been mentioned in another connexion in the introduction to homily IX (I. 376, n.), is now attributed to the unidentified author of the pseudo-Ambrosian commentary on thirteen epistles of St. Paul (*PL* XVII. 45–508), who has been called 'Ambrosiaster' since the sixteenth century. His writings have been dated about A.D. 370–85. For recent bibliography see E. Dekkers, *Clavis Patrum Latinorum*, 2nd ed., Steenbrugge, 1961, pp. 40–42.   [3] See above, p. 673.

THE TEXT

We spræcan ǽr be wiccan, nu wille we eow secgan
sum þing swutolicor be heora scincræfte,
and be þam drymannum þe bedydriað þa unsnoteran.
Mannum is eac to witenne þæt manega drymenn maciað
menigfealde dydrunga þurh deofles cræft,   5
swa swa wisceras oft doð, and bedydriað menn
swilce hi soðlice swylc þing dón,
ac hyt is swaþeah dydrung mid deofles cræfte,
and gif hwa hyt bletsað, þonne ablinð seo dydrung.
Be þam we magon secgan sume soðe bysene.   10
Macharius wæs gehaten sum halig fæder
on westene wunigende, fela wundra wyrcende,
munuclifes mann; þa wearð an mæden forbroden

Text based on R (CCCC 178), pp. 97–101. Collated with S (Hatton 116),
pp. 359–65. In both MSS. the lines are added to *De Auguriis*, *LS* xvii, after
line 267 of Skeat's text, replacing the original conclusion, 268–71. Lines 5–35 of
the addition were appended to *LS* xxi in W (Cotton Julius E. vii), f. 103^{rv}, and
were printed by Skeat as indicated below. W has been freshly collated.

1 *Marginal heading in* R: BYSNE BE DRYMANNU*M AND* BE ANU*M*
GODAN M*EN*, MACHARI*US* GEHAT*ÆN*.   1 spræcon *S*.   2 swutel-
licor *S*.   3 -dyder- *S* (*similarly* 5, 6, 8, 9, 14).   4 Mannum] *Here
begins the 'Item Alia' appended to 'Natale Sancti Swyðuni, Episcopi', LS* xxi.
464–95, printed by Skeat from W, *f. 103^{rv}*.   drymen *SW*.   5 mænig- *S*.
6 wischeras *W*.   7 swylce *SW*.   þincg *W*.   8, 9 hit *SW*.   9 ablynð *W*.
10 magan *W*.   bysne *SW*.   12 wæstene *SW*.   13 man *W*.

Glosses in R *and* S, *Latin*: 1 *marg.* exemplum de incantatoribus *R*.   2 scincræfte: incantatio*ne* R, incantationibus *S*.   3 drymannum: incantatoribus
R, magis *S*.   bedyderiað: obceca*nt* S.   unsnoteran: imprudentes *R*.
4 drymenn: incantatores *R*, magi *S*.   5 dyderunga: transfigurationes *S*.
9 ablinð: cessat, desinit *S*.   12 westene: deserto *R*.   13 *marginal heading*:
de puella incantata *R*.   forbroden: transfigurata *S*.
ME: 3 bedydriað: biwicheþ *R*.

Sources. 13–34 [*Rufinus, Hist. Monachorum, cap. XXVIII*, '. . . *de Macario
Ægyptio*'] Cujusdam in vicino oppido patris familias virgo filia per phantasias
magicas videbatur hominibus in equinum animal versa, ut putaretur equa esse,
et non puella. Hanc adduxerunt ad eum. Tunc ille perconctatus, quid vellent?
aiunt parentes eius: Equa hæc quam vident oculi tui, puella virgo et filia nostri
fuit, sed homines pessimi, magicis artibus in animal hoc quod vides mutaverunt
eam. Rogamus ergo, ut ores Dominum, ut commutet eam in hoc quod fuit.

þurh drymanna dydrunga, gedwymorlice swaþeah.

þæt mæden wæs swa forbroden swylce heo án myre wǽre,   15
7 eallum þam þuhte þe hire on locodan
swylce heo myre wære, na mennisces gecyndes.
Ða læddan hyre magas hy to Macharie,
7 he sona ahsade hwæt hi woldan mid þam.
þa magas hym cwædon tó, þeos myre þe þu gesy[h]st   20
wæs ure dohtor, arwurðe mæden,
ac awyrgede drymenn awendon hy to myran.
*Nu bidde we þe, leof, þæt ðu gebidde for hy,   *p. 98
and hy eft awénde to ðam þe heo ær wæs.
Macharius þa cwæð to hyre magum þus: 25
Ic geseo þis mæden on menniscum gecynde,
and heo nis na awend swa swa ge wenað þæt heo sý,
and heo nan þing on hyre næfð horses gecyndes;
ac on eowrum gesihðum hit is [swa] gehiwod
þurh þæs deofles dydrunge and hys drymenn leaslice.   30
Macharius þa gebæd for þæt mæden God,
and mid ele [ge]smyrede, and mid ealle adræfde

---

14 dydrunge W.   -dwimor- SW.   16 locodon SW.   17 swilce W.
myre] an myre S.   mænnisces S.   18 læddon S; leddon W.   hire SW.
magos S.   hi SW.   19 axode SW.   hwet S.   woldon SW.   20 magos
S.   him SW.   þeos] no capital in MSS.   gesyhst] gesyhðst R; gesihst SW.
22 awyrigde W; awyrgde S.   drymen S.   hi SW.   myren S.   23 gebidde]
gebide W.   hi SW.   24 hi SW.   25 cweð S.   hire SW.   magon S.
26 mænniscum S.   27 nis] om. S.   si S.   28 þincg W.   hire SW.
29 swa] sic SW; geþuhð and R.   30 þæs] om. S.   dyderunge S.   his SW.
32 ge-] sic SW; om. R.   -smyrode W.

Glosses in R and S, Latin: 14 drymanna dydrunga: incantationibus R, magica
incantatione S.   gedwymorlice: fantasma RS.   15 an: una R.   myre:
equa S.   17 na: non RS.   mennisces gecyndes: hominis nature R.
18 magas: parentes RS.   19 he: ill(e)? R.   ahsade: inquisiuit R.   þam:
illa RS.   20 magas: parentes R.   þeos: ista R.   gesyhðst: vides R.
21 arwurðe: venerabilis RS, honesta S.   23 leof: domine R.   hy: illam R.
27 na: non S.   ge: vos R.   29 gehiwod: fictum R; fingitur, simulatur
RS (simil-).   30 leaslice: fallaciter R.   31 god: deum R.   32 ele:
oleo R.   adræfde: eiecit RS, expulit R.

At ille ait: Ego hanc quam ostenditis mihi puellam video, nihil in se pecudis
habentem: hoc autem quod dicitis, non est in eius corpore, sed in oculis in-
tuentium. Phantasiæ enim dæmonum sunt istæ, non veritas rerum. Et . . . orare
Dominum coepit, . . . et post hoc perungens eam oleo in nomine Domini, omni
fallacia visus expulsa, virginem videri omnibus, ut etiam sibi videbatur, effecit.

þæs deofles gedwymor þurh his Drihtnes naman,
swa þæt hi ealle gesawan þæt heo ansund wæs.
Swylce synd þa dydrunga þæra drymanna.   35
  Eac swylce we rædað on þære gerecednysse
on þæra Cyninga Bocum, swa swa hyt gecweden is,
þæt Saúl se cyning on his unsiðe
þa þa hym God gram wæs for hys gramlicum dædum,
become to anre wiccan, wolde witan þurh hi   40
hu him sceolde gelimpan, hwæðer þe líf þe deað,
síge oððe fléam on hys fyrdunge,
þa þa he feohtan ongan wið ða Philisteos
on Gelboes múnte mid mycelre fyrdunge.
  Nu segð se wyrdwritere þæt seo wicce sceolde   45
aræran þa of deaþe þone Drihtnes witegan
Samuhel geháten, haliges lifes mann,
and he sceolde secgan Saule þam cyninge
þæs þe he befrán on hys frecednysse.
  Ac Augustinus se wisa wiðcwyð þyssere leasunge,   50

---

33 þæs] *sic MSS.*; þas *Skeat.*   gedwimor *SW.*   34 gesawon *W*; ge-
segon *S.*   35 dyderunga *S.*   þæra] þære *W.*   drymanna] *Here ends the
correspondence with W, which adds three concluding lines from the end of the preced-
ing homily.*   36 -nesse *S.*   37 hit *S.*   39 him *S.*   his *S.*   41 hweþer *S.*
42 his *S.*   fyrdinge *S (and* 44).   45 sægð *S.*   47 samuel *S.*   gehaten]
wæs gehaten *S.*   49 his *S.*   -nesse *S.*   50 Ac] *sic S*; *no capital in R.*
þissere *S.*

  Glosses in R and S, Latin: 33 gedwymor: fantasma *R.*   34 ansund: sospes, incolumis, integer *R.*   36 Eac swylce: similit*er S.*   gerecednysse: rela-
tione *RS.*   37 on þæra cyninga bocum: i*n* libro regum (*marginal heading*)
R.   38 unsiðe: exitu (*!*) *R.*   39 gram: irat*us R.*   *margin,* relatio bona
de saul *R.*   40 become: deuenit *S.*   42 sige: victoria *RS.*   fleam:
fuga *RS.*   on: i*n R.*   fyrdunge: excercitu *RS*; itineratione (*?*)*R*, itinerando *S.*
43 ongan: incepit *R.*   44 fyrdunge: excercitu *S.*   acie *S.*   45 wyrdwritere: ortodoxus *S.*   46 aræran: suscitare *R.*   þa: tunc *RS.*   49 befran
inquisiuit *S.*   frecednysse: periculo *RS.*

---

  36 sqq. [*The story is in I Reg.* (*I Sam.*), *xxviii. 4–25, with the sequel, of Saul's
death, in xxxi; but Ælfric's account is too free to justify quotation except at the few
points indicated below.*]
  50–54 [*ps.-Augustine, Quæstiones Veteris et Novi Testamenti; ex Vet. Test.
Quæst. xxvii, § 1*] Quomodo enim fieri poterat, ut arte magica attraheretur vir,
et nativitate sanctus, et vitæ operibus iustus? aut si non attractus est, consensit?
Quod utrumque de viro iusto credere adversum est. Si enim invitus adductus est,
nullum suffragium habet iustitia; si voluntarius autem, amisit meritum spiritale
quod positus in carne quæsiverat. [*For the reference to Abraham's dwelling, see the
passage cited below for 66–74.*]

and segð us to soðan þæt se soðfæsta witega,
þe on Abrahames wununge wæs gefyrn gebroht,
ne mihte þurh þone wiccecræft eft to worulde siðian,
ne þances ne unþances, þæt he hyre to spræce.
Hit is swa gesæd on þære ge*setnysse,   *p. 99
swa swa Saul se cyning þa gesihðe oncnéow,   56
for þam þe he wende þæt he þone witegan
Samuhel gesawe; ac hit wæs sylf se deofol
on hys gelicnysse þe hyne swa forlærde.
We secgað eac to soðan þæt nan scincræft ne mæg,   60
ne furþan se deofol sylf, nænne deadne aræran,
for þam ðe seo dæd is ures Drihtnes anes,
þæt he ða deadan arære swa swa he dyde him sylf
and eac þurh his halgan her on þysum life,
se þe ís soð Scyppend sawla and lichamena.   65
Ac se deofol gehiwode hine sylfne swa
on þæs witegan gelicnysse, and to þære wiccan spræc,
and sæde þam cyninge, þu scealt beon mid me
nu tomergen on minre wununge.

51 sægð S.   53 eft] om. S.   54 hyre to] to hire S.   sprece S.
55 gesæd] geræd S.   -nesse S.   57 þan S.   58 samuel S.   gesawe]
gesege S.   wes S.   59 his S.   -nesse S.   hine S.   61 ne ... sylf] om. S.
62 þan S.   64 þisum S.   65 lichamana S.   66 Ac] no capital in MSS.
67 þes S.   -nesse S.   spræc] gesprec S.   68 þu] no capital in MSS.

_____

   Glosses in R and S, Latin: 52 gefyrn: olim R.   53 eft ... siðian: redire R.
54 spræce: loqui (sic) R.   55 gesetnysse: institutione R.   56 swa swa:
sicut R.   þa: illam R.   gesihþe: visionem S.   59 forlærde: decepit R;
seduxit S.   60 scincræft: incantatio RS.   61 ne furþan: nec eciam R.
62 dæd: actio R; mors (dæd altered to dæð) S.   64 her: hic R.
66 gehiwode: finxit RS; dissimulauit R, similauit S.   67 witegan: pro-
fete R.

_____

   55–59 [Ibid., § 3] Historicus enim mentem Saul et habitum Samuelis descrip-
sit, ea quæ dicta et visa sunt exprimens; prætermittens, si vera an falsa sint.
Quid enim ait? Audiens in quo habitu esset excitatus, Intellexit, inquit, hunc esse
Samuelem (I Reg. xxviii. 14) . . .; et putans Samuelem, adoravit diabolum.
   60–65 [Independent.]
   66–74 [ps. -Augustine §§ 3, 4] Et quomodo homo Dei, qui cum Abraham in
refrigerio erat, dicebat ad virum pestilentiæ, dignum ardore gehennæ, Cras mecum
eris? (I Reg. xxviii, 19, inexactly). Subtilitatem fallaciæ suæ prodidit improvidus
Satanas, quia . . . virum peccatis pressum, cum magna distantia peccatorum et
iustorum sit, cum Samuele iustissimo futurum mentitus est. Verum potest videri
si de Samuelis nomine taceatur, quia Saul cum diabolo futurus erat. Ad eum
enim transmigravit, quem adoravit.

Her we magon tocnawan þæt se cyning sceolde   70
for hys manfullum dædum to þam deofle becuman,
and [for] þam wiccecræfte mid him á wunian,
for þam ðe he næs na wyrðe þæt he wununge hæfde
on Abrahames wununge mid þam witegan Samuhele.
Ða feoll se cyning mid fyrhte fornumen   75
to ðæs deofles fotum þe hyne bedydrode,
wende þæt hit wære se witega Samuhel,
and hyne to hym gebæd mid gebigedum limum;
ac gyf hyt se witega wære, he wolde him forwyrnan
þæt he to hym ne gebæde, his Hælende on teonan;   80
for þam þe man sceal hyne gebiddan to þam Hælende ánum,
and hym ánum þeowian, se ðe ana is G[o]d.
þæs gewilnað se deofol þæt man hyne wurðige,
and to him gebidde, þæt he hæbbe anweald
ofer þa gedwolan þe hys gedwyldum gelyfað,   85
swa swa þa hæðenan dydan þe hyne wurþodan for god,
and forletan heora Scyppend þe hy gesceop to mannum;
and swa swa Saul dyde on þære deoflican gesihðe,
þæt he fullice wære *forwyrht to þam deofle.   *p. 100
Saul þa syððan æfter þære deoflican gesihðe   90

---

71 his S.   deofle] deoflum S.   72 for] sic S; to R.   73 þan S.
76 hine S.   bedyderode S.   77 samuel S.   78 hine S.   him S.
79 gif hit S.   forwyrnen S.   80 him S.   81 mann S.   sceall S.
hine S.   82 him S.   God] god S; gód R.   83 hine S.   85 his S.
gedwildum S.   gelefað S.   86 dydon S.   hine S.   wurþodon S.
87 forlæton S.   hi S.   gescop S.   89 forwyrht] sic RS, but R has small
o above y.   90 siððan S.

Glosses in R and S, Latin: 71 manfullum: iniquis R.   72 á: semper R.
75 mid fyrhte fornumen: timore consumptus R.   78 gebæd: adorauit R.
gebigedum: flexis R.   80 gebæde: genuflecteret R.   teonan: contumelia
RS.   81 gebiddan: adorare R.   83 þæs: hoc RS.   gewilnað:
desiderat S.   85 gedwyldum: errorem, erroribus R; errores S.   88 gesihðe:
visione R.   89 forwyrht: damnatus R.   90 gesihðe: visionem R.

75–78 [I Reg. xxviii. 20] Statimque Saul cecidit porrectus in terram; ex-
timuerat enim verba Samuelis. [Earlier, verse 14] Et intellexit Saul quod Samuel
esset, et inclinavit se super faciem suam in terra, et adoravit.

77–85 [ps.-Augustine, § 3] Putans Samuelem, adoravit diabolum, ut fructum
fallaciæ suæ haberet Satanas. Hoc enim nititur, ut adoretur quasi Deus. Si enim
vere Samuel illi apparuisset, non utique vir iustus permisisset se adorari, qui
prædicaverat Deum solum esse adorandum.

90–96 [I Reg. xxviii. 25] Cum comedissent surrexerunt [Saul et servi eius], et
ambulaverunt per totam noctem illam. . . . [xxxi. 1] Philisthiim autem pugnabant

gewende to hys fyrde fram þære wiccan huse,
and þa Philiste[i] fuhtan fæstlice þæs on merigen
wið Saul þone cyning, and ofslogan hys fyrde
and hys þry suna, and he sylf þa feoll
úppon his wæpne and gewat swa of lífe   95
to þam swicolan deofle, swa swa he him ǽr sæde.
  Nu wundrað gehwá hu se deofol wiste
þæt Saul sceolde sweltan þæs on merigen,
ac he wat gehwæt þæs þe gewurþan sceal
þurh hys scearpe andgit þæs engellican gecyndes,   100
oððe þurh Godes geþafunge þæs ðe ús dyrne is,
oððe þurh gebicnunge þæs mannes nebwlitan;
for ðam þe he wæs gefyrn, and fela hæfð gesewen,
and wide and side færð, and cann fela searacræfta.
Paulus cwæð be hym on sumon his pistole: 105

---

91 his S.   92 Philistei] philisteos RS.   fuhton S.   93 þone] þoñ
as if þonne S.   ofslogon S.   his S.   94 his S.   þreo S.   sunu S.
96 ær sæde] sæde ǽr S.   98 swyltan S.   99 sceall S.   100 his S.
102 gebicnungæ S.   103 gesegen S.   105 cweð S.   him S.

Glosses in R and S, Latin: 94 þry suna: iii filios R.   95 wæpne: armis S.
gewat: obiit R.   97 gehwa: aliquis S.   wiste: sciret R.   99 gehwæt:
aliquid S.   100 andgit: intellectum RS.   engellican gecyndes: angelice
nature S.   101, 102 oððe: vel S.   101 geþafunge: permissione RS.
þæs: ea S(!)   þæs ðe: qui R (!).   102 gebicnunge: nutu RS; vel singno S.
nebwlitan: faciei S.   103 gefyrn: olim R; diu S.   104 searacræfta:
machinas R, machina S; ingenia R.

---

adversum Israel, et fugerunt viri Israel ante faciem Philisthiim, et ceciderunt
interfecti in monte Gelboe. [2] Irrueruntque Philisthiim in Saul et in filios eius,
et percusserunt Ionathan, et Abinadab, et Melchisua, filios Saul. . . . [4] Arripuit
itaque Saul gladium, et irruit super eum.
  97–104 [ps.-Augustine, § 2] Sed hoc quosdam fallit, quod de morte Saul et filii
eius non sit mentitus: quasi magnum sit diabolo, ante diem occasum corporis
prævidere, cum signa quædam soleant apparere morituris; quippe a quibus Dei
protectio amota videtur. Quanto magis diabolus quem angelica maiestate sub-
limem prophetica oracula fuisse testantur. [For 101 cf. Augustine, De Diversis
Quæstionibus ad Simplicianum, II. iii. 3] Cum enim vult Deus, etiam per infimos
infernosque spiritus aliquem vera cognoscere, temporalia dumtaxat atque ad
istam mortalitatem pertinentia, facile est. . . . Tantum autem audiunt, quantum
omnium Dominus atque moderator vel iubet vel sinit. [For 101–4 cf. Isidore,
Etym. VIII. xi] Præsciunt [dæmones] futura multa, unde et solent responsa
aliqua dare. Inest enim illis cognitio rerum, plusquam infirmitati humanæ,
partim subtilioris sensus acumine, partim experientia longissimæ vitæ, partim
per Dei iussum angelica revelatione. [See note on 102–4.]
  105–12 [Cf. ps.-Augustine, § 1] Hoc est præstigium Satanæ, quo ut plurimos
fallat, etiam bonos in potestate se habere confingit. Quod Apostolus inter cætera

Transfigurat se in angelum lucis:
He abryt hine sylfne to scinendum engle,
þæt he mid hys lotwrencum þa geleaffullan fordó,
ac he ne mæg þa fordon þe on Drihtne truwiað.
Be þam ylcan cwæð eft se apostol þuss: 110
An ignoratis altitudinem Satane?
Oððe nyte ge lá þæs sceoccan deopnysse?—
for þam þe we ne cunnan tocnawan þa deopnysse
hys searacræfta hys swicolan modes;
ac his miht nis naht wið þæne ælmihtigan Crist,   115
þe us ealle bewerað wið hys wodnysse æfre,
gif we mid geleafan and mid lufe hyne sécað.
Gyt farað wiccan to wega gelæton,
and to hæþenum byrgelsum mid heora gedwimore,
and clipiað to ðam deofle, and he cymð hym tó   120
on þæs mannes gelicnysse þe þær lið bebyrged,
swylce he of deaðe aríse; ac heo ne mæg þæt dón,
þæt se deada aríse þurh hyre drycræft.
*Deofolgild and drycræft, wiccecræft and wiglunga   *p. 101
synd swyðe andsæte urum Hælende Criste,   125
and þa ðe þa cræftas begað syndan Godes wiðe[r]sacan,
and hy soðlice belimpað to þam swicolan deofle,
mid hym æfre to wunigenne on þam ecum witum.

---

108 his *S.*   109 drihten *S.*   110 cweð *S.*   þus *S.*   112 -nesse *S.*
113 *entire line om. S.*   114 his (*twice*) *S.*   116 his *S.*   -nesse *S.*
117 hine *S.*   118 gelætum *S.*   119 heþenum *S.*   gedwimoræ *S.*
120 clypiað *S.*   him *S.*   121 -nesse *S.*   122 swilce *S.*   123 hire
S.   124 -gyld *S.*   125 swiðe *S.*   126 syndon *S.*   wiðer-]*sic S*;
wiðes- *R.*   127 hi *S.*   128 him *S.*   *after* witum] a buton ende *S.*

Glosses in R and S, Latin: 107 abryt: transfig*ur*at, fing*it*, simulat *R.*
108 lotwrencum: machinis *RS.*   fordo; *perdat R.*   109 þa: illos *R.*
fordon: *perdere R.*   truwiað: *confidunt RS*; sperant *R.*   112 deopnysse:
altitudin*em RS.*   113 tocnawan: discer*nere R.*   114 searacræfta:
incantationes *S.*   modes: *animi R.*   115 wið: *contra RS.*   118 wega
gelæton: biuio *R.*   119 gedwimore: fantasma *RS.*   121 gelicnesse:
similitudine *S.*   124 Deofolgild: idolo*rum* seruit*ium R*; idolu*m S.*   drycræft: incantatio *R.*   125 andsæte: hodiosa *R*, odiosa *S*; detestanda *RS*;
exosa *R.*   126 begað: excercent *RS.*   wiðersacan: adu*er*sarii, rep*ro*bi *R*:
apostate *S.*

---

ait, *Ipse Satanas transfigurat se in angelum lucis* (II *Cor. xi. 14*)....[§ 2] De cuius
magnitudine Apostolus ait, *An ignoratis altitudinem Satanæ?* (*Apoc. ii. 24*; *see
note on line* 111).

NOTES

4. *eac.* On the inappropriateness of this word in its present context see the introductory comment, p. 787.

6. *wisceras.* This word is spelled *wischeras* in W, from which Skeat printed the present passage at the end of *LS* xxi. He defined the word in his translation as 'diviners'; Toller, in his Supplement, taking it from Skeat, and giving hesitantly the nominative singular as *wischere*, suggested 'wizard'. The context makes these guesses plausible, though perhaps the emphasis should be placed squarely on spell-binding by some such word as 'enchanter' or 'sorcerer'. The etymology of the word, listed as *wischere* by Holthausen also, is passed over by him as unknown, and its uniqueness makes any guess hazardous. The spelling *wisceras*, however, in MSS. R and S, here brought into notice for the first time, suggests a direct connexion with OE *wīsc* or *wȳsc*, f. 'wish'. One might explain *wiscere* as an agent-noun formed directly from a combination of *wīsc-* and *-ere*, and applied to any practitioner of magical arts who claimed the power to bring about the satisfaction of wishes. But if the word is an old one, as seems probable, it may be derived from less everyday associations of *wȳsc*. It is to be noted that the ON cognate *ósk* appears in weak form as one of the names of Odin, *Óski*, in the *Grímnismál*, stanza 49, and that *ósk-mær*, f., defined as 'chosen maid' by Cleasby–Vigfusson, but possibly rather 'maid who governs choice' or 'maid of the God Wish', is a name for a Valkyrie. The word *wishmay* recorded by the *OED* seems to be merely a translation of the ON, but the *OED* indicates an association of *wish* with magic which may be much more ancient than the citations. See *wish*, v., 7; *wish-hounds*; *wishing*, d; and perhaps *wisht*, 2, though the *OED* says this is of unknown origin.

7. *swilce hi soðlice swylc þing don.* The antecedent of *swylc* is indefinite. Skeat translates, 'as if they would verily perform a desired matter', probably taking the literal sense as equivalent to 'such and such a thing'. Perhaps 'such a thing (as they pretend)' may equally well be meant.

45, 48. Ælfric's use of *sceolde* here calls attention to a misunderstanding on the part of the Biblical historian, who supposed, like Saul himself, that the witch had raised the prophet Samuel, or at least (as Ælfric's source suggests) chose to tell the story as it appeared to Saul without committing himself as to its truth or falsity. See the Glossary under *sceolan*, b.

102–4. This explanation of the devil's foreknowledge, whether or not it owes something to Isidore, corresponds in part to a passage in Ælfric's life of St. Maur, *LS* vi. 327–9, where an angel makes the statement:

Witodlice se deofol wat towerde ðing,
hwilon, na symle, þurh sume gebicnunge,
be þam þe he oft geseah, þeah þe he sylf leas sy.

Note the word *gebicnunge* in the same sense, 'indication', as in our line 102. Skeat has 'token' in his translation of the passage above, and this is the nearest meaning listed in BT and Hall–Meritt. It is fairly close to the mark, but 'indication' better conveys the verbal force of the word. In his *Grammar*, Ælfric translates *indicativus* by *gebicniendlic* (ed. Zupitza, p. 124/14). Cf. also *gebycnode*, xxviii. 5.

111. *An ignoratis altitudinem Satane?* Ælfric supposes that the 'apostolus' of the Latin text is St. Paul, as before; but Ambrosiaster is actually referring to St. John and is slightly misquoting *Apoc*. ii. 24. This is made clear by two other passages. In *Quæstio* cii, § 19, Ambrosiaster gives at length *Apoc*. ii. 18–26 in an Old Latin form, and verse 24 includes the words, *Vobis autem dico . . . qui hanc doctrinam non habetis et ignoratis altitudinem Satanæ* (*CSEL* L. 214; *PL*. xxxv. 2309). That the question he attributes to the apostle is a modification of this same verse seems evident from Ambrosiaster's commentary on *Romans* viii. 38, 39, where we find a more explicit attribution of the same words: *De qua dicit Ioannes apostolus: An ignoratis altitudinem Satanæ?* (*PL* xvii. 130). The modern editors of Ambrosiaster's *Quæstio* xxvii have supposed, like Ælfric, that St. Paul was at least partly in view, and have referred to *II Cor*. ii. 11, *ut non circumveniamur a Satana: non enim ignoramus cogitationes eius*, either alone (as in Migne) or in conjunction with *Apoc*. ii. 24 (as in Souter); but the latter text alone is recognized by P. Sabatier, who cites all three passages from Ambrosiaster in his note on the Old Latin readings of the verse (*Bibliorum Sacrorum Latinæ Versiones Antiquæ*, Paris, 1751, III. 996).

118. *wiccan*. Ælfric's use of *heo* in 122 seems to show that he was thinking of female witches only. I know of no instance of his use of the weak masculine *wicca* instead of the weak feminine *wicce*. See Glossary, *wicce*.

124. *Deofolgild and drycræft, wiccecræft and wiglunga*. The alliterative pairing here resembles Wulfstan's technique, but notice the repetition of *cræft* in the middle, the difference between *dry* and *wicce-* being essentially, I think, between male and female

XXX

FROM DE VIRGINITATE

HERE are printed two consecutive but not very closely related passages that constitute the unedited remainder of a compilation in MS. V (CCCC 419). It is entitled *De Virginitate*, but the title is somewhat inaccurate even for the beginning, and it applies to only eight of the lines edited here. The piece consists of three originally unconnected passages by Ælfric (if we count as one passage two excerpts from the same homily), and a fourth passage also by him that has survived here only, but was probably, like the rest, excerpted from some longer piece rather than composed for the occasion. V gives no indication in the heading of the day or season for which the homily was intended, and it must, therefore, be classed as *quando volueris*, but there is some evidence, as I shall explain later, that the compiler had in mind the harvest season and either the assumption of the Virgin (15 August) or her nativity (8 September). A brief analysis of the compilation as it stands in V, pp. 347–66, will reveal something of its character:

1. Pp. 347–52/17. An excerpt from the *Letter to Sigefyrth*, Assmann II. 132–88. In this section Assmann's text includes additional passages that appear only in our H among the manuscripts he has used. These additional passages are also in V. The excerpt, written in Ælfric's rhythmical style, presents the topic of the three estates pleasing to God: lawful marriage, widowhood, and virginity, connecting these three with the good soil which, in the parable, brought forth fruit, some thirty, some sixty, some a hundred fold, and with the correspondingly multiplied heavenly rewards.

2. Pp. 352/17–354/19. Two excerpts from *De Doctrina Apostolica*, our XIX. 34–42 and 53–60, which have been collated for that piece. They are in non-rhythmical prose. The first contrasts the 'increase and multiply' of *Genesis* with Christ's strict demands for marriage. The second forbids anyone to break a vow of chastity in God's service once it is made, and applies this particularly to children

whose parents have vowed on their behalf, pointing to the com-
mandment of obedience to parents. Since these two excerpts
merely qualify and elaborate the original topic, everything up to
this point could be adequately described by the alternative title
given to the expanded Assmann II in H: not *De Sancta Virginitate*,
but *De Tribus Ordinibus Castitatis*. But in the two sections that
remain we proceed by an unsteady bridge to a very different range
of topics.

3. Pp. 354/19–361/16. The first seventy-four lines below, the
rhythmical portion of our text. It has survived nowhere else, so
far as I know, but I think it can hardly have been composed to fill
the place assigned to it here, because it does not bring the earlier
passages into intelligible relation to a larger theme; it leads away
from them and ends abruptly without any attempt to prepare us
for what follows. Within it, on the other hand, there is an intelligible sequence. Beginning with the topic of obedience, in which the
warning to proud virgins (as explained in the notes) is a not very
clearly related parenthesis, it asserts as its major theme that, as
Samuel maintained, obedience to God is better than offerings.
This theme could easily have been related to the earlier themes,
for Ælfric often speaks of virginity as an offering made to God (as
at Assmann III. 232–7, and our XIX. 48–52, a passage skipped by
the compiler), and the offering of children to God by their parents
is explicitly mentioned. But nothing is made of this. As the passage
proceeds, on the other hand, we have an extension of the theme by
a direct consideration of almsgiving and the spirit by which it can
be made a suitable offering to God; and so from this, very briefly,
to other acts of worship—to fasting and prayer. A new theme,
Nesciat sinistra tua quid faciat dextera tua, is closely related to the
old and helps to draw the whole section together into a unified
though progressive sequence. As part of a larger treatment of how
God is to be loved and worshipped (still including, perhaps, some
discussion of virginity) this passage might be clear and effective.
It seems muffled and even disconcerting because of its lack of con-
cord with its neighbours.

4. Pp. 361/17–366. The final, non-rhythmical section of our
text, 75–114, is a more or less independent discourse on tithes and
first-fruits. It appears also in MS. R, where it is added to Ælfric's
homily for the twelfth Sunday after Pentecost, just a few sentences
later than the addition on Theodosius and Ambrose that has been

FROM DE VIRGINITATE

edited above as no. xxvi. The passage on tithes is preceded in R
by a linking sentence (quoted below in the apparatus at line 75)
that is probably Ælfric's and indicates that on some occasion at
least he found it convenient to attach the passage to the homily.
It is self-contained except for the linking sentence and might have
been attached to a number of homilies. The unstated connexion
here is the theme of offerings introduced in section 3.

If we seek for a rationale behind this compilation beyond the
mere fact that each section after the first has some relation, however tenuous, with a theme in the section immediately preceding,
we shall find it, I think, not in any ingenious synthesis of its
various topics (for although a synthesis could have been made,
none is even implicitly supplied) but, as I have already intimated,
in a combination of topics that would fall together at or near one
of the feasts of the Virgin during the harvest season. The first
section and the last furnish the important clues.

The topic of the first section, the three estates pleasing to God,
or the three orders of chastity, would seem to be most appropriate
for one of two periods in the year, to judge by Ælfric's own
example and by that of certain manuscripts. Assmann II, though
written first as a letter, occurs as a homily in three manuscripts.
In O, it is assigned to the second Sunday after Epiphany; in N,
to the fourth Sunday; in H (where it is enlarged) it bears a non-
seasonal title (*De Sancta Virginitate vel de Tribus Ordinibus
Castitatis*) but is placed with the homilies for the assumption of
of the Virgin. The assignment in N is erratic, a mere blunder;[1] but
that in H is obviously appropriate and that in O is intelligible.
Ælfric himself mentions the three orders of chastity in his homily
for the second Sunday after Epiphany in the Second Series (*CH*
II. iv), and that is natural because the gospel-text for that day is
the wedding at Cana in Galilee, *John* ii. 1–11. For the present
compilation, however, the choice would fall on either the assumption or the nativity of the Virgin, not because of any indication in
the first section alone, but because of what seems to be implied by
the fourth.

Ælfric's own choice of a day on which to talk about tithes was
once, at least, the twelfth Sunday after Pentecost, as shown by
MS. R. It is a reasonable choice, for the twelfth Sunday will usually
fall some time in August when the harvest is beginning. Cæsarius

[1] See the description of N, Introduction, I. 49.

of Arles preached his sermon on tithes earlier, near midsummer,[1] but August or even early September would seem as good. According to a law of Edgar's reign, the tithe on the young of cattle had to be paid by Pentecost, that on the fruits of the earth by the autumnal equinox.[2] An admonition from the pulpit a few weeks in advance of the equinox would thus be timely, and the feast of the assumption on 15 August, or a Sunday very close to it, might seem a better time than the twelfth Sunday, which changes its date from year to year. Probably the Virgin's nativity on 8 September would be less satisfactory, but I include it as a marginal possibility. Either of these feasts might prompt a discussion of both chastity and tithes, and the other topics of the compilation would follow easily enough. Obedience and humility are readily associated with virginity, and the general topic of offerings to God will include tithes. For Ælfric himself, though nothing is said of the matter in the compilation, virginity itself is an offering. If the compilation showed any sign of subtlety, one could go further; for the opening discussion of the three orders of chastity refers to the parable of the sower and represents the three orders as a harvest.

The question remains whether we are to believe that Ælfric himself put these pieces together. It is probably impossible to be certain that he did not, for one cannot expect unfailingly high standards of organization from so prolific and so practical an author. But MS. V shows no concern for the authorship or the textual authority of its homilies, and this compilation is so pedestrian that I am inclined to attribute it to some less gifted preacher. Whoever it was had access, however, to a range of Ælfric's work in a textually late form. The expanded version of Assmann II represented by the first section must have been composed late in Ælfric's career, because the *Letter to Sigefyrth* as first issued names him as abbot. Very likely the unique third section, lines 1–74 below, is also late. Sections 2 and 4, on the other hand, since they represent Ælfric's early style, may be leftovers from his early career, as I have already suggested in the introductions to xix and xxvi, pp. 614 and 760.

The two sections here edited are best considered by themselves,

---

[1] *Sermo* xxxiii, *De Reddendis Decimis: Ante Natale S. Iohannis Baptistae* (24 June). See *Caesarii Arelatensis Sermones*, ed. Morin, *CCSL* ciii. 142 sqq.

[2] II Eadgar 3, Liebermann, *Gesetze*, I. 196. Repeated in VIII Æthelred 9, p. 265.

apart from their function in the compilation. The first, indeed, seems to imply a larger structure now lost. If so, it may have followed some inclusive source that I have not found. I have had to be content with identifying Biblical quotations and a few bits from Augustine. The section on tithes and first-fruits has rather close connexions with a short version of the sermon by Cæsarius that was mentioned above. The short version, printed in Migne, *PL* LXVII. 1078 sq., is quoted as a source rather than the long one, even when the two agree, because at a few points where they differ it is closer to Ælfric. For certain details of the correspondence, and also for certain parallels between Ælfric's teaching and the laws, the notes should be consulted. I suspect there are several sources I have not encountered.

THE TEXT

[A. Obedience better than Offerings; Humility in God's Service]

Ure Hælend Crist *wæs gehyrsum his Fæder,   *p. 355
swa þæt he sylfwilles hine sealde to deaðe
for ure alysednesse mid micelre lufe.
Nu sceal ælc bearn beon his fæder underþeod
to þæs Hælendes willan, ac he ne sceal na swaþeah   5
his ræde folgian gif he him misræt for Gode,
ne his wissungum, gif he hine wemð fram Criste.
    Ða þe on mægðhade and on modes clænnesse
heora lif libbað, locien hy georne
þæt hy þa ne forseon þe on sinscipe wuniað,   10
for ðan þe þæt eadmode wif, swa swa Augustinus cwæð,
bið betere ætforan Gode *þonne þæt modige mæden.   *p. 356
For ðam mot seo eadmodnes beon mid þære clænnesse
þæt se mægðhad mage þa miclan geþincðe habban
þæs hundfealdan wæstmes, swa swa se Hælend cwæð.   15
    And æfre to Godes bebodum man sceal beon gehyrsum,
[and] þam gastlican ealdre þe him for Gode wiss[a]ð.
Be ðam cwæð Samuel to Saúle þam cynge
þa þa he Godes hæse and his wissunge forseah:
Melior est enim obedientia quam uictima: 20
Betere is soðlice seo gehyrsumnes
þonne seo onsægednes, þæt syndon *offrunga;   *p. 357

Text of both passages based on V (CCCC 419), pp. 354–66. For the first,
lines 1–74, this is the only surviving copy. The second is collated with R
(CCCC 178), pp. 124–6.

17 and] *not in MS.*   wissað] wissiað *MS.*

SOURCES. 11–12 [*Augustine, Sermo CCCLIV, cap. ix*] Quid enim prodest cui
inest continentia, si dominatur superbia? . . . Non dubito præferre humilem
mulierem virgini superbæ.
    14–15 [*Cf. Matth. xix. 29*] Et omnis qui reliquerit domum, vel fratres, aut
sorores, aut patrem, aut matrem, aut uxorem, aut filios, aut agros, propter
nomen meum, centuplum accipiet, et vitam æternam possidebit.
    20–28 [*I Reg. (I Sam.) xv. 22*] Melior est enim obedientia quam victimæ; et
auscultare magis quam offerre adipem arietem; [*23*] quoniam quasi peccatum
ariolandi est, repugnare; et quasi scelus idololatriæ, nolle acquiescere.

and betere is to heorcnienne þæs Hælendes willan
þonne him to offrigenne ænige oðre lac;
for ðan þe hit soðlice is, swa swa Samuel sæde,   25
swylce hæðenscipe, and swylc swa is deofolgyld,
þæt se man wiðrige ongean Godes willan,
and nelle gehyrsumian his hæsum nateshwon.
    Ðis is nu gesæd sceortlice þus,
and we sæcgað gyt þæt we sceolan god dón   30
on urum ælmesdædum þam ælmihtigum Gode to lofe,
se ðe ure lytlan lac mid lufe underfehð,
gif we mid godum willan hy Gode betæcað,
and on his þearfum *her hy aspendað.   *p. 358
He sceawað þæs mannes heortan swiðor þonne his lac,   35
for ðam þe him nan neod nis ure lytlan sylene,
se ðe ægðer hæfð on his anwealde symble
heofonan and eorðan, and þæt þæt him on wunað;
ac he forgeaf us mannum middaneardlice þing
us sylfum to bryce, and þæt we hine oncnawan   40
mid þam eorðlicum þingum him to wyrðmynte,
and he us forgylt eft be hundfealdum
swa hwæt swa we her doð for his lufan to góde.
Gif þu oncnawst þinne Drihten on þinum ælmesdædum
be ðinre lyt*lan mæðe on wanhalum mannum,   *p. 359
hit fremað þe sylfum on þam selran life,   46
and Gode naht ne hearmað þeah ðe þu hine forgite;
God girnð þære godnysse þines gódan modes,
na þinra æhta, se ðe ah ealle þing.
Gif þu hwæt dest him to lofe on his lacum mid cyste,   50
þu geswutelast þine gódnessa swa mid þære dæde.
Gif þu þonne nan gód for Gode don nelt,
þu geswutelast þa uncyste þines yfelan modes,
and seo yfelnes þe fordeð on ecnysse wið God.
    Be ðam þe se Hælend on his halgan godspelle cwæð,   55
Nesciat sinistra tua quid faciat dextera tua,   *p. 360
Nyte þin wynstre hand hwæt þin swiðre hand dó,
us nis na to understandenne be ðam stæflicum andgite,

56 [Matth. vi. 3, as given.]
56–65 [Augustine, De Serm. Dom. in Monte, II. 8] Nihil consequentius sinistra videtur significari, quam ipsam delectationem laudis. Dextera autem significat intentionem implendi præcepta divina. Cum itaque conscientiæ facientis eleemosynam miscet se appetitio laudis humanæ, fit sinistra conscia operis dexteræ.

ac be þam gastlicum andgite, þæt we for Godes lufan
ure ælmessan don, na for idelum gylpe. 　　　　　　　　60
Seo wynstre hand getacnað þissere worulde gylp.
Nu se ðe ælmessan dælð þam Ælmihtigan to lofe,
he dæ'l'ð soðlice mid þære swiðran handa.
And se ðe for idelum gylpe his ælmessan dælð,
he dælð witodlice mid þære wynstran handa. 　　　　　65
Gif seo *swiðre hand bið seoc oððe untrum, 　　　　　*p. 361
wel he mot dælan mid þære wynstran handa,
gif he þone idelan gylp eallunga onscunað.

Ealswa be fæstenum: gif we fæstað eawunga
on gebodenum fæstenum, and þonne we us gebiddað 　　70
betwux oðrum mannum, æt mæssan and æt tidsangum,
eall hit bið diglice gif we hit doð butan gylpe,
urum Hælende to lofe, þæt we habban þa mede
on þam soðan life on ecere gesælðe.

[B. First-fruits and Tithes]

God sylf bebead on þære ealdan á, and eac manað on þære 75
niwan, þæt ælc Cristen *man sceal glædlice syllan Gode his frum- *p. 36
wæstmas, and his teoðunge ealra þæra wæstma þe him God to þam
geare forgifð, and ealre þære geoguðe þe him of his orfe acenned
bið, and ealra þara goda þe him God to þam geare foresceawað,
to þy þæt he mid gesundfulnysse and Godes bletsunge þara nigen 80

75 *In V this passage follows directly upon the preceding with no sign of a break.
In R it is added independently to Ælfric's 'Domc. XII Post Pent.' (cf. no.* xxvi
supra) with an introductory sentence: Ge hyrdon nu þæt þiss godspell hrepode
hwæthwega be þære teoðunge þe man Gode syllan sceal; be þam we willað eow
sceortlice secgan. 　　75 *marg. an early heading,* BE TEOÐUNGE *R.*
76 syllan Gode] gode syllan *R.*　　hys *R.*　　　77 hys *R.*　　hym *R.*　　　78 geogoðe *R.*　　　79 góóda *R.*　　hym *R.*　　　80 þi *R.*　　þæra *R.*　　nigon *R.*

Glosses in R, Latin: Sentence preceding line 75: Ge: vos. 　　hrepode: tetigit.
hwæthwega: par*um. In the margin as headings*: De decima; de decimis. 　　75
manað: admon*et.*　　　76–77 frum*wæstmas: primicias.*　　77 wæstma: fructu.
78 geogoðe: iuuencula*m, pr*imitias.　　acenned: natus.　　80 gesundfulnysse:
sospitate.
ME: 75 á: lawe.

69–74 [*Augustine, ibid. II. 10*] *Et cum oratis*, inquit, *non eritis sicut hypocritæ,
qui amant in synagogis et in angulis platearum stantes orare, ut videantur ab
hominibus (Matth. vi. 5). Neque hic videri ab hominibus nefas est; sed ideo hæc
agere ut videaris ab hominibus.* [*See note.*]
75–85 [*See notes.*]

dæla brucan mote; for ðam þe hit stent on halgum bocum þus
awriten: *Si quis primitias retinuérit, aut decimas de laboribus suis,*
maledictus sit in omni domo sua. Ðæt is on Englisc, swa hwa swa
his frumwæstmas *oððe teoðunge his agenre tilðe Gode ætbret, *p. 363
þæt he bið awyrged on ealre his hiwrædene. Eft is awriten, gif þu 85
æthæfst Gode þa teoðunge, þæt his rihtwisnes benæmð þe þara
nigon dæla, and læt þe habban þone teoðan dæl. Se ælmihtiga
God, þe us ealle þing forgifð, wile habban æt us þa teoþunga his
agenre gife, na for his neode, ac for ure, him to wyrðmynte and us
to þearfe, for þære gehyrsumnysse, swa swa he behet þurh his 90
witegan, þus cweðende: Betæcað *me eowre teoðunge glædlice *p. 364
butan elcunge, and afandiað min swa, cwæð God, hwæðer ic
eow forgife syððan rénscuras, and gode gewideru, and wæstmas
oð fulre genihtsumnesse. Ða twegen dælas þære teoþunge man
sceal betæcan Godes þeowum into þam mynstre þær þær he to 95
hyrð, þær þær he his Cristendom hæfð, and þone þriddan dæl
man sceal dælan þearfum, and wuduwum, and steopcildum, and
ælþeodigum mannum; for ðam þe seo teoðung is Godes dæl, and

81 hyt *R.*   83 maledictus] maledic *R.*   englis *R.*   84 hys (*twice*) *R.*
teoðunga *R.*   ætbret] ætbrytt *R.*   85 hys *R.*   gyf *R.*   86 teoðunga *R.*
his] *preceded by* is erased *V.*   -nyss *R.*   88 his] hys *R.*   89. hym *R.*
wurð- *R.*   90–91 þurh his witegan] *written a second time and crossed out, V.*
hys *R.*   91 teoþunga *R.*   92 ælcunge *R.*   æfandiað *R.*   93 gewyderu
R.   94 genyhtsumnysse *R.*   þæra teoþunga *R.*   95 innto *R.*   96
hyrð] gehyrð *R.*   þær þær] þær þæ *R.*   hys *R.*   97 wydewum *R.*   *second*
and] *om. R.*   98 ælþeodegum *R.*

Glosses in R, Latin: 81 brucan: frui.   84 ætbrytt: aufert.   85 hiwrædene: domo.   86 æthæfst: retines.   his rihtwisnyss: iusticia sua.
benæmð: detine*t*, aufert.   89 gife: gracie.   92 ælcunge: dilat*i*one,
mora.   93 wæstmas: fruct*us*.   94 oð: us*que*.   genihtsumnysse:
vbertate.   98 ælþeodegum: peregrinis.
ME: 90 þearfe: neode.   97 þearfu*m*: neodfule.

85–87 [*Cæsarius, De decimis, PL LXVII. 1079*] Hæc enim est Domini
iustissima consuetudo, ut si tu illi decimam non dederis, tu ad decimam re-
voceris.
87–90 [*Ibid., earlier*] Non eget Dominus Deus, non præmium postulat, sed
honorem; Deus enim noster, qui dignatus est totum dare, decimam a nobis
dignatur repetere, non sibi, sed nobis, sine dubio profuturam.
91–94 [*Mal. iii. 10*] Inferte omnem decimam in horreum, et sit cibus in domo
mea; et probate me super hoc, dicit Dominus: si non aperuero vobis cataractas
cæli, et effudero vobis benedictionem usque ad abundantiam. [*11*] . . . Et non
corrumpet fructum terræ vestræ. [*Quoted by Cæsarius.*]
94–98 [*See note.*]
98 sq. [*Cf. Num. xviii. 20 sqq., and Deut. xiv. 28 sq.*]

he sylf hy betæhte þam þe him synderlice þeowiað. Ælcum *men *p. 3⁕
þe ænige tilunge hæfð, oððe on cræfte, oððe on mangunge, oððe 100
on oðrum begeatum, ælcum is beboden þæt hy þa teoðunge Gode
glædlice syllan of heora begeatum oððe cræftum þe him God
forgeaf. Se ðe næfð butan an cealf on geoguðe, oððe an lamb, he
do swa micel to Godes lacum þærfore swa þær to teoþunge gebyrige, þæt is se teoða dæl þæs þe hit wyrðe is. Frumwæstmas 105
hatað sume men ælmes-æcer, se ðe us ærest geripod bið of þam
man sceal don ælmessan be his mihte, and *bletsian þone niwan *p. 3⁕
hlaf, and onbyrige ærest se Godes þeowa þæs hlafes, and ealra
þara oðra wæstma, ær þam þe se hlaford his onbyrige. Frumwæstmas synd eac swa hwæt swa us ærest on geoguðe acenned bið, and 110
þæt is eall geteald to Godes lacum, þeah ðe hit eow ungewunelic
sy. On þissum þingum and on eallum oðrum begeatum we scylon
wurðian urne Drihten þe us ða gód foresceawað, se ðe leofað and
rixað á in ealra worulda woruld á butan ende. Amen.

99 hy] hi *R.*   hym *R.*   menn *R.*   101 hy] hi *R.*   teoðunga *R.*
102 syllon *R.*   hym *R.*   103 geogoþe *R.*   104 mycel *R.*   105 hyt *R.*
wyrð *R.*   106 menn *R.*   107 hys *R.*   109 þara] *om. R.*
hys *R.*   onbyrige] onbite *R.*   109–10 Frumwæstmæs *R.*   110 iuguðe
R.   111 hyt *R.*   112 si *R.*   þisum *R.*   oðrum] urum *R.*   sceolan
R.   113 góód *R.*   114 rihsað *R.*   in ealra . . . ende] on ecnysse *R.*

Glosses in R, Latin: 99 synderlice: specialit*er.*   þeowiað: seruiu*nt.*   100
cræfte: arte.   mangunge: m*er*catu, negociatio*ne.*   103 geogoþe: etate.
104–5 gebyrige: decet.   105 Frumwæstmas: pr*i*micie.   106 geripod:
mat*ur*us.   108 onbyrige: Gustare.   þeowa: s*er*uus.   þæs: ill*i*us.   109
wæstma: fruct*us.*   onbite: *com*medat.   110 acenned: natus.

ME: 106 ælmes-æcer *repeated in margin as* ælme aker.   108 onbyrige:
eten.

99–103 [*Cæsarius, loc. cit.*] De negotio, de artificio, de qualicumque operatione
vivis, redde decimas.

NOTES

1–7. This first paragraph follows immediately after XIX. 53–60, in
which the obligation to obey one's parents is given as the reason why
children whose parents dedicate them to a life of celibacy in God's service
may not afterwards repudiate the vows made on their behalf. Obedience
to earthly parents is now qualified by the higher requirement of obedience
to God, which is elaborated in lines 16–28. Thus the transition from the
previous excerpt is easy, though I hesitate to believe that the present
passage was written expressly as a continuation.

8–15. These lines interrupt the otherwise orderly discussion of obedience, but before we conclude that the compiler thrust them in from some other context we must recognize their latent relevance, which might seem much greater if we knew what had originally preceded line 1. The comparison of the proud maiden with the humble wife is more fully developed in Assmann III, *Nativitas S. Mariae Virginis*, 383–420, where, at 396 sqq., the closely allied virtues of obedience and humility are brought together:

> Betere bið þæt wif, þe wunað on sinscipe,
> Gode a gehyrsum to his halgum bebodum
> and eadmod on heortan, . . .
> þonne þæt mæden beo, þe modig bið on heortan
> and Gode ungehyrsum.

Now the whole passage in Assmann III appears to be drawn partly from Augustine's *Sermo* CCCLIV, in which he states very explicitly why a humble wife is better than a proud virgin, and partly from his treatise, *De Bono Coniugali*, cap. xxiii, where he maintains that obedience is a greater virtue than continence, and an obedient wife is better than a disobedient virgin, though at the end of this treatise he also mentions the danger that virgins may be proud. (The partial dependence on *De Bono Coniugali* is shown most clearly by the comparison of a healthy Zacchæus and a diseased Goliath at Assmann III. 409–12, which is obviously prompted by cap. xxiii. 29: *Melius est autem habere omnia bona vel minora, quam magnum bonum cum magno malo: quia et in corporis bonis melius est habere Zacchæi staturam cum sanitate, quam Goliæ cum febre. PL* XL. 393.) Thus in Augustine there is a very clear and emphatic association between obedience and humility with respect to wives and virgins, an association that has become almost parenthetical in Assmann III and is not explicitly mentioned here. Again, in warning virgins not to despise wives he reminds them explicitly that in doing so they are showing disrespect for their parents. For example, he says in *Sermo* CCCLIV, cap. viii (*PL* XXXIX, 1567): *Usque adeo continentes homines plerumque superbiunt, ut non solum quibuscumque hominibus, sed etiam parentibus ingrati sint, et adversus parentes extollantur.* Hence, there is latently a greater connexion than appears on the surface between obedience to parents and the warning to virgins not to despise those that are married. All this might have been clear if a preceding passage omitted by the compiler had laid down the main themes.

29–54. This passage, emphasizing the all-importance of the spirit behind the giving of alms, elaborates a theme Ælfric has treated several times before. Cf. *CH* I. 580/5–584/25, including the statement, 'God sceawað þæs mannes heortan, and na his æhta' (580/16), which line 35 here almost repeats. Also, partially, *CH* II. 106/7–17, and our XVI. 163–98.

55–60. I have punctuated these six lines as a single sentence, in accordance with the grammar. The manuscript has a full stop after the quotation and starts a new sentence with a capital at 58.

69–74. If Ælfric was building on Augustine's comment as quoted, he altered the emphasis in order to justify the ecclesiastical observances of his day. Perhaps his reference to fasting as well as praying was prompted by his remembering the Pharisee of the parable who boasted in his prayer of having fasted and paid tithes (*Luc.* xviii. 12).

75–81. The basic scriptural texts behind this freely composed generalization include *Exod.* xxii. 29 and xxiii. 19 for first-fruits; *Lev.* xxvii.30–33 and *Deut.* xiv. 22–28 for tithes. Ælfric has apparently been influenced, however, by the short version of Cæsarius's sermon on tithes printed by Migne, *PL* LXVII. 1078 sq., which, unlike the long version printed by Morin as *Sermo* XXXIII, masses a number of quotations at the beginning. The first of these quotations may be partly responsible for Ælfric's adding, *and eac manað on þære niwan* (75), since it is represented as a saying of Jesus: 'Dominus dicit in Evangelio: *Omnem decimationem vestram distribuite.*' I cannot find these words anywhere in the gospels, though Jesus recommends much more drastic distributions (as at *Matth.* xix. 21; *Luc.* xii. 33), and also affirms his acceptance of the Old Law in the Sermon on the Mount (*Matth.* v. 17–19). The quotations that follow in Cæsarius are readily identified, and some of these have been put to use by Ælfric, especially the passage in *Malachi* iii. 10 sq., which he paraphrases in lines 91–94. The next quotation, *Hebrews* vii. 5, is not directly used but may have helped to assure him that tithes were approved in the New Testament. It is coupled with St. Paul's saying in *II Corinthians* ix. 7: *Hilarem enim datorem diligit Deus,* and this is backed up by a long quotation recommending cheerful giving from *Ecclesiasticus* xxxv. 11–13. These two quotations help to explain Ælfric's *glædlice* in lines 76, 91, and 102. Immediately after the quotations, Cæsarius continues: 'Quod si decimam dederis, non solum abundantiam frugum recipies, sed etiam sanitatem corporum consequeris.' Hence, probably, Ælfric's *mid gesundfulnysse,* 80.

81–85. I have not been able to trace this Latin malediction, though it might be deduced from the all-inclusive maledictions of *Deut.* xxviii. 15 sqq. It might also have been suggested by the verses in *Malachi* just preceding those that Ælfric paraphrases in lines 91–94, particularly if Ælfric had come upon the following passage in an admonition on tithes and first-fruits from the *Concilium Forojuliense* of St. Paulinus, Patriarch of Aquileia (*PL* XCIX. 302):

> Sed quia indignatio et ira Dei manet super gentem vel populum, qui hoc Domini præceptum toto corde et bona voluntate non adimplet, supra præmiserat, dicens: *Si affiget,* inquit, *homo Deum, quia vos configitis me? Et dixistis: In quo configimus te? In decimis et in primitiis vestris. In penuria vos maledicti estis, et me vos configitis gens tota* (*Mal.* iii. 8, 9).

Since Ælfric does not usually invent Biblical quotations, however, it seems probable that he found the malediction in some unidentified source.

85–87. Ælfric's reference to God's *rihtwisnes* seems to reflect Cæsarius's adjective *iustissima*. In the longer version of his admonition, Cæsarius deduces that God takes away the nine parts from those who withhold the tenth by such means as are suggested by the passage in *Malachi*: that is, by droughts, frosts, and pests. (*Caesarii Sermones*, ed. Morin, *CCSL* CIII. 144 . The idea appears also in one of the laws of Æthelstan:

> Us is to ðencanne, hu ondrislic hit on bocum gecweden is: 'Gif we þa teoðunga Gode gelæstan nellað, þæt he us benimað þara nigon dæla þonne we læst wenað, and eac we habbað þa synne to eacan.'

The Latin version of the threat is closer to Cæsarius and Ælfric:

> Si decimam dare nolumus, ut auferantur nobis novem partes, et decima sola relinquatur.
> (I Æthelstan 3, Liebermann, Gesetze, I. 146, 147.)

Liebermann calls attention to a milder statement of the idea in the report of a synod of 786:

> Plerumque contingit, ut qui decimam non tribuit, ad decimam rever-
> titur.   (Haddan and Stubbs, *Councils*, III. 456.)

In subsequent laws something like this threat is to be carried out by the joint action of certain specified reeves and the priest of the minster, who will take by force the tenth part that has been withheld, allow to the offender a ninth part of the remainder, and divide the other eight parts between the landlord and the bishop.
(II Eadgar 3, 1 and VIII Æthelred 8, Liebermann, I. 196, 265.)

91 sq. Ælfric's *glædlice butan elcunge* is not derived from Malachi. The *butan elcunge* is perhaps a reminiscence of *Exod.* xxii. 29: *Decimas tuas et primitias tuas non tardabis reddere*. On *glædlice* see the note on 75–81 above.

94–98. Payment of tithes to the minster to which a man belongs is established as law in II Eadgar 1. 1:

> And man agife ælce teoðunge to þam ealdan mynstre, þe seo hernes tohyrð.   (Liebermann, I. 196.)

The threefold division is prescribed first as a law in VIII Æthelred 6:

> And be teoðunge se cyng and his witan habbað gecoren and ge-cweden, ealswa hit riht is, þæt ðridda dæl þare teoðunge, þe to circan gebyrge, ga to ciricbote and oðer dæl þam Godes þeowum, þridda Godes þearfum and earman þeowetlingan.   (Liebermann, I. 264.)

This law may have been decreed some years after the passage in Ælfric was written.

101, 102. *begeatum*. Ordinarily the word *begeat* means either 'attainment, acquisition' (BTS, I) or 'what is acquired, possessions, property' (BTS, II), and Ælfric elsewhere uses the word in both these meanings.

Below, line 112, the second meaning is satisfactory; but here, where *begeatum* is treated as somehow parallel to *cræfte* or *cræftum* and *mangunge*, some such meaning as 'gainful activity' or 'means of acquisition' seems called for.

106. *ælmes-æcer*. Cited from this passage by Napier in *COEL*. The metaphor is not otherwise known. The injunction to give alms from first-fruits occurs in *CH* II. 102/9–11, where Ælfric is quoting *Proverbs* iii. 9:

> Arwurða ðinne Drihten mid þinum æhtum, and of ðinum frumwæst-mum syle ðearfum.

114. *in ealra worulda woruld*. The preposition *in* occurs here in MS. V instead of the normal WS *on*. It is certainly not to be attributed to Ælfric. The scribe of this part of V was probably responsible, since he copied a number of texts by other authors, in one of which *in* is regular. See the description of V in the Introduction, I. 82, where in line 22 the number 111 should be 114, and the statement in line 23 should be modified to include another instance of *in* at XXIII. 171. The latter instance also is to be attributed to the scribe, who is responsible for several other Anglian forms (see above, p. 735). There is a lonely *in* for *on* in Ælfric's homily for the second Sunday in Advent as edited by Thorpe, *CH* I. 618. Thorpe was there printing not from his standard manuscript, K, but from F (CCCC 162), which is not quite so faithful to Ælfric. In the present passage R's *on ecnysse* is probably correct, for although Ælfric uses *on ealra worulda woruld*, he seems not to use it after *a*. The combination *a on ecnysse*, on the other hand, is very common.

GLOSSARY AND WORD-INDEX
INCLUDING PROPER NAMES

APART from Latin quotations, which are indexed in the Introduction, pp. 172–7, all words that occur in the text are listed, and all but certain very common ones, chiefly conjunctions, prepositions, pronouns, and the various forms of the substantive verb *beon-wesan*, are completely indexed. Even for *beon-wesan* an effort has been made to include all the different forms, and for the common but protean *habban* and *don* to include both forms and the full range of meanings. Nouns, adjectives, and adverbs are not fully indexed if, like *God, Crist, mann, ælmihtig, halig, a, swipe*, they occur frequently and without troublesome variations of meaning. Ordinarily the frequency of such words is roughly indicated by presenting the full count of their appearances in consecutive homilies, starting with the first, before cutting off the list with 'etc.' Certain common words receive much fuller, though incomplete, treatment in order to exhibit various forms: for instance, *halig*, of which the inflected forms are standardized in the manuscripts in a pattern not clearly indicated in the grammars. Others, such as *casere* and *apostol*, are given full treatment for their possible usefulness as a guide to persons and topics. The prepositions are treated unevenly. I had intended at first to treat all of them as summarily as I have even now treated *to*, but found with several of them (notably *be, fram, mid, of, on*, and *wip*) enough perplexing or rare uses to make it seem desirable to enumerate shades of meaning, and sometimes to refer these to the definitions in Bosworth–Toller or the *Oxford English Dictionary*. In addition to proper names, unassimilated common nouns and adjectives from foreign languages are listed if they are introduced as individual words, not merely as parts of quotations.

Forms are cited only for particular reasons. Normally the occurrences of a word are listed by homily and line after the main entry in numerical sequence without regard to variations of inflexion. If there are particular forms that require notice these are included in brackets after their line-numbers. For strong verbs, however, the particular forms that occur are specified and these forms are entered separately with cross-references if they are alphabetically distant from their infinitives. Irregularities of form in the weak verbs, even if they conform to well-known phonological laws, are cited whenever it has seemed that they might cause confusion. All verb-forms, except purely adjectival participles, are entered under their infinitives, even though some of the preterite–present infinitives (those enclosed in square brackets) are not on record for Old English.

Entries are alphabetically arranged, except that all words beginning with the prefix *ge-* are listed according to their unprefixed forms. The digraph *æ* is treated like *ae*, following *ad*; *ð* is replaced by *þ*, which is treated as a separate letter between *t* and *u*.

With the exception of the substitution of *þ* for *ð*, the stems of the entries are spelled just as they appear in the text. When there is more than one spelling, cross-references are used to refer the reader to the preferred spelling. Occasionally, when a word appears with an unusual or ambiguous spelling, the usual dictionary form or a form indicating its derivation is placed immediately after it, enclosed in quotation marks and brackets. Final consonants that are doubled before inflexional endings are entered uniformly as double even though they often appear single in the text: so, for example, *mann, eall, full*. Similarly the suffix that appears variously as *-nyss, -nys, niss, -nis, -ness, -nes*, is standardized in accordance with its most frequent spelling in these manuscripts as *-nyss*. No notice is taken of the accents in the manuscripts (though the accents of the basic manuscripts have been included in the text), but the long vowels are distinguished by macrons according to the modern grammars unless a manuscript spelling is reported as such, words or phrases are quoted in illustration of a meaning, or reference is made to a dictionary entry. Vowels of foreign names are left unmarked even though their quantities can often be surmised.

An asterisk calls attention to a word or a particular meaning for which the only evidence so far adduced from Old English documents is in the homilies here edited. Among these asterisked words and meanings are some that have already been recognized in dictionaries, as the following list will show:

1. A number of words appear in BTS and Hall (reprinted in Hall–Meritt) with citations originally supplied by A. S. Napier in his article, 'Contributions to Old English Lexicography', *Transactions of the Philological Society*, 1903–6, pp. 265–352. Napier drew words from the pieces here numbered IV, VII, VIII, IX, XI, XII, XIV, XVI, XIX, XXI, XXII, and XXX as they stand in the manuscripts called P, R, T (Hatton 113, 114), U, and V (CCCC 419) in this edition. Words otherwise unrecorded are *ælmesæcer* (incorrectly assigned by Hall to an earlier publication of Napier's in *Anglia* XI), *cæpse, Candelmæssedæg, gedrinca* (redefined in BTS), *dumbnyss, fleamdom, forþmann, fuhtian, hundteontigwintre, idellic, ome* (less probably *oma*), *samweaxen, sceoccen, geseþnyss, ge-unblissian, ungedwimorlice, unhetol, unmæpfull*. Words previously recorded but with otherwise unrecorded meanings are *aberan* (sense b), *hama, hefigmod*.

Other rare but not unique words and meanings cited by Napier are *belyfan, cuplic* (sense b), *fiscnoþ, Frigeniht, inmede, sceawere* (incorrectly assigned by Hall, as above), *unhearmgeorn, wæterstream.* He included also the accusative plural *fotlæsta* in XXI for its gender. Toller included the words at the beginning of the alphabet (a–c) in his 'Additions and Corrections'; the others he was able to include in the main entries of BTS.

2. Toller called attention to four other words found only in these homilies. He cited *unfæderlice* in BT from Kemble's edition of the first part of our XXI, and in BTS from Napier's edition of Wulfstan's revision of the same passage, which hardly constitutes a second occurrence. He cited *wischere* (here *wiscere*) in BT from Skeat's edition of the *Lives of Saints,* for this portion of our XXIX is a mere repetition of the same passage. After the publication of BTS, in an article in the *Modern Language Review,* XVII. 165 sq., he listed *astæppan* from a quotation given by Napier (from our XXI as in MS. R) in illustration of another word, and *behegian* from the opening lines of our III as quoted in Wanley's *Catalogus.* These words were included in Hall's third edition and are reprinted in Hall–Meritt.

3. The following words are not listed in the dictionaries of Sweet, Bosworth–Toller, or Hall–Meritt: *æfning* (a mere variant of the familiar *æfnung*), *amberlice, berian* (except as a past participle), *ceping, deafnyss, dyrne-ceorl, eall-sweart, eorþteolung* (probably not Ælfric's word), *eunuchi* (still Latin in form), *feohte-god* (though this was printed as a compound by Unger in his edition of the first part of XXI), *fore-don* (probably better regarded as two words), *fullcyþan, hwylc-eower* (perhaps a nonce-formation), *lissian, miswyrcan, sceamigendlic* (in a passage not by Ælfric), *sundorrunung, swyre, þærfore, þryfyrclede, þurh-hlynnan* (conjectural), *undigol, untimæt, utlice, gewiss* as an adverb, *wiþerrædlice.*

4. The following words, already recorded and sometimes very familiar, have meanings in these homilies that differ from those given in the dictionaries: *abredan* (b), *ahlyttrian* and *hluttrian, and* with the supposedly Middle English meaning 'if', *asmeagan* (c), *begeat* (a), *behypan, bepæcan* (b), *biscopstol, biter, buc, burhwita, cræft* (d), *Cristendom* (d), *cyst* (b), *dream* (b), *drifan* (?), *dynt* (?), *earnung, faru* (d), *geforþian, forwyrnan* (d), *geancyme, geomrian* as a transitive verb, *gladian* (with *to*), *grama* (b), *habban* (I, k), *hæftnyd, healdan* (k), *hoc, gehradian, huxlice* (b), *leap, ofcuman, slean* (b), *smealice, stæþþig, getæcan* (b), *talian, toferian, getrywsian, tweonung, þærwiþ, þrafian, wel* (e), *weler* (b), *geworht, wyrcan* (e). Most of these unrecorded meanings are readily inferred from

meanings already recorded or, for compounds, from the separate elements. On the problematical *weler*, as it is used at XXI. 445, there is an elaborate note, pp. 720 sqq. above.

5. The combination *gehwær and þær*, listed under *gehwær*, seems to be idiomatic and is not registered in the dictionaries.

A few other words have meanings so slightly modified from those on record that it has seemed unnecessary to distinguish them with asterisks.

ABBREVIATIONS

The classes of strong verbs are indicated by arabic numbers from 1 to 7; of weak verbs, by roman numbers from I to III; preterite present and anomalous verbs by pret. pres. vb. and anom. vb. respectively. Nouns are indicated by a following m., f., or n. for masculine, feminine, or neuter; the other parts of speech by the usual abbreviations, adj., adv., pron., etc. Inflexions of nouns are indicated by case and number: ns. for nominative singular, dp. for dative plural, etc.; inflexions of adjectives by case, number, and gender: nsn. for nominative singular neuter, etc. (usually only case and number in the plural); conjugational forms of verbs, when finite, by tense, person, and number: pret. 2s. for preterite, second person singular (sometimes without person in plural, as pret. pl.), to which subj. is added if the mood is subjunctive (optative) rather than indicative. Other verb-forms are marked imp. sg. for imperative singular, dat. inf. for dative infinitive, pres. part. for present participle, pp. for past participle.

BT, *An Anglo-Saxon Dictionary*, by J. Bosworth and T. N. Toller, Oxford, 1898, including *Supplement* unless contrasted with next item.

BTS, The Bosworth–Toller *Supplement*, by T. N. Toller, Oxford, 1921, with Add., the Additions and Corrections.

Cpb, A. Campbell, *Old English Grammar*, Oxford, 1959. Corrected reprint, 1962. Cited by paragraph.

Hall, Hall–Meritt, *A Concise Anglo-Saxon Dictionary*, by John R. Clark Hall, 4th ed., with a Supplement by Herbert D. Meritt, Cambridge, 1960.

Holt. or Holthausen, *Altenglisches etymologisches Wörterbuch*, von F. Holthausen, Heidelberg, 1934. 2nd ed., 1963.

MED, *Middle English Dictionary*, ed. by H. Kurath and S. M. Kuhn, and others. Michigan, 1952– (in progress).

MLR, *Modern Language Review*.

OE, Old English.

OED, *Oxford English Dictionary*.

ON, Old Norse.

S–B, Sievers–Brunner, *Altenglische Grammatik nach der angelsächsi-*

schen Grammatik von Eduard Sievers, neubearbeitet von Karl Brunner. 3rd. ed., Tübingen, 1965.

Sweet, *The Student's Dictionary of Anglo-Saxon*, by Henry Sweet, Oxford, 1896. (This dictionary, though issued in later impressions, antedates the important contributions of Napier and Toller, so that it is seldom cited, though now and then useful for a definition.)

The formula, 'cited by Napier', refers to his 'Contributions to Old English Lexicography', *Transactions of the Philological Society*, 1903–6, pp. 265–352, described above.

For 'Napier's Wulfstan', and for certain works of Ælfric—referred to either by abbreviated title, not here italicized (CH, Grammar, LS, O. E. Hept., ONT) or by editor (Assmann, Belfour, Brotanek, Warner)—see the principal Table of Abbreviations at the beginning of Volume I.

A

ā, adv. *ever, always*. i. 385; vii. 180; x. 33, 79, 124; etc.—in phrases meaning *for ever*: ā būtan ende, i. 166; iv. 115; etc. ā tō worulde, ii. 262; v. 290; vi. 153 (spelled aa), 373; etc.; ā (...) on ēcnysse, iv. 172, 298; ix. 218; x. 210; etc.

Aaron, brother of Moses. i. 369; xx. 222, 243, 263, 271, 288, 367; xxi. 218 (gs. -es).

abād, see abīdan.

abæd, abædon, see abiddan.

abær, abæron, see aberan.

abāt, see abītan.

Abbacuc, *Habbakuk* the prophet (Dan. xiv. 32). xxi. 465, 470, 473, 476, 482.

abedene, see abiddan.

abelgan, 3, w. dat. *to make angry, offend*. pres. 3s. subj. abelge, ii. 239; pret. 1p. abulgon, xv. 142; pret. 3s. subj. abulge, xxi. 539. [Cf. gebelgan, ge-æbylgan.]

aberan, 4. (a) *to bear, sustain, hold up*. inf., xxii. 5; pret. 3s. abær, iv. 280, 290; pret. 3p. abæron, xia. 109. *(b) to do without*. inf., vii. 41. [Unique in sense (b); cited by Napier. Cf. beran.]

aberstan, 3. with ūt, *to burst out*. inf., xiv. 166. [Cf. berstan.]

abīdan, 1. (a) trans., *to await, expect*, *wait for*. with acc., xi. 257; with clause, iii. 65; with gen. of person and clause, iii. 77 (*I expected of them that* ...); with acc. or gen., iii. 79; with gen., xix. 184. (b) intrans., *to wait*. v. 10. [Forms: inf., xi. 257; pres. 2p. abīde gē, xix. 184; pret. 1s. abād, iii. 65, 77, 79; 3s., v. 10.— Cf. oferbīdan.]

abiddan, 5. (a) w. acc. or clause, *to pray for, ask for, pray* (that). i. 231, 236; viii. 82, 85, 126; xv. 178, 184; xvii. 99 (with two accs., person [usually æt with dat.] and thing; see note); xxvii. 19. (b) w. acc., *to get by asking, obtain*. viii. 73; xvi. 120; xxi. 466 (pp., *obtained, called in*); xxii. 90. [Meanings (a) and (b) not always distinct.— Forms: inf., viii. 85 (3 more); pret. 3s. abæd, i. 231 (6 more); pret. 3p. abædon, viii. 73; pp. ap. abedene, xxi. 466. Cf. biddan, gebiddan.]

Abiron, a rebel against Moses (Num. xvi. 1). xx. 220, 251.

Abisai, one of David's officers (II Reg. [= II Sam.] xxi. 17—A.V. *Abishai*). xxii. 42.

abītan, 1. (a) w. acc., *to devour*. pret. 3s. abāt, xxi. 106; pret. 3s. subj. abite, xxi. 109; pp. np. abitene, xxi. 492. (b) w. gen., *to taste, partake of*. pret. 3s. abāt, xxi. 410, 448. [Cf. bītan.]

ablendan, I. *to blind.* pret. 3s.
ablende, iv. 62; pp. **ablend**, as
adj., i. 297; iv. 6; xx. 210.

ablinnan, 3. *to cease.* pres. 3s.
ablinþ, xxix. 9.

Abraham. gs. **Abrahames**, vi. 361;
xviii. 66; xix. 110; xxi. 213; xxix.
52, 74; ds. **Abrahame**, xx. 146.

abrecan, 4. with **ūt**, *to break out,
break forth.* pres. 3p. **abrecaþ**, xiv.
130. [Cf. **tobrecan**.]

abrēdan ('-bregd-'), 3. (a) *to take
away, take up, draw up.* pres. 1s.
abrēde, iii. 68; pp. **abrōden**, xii.
132. *(b) *to change, transform.* pres.
3s. **abrŷt**, xxix. 107 (Lat. *transfigurat*); pp. **abrōden**, viii. 192;
xii. 163. [Meaning (b) not in dict.
but see BTS, 'bregdan'.—Cf. **brēdan**.]

abroþen, adj. (pp. of 'abrēoþan') *de-
generate.* iii. 66.

abūgan, 2. *to bow, incline.* inf., iv.
256. [Cf. **būgan**.]

abulg-, see **abelgan**.

abūtan, adv. *around, about.* xv. 183;
xviii. 116.

ac, conj. *but.* i. 50, etc. (15 times);
ii. 92, etc. (12 times); iii. 44, 72,
110, 119, 130; iv. 14, etc. (21 times);
etc.

acennan, I. *to give birth to, bring forth.*
pret. 3s. acende, xia. 72; every-
where else as pp. acenned, *born*:
i. 50, 270 (**acende** for np. **acennede**), etc. (10 times); ii. 96; vi.
121, 229; viii. 60; xia. 60, 202 (asm.
-ne), 213, 226; xii. 9, etc. (14
times); xix. 43; xxi. 16, 17, 189;
xxx. 78, 110. [Cf. **cennan**.]

acennednyss, f. *birth, nativity.* (a)
as an event (esp. the birth of Christ).
i. 2, 114; xi. 7, 20; xia. 76, 83, 94.
(b) as the act or process of being
born, physically or spiritually. vi.
254; xii. 71, 79, 83, 118, 119, 123,
142, 144.

acōlian, II. *to grow cold.* xviii. 333, 343.

ācsian, see **āxian**.

acucian, II. *to come to life, revive.*
vi. 141; xi. 303.

acuman, 4. (a) *to bear, endure, withstand.* inf., ix. 210. (b) *to come away,*

come forth (from). inf. **acumen** (for
-an), xxiii. 82. [Cf. **cuman**.]

acwelan, 4. *to die, perish.* pres. 3p.
acwelaþ, xii. 108.

acwellan, I, pret. **-cweald-**. *to kill,
destroy.* iii. 128; vii. 110; viii. 137;
ix. 191; xi. 380; xiv. 141; xviii.
352; xx. 113, 116, 132; xxi. 112,
237, 247, 443, 454, 566; xxii. 93;
xxvii. 35.

Adam. i. 189; iv. 194; xi. 95, 500;
xia. 48, 148; xx. 341; xxi. 29, 33,
43, 79; gs. **Adames**, i. 203, 204;
iv. 190; vii. 182; x. 198, 203; xii.
134; xvii. 86; xxi. 58; ds. **Adame**,
ii. 242.

adēafian, II. *to become deaf.* xvii. 86.
[Hitherto recorded from one gloss
(BT) and one passage in Leech-
doms (BTS).]

adela, wk. m. *mud, dirt, filthy place.*
i. 421; xvii. 261.

adeorcian, II. *to grow dark.* xviii.
260, 399.

adīlegian, adŷl-, II. *to destroy, blot
out.* vi. 281 (*purge away?*); xii. 136;
xix. 70; xxii. 93; xxv(*c*). 16
(adilig-).

ādl, f. *disease, infirmity, sickness.* xvii.
9, 15.

ādlig, adj. *sick, diseased.* np. as noun,
ii. 68.

adōn, anom. vb. *to put away, take
away.* inf., xiii. 179 (with **aweg
fram**); pret. 3s. adyde, xxiii. 130
(with **of**). [Cf. **dōn**.]

adrǣfan, I. *to drive away, drive out.*
iv. 9, etc. (14 times); vii. 184; viii.
105; ix. 180; xvii. 9, 127, 235, 256,
296; xxi. 574, 604; xxix. 32.

adrencan, I, trans. *to submerge,
drown.* xviii. 15 (pret. 3s. **adrencte**);
xxi. 37; xxiii. 168 (inf. **adrencean**,
used absolutely), 202.

adrēogan, 2. *to pass, spend* (time).
pres. 3p. **adrēogaþ**, xiv. 131; pret.
3p. **adrugon**, xi. 387.

adrīfan, 1. with **aweg**, *to drive away.*
pres. 3s. **adrīfþ**, x. 39. [Cf. **drīfan**.]

adrincan, 3, intrans. *to drown, be
drowned.* pret. 3s. **adranc**, i. 238;
3p. **adruncon**, xvii. 239; pp.
adruncen, xi. 333. [Cf. **drincan**.]

adumbian, II. *to grow dumb.* pret. 3s. adumbode, xvii. 91.

adūn(e), adv. *down, downward.* adūn, xiii. 212; adūne, xx. 48; xxi. 339.

adwǣscan, I. *to quench, blot out.* ii. 102 (pret. 3s. adwǣscte); xviii. 283; xx. 77; xxi. 564, 647; xxii. 49; xxvi. 26.

adȳdan, I. *to destroy, kill.* xxiii. 168 (used absolutely); xxvii. 45 (pret. 3s. adȳdde).

adyde, see adōn.

adȳlegian, see adīlegian.

ǣ, f. *law;* esp. the divine law, old and new, according to the two Testaments. Invariant form, ns., ds., as., i. 464; ii. 44, etc. (8 times); iii. 54, 90, 102; iv. 148, 261, 265; vii. 68; xv. 27, etc. (5 times); xviii. 66; xx. 33, etc. (5 times); xxiv. 4; xxvi. 109; xxx. 75.

ge-ǣbylgan, I. *to exasperate, offend.* pp. np. geǣbyligde, xxi. 451. [Cf. abelgan.]

ǣc, see ēac.

ǣcer, m. *field, cultivated land.* xviii. 28, 35, 141, 163, 202, 242, 312; xxi. 241. Godes ǣcer, *the church.* xviii. 145, 146. [Cf. ælmes-ǣcer.]

ǣfen, n. or m. *evening.* xxi. 314, 413.

*ǣfning, f. *evening.* ds. ǣfninge, xxiii. 90. [This spelling not recorded in dict., probably scribal; Ælfric elsewhere has the usual 'æfnung'.]

ǣfre, adv. *ever.* i. 153, 160, 165; ii. 83, 286; iii. 55, 178, 181, 184; iv. 168, 170, 202; v. 67, 187, 188; etc.

æfstan, see efstan.

æftemyst, adj. *last, hindmost.* xi. 298 (v.l. -mest).

æfter, prep. w. dat. *after.* (a) with verbs of motion, *following, behind.* vi. 71; xii. 206; xxiii. 134. (b) marking an object of desire, (*with longing*) *after, for.* xx. 84; xxi. 277. (c) temporally, *subsequent to* a specified event or period. i. 24, 204; ii. 22, 35, 117, 125; iv. 115, 244; v. 200, 235; vi. 152; vii. 129, 138, 157, 158, 190; etc.; *at the end of* a specified interval. xxiii. 205; *in succession to* someone in office. xxi. 643. (d) *following the example or*

guidance of, according to, in accordance with.* ii. 44, 61, 213; iv. 65; v. 107; ix. 57; xia. 68, 70; xix. 102, 112; xx. 245, 298.—æfter þam þe, conj. *after (the time when).* ix. 162. [Cf. hēr-, þǣr-æfter.]

æftergenga, wk. m. *successor.* v. 266; vi. 324.

æfteweard, adj. as noun, ds. in phrase on æfteweardan, *in the latter part, at the end.* xv. 141.

æftra ('æfterra'), comp. adj. *second, next.* xx. 261.

ǣghwār, adv. *everywhere.* xxii. 4.

ǣgþer, pron. adj. *each (of two), both.* as adj., xi. 314; xii. 214; xiv. 57, 58; as indecl. pron., vi. 267; xv. 137; xxx. 37.—ǣgþer ge ... ge, conj. *both ... and.* i. 3; ii. 202; iv. 285; vii. 17, 74; x. 73; xi. 11, 147; xia. 80; xiv. 156; xv. 166; xvii. 214; xix. 2, 82; xxv(a). 16.

ǣht, f. *possessions, goods, property.* i. 105; v. 201; xi. 357; xvi. 50, 55, 69, 176, 184, 248; xxiii. 41; xxx. 49.

ǣhtemann, m. *serf.* xxiii. 39. [See note.]

ǣlc, pron. adj. *each.* as adj., i. 42, 273, 328, 331, 334; iii. 109, 113; iv. 18, 98; v. 189; vi. 143; etc.—after būtan, *any.* viii. 149; ix. 134; x. 72; xi. 317; etc.—as pron., ii. 203; v. 26, 137, 143; vi. 60, 358; ix. 169; x. 89; etc.—ǣlc ... ān, *each one.* i. 382.— ǣlc þing, *everything.* xi. 564; xv. 217.—ǣlce dæge (instr.) *every day.* ii. 227; vi. 120; xxi. 359, 461; ǣlce gēare, xvi. 235; ǣlce dæg (instr. with endinglesslocative), xv. 47 (twice); xx. 14, 106.

ælfremed, adj. with fram, *estranged, separated.* xiv. 139 (nsm. or uninfl. for asm.); xxi. 164.

ǣlic, adj. *of law, prescribed by law.* ii. 66; xi. 24; xia. 98.

*ælmesǣcer, m. *ground of which the yield was given as alms, first-fruits.* xxx. 106. [Unique in this passage. Cited by Napier.]

ælmesdǣd, f. *gift of alms, charitable deed.* ii. 90 (ælmys-); xi. 211, 367; xxx. 31, 44. [Omitted from BT, hence dated too late, 1175, by

ælmesdǽd (*cont.*)
OED; BTS has several quotations, earliest from OE Bede.]

ælmesse, ælmysse, wk. f. *alms, almsgiving.* xi. 382, 431; xiii. 108; xv. 216; xvi. 158, 166, 188, 269; xvii. 200; xviii. 125; xix. 117; xxvii. 121; xxx. 60, 62, 64, 107.

ælmihtig, adj. *almighty.* as adj., i. 30, etc. (11 times); ii. 18, 92, 144, 214, 290; iii. 125; iv. 166, 168, 170, 297; v. 128; vi. 117, 209, 228, 241, 256, 279; etc.—wk. with def. art. as noun, ii. 243; viii. 113; x. 153; etc.

ælþēodig, adj. *foreign.* v. 115; xxi. 453 (nsm. wk. -þeodega); xxvii. 51; xxx. 98.

ælþēodignyss, f. *foreign parts, foreign travel,* iii. 8.

æmtig, æmptig, adj. *empty.* iv. 228, 241; x. 167; xviii. 247, 327; xxi. 254.—with **fram** or gen., *devoid of, free from.* ii. 149; iv. 244; xvi. 109 (gen.); xviii. 93, 99, 342.

ænde, see **ende.**

æne, adv. *once.* xi. 214, 215; xiv. 150; xix. 53—**syþþan . . . æne,** *when once, as soon as.* xvii. 92.

ænig, pron. adj. *any.* as pron., i. 163; vii. 157; ix. 45; xi. 551.—as adj., i. 173; v. 74; viii. 69, 98; ix. 79, 109; x. 193; xi. 278, 321, 327; xv. 19, 46, 191, 211; xvi. 104, 191, 201; xviii. 359; xix. 49; xx. 36, 55 (**æni**), 125, 274; xxiii. 60, 63, 123, 139; xxiv. 10; xxv(*a*). 8; xxvii. 12, 104 (?); xxx. 24, 100.—**ænig þing,** n. *anything.* xiv. 136; inflected and separated, xviii. 79; as adv., *in any way, at all.* vi. 208.

ænlic, adj. *wondrous, excellent, beautiful.* xi*a*. 20; xviii. 82; xx. 173.

ænlīce, adv. *excellently, marvellously.* xxi. 527.

ænlȳpig, adj. *single.* ix. 35 (np. as noun, *individuals,* a use not previously recorded;—v.l. -līp-).

ænne, see **ān.**

a-ēode, see **agān.**

ǽr, adv. *before* (in time). i. 106, 261, 442; ii. 30, 37, 89, 164, 247, 256; iii. 106, 115, 155; iv. 49, 75, 248; etc. —conj. *before, sooner than.* w. subj.,

xv. 210 (after correl. adv.); xvi. 247; xviii. 396; xix. 151; xxi. 188; w. verb to be inferred, xiii. 176.—**on ǽr,** adv. *at an earlier time, before.* i. 253; iv. 69; xi. 259; xviii. 72; xxi. 109, 130, 197.—**sīþ and ǽr,** (*later and earlier,*) *at any time, ever.* xix. 180.—comp. **ǽror,** *earlier.* iv. 266; ix. 211; x. 198; xi. 253, 469; xii. 129.—sup. **ǽrest,** *earliest, first.* i. 11; ii. 181; v. 280; vii. 51; viii. 132; ix. 131 (**ǽrist**); xi. 6, 260, 456; xi*a*. 227; etc. (24 more).

ǽr, prep. w. dat. *before* (in time). i. 447; ii. 177; v. 142, 235; ix. 90; x. 148; xi*a*. 203; xiv. 150; xviii. 66, 385; xx. 303; xxi. 73; xxv(*a*). 20.— **ǽr þam þe, ǽr þan þe,** conj. *before.* w. ind., ii. 230; vii. 63; viii. 21; x. 149; probably w. ind., vii. 191 (after correl. adv.); xviii. 349; xxi. 339; w. subj., ii. 96; v. 78; vii. 95, 205; viii. 60; ix. 165; x. 22, 182; xi. 178, 380, 532; xi*a*. 58; xii. 129; xviii. 281; xix. 23; xxx. 109; probably w. subj., xix. 222.—**ǽrþam,** conj. *before.* xxi. 60 (probably w. ind.). —**ǽrþan,** adv. *before that, up to that time.* xvi. 105; xxi. 461.

ǽr, adj. *early.* perhaps latent as asm. in **ǽrne-mergen,** q.v.—comp. **ǽrra,** *earlier, former.* ii. 237; xvii. 116; xx. 2; xxii. 2.—sup. **ǽrest,** *first.* gsm. wk. **ǽreston,** xxi. 218.

ǽren, adj. *made of brass, brazen.* xii. 228, 230, 233; xx. 325, 337, 348; xxi. 375, 562, 584; xxvi. 19.

ǽrende, n. *errand, message.* viii. 140, 146, 149.

ǽrendraca, wk. m. *messenger, reporter.* xx. 171, 195.

ǽrist, m. or n. *resurrection.* ii. 253; v. 200, 235; vi. 56, 58, 135, 136, 137, 356; vii. 112, 157, 190; x. 149; xi. 477; xii. 191; xiv. 151, 162; xvi. 171.

ǽrist, adv., variant of **ǽrest;** see **ǽr,** adv.

ǽrnemergen, m. *the twilight period before sunrise, dawn, daybreak.* **on ǽrnemergen,** xiii. 193; xxi. 225, 396, 411; xxiii. 88, 93. [On the question whether this should be treated as one word or two, see note on xiii. 193.]

ge-æswician, II. *to offend, cause to stumble, tempt to evil.* ix. 12, 172, 174. [Cf. **swician**.]

æt, prep. w. dat. *at.* (a) of position or location close to an object, in or near a place, *at.* v.110, 202; vi. 50, 73, 306; viii. 122; xi*a*. 163; xv. 19, 191; xviii. 201; etc., including xxi. 586, 590, these two with admixture of sense (c). (b) of offensive action directed *at* or *against* an object. iii. 148. (c) designating the person *at* whose hands something is sought, asked, merited, received, or taken now usually *from.* i. 231, 363; v. 119; viii. 30, 57, 74, 126; ix. 52; x. 32; xi. 367; etc.; of being baptized, *at the hands of, by.* xxiii. 37, 45. (d) *at* a particular time, in the phrases, **æt fruman** and **æt nēxtan**: see **fruma** and **nēxt**.

ǣt, m. *food.* xxi. 51, 322. [Cf. **un-tīma-ǣt**.]

æt, **ǣte**, **ǣton**, see **etan**.

ætberstan, 3, w. dat. *to escape from, break away from.* inf., xviii. 80; pres. 3s. subj. **ætberste**, xi. 167; 3p. subj. **ætbǣrston** (v.l. -ber-ston, -an), vi. 147. [Cf. **berstan**.]

ætbrēdan ('-bregd-'), 3. *to take away, carry off.* pres. 3s. **ætbrēt**, xxx. 84; 1p. **ætbrēdaþ**, i. 256; pret. 3s. **ætbrǣd**, iv. 192; pp. **ætbrōden**, iii. 36, 156, 158. [Cf. **brēdan**.]

æteowan, -īwan, -ȳwan, I. (a) trans., *to show, reveal.* iii. 67; iv. 16, 91; xi. 292, 393, 395; xviii. 24, 384; xix. 203, 207; xxi. 425; xxiii. 121. (b) intrans., *to appear.* xx. 180, 247, 268. [See next entry.]

æteowian, II. *to demonstrate.* pres. 2p. **æteowiaþ**, w. þæt-clause, xxi. 384. [A variant of 'æteowan: S–B 408, Anm. 14, 15; Cpb 753. 6 and n. 2, 764.]

ætflēon, 2. *to flee away, escape.* pres. 3p. subj. **ætflēon**, vi. 148. [Cf. **flēon**.]

ætforan, prep. w. dat. *before, in the presence of, prior to.* i. 307; iii. 99; iv. 140; vii. 93; viii. 20; xi. 49, 290;

xi*a*. 155; xiii. 220; xv. 7, 22, 58, 194; xvi. 115, 222; etc. (17 more).

ætgædere, adv. *together.* xviii. 33, 35, 90, 110, 141, 251, 367; xxiii. 75, 98, 99.

æthabban, III. *to retain, withhold.* pres. 2s. **æthæfst**, xxx. 86. [Cf. **habban**.]

ætīwan, see **æteowan**.

ge-ætrian, II. *to poison.* xx. 317.

ætsacan, 6. *to deny.* pret. 3s. subj. **ætsōce**, v. 231.

ætsomne, adv. *together, at once.* ix. 29; xxii. 4.

ætspurnan, 3. *to strike against, stumble.* pres. 3s. **ætspyrnþ**, vi. 26, 28, 344; 3p. **ætspurnaþ**, iii. 147.

ætstandan, 6. *to stand still, cease.* pret. 3s. **ætstōd**, xi*a*. 110. [Cf. **standan**.]

ætwindan, 3, w. dat. *to escape.* inf., xi. 199; xvii. 275; pres. 3s. **ætwint**, xv. 148; 3p. **ætwindaþ**, xi. 136. [Cf. **bewindan**.]

ætȳwan, see **æteowan**.

æþelboren, adj. *nobly born, distinguished.* xxiii. 55.

æþele, adj. *noble, distinguished, excellent.* xii. 26; xx. 188, 200; xxi. 543; xxvi. 7.

æþeling, m. *prince,* applied to the Son of God. i. 405; xi. 23; xi*a*. 59, 97.

æþryt, adj. *wearisome, troublesome.* vi. 205.

æx, f. *axe.* xxi. 546.

afæstnian, II. *to infix, fasten.* vii. 100; xxiii. 190 (inf., -en for -an). [Cf. **gefæstnian**.]

afandian, II. *to try, test.* w. gen. of person and clause, xxx. 92; w. uncertain case, x. 49; xx. 353. [Cf. **fandian**.]

afeallan, 7. *to fall down, fall off.* inf., xxi. 540; pret. 3p. **afēollon**, xi*a*. 28; pret. 3s. subj. **afēolle**, vi. 352. [Cf. **feallan**.]

afēdan, I. *to feed, nourish.* xi*a*. 119, 123; xiii. 50 (pres. 3s. **afēt**); xviii. 350 (pp. np. **afēdde**, *brought up*); xx. 5, 13, 370; xxi. 89. [Cf. **fēdan**.]

afeormian, II. *to cleanse, purge, purify.* xi. 187, 226, 228; xv. 155; xviii. 81.

afindan, 3. *to find, discover.* inf., x. 194; pres. 3s. **afint,** iv. 46, 240; pret. 3s. **afunde,** xiv. 182; xxiii. 125; 3p. **afundon,** i. 194; pp. **afunden,** xviii. 97 (np. -e); xxi. 155 (np. -e, *to be found, known*), 331. [Cf. **findan.**]

aflīgan, aflȳgan, I. *to expel, put to flight.* iv. 32, 133; xi. 173; xia. 107; xxi. 111, 513, 593, 613, 626, 636; xxii. 20.

afyllan¹ (EWS 'afiellan'), I. *to fell, cut down, kill.* xxii. 65.

afyllan,² I. *to fill.* i. 24; xi. 58, 103; xia. 38, 175; xiv. 28, 189; xv. 78; xvii. 287; xviii. 323, 370; xix. 174; xx. 155 (pp. ap. **afyllode,** v.l. -ede). [Cf. **ġefyllan.**]

afyrhtan, I. *to frighten, terrify.* pp. **afyrht,** xiii. 224; xiv. 33, 35, 207, 209; xvii. 210, 240; xx. 177, 254; xxiii. 96, 118.

afyrsian, II. *to remove.* vii. 48; xx. 321.

aġān, anom. vb. (a) *to go forth, go out.* pret. 3s. **a-ēode,** x. 165. (b) impers. *to befall.* pret. 3s. **a-ēode,** xix. 158; xxvii. 28. [Cf. **ġān.**]

āgan, pret. pres. vb. *to own, have, owe.* dat. inf. **āgenne,** xvi. 56; pres. 2s. **āhst,** xvi. 21, 128; 3s. **āh,** vii. 179; xvi. 40; xix. 117; xxx. 49; 3p. **āgon,** xiii. 183 (*ought*); pret. 3s. **āhte,** xxvi. 9; 3p. subj. **āhton,** xxi. 182. [Cf. **nāgan.**]

āġēaf-, see **aġifan.**

aġeldan, see **aġyldan.**

āgen, adj. (always decl. strong). *own, proper.* i. 86, 254, 257, 362; ii. 159; iii. 111, 113, 124, 126, 139; vii. 6, 129; viii. 98; ix. 35, 59, 62, 63; etc. —absolute in pl. as noun, *own people,* i. 46, 344 (twice in each).

aġēotan, 2. (a) *to pour out.* pp. **agoten,** vii. 223. (b) *to shed* (blood). inf., xxvi. 67. (c) *to found or cast* (metal). pp. **agoten,** xx. 43, 50; xxi. 375.

aġifan, agyfan, 5. *to give, give up, pay.* inf. **agifan,** xvi. 28, 145; pres. 3p. **agyfaþ,** iii. 29, 138; 1p. subj. **agyfan,** iii. 183; pret. 3s. subj. **aġēafe,** xxvii. 20; 3p. subj. **aġēafon,** iii. 91. [Cf. **ġifan.**]

agrafan, 6. *to carve, sculpture.* pp. np. **agrafene,** xv. 76.

Agustinus, see **Augustinus.**

agyfan, see **aġifan.**

aġyldan, -ġild, -ġeld-, I. *to pay back, repay.* xiii. 114, 115. [Cf. **ġyldan.**]

aġyltan, I. *to offend, sin, do wrong.* xv. 40, 200; xviii. 320; xxi. 45 (pp. **agylt**), 60 (pret. 3s. **agylte**).

āh, see **āgan.**

ahangen, see **ahōn.**

ahēawan, 7. *to cut off.* pp. np. **ahēawene,** xxi. 232. [Cf. **tohēawan.**]

ahebban, 6. *to lift up, exalt.* inf., vi. 295; xx. 223; xxvi. 65; d. inf. **ahebbenne,** xii. 40, 221; pret. 3s. **ahōf,** xii. 39, 220; 3p. **ahōfon,** vi. 91; 3s. subj. **ahōfe,** viii. 114; pp. **ahafen,** xii. 235. [Cf. **hebban.**]

***ahlyttrian, ahluttrian,** II. *to strain out* (impurities from a liquid). xiii. 164. [This meaning not in dict. Cf. **hluttrian.**]

ahnexian ('-hnesc-'), II. *to soften* (trans.). xix. 33. [This meaning in BTS though not in Hall.]

ġe-āhnian, II. *to appropriate.* xviii. 297.

ahōf, ahōf-, see **ahebban.**

ahōn, 7, trans. *to hang.* pp. **ahangen,** xia. 137. [Cf. **hangian.**]

ahrǣred, see **arǣran.**

ahreddan, I. *to set free, save, rescue.* ix. 61; xi. 267; xiv. 205 (pres. 3s. **ahret**); xvii. 251; xviii. 29, 241, 311; xx. 3, 340; xxi. 296, 319.

āhsian, see **āxian.**

āhst, see **āgan.**

āht, n. *aught, anything, something.* xvi. 16, 20, 123, 127; xviii. 29.

āht, adv. *at all, by any means.* x. 110.

āhte, āhton, see **āgan.**

āhwǣr, āhwār, adv. *anywhere.* i. 191; vii. 186; xvi. 14, 102; xvii. 167.

āhwider, āhwyder, adv. *in any direction.* iii. 108; xviii. 80.

a-īdlian, II. *to void, annul.* xix. 18.

alǣdan, I. *to lead, lead away.* xvii. 115; xviii. 21 (pp., **alǣd**), 73. [Cf. **lǣdan.**]

alǣtan, 7, with **ūt**. *to let (a ship) go out*. inf., xiv. 16, 108. [Cf. **lǣtan**.]

aldlic, see **ealdlic**.

alecgan, I. *to put down, allay, suppress*. inf. xx. 230; pres. 3s. subj. **alecġe** (v.l. **alecġe**), xviii. 173; pret. 3s. **alēde**, xx. 67. [Cf. **lecgan**.]

alēfian, II. *to injure, enfeeble*. pp. np. **alēfode**, ii. 26, 68 (as noun), 71.

alēogan, 2. *to deny, leave unfulfilled*. pp. **alogen**, xi. 150; xviii. 47. [Cf. **lēogan**.]

Alexander. *Pope Alexander I*, ca. 106–115, identified in legend with Alexander the martyr, whose day is May 3. xxiii. 2, 30, and *passim*; gs. **Alexandres**, 101; ds. **Alexandre**, 25; as. uninfl., 165; **Alexandrum**, 95, 174, 206.

Alexandria, the city in Egypt. ds., xxi. 563.—**Alexandria-burh**, f. *the city of A.* ds. -**byriġ**, xxi. 521.

alīhtan, I. (a) *to lighten, alleviate*. xxii. 3. (b) *to dismount*. xxvii. 95? (see **līhtan**).

all, alle, see **eall**.

alogen, see **alēogan**.

alȳfan, I. *to allow, grant*. xxvi. 93. [Cf. **lȳfan**.]

alȳsan, I. *to set free, deliver, redeem*. i. 409 (**alȳsende** for d. inf. **alȳsenne**?); ii. 93, 99; iii. 127, 129; iv. 193; v. 109, 112, 289; vi. 280, 342; vii. 125, 170; etc. [Cf. **tolȳsan**.]

alȳsednyss, f. *deliverance, redemption*. ii. 249; iii. 181; v. 197, 242; vi. 264; vii. 112; xi. 9, 45; xi*a*. 78, 152; xviii. 61; xxx. 3.

alȳsend, m. *redeemer*. i. 409 (ds. for d. inf. **alȳsenne**?); iv. 268 (uninfl. ds., v.l. -**e**); xi*a*. 74; xxi. 347; xxiii. 147.

Amalech, *Amalek*, the desert king and his descendants, enemies of Israel (Ex. xvii). xxii. 88, 91.

amānsumian, II. *to excommunicate*. xix. 63; xxvi. 138.

*****amberlīce**, adv. *fittingly, appropriately*. iii. 141. [Unique. See note.]

Ambrosius, *St. Ambrose*, bishop of Milan, d. 397. xxvi. 38, 48, 108.

amen, borrowed from Lat. (ultimately Hebrew) as a concluding formula. At end of each full homily, i–xxi, and of xxx. Concludes paragraphs at xviii. 216; xxi. 11. When the word occurs in the Vulgate gospels as part of a speech it is translated by **sōþ**, *verily*. See **sōþ** below.

ametan, 5. *to measure, mete out*. pres. 2p. **ametaþ**, xiii. 18, 119; pp. **ameten**, xiii. 18, 119; np.—**e**, *filled to the proper measure* (?), xvi. 23, 130.

amētan, I. *to paint, decorate*. xv. 77.

Ammonisc, adj. *Ammonite* (cf. next entry). wk. pl. as noun, xxii. 25.

Amon, *Ammon*, ancestral king of the Ammonites, here used for the tribe (II Reg. x, 'Filii Ammon'). xxii. 19.

amyrran, I. *to injure, destroy*. xvii. 291; xxiii. 178.

an, prep., see **on**.

ān, pron. adj., strong decl. (a) before a noun, emphatic, *one, a single*. i. 76, etc. (11 times); ii. 132, 135, 137, 291; iii. 146; iv. 168, 170; vi. 120, etc. (7 times); vii. 209, 226; etc.— the noun understood, xi. 500, 501.— unemphatic, *a certain, a*. i. 431; ii. 11; iii. 6 (twice); v. 12; vi. 176, 182 (twice), 229, 302, 304; etc.—(b) after a noun or pron., *alone*. gsm., gsn. **ānes**, iv. 207; xxix. 62; dsm., dp. **ānum**, i. 133, 141, 143; vi. 229, 254; xi. 132; xi*a*. 28, 202; xx. 360 (**twām mannum ānum**); xxix. 81, 82; asm. **ǣnne**, iii. 55; xx. 139; nap. **āne**, vi. 320 (**þā āne**, *those alone*); xx. 200 (**hī āne twēgen**, *they two alone*)—elliptically, **þiss ān līf**, *this one life (alone)*, xxiii. 65; similarly, xx. 88.—(c) as pron., *one* (*person, being*, or *thing*). ii. 125, 126, 134, 258; viii. 186, 194; xi. 429, 450; xi*a*. 13, 214; etc.—with noun in apposition, **mid ānum his þeiġne**, xxiii. 53.—with part. gen., vii. 5; xii. 2, 53; xvi. 21, 128; xviii. 32, 87, 91; xxvi. 85.—correl. with **ōþer**, (*the*) *one ... the other*, ii. 116; xi. 130; xviii. 32, 87, 91; xix. 193; **sē ān**, xviii. 36, 105, 142, 196; **sēo ān**,

ān (*cont.*)

xviii. 34, 111, 140; in pl., **ge þā āne ge þā ōþre**, *both one sort and the other*, xii. 115.—**on ān**, adv., *together, continuously*, xi. 44; xi*a*. 151; xx. 42. [The asm. usually **ǣnne** as at i. 251, **ānne** occasionally as at iii. 6.—Cf. **ǣne** above and **āna** next below.]

āna, indecl. adj. and adv. *alone, only* (orig. nsm. wk. of **ān**?). (a) following a sing. subject, masc., i. 182, 384; vi. 240, 262; viii. 202; xi. 88; xi*a*. a, 198, aa6; ɪɪii. ao6; xx. 37, 189, 415; xxi. 91, 98, 666; xxvi. 9, 62; xxvii. 51; xxix. 82; fem., **sēo þe āna**, xi. 11; xi*a*. 80; neut., **þæt wīf āna**, xiii. 220; **folc, þe āna**, xxi. 212.—(b) following a plural subject, **hī āna**, iii. 59; **þā gōdan āna**, xi. 353.—(c) following a plural noun in appositional phrase, nom., **nā twēgen menn āna**, xviii. 108; acc., **þā nacedan word āna**, viii. 52. [In (a) the word may be taken as adj. *alone* or adv. *only*, since uninflected **ān** is not used after a noun; in (b) adverbial *only* seems more likely since adjectival plural **āne** occurs as an alternative; in (c) the meaning is strongly adverbial.]

anam, see **animan**.

anbidian, and-, II. *to await, expect.* w. gen., ii. 27, 28, 140, 172; xi. 153; xxvii. 29. w. **oþþæt** and clause, vi. 330.

āncenned, adj. *only begotten.* i. 53, 73, 139, 386, 428; vi. 117, 233, 241; xi*a*. 16, 54. [Cf. **cennan**.]

ancersetla, wk. m. *hermit.* xxvii. 26.

ge-ancsumian, II. *to trouble, perplex.* xxi. 599. [Cf. **angsumnyss**.]

and, conj. *and.* (Almost always 7 in the manuscripts except at beginnings of sentences, where it is often spelled out and capitalized.) *An apparent instance of the conditional *and*, meaning *if*, with subjunctive, at xv. 52 (see note) and possibly 140.

anda, wk. m. *grudge, enmity, envy.* xi. 103, 110, 551; xi*a*. 38.

andbid-, see **anbid-**.

andetnyss, f. *confession.* vi. 141; xvii. 108, 179; xix. 247; xxvii. 120.

andettan, ge-andettan, I. (a) *to confess* wrong-doing (to a priest). with **ge-**, xi. 196; xiii. 230 (pres. 3s. **geandet**); xix. 131, 143, 150, 153, 154, 244 (pret. 3p. **geandettan**); without **ge-**, xi. 398; xxvii. 7, 115. (b) *to avow* a belief. without **ge-**, xvii. 134. (c) *to acknowledge, declare belief in* a person. with **ge-**, xxi. 26; without **ge-**, xvii. 173.

andfenge, adj. *acceptable.* xv. 219; xvi. 198.

andgit, -gyt, n. (a) *meaning, sense, interpretation.* i. 58; ii. 60, 61, 188; iii. 47; iv. 58, 65; v. 100; vii. 201; viii. 53, 55; ix. 73; xi. 4; xii. 224; xiii. 35, 162 (**be þam ylcan andgite**, *in the same sense*); xvi. 86, 150; xvii. 49, 279; xviii. 271, 272; xix. 21; xx. 334; xxx. 58, 59. (b) *understanding, intelligence, faculty of perception.* iii. 59; ix. 140; xii. 45; xiii. 142 (**on micclum andgyte**, *in largeness of understanding, intellectual power*); xvi. 43, 51, 62; xvii. 126; xviii. 315; xx. 274; xxix. 100.

andian, II. *to feel envy, resentment.* ii. 123.

andluman, wk. m. pl. *utensils.* xxi. 519 (v.l. **andlaman**). [See BTS, 'andlóman' and 'gelóman'; OED 'loom', sb. 1.]

andrysne, adj. *terrible.* xi. 349.

andsǣte, adj. *hateful, repugnant.* viii. 66; xvi. 201; xvii. 195 (?); xxvii. 28; xxix. 125.

andsund, see **ansund**.

andswarian, II. *to answer.* xi. 418. [See also **andwyrdan** below.]

andswaru, f. *answer.* ns., xxvii. 70; ds., **tō andsware**, iii. 135; v. 14, 34; xi*a*. 67; xvi. 179.

andweard, anweard, adj. *present, of this world, earthly.* v. 188; xiv. 62; xvi. 42 (-werd-), 95; xx. 348, 385; xxi. 377 (-wyrd-, v.l. -werd-, -weard-).

andweardnyss, f. *presence.* iii. 109; with reference to Christ's bodily presence on earth, **on hys and-**

weardnysse, *while he was present*,
ii. 158; vi. 327.

andwyrdan, I. *to answer*. inf., iii.
141; xxi. 595; pres. 3s. andwyrt,
xi. 426 (v.l. -wyrd, -weardaþ,
-swaraþ), 448; 3p. -wyrdaþ, xi.
444; pret. 3s. -wyrde, ii. 33, 47; iv.
54, 287; v. 17, 25, 30, 59, 71, 226;
vi. 11, 24, 57, 62; etc. (32 more);
-werde, xxi. 365; pret. 3p. -wyr-
don, -wyrdan, ix. 66; xviii. 37,
203; xxi. 252.

ge-andwyrdan, I. *to answer*. inf.,
ii. 275; xxi. 598.

ānēgede, -ēagede, adj. *one-eyed,
blind of one eye*. np., xi. 322. [See
BTS, 'an-eged', for evidence of
nom. sing. ending in '-e'.]

ānfeald, adj. *single, simple*. ii. 60;
xi. 244; xvii. 279; xviii. 271.

ānfealdlīce, adv. *singly, simply*. iii.
46; xviii. 315.

anginn, angynn, n. (a) *beginning*.
i. 28–155 (16 times); ix. 11, 151; x.
102; xi. 28, 411; xia. 44, 128, 200,
203; xii. 98; xiii. 234; xiv. 84, 141;
xvi. 85; xviii. 347; xix. 34; xxi. 15,
16.—(b) *undertaking*. ix. 148.—
(c) *action, behaviour*. xii. 51; xv.
168; xx. 80, 211, 246; xxvii. 90.
[Spelled with y only at i. 28; xia.
44.]

angsumnyss, f. *distress*. xxvii. 99.
[Cf. ge-ancsumian.]

animan, 4. *to take (away)*. pret. 3s.
anam, vii. 182; xia. 147. [Cf.
niman.]

anlīcnyss, f. *likeness, image, idol*. viii.
105; xia. 48; xvi. 65; xx. 351; xxi.
190, etc. (24 times); xxiv. 14; xxvi.
19.

ānmōdlīce, adv. *unanimously, with
one accord*. xxi. 282, 343, 391.

ge-ann, see ge-unnan.

Anna, the widow who prophesied of
Christ (Luke ii, 36–38). xi. 27; xia.
101.

ānnyss, f. *unity*. i. 166; ii. 127, 128;
vi. 266; viii. 194; ix. 107; xia. 219;
unanimity, agreement, xvi. 250, 255.

ānrǣde, adj. *concerted, constant, un-
wavering, resolute*. iv. 112, 283; ix.
70; xviii. 193; xx. 54; xxii. 97;

xxvi. 40.—ānrǣdra, comp., ii. 4
(np. -an). [Ælfric elsewhere uses
ns. ānrǣde with final -e, as here
at xxvi. 40. Cf. BTS, 'an-ræd'.
That he understood the first syllable
as ān 'one' is suggested especially
by iv. 282–3.]

ānrǣdlīce, adv. *resolutely, without
hesitation*. ii. 47; xxi. 365.

ānrǣdnyss, f. *constancy, singleness of
mind, resolution*. ix. 141, 153; xv.
229; xx. 353; xxvi. 135.

ansund, adj. *sound, entire, perfect;
unimpaired, undiminished; in good
health, safe and sound*. i. 426; ii.
109; vii. 144, 155; xi. 324; xvi. 162
(np. andsunde); xix. 155; xxi. 65,
486; xxiii. 19; xxix. 34.

ansȳn, n. *countenance, face*. xi. 541
(twice); xxiii. 103; xxvii. 92 (gs.
ansȳnes, supporting neuter rather
than feminine gender).

Antecrist, m. *Antichrist*. ns., xviii.
289, 296, 403; xxviii. 11; gs. -es,
xviii. 89, 356, 387; xxviii. 8.

antimber, n. *material*. i. 261; xxi.
193, 528, 532. [See BT, BTS,
'ontimber': several citations from
Ælfric, all with 'an-'.]

anþræc, adj. *horrible, dreadful*. nsn.,
xix. 174. [See BT, BTS, 'onþræc':
seven citations, all from Ælfric, all
dat. 'anþræcum' or 'andþræcum'.
This unique example of the nominative disposes of BT's alternative,
'anþræce'.]

anweald, m. *power, rule, authority,
sway*. i. 47, 350, 354, 363; iv. 189
(and-); vii. 61, 126, 170, 177, 183;
ix. 53; x. 198; xia. 136; xiii. 185;
xvii. 302, 313; xx. 225; xxi. 30;
xxii. 5; xxvi. 29, 56, 138; xxvii. 3;
xxix. 84; xxx. 37.—spelled anwald,
xxi. 369, 453; xxiii. 50.

ānwilnyss, f. *self-will, obstinacy*. ix.
57, 79, 203; xiv. 104; xxvi. 71.

Apocalypsis, The Revelation of St.
John. ds. Apocalypsi (? last three
letters lost), i. 11.

Apollo. xxi. 582, 616.

apostol, m. *apostle*. ns., (referring to
Paul) i. 107; ii. 168, 198; xi. 538;
xv. 169; xvii. 159; xviii. 301; xix.

apostol (*cont.*)
70, 74, 105; xx. 390, 422; xxix. 110;
(referring to Peter) xiv. 10, 75.—np.
apostoli, i. 429; v. 199, 260; vi.
324, 338, 349; viii. 250; xxi. 515;
apostolas, iv. 126 (9 more); ap.
apostolas, v. 266 (11 more); gp.
apostola, v. 202; dp. **apostolum**,
i. 317 (23 more); the plural forms
occur in i, ii, iv–xi, xi*a*, xiii–xvi,
xviii, and xxi.
ār, f. *mercy*. i. 231.
ār, n. *brass, copper.* xx. 328; xxi. 520.
aræfnian, II. *to endure.* vii. 25,
188.
arǣran, I. (a) *to raise* (from the
ground), *erect, build.* viii. 106; xii.
230; xiv. 95; xxi. 194, 525.—(b) *to
raise* (from death to life). vi. 109,
etc. (17 times); vii. 92, 107, 108;
viii. 75; xi. 48, 315, 336, 521; xi*a*.
114, 157, 167 (undecl. pp. **arǣred**
for np. **arǣrde**); xxiii. 23, 29, 100;
xxix. 46, 61, 63.—(c) *to raise* (the
soul from sin). vi. 193, 210, 298,
371. (d) *to set up, establish* (a
religion, a doctrine, etc.). xiv. 233
(pp. **arǣred**, MS. **ahred** alt. to
ahrǣred); xviii. 174, 285; xxi. 72;
xxvi. 27.
arās, see **arīsan**.
arc, m. *the ark* of Noah. xviii. 13, 16.
[Apparently Ælfric uses this form,
for Noah's ark exclusively. See BT,
'arc', BTS, 'earc'.]
arcam Domini Lat. phrase treated
almost as proper name and inflected
(asf.) as part of Ælfric's sentence;
translated as **Drihtnes scrīn.** xxi.
216.
ardlīce, adv. *quickly.* ii. 273; v. 69;
viii. 140; xxi. 334, 405, 482, 550;
xxiii. 57, 77, 109; xxvii. 61.
ārfæst, adj. (a) *virtuous, pious.* v. 187;
xi. 426. (b) *merciful, gracious.* xi. 159,
418.
ārfæstlīce, adv. *piously.* ii. 172.
ārfæstnyss, f. (a) *piety.* ix. 142;
(b) *mercy.* xi. 152; xix. 134, 247.
ārian, II. *to be merciful to, spare.*
xxvii. 40.
arīsan, I. *to arise.* (a) *to get to one's
feet, stand up.* ii. 38, 185, 186, 193;

vi. 68, 72; xvii. 211; xix. 190. (b)
to arise from death. ii. 110, 251,
253; vi. 55, 56, 119; vii. 55, 120,
123, 129, 143, 159; ix. 159, 162; x.
156; xi. 40, 46, 298, 332, 340; xi*a*.
143, 153; xvi. 80, 172; xviii. 419;
xxi. 502; xxiii. 31; xxix. 122, 123.—
from the death of the soul caused
by sins, vi. 139; from the mire of
sins, vi. 206. (c) *to rise up* in revolt.
xx. 217. (d) *to come into being, appear.*
xvii. 205; xviii. 256, 332, 379.
[Forms: inf., ii. 186; xi. 332; imp. sg.
arīs, ii. 38, 185; pres. 3s. **arīst**, ii.
110; vi. 55, 56, 139; xi. 340; xviii.
332, 419; 1p. **arīsaþ**, vii. 159; xvi.
172; 3p. xi. 298; xviii. 256, 379; 3s.
subj. **arīse**, vi. 206; xxix. 122, 123;
pret. 3s. **arās**, ii. 251 (20 more);
3p. **arison**, xix. 190; xx. 217;
pret. 3s. subj. **arise**, ii. 193; vi.
119.—Cf. **ģerīsan**.]
ārlēas, adj. *impious.* iv. 274; x. 191;
xi. 269, 451, 466; xviii. 289, 424 (as
noun), xix. 216; xxvii. 41.
ārlēasnyss, f. *impiety, wickedness.*
ii. 169; xxiv. 9.
arn, see **yrnan**.
Arrius. *Arius* the heretic, d. 336.
x. 159.
ārwurþe, ārwyrþe, adj. *honourable,
venerable.* iv. 289; xx. 243, 324;
xxi. 139, 190, 545, 632; xxiii. 54,
154, 199; xxix. 21.—comp., np.
ārwurþran, xxi. 651; sup., nsm.
ārwurþust, xxi. 122.
ārwurþian, ģe-ārwurþian, II. *to
honour, reverence, do honour to.*
without **ģe-**, vii. 180; xxi. 353; xxv
(a). 3, 4. with **ģe-**, xi. 544. [Cf.
wurþian.]
ārwurþlīce, adv. *reverentially,
solemnly.* xxi. 223, 254.—comp.
arwurþlīcor, xxi. 181.
ārwurþnyss, f. *reverence.* vi. 5; xxiii.
128.
ārwyrþe, see **ārwurþe.**
asǣde, see **asecgan.**
asceacan, 6. *to shake off.* imp. sg.
asceac, ii. 189.
ascirian, ascyrian, I (II). *to dissever,
separate.* inf. **ascyrian**, xvii. 196;
pp., nsm. **ascyred**, xxvi. 76; np.

ascirode (v.l. -ede), xi*a*. 37. [Cf. bescirian.]

ascūfan, 2. *to push away, remove*. inf., xiv. 12, 77; pret. 3s. ascēaf, viii. 116. [Cf. bescēofan.]

ascyrian, see ascirian.

asecgan, III. *to say out, tell, narrate*. pret. 3s. asǣde, xxi. 632. [Cf. secgan.]

asendan, I. *to send*. i. 37 (pp. asend), 299, 301; ii. 18 (pret. 3s. asende), 230 (pres. 3s. asent); iii. 126; v. 76, 241; vi. 96 (pret. 2s. asendest), 285; vii. 9, 15 (pres. 1s. asende), 33, 65, 81; etc.—spelled with æ for e in variants from MS. U at vii. 9 and frequently in viii–x; from MS. N at vii. 81; from MSS. C and (without prefix) G at xxi. 328. [Cf. sendan.]

asēon, 5. *to look upon*. inf., xx. 408. [See note on construction. Cf. gesēon.]

Asia, the continent. gs. Asian, i. 20.

asmēagan, II. (a) *to imagine, conceive, think*. i. 136 (pp. asmēad); xv. 116. (b) *to scrutinize*. viii. 247. *(c) *to design* (?). xxi. 191 (pret. 3p. asmēadan). [Meaning (c) not recorded; see note on the passage. Cf. smēagan.]

asolcen, adj. (pp. of 'aseolcan', 3) *sluggish, idle, dissolute*. xvi. 117 (wk. as noun, *sluggard*); xviii. 193.

asolcennyss, f. *sloth, laziness*. iv. 251; xix. 129.

aspendan, I. *to spend, squander, dissipate*. xvi. 6, 50, 69, 70 (pres. 3s. aspent), 89; xxx. 34.

aspringan, 3. *to spring forth, spread*. pret. 3s. asprang, xvii. 11.

assa, wk. m. *ass*. i. 271; ii. 272.

*astæppan, 6. *to imprint* (a footstep). pp. ap. astapene, xxi. 420. [Unique in this passage. Quoted by Napier, p. 344, from MS. R but defined by Toller, MLR, XVII. 165. Cf. stæppan.]

astellan, I. *to establish, ordain*. pret. 3s. astealde, xii. 72; xix. 49.

astīgan, 1. (a) *to ascend*. inf., v. 174; pres. 3s. astīhþ, xii. 35, 197; pret.

3s. astāh, i. 435; vii. 36, 64; viii. 223; xi. 47; xi*a*. 154; xii. 203, 206; xix. 124; xxi. 503; 3p. astigon, xx. 204. (b) *to descend*. imp. sg. astīh, xx. 48; pres. 3s. subj. astīge, xviii. 240, 310; pret. 3s. astāh, ii. 92; xii. 36, 198, 202, 217; xx. 52. (c) *to embark*. pret. 3s. astāh, xiv. 11, 76. [Cf. stīgan.]

astreccan, I. *to stretch out*. ii. 86, 87 (pret. 3s. astrehte), 89; xxvi. 130 (pp. astreht).

astyrian, I and II. *to arouse, stir up*. as wk. II, ii. 122; xviii. 263, 402; xx. 165; xxii. 31; as wk. I, xviii. 405 (pp. np. astyrede); xx. 89 (pp. astyred). [Cf. styrian.]

aswāpan, 7. *to sweep (off), clean*. pp. aswāpen, iv. 240.

asyndrian, II. *to separate, divide, dissever*. xi*a*. 35; xviii. 429.

atelic, adj. *dire, terrible*. xvii. 267; xix. 181, 186, 197.

atēon, 2. *to draw (out)*, with limiting adverbs (up, ūt) and/or prepositions (of, fram, tō). inf. ii. 273; xii. 128; xiii. 157; xiv. 69; xxi. 334, 490; imp. sg. atēoh, xiii. 31, 172; pres. 2s. atȳhst, xxvii. 41; pres. 1s. subj. atēo, xiii. 28, 150; 2s. subj., xiii. 33, 174. [Cf. tēon.]

atēorian, II. *to fail, come to an end*. ii. 237; xx. 100.

attor, n. *poison*. xii. 233; xvii. 94; xx. 337. [Orig. 'ātor', S–B 138. 1.]

aþenian, I. *to stretch out*. xxiii. 191.

aþēostrian, II. *to become dark, obscured, eclipsed*. xviii. 261, 400.

āþer or āþor, pron. *either*. ix. 45 (dsn. āþrum). [Ælfric has the acc. sg. at LS xxv. 68, where it is spelled 'aþor'. See BTS 'ahwæþer' and OED 'outher'.]

aþwēan, 6. *to wash, cleanse*. inf., xvii. 263; pres. 3s. aþwyhþ, xii. 93, 105; pret. 3s. aþwōh, vi. 307; pp. aþwogen, xii. 73 (np. -e), 133 (v.l. aþwægen). [Cf. þwēan.]

Augustinus, Agustinus, *St. Augustine*, bishop of Hippo. i. 55; ii. 61; xxix. 50; xxx. 11.

Aurelianus, a general under Trajan, said to have posed as emperor after

Aurelianus (*cont.*)
the latter's death. xxiii. 47, 49, 161
(ds. **Aurelian**), 184, 190, 198.

awǣgan, I. *to destroy, nullify, invalidate.* xiii. 95; xix. 54; xxi. 147;
perhaps also i. 237, but see **awecgan**. [Cf. **wǣgan.**]

awǣndan, see **awendan**.

aweccan, I. *to awaken.* vi. 31. [Cf. **awreccan.**]

awecgan, I. trans., *to move, sway.*
pret. 3s. **awǣgde**, altered to
awegde, i. 237. [Form and meaning doubtful; see **awǣgan.**]

awēdan, I. *to be mad, rage.* xvii. 243.
[Cf. **wēdan.**]

aweg, adv. *away.* iii. 108; iv. 262;
viii. 97, 105; x. 39; xiii. 180, 227;
xvii. 295; xviii. 30; xx. 254; xxi.
626; xxii. 34; xxiii. 153 (**aweig**);
xxvi. 70; xxvii. 47.

awendan, **awǣndan**, I. (a) trans. *to
turn, change, convert, pervert.* i. 187
(pp. np. **awend**[e]), 196, 404); ii.
108; viii. 15, 19, 83, 129; xi. 42;
xia. 30, 112 (pret. 3s. **awende**), 145;
xii. 152, 155 (ellipsis of object); xv.
36, 101 (pres. 3s. **awent**); xvi. 51,
62, 265; xvii. 116; xxi. 662; xxvi.
10, 102; xxix. 22, 24 (pres. 2s. subj.
awende), 27. (b) refl., *to turn oneself, change, turn.* xvii. 119; xix. 24.
(c) intr. *to change, deviate.* viii. 191;
xx. 18.—spelled with **æ** for **e** at
xvi. 265 (MS. U) and in variants
from U at viii. 15, 19, 83, 191 and
from C at xix. 24 and xxi. 662.
[Cf. **wendan.**]

awendedlic, adj. *changeable, mutable.*
xxiii. 58. [Manuscripts of other
Ælfric texts have both 'awended-'
and the more logical 'awendend-'.]

aweorpan, see **awurpan**.

awēstan, I. *to lay waste.* iii. 71; xxi. 241.

awlǣtan, I. *to disfigure, deform.* pp.
awlǣtt, xxiii. 103. [BTS cites two
other examples from Ælfric. Cf.
wlatian.]

aworpennyss, f. *confusion, destruction.* iv. 103.

awreccan, I. *to arouse, awake.* i. 227;
ii. 137; xvii. 209 (pret. 3p. **awrehton**). [Cf. **aweccan.**]

awrītan, 1. *to write* (*down*), *say in
writing, record.* inf., xvi. 24, 131;
pres. part. **awrītende**, i. 155; pres.
1p. **awrītaþ**, i. 61; pret. 3s. **awrāt**,
i. 4, 70, 107, 144; ii. 168; iii. 57;
iv. 136; vii. 4; etc. (17 more); 1p.
awriton, xxii. 79; 3p., i. 17; xvii.
310; xxi. 148; **awritan**, xxii. 1;
pret. 3s. subj. **awrite**, i. 21; pp.
awriten, ns. xi. 469 (11 more);
np. **-e**, iv. 145 (8 more); ap. **-e**,
xix. 179; asm. **-e** for **-ne**, xxi. 342.
[Cf. **wrītan.**]

awurpan, **aweorpan**, **awyrpan**, 3.
(a) where the purpose is simply to
be rid of the object, lit. or fig., *to
cast off, out, aside.* iii. 32; iv. 265;
viii. 134; xiii. 158; xvi. 235, 237;
xix. 18; xxvi. 10. (b) where the
object is purposefully directed, *to
cast out* (nets for fish). xiv. 18, 22,
110, 118 (twice), 159, 168, 170.—
with **in**, **intō**, *to cast in, into.* xi. 467.
xviii. 431; xxi. 293, 335, 337, 491;
—with **on** and acc., *to cast at.*
xiii. 216. [Forms: inf. **aweorpan**,
xiv. 18 (v.l. **awyrpan**); **awurpan**,
xiv. 110 (5 more); pres. 1s. **awurpe**,
xiv. 22, 118; 3s. **awurpþ**, xvi. 235;
3p. **awurpaþ**, xviii. 431; 2s. subj.
awurpe (v.l. **aweorpe**), xiii. 158;
3s. subj. **awyrpe**, xiii. 216; pret. 1s.
awearp, xix. 18; 3s., viii. 134
(2 more); 3p. **awurpon**, iv. 265 (2
more); pp. **aworpen**, iii. 32 (2
more). Cf. **wurpan.**]

awyrdnyss, f. *corruption.* xi. 321.
[For this meaning see BTS.]

awyrged, adj. (pp. of 'awyrgan')
accursed, damned. xi. 437 (**awyrged-**), 452, 457; xia. 30, 41; xvii.
250, 254, 288; xviii. 58; xix. 20, 22;
xxix. 22; xxx. 85.

axe, wk. f. (*burnt*) *ash.* xvii. 63; xxi.
403, 422.

āxian, **ācsian**, **āhsian**, II. *to ask.* ii.
49, 266, 271; viii. 48, 243, 249; xiii.
213; xviii. 3, etc. (8 times); xx. 221;
xxi. 249, etc. (7 times); xxiii. 54,
122, 208; xxvi. 88; xxix. 19; pres.
part., dp. **þam āxiendan**, *to those
who asked*, xxi. 252. [Cf. **ofāxian**
and next entry.]

ġe-āxian, II. *to learn, discover.* vi. 16; xx. 410.

B

Baal, pagan god identified with **Beel** and **Beelzebub**, iv. 77.

Babilon, Babilonia, *Babylon.* ds. Babilone, xxi. 354; **Babilonian,** xxi. 468 (where the city is meant, not the country). [For **Babilonia** see Napier's Wulfstan, p. 194.]

Babilonisc, adj. *Babylonian.* np. wk. as noun, xxi. 433, 451.

bæc, n. *back.* ii. 41; xiii. 57. [Cf. underbæc.]

(ġe)bæd, (ġe)bæde, (ġe)bǣdon, see **biddan, ġebiddan.**

bæftan, prep. w. dat. *after, behind.* xviii. 103; xx. 192.—adv. *after-wards*, in the combination **hēr bæftan**, see **hēr.**

bǣr, f. *bier.* vi. 190.

bær, ġebær, bǣre, bǣron, see beran, ġeberan.

bærst, see berstan.

bæþ, n. *bath.* x. 171 (ds. **bæþe**), 175 (ds. **baþe**).

ġeband, see **ġebindan.**

be, prep. w. dat. I. indicating the place where something is found or whence it is derived, *in* or *from* (*the writings of*). iv. 57. [Cf. OED, 'by', prep., 3. c.] II. *about, concerning, of, with respect to.* (a) after verbs of knowing, thinking, judging, saying, seeing, hearing, etc., i. 2, etc. (26 times); ii. 2, 31, 84, 96; iii. 30, etc. (11 times); iv. 27, etc. (5 times); etc. (about 129 more). (b) after impersonal **hū hit wæs**, *with respect to, with.* xviii. 62, 63, 64. (c) after **þrēaġan**, marking the abstract grounds of censure, *with respect to* (?). vii. 17–22, 74–85, 162, 171 (14 times). (d) marking the object of an accusation (**wrōht**), *concerning, against.* xiii. 207. [Cf. OED, 'by', prep., 26. d.] III. *by, according to, in.* (a) indicating a model, pattern, rule, or standard of action

(a command, someone's will or decision, consent, advice, an outline, an example, etc.), *according to, in accordance with, by.* i. 283; ii. 20, 67; viii. 114, 141; ix. 47 (twice); x. 209; xi. 257, 277, 278, 399; xii. 228; xiii. 86 (**be endebyrdnysse,** *in order*), 162 (**be þam ylcan andġyte,** *with the same meaning*); xiv. 220; xv. 205; xvii. 49 (like xiii. 86), 152 (**be þǣre ylcan dǣde,** *in imitation of that same deed*); xviii. 6 (**be cēpinge,** *in accordance with observation*), 122, 124, 320; xix. 48, 121; xxii. 33, 92; xxx. 58 (**be þam stæf-licum andġite**), 59 (**be þam ġāstlicum andġite**). (b) indicating the standard of judgement for a pronouncement, *by, according to, in,* xix. 88. (c) marking that which regulates or determines the specified action or condition by its quantity or quality, *in proportion to, according to.* i. 218; vi. 216; xi. 127, 184, 460, 496, 548; xia. 165; xii. 45; xiii. 122; xvi. 163, 164; xviii. 26, 50, 315; xxi. 667; xxx. 45, 107. (d) indicating the degree or extent of difference or fulfilment, *by, in.* v. 161; xi. 514, 569 (**be twȳfealdan,** *doubly*); xiii. 108; xvi. 159, 178; xxi. 59, 63 (**be fullan,** *in full*); xxx. 42. IV. indicating the medium or means, *by.* (a) a means of knowing, vi. 258. (b) a means of living, xvi. 266; xxi. 376. (c) the part by which an action is applied to the whole, xxi. 473 (**be þam feaxe**). V. *by reason of, in consequence of.* xxi. 58.—be þam þe, rarely be þan þe, conj. (a) *concerning which* or *whom.* xiv. 150; xvii. 159; xxii. 50. (b) *concerning that which.* xxx. 55. (c) *according to that which* (sometimes translatable by a mere *as*): where **þe** is subject or complement of the following verb, i. 382; iv. 162; ix. 122; xxi. 193 (**be þam þe heora mihta wǣron,** *according to what their powers were*), 205 (**be þam þe his wurþ wæs,** *according to what his value was*); where **þe** is object, vii. 161; xi. 210,

be (*cont.*)
219, 231, 515; xi*a.* 170; xv. 149;
xvi. 107, 203; xxii. 81; xxiii. 61;
xxvii. 94. (d) where þe is oblique-
ly related to the following verb,
according as, as. i. 383; x. 117; xi.
71, 230, 550; xi*a.* 187; xxi. 63, 204.
(e) where þe, like þæt, introduces
a clause explaining þam, *to the*
extent that, in so far as, in that.
x. 151, 154, 155 (note the parallel
on þam þe in 156).

bēad, see **bēodan.**

bēah, ġebēah, see **būgan.**

bealdlīce, adv. *boldly.* i. 313; xxi. 47.

bēam, m. *beam, piece of wood.* xiii.
25, etc. (8 times).

bearn, n. *child, offspring.* i. 48, 351,
353, 355, 362, 400; v. 25; xii.
138; xvi. 32, 34, 215, 217; xvii.
74 (conject.); xix. 54, 55, 56, 57,
107, 112; xxi. 336, xxx. 4.

bearnēacniġende, adj. (pres. part.)
pregnant. xix. 113.

bearntēam, m. *procreation of chil-*
dren. i. 393.

bēatan, 7. *to beat, strike.* pres. part.
bēatende, xvii. 226; pret. 3s. **bēot,**
xxvi. 131.

bebēodan, 2. *to bid, command,* w.
acc. object, a clause, or dat. inf.; or
absolute; often also w. dat. of person. pres. part., nsm. **bebēodende,**
ix. 97; pres. 1s. **bebēode,** xix.
99; 3s. **bebȳt,** iii. 102; xix. 100; xx.
404; **bebȳtt,** xvii. 302; pret. 3s.
bebēad, ii. 54, 184; viii. 70; xi. 25,
105; xi*a.* 99; xiii. 37, 203; xv. 9, 34,
67, 103, 125; xvi. 226; xvii. 39, 180,
189; xx. 369; xxx. 75; pp. **beboden,**
xv. 80, 90; xxvii. 63; xxx. 101. [Cf.
bēodan.]

bebindan, 3. *to bind fast.* pret. 3s.
subj. **bebunde,** xix. 50. [Cf.
ġebindan.]

bebod, n. *command.* as., x. 28, 206;
xi. 105; xi*a.* 50; xii. 134; xvii. 88;
xxi. 32, 35, 44, 45; xxiv. 8; ds.
bebode, x. 209; xix. 50; np.
beboda, xv. 29, 34; ap. **beboda,**
ii. 78, 146; iii. 102; xv. 67, 103, 105;
xviii. 188; xix. 7, 29; xx. 279; 281;
bebodu, xv. 9, 125; dp. **bebodum,**

ii. 142; xv. 37, 172; xvii. 117; xix.
8, 33; xx. 356; xxx. 16.

bebrūcan, 2. *to consume* (*food*). pp.
np. **bebrocene,** xxi. 397. [BTS
cites once from Greg. Dial. and
once with different meaning from
pseudo-Ælfric, LS XXIII B. Cf.
brūcan.]

bebyrgan, I. *to bury.* pret. 3s.
bebyrġde, xxiii. 200; pp. **be-**
byrġed, vi. 43, 44, 88, 168, 197;
x. 155; xi. 38; xi*a.* 140, 142; xxiii.
195; xxix. 121.

bebȳt(t), see **bebēodan.**

bēc, see **bōc.**

becēapian, II. *to sell.* v. 201.

beclȳsan, I. *to confine.* pp. np.
beclȳsede, xi. 507; irreg. **be-**
clȳsode, xxiii. 171.

becuman, 4. intr. *to come* (the prefix
implying arrival). (a) absolute, *to*
come, come to pass, come to be. vii.
217; viii. 96; ix. 14, 187; xi*a.* 40.
(b) w. dat. of person, *to come to,*
befall. ii. 129, 131; ix. 212; x. 163;
xi. 117, 122, 130, 131, 201, 275,
283; xviii. 84; xx. 106, 341; xxii.
82. (c) w. **on** and acc. (place or
person), *to come into, in unto.* i. 43,
329; iv. 33, 134, 174; w. **on** and dat.
of person, *to come upon,* xxiii. 119.
(d) w. **ofer** and acc., *to come upon,*
overwhelm. xviii. 14; **ofer** w. dat.,
to come over, extend over, xviii. 306.
(e) w. **tō** and dat. of person, *to come*
to, visit. x. 5, 25, 36, 188; xxix. 40,
71. (f) with a destination, stopping-
place or stage of a journey (lit. or
fig.), object of aspiration or desire
indicated by adv. or prep. phrase
(**tō, intō**), *to come to, arrive at,*
attain (*to*), *enter into.* with personal
subject, vii. 204, 205; xi. 141, 233,
545; xii. 121; xiii. 71, 191; xiv. 165;
xv. 5, 56; xix. 18, 252; xx. 118, 187,
201, 306; xxv(*a*). 15, 19; xxv(*c*).
17; with impers. subject, ii. 241
(**hwǣr hit eal becume,** *where it*
all gets to, i.e. *what becomes of it all*);
xiv. 113; xxi. 246; xxvi. 139 (**hym**
becōm tō hǣle, *came to salvation*
for him, i.e. *became his salvation*).—
twice under (c) above, once under

(f), the manner of coming is indicated by an adj. or pp. in agreement with the subject: i. 43 and 329 (on **middanġeard becymþ** to **menn ġeboren,** *comes into the world born as man*); xx. 118 (**becōm cucu to lande,** *came to land alive*). [Forms: inf., vii. 204; xx. 187, 201; xxiii. 119 (-en); xxix. 71; pres. 3s. **becymþ,** i. 43 (20 more); 1p. **becumaþ,** x. 5, 36; 2p., xv. 5, 56; 3p., ix. 212 (6 more); 3s. subj. **becume,** ii. 241; vii. 205; xi. 141, 275; pret. 1s. **becōm,** xix. 18; 3s., ii. 131 (11 more); 3p. **becōmon,** vii. 217; xviii. 84; xx. 306; 3s. subj. **becōme,** xxix. 40.—Cf. **cuman.**]

ġebed, n. *prayer.* viii. 66, 147, 153, 155; xi. 165; xv. 198, 215; xvii. 201; xxii. 76; xxiii. 30, 95.

Beda, *Bede.* xix. 137, 208.

bedǣlan, I. w. gen., *to deprive of.* xii. 46 [Cf. **dǣlan.**]

bedd, n. *bed.* ii. 38, 49, 50, 211; xviii. 31, 86, 90, 92, 106, 201.

bedding, f. *bedding, bed.* ii. 46.

bed(d)rida, -ryda, wk. m. and adj. *bedridden (man),* as noun, ii. 28, 139, 147, 184, 192; xiα. 104.—as adj., xvii. 13.

bedecian, bedician, II. *to beg.* xvi. 14, 102, 108, 118. [BTS cites Ælfric in Assmann, 1. 230.]

bedelfan, 3. *to dig round.* pp. **bedolfen,** iii. 72. [Cf. **delfan.**]

bedīġlian, II. *to conceal.* ix. 44.

bedydrian, II. *to delude.* xxix. 3, 6, 76.

bedyppan, I. *to dip, immerse.* xii. 127, 131.

Beel, Bel, pagan god; in iv, spelled **Beel,** then **Bel,** and identified with **Baal** and **Beelzebub;** in xxi, from Daniel, uniformly spelled **Bel,** and not otherwise identified. iv. 77, 84; xxi. 355, 360, 361, 364, etc. (17 times).

Beelzebub, a devil mentioned at Luke xi. 15 and identified with the pagan god **Baal** or **Beel.** iv. 14, 24, 74, 83, 117.

be-ēode, be-ēodan, see **beġān.**

befeallan, 7. with **on** and acc., *to fall into.* inf., xix. 132; pres. 3s. **befylþ,** ix. 175; 3p. subj. **befeallon,** xix. 91; pret. 1p. **befēollon,** xvii. 141. [Cf. **feallan.**]

befōn, 7. *to envelop, surround, invest.* pret. 3s. **befēnġ,** ix. 132; pp. **befangen,** ii. 65; vi. 101; viii. 208; xi. 9; xiα. 78; xiii. 199; xvi. 236. [Cf. **fōn.**]

beforan, prep. w. dat. *before, in front of.* xiv. 103; xxi. 393; xxvii. 110–18 (8 times); marking relative order, *in advance of,* xvi. 158.—adv. *before, earlier,* in the combination **hēr beforan,** see **hēr.**

befrīnan, 3. *to ask.* (a) followed by a question, direct or indirect, inf., v. 62; pres. 3s. **befrīnþ,** vii. 10; and with acc. of person, pret. 3s. **befrān,** ix. 64; xvi. 8, 91; xvii. 232. (b) absolute (the question implicit), dat. inf. **befrīnenne,** vii. 34. (c) w. gen., *to ask about.* pret. 3s. **befrān,** xxix. 49; 3p. **befrūnon,** xxi. 590. [For constructions with gen. see BTS, 'befrinan', III, and 'frignan', (3 b α).]

befȳlan, I. *to befoul, defile.* i. 421 (prefix obliterated), 425; v. 129; xii. 92; xvii. 264.

beġān, anom. vb. *to go about, attend to, engage in, perform, practise.* pres. 3p. **beġāþ,** xi. 281; xviii. 94, 114; xxix. 126; pret. 1s. **be-ēode,** xix. 19; 3p. **be-ēodan,** xviii. 19. [Cf. **ġān.**]

beġeat, m. *(a) gainful activity* (?). xxx. 101, 102 (see note). (b) *acquisitions, gains.* xxx. 112. [For previously recognized meanings see BTS, 'be-geat' and OED, 'beget', sb. The diphthong should be short, as in Holthausen, 'ġeat 2'. Cf. **beġytan.**]

bēġen, adj. pron. m. *both.* nom. **bēġen,** ix. 116; x. 6, 37, 42; xiii. 21, 125; xx. 267; xxvi. 104; acc. **bēġen,** ix. 125; gen. **bēġra,** vi. 234, 236, 238, 246, 257; ix. 113; x. 41; xiα. 13, 221; dat. **bām,** vi. 235, 240; vii. 211 viii. 121, 188, 189; ix. 112; x. 72, 94; xiα. 211, 213; xxi. 18. [Only the masc. represented. Cf. **bū-tū.**]

begeondan, prep. w. dat. *beyond.* xvii. 79.

beginnan, 3. *to begin.* w. tō and dat. inf. except xx. 68, w. uninfl. inf. only: pret. 3s. **bēgan(n),** v. 219; xxi. 624; 3p. **begunnon,** xx. 45, 68, 307. [Cf. **unbegunnen, onginnan.**]

begyrdan, I. *to gird.* pres. 3s. **begyrt,** xxv(*a*). 12.

begytan, begitan, 5. (a) *to get, obtain, gain possession of.* dat. inf. **begytenne,** xx. 160; pres. 3p. **begytaþ, -git-,** xviii. 165, 220; prct. 3s. **begeat,** xxii. 35. (b) *to bring about.* pret. 3p. **begēaton,** xix. 64. [Cf. **forgytan, undergytan.**]

behāt, n. *promise, vow.* xi. 150; xxii. 98.

behātan, 7. *to promise.* (a) intrans. after **swā swā,** pret. 3s. **behēt,** viii. 227; xxx. 90; and w. dat. of person, iii. 186; iv. 238; vii. 66, 135; viii. 9; x. 138; xi. 142, 526; xii. 238; xv. 38; xx. 146. (b) w. acc. object or clause and dat. of person, pres. 3s. **behǣt,** xix. 53 (v.l. **behat** alt. to pret. **behet**); 1p. **behātaþ,** xxii. 98; pret. 3s. **behēt,** v. 135; vii. 158; xii. 204; xv. 114, 118; xix. 66, 248; xx. 382; pret. 3s. subj. **behēte,** xi. 145; perf. **hæfþ behāten,** xi. 151. (c) pp. **behāten** in passive w. dat. of person, xi. 141; xv. 112 (nsn. followed by plural subject), 121; xx. 188, 376 (subject a clause). [See also next entry. Cf. **hātan.**]

behāten, adj. (pp. of **behātan**), with **eard** or **land,** (*the*) *promised* (*land*). xx. 145, 362, 372.

behēafdian, II. *to behead.* ix. 196; xxiii. 194, 198 (inf. -en).

behealdan, 7. (a) w. acc. object or indirect quest., *to behold, contemplate, have regard for, consider.* inf., xx. 345; pres. 3s. **behylt,** v. 182; 1p. **behealdaþ,** vi. 114; pret. 3s. **behēold,** xxvii. 87. (b) intrans., *to look.* pret. 3s. **behēold,** xxi. 421. (c) intrans. w. clause of purpose, *to keep watch, take care.* inf., xxi. 50. [Cf. **healdan.**]

*****behegian,** II. *to hedge in, enclose.*

iii. 5, 81. [Unique in this passage. Cited by Toller from Wanley's Catalogus, MLR, XVII. 166.]

behōfian, II. (a) with object in gen., *to have need of, require.* xi. 165, 341; xviii. 117; xix. 5; xxiv. 10. *****(b) with gen. **þæs** and a clause, *to need to, be well-advised to* (do such and such). ix. 46. [Meaning (b) not explicit in dict.]

behrēowsian, II. *to rue, repent of.* vi. 192, 225, 260, 297; x. 86. part. adj. **behrēowsiende,** *penitent.* vi. 276; as noun, xxvi. 117.

behrēowsung, f. *repentance, penitence.* xi. 197 (ds. **berēowsunge**); xix. 143, 151, 222, 244.

behȳdan, I. *to hide.* ix. 40, 44; xi. 391.

*****behȳpan,** I. *to heap up.* xiii. 57 (pres. 3s. **behȳpþ,** but with v.l. **behefþ** as if from *****behebban,** probably a mere blunder). [This meaning not in dict., but BTS has it for 'behipian', II, based on the gloss 'behypedan' cited in Napier's Anecdota Oxoniensia.]

Bel, see **Beel.**

belādung, f. *excuse.* xx. 419, 421.

belǣwan, I. *to betray.* vi. 351; vii. 3; xiv. 135.

gebelgan, 3. refl., *to become angry.* pret. 3p. **gebulgon,** iii. 171. [Cf. **abelgan.**]

belimpan, 3. with tō, *to belong to.* pres. 3s. **belimpþ,** v. 98; vi. 254, 255; 3p. **belimpaþ,** xxix. 127. [Cf. **gelimpan.**]

belūcan, 2. (a) *to lock, shut* (*fast*). iii. 99; vi. 273; xv. 187; xxi. 329, 394, 630; xxiii. 80, 115; xxvi. 96. (b) *to lock in, imprison, enclose, include.* i. 84; ii. 141, 202; xi. 482, 488; xviii. 200; xxiii. 124. (c) *to conclude.* xi. 76; xia. 192. (d) with **wiþūtan,** *to exclude, shut out* (*from*). xvi. 114; xviii. 104, 139, 199, 217. [Forms: inf., xi. 488; imp. sg. **belūc,** xxi. 394; pres. 3s. **belȳcþ,** ii. 202 (2 more); 1p. **belūcaþ,** xi. 76; xia.192; 2p., iii. 99; pret. 3s. **belēac,** ii. 141 (3 more); pp. **belocen,** i. 84 (9 more); **belocan,** xxiii. 115.—Cf. **unlūcan.**]

belȳfan, I. *to believe.* xxi. 488. [This
instance, with others in Ælfric, was
cited by Napier to show use in early
11th century. BTS has the other
examples. Cf. gelȳfan.]

bemǣnan, I. *to bewail, lament.* ii.264;
xxi. 611; xxvi. 41. [Cf. mǣnan,
to mean, considered by Holthausen
to be etymologically related; but
see OED, 'moan', sb.]

bēn, f. *prayer, request, petition.* viii.
85, 97; xiv. 199; xxi. 304.

benǣman, I. (a) w. dat. of person, *to
take* something *away from* someone. iv. 5 (**him wæs benǣmed his
gesihþ and sprǣc,** *his sight and
speech had been taken away* from
him). (b) w. gen. of thing, *to deprive*
someone *of* something. xxi. 57; xxx.
86. [The first construction is not
illustrated in BT.]

bend, m. *bond, fetter* (lit. or fig.). iv.
61 (gs. **bendas,** v.l. -es); vi. 104;
xvii. 37, 169; xxi. 329; xxiii. 52, 56;
xxvi. 72, 91, 100, 107, 115, 126.

bēo, wk. f. *bee.* np. **bēon,** i. 270.

bēodan, 2. *to command.* w. acc. object
or clause and (3 times) dat. of person, pres. 1s. **bēode,** iii. 74; pret.
3s. **bēad,** i. 23; ix. 106; xv. 83; xix.
55. [Cf. bebēodan, forbēodan,
and next entry.]

gebēodan, 2. *to ordain, prescribe.* pp.
dp. gebodenum, xxx. 70.

bēon-wesan, anom. vb. *to be.*—
forms, one example each: inf. **bēon,**
i. 136; **wesan,** i. 190 (once only);
d. inf. **bēonne,** i. 48; imp. sg. **bēo,**
ii. 195; pl. **bēoþ,** xvi. 228; pres. 1s.
eom, i. 69; **bēo,** xvi. 100; 2s. **eart,**
ii. 55; **bist,** xvi. 169; **byst,** vi. 193;
3s. **is,** i. 28 (once **his,** xxvii. 114);
ys, iii. 21; biþ, i. 393; byþ, vi. 225;
pl. **synd,** i. 50; **syndon,** i. 31
(rarely **sint,** ii. 285; **synt,** v. 78);
bēoþ, i. 95; pres. subj. sg. sī, i. 159;
sȳ, ii. 290; **bēo,** i. 163; pl. **syndon**
(not 'sȳn'), i. 162 (also viii. 197;
xi*a*. 218); **bēon,** ii. 3.—pret. 1, 3s.
wæs, xi. 414; i. 28; 2s. wǣre, xvi.
212; pl. wǣron, i. 191; pret. subj.
sg. wǣre, i. 108; pl. wǣron, xi.
307—negative forms, pres. 3s. **nis,**

i. 32; **nys,** iv. 39; pret. 1, 3s. **næs,**
vi. 38; i. 41; pl. **nǣron,** vi. 319;
pret. subj. sg. **nǣre,** i. 314; pl.
nǣron, xxv(*b*). 4.—þæt is, i. 28
(frequent); pl. þæt syndon, i. 340;
þæt synd, i. 400. [As with other
verbs, certain scribes occasionally
substitute -an for -on: e.g. syndan,
xxix. 126; wǣran, xxi. 63.—Cf.
fore-bēon.]

beorcan, 3. *to bark.* inf., xviii. 176.

beorg, m. *mountain, hill.* xxi. 138.

gebeorgan, 3. *to guard, protect.* pres.
1p. gebeorge wē, xxvii. 10.

beorht, adj. *bright.* xi. 290.—comp.,
nsf. beorhtre, xxi. 59; np. beorht-
ran, xi. 515.

beorhte, adv. *brightly.* i. 442; xi. 571;
xix. 167.

beorhthwīl, f. *moment, twinkling of
an eye.* xxi. 492 (v.l. **bearhtm-**).
[Several instances recorded in BTS
from Greg. Dial. and glosses; also
this passage cited by Napier and
printed by Warner from MS. G.]

beorhtnyss, f. *brightness.* vii. 71;
xi. 261, 324, 531; xxi. 57, 61, 63, 83.

gebēorscype, m. *feast, eating and
drinking.* xx. 45.

bēot, see **bēatan.**

gebēot, n. *boast.* only in **mid ge-
bēote,** *with boastful speech, pre-
sumptuously,* xx. 210.

bepǣcan, I. (a) *to deceive.* xxi. 78.
*(b) *to defraud.* xix. 93 (Lat.
fraudare). [BTS implies meaning
(b), citing 'bepæcst *defraudas*' from
Lib. Scint., ed. Rhodes, p. 109/8.]

bepǣcend, m. *deceiver, seducer.* as.
xvii. 92; np. bepǣcendras, xxi.
289. [See S–B 286, Anm. 3; Cpb
633.]

berǣdan, I. *to take by treachery.* iii.
43, 165; vi. 336. [See BTS, 1a,
where Ælfric is cited for this meaning. Cf. rǣdan.]

beran, 4. (a) *to bear* a burden, *carry.*
inf., ii. 194; xxi. 468; imp. sg. **ber,**
ii. 39, 185, 195; pl. beraþ, ii. 200;
pres. 3p. beraþ, xi. 290; 1p. subj.
beron, ii. 208 (MS. **bǣron**); pret.
3s. bær, ii. 41, 211; xi. 22; xi*a*. 96;
xx. 256; xxi. 466, 474; xxiii. 32;

beran (*cont.*)

3p. **bǣron**, xxi. 433; xxvii. 93; pp. **geboren**, *conveyed* (?), xxii. 36. —(b) *to bear* fruit. pres. 3s. subj. **bere**, xix. 23; pret. 3s. subj. **bǣre**, iii. 65. [Cf. **a-**, **for-**, **to-beran**, and next entry.]

geberan, 4. *to bear* a child. pret. 3s. **gebær**, i. 418; iv. 52, 271; v. 196; pp. **geboren**, *born*, i. 43, 329, 458; viii. 200; xvii. 3; xxi. 106; xxvi. 84. [See also preceding entry.]

berēafian, II. *to despoil*. xxiv. 7. [Cf. **rēafian**.]

beren, adj. *of barley*. xia. 121. [Ælfric uses the word in describing the same miracle, CH I. 182/12 and 188/4.]

berēowsung, see **behrēowsung**.

***berian**, I (and II). *to beat, knead* (?). pret. 3s. **berode** (v.l. **berede**), xxi. 446. [Hitherto recorded only as pp.; see BT and BTS, 'gebered'; OED, 'berry', v. 1; and the note on this passage.]

berie, wk. f. *berry, grape, fruit*. iii. 66; xvi. 134; xx. 155.

bern, n. *barn*. v. 261.

berstan, 3. *to burst*. pret. 3s. **bærst**, xiv. 24, 127, 152, 161. [Cf. **a-**, **æt-**, **to-berstan**.]

berȳpan, I. *to rob*. xiii. 59.

besāwan, 7. *to sow*. pres. 3s. **besǣwþ**, ix. 121. [Cf. **sāwan**.]

bescēawian, II. *to observe, look upon*. xvi. 233; xxvi. 63. [Cf. **scēawian**.]

bescēofan, 2. *to thrust, throw*. inf., xxi. 313 (MS. G, **bescufen**). [Cf. **ascūfan**.]

bescīnan, I. *to shine upon, illuminate*. pres. 3s. **bescīnþ**, i. 294; viii. 233. [Cf. **scīnan**.]

besciran, 4. *to shave, give the tonsure*. pp. **besceoren**, *tonsured*, viii. 133.

bescirian, I. *to cut off, discharge, deprive of office*. pp. **bescired**, xvi. 12, 100. [Cf. **ascirian**.]

besencan, I. *to* (*cause to*) *sink*. ii. 176; xi. 456 (pp. np. **besencte**); xiv. 138, 193; xviii. 57; xxi. 70.

besēon, 5. intrans., *to look*, with limiting adverbs or prepositions (**in**, **intō**, **on**, **tō**, **þǣrtō**). dat. inf. **be-sēonne**, xxi. 536; pres. 1p. **besēoþ**, xii. 235; pres. 3s. subj. **besēo**, xx. 327; pret. 3s. **beseah**, xvii. 32, 135, 138; xxi. 485 (**intō**, *into it*); 3p. **besāwon**, xii. 231; xx. 331; xxi. 414. [Cf. **gesēon**.]

besettan, I. *to set, impose, place*. ix. 197; xvi. 264. [Cf. **settan**.]

besittan, 5. *to be stationed around, surround*. pret. 3p. **besǣton**, i. 234; vii. 119. [Cf. **sittan**.]

beswīcan, I. *to deceive, seduce, betray*. dat. inf. **beswīcenne**, xvii. 97; xviii. 257; **-anne**, xviii. 380; pres. 3s. **beswīcþ**, xxiv. 6; 3p. **beswīcaþ**, xviii. 390; pret. 3s. **beswāc**, xi. 104; xia. 49; xvi. 231; xxi. 79; 3p. **beswicon**, iv. 112; xxi. 197; 3p. subj., ii. 124; pp. **beswicen**, ix. 176; xix. 157. [Cf. **geswīcan**.]

beswincan, 3. *to labour upon*. pret. 2p. and 3p., **beswuncon**, v. 86, 254 (two in each line). [Cf. **swincan**.]

beswingan, 3. *to flog, beat, scourge*. inf., xxiii. 167 (**-en**); pret. 3s. **beswang**, xx. 111; 3p. **beswungon**, iii. 13, 120; ix. 182.

besylian, II (orig. I). *to sully, defile*. pres. 3s. **besylaþ**, xiii. 233.

besyrwan, I. *to deceive, ensnare*. iii. 95, 172; xxi. 305. [Cf. **syrwan**.]

bet, comp. adv. *better*. vi. 299; xii. 232.—**betst**, sup. adv. *best*. ii. 196.

betǣcan, I, pret. **betǣhte**, pp. **betǣht**. (a) *to give, assign, commit, entrust*. i. 204; vi. 187, 194 (pres. 3s. **betǣcþ**); xi. 522, 524 (pres. 3s. **betǣchþ, betǣhcþ**); xiv. 204; xvi. 41; xxii. 77; xxx. 33, 91, 95, 99. (b) *to consecrate, dedicate*. xix. 57; xxi. 635. (c) *to consign, surrender* (a person). xiii. 53; xvii. 267; xxi. 429, 456 (pres. 2s. subj. **betǣce**, as imp.; MS. G has imp. **betǣh**), 458. (d) *to lease, let out*. iii. 7, 28, 89, 107, 137. (e) *to give up, resign* (an office). xvi. 9, 92 (imp. **betǣc**), and with clarifying **fram mē**, 18, 125. [Meanings (d) and (e) not explicit in BT. Cf. **tǣcan**.]

bētan, **gebētan**, I, pret. **gebētte**, pp. **gebēt(t)**. (a) *to make amends* *for*, *compensate for*. vi. 222; xi. 175, 220, 222, 395; xv. 18, 99, 124, 136, 156, 157; xviii. 123; xx. 295, 302; xxv(*a*). 20; xxvii. 8, 14, 115, 123. (b) intrans. or elliptical, *to make amends*. vi. 214. (c) *to amend, reform* (one's own sin), xiii. 169; (another's sin), xix. 212; (a person), xvi. 275. [Without prefix only at xviii. 123; xxvii. 7, 115. Cf. **dǣdbētan, ungebĕtt**.]

betellan, I. *to speak about, testify about*. xi. 403. [Cf. **tellan**.]

betera, comp. adj. *better*. xii. 89, 164 (dsm. with strong ending -**um**); xvi. 207; xxi. 629; xxvii. 109; xxx. 12, 21, 23.—**swā betere** (nsn.) **swā wyrse**, *whether it is better or worse, for better for worse*. xi. 484.—**tō beteran**, *for the better*. ix. 77; xv. 101. —**þæt betere**, n. *the better, what is better*. as., xx. 399; gs., i. 224.

beterung, f. *improvement*. viii. 13; x. 112; xii. 171; xiv. 225; xx. 397.

Bethania-wīc, Bethanian wīc, f. *the village of Bethany*. vi. 3, 44 (endingless locative, **wīc**, twice). [For gender and form, cf. 'to anre wic', CH I. 402/22 and II. 382/13. For the form see S–B 237, Anm. 2; Cpb 572.]

Bethleem, Bethlehem. uninfl. ds., xvii. 4.

Bethsaida. (a) the pool in Jerusalem called also Bethesda. ii. 11. (b) the city in Galilee condemned for unbelief (Matth. xi. 21). xvii. 58, 59.

betst, see **bet**.

betwux, betweox, betwyx, prep. w. dat. *among, between*. ii. 100; iv. 177; v. 270; vi. 111; xvi. 188, 250, 253; xxi. 124, 139, 486, 533; xxii. 45; xxx. 71. —**betwux þām**, *meanwhile*. v. 11, 70, 225. **betwyx þisum**, *meanwhile*, xvi. 15, 122.

betwȳnan, prep. w. dat. *among, between*, directly following a personal pronoun in dp., ii. 200, 204, 208; iii. 42, 164; v. 73; vi. 235; xvii. 300; xx. 85, 166.

beþencan, I. (a) *to take thought for,*

plan. pp. **beþōht**, i. 469. (b) refl., *to bethink oneself, take heed*. inf., xvi. 97. [Cf. **þencan**.]

bewerian, II (orig. I). *to guard, protect, defend*. i. 226; xiii. 93; xvi. 240; xxi. 315; xxii. 78 (pret. 3s. **bewerode**); xxix. 116 (pres. 3s. **beweraþ**). [Cf. **werian**.]

bewindan, 3. *to wind* (*about*), *wrap*. inf., xvi. 241; pres. 3s. **bewint**, xi. 339; pp. **bewunden**, vi. 100 [Cf. **ætwindan**.]

bewitan, pret. pres. vb. *to govern*. pret. 3s. **bewyste**, xxiii. 12. [Cf. **witan**.]

bewrēon, 2 (orig. 1). *to cover over, hide*. pres. 3s. subj. **bewrēo**, xxvii. 120; pret. 3s. subj. **bewruge**, xxvii. 119. [Not recorded from Ælfric in BT. Cf. **onwrēon**.]

bewyrcan, I. (a) *to build around, surround*. pret. 3s. **beworhte**, ii. 12; pp. **beworht**, ii. 63. (b) *to cover over, adorn*. pp., xxi. 530. [Cf. **wyrcan**.]

bewyste, see **bewitan**.

Bibliotheca, *the Bible*. ds. -**n**, xxii. 9.

bicgan, gebicgan, I. *to buy*. inf. **gebicgan**, xvi. 113; pres. 3p. **bicgaþ**, xix. 77; pret. 3p. **bohtan**, xviii. 18; 3p. subj. **bohton**, v. 10.

bīcnian, gebīcnian, II. (a) *to beckon*. xiv. 24, 176. (b) *to indicate*. xxviii. 5 (**gebȳcnode**).

gebīcnung, f. *indication*. xxix. 102. [See note.]

biddan, 5. (a) intrans. or absolute, *to ask, entreat, pray*. ii. 200; viii. 33, 37, 61 (first), 70, 159, 163, 179, 181 (twice); xv. 171, 180; xxiii. 104; and with **for**, *on behalf of*, xi. 172. (b) *to ask, entreat* someone (acc.)— what is sought not included, v. 19, 70, 225; viii. 38, 206, 209 (with **for**, *on behalf of*); xv. 43; xx. 207, 323; xxi. 637; xxiii. 137;—what is sought introduced by **þæt**, i. 20; v. 92; vi. 278, 370; viii. 80, 113; xvii. 27, 234, 244; xxiii. 28, 174; xxvi. 99, 106, 114; xxix. 23;—what is sought in gen., *to ask* someone *for* something, v. 14; vi. 54. (c) without mention of person entreated, what is sought in

biddan (*cont.*)

gen. or acc., *to ask for, pray for*
something;—gen., vii. 121 (gen.
explained by a clause); viii. 164; xx.
82; xxi. 227, 634; xxiii. 36—gen. or
acc., xv. 42; xix. 247;—acc., viii. 32,
158, 161;—what is sought introduced by **þæt**, *to ask that, pray
that*, v. 282; xvii. 101, 236; xviii.
246, 326; xix. 150, 221. (d) *to ask
for* something (gen. or acc.) for oneself (reflex. dat.) or another (dat.).
viii. 61 (second), 63, 69 (**yfeles
ǣnigum ōþrum menn**); xvii.
273. (e) *to obtain* something (acc.)
for oneself (dat.) by asking. xvi.
113. (f) constructions c or d with
person *from* whom something is
sought introduced by **æt**. v. 118
(c, with acc. or gen. or inf. object);
xviii. 342 (c, with a clause); xxi. 303
(c, with acc.); viii. 29, 56; ix. 52;
xxvi. 132 (these four, d).

[Forms: inf., v. 14 (11 more); pres.
part. **biddende**, xxi. 634; xxiii. 36;
imp. sg. **bide**, viii. 63; xv. 171; pl.
biddaþ, viii. 33, 163; xviii. 246,
326; pres. 1s. **bidde**, ii. 200 (4
more); 2s. **bitst**, vi. 54; viii. 69, 70;
3s. **bit(t)**, viii. 61 (twice), 209; 1p.
biddaþ, xv. 43; **bidde wē**, xxix.
23; 2p. **biddaþ**, viii. 29, 37, 56,
179; 3p. viii. 181 (twice); xx. 82;
pret. 1s. **bæd**, xxiii. 174; 3s., v. 118
(11 more); 2p. **bǣde gē**, viii. 32,
158; 3p. **bǣdon**, i. 20 (13 more);
pret. 2s. subj. **bǣde**, v. 19; 3s.
subj., xxi. 227, 303—Cf. **abiddan**,
esp. sense (b) for sense (e) above,
and next entry.]

gebiddan, 5. *to pray* (used only of
formal prayer to a deity, generally
intrans. or reflex. as in a, b, c). (a)
absolute, *to pray*. v. 43, 55, 173; and
reflex., v. 41, 163, 175, 180, 191;
xxvi. 45; xxx. 70. (b) with **for** and
acc. or dat., or **fore** and dat., *to
pray on behalf of* someone. xi. 237;
xvii. 109; xix. 226; xx. 273, 323;
xxvi. 115; xxix. 23. (c) with **tō**, *to
pray to*. v. 53, 54, 171, 172; xviii. 298;
xx. 51; xxix. 80, 84; and reflex., v. 45,
51, 169; xviii. 283; xix. 94; xxi. 196,

309, 360, 362, 364, 437, 439; xxix.
78, 81. (d) trans., *to pray to, sup-
plicate, worship*; the object God,
xxvi. 94; and with **for**, *on behalf
of*, xx. 76; xxix. 31; the object a
clause, v. 48 (first), 166 (first); and
with reflexive (dat.?) pron., v. 48
(second), 166 (second), 192. [Forms:
inf., v. 41 (6 more); dat. inf. **-enne**,
v. 43, 173; **-anne**, v. 55 (3 more);
imp. sg. **gebide**, xxi. 437; xxvi. 115;
pres. 1s. **gebidde**, xxi. 439; pl. **ge-
biddaþ**, v. 45 (15 more); pres. 2s.
subj. **gebidde**, xxix. 23; 3s. subj.,
xxix. 84; 3p. subj. **gebiddan**, xviii.
298; xix. 94; pret. 3s. **gebæd**, xx.
76 (6 more); 3p. **gebǣdon**, v. 191
(2 more); pret. 3s. subj. **gebǣde**,
xxix. 80.]

biddend, m. *petitioner*. nap. **bidden-
dras**, v. 51, 53, 169, 171. [Cf. S–B
286, Anm. 3; Cpb 633.]

gebīgan, I. trans. (a) *to bend*. xxi.
309; xxix. 78. (b) *to turn*. xxi. 186.
(c) *to humble*. vi. 278. (d) *to convert*.
v. 246; viii. 78; x. 104; xi. 64;
xia. 181; xiv. 94; xviii. 149, 178,
349; xx. 391; xxiii. 10. [Cf. **būgan**.]

bīgels, m. *arch, vault*. xxi. 533. [BTS
cites Ælfric twice.]

biggeng, **bīgeng**, **-gencg**, m. *worship, (religious) practice*. iii. 56; iv.
238; v. 121, 127; xi. 387; xxi. 7,
121, 390, 515 (ap. **-as**, glossed *cultores* by mistake), 571; xxiii. 165;
xxvi. 11, 14, 18.

biggenga, **bīgenga**, wk. m. *wor-
shipper*. iv. 83 (np. **bīgengas** for
-an); xxi. 163, 290, 379, 449, 455,
495, 509, 539, 568, 585, 598.

bigleofa, wk. m. *sustenance, food,
means of subsistence*. i. 209; v.
203; xvi. 192; xx. 130, 133; xxi.
462, 612.

bigspell, **bīspell**, n. *parable*. ii. 271;
iii. 1, 2, 40, 162, 171; viii. 34, 35,
46, 167, 168, 170, 173, 238; xiii.
19, 123, 126; xvi. 3.

gebīgþ, see **gebīgan**.

gebīhþ, see **būgan**.

bilewit, **byle(h)wit**, adj. *innocent,
simple, sincere*. nsf. **bylewit**, xvi.
249 (corrected from **bylehwite**,

v.l. **bilewite**); np. **bylehwite**, xvi.
229 (v.l. **bilewite**).

bilewitnyss, f. *innocence, simplicity.*
xvi. 226 (bilehwit-, v.l. bilewit-),
257 (bylewit-).

gebindan, 3. *to bind.* pres. 3s. subj.
gebinde, vii. 105; pret. 3s. **geband**,
xxvi. 72; pp. **gebunden**, xxvi. 75;
ap. **gebundene**, v. 275 (so MS. H;
F improperly -**enne**); xxi. 196. [Cf.
bebindan, unbindan.]

binnan, binnon, prep. w. dat. *within.*
i. 20; ii. 20, 54; v. 191; xvi. 139;
xvii. 201; xx. 8, 267; xxi. 303, 585.

gebirian, see **gebyrian**.

bisceop, biscop, m. (a) *bishop.* i. 20,
55; viii. 101, 111, 125; xiv. 203;
xviii. 123, 154; xx. 276; xxi. 575,
610, 632, 637, 640, 644; xxvi. 38,
etc. (9 times). (b) *high priest* of the
Jews: applied to Aaron as first
bishop. xx. 243, 244, 287; xxi. 218.

bisceopealdor, m. *high priest* of
the Jews. iii. 40, 162.

biscophād, m. *office of bishop, epi-
scopate.* xxi. 645.

*****biscopstōl**, m. *episcopal seat, cathe-
dral.* xxvi. 46. [This sense not in
dict.]

bismer(-), see **bysmor(-)**.

bītan, 1. *to bite.* pret. 3p. **biton**, xxi.
47. [Cf. abītan.]

*****biter**, adj. *bitter* to the taste, like
undeveloped fruit; here applied to
death in childhood, translating *acerba*
(i.e. *painfully early*). xi. 113, 115.
[This figurative use not in dict.]

biterlīce, adv. *bitterly.* xxvi. 80, 131.

biternyss, f. *bitterness, grief.* xvi. 253
(byter-).

bitst, bit(t), see **biddan**.

blǣd, m. *blast* of wind. xi. 335; xvii.
207. [The instance in xvii already
cited in BTS from CH.]

blāwan, 7. (a) intrans., *to blow.* pres.
part. **blāwendan**, asm. wk., xia.
109; pret. 3s. **blēow**, vii. 56. (b)
trans., *to blow* a trumpet. pres. 3s.
blǣwþ, xi. 297; 3p. **blāwaþ**, xviii.
418.

blētsian, geblētsian, II. *to bless.* i.
130; xi. 409; xv. 178; xxix. 9; xxx.
107.

blētsung, f. *blessing.* xi. 26; xia. 100;
xxx. 80.

blēwþ, see **blōwan**.

blind, adj. (a) *blind.* ii. 76; xxiii. 20,
24.—absolute in pl., *blind persons.*
ii. 26, 69; xia. 104; xvi. 169.—wk.
w. def. art. as noun, *the blind (man).*
i. 294, 295; vi. 84; xiii. 20 (twice),
124 (twice). (b) *dark.* xiii. 21, 125.

blindnyss, f. *blindness.* iv. 62.

bliss, f. *bliss.* v. 264; viii. 33, 44, 163,
164, 165, 236; x. 138; xi. 156, 157,
243, 244, 255, 264, 485, 505, 561;
xvi. 214; xviii. 439; xxi. 33; xxvii. 78.

blissian, II. *to rejoice.* ii. 182; v. 83,
251, 263; vi. 37, 115; x. 19, 139,
144; xi. 107, 205, 255; xix. 77
(twice); xxv(c). 14. [Cf. **ge-unblissian**.]

blīþe, adj. (a) *joyous, glad.* xxiii. 26.
(b) *gentle, kind.* xx. 409.—adv.
joyously, gladly. iv. 290; xxiii. 32.

blīþelīce, adv. *blithely, joyously.* ii.
211.

blōd, n. *blood.* i. 49, 391, 393; viii.
126; xxvi. 66.

blōwan, 7. *to blossom, flower.* pres.
3s. **blēwþ**, xix. 22.

bōc, f. *book.* (a) singular, referring to
some part of the Bible, xii. 100; xv.
154; Book of Life, xi. 468, 471;
xxv(c). 16, 17; *Vita Patrum*, xix.
62; xxvii. 17, 83; *Liber Regum*, xxi.
210; *Hist. Tripartita*, xxii. 60, 67;
unnamed books in a vision, xix. 167,
169, 172, 176, 178, 181, 184. (b)
Crīstes bōc, *(the) Gospel.* i. 26;
ii. 6; v. 233; vi. 170; viii. 24; ix.
129; xvii. 280; xviii. i. 226. (c)
plural in references, specific or
general, to books of the Bible, or
vaguely to other written authority.
ii. 66, 142, 228; iii. 31, 50, 56; iv.
166; vii. 200; viii. 170; ix. 36; x. 164;
etc. (37 more). [Forms: ns., vi. 170 (7
more); as., i. 26 (7 more); ds.
bēc, ii. 6 (11 more); nap. **bēc**, ii.
142; iii. 56 (19 more); gp. **bōca**,
xix. 102; dp. **bōcum**, ii. 66 (25
more).]

bōcere, m. *scribe.* pl., referring to the
Jewish scribes, iii. 89, 97; xiii. 197;
xv. 8, 59, 60.

bōclic, adj. *of books*, esp. *scriptural, biblical, canonical.* ii. 3; iii. 158; xix. 112.

gebodenum, see **gebēodan**.

bodian, II. *to tell, proclaim, preach.* i. 313; v. 215, 219; vii. 30, 72, 220; viii. 175; ix. 136, 156, 183, 192; xvii. 7, 247; xviii. 178, 184.

bodung, f. *preaching, message.* ix. 158, 184; xi. 62; xia. 66, 179.

bohton, -an, see **bicgan**.

geboren, see **geberan**.

bōsm, m. *bosom*, xia. 204; xiii. 14, 109.

bōt, f. *amends, atonement, penance.* xv. 52, 139; xxvi. 123, 124.

brād, adj. *broad.* viii. 120; xi. 462, 468, 506, 511; xiv. 4; xviii. 80, 432; xxi. 290, 533.

brāde, adv. *broadly, far and wide.* ii. 77.

brǣd, f. *breadth, width.* xiv. 44.

brǣþ, m. *odour.* xvii. 161, 162.

brastlian, II. *to crackle, roar* (as a fire). xi. 462.

brēdan ('bregdan'), 3. *to weave, tie.* pres. 3s. **brȳt** (v.l. **brytt, bret**), xi. 164 (fig. of the devil's knotted snares: cf. Beow. 2167). [Cf. **abrēdan, ætbrēdan, forbrēdan**.]

brēme, adj. *famous, glorious, noble.* i. 241; xxvi. 39.

brēmel, m. *bramble.* iii. 72.

brēost, n. *breast.* np. **þā brēost**, iv. 53, 272, 280; as. or ap. **brēost**, i. 7; vii. 148; xxvi. 131. [The word is often used in the plural where modern English has the singular; the evidence here is uncertain.]

brice, see **bryce**.

bringan, gebringan, 3, I, pret. **brōht-**, trans. *to bring.* (a) *to bring* something, material or immaterial, to a person (dat.), i. 466; v. 74; xi. 14; xia. 88; xix. 167, 184; the person not specified, xvi. 191, 192; the person linked with a dat. inf. of purpose (**him to sceawienne**), xx. 150, 154; to a person (dat.) and a place (**tō** w. dat.), xxi. 138; to a place (**tō** w. dat.), xxi. 592. (b) *to bring, lead, conduct, convey* a person, a soul, a body to (**tō**) a person, place, state, or condition. iv. 3, 180;

vi. 152; xiii. 198; xiv. 58 (**of**, *from* and **tō**); xvii. 13, 25, 101; xviii. 420; xix. 232 (**tō dēaþe**, *to the point of death*); xx. 174; xxi. 201, 290 (**intō**); xxiii. 108; destination omitted, xvii. 39, 180; xxi. 336; xxiii. 109. (c) w. acc. of person and **on** w. dat., *to cause to be in* a place or state, *bring to, reduce to, put in, put to.* ii. 261; vi. 286; xi. 506; xia. 106; xx. 214; **on** w. acc., *into*, xxi. 160; xxiii. 51, xxix. 52 (or dat.). (d) w. **aweg**, *to take away (with one).* xviii. 30. (e) *to bring about, induce* a state or quality (acc.) in a person (**on** w. dat.), xii. 171. [(a) without pref. exc. i. 466; (b) with pref. exc. xxiii. 108, 109; xvii. 39, 180; the rest with pref.—Cf. **forþbringan**.]

broc, n. *affliction, disease.* ii. 268.

gebrocian, II. *to hurt, afflict.* ii. 25, 280.

brōga, wk. m. *terror.* xviii. 79.

brōht(-), gebrōht(-), see **bringan**.

brosnian, II. *to decay.* ii. 107 (pres. part. **brosnigenda**, *perishable*).

brōþor, brōþur, m. *brother* (undecl. in sing. exc. dat.). voc. s., xiii. 28, 150; ns., i. 369; vi. 4. 52, 55, 76; xv. 20, 192, 203; xx. 367; xxi. 152, xxii. 43; as., vi. 16, 109; xv. 14, 130, 206; xx. 288; gs., vi. 48; xiii. 25, 33, 147; xviii. 66; ds. **brēþer**, xiii. 27, 149; xv. 23, 143, 195. [Plural only as in next entry.]

gebrōþra, coll. pl., m. (orig. n.). *brothers.* (a) sons of the same parent(s). viii. 119; xiv. 210; xxi. 109. (b) Christians or men generally or saints, as sons of God, brothers of Christ. i. 387, 388; xi. 257, 429; xvi. 253; xxi. 6; xxvii. 7 (the last two the preacher's congregation). (c) monks. xix. 212, 220, 221. [**gebrōþra** 11 times, nva. and gp.; **gebrōþrum**, dp., xvi. 253; xix. 220.—variants without prefix at xi. 257 and xxi. 109.]

brūcan, 2, w. gen. *to enjoy, partake of.* inf., i. 218; v. 125; xiii. 62; xxx. 81; pres. part. **brūcende**, viii. 161; pres. 3p. **brūcaþ**, xix. 78; 3p. subj. **brūcon**, xix. 79. [Cf. **bebrūcan**.]

bryce, brice, m. (a) *use, enjoyment.*
xxi. 92; xxx. 40. (b) *useful thing,*
fruit. i. 209 (ap. bricas, *good things*).

brȳdguma, wk. m. *bridegroom.* xvi.
111.

brym, m. *sea.* xvii. 220 (sea of Galilee). [Distinct from 'brim', n. See
BTS, 'brymm', and Holthausen.
BTS cites this passage from CH as
printed by Thorpe.]

bryne, m. *burning, flame, heat.* xi.
479; xviii. 77; xx. 270; xxi. 87.

brȳt, see brēdan.

*būc, m. *trunk* of the body. xxi. 559.
[This meaning not recorded for OE.
See note.]

būgan, gebūgan, 2. (a) of bodily
action, *to stoop.* pret. 3s. bēah, xiii.
212. fig., with tō, *to bow, incline,
submit to* a god, a faith, a rite, etc.
inf. gebūgan, viii. 68; pres. 3s.
gebīhþ, iv. 68 (v.ll. gebȳgþ,
gebȳhþ); 3p. gebūgaþ, xiv. 128,
132; pres. 3s. subj. būge, xxi. 343;
3p. subj. gebūgon, xxiii. 141; pret.
3s. bēah, xxi. 282; xxii. 51; gebēah,
xxvi. 5; 3p. bugon, v. 117; xxi. 294;
gebugon, vi. 222; xix. 242; xxi.
516, 571; xxvi. 8; pret. 3s. subj.
gebuge, xix. 221; 3p. subj. gebugon, vii. 133; pp. gebogen,
xxiii. 164. [Cf. a-, for-būgan and
gebīgan.]

gebulgon, see gebelgan.

gebund-, see gebindan.

būr, n. (*private*) *chamber.* xxvi. 80 (the
emperor's private apartment).

burh, f. *walled town, fortress, city.* gs.
byrig, v. [88]; ds. byrig, ii. 10;
v. 3, 9, 11, 65, 113, 215, 218; vi. 182;
xvii. 3, 4, 57, 58, 240; xviii. 21; xxi.
354, 432, 474; xxiii. 12; xxvii. 23,
25, 49, 85; as. burh, xiii. 192; xxi.
471, 558; byri (!), xxiii. 12; nap.
burga, xvii. 51; xx. 110, 161; xxi.
243, 245; dp. burgum, iii. 82 (*fort-
resses, fortified towns*); xvii. 53; xxi.
255, 563; burhgum, xxi. 272. [Em-
phasis on fortification only at iii. 82;
xx. 161; and perhaps xx. 110.
Cf. Alexandria-, Capharnon-,
Mediolana-burh, and hēafodburh; also inburh.]

burhscīr, f. *city, township.* xvii. 24 (?),
80 (see Tȳn Burhscīra); xviii. 21,
23, 70.

burhware, mp. *citizens.* v. 65, 219.

burhwaru, f. *citizens, townsfolk* (collectively). v. 69, 88, 92, 246, 279;
xviii. 68; xxii. 36.

*burhwita, wk. m. (*city councillor*),
senator (of Rome). xxiii. 10, 11.
[This specific application not in dict.]

būtan, būton, prep. w. dat. (a)
without. i. 32, 153, 166, 417, 426;
ii. 128; iv. 115; v. 104, 154, 203,
237 (twice), 238; vi. 151; vii. 145,
146, 148, 152; etc. (for particular
combinations see ā and ǣlc).
(b) after eall, *except.* xviii. 15; xx.
360; and with obj. clause instead of
dat., xxiv. 13.—after a specific number, *not counting.* xia. 120; xx. 12.—
conj. (a) subordinating, w. subj.,
unless. i. 325, 396; ii. 207; iii. 49;
v. 100; vi. 141; x. 53, 109; xii. 6,
9, 58, 68; etc. (b) co-ordinating,
after negatives, *but, except.* i. 191,
335; xi. 517; xii. 36, 198; xiii. 85;
xviii. 79, 434; xix. 112; xx. 37, 88,
119, 189, 199; xxi. 95, 304, 665,
675.—with ellipsis, ne . . . būtan,
only. vii. 79, 209; xxx. 103. [Some
scribes have a tendency to spell the
prep. butan and the conj. buton,
but there is no general rule.]

butere, wk. f. *butter.* xvi. 135.

būtū, būta, adj. pron. common gender (orig. n.). *both.* acc. n. būtū,
xiv. 188; būta, xiv. 27; nom. acc. f.
būta, xiv. 175; xxi. 116. [Cf. bēgen,
twēgen.]

gebȳcnian, see bīcnian.

bydel, m. *herald, proclaimer, minister.*
i. 309; v. 221; vii. 72; ix. 191; xx.
276, 281; xxiii. 73; xxviii. 5.

gebyldan, I. *to embolden.* pret. 3s.
gebylde, xi. 62; xia. 179; pp. np.
gebylde, vii. 214; ix. 152.

bylewit, bylehwit, see bilewit.

bȳme, wk. f. *trumpet.* xi. 297 (as.
bȳman, v.l. bȳme); xviii. 418; xx.
32.

gebyrd, f. or n. (*birth*), *parentage.*
xiv. 213 (dp. -um).

gebyrdtīd, f. *time of birth.* xxvi. 83.

byrgels, m. *tomb.* xxix. 119.

byrgen, f. *tomb, place of burial.* ii. 249; vi. 73, 85, 133, 134; vii. 119, 120; xv. 76 (np. **byrgenu,** v.l. **birgena**); xvii. 223, 226; xviii. 420. [The n not doubled before a vowel except at vi. 73, 85.]

gebyrian, gebirian, II (orig. I). (a) with **on** or **tō,** *to be (meant) for* a particular time, *pertain to, belong to* a particular ceremony. ii. title (and in titles of iii, vi in MS. H); x. 106; xvii. 19. (b) with **tō,** *to be fitting for* the payment of an obligation xxx 104–5. (c) impers. w. dat. of person and clause as subject, *to be incumbent on, behove.* xii. 19, 141.

byrnan, 3, intrans. *to burn.* pres. part. **byrnende,** variously inflected, v. 275; vii. 71; xi. 473; xx. 315; xxi. 294; pres. 3s. **byrnþ,** xvi. 139; 3p. **byrnaþ,** xi. 473, 475; xviii. 432. [Cf. **forbyrnan** and **forbærnan.**]

byrst, f. *bristle.* xxi. 446.

byrþen, f. *burden.* ns. xix. 177 (**swylce mannes byrþen,** *as big as a man could carry*); as. **byrþene,** xiii. 57 (generic sing. for pl.); ap. **byrþena,** ii. 200, 208; xxii. 3.

bȳsen, f. *example, pattern, model.* ix. 31, 74, 78, 80, 81, 177; xiii. 133, 136, 189; xv. 111; xvi. 156; xvii. 190; xix. 136; xx. 398; xxix. 10— ap. **bȳsne** (as. in form), xxii. 11 and perhaps xxvii. 15. [Cf. **forebȳsen.**]

bysgu, f. *occupation, labour.* ap. **bysga,** xxii. 86.

bysmor, n. or m. *disgrace, scandal, shame.* xvi. 108; xxi. 163, 386.

bysmorfull, bismer-, adj. *disgraceful, ignominious.* vi. 168; xxi. 495.

gebysmorian, II. *to mock, put to shame.* pret. 2s., **gebysmrodest,** xxiii. 164.

bysmorlic, adj. *shameful, ignominious.* x. 164; xx. 110, 288; xxi. 568.

bysmorlīce, adv. *shamefully, ignominiously.* xviii. 69.

bȳsnian, gebȳsnian, II. *to teach by example, set an example.* xiii. 140; xviii. 160.

gebȳsnung, f. *example, pattern.* ix. 175; xvi. 275; xxi. 645.

byternyss, see **biternyss.**

bytlian, II. *to build.* xi. 281; xviii. 19 (pret. 3p., **byttlodan**).

C

***cæpse,** wk. f. *box.* xxi. 260. [Unique in this passage. Cited by Napier.]

cāflīce, adv. *boldly.* xxvii. 95.

campian, II. *to do battle.* xi. 149.

***Candelmæssedæg,** m. *Candlemas day.* xi. 21; xia. 95. [Here only. Cited by Napier.]

cann, see **cunnan.**

Capharnon-burh, f. *the city of Capernaum* in Galilee. xvii. 281 (ds. -byrig).

cāsere, m. *Cæsar, emperor.* viii. 133, 135, 143, 150; xxi. 543, 561; xxii. 51, etc. (8 times); xxiii. 13, 42; xxvi. 8 (kaserum), 17, etc. (15 times); xxviii. 9, 10.

ceald, adj. *cold.* xvi. 195.

cealf, m. *calf.* xxi. 264, 266, 277; xxx. 103.

cearf, see **ceorfan.**

gecēas, see **gecēosan.**

cēast, f. *strife, contention.* viii. 123 (np. **cēastu**); xx. 266; xxvi. 30.

ceastergewaran, wk. mp. *citizens.* v. 222; xvii. 242; xxvi. 35.

cempa, wk. m. *warrior.* xxvi. 44.

cēne, adj. *bold, brave.* xxii. 13, 68.

cēnlīce, adv. *boldly.* ix. 136.

cennan, I. *to conceive.* xia. 64. [Cf. **acennan, ge-edcennan, āncenned.**]

cenning, f. *conceiving, bearing* (of children). i. 394.

Cēnred, Kēnred, king of the Mercians, 704–9 (Bede's Coenred). xix. 139, 149.

ceorfan, 3. *to cut.* pret. 3s. **cearf,** xxi. 550. [Cf. **forceorfan.**]

ceorian, II. *to murmur, complain.* ii. 212; vi. 369; xx. 68, 79, 83, 186.

ceorlfolc, n. *common people.* xx. 12. [Hitherto recorded only from Ælfric's Grammar, defining *vulgus,* Zupitza, p. 28/21. See note.]

ceorlian, II. *to take a husband.* xi.

282, 319; xviii. 12; xix. 74, 83, 87, 92.

ceorung, f. *murmuring.* xx. 72, 105, 166, 218, 264, 307, 314, 393.

ġecēosan, 2. *to choose.* pres. 3s. ġecȳst, xx. 228; 3s. subj. ġecēose, xix. 49; pret. 3s. ġecēas, xiv. 185, 228; xx. 244; 3p. ġecuron, xvii. 260; xix. 67; pret. 3s. subj. ġecure, xx. 242.—pp. ġecoren, *chosen.* np. -e, xviii. 96, 132; xxi. 189; referring to God's elect, wk. as adj., xiv. 167; xviii. 258, 267, 294, 368, 381, 415, 421; after his, Godes, or dem., as noun, i. 356; v. 132; x. 203; xi. 344, 517; xiv. 57, 128; xviii. 252, 375; xxv(c). 13. [Cf. wiþercoren.]

cēpan, I. (a) *to desire, seek after* (w. gen.). xx. 387. (b) *to be mindful of, intent on* (w. gen.). iv. 207; xiv. 97; xix. 82. (c) *to take heed* (w. clause of purpose). xix. 93. (d) *to keep watch of, spy on* (w. gen.). xxi. 310. (e) *to discover* by observation (w. ind. question). xviii. 44.

*cēping, f. *observation.* xviii. 6. [Not in dict.]

Chaldea rīce, n. *the kingdom of the Chaldeans.* xxi. 293. [Chaldea, gp., suggests np. Chaldei; cf. Iudei.]

Chaleph, *Caleb* (Num. xiv, 6). xx. 170, 189, 199, 360 (ds. uninfl.).

Chananēisc, adj. *Canaanitish.* xx. 212.

Chore, *Korah,* a rebel against Moses (Num. xvi. 1). xx. 220, 237, 256.

Christus, cited as a Greek form, v. 208. [Cf. Crīst.]

cīdan, I, w. dat. *to chide.* iii. 96; xv. 65, 71, 167, 171; xvii. 53; xx. 307.

cild, n. *child.* nas., xii. 87, 88, 120, 131; xvii. 153; xix. 3, 20; xxiii. 31; gs. cildes, xvii. 154, 155; xix. 22; xxiii. 16, 27; ds. cilde, xia. 69, 70; nap. cild, xi. 147, 319, 380; xii. 106, 109, 112, 135; xviii. 321; xx. 169; np. cildra, xx. 190; gp. cildra, vii. 101; cilda, xxi. 423 (v.l. -ra); dp. cildum, xi. 115, 498; xia. 120; xx. 12, 252; xxi. 406; xxiii. 38.

cildhād, m. *childhood.* iv. 280; viii. 59; xi. 307, 311.

cildlic, adj. *childish, of a child.* xix. 19.

cining, cing, see cyning.

clǣne, adj. *clean.* (a) *without taint of sin, pure, chaste.* i. 6, 459; iv. 216, 234 (as noun); xi. 189; xvi. 56; xix. 50, 57, 82; xxi. 571; xxiii. 197; xxvi. 11. (b) of animals, *wholesome* for food. i. 212.

clǣnheort, adj. *pure in heart.* iv. 215 (dp. -um w. def. art. as noun).

clǣnlīce, adv. *with purity, chastely.* xix. 94; xxi. 638.

clǣnnyss, f. *purity, virginity, chastity.* xi. 148; xix. 49, 53, 67; xxi. 165, 510; xxv(a). 17; xxx. 8, 13.

ġeclǣnsian, II. *to cleanse.* i. 424; iv. 70, 242; xviii. 83; xix. 118.

cleofian, II. *to stick.* pret. 3s. cleofode, xx. 101 (v.l. clifode).

clif, n. *cliff.* viii. 108.

clypian, clip-, II. (a) intrans. *to cry out.* xix. 161, 163, 199; xxi. 415, 487; xxvii. 99 (uncertain constr.).— with upp, *to call upwards.* xxvii. 67. —introducing direct discourse, *to cry out, proclaim, call.* vi. 97; xvii. 229; xxi. 324; and with tō and dat. of person, xxi. 476. (b) intrans. w. tō and dat. of person, *to call to someone from a distance.* i. 448, 452; xi. 527; xxiii. 151; xxv(c). 3. —*to call to* for help, *call upon, appeal to, invoke.* v. 184; vi. 291; ix. 46; xx. 75; xxi. 601; xxiii. 84; xxix. 120.—(c) trans. *to cry out, proclaim, say.* iv. 50, 269; xvii. 288. (d) trans. *to call, summon.* v. 33; vi. 66, 67; xvi. 94; xxiii. 149. [Uniformly clyp- except clip- at xxix. 120 and occas. cleop- in variants.]

clypung, f. *cry, supplication.* viii. 156.

clȳsing, f. *enclosure.* xix. 198.

cnapa, wk. m. *boy.* xii. 120 (giving progression in age: cild, cnapa, cniht); xxi. 566; xxiii. 15 (seofon wintra).

cnēow, n. *knee.* xiv. 30, 196; xxi. 308.

cnēowian, II. *to kneel.* xxiii. 30.

cniht, m. (a) *young man.* vi. 182; xi. 169, 172, 174; xii. 121; xviii. 12; xix. 102; xxi. 292. (b) *servant, retainer.* iv. 105.

cnotta, wk. m. *knot.* xi. 164.

gecnyrdnyss, f. *diligence, zeal.* xix. 9.

coccel, m. *cockle, weeds.* v. 269.

col, n. *coal.* x. 175.

cōm(-), see **cuman.**

consolator, cited as Latin name for the Holy Spirit. x. 84.

Constantinus, *Constantine* the Great. xxii. 51; xxvi. 7.

gecoren, see **gecēosan.**

gecorennyss, f. *choice, election.* xix. 48.

corn, n. (a) *kernel* of wheat or other cereal grass. xix. 23. (b) collectively, *corn, grain.* viii. 131; xxi. 166.

Corozaim. *Chorazin,* a town near Capernaum, condemned by Christ (Matth. xi. 21). xvii. 57, 59.

costnian, II. *to try, tempt.* xi. 31; xia. 131.

costnung, f. *temptation.* viii. 182; xi. 149; xiv. 191, 205.

coþu, f. *disease, sickness.* xiii. 2.

cræft, m. (a) *skill, artistry, contrivance, cunning.* iii. 85; xviii. 389; xxi. 191, 202, 526, 537 (or *power?*); xxv(*b*). 1; xxix. 5, 8. (b) an *art, craft, skilled occupation.* xix. 55; xxx. 100, 102; *magic art,* xxix. 126. (c) *work of art, creation.* xia. 208. *(d) artist's *idea, conception, design.* i. 281 (see note). [Meaning (c), in Ælfric's use, verges on (d). Cf. his Hexameron, ed. Crawford, lines 36–38, which Crawford mistranslates.]

gecrammian, II. *to cram, stuff.* xiii. 16, 111.

Creta, the island of *Crete.* xxi. 104.

Crīst, m. *Christ.* i. 6, etc. (10 times); ii. 6, etc. (10 times); iii. 95, etc. (5 times); iv. 7, etc. (16 times); etc. —np. **Crīstas,** xviii. 255, 378, 386. —**Crīstes bōc,** see **bōc.** [Cf. *Christus.*]

Cristen, adj. *Christian.* iv. 179, 237, 284; viii. 132; ix. 49; xi. 81, 372, 432, 433, 536, etc.—pl. as noun, iii. 160; xi. 390, 406, 434; xiv. 140, 163; etc.

Cristendōm, m. (a) *Christianity.* iv. 237; x. 102; xiv. 141; xviii. 281, 347; xxii. 51; xxiii. 141; xxvi. 5. (b) w. def. art., *the Christian faith.* xiv. 232; xviii. 158, 285; xix. 120; xxi.

648; xxvi. 6. (c) *Christendom:* body of persons and territories under Christian rule. xiv. 114, 181. *(d) *Christian supervision* (of the individual by his local minster). xxx. 96. [Meaning (d) not in dict.]

cristnian, II. *to christen.* xxi. 638.

crocc, f. or **crocca,** wk. m. *crock.* dp. **croccum,** xx. 127. [Ælfric has '*olla* crocca' in his Grammar, Zupitza, p. 25/7.]

cū, f. *cow.* nap. **cȳ,** xxi. 261, 265, 275.

cucu, ('cwic'), adj *quick, alive.* ns., vi. 193; vii. 120, 122; xia. 168; xviii. 419; xx. 118; xxi. 436, 548; dsm. **cucum,** xi. 273; np. **cuce,** i. 270; xi. 299, 300, 392; xia. 166; xx. 253; wk. w. def. art. as noun, np. **cucan,** xi. 302.

culfre, wk. f. *dove.* xvi. 229, 249.

cuma, m. *stranger, guest.* x. 38, 40; xi. 414, 422, 441, 446; xvi. 174.— **cumena hūs,** n. *guest-house.* ds., xxvi. 105. [Lat. *in salutatorio,* 'in the audience-chamber', but the OE is glossed *in domo hospitum.* See BT, 'cuma'.]

cuman, 4. *to come.* i. 18, etc. (11 times); ii. 21, etc. (9 times); iii. 26; iv. 36, etc. (7 times); v. 3, etc. (17 times); vi. 43, etc. (15 times); vii. 14, etc. (13 times); etc., including the following relatively uncommon uses: (a) with **of,** *to come from, be derived from.* i. 271–4; ii. 232–3. (b) with dat. of person, *to come to, befall* someone. xx. 90. (c) with **tō,** *to come to, result in:* **cymþ heora sacu him tō aworpennysse,** *their strife will result in their destruction.* iv. 103. (d) **cuman tō mannum,** *to be born;* said of ordinary children, xx. 114, and also, with additional literal significance, of Christ, i. 18; vi. 64; xi. 8; xia. 77; xxi. 656; see note on i. 43. (e) **cuman under iuce,** *to be put under a yoke.* xxi. 261. (f) **cuman æfter, sīþ,** *to come (into the world) at a later time (than).* xxi. 650, 652. [Forms: inf., xvii. 10 (7 more); pres. part. **cumende,** xviii. 264, 408; imp. sg. **cum,** v. 34; vi. 81, 98;

pl. **cumaþ**, v. 66, 157; xi. 409; pres. 1s. **cume**, ii. 36; x. 18, 136; 2s. **cymst**, xv. 24, 196; xxiii. 110; 3s. **cymþ**, ii. 37 (51 more); 1p. **cumaþ**, xia. 166; 3p., i. 271 (10 more); pres. 1s. subj. **cume**, xxiii. 89; 3s., v. 78 (7 more); pret. 1s. **cōm**, viii. 42, 219; 2s. **cōme**, vi. 64 (8 more); 3s. **cōm**, i. 18 (68 more); 1p. **cōmon**, xi. 425; 2p., xi. 417; **cōme gē**, xi. 443; 3p. **cōmon**, i. 373 (25 more); **cōman**, xxi. 230, 310; pret. 3s. subj. **cōme**, ii. 21 (8 more); 3p. subj. **cōmon**, xiv. 26, 178; xx. 232; pp. **cumen**, vi. 49; vii. 79; xxiii. 127 (ap. **-e**).—Cf. **a-**, **be-**, **of-**, **ofer-cuman** and next entry.]

ġecuman, 4. *to come.* imp. sg. **ġecum**, xxiii. 74.

cunnan, pret. pres. vb. (a) w. inf., *to be able, can.* pres. 3s. **cann**, i. 283; 1p. **cunnan**, xxix. 113; 2p. **cunnon**, iii. 48. (b) w. acc., *to be acquainted with, know.* pres. 1s. **cann**, xxvi. 101; 3s., xv. 75; xxix. 104; 3p. **cunnon**, ix. 17, 200; xvi. 218; pres. 1s. subj. **cunne**, xxiii. 66; 3s. subj., ix. 41; pret. 3s. **cūþe**, v. 233; xiii. 142; 3p. **cūþon**, vii. 200; ix. 193; xi. 234 (twice), 372, 386; xv. 63; pret. 2s. subj. **cūþest**, v. 18, 130; 3s. subj. **cūþe**, iv. 255; xii. 142; 3p. subj. **cūþan**, xxi. 90. (c) absolute, *to understand.* pret. 1s. **cūþe**, xix. 17 (translating *sapiebam*).

cunnian, II. (a) *to seek to know, look to see.* x. 192; xxi. 230. (b) *to try.* xxi. 442; xxiii. 82 (inf., **-en** for **-an**). [Meaning (a) is a slight extension of BTS, 'cunnian', III. 1.]

ġecure, **ġecuron**, see **ġecēosan**.

cūþ, adj. *known.* ii. 219; vi. 161, 190; viii. 183; ix. 89, 211; xi. 273, 380; xviii. 44. [Cf. **fullcūþ**.]

cūþ-, pret. forms, see **cunnan**.

cūþlic, adj. (a) *evident.* i. 444. (b) *certain.* ix. 8, 87 (asf. or adv.?). [Napier cited passage in ix to illustrate meaning (b). Accepted in BTS Add.]

cūþlīce, adv. *clearly, openly.* i. 448; ii. 73; xx. 232.

(ġe)cwǣd-, **ġecwǣd-**, **(ġe)cwæþ**, see **cweþan**.

cwalu, f. *violent death.* iv. 264.

cwealm, m. *death, pestilence.* xxi. 244, 246, 269.

cwealmbǣre, adj. *deadly, murderous.* xix. 173.

cweartern, **cwartern**, n. *prison.* xi. 417, 425, 443, 447; xxiii. 51, 69, 71, etc. (16 times).—unbroken **cwart-** is peculiar to the scribe of xxiii.

ġecweden, see **cweþan**.

cwellere, m. *killer.* xxiii. 161, 202, 205.

ġecwēman, I, w. dat. *to please.* ix. 54; xi. 124, 140 (pret. 3s. subj. instead of pres.?), 185, 366; xviii. 138; xix. 80, 81.

ġecwēme, adj., w. dat. *agreeable, pleasing, acceptable to.* iv. 215, 234; xia. 149; xviii. 96; xix. 67.

ġecwēmednyss, f. *pleasure, satisfaction.* Gode tō ġecwēmednysse, *for God's satisfaction,* xxi. 646.

cweþan, **ġecweþan**, 5. (a) w. acc. or clause, or direct discourse, or absolute, *to say, speak.* inf., **cweþan**, xviii. 119, 143; xxi. 436; pres. part. **cweþende**, i. 444; iv. 136; v. 70, 225; vi. 66; etc. (9 more); imp. pl. **cweþe gē**, v. 68; pres. 1s. **cweþe**, xxiii. 73; 2s. **cwist**, xxiii. 60; 3s. **cwyþ**, **cwiþ**, **cweþ**, i. 225; iv. 44 (MS **cwæþ**, v.ll. **cweþ**, **cwyþ**), 235; vi. 218, 269; etc. (6 more); **ġecwyþ**, vi. 226; viii. 95; xv. 15, 143, 173; 1p. **cweþaþ**, i. 77, 281, 472; xia. 234; xii. 241; **cweþe wē**, xx. 406; 3p. **cweþaþ**, xviii. 7; pret. 2s. **cwǣde**, v. 36; xxiii. 97; 3s. **cwæþ**, i. 108; etc. (30 times in i–iv); **ġecwæþ**, iv. 220; xii. 78, 213; xv. 3, 29; xvi. 116, 121; xvii. 163; xviii. 392; xxiii. 117, 192; 1p. **cwǣdon**, iii. 155; 3p., i. 410, 454; ii. 44; iii. 20, 26; v. 95, 285; vi. 21, 32, 73, 80; etc. (15 more); **ġecwǣdon**, xxi. 242; pp. **ġecwǣden**, v. 84; **ġecweden**, v. 252; x. 150; xiii. 120; xviii. 322; *spoken of, mentioned,* xviii. 88, 128 (np. **-e**), 189 (np. **-e**),—(b) w. acc. and compl. noun, *to call, name, interpret.* pres. 1p. **cweþaþ**, xi. 21;

cweþan, ġecweþan (cont.)
xia. 95; and in passive w. compl. or swā, pp. ġecweden, v. 206; viii. 62; xiii. 144; xiv. 88; xx. 306; xxix. 37. (c) in passive when subject anticipates unexpressed complement, pp. ġecweden, so-called. viii. 2; xi. 115. [Cf. wiþcweþan.]

cwyde, m. discourse, homily. xx. 2.

cwylmian, II. to suffer. vi. 158; xi. 390, 489, 507.

cwylminġ, f. suffering, tribulation. xviii. 352; xxi. 71, 291.

cwyrn, f. hand-mill, mill. xviii. 33, 110, 113, 115, 201.

cȳ, see cū.

cȳdd-, ġecȳdd, see cȳþan.

cyle, m. chill, cold, coldness. xvi. 117; xxi. 41, 583.

cymst, cymþ, see cuman.

ġecynd, n. nature, kind. i. 333 (natural capacity), 412; v. 107; vi. 249; viii. 196; x. 94; xi. 87; xia. 19, 212; xii. 103, 162, 214; xvii. 259; xix. 30 (twice); xxi. 24, 510; xxvi. 57; xxix. 17, 26, 28, 100.

ġecyndelic, adj. natural. xi. 114, 117; xxi. 52.

cynecynn, n. royal family. v. 196.

cynedōm, m. kingly rule, kingdom. xxi. 351; xxvi. 16, 103; xxviii. 9.

cynehlāford, m. royal lord, king. iv. 102.

cynerīce, n. kingdom. iv. 18, 98, 104.

cyninġ, m. king. (a) with reference to various earthly kings, i. 229, 241, 371; ii. 12; iv. 101; ix. 46–55, 137; xi. 13; xia. 87; xviii. 187; xix. 9, 139–63; xx. 116, 406, 409; xxi. 293–493, 516; xxii. 1–46, 85; xxvi. 1; xxix. 38–93; xxx. 18 (ds. cynġe). spelled cining, xxi. 323, 327; cing, xxi. 306, 311, 391. (b) with reference to God, v. 196 (Kyning); xi. 426; xxvi. 62.

Cyninġa bōc, f., w. def. art. þǣra. Book of Kings. xxii. 15; xxix. 37. [These references are to the first two books of Kings in the Vulgate, I and II Samuel in A.V. See also Liber Reġum below.]

cynn, n. (a) kindred, tribe, race, nation. i. 348, 459; iv. 130, 181; v. 115, 195, 199; vii. 79; x. 198, 203; xia. 149; xvii. 86; xx. 58, 132, 163; xxii. 93. (b) species, kind, nature. i. 373 (gp. cynna, governing noun obliterated); vi. 161; xi. 227; xvi. 73; xix. 10, 24; xx. 17.

cynren, cynryn, n. kindred, generation. xvi. 33, 216.

cyrce, cyrice, wk. f. church. iii. 144; xi. 3, 66; xia. 183; xiv. 95; xvi. 83, 139; xix. 228; xxiii. 18, 160; xxvi. 76, 94, 129.

cyre, m. free will, choice. iii. 111, 113.

cyrr, m. (turn), time, occasion. xiv. 158.

cyrran, I. to turn, return. iv. 263; xvii. 265; xviii. 243, 313.

ġecyrran, I. (a) of physical movement, to turn, return. xx. 167; xxi. 277, 579, 582. (b) of spiritual change, to turn (from sins) to God. xi. 196; xiii. 51, 77; xv. 42, 54, 161; absolutely or elliptically, to turn from one's (evil) ways, change (for the better), be converted. xiii. 53; xv. 51; xix. 223, 241.

ġecyrrednyss, f. conversion. iv. 66.

Cyrus, king of Persia. xxi. 351, 442.

cyst, f. (a) generosity, munificence. i. 212; xvi. 46; xxx. 50. *(b) bountiful gift(s), bounty. i. 257. [Meaning (b) a concretion of (a); cf. BTS, II, excellent thing, and III, liberality, etc.]

ġecȳst, see ġecēosan.

cystiġ, adj. bountiful, generous. i. 257; xvi. 193.

cystiġnyss, f. liberality, bounty. i. 352, 389; xvii. 72.

cytel, m. kettle, cauldron. xxi. 518.

cȳþan, I, pres. 3s. cȳþ, pret. cȳdd-, pp. ġecȳdd. (a) w. acc. object or clause or both, often w. dat. of person, to make known, show forth, tell, declare, proclaim. i. 229 [double construction; see also sense (b) below], 389; ii. 121, 288; iii. 109; v. 58, 222, 233; vi. 328; vii. 28, 120, 215, 217; ix. 32; xia. 57, 64; xiv. 143; xvii. 42, 131 (construction uncertain), 183, 246; xix. 152; xxiii. 42, 71, 161.—cȳþan ġecȳþnysse, to give testimony, testify. i. 39, 41,

304, 310; v. 90, 224; ix. 8, 10, 87, 115, 130, 150.—(b) absolute after swā swā, *to testify*. xi. 81; xxii. 15; and w. dat. of pers., *to tell*, xii. 173; xvi. 183; xviii. 226; xxi. 646; with sense (a) also, i. 229. (c) intrans., w. be or embe, *to tell of, testify about.* i. 9, 114; v. 256; xvii. 241; and w. dat. of person, v. 285; viii. 36, 169, 175. [Cf. full-cȳðan.]

cȳþnyss, f. *testimony*. xia. 57.

ᵹecȳþnyss, f. (a) *testimony*. i. 39, 40, 41, 302, 304, 305, 310; v. 90, 224, 286; ix. 8, 10, 87, 115, 124, 130, 150; xii. 30, 176. (b) *testament* (Old or New), *dispensation.* ix. 165, 193; xix. 36.

cȳþþ, f. *kinship, friendship, acquaintance*, in the phrase, habban cȳþþe tō, *to have friendly relations with, be on good terms with.* xi. 385; xvi. 47. [In Ælfric's period there is evidence for ns. 'cyþ(þ)', not for 'cyþþu'.]

D

dǣd, f. *deed.* ii. 187, 197, 286; iv. 200; vi. 169, 200, 267; ix. 39; x. 35; xi. 124, 373, 394, 404; xia. 165; xiii. 120, 122, 205; xiv. 37, 137, 215; etc.

dǣdbētan, I. *to do penance.* pres. part. as adj., dǣdbētende, *penitent*, vi. 251. [Cf. bētan and next word.]

dǣdbōt, f. *penance.* iii. 149; iv. 68; vi. 142, 215; xi. 399; xia. 10; xii. 154; xv. 162; xvi. 95; xvii. 63; xix. 118, 147, 201; xxvi. 118; xxvii. 120.

ᵹedæftan, I. *to arrange, put in order.* pp. ᵹedæft, iv. 46, 241.

dæᵹ, m. *day, time.* i. 23, 207, 326; ii. 43, etc. (12 times); vi. 22, etc. (9 times); vii. 139; viii. 37, 142, 179, 180, 181; ix. 159; x. 43; etc.— on dæᵹ, *in the daytime, by day*, w. endingless locative (less probably acc.), vi. 26, 344 (cf. on dæᵹe, i. 207; viii. 181; and see niht below); for ǣlce dæᵹ, sume dæᵹ, see ǣlc, sum.—se miccla dæᵹ, *the*

great day (of the Judgement). iv. 128; xi. 247, 283.—dæᵹes, adv. *by day.* xii. 50, 65; xvii. 226; þæs ylcan dæᵹes, *on the same day*, xix. 249.

dæᵹhwamlīce, adv. *daily.* iv. 64; vi. 138; xi. 149, 254; xxi. 356, 373.

dæᵹrēd, dæᵹerēd, n. *daybreak, dawn.* i. 306; xxi. 323.

dǣl, m. *portion, part.* iv. 195; viii. 111; xvi. 177; xx. 74; xxvii. 9; xxx. 81–105 (7 times).—be sumum dǣle, *partly.* v. 161.

dǣlan, I. (a) trans. *to distribute.* xvi. 158, 176, 269, 292; xxx. 62, 64, 97; trans. or absolute, xiii. 13, 106; xvi. 273. (b) intrans. or absolute, *to distribute, give alms.* xiii. 15, 107, 110; xxx. 63, 65, 67. [Cf. be-, to-dǣlan.]

ᵹedafenian, II, impers. *to be fitting.* iii. 104; v. 43; ix. 185; xii. 40, 221; w. dat. of person, *to be fitting for*, i. 53, 416, 428; v. 55, 173; xix. 11; xxi. 234.

Dagon, a god of the Philistines. xxi. 224, 228, 231 (gs. Dagones), 233.

Danihel, Daniel, the prophet. xviii. 234, 278; xxi. 300–490 *passim*, including gs. Daniheles, 344, 429, and ds. Danihele, 318, etc.

Darius, king of the Medes. xxi. 302 (gs. Daries), 306 (ds. Dariᵹe), 311, 318, 323.

daru, f. *impairment.* ix. 134.

Dathan, a rebel against Moses (Num. xvi. 1). xx. 220, 231 (ds. uninfl.), 250.

Dauid, *David.* i. 459 (gs. -es); xxii. 13, 18, 24, 30, 32, 33 (ds. -e), 41, 44, 50; xxvii. 72.

dēad, adj. *dead.* vi. 52, etc. (12 times); x. 156, 157, 158; xi. 273, 307, 330. —absolute as noun, ap. ealle dēade, vi. 128; nænne dēadne, asm., *no dead person*, xxix. 61 (where either nænne or dēadne may be regarded as a sb.).—wk. as noun, *dead (person).* sg., vi. 188, 190, 196; xi. 339; xxix. 123; pl., vi. 211, 318; vii. 92, 107; viii. 75; xia. 114; xxix. 63.

dēadlic, adj. *mortal.* xi. 98, 106; xia. 51; xvii. 87.—ap. wk. as noun, i. 135.

dēaf, adj. *deaf*. ii. 80; xvii. 26, 85.—
wk. w. def. art. as noun, *the deaf
(person)*. sg., xvii. 83, 99; pl., xvii.
44, 185.
*dēafnyss, f. *deafness*. xvii. 150.
[Not in dict. First example in OED
and MED dated 1398.]
dearst, see durran.
dēaþ, m. *death*. ii. 108, 110, 114, 251;
iv. 193; vi. 12, etc. (21 times); vii.
55, etc. (11 times); etc.
dēaw, m. or n. *dew*. xx. 15.
delfan, 3. *to dig*. (a) trans., inf., iii. 5.
(b) intrans., inf., xvi. 13, 101, 103.
[Cf. bedelfan.]
dēma, wk. m. *judge*. iv. 125, 128; vii.
104; xi. 197, 418, 435, 444, 448.
dēman, gedēman, I. (a) intrans. or
absolute, *to judge*. xiii. 10 (first), 87
(first), 89, 92. w. clause, *to decree*.
xxi. 302. (b) intrans. w. dat., *to
pass judgement on, judge* someone.
xi. 359, 363 (second), 369 (first);
xia. 164 (d. inf. dēmende for dē-
menne); xiii. 81, 102; xv. 221;
xviii. 25, 45, 50, 385. (c) impers.,
is (wæs, biþ) gedēmed, w. dat. of
person, someone *is (was, will be)
judged, sentenced, doomed*. vii. 22,
171, 181; xi. 363 (first), 369 (second),
383, 460. (d) trans. *to pass judgement
on, judge* a matter brought to trial.
xiii. 91 (see note).—w. dōm as
object, *to pronounce judgement*. iii.
139; xiii. 75 (ge-), 78 (ge-). (e)
trans., pp. in passive w. person as
subject, *judged*. np. gedēmede,
xiii. 10 (second), 87 (second). [Pre-
fix ge- only in pp. and twice in
xiii as indicated under (d).—Cf.
fordēman.]
dene, f. *valley*. v. 177, 179. [Ælfric
MSS. regularly have dene for denu
in nom. but follow strong declension. See BT and BTS.]
Denisc, adj. *Danish*. xxi. 125.—on
Denisc, *in (the) Danish (language)*,
xxi. 140, 177.—wk. pl. as noun, þā
Deniscan, *the Danes*. xiv. 132; xxi.
141.
dēoflic, dēofollic, adj. *devilish, of the
devil(s)*. iv. 61, 210; v. 121; xvii.
240 (deofel-); xviii. 296; xix. 194;

xxi. 234; xxvi. 12, 15, 18; xxix. 88,
90.
dēoflīce, adv. *devilishly*. iv. 6 (v.l.
dēofollīce).
dēofol, m., pl. dēoflu, dēofla, n.
devil, the devil. i. 187; iv. 8, 13, 23,
etc. (33 times); vi. 282, 284; vii.
125, 126, 170, 173, 177, 181, 184,
185; viii. 136, 139, 141, 144; ix. 62;
x. 190, 197; etc.—references to
Satan sometimes have def. art. (e.g.
se dēofol, iv. 62; x. 197), sometimes not (e.g., dēofol, iv. 188, 204;
dēofle(s), iv. 239, 254).
dēofolgyld, -gild, n. (a) *idol, pagan
god, image of the devil*. iii. 60; viii.
134 (ap. ?); xviii. 234, 278, 282, 300.
(b) *devil-worship, idolatry*. xviii.
296; xxix. 124; xxx. 26.
dēofollic, see dēoflic.
dēop, adj. *deep* (lit. or fig.). v. 21;
xia. 208; xiv. 59; xix. 215; xxiii.
203 (dsf. dēoppre).—comp., dsf.
dēopran, xxvi. 71.
dēoplic, adj. *deep-witted, subtle*. i.
258. [This shade of meaning not
well illustrated in BT, BTS.]
dēopnyss, f. *depth, profundity*. i. 58;
iii. 159; v. 99, 101, 159, 177; xxix.
112, 113.
dēor, n. *animal*. i. 211; xi. 333; xxi.
349, 486, 490, 493.
deorc, adj. *dark*. iv. 224; xi. 488;
xxvii. 31.
dēorwurþe, -weorþe, -wyrþe, adj.
precious. vi. 6, 309; xvi. 140; xxi.
371. [Cf. dȳre.]
derian, II (orig. I) w. dat. *to injure*.
ii. 112 (pres. 3s. deraþ); iii. 72; vi.
290; vii. 186; xi. 560; xv. 204, 211;
xvi. 161, 254; xvii. 150, 298; xxi.
36, 40, 330, 349.—pres. part. derigende, as adj., *malignant*. xviii.
195. [Cf. ungederod.]
dēst, dēþ, see dōn.
Didimus, surname of Thomas, the
disciple. vi. 40.
dīgol, dīgel, adj. *secret, mysterious,
obscure*. i. 58; ii. 218, 285; iii. 1;
xii. 145; xiii. 91; xvii. 188; xx. 334.
sup., ap. wk., dīglostan, xviii.
41.
dīgollīce, dīgel-, dīglīce, adv.

secretly. v. 73; vi. 163, 177; xii. 50, 65; xviii. 182; xxx. 72.

dīgolnyss, dīgel-, f. (a) *hidden meaning, mystery.* iii. 48; xviii. 316. (b) *hiding place, covert.* iv. 223. (c) *secret thought.* xvii. 202. (d) **on dīgelnysse,** *in secret.* ix. 30; xvii. 200.

diht, n. *direction, disposition, fiat.* i. 283; ii. 20, 67, 153, 226, 238; xi. 277, 399, 483; xx. 211.

gedihtan, I, pret. **gedihte.** (a) w. dat., *to direct, give direction to.* xxi. 93. (b) w. acc., *to dispose.* xia. 208. [For (b), cf. CH II. 206/16, correctly translated by Thorpe— probably not so exactly *construct, make,* as in BTS, (6).]

discipul(us), m. *disciple.* np. **discipuli,** v. 9, 73; vi. 32; dp. **discipulum,** xx. 282.

dohtor, f. *daughter.* nas., vi. 176; xxiii. 102, 121, 136, 196; xxix. 21; **dohter,** xxi. 150, 154; gs. **dohter,** xxiii. 132; dp. **dohtrum,** xix. 70.

gedohtra, fp. *daughters* of the same parent(s). xxi. 115 (v.l. **dohtra**).

dolhswaþu, f. *scar.* vii. 142.

dollīce, adv. *rashly, foolishly.* xiii. 78 (v.l. **dwollīce,** q.v.).

dōm, m. (a) *judgement, (a judge's) sentence.* ii. 285; iii. 103, 139; vii. 18, 22, 75, 171; xiii. 75, 78, 88; xv. 12, 13, 128, 129, 131, 132, 138; xvi. 75; xix. 230; xxi. 429. (b) *right judgement, justice.* iii. 77; xiii. 101. (c) *the (Last) Judgement.* xi. 275, 401, 519; xvi. 96, 98; xviii. 25, 413.

Dōmes-dæg, m. *Doomsday.* ii. 110; iv. 115; vi. 152; vii. 108, 159; xi. 199, 254, 315; xii. 109; xiv. 190; xvi. 172; xvii. 65; xviii. 5, 75; xix. 253; xxi. 62, 68; xxvii. 111, 116, 119.

dōmsetl, n. *judgement seat.* xi. 355 (-settl-), 358 (-setl-).

dōn, gedōn, anom. vb., pres. 2s. **dēst,** 3s. **dēþ,** pret. **dyd-;** pp. **gedōn;** the prefix optional for the other forms, occurring only as indicated below. I. trans. (a) *to do, perform, effect, practise.* iii. 67, 104, 133; vi. 138, 162, 215, 267, 326

(first); ix. 16, 23, 146, 199; xi. 381 (also means *give,* sense d), 427, 428; xi*a.* 10; xiii. 231; xv. 217; xvi. 11, 100, 107; xix. 101, 170; xxi. 94, 497, 618 (twice); xxiii. 139 (þanc **dōn,** *to do a kindness,* Lat. *præstare beneficium,* perhaps coloured by *give thanks;* cf. sense d), 183; xxix. 7, xxx. 57, 72; and w. prefix, xi. 399; xv. 204, 211 (both **unþanc gedōn,** *to do an ill turn*); xvii. 43, 62, 184, 191 (? object obliterated); xxvi. 42; and pp. **gedōn,** iii. 34; x. 23, 183; xx. 261; xxvi. 52. (b) *to put.* ii. 35; vi. 86 (w. **of,** *put* or *take off from*); xvii. 30, 120; xxiii. 132; and w. prefix, iv. 264 (**tō cwale gedydon,** *put to death*); xix. 55 (**tō cræfte,** *to an occupation*). (c) *to put to use for* (**tō**). xvi. 137, 140. (d) *to put forth, give* alms, goods, etc. xi. 431, 432; xiii. 13, 106, 113, 116; xvi. 154, 158; xvii. 200; xviii. 125; xxi. 373; xxv (*c*). 9, 10; xxvii. 9; xxx. 30, 43, 50, 52, 60, 104, 107; and w. prefix, xvi. 273; used absolutely, without prefix, xvi. 156, 163, 164, 165.—*to do* or *give* honour. i. 380.—*to give, confer* forgiveness. vi. 251; and w. prefix, x. 87.—*to give, administer* the Christian religion. xviii. 158.— see also sense a, above, for xi. 381 and xxiii. 139. (e) w. clause as object, *to cause, bring it about that.* vi. 83; viii. 176; xvii. 188; xxiii. 66, 170; and w. anticipatory pron. object **þæt,** xxix. 122; and w. prefix, xvii. 44, 45, 185, 186; xix. 109; xxiii. 140. (f) w. complementary adj., *to make* someone such and such; xxiii. 55 (reflex.); and w. prefix, xvi. 71 (reflex.); xvii. 83. (g) w. complementary inf., *to make* someone *do* something, *cause* him to do it. xxv (*a*). 13. II. intrans. *to do, act.* (a) w. adv. or adv. phrase of manner (**hū, swā,** prep. **be . . . ,** etc.), ii. 207 (**swā . . . þæt**); iii. 17, 25; v. 127; viii. 249; ix. 63, 82 (twice), 186; x. 28, 206; xii. 185; xiii. 190; xiv. 140, 220; xv. 205; xvi. 237, 243; xvii. 106, 152; xviii. 170; xix. 126; xx. 246, 291, 404; xxi. 93, 250, 307;

dōn, gedōn (*cont.*)
xxiii. 77; and w. prefix, xv. 110 (adv. implicit); xvi. 31, 206. (b) after conj. swā swā, like III below, but with broader reference, vi. 326 (second; or trans. as in I. a, with ellipsis of object); vii. 55; viii. 76; ix. 54, 181; xiv. 107, 132; xv. 167; xvi. 132; xvii. 265; xix. 120 (second); xx. 395; xxi. 54; xxix. 6, 86, 88. III. *to do*, as substitute for a preceding verb (which governs the construction, trans. or intrans.). after conj. swā swā, v. 234, 277; vi. 298 (w. acc.); vii. 70; viii. 250; ix. 133; xvii. 84 (w. acc.), 96; xix. 110; xx. 216; xxi. 65, 596, 623; xxix. 63; after single swā, xxvii. 117 (for impersonal sceamode w. dat. of person); after comp. adv. and þonne, xix. 120 (first). [Cf. a-, for-, fore-, un -dōn.]

dorst-, see durran.

draca, wk. m. *dragon*. i. 242; xi. 169, 173, 176; xxi. 48, 432, 441, 444, 447, 449, 454.

dragan, 6. *to drag, draw*. pret. 3p. drōgon, xxi. 558.

dranc, see drincan.

drēam, m. (a) *music*. xx. 32. *(b) *choir* of singers. xxvii. 72. [Meaning (b) not in dict. See note.]

dreccan, gedreccan, I, pret. dreht-, pp. gedreht. *to afflict, torment*. i. 198, 222; iv. 4, 9; v. 101; xi. 203, 491, 560 (pres. 3s. drehþ); xia. 107; xvii. 128; xxvii. 44.

gedrecednyss, f. *affliction*. xxi. 281.

gedrēfan, I. *to afflict, trouble*. vi. 79; x. 16, 130, 132; xviii. 360.

gedrēfednyss, f. *tribulation, trouble*. v. 184; xviii. 248, 260, 345, 399.

dreht-, gedreht(-), see dreccan.

drēorig, adj. *sad, dejected, sorrowful*. vi. 185; xi. 435.

drēoriglīce, adv. *sorrowfully*. xxvi. 79. [Two similar passages from Ælfric cited for this word in BTS.]

*drīfan, 1. *to promote, further* (?). inf., xiii. 96; see note. [Cf. a-, oferdrīfan.]

Drihten, m. *lord, the Lord*. i. 102,
134, 418; ii. 4, 80, 144, 248, 253; iii. 1, 149, 159; iv. 12, etc. (15 times); v. 179, 231; vi. 6, etc. (12 times); vii. 181; etc. [Reserved for God, esp. Christ, but once applied to Christ by his disciples, vi. 32. The spelling with *i* has entirely superseded that with *y*.]

drihtenlic, adj. (a) *lordly, divine*, in the phrase, þurh his drihtenlican mihte. vi. 128, 211; vii. 92, 107; xia. 114, 167; xxi. 502. (b) *of the Lord*. i. 1; xviii. 41 (i.e. spoken by the Lord). [For Ælfric's use of the formula in (a), see BTS.]

drinca, wk. m. *drink*. perhaps gs. drincan, v. 118; as. drincan, xi. 413; but both may be infinitives: see drincan.

*gedrinca, wk. m. *drinking companion, table companion*. xxi. 352 (glossed *pincerna*, 'cupbearer', in MS. R but translates *conviva*). [Unique in this passage though already in print in Warner's ed. of MS. G. Cited by Napier from R as 'cupbearer'. Correct meaning in BTS.]

drincan, 3. *to drink*. inf., v. 13, 17, 19, 118 (?), 123, 126, 152; xi. 413 (?); xvi. 194; pres. part. drincende, vii. 193 (nsm. for asm.); pres. 3s. drincþ, v. 26, 27, 137, 138; xxi. 373; pres. 3s. subj. drince, v. 143; pret. 3s. dranc, v. 24, 236, 237; vii. 136, 150; 1p. druncon, ix. 161; 3p., xviii. 11, 18; xxi. 409. [For the questioned infinitives, v. 118 and xi. 413, see drinca. Cf. adrincan.]

drōgon, see dragan.

drohtnung, f. *conduct, mode of behaviour, conversation, life*. ii. 133; xvi. 104; xxv (c). 12 (Lat. *conversatio*).

dropian, II. *to drip*. xxvi. 66.

dropmǣlum, adv. *drop by drop*. xix. 31. [BT has one example only, from Ælfric.]

druncennyss, f. *drunkenness*. v. 237; xvi. 76; xix. 210.

druncon, see drincan.

drȳcrǣft, m. *magic art, sorcery*. i. 258; viii. 136; xxix. 123, 124.

drȳmann, m. *magician*. i. 258; iv.

139; xi. 377; xvii. 96; xxix. 3, 4, 14,
22, 30, 35.

dūfan, 2. *to be immersed, sink.* pret.
3p. dufan, xiv. 28; dufon, xiv. 189;
pret. 3s. subj. dufe, xii. 129.

dugoþ, f. *army, host.* i. 238.

dum(b), adj. *dumb.* iv. 6; xvii. 26, 33,
85, 99, 136; xviii. 176.—wk. w. def.
art. as noun, *the dumb (person).* xvii.
45 (dp. -an), 83 (asm. -an), 186
(MS. not fully legible). [Spelled
with b except at xvii. 26 and 33.]

*dumbnyss, f. *dumbness.* iv. 61.
[Unique in this passage. Cited by
Napier. OED's first quotation
dated 1380.]

dūn, f. *hill, mountain.* i. 431; xvii. 226,
235; xviii. 238, 308; xx. 204.

[durran], pret. pres. vb. *to dare, presume.* pres. 2s. dearst, xxvi. 68; 1p.
durran, vi. 367; xviii. 186; 1s.
subj. durre, xxvi, 112; pret. 2s.
dorstest, xxiii. 186; 3s. dorste,
xii. 50, 65; xxi. 39, 48; 3p. dorston,
iii. 128; xvii. 256 (elliptical w. prep.
intō, *dared go into*); xix. 226; 3s.
subj. dorste, xi. 143.

duru, f. *door.* as. duru, xv. 183, 184,
187; xxi. 394, 405, 412, 414, 425;
xxiii. 80, 116; ds. dura, xxi. 231.

dūst, n. *dust.* ii. 108; xi. 334, 335; xx.
67.

dwelian, II. *to err.* i. 151; iv. 276;
xxi. 374.

gedwimor, gedymor, n. (a) *(magical)
illusion.* xxix. 33. (b) *delusive magic.*
xxix. 119. (c) *falsehood, delusive lie.*
xxi. 589.

gedwimorlīce, adv. *illusorily.* xxix.
14 (-dwymor-).

gedwola, wk. m. *heretic.* i. 154, 410,
413; ix. 170; x. 159, 163, 170, 172;
xviii. 295; xxvi. 26; xxix. 85.

dwollīce, adv. *heretically, in error, in
folly.* xvii. 253; xviii. 11. [Cf. dollīce.]

gedwolmann, m. *heretic.* i. 151; iv.
276; vi. 221.

gedwyld, n. *error, heresy.* v. 121,
231; ix. 16, 171, 199; x. 163, 172;
xii. 153; xiii. 132; xiv. 131; xv. 168;
xviii. 295; xx. 67; xxi. 123, 141,
160, 564, 592, 658; xxvi. 26; xxix. 85.

gedwymor-, see gedwimor-.

dyd-, gedyd-, see dōn.

dydrung, f. *delusion* practised by
sorcerers. xxix. 5, 8, 9, 14, 30, 35.

dynt, m. *blow;* or the **impression* of
a blow? xix. 194. [Cf. BTS, 'dynt',
I, II.]

dȳpe, wk. f. *the deep (sea).* xiv. 17, 109.

dȳre, adj. *dear, beloved.* xxi. 224, 306.
—sup., dȳrost, xxi. 497. [Cf.dēor-
wurþe.]

dȳrling, m. *(dearly) loved one.* ii. 5.

dyrne, adj. *secret, hidden.* ii. 102; xiii.
179; xvii. 33, (136); xxi. 604; xxix.
101.

*dyrne-ceorl, m. *secret lover.* xix. 38.
[Not in dict. See note.]

dyrstelīce, adv. *boldly, with temerity.*
xxiii. 186.

dyrstig, adj. *presumptuous.* iii. 128;
xii. 51; xv. 168; xx. 77, 80, 246;
xxvi. 111.

dyrstignyss, f. (a) *effrontery, presumption.* vii. 96; xiii. 89; xvii. 93;
xx. 250, 258; xxvi. 68. (b) *presumptuous deed.* xxvi. 52.

gedyrstlǣcan, I. *to presume.* vi. 295;
xviii. 186. [Cf. -lǣcan.]

dyselīce, see dyslīce.

dysig, adj. *foolish.* only as noun,
various spellings: i. 413 (se dy-
sega); xiii. 131 (þam dysigan);
xxi. 653 (þa dysgan, v.l. dysegan).

dysig, n. *foolishness.* xii. 153; xix. 22.

dyslic, adj. *foolish, stupid.* xx. 211.

dyslīce, adv. *foolishly.* vi. 221 (dyse-),
295; xix. 141, 210.

E

ēa, f. *river.* ds., viii. 107; xi. 16; xia.
90; xiv. 45.

ēac, adv. *also.* i. 19, etc. (13 times); ii.
60, etc. (7 times); iii. 13, 74, 95, 96,
105; iv. 15, etc. (6 times); v. 289;
vi. 41, 84, 125; vii. 69, 127, 142,
150; etc.—spelled æc at i. 324.—
ne ēac, *nor . . . either,* vi. 341; x.
56; xia. 34.—ēac swā, *also,* xxiv. 4.
—ēac swilce, ēac swylce, *likewise,* i. 399; iv. 131, 145, 241, 296;
viii. 299; ix. 161; etc.

ēacnian, II, intrans. *to be pregnant.*
pres. part., dp. as noun, þam
eacniendum, *to the pregnant,* xviii.
244, 318.

ġe-ēacnian, II, trans. *to make greater,
increase.* xiii. 107; xviii. 325 (?),
xxiv. 2.

ēadiġ, adj. *blessed.* ii. 173; iv. 52, 271,
279, 289, 291, 293; xiv. 165; xvi.
169; xvii. 163; xix. 231.—comp.,
np., ēadiġran, iv. 54, 287.

ġe-ēadmēttan, I. *to humble.* xxvi. 2
(pp. ġeēadmēt, -mētt).

ēadmōd, adj. *humble.* vi. 353; xxx.
11.—wk. w. def. art. as noun, v.
182.—comp. np. ēadmōdran, ii.
283.

ēadmōdlīce, adv. *humbly.* xiv. 31,
197.

ēadmōdnyss, f. *humility.* v. 179, 180;
xii. 170; xxvi. 106, 129, 136, 139;
xxx. 13.

ēage, wk. n. *eye.* i. 13, 324; vi. 92; xiii.
25, etc. (14 times, ds. ēagan, for
which MS. H usually has strong
ēaġe); xv. 115; xxi. 207; xxiii. 26
xxvi. 63. [Cf. ēhsȳnes.]

eahta, num. *eight.* ii. 29, 139; xviii.
15; xix. 127; xxvi. 81.

eahtēoþa, wk. adj. *eighth.* iv. 251
(nsf. eahtēoþe, v.l. eahtoþe).

ēalā, interj. *O, lo.* (a) as a vocative,
preceding þū, ġē, Hǣlend, *O thou,*
etc. i. 102; xi. 419, 445; xiv. 19,
115; xvi. 211; xvii. 210, 229; xxi. 6,
479, 488; xxiii. 85, 137, 187; xxvi.
48. (b) as an exclamation expressing
wonder, preceding hū mycel, *O,
how great.* xix. 230. (c) asseverative,
O yes, behold, indeed. xvii. 292.

eald, adj. *old.* (a) applied to a man,
advanced in years. xi. 26; xia. 100;
xii. 11, 75; xxi. 422; as an epithet
of Saturn, *the old one,* xxi. 178.
(b) applied to institutions or beings
still in existence but dating far back
into the past, or without beginning,
*long in existence, long-established,
ancient, primeval.* ii. 226 (applied to
the divine ordinance by which the
world was created); vii. 125; xi.
103; xxi. 79 (these three applied to
the devil, as having lived from the
beginning); xxi. 15 (eall swā eald
swā, *just as ancient as,* said of the
Son as coeternal with the Father).
(c) of impermanent things or institutions, *dating from a former age,
ancient.* vii. 200 (books); xxi. 564
(a heretical religion). (d) in expressed or implied contrast to nīwe,
earlier, former. xvi. 235 (a snake's
skin); applied esp. to the law of
Moses, the Old Testament, the
customs and observances of the
Jews, ii. 14, 256; iii. 87; iv. 148;
vii. 68; ix. 165; xv. 27, 63; xx. 245;
xxx. 75; to pre-Christian days,
xviii. 281; ancient days, xxi. 525;
and to men of a former age, xx.
163; xxi. 148; xxii. 2; esp. to men
in general or the Jewish people
before the Christian era, i. 464;
iv. 149; xv. 10, 61, 126. [For comp.
and sup. see yld-.]

ealdian, II. *to grow old.* xxi. 64 (said
of the moon, as waxing and waning.)
[Cf. forealdian.]

ealdlic, adj. *old(-seeming)* in a specified aspect. xxiii. 7 (ald-).

ealdor, m. (a) *prince,* Lat. *princeps.*
vii. 23, 172, 173; x. 25, 188, 191;
xii. 2, 53. (b) *head* of a household
(hiredes ealdor, Lat. *pater familias*). iii. 4, 51, 115, 133. (c) *author,
originator,* Lat. *auctor.* xi. 464.
(d) *a (spiritual) superior.* xx. 291;
xxx. 17.

ealdordōm, m. *sovereignty, authority.*
vii. 175; xviii. 166.

ealdormann, m. (a) *prince, nobleman*
of the highest rank, *great lord.* ix.
137; xxii. 7, 10. (b) *ruler* of the
synagogue (*archisynagogus*). vi. 176.

ealdorscype, m. *position of authority.*
xx. 293.

eall, adj. and sb. *all.* i. 16, etc. (15
times); ii. 132, etc. (16 times); iii.
48, 60, 154, 159, 160; etc.—pl. as
noun, *all men,* i. 40, 305; xi. 392,
400; xiii. 46, 81; xvii. 8; xx. 99;
perhaps elliptically, *all (ye),* v. 157;
(us) all, vi. 370; w. preceding gen.,
all (of), iv. 278.—neut. sg. as noun,
all, xiii. 116; and w. gen., *all of,*
xvii. 5; pl. ealle, *all things* (?), xxi.

632 (v.l. **eal**, *everything*).—spelled **alle**, xxiii. 140; np. **ealla** for regular **ealle**, xxiii. 201. [See also **mid ealle** under **mid**, **ealle þing** under **þing**.]

eall, adv. *fully, entirely, all*; before **swā**, *just*. i. 45, 54, 223, 456; ii. 154; xi. 300, 487, 513; xiii. 9, 38; xvi. 132, 249; xviii. 24, 75, 85, 370; xx. 67; xxi. 14, 16; xxiii. 115 (**all**); xxv(*b*). 1, 2; xxvii. 114, [See also the loose compounds below, with **eall**, adv., plus adj.]

ealles, adv. *altogether, in all, entirely*. ii. 246; xii. 45; xvii. 142, 175; xxiii. 39.

eall-gōd, adj. *entirely good, infinitely good*, characterizing God in contrast to man. xvii. 104. [BTS cites a closely parallel instance from Ælfric, now in O.E. Hept., ed. Crawford, p. 18/65, where the expression is printed as two words. BTS notes the later parallels in OED under 'all-good'.]

eall-hwīt, adj. *entirely of white, all-white*. xxiii. 172. [BT cites a charter, BTS a gloss.]

eall-nīwe, adj. *entirely new*. xi. 510 (twice); xiv. 101; xvi. 236. [Ælfric cited twice in BT and BTS.]

eallswā, ealswā, adv. *also, likewise*. xvi. 274; xvii. 278; xxx. 69. [Cf. **eall**, adv., w. **swā**.]

*****eall-sweart**, adj. *all-black, entirely of black*. xxvii. 92. [Not in dict. Cf. **eall-hwīt**.]

eallunga, adv. *entirely, altogether*. xv. 7, 58; xxx. 68.—with negative, *at all*. x. 26, 189.

eallwealdend, m. w. def. art., *the Omnipotent*. viii. 234. as adj. qualifying God, *omnipotent, all-ruling*. vi. 258; viii. 245. [Cf. **þrymwealdend**.]

eallwealdende, adj. *all-ruling*. dsm. wk. **eallwealdendan**, xxvii. 11.

ealu, n. *ale*. xx. 26.

eard, m. *land, country, region*. iii. 53, 58; v. 79, 247; xi. 141, 143, 145; xvii. 1, 235, 282, 305; xx. 154, 159, 173, 174, 188, 191, 205, 374; xxi. 43, 241; xxii. 92.

eardian, II. *to dwell, live* (in a specified region). i. 211; x. 90; xviii. 67; xxi. 104.

eardungstōw, f. *dwelling-place*. ix. 518; xvi. 38, 153, 261. [w. ref. to heavenly habitations exclusively, corresponding to *mansiones* and *tabernacula*.]

ēare, n. *ear*. xv. 116; xvii. 30, 35, 36, 120, 151, 154, 168.

earfoþe, adj. *hard, grievous, difficult*. xi. 201, 203; xiv. 105; xx. 159.

earfoþnyss, f. *hardship, difficulty*. v. 175; ix. 148, 211; xi. 158; xia. 73; xix. 64; xxi. 66; xxvii. 65.

earm, m. *arm*. vii. 155.

earm, adj. *poor, miserable, wretched*. i. 195; ii. 90; iv. 60 (asm. wk. **earmann**, v.l. **earman**); xi. 349, 352, 448, 474; xvi. 187; xvii. 297; xviii. 55; xix. 197, 236; xxi. 199, 596; xxvi. 93; xxvii. 98 (?).—wk. w. art. as noun, *the poor man*, ii. 32; pl., *the poor*, xiii. 61; xv. 216.

earming, m. *poor wretch*. ii. 36; xi. 101, 451; xix. 199; xxiii. 187 (**erming**). [The Anglian spelling in xxiii corresponds to the mutated form, LWS 'yrming'.]

earmlīce, adv. *wretchedly, miserably*. x. 166; xix. 158; xxi. 248, 599.

earn, m. *eagle*. i. 12, 14, 15; xviii. 39, 205, 210, 211.

ge-earnian, II. *to earn, merit*. (a) w. acc., i. 203, 219; xi. 53, 219, 231, 367 (**æt Gode**, *from God*); xia. 161, 170; xvi. 199; xvii. 147; xx. 81, 399; xxvii. 6, 10. (b) w. clause, xxi. 66. (c) w. gen., xi. 224, where the genitive may be vaguely partitive: **hē his ne geearnode ǣr**, *he had not merited any of it* (the benefit of intercession). [BTS records only one instance of 'ge-earnian' with genitive, Paris Psalter, vii. 3, where the partitive idea may also be present. The unprefixed verb often takes the genitive.]

*****earnung**, f. *earning* (of recompense by present action). xvi. 106. [This meaning not precisely illustrated in BT or BTS, but cf. BTS, I.]

ge-earnung, f. *desert* (good or bad).

ge-earnung (*cont.*)
xi. 496, 548; xviii. 50; xxvii. 88.

ēastdǣl, m. *eastern quarter, the east.*
xi. 14; xia. 88; xvii. 78; xviii. 9; xxi. 185; xxiii. 127 (ēst-).

Ēasterdæg, m. *Easter Sunday.* xi. 40; xix. 123; xxiii. 41 (Ēastor-).

Ēastre, wk. f. (usually pl. in WS). *Easter.* dp. **Ēastran**, ii. 177; **Ēastron**, viii. 20.

ēaþ, comp. adv. *more easily.* viii. 15; ix. 210; xv. 136; xvi. 86.

ēaþe, adj. *easy.* xv. 99 (comp., nsn. **ēaþre**).

ēaþe, adv. *easily.* i. 240; vi. 127; vii. 53, 191; xiii. 65; xv. 50; xviii. 42, 317; xix. 109, 146; xx. 24.

ēaþelic, adj. *slight, insignificant.* xiii. 182.

ēaþelīce, adv. *easily.* ii. 135; vii. 36; xi. 101, 487; xia. 113; xvii. 224; xx. 13, 176; xxi. 438, 574.

ēawbryce, adj. *adultery.* xvi. 73. ['ēaw-' = 'ǣ(w)-'. Cf. ǣ.]

ēawfæst, adj. *pious, devout.* xix. 121. ['ēaw-' = 'ǣ(w)-'. Cf. ǣ.]

ēawunga, adv. *openly, publicly.* xxx. 69.

Ebreisc, adj. *Hebrew.* on Ebreisc, *in* (*the*) *Hebrew* (*language*), v. 208.

ecclesia, Lat., introduced for definition, xiv. 88.

ēce, adj. *eternal.* i. 220; ii. 113, 174, 183; iii. 154, 178, 185, 187; v. 30, 82, 141, 149, 250, 264; vi. 150, 317, 372; vii. 126, 134; etc.

ēcelīce, adv. *eternally.* vi. 157; xi. 475; xxiii. 59.

ecg, f. *edge.* xx. 213.

ēcnyss, f. *eternity.* on ēcnysse, *for ever,* i. 470; ii. 290; iv. 172, 298; v. 27, 138, 149; vi. 61, 359; etc. [Cf. ā.]

ge-edcennan, I. *to regenerate.* pp. **geedcenned**, *born again,* xii. 13, 14, 77, 96. [Cf. cennan.]

ge-edlǣcan, I, pp. -lǣht. *to repeat, renew.* xii. 80, 84; xvi. 84; xvii. 47, 268, 270, 274. [Cf. -lǣcan.]

edlēan, n. *reward, retribution.* ii. 172; xia. 169; xiii. 17, 112; xvi. 106; xxiv. 11.

ednīwe, adj. *renewed, new.* ii. 227;

xx. 14, 106 (less probably, in view of 14, adv., *anew, freshly*). [See BTS for doubtful status of adv. and for other examples of Ælfric's sometimes ambiguous usage.]

ge-ednīwian, II. *to renew.* ii. 222, 235; xi. 135, 513; xviii. 82.

Edom, the land skirted by the Israelites in their journey (Num. xxi. 4). xx. 306.

edwist, f. *substance.* i. 460.

Efa, Eua, *Eve.* iv. 194; xia. 48, 148; xxi. 29 (all as. -an).

ge-efenlǣcan, I. *to make like, match.* xviii. 126 (pp. np. -lǣhte). [Cf. -lǣcan.)

effeta, Aramaic *ephphatha* 'be opened' (Mark vii. 34). xvii. 34, 137, 149, 155.

efne, adv. and interj. (a) with adv. of time, *even, just*: efne þā, *just then,* xxvii. 49; and with some exclamatory force, xvii. 205 (Lat. *ecce*); xix. 173 (Lat. *tum subito*); efne þā þā, *just as,* xvii. 221 (Lat. *statim*). (b) *lo, behold* (Lat. *ecce*). ii. 55; iii. 78; v. 79; viii. 45, 237; xviii. 7; xxi. 486.

efstan, I, pret. 3s. efste. *to hasten.* v. 215, 218; xi. 139 (æf-), 157; xiv. 6; xxi. 620.

ge-efstan, I. *to hasten.* xviii. 29.

eft, adv. *afterwards, again.* i. 11, 67, 77, 98, 189, 434, 441; ii. 53, 104, 109, 158, 181; iii. 9, 15, 122; iv. 125, 127, 257, 263; etc.

ege, m. *awe, fear, dread.* viii. 133; ix. 143; xiii. 96; xiv. 31, 197; xxi. 208; xxvi. 3; xxvii. 13.

egefull, adj. *awe-inspiring.* xxi. 103.

egeslic, adj. *terrifying, terrible, awesome.* xi. 169, 204, 349; xv. 71; xvii. 128; xviii. 77, 371; xix. 191; xx. 30, 317; xxi. 536; xxvii. 31.

egeslīce, adv. *terribly, dreadfully.* xi. 328; xx. 194, 358.

Egipte, Egypte, pl. *Egyptians.* only in gp. with **land**, i. 259; iii. 58 (MS. **Egiptan**); iv. 140; xx. 86, 108, 167, 310; xxi. 521.

Egiptisc, Egyptisc, adj. *Egyptian.* i. 229; xxi. 522, 538.

eglian, II. *to ail, trouble.* viii. 166.

ēhsȳnes, adv. *visibly.* x. 174 (v.l.

eah-). [BTS, 'eagsynes', cites two examples from Ælfric. Cf. ēage.]

ēhtan, I, pret. 3s. ēhte, w. gen. *to persecute.* xxv(c). 3, 5, 6 (twice).

ēhtere, m. *persecutor.* ix. 179; xviii. 184.

ēhtnyss, f. *persecution.* ix. 197; xi. 159 (v.l. hæftnyssum); xiii. 138; xviii. 89, 306, 347, 403; xix. 231.

elcung, f. *delay.* xxx. 92.

ele, m. *oil.* xvi. 23, 130, 132, 135; xx. 379; xxix. 32.

elebēam, m. *olive-tree.* xvi. 133.

elles, originally gsn. of an adj. *other* used absolutely, appearing historically in various idiomatic constructions (see OED, 'else'). (a) used adjectivally, *of another sort, different.* viii. 193 (perhaps an elliptical use: cf. OED, 'else', 1. c.). (b) used adverbially, *differently, in another manner,* xix. 106; *for another reason,* xxi. 270. (c) conj. adv., *or else, otherwise.* xxi. 456 (Lat. *alioquin*).

emb-, embe(-), see ymb-, ymbe(-).

emlīce, adv. *equally, alike.* xviii. 113.

Enach, Anak, progenitor of giants feared by the Israelites (Num. xiii. 34). xx. 163 (gs. Enaches).

ende, m. *end, conclusion.* v. 271; vi. 271, 372; viii. 225; x. 204; xia. 200; xii. 185, 208; xiii. 53 (ænde), 81, 234; xviii. 138, 223, 289, 391; xix. 241, 242; xx. 60, 426; xxv(a). 20; xxvii. 106.—ā būtan ende, *for ever.* i. 166; iv. 115; xi. 574; xviii. 439; xxx. 114.

ge-endebyrdan, I. *to put in order, place.* xi. 548 (pp. np. geendebyrde).

endebyrdnyss, f. (a) *order:* be endebyrdnysse, *in order.* xiii. 86; xvii. 49. (b) *sequence of events.* xi. 459. (c) *class.* xviii. 200.

endelēas, adj. *endless.* vi. 158, 227, 317; xxi. 71, 496.

endelēaslīce, adv. *endlessly.* vi. 313.

endemes, -ys, adv. (a) combined with eall: *all without exception,* vii. 83; x. 91, 115; *all in a body,* xvii. 238; *all with one accord,* xx. 75; *all in procession, one after another,* xiii.

219. (b) alone: *in a body, one and all,* xx. 96, 204; *with one accord, all alike,* xviii. 231, 275; xx. 233.

endenēxt, -nȳhst, adj. *last, final.* vi. 57; xviii. 46, 100, 344; xix. 207; xx. 398 ('last men', men of the sixth and last age of this world); xxi. 180 (-nexþ).

ge-endian, II. (a) trans., *to bring to an end.* vi. 156, 314; xvi. 285; xix. 47. (b) intrans., *to end, make an end, die.* i. 455; iv. 254; viii. 180; xi. 193, 382, 568; xviii. 134; xix. 135, 250; xx. 365, 367; xxvii. 89 [Cf. unge-endod.]

ge-endung, f. *ending, conclusion.* v. 268; vi. 130; xi. 278; xii. 115, 226; xvii. 278; xviii. 49, 231, 275; xx. 303; xxi. 668.

engel, m. *angel.* i. 89, 186, 192, 201; ii. 18–125 (8 times); iii. 82; v. 271; viii. 60, 178; x. 90; etc.

engellic, adj. *angelic, of angels.* xxix. 100.

Engle, pl. *the English.* xiv. 98 (on Engla þēode, *in the English nation*).

Englisc, adj. *English.* i. 28, 179; xiv. 90, 132; xv. 224; xviii. 331; xx. 424. —on Englisc, *in (the) English (language).* iv. 177; v. 209; viii. 50; x. 85; xi. 113; xia. 95; xv. 94; xvii. 34, 46, 137; xviii. 151, 428; xx. 335; xxii. 58; xxv(c). 5, 14; xxx. 83.

ent, m. *giant.* xx. 162, 163; xxi. 74, 101; xxii. 40, 43.

ēode, ēodon, see gān.

eornost, n. *seriousness.* only in phrase, on eornost, *seriously, in earnest.* viii. 91; xvi. 268; xxii. 97; xxiii. 166.

eornostlīce, adv. (a) *therefore* (Lat. *ergo*). vi. 107; ix. 100; xiii. 9, 38; xviii. 259(?), 382(?). (b) *truly, indeed* (Lat. *autem*). xviii. 246, 326.

ēorod, n. or f. *(troop), legion.* xvii. 233, 249.

eorþe, f. *(the) earth.* i. 72, etc. (8 times); v. 197; vii. 54; xi. 61, 237, 263, 510, 516, 527; xia. 45, 178; xii. 192; xiii. 213, 217; xviii. 81, 269, 305, 417; xix. 35; xx. 249; xxi. 89, 368, 407, 528, 541, 549; xxx. 38.

eorþland, n. *arable land.* viii. 127

eorþland, (*cont.*)
(v.l. **yrþ-**), in contrast to fishing
grounds. [BT and BTS, 'irþland';
Hall, 'yrþ-'. Unmutated 'eorþ-' is
recorded but rare.]
eorþlic, adj. *earthly.* viii. 83; xia. 228;
xii. 32, 186, 189, 192; xiii. 46; xv.
113; xvi. 269; xvii. 142; xix. 9; xx.
378, 389; xxi. 30; xxvii. 113; xxx.
41.
***eorþteolung,** f. *agriculture.* xviii.
152(MS. P, probably non-Ælfrician
—see **tilung** and note). [Unique;
BT, BTS have 'eorþtilþ'.]
ēow, see **þū.**
ēower, poss. adj. *your.* ii. 4, 200; iii.
35, 101; iv. 26, 119, 125; vii. 39, 48;
etc. [For the pronoun see **þū.**]
erian, II (orig. I). *to plough.* viii. 130;
xvi. 117; xviii. 35, 141.
Ermen, see **Hermes.**
erming, see **earming.**
ēstdǣl, see **ēastdǣl.**
ēstfull, adj. (*full of grace*), *devout.* ix.
123.
ēstmete, m. (pl. **-mett-**). *dainty*
(*food*), *delicacy.* xvi. 136; xx. 87, 135.
etan, 5. *to eat.* inf., v. 17; xx. 312;
xxv(c). 8; d. inf. **etenne,** v. 72;
etanne, v. 227; pres. part. **etende,**
vii. 193 (uninfl. asm.); imp. s. **ett,**
v. 71, 226; pres. 3s. **et,** xvi. 135;
ytt, xxi. 384; 1p. **etaþ,** xvi. 135;
pret. 3s. **æt,** v. 228, 236, 237; vii.
136, 150; xx. 19; xxi. 377 (MS. R
yt), 481 (MS. R e(a)t?); pl. **æton,**
ix. 161; xviii. 11, 18; xx. 99; xxi.
408; 3s. subj. **ǣte,** v. 231, 234; 3p.
subj. **ǣton,** xi. 333.
ge-etan, 5. *to eat, consume.* pres. 3s.
ge-et, xiii. 232; **ge-ytt,** xxi. 398.
ēþel, m. or n. *country, native land.*
xvii. 282.
Eua, see **Efa.**
Euentius, a priest martyred with
Pope Alexander I. xxiii. 4, 127 (as.
-um).
***eunuchi,** mp. *eunuchs.* xix. 43,44,45.
[Lat. form from Vulgate; OED and
MED date English forms after 1400.]
exl, f. *shoulder.* vii. 155.
Exodus, the Biblical book. xxii. 88.
Ezechiel, the prophet. i. 11.

F

fācenfull, adj. *deceitful, fraudulent.*
xxi. 134.
fācn, n. *deceit, fraud.* xvi. 155, 201;
xxi. 416.
gefadian, II. *to arrange, dispose.* ii.
161; ix. 38; xxi. 526.
fæc, n. *space of time, while.* xxvi. 43.
fæder, m. (uninflected in sing.) *father,*
i. 65, etc. (11 times); ii. 233 (twice),
290; iii. 130, 178; iv. 155, 165, 169;
etc. (usually God the Father;
occasionally human fathers, e.g. ii.
233; v. 23; Adam, xi. 95; a religious
elder, xxix. 11; np. **fæderas,** v. 40;
þā hālgan fæderas [Biblical and
ecclesiastical?], xi. 82).
fæger, adj. (a) *beautiful.* viii. 53 (fig.);
xi. 248; xiv. 41; xvi. 138; xxi. 198.
(b) of words, *fair, pleasing, cheerful.*
x. 131. (c) of spiritual attainments,
fair, resplendent. xviii. 144.
fægere, adv. (a) *with decorum, properly.* ix. 38. (b) *graciously.* xiv. 217.
fægernyss, f. *beauty.* xia. 20.
fægnian, II. w. gen., *to exult, rejoice*
in. xx. 44; xxi. 333.
fær, n. (a) *journey.* x. 133; (b) *course of*
life, proceedings. i. 469; ix. 137.
færeld, n. or m. (a) *journey.* xx. 354,
365; (b) *course of life, progress.* xi.
84.
fǣringa, adv. *suddenly, unexpectedly.*
ix. 212; xxvii. 118.
fǣrlic, adj. *sudden, unexpected.* ix. 212;
xv. 135; xviii. 8; xx. 270; xxi. 87,
237, 247.
fǣrlīce, adv. *suddenly, unexpectedly.*
x. 174; xi. 334, 512; xvii. 205; xviii.
8, 14, 20, 76, 262, 401; xix. 144,
171, 173; xx. 255; xxi. 38, 467, 613;
xxiii. 138.
fæst, adj. *fast, firmly fixed, secure,*
constant. ii. 13; iv. 34, 183 (both
asf. **fæste,** or adv.); xix. 243; xxii.
99 (np. **fæste**).
fæstan, I, pret. 3s. **fæste.** *to fast.* ii.
152, 154, 158, 177; xi. 30; xia. 130;
xxx. 69.
fæste, adv. *fast, firmly, securely.* iv. 34,
183 (or both may be asf. of **fæst**);
xxiii. 115.

fæsten, n. *fast* (act or period of fasting)
i. 23, 24; ii. 156, 165, 167 (fig.), 177;
xxx. 69, 70.

fæstlīce, adv. *resolutely, vigorously.*
xxix. 92. [Cf. BTS, 3.]

gefæstnian, II. *to fasten, fix, make
fast.* i. 82; vii. 141; xi. 35; xiₐ. 138;
xxi. 533. [Cf. afæstnian.]

fæt, n. *vessel: drinking-vessel,* v. 124,
126 (dp. fatum); any household
vessel, utensil, xviii. 30 (gp. fata).

fætels, m. *container, receptacle.* xxi.
260.

fǣt(t), adj. *fat, unctuous.* xvi. 138 (referring to the consistency of oil).

fæþm, m. *fathom.* xxi. 532.

fandian, II. (a) w. gen., *to tempt.* iv.
91, 96; xiii. 206; xx. 103. (b) *to
investigate, search* (intr.). xxiii. 125.
[Cf. afandian.]

fandung, f. *trial, test.* ii. 284; xx. 31.

fant, m. *(baptismal) font.* xii. 132.

faran, 6. (a) *to fare, go.* ii. 8, 106; iii.
99, 100, 108; iv. 42, 44, 213, 235; etc.
(b) *to take one's way in life, be, behave.* ii. 79, 149; xxi. 625. (c) faran
be, *to go by, act in accordance with.*
ix. 47; xxii. 33. [Present stem only
is represented: inf., ii. 8, etc. (20
times); d. inf. farenne, xxi. 617;
part. farende, ii. 79; xvii. 22; xx.
364; xxvi. 44; imp. sg. far, viii. 93;
xv. 22 (fær), 194; xvii. 245; imp.
pl. faraþ, ix. 100; fare ge, xx. 207;
pres. 1s. fare, vii. 9, etc. (7 times);
viii. 43, 220; x. 18, 20, 136, 140;
pres. 3s. færþ, ii. 106, 149; iii. 108;
iv. 42, 213; vi. 316, 344; xi. 519;
xxi. 625; xxix. 104; pres. pl. faraþ,
iii. 99; xi. 209, 453; xii. 113, 209;
xviii. 304, 389, 428; xxi. 184; xxix.
118; pres. 1s. subj. fare, vii. 10,
13, 46; xxiii. 89; 3s. fare, viii. 97;
ix. 47; xii. 22, 148; xxiii. 153.—
preterite replaced by that of fēran,
q.v. See also for-, forþ-, misfaran and for-, forþ-, to-fēran.]

Farao, see Pharao.

faru, f. (a) *journey.* xx. 70; xxi. 609.
(b) *course of life, progress.* ix. 155.
(c) the *troops* of a general on the
march. xxiii. 49. *(d) *equipment* or
freight of a vehicle on a journey. xxi.

274 [Meaning (d) not in dict. but
see BTS, III, 4 and IV. Also OED,
'fare', sb.¹, esp. 1c and 5b.]

fata, fatum, see fæt.

feala, see fela.

feallan, 7. *to fall.* inf., xxi. 339; pres.
3s. fylþ, ii. 272; iii. 38, 152, 153;
fealþ, iv. 20, 100; 3p. feallaþ, xiii.
21, 125; xviii. 262, 401; pres. 3s.
subj. fealle, iii. 150, 151; 2p. subj.
feallon, xx. 209; pret. 3s. fēoll
vi. 75; xiv. 30, 196 (fēol); xvii. 228;
xxi. 308, 549, 634; xxiii. 36, 118;
xxix. 75, 94; 3p. fēollon, xvii. 255;
xx. 102, 198; pret. 3s. subj. fēolle,
xxi. 50. [Cf. a-, be-, of-feallan.]

gefearhsugu, f. *sow in farrow.* xviii.
323. [BT, BTS cite two glosses
only.]

fearr, m. *bull.* i. 269. [BT and Hall
give *ox* also but without supporting
evidence. *Bull* is likelier here.]

fēawa, pron. adj. *few, a few.* (a) as
adj., nap. fēawa, xix. 170, 171; dp.
fēawum, vi. 22; xiₐ. 124; xxi. 100;
xxiii. 62; xxvi. 16. (b) as pron., np.
fēawa, vi. 144; xi. 119; ns. fēawa
w. part. gen., xviii. 172.

feax, fex, n. *hair (of the head).* vi. 7,
308; xxi. 297, 473.

feccan, gefeccan ('fetian'), I, pret.
fette. *to fetch, obtain, bring.* i. 388;
v. 12; x. 137, 202; xxiii. 129.

fēdan, I. *to feed* (trans.) xi. 420; xviii.
245, 319 (pres. part, as noun, fēden-
dum, Lat. *nutrientibus*), 321; xix. 3
(pres. 3s. fēt), 4 (pres. 2s. fētst);
xxi. 356; xxv(b). 3. [Cf. afēdan.]

gefēgan, I. *to join, unite.* iii. 144.

fēhst, see fōn.

fela, feala, indecl. pron. and adj. *many,
much.* i. 47, 145, 350; ii. 25, 246;
iv. 30, 123; vi. 202; vii. 24, 80, 93,
187, 189; viii. 23; etc.—usually
treated as pron. w. part. gen. but
alone as a pl., *many (people),* i. 47,
350 (both swā fela swā, *as many
as, all those who*); ii. 246.—occasionally as adj., e.g., vii. 24, 187,
189; viii. 23; x. 24, 185; where
MSS. vary between fela þinga and
fela þing.—construed as a singular
in ēower fela nāt, *many of you know*

fela (*cont.*)
not, xviii. 63.—spelled **feala** at xx. 38, 87, 103, etc.

feld, m. *field, open land.* only as ds. **felda**. viii. 129; xx. 149, 378.

fell, n. *skin.* xvi. 236.

(ge)fēnge, (ge)fēngon, see **fōn.**

fenlic, adj. *of the fen, miry.* xvii. 261.

feoh, n. (*material*) *goods, wealth, money.* xvi. 20 (ds. **fēo**), 127, 263, 265, 266, 269; xxiv. 2, 5, 8, 10 (gs. **fēos**).

gefeoht, n. *fight, battle.* viii. 124; ix. 209, 213; xxi. 129, 132 (twice); xxii. 39, 40, 48, 75.

feohtan, gefeohtan, 3. (a) *to fight.* inf. **feohtan**, xxix. 43; pret. 3s. **feaht**, xxii. 64; **gefeaht**, xxii. 19; pret. 3p. **fuhton**, xxi. 211; **fuhtan**, xxix. 92. (b) trans., *to win.* pret. 3p. **fuhton**, xxi. 215 (v.l. **gefuhton**, the normal form in this meaning). [Cf. **onfeohtan**.]

*****feohte-god**, m. *war-god.* xxi. 171. [Not in dict., though Unger rightly printed it as one word in his text of MS. W.]

fēol(l), fēolle, fēollon, see **feallan.**

fēond, m. *enemy, devil.* xi. 167, 168; xv. 82 (ap. **fȳnd**), 86; xx. 116, 209, 380; xxi. 284; xxii. 10, 20 (as. **fȳnd** for **fēond**; see note).

fēondlic, adj. *devilish, fiendish.* xi. 173; xviii. 290, 389; xxi. 590; xxii. 31.

feorh, m. or n. *life.* xxii. 48.

feorr, adv. *far.* iii. 108; viii. 93.

feorran, adv. (a) *from afar.* xx. 95. (b) *far away*, xvii. 141 (conjectured reading).

fēorþa, wk. adj. *fourth.* vi. superscription (MS. H), 43; viii. 81; ix. 129; xi. 384; xxi. 172.

fēorþling, m. (*fourth part*), *farthing.* xvi. 187.

fēower, num. *four.* ii. 161; v. 78; vi. 88; xi. 36, 360; xia. 123, 138; xviii. 268 (feowor), 416; xix. 125, 126.

fēowerfeald, adj. *fourfold.* only in phrase, **be fēowerfealdum**, *quadruply.* xvi. 178.

fēowertēogoþa, wk. adj. *fortieth.* xi. 20, 46; xia. 94, 153 (-teogeþ-).

fēowertig, num. *forty.* (a) as sb., without ending, acc. of extent of time w. part. gen. **daga, gēara, wintra**. ii. 152, 159; vii. 139; xi. 30; xia. 130; xx. 5, 42, 354, 364.—dp. after prep., **tō þam twām lǣs fēowertigum**, *to the two-less-than-forty.* ii. 146. (b) as adj., dp. **-um**, xxi. 356. [Ælfric's Grammar has 'duodeviginti twam læs twentig,' ed. Zupitza, p. 287, showing that the dative in ii. 146 is not due to 'læs'.]

fēowertig-getel, n. *the number of forty.* ii. 148 (v.l. -**getæl**).

fēowertȳne, num. *fourteen.* xx. 270.

gefēra, wk. m. *companion.* vi. 40; vii. 34; ix. 20; xiv. 25, 33, 177, 207; xvi. 250; xviii. 388; xx. 189, 231.

fēran, I (only in pret., replacing strong pret. of **faran**, q.v.). (a) *to fare, go.* **fērde**, pret. 1s., viii. 41, 42, 214, 219; pret. 3s., i. 388; iii. 8, 92, 106; iv. 45, 236, 262; vi. 42, 331; etc. (12 times more); pret. 3s. subj., vi. 335; **fērdon**, pret. 2p., v. 87, 255; pret. 3p., iii. 173; xi. 63; xia. 180; etc. (7 more); pret. 3p. subj., xxiii. 175.—(b) *to take one's way in life, behave.* pret. 3p. **fērdon**, xviii. 102. [Cf. **ge-, for-, forþ-, to-fēran**, all in pret. only.]

gefēran, I. *to attain, gain.* xxii. 27 (pret. 3s. **sige gefērde**). [The same phrase used by Ælfric in LS, xxv. 730, but at 721 is an exceptional 'sige gefor'.]

ferian, II (orig. I), pp. **geferod, -ed.** *to carry, convey, transport.* vi. 178, 183, 189; xii. 101; xxi. 221, 245, 262, 482; xxvii. 79. [Cf. **toferian**.]

fers, n. or m. *verse, sentence.* i. 84.

fersc, adj. *not salt, fresh.* xiv. 44.

fēt, see **fōt.**

fēt, fētst, see **fēdan.**

fette, gefette, see **feccan, gefeccan.**

feþerfēte, adj. *four-footed.* ii. 236.

fex, see **feax.**

ficsian, fixian, II. *to fish.* xiv. 8, 61, 148. [Cf. **fisc**, etc., below.]

ficsnoþ, see **fiscnoþ.**

fīf, num. *five.* ii. 13, 63, 66; iii. 56; v.

37; xi*a*. 119, 121; xviii. 21, 23, 70; xxi. 184, 243–73 (8 times).

fīfta, wk. adj. *fifth*. xxi. 174; xxiii. 6.

fīftēne, num. *fifteen*. vi. 45.

fīftig, num. *fifty*. ii. 178; xvi. 24, 131; xxiii. 40 (**fīfti**).—used as sb. with part. gen. or alone, acc. or nom. without ending. [Cf. fēowertiġ.]

findan, 3. *to find*. inf., ix. 34; xxii. 69; pres. 3s. fint, iv. 43, 214, 234; pret. 3s. funde, x. 194; xxi. 565; xxvii. 49; pret. 3p. fundon, xxi. 161, 226; xxvi. 105. [Cf. afindan.]

finger, m. *finger*. i. 264, 266; iv. 32, 133–60 (8 times); xiii. 212; xvii. 30, 120, 121, 153; xxi. 220.

fisc, fix, m. *fish*. i. 210 (?); ii. 236; xi*a*. 121, 124; xiv. 23, 28, 38, 126, 149, 160, 189, 216, 223; xx. 87. [Cf. ficsian above.]

fiscere, m. *fisherman, fisher*. xiv. 8, 10, 66, 72, 75, 228.

fiscnoþ, ficsnoþ, fixnoþ, m. (a) *fishing-ground, fishery*. viii. 120, 124, 128, 130; xiv. 3, 41, 66. (b) *fishing, catching of fish*. xiv. 18, 47. (c) *catch, draught of fishes*. xiv. 29, 35, 152, 154, 162, 195, 209. [Napier cited these passages, with definitions, as registered in BTS.]

fix, see fisc.

fixian, see ficsian.

flǣsc, n. *flesh, meat*. i. 49, 51, 217, 269, 271, 272, 391, 398 (twice), 403, 404; xi. 9; xi*a*. 78; xii. 16 (twice), 116 (twice); xx. 101, 127; xxi. 107, 369 (Lat. *carnis*, 'fleshly creatures').

flǣsclic, adj. *fleshly*. xii. 137; xx. 123, 297.

flǣscmete, m., pl. -mett-. *flesh* (for food), *animal food*. xx. 84, 85, 92 (-mætt-).

flēa, wk. m. or f. *flea*. i. 227; xxi. 47.

flēam, m. *flight* (of a defeated force). xx. 214 (**on flēame ġebrōhton**, *put to flight*); xxix. 42.

*flēamdōm, m. *the condition of a a fugitive*. mid flēamdōme, *as a fugitive*. xxii. 34. [Unique in this passage. Cited and defined by Napier.]

flēogan, flēon, 2. *to fly*. part. flēogende, xx. 95; xxi. 467; pres. 3p.

flēoþ, i. 270; pret. 3p. flugon, i. 233; xx. 96; xxi. 198. [Cf. flēon below.]

flēoġe, wk. f. *fly, any winged insect*. i. 230; iv. 82, 84 (twice), 85.

flēon, 2. *to flee*. pres. 3p. flēoþ, xviii. 238, 308; pret. 3s. flēag, xx. 254; flēah, xxi. 626; xxii. 34; pret. 3p. flugon, xvii. 240; xx. 267. [Already some confusion with flēogan. Cf. ætflēon.]

flēwþ, see flōwan.

flītan, 1. *to make accusations* (against). inf., xx. 262.

flocc, m. (*flock*), *troop, multitude*. xi. 360; xix. 190.

floccmǣlum, adv. *in flocks, multitudes*. xxi. 553.

flōd, n. (a) *body of water, water*. i. 210; xiv. 48, 61; (b) *stream, river*. v. 145. (c) (Noah's) *flood*. xviii. 10, 14, 61, 63; xxi. 73, 75.

flōr, f. or m. *floor*. ds. flōre, v.l. flōra, xxi. 226, 420, 426; xxvi. 64, 87, 130; as. flōr, xxi. 404 (two MSS. treat as fem., two as masc.), 553 (fem.); as. flōre, xxi. 403 (v.l. flōr, twice fem., once masc.). [Orig. fem. *u*-stem, ds. 'flōra', as. 'flōr'.]

flot, n. *deep water, sea*. on flot, *afloat, at sea*. i. 245 (?)

flōwan, 7. *to flow*. part. flōwende, xx. 26; pres. 3s. flēwþ, xiv. 45; 3p. flōwaþ, v. 145. [Cf. oferflōwan.]

flugon, see flēogan and flēon.

flyht, m. *flying, flight*. xxi. 475.

fōda, wk. m. *food*. xiii. 46.

folc, n. *folk, people, nation*. i. 449; ii. 65, 85, 95, 97, 122; iii. 45, 81, 144, 145, 167; iv. 30, 31, 123, 132, 149, 179, 261, 262, 284; etc.

folgere, m. *a follower*. vii. 8, 165; viii. 44, 236; ix. 4; x. 101; xii. 143; xiv. 228.

folgian, II. (a) w. dat. *to follow* a moving object. xxi. 279. (b) w. dat. *to follow, serve* a person or a doctrine. i. 449; iv. 126; v. 202; vi. 184, 350; x. 101; xi. 49, 123, 354; xi*a*. 155; xii. 204; xiii. 145; xiv. 40, 65 (doctrine), 227, 230 (both doctrine and person); xvi. 185; xxi. 570. (c) w. dat. *to follow* advice. xxx. 6.

folgian (*cont.*)
(d) w. **æfter**, *to follow after* someone who has departed. xii. 208. [Cf. **fylgan** and S–B 417. 2, Anm. 7; Cpb 763, n. 4.]

folgoþ, m. *employment, service.* xvi. 10, 93.

fōn, **gefōn**, 7. (a) trans., *of fish or* birds, fig. *of men, to take, catch.* inf. **gefōn**, xiv. 219; pres. 2s. **fēhst**, xiv. 38, 216; pret. 2s. **fēnge**, xiv. 38, 216; 3s. **gefēng**, xiv. 221, 223; xx. 97; pret. 1p. **gefēngon**, xiv. 21, 117; 3p , xiv. 160; **fēngon**, xiv. 148. (b) **fōn tō**, w. dat. inf., *to take to, begin to.* pret. 3p. **fēngon**, xxi. 100. —w. dat. *to take up,begin to do.* inf., xix. 147;—*to accept.* pret. 3p. **fēngon**, xxi. 271.—*to succeed to a position* or *office.* pret. 3s. **fēng**, vi. 352 (w. **þær** instead of dat.); xxi. 351; xxvi. 16. (c) **fōn tōgædere**, *to join together* (to do something). imp. pl. **fōþ**, xxi. 255. [Cf. **be-**, **for-**, **on-**, **under-fōn**.]

for, prep. *for.* (a) w. dat., *because of, on account of, for the sake of.* i. 116, 206, 223, 266; ii. 127, 212, 219, 280, 282, 284 (twice); iii. 131, 132; iv. 79, 161; v. 90, 94, 95, 127, 177, 264; vi. 13, etc. (9 times); etc. (b) w. dat., *in spite of, in opposition to.* iii. 173. (c) in a temporal sense, w. dat. and **nū**, *before, since, ago*: **nū for fēawum dagum** (**gēarum**), *only a few days* (*years*) *ago.* vi. 22; xxiii. 62. (d) w. acc., *for the sake of, on account of.* viii. 64; x. 133; xxix. 23, 31. (e) w. acc., marking estimate formed, character attributed, *for, as.* iii. 45, 167; xiv. 175; xxi. 82, 88, 128, 154, 209, 434, 663; xxiii. 163; xxix. 86.—**for þam** (**þan, þon**) **þe**, conj. *for, because.* i. 87, etc. (8 times); ii. 72, etc. (7 times); iii. 45, etc. (8 times); etc.—the spelling **þon** occurs chiefly in the late manuscripts; **þæm** at xxi. 15.—**for þam** (**þan, þon**), conj. without **þe** occurs occasionally, e.g. vi. 140, 296 and in MS. F at ii. 120; v. 48, 167, 193.—**for þam . . . þæt**, *in order that.* xxx. 13. [Cf. **forþam**, adv. and **forþi**.]

for, adv. *too, very.* xxi. 511 (**for langsum**). [Cf. **fornēan, foroft, forþearle.**]

foran, adv. *in advance.* vii. 217.

forbærnan, I, trans. *to burn up, consume.* x. 175; xi. 334; xviii. 23, 70; xx. 73, 256, 269; xxi. 559; xxiii. 138; used absolutely, xxiii. 169. [Cf. **forbyrnan.**]

forbēodan, 2. *to forbid.* w. acc. object or clause (absolute at xx. 206); 5 times with dat. of person; inf., xiii. 130; pres. 3s. **forbȳt**, xxiv. 4; 3p. **forbēodaþ**, xiii. 651 prot. 3o. for **bēad**, xia. 117; xiii. 88; xvii. 198; xx. 206; xxvi. 14; pret. 3p. **forbudon**, ix. 182. [Cf. **bēodan.**]

forberan, 4. *to endure, suffer, sustain.* inf., ii. 204; xiii. 139; xxvi. 137; imp. s. **forber**, ii. 196; pres. 3s. **forberþ**, xi. 484 (v.l. **forbyrþ**). [Cf. **beran.**]

forbrēdan ('-bregd-'), 3. *to change for the worse, transform.* pp. **forbrōden**, xxix. 13, 15. [So defined by BTS from this passage as printed by Skeat. Cf. **brēdan.**]

forbūgan, 2. *to refrain from.* inf., ii. 260; xi. 100, 102; pres. 1p. subj. **forbūgon** (?), xvii. 192. [Cf. **būgan.**]

forbyrnan, 3, intrans. *to burn, be consumed by fire, burn up.* inf., xi. 476; pret. 3p. **forburnon**, xx. 257; pp. **forburnen**, xviii. 83. [Cf. **forbærnan** and **byrnan.**]

*****forc**, f. *a pitchfork.* as. **force**, xxvii. 34, (42). [BT and BTS give 'forca', wk. m., and 'force', wk. f., but this seems to be str. f. The dp. 'forcum' cited by BTS from Ælfric might be any of these.]

forceorfan, 3. *to cut off.* inf., xix. 61; xxiii. 185, 193; pp. **forcorfen**, xxi. 231. [Cf. **ceorfan.**]

fordēman, I. *to condemn.* vii. 104; xi. 213, 504; xia. 51; xiii. 11 (twice), 99 (twice), 223, 225, 226; xviii. 219; xix. 217. [Cf. **dēman.**]

fordōn, anom. vb. (a) *to bring to ruin, destroy.* inf., iv. 203; xiii. 94; xviii. 374; xxix. 109; d. inf. **fordōnne**, xvii. 291; pres. 3s. **fordēþ**, iii. 27, 136; xxii. 101; xxx. 54; 3p. **fordōþ**, xviii. 324; pres. 3s. subj. **fordō**,

xxix. 108; pret. 3s. **fordyde**, xix. 141; 3p. **fordydon**, xxi. 241; pp. **fordōn**, xi. 501; xx. 253 (np. -e). (b) *to corrupt.* pp. **fordōn** as adj. *corrupt, depraved.* vi. 302; xi. 191, 223; xxiii. 143. [Cf. **dōn.**]

fordrūgian, II. *to dry up.* ii. 83.

fordwīnan, 1. *to vanish.* pres. 3p. **fordwīnaþ**, xxviii. 13. [BT cites from CH I. 592/12; II. 504/4.]

fordyttan, I. *to obstruct.* xv. 184.

fore, prep. w. dat. *for the sake of, in support of, on behalf of*; placed after its pron. object and immediately before verb. xi. 212, 223 (or as prefix both times, **foredēþ**?), 230 (or as prefix, **forebēoþ**?); xvii. 109; xix. 226. [Perhaps also xi. 166 and xviii. 162: see **foreþingian.**]

forealdian, II. *to grow old.* ii. 113. [Cf. **ealdian.**]

?***fore-bēon**, anom. vb. *to be supporter of, be for* (someone). pres. 3p. **forebēoþ**, xi. 230 (but probably two words: see **fore**). [Note Ælfric's Grammar, ed. Zupitza, p. 200, '*præsum* ic fore eom'. Cf. **bēon.**]

forebȳsen, f. (*premonitory*) *example.* xxvii. 107. [BT cites only one instance, late OE. See MED, 'forebisne', and cf. **bȳsen.**]

?***fore-dōn**, anom. vb. *to do* (something) *on behalf of* (someone). pres. 3s., **foredēþ**, xi. 212, 223 (but probably two words: see **fore** and **dōn**).

foresǣd, adj. (pp. of **foresecgan**). *aforesaid.* i. 36, 293; ii. 24, 263; iii. 10; vii. 8; xi. 228, 428; xia. 160, 215; etc.

forescēawian, II. *to foresee, preordain, provide.* i. 253; xi. 259, 342; xviii. 76; xxx. 79, 113. [Cf. **scēawian.**]

forescēawung, f. *foresight, providence.* xi. 279.

foresecgan, III. *to predict, mention before.* iii. 142; xi. 361 (þe wē hēr **foresǣdon**, *that we have just mentioned*; or as two words, hēr fore **sǣdon**?); xx. 237. [Cf. **foresǣd** above and **secgan.**]

forestīhtung, f. *predestination.* xi. 472.

foreþingian, II. *to intercede for.* xi. 166; xviii. 162. [Both instances can be taken as two words: see **fore** and **þingian.**]

foreþingung, f. *intercession.* xi. 242.

forfaran, 6. *to go astray, perish.* pres. 3p. **forfaraþ**, ii. 246. [Cf. **faran.**]

forfēran, I (only in pret.). *to go astray, perish.* i. 194, 245; viii. 138. [Cf. **fēran.**]

forfōn, 7. *to forestall.* inf., xv. 135. [Cf. **fōn.**]

forgǣgan, I. *to transgress.* i. 186; xxvi. 109.

forgǣgednyss, f. *transgression.* i. 189; iv. 190; xii. 134; xvii. 88.

forgifan, -**gyfan**, 5. (a) *to give.* inf. **forgyfan**, i. 390; **forgifan**, vii. 54; pres. 3s. **forgyfþ**, v. 132; 3s. subj. **forgyfe**, vi. 372; pret. 3s. **forgeaf**, i. 47, 213, 215, 350; v. 5, 24; vii. 61, 183; pp. **forgyfen**, v. 150;—etc. (b) *to forgive.* inf., vi. 259; vii. 60; pres. 3s. **forgyfþ**, vii. 106; pp. **forgyfen**, vi. 225, 242 (np. -e), 311 (np. -e); np. **forgifene**, vii. 59, 60;—etc. [Cf. **gifan.**]

forgife(n)nyss, -**gyf-**, f. *forgiveness.* i. 97; iii. 148; vi. 219, etc. (8 times); vii. 58; x. 87; xi. 202; etc.

forgyldan, -**gildan**, -**geldan**, 3. trans. or intrans., w. dat. of person if mentioned. *to pay for, requite, repay.* inf. **forgyldan**, xvi. 178; pres. 3s. **forgylt**, xiii. 108; xvi. 271; xxi. 667; xxx. 42; pres. 3s. subj. **forgilde**, xvii. 202; 3p. subj. **forgeldon** (v.l. -**gyldon**), xvi. 170; pp. **forgolden**, xvi. 171 (future passive, with **biþ**, *it shall be repaid*). [Cf. **gyldan.**]

forgytan, -**gitan**, 5. *to forget.* pres. 2s. subj. **forgite**, xxx. 47; 3p. subj. **forgytan**, xiii. 187. [Cf. **be-**, **under-gytan.**]

forhabban, III, refl. *to restrain oneself, abstain.* ii. 169; xix. 45 (see note). [Cf. **habban.**]

forhæfednyss, f. *self-restraint, continence.* xix. 116; xxi. 639 (-**hæfd-**).

forhogian, II. *to scorn, neglect.* xix. 13, 27. [Cf. **hogian.**]

forhtian, II. *to be afraid.* x. 16, 130, 142.

forhtlīce, adv. *timidly.* vi. 308.

forlǣdan, I. *to mislead, seduce.* iv. 69; xxi. 200. [Cf. **lǣdan.**]

forlæg, see **forlicgan.**

forlǣran, I. *to lead astray, deceive, seduce.* i. 259; xia. 42; xvi. 234; xx. 342; xxix. 59. [Cf. **lǣran.**]

forlǣtan, 7. (a) *to let go, leave, relinquish, abandon, forsake, neglect.* inf., xiv. 203; xvii. 274; xix. 25, 108. d. inf. **forlǣtenne,** vii. 40; **forlǣtene,** iii. 105; pres. 1s. **forlǣte,** viii. 43, 220; 2s. **forlǣtst,** xxi. 480; xxiii. 56; 3s. **forlǣt,** iv. 69, 216; x. 54; xviii. 103; xix. 38; 1p. **forlǣtaþ,** i. 221; 2p., iii. 101; 3p., xiv. 206; pres. 3s. subj. **forlǣte,** x. 53; xix. 95, 98; 1p. subj. **forlǣton,** ix. 148; pret. 3s. **forlēt,** v. 64, 214, 220; viii. 223; x. 125; xix. 211; xxi. 640; xxiii. 115; 3p. **forlēton, -an,** i. 187; xi. 356; xia. 36; xiv. 40, 145, 227, 229; xv. 102, 108; xvi. 184; xviii. 126; xxi. 84, 280, 413; xxix. 87; pret. 3s. subj. **forlēte,** v. 121; pp. **forlǣten,** x. 52; xviii. 32–217 (12 times); xix. 39; xxiii. 43. (b) *to leave* something (acc.) *to* someone (dat.). pres. 1s. **forlǣte,** x. 14, 121. [Cf. **lǣtan.**]

forlegen, adj. (pp. of **forlicgan**). *adulterous.* xiii. 209.

forlēosan, 2. *to lose.* pres. 3s. subj. **forlēose,** vi. 208; 1p. subj. **forlēoson,** xvi. 248; pret. 3s. **forlēas,** x. 197; xxi. 46; pp. **forloren,** vii. 160. [Cf. **forloren,** adj.]

forlicgan, 5. *to lie with* (illicitly). pret. 3s. **forlæg,** xxi. 116. [Cf. **forlegen** and **licgan.**]

forliger, forlīr, n. *adultery, fornication.* iv. 250; xiii. 199, 202; xv. 97; xvi. 73; xix. 91.

forliger, forlīr, m. *adulterer, fornicator.* xi. 379; xix. 39, 40; xxiii. 144.

forloren, adj. (pp. of **forlēosan**). *(spiritually) lost, abandoned.* vi. 203.

forma, wk. adj. *first, earliest.* ii. title; xi. 361, 411. [Cf. **fyrmest.**]

formolsnian, II. *to rot away, decay.* xi. 246.

fornēan, adv. *very nearly, almost.* xiv. 28, 189.

forniman, 4. *to seize, possess, take away.* pp. **fornumen,** ii. 108; xvii. 255; xxix. 75. [Cf. **niman.**]

foroft, adv. *very often.* ii. 241; vi. 296; xi. 201, 205; xiii. 65, 141; xvii. 96; xviii. 410; xix. 31, 242; xx. 357.

forrotodnyss, f. *corrupt matter, rottenness.* xv. 78.

forsǣd, see **forsecgan.**

forsāwe, forsāwon, see **forsēon.**

forscruncen, adj. (pp. of 'forscrincan'). *shrunken, withered away.* ii. 69, 82.

forscyld(e)god, adj. (pp. of 'forscyldigian'). *condemned, guilty.* xi. 448, 492; xiii. 204; xvii. 271; xviii. 69; xix. 246; xxiii. 146.

forseah, see **forsēon.**

forsearod, adj. (pp. of 'forsearian'). *dried up.* ii. 87.

forsecgan, III. *to defame, accuse.* pp. **forsǣd,** xvi. 5, 88. [Cf. **secgan.**]

forsēon, 5. *to despise, scorn, neglect.* inf., vi. 296; pres. 3s. **forsyhþ,** vi. 272; xx. 280, 286, 291, 294, 407; **forsihþ,** viii. 156; xiii. 48; xx. 286; pres. 1p. **forsēoþ,** xx. 300; 3p., ii. 176; vi. 277; xiii. 78; xxi. 70, 508; pres. 3s. subj. **forsēo,** xix. 30; 1p. subj. **forsēon,** xiv. 107; 3p., xviii. 299; xxx. 10; pret. 3s. **forseah,** xix. 146; xx. 410; xxi. 361; xxvi. 26; xxx. 19; 3p. **forsāwon,** i. 345; iii. 95; xi. 192, 294, 357; xviii. 55 (-an); xx. 105, 233, 260, 287; xxi. 81; pret. 3s. subj. **forsāwe,** xxi. 312. [Cf. **gesēon.**]

forsewennyss, f. *contempt.* i. 198; xx. 238, 280, 289; xxvi. 36 (**for his f.,** *for contempt of him*).

forsihþ, see **forsēon.**

forstelan, 4. *to steal, carry off.* inf., xvi. 160; xxii. 45.

forswǣlan, I. *to burn, burn up* (trans.). xxi. 297.

forswelgan, 3. *to swallow up.* pres. 3p. **forswelgaþ,** xiii. 165; pret. 3s. **forswealh,** xx. 250.

forsweorcan, 3. *to grow dark.* pres. 3s. **forsweorcþ,** xi. 285; pp. **for-**

sworcen, xxvii. 102. [Cf. ǥe-
sweorcan.]

forsworen, adj. (pp. of 'forswerian').
perjured, forsworn. xi. 378; xxiv. 1.
[Cf. swerian.]

forsyhþ, see forsēon.

fortredan, 5. *to tread down, trample
on.* inf., vii. 185; pres. 1p. subj.
fortredon, xiv. 106; pp. fortreden,
iii. 70. [Cf. ǥetredan.]

forþ, adv. (a) *forth, on, onward, out,
into view.* vi. 42, 99, 178; viii. 146;
xi. 453; xxi. 266; xxii. 70. (b) *from
that time forth, on,* marking the continued action of a verb: ǥǣþ forþ,
goes on, continues, xviii. 181; ǥefylþ
forþ, *goes on filling,* xiv. 190. (c)
with other adverbs: forþ on, *onward, further,* i. 275; forþ
ǥīt, ǥīt forþ, *still further,* x. 181,
184; xiii. 86; for heonon forþ see
heonon.

forþam, for þam, forþan, adv. *for
that, for that reason, therefore.* iv.
125; xiii. 223; xiv. 168; xviii. 360.
[Cf. forþī; for conj. for þam (þe)
see for.]

forþbringan, 3, I. *to bring forth.* iii. 66
(pret. 3s. -brōhte). [Cf. bringan.]

forþearle, adv. *very much, greatly.* ii.
71; iv. 14, 74; v. 232; xxi. 569;
xxiii. 103.

forþfaran, 6. *to depart, die.* only as
pp., forþfaren, *dead.* ii. 248; vi. 34,
37, 99, 331. [Cf. faran.]

forþfēran, I. *to depart, die.* pret. 3s.
-fērde, xix. 144 (subj.); xxiii. 14.
[Cf. fēran.]

forþī, forþȳ, forþiǥ, adv. *for that
reason, therefore.* ii. 24, 165; iii. 35;
iv. 159; v. 161; vi. 155, 337; viii.
158; etc.—spelled -þiǥ at xiv. 172;
xv. 152; xxvii. 65.

*ǥeforþian, II. *to send forth.* xxi. 274.
[This meaning not in Hall, and not
in BT or BTS under 'geforþian';
but one instance in BTS under
'forþian'.]

*forþmann, m. *man of rank.* xix. 138.
[Unique in this passage. Cited by
Napier.]

forþon, adv. see furþon.

forþsīþ, m. *going forth, decease.* xi.

C 2710 2

127, 164, 167, 171, 181, 182, 205,
209; xv. 123; xvi. 37, 153, 260; xix.
243; xxvii. 14, 33, 87, 89.

forþstæppan, 6. *to proceed, step forth.*
inf., ii. 210; pres. 3s. forþstæpþ,
ix. 7, 86, 111, 112. [Cf. stæppan.]

forþtēon, 2. *to draw forth, bring forth.*
pret. 3s. -tēah, xix. 176. [Ælfric
has 'forþteah' at Gen. i. 12. The
prefix rather than the adv. seems
especially likely here in view of the
Lat. *proferens.* Cf. tēon.]

forþȳ, see forþī.

forwandian, II. *to reverence.* iii. 19.
[Cf. wandian.]

forwrēgan, I. *to accuse, calumniate.*
xxi. 491. [Cf. wrēgan.]

forwurþan, 3. *to perish, be destroyed.*
pres. 3p. forwurþaþ, xi. 389; xx.
426; pret. 3s. subj. forwurde,
xviii. 74, 251, 367. [Cf. wurþan.]

forwyrd, f. or n. (a) *destruction, ruin.*
ix. 80; xi. 108; xiv. 134; xviii. 293;
xix. 251; xxi. 157. (b) *place of dam-
nation.* xix. 188.

forwyrht, adj. ('forworht', pp. of
'forwyrcan'). *made forfeit by evil-
doing, damned.* xxix. 89 (glossed
damnatus). [Cf. BTS, 'forwyrcan',
II, IIa, III.]

forwyrnan, I. (a) *to deny* something
(gen.) to someone (dat.). viii. 148;
xi. 449, 450; xxvi. 47; xxvii. 22.
(b) *to restrain, prevent* someone
(dat.) from doing something (neg.
clause of purpose). iv. 142 (clause
omitted); xxvi. 53. (c) *to forbid,
prohibit* (same constr.). xxix. 79.
*(d) *to keep off, withhold* something
(acc.). viii. 81. [Meaning (d) not
clearly illustrated in BT, BTS,
though perhaps close to Beow. 1142,
'he ne forwyrnde woroldrædenne'.]

fōstor, m. *feeding.* xviii. 325.

fōstormōdor, f. *foster-mother.* xxiii.
16, 32 (foster-).

fōt, m. *foot.* v. 202; vi. 7 (ap. fēt), 75,
101, 306, 307, 344; vii. 141, 146;
xvi. 13, 101; etc.

fōtcops, m. *foot-fetter.* xvii. 224, 225.
[BT cites this instance from
Thorpe's text of CH; BTS gives
other instances in Ælfric.]

B b

fōtlǣst, f. *footprint.* xxi. 420 (ap. fōt-lǣsta). [This form cited by Napier to call attention to its gender.]

fracod, adj. *infamous, indecent, abandoned.* vi. 169; xi. 379; xxi. 151, 513.

fracodnyss, f. *abomination.* xxi. 496, 567.

gefrǣtewian, II. *to adorn.* iv. 245; viii. 53; xi. 248 (-fret-, v.l. -frǣt-).

fram, once from (xviii. 84), prep. w. dat. *from.* (a) indicating whence there is motion or direction, literal or figurative (going or coming, sending, leading, taking away, raising, driving, separating, etc.). i. 37, 299, 301 (these three can also mean *by*); iii. 58, 68; iv. 9, 208, 257, 262; vi. 281, 371; vii. 14, 46, 52, 133; etc. (b) indicating that *from* which one refrains or is cut off or excluded. ii. 169, 170; xi. 133 (losaþ fram, *is lost from*); xvi. 114 (fram Crīste, perhaps also *by*); xviii. 341; xix. 45; xxvi. 76. (c) indicating that *from* which one is healed, cleansed, saved, released. ii. 23 (*from* w. hāl, *by* w. gehǣfd; see note), 97, 105, 118, 268; iv. 60, 61, 62, 70, 242; vii. 126; xia. 136; etc. (d) indicating that (good or bad) *from* which there is turning, change, correction. xii. 163; xiii. 132; xv. 54, 161; xvi. 63; xvii. 116; xxi.295. (e) with adjectives signifying lack, difference, estrangement: w. ǣmtig, *devoid of, free from.* ii. 149; iv. 244; xviii. 93, 99, 343; w. ælþēodig, *alien from.* v. 115; w. ælfremed, *estranged from*, xiv. 139 (twice); xxi. 164. (f) indicating a past event or period *from* which an interval of time is measured. i. 469; ii. 242 (fram Adame, *from Adam's time*); viii. 59; ix. 11, 151, 155; xi. 20, 411; xia. 94; xviii. 84; xxi. 525. (g) of source, indicating *from* whom something is acquired. xiii. 185. (h) of agency, indicating the person or thing whence action proceeds, now usually *by.* i. 136, 192; ii. 23 (w. gehǣfd; see above, sense c), 265; viii. 60; x. 52; xi. 15; xia. 89; xii.

229; perhaps xvi. 114 (see above, sense b); xxiii. 195; xxvii. 63.)

frec, adj. *greedy, voracious.* xxi. 493.

frēcednyss, f. *danger, peril, harm.* vi. 335; xiv. 191; xviii. 245, 319, 321; xxix. 49.

frēcenfull, adj. *perilous.* vi. 316. [Cf. BT and Hall, Suppl.]

gefrēdan, I. *to feel, perceive.* i. 266; xi. 218 (pres. 3s. gefrēt), 479, 486; xxi. 547; xxv(c). 2, 6; xxvi. 90.

frēfrian, gefrēfrian, II. *to comfort.* vi. 48, 186, 253; vii. 42; x. 85, 131; xia. 7; xiv. 217; xx. 82; xxiii. 120; xxvi. 85.

frēfrigend, m. *comforter* (the Holy Spirit). x. 85.

fremfull, adj. *benignant.* xviii. 195.

fremian, II (orig. I). *to be of advantage* to someone (dat.), *avail, benefit.* impers., vii. 12, 44, 47; xi. 223, 272; xix. 202; xxx. 46; pers., xi. 160.

gefremian, gefremman, II, I. *to perform.* v. 67 (pret. 1s. gefremode), 91; vi. 164 (pres. 3s. gefremaþ); x. 46; xi. 406; xii. 60, 126; xv. 97; xvi. 208; xvii. 60, 62, 187; xviii. 362 (inf. gefremman); xix. 180; xxvi. 50.

fremming f. *performance.* vi. 175, 181 (-incge); ix. 147; x. 31, 34, 46; xii. 154.

fremu, f. *advantage, use.* ix. 45.

frēo, frīg, adj. *free.* xix. 86 (nsf. frīg); xxiii. 153 (nsm. frēo), 173 (np. frīge).

gefrēogan, II. *to set free.* xxiii. 40 (pret. 3s. gefrēode).

frēolīce, adv. *freely.* ii. 267.

frēols, m. or n. *festivity, festival.* ii. 43, 183, 255.

frēolsdæg, m. *feast day.* ii. 267; xviii. 339.

frēolsian, II. *to celebrate, keep as a feast.* ii. 218, 263; xvi. 78; xxi. 174.

frēolslīce, adv. *festively, joyfully.* ii. 178.

frēond, m. *friend.* vi. 30; viii. 64; xi. 139, 153, 230 (np. frȳnd), 239, 271, 272; xv. 82 (ap. frȳnd), 85 (ap. frēond, v.l. frīnd both times); xvi. 15, 36, 122, 150, 155, 259; xvii. 106.

frēondrǣden, f. *friendship.* xvi. 147.

Fricg. *Frigg,* the Scandinavian goddess, wife of Odin, corresponding to OE Frīg as in Frīgedæg. xxi. 177 (v.l. frycg, fricge).

frīg, see frēo.

Frīgedæg, m. *Friday.* ii. title (and in titles of iii, v, vi in MS. H); xi. 36. (Langgan Frīgedæge, *Good Friday*).

Frīgeniht, f. *Thursday night.* viii. 20. [This instance cited by Napier with two other examples. BTS has these and a fourth.]

friþ, m. or n. *peace, protection.* xxi. 227.

frōfor, f. (?) *comfort, help.* ix. 213; xxi. 172, 179.

frōforgāst, frōfer-, m. *Spirit of comfort, Comforter, Paraclete.* vi. 253; vii. 14, 46, 52, 54, 57; ix. 5, 84, 112; x. 11, 80; xia. 7.

from, see fram.

fruma, m. *beginning.* only in æt fruman, *at first.* ii. 226; xiii. 143; xvi. 173; xvii. 145; xix. 34.

frumsceapen, adj. *first created, first.* xi. 94; xvi. 231.

frumwæstmas, mp. *first-fruits.* xxx. 76, 84, 105, 109.

frymþ, m. (?) *beginning.* fram frymþe, i. 469; ix. 155; xi. 82, 472; xviii. 84; on frymþe, xxi. 188.

frȳnd, see frēond.

fugel, m. *bird, fowl.* i. 210; ii. 236; xx. 87.

fugelcynn, n. *bird-tribe, species of birds.* xx. 95.

fūht, adj. *damp, moist.* iv. 223.

*fūhtian, II. *to be moist, drip.* iv. 229. [Unique in this passage. Cited by Napier.]

fūl, adj. *foul.* i. 421; ii. 190; iv. 44, 82, 229, 235, 245, 262; v. 129; xi. 374, 379, 384; xiii. 199; xvi. 68; xvii. 268; xviii. 74, 373; xxi. 121, 161, 565, 570, 593; xxvi. 14.

fūle, adv. *foully.* i. 269; vi. 169, 198. comp., fūlre, xvi. 68 (or adj., -re for -ra).

full, adj. *full, filled, complete.* viii. 33, 163, 165; xia. 105, 122, 125; xii. 236; xiv. 186; xx. 102; xxx. 94.—

with gen. pl., *full of.* xiv. 23, 126, 149.—with mid, *filled with.* i. 54, 456.—be fullan, *fully.* xxi. 63.

full, adv. *completely, to the full.* (a) ful gōd, *entirely good.* xi. 187 (np. gōde). (b) ful strang, *at full strength.* xx. 371. (c) ful sōþ, adv. *with perfect truth.* viii. 244. [In other expressions the adverb has been treated as a prefix, presumably with subordinate stress. Cf. the next five entries and fullweaxan.]

full cūþ, fulcūþ, adj. *well-known.* xi. 111; xii. 79; xiv. 114; xxi. 292.

*fullcȳþan, I. *to utter completely, declare in full.* i. 131. [Not in dict. Cf. cȳþan.]

fullfremed, ful-, adj. *complete, perfect.* i. 118; xiii. 23, 135, 145; xix. 115; xxi. 654.

fullfremedlīce, adv. *completely, perfectly.* xxi. 641.

fullfremednyss, f. *perfection, completeness.* ii. 149 (ful-) ; xviii. 120, 144.

fullian, II. *to baptize.* i. 308; iv. 232; ix. 101; xii. 87; xvii. 153.

gefullian, II. *to baptize.* pret., xi. 65; xia. 182; xxiii. 202; pp. gefullod, vi. 195; ix. 106; xi. 15, 503; xia. 89; xii. 89, 113, 126; xxi. 641; xxiii. 37, 45, 157, 158; gefulled, xxiii. 153, [Cf. ungefullod.]

fūllīce, adv. *foully.* xi. 374; xvii. 264; xxi. 103, 116, 158.

fullīce, adv. *fully.* ii. 148; v. 284; xia. 71; xxvi. 81; xxix. 89.

fulluht, n. *baptism.* i. 401; iv. 243, 244; vii. 133; xi. 18; xia. 92; xii. 72, 85, 94, 101, 104, 124, 133, 193; xvi. 140; xvii. 175; xxi. 8, 634; xxiii. 36; xxvi. 5.

fulluhtere, m. *baptist* (confined to John the Baptist). i. 437; ix. 67; xi. 15; xia. 89.

fullweaxan, 7. *to grow to maturity.* xi. 310 (pret. 3s. subj. fulwēoxe); xii. 111 (pret. 3p. subj. fulwēoxon). [Hall cites the form at xii. 111 from Belfour's text. Otherwise recorded only as pp., 'fulweaxen', *full-grown.* Cf. weaxan.]

fūlnyss, f. *foulness, filth.* i. 415; iv. 219; xvii. 261.

fulstan, see **fylstan.**

fultum, m. *help, support.* i. 60, 215, 264; ii. 159; ix. 51; xi. 162; xiv. 164, 233; xx. 82, 160; xxi. 171; xxii. 6, 69; xxvi. 25.

fultumian, II. *to help, support, assist.* xiv. 26, 178 (dat. inf. -**igenne**); xxi. 131 (v.l. **gefultumian**).

fulweoxe, fulweoxon, see **fullweaxan.**

funde, fundon, see **findan.**

fundian, II. *to direct one's course.* xxv(c). 18.

fundung, f. *departure.* viii. 23; ix. 4; x. 133.

furlang, n. *furlong.* vi. 45.

furþon, forþon, furþan, adv. *even, indeed.* i. 173, 251, 415; v. 126; vii. 160; xi. 504; xviii. 336; xix. 241; xx. 7, 26; xxi. 48, 297, 339; xxix. 61.

furþor, adv. *further (than), ahead (of).* v. 23; xi. 556; xiii. 22, 134.

fūs, adj. *ready to depart, eager* or *in haste to go* (sometimes best translated by an adverb). x. 76 ('speedily') 143 ('close to going'); xx. 207 ('eagerly').

gefylc(e), n. *band of men, host.* xi. 360 (np. **gefylcu**), 361 and 384 (both ns. **gefylc,** v.l. **gefilc, gefylce**).

fylgan, fylian, I, w. dat. *to follow.* i. 290; vi. 347 (both pres. 3s. **fyligþ, filigþ**); x. 146 (inf. **fylian**); xii. 206; xvii. 204 (both pret. 3p. **fyligdon**); xxii. 33 (**fylian**). [Cf. **folgian.**]

gefyllan, I. *to fulfil, perform, fill, complete.* i. 467; ii. 79, 201, 205, 207; v. 77, 241; vi. 353; ix. 24, 190; x. 64; xiii. 49; xiv. 186, 190; xv. 106; xvi. 202; xix. 35; xx. 144, 373. [Cf. **afyllan².**]

gefylsta, m. *helper.* xv. 224.

fylstan, fulstan, I, w. dat. *to support, help.* ii. 203; xvii. 109; xxii. 78 (pret. 3s. **fylste**).

fylþ, f. *filth, impurity, unclean practice.* i. (423); xviii. 84, 371; xxi. 497, 568.

fylþ, see **feallan.**

fynd, see **feond.**

fȳr, n. *fire.* ii. 180; v. 275; vii. 71; ix. 132; x. 97, 174; xi. 58, 226, etc. (16 times); etc.

fyrd, f. (*national*) *army, host* (applied in xx to the Israelites on the march to the promised land). xx. 11, 60, 96; xxii. 20, 77; xxix. 91, 93.

fyrdian, II. *to go on a military expedition, march.* xxi. 129. [BTS cites this passage from Wulfstan's adaptation in MS. T.]

fyrding, f. (a) *an army* (called out for a campaign). xxii. 53 (ds. -**incge**); xxix. 44 (ds. -**unge,** v.l. -**inge**). (b) *an expedition, campaign.* xxix. 42 (ds. -**unge,** v.l. -**inge**).

fyrdlāf, f. *remnant of an army.* xx. 214 (ds. where as. is to be expected: see note). [BTS cites one passage only, LS xxv. 377.]

fȳren, adj. *fiery.* xx. 316.

fyrhtu, f. *fright, dread.* xvii. 255; xxix. 75.

fyrlen, adj. *distant, remote.* iii. 8, 92, 107 (asm. **fyrlen[n]e**); ix. 100; xiv. 180; xxi. 77.

fyrmest, adj. (sup. of **forma**). *first, chief;* wk. as noun, *the foremost, the leader,* xia. 32; xvi. 136, 174; xix. 176; xxi. 158, 523.

gefyrn, adv. *long ago, formerly.* i. 467; ii. 151, 190; xv. 9, 61, 125; xvii. 62; xviii. 10; xx. 146; xxvi. 21; xxix. 52, 103.

fyrnlic, adj. *former.* vii. 133; xi. 503.

fyrnlīce ('firen-'), adv. *sinfully, wickedly.* xvii. 268.

fyrst, m. or n. *period, space of time.* viii. 142; xviii. 372; xix. 147; xx. 7, 8; xxi. 73; xxiii. 205.

fyrþrian, gefyrþrian, II. *to further, advance, benefit.* xi. 162 (inf. -**iun**); xx. 112; xxii. 69.

G

Gabriel, the angel. xia. 62; xxvii. 55, 60 (**Gabrihel**).

gegada, wk. m. *comrade, companion.* xia. 34; xx. 238.

gaderian, gegaderian, II. (a) trans. or absolute, *to gather, unite.* iv. 40, 56, 199, 211; v. 82, 250, 261, 273; xi. 343; xii. 211; xvi. 134; xvii. 74; xviii. 212 (pp. np. **gega-**

dorade), 267, 415. (b) refl. *to come together.* xviii. 211. (c) refl. w. **eft**, *to be reunited, reconciled.* xix. 101. (d) intr. *to gather.* xviii. 39 (pres. 3p. ġadriaþ), 205 (ġaderiaþ).

ġegaderung, f. *gathering, assembly.* xiv. 90 (translating **Sinagoga**).

ġærs, n. *grass.* xix. 23.

ġærstapa, wk. m. *grasshopper, locust.* i. 235; xx. 164.

ġafol, n. *interest, usury.* xxiv. 5, 8, 11.

ġāl, adj. *lustful.* xxi. 113.

Galileisc, adj. *Galilean, of Galilee.* xiv. 42; xvii. 2, 23(?), 282.

Gallicanus, a general under Constantine the Great. xxii. 52, 56.

ġālnyss, f. *lust, wantonness.* i. 415 (?); iv. 229; xi. 317; xxi. 151.

ġamen, n. *sport, merriment.* xxi. 551.

ġān, anom. vb. *to go, walk, proceed.* inf., ii. 49, etc.; pres. 2s. ġǽst, xxi. 396; xxvi. 64; 3s. ġǽþ, i. 291, 306; etc.; 3p. ġāþ, vi. 134;p ret. 3s. ēode, i.438; etc.; 3p. ēodon, v. 9; ēodan, xxvi. 104; etc. [26 times in i–vii. Cf. a-, be-, ofer-, þurh-ġān and next entry.]

ġeġān, anom. vb., w. dat. of pers. *to attain to.* inf., vi. 283. [BTS, II. 1, with examples from Ælfric.]

ġang, m. *privy.* x. 166.

ġangan, 7. *to go, walk,* occas. *come.* pres. part. ġangende, ii. 39, 211; xx. 120 (mid fōtum, *on foot*); imp. sg. ġang, ii. 185; v. 33; xiii. 227; xvi. 214; xxiii. 109; pres. 1s. ġange, xxiii. 72; pres. 3s. subj. ġange, vii. 118 (ġange of, *descend from*); xix. 130; xx. 56 (*come*). [Apparently substituted in these forms for the corresponding forms of ġān.]

Gangwuce, wk. f. *Rogation Week.* xi. 51; xia. 159; xix. 123.

ġārsecg, m. *ocean.* xia. 46.

ġāst, m. *ghost, spirit.* (a) the Holy *Spirit.* i. 25, 75, etc. (9 times); ii. 179, 291; iii. 179; iv. 135, etc. (8 times); v. 131, 132, 146, 210; vi. 218–82 (16 times); vii. 26, etc. (10 times); etc. (b) abstract *spirit,* or a living person's spirit. i. 399

(twice); v. 52, 54, 55, 170, 172, 173; vi. 79; etc. (c) a demonic *spirit.* iv. 41, etc. (9 times); etc.

ġāstlic, adj. *spiritual.* i. 10, 400; ii. 61, 259; iv. 65; v. 242; vii. 202; viii. 55; ix. 119; x. 110; etc.

ġāstlīce, adv. *spiritually.* xvi. 202.

ġata, see ġeat.

ġe, conj. *and.* i. 173.—usually as corr., *both . . . and.* i. 348; ii. 236 (three times); iv. 129, 149, 181–2; v. 235; vii. 148; etc. [Also with ǽgþer, q.v.]

ġē, see þū.

ġealla, m. *gall, bile.* xvi. 249.

*ġēancyme, m. *return.* xxi. 633 (glossed *reditu*). [This meaning not in dict., which gives *meeting*; but see BT, BTS, 'ġeancyrr,' meaning both *meeting* and *return.*]

ġēar, n. *year.* viii. 81; xi. 5, 90; xvi. 235 (is. ǽlce ġēare); xviii. 329, 369 (ap. ġēar); xix. 21; xx. 5, 354, 366; xxii. 25; xxiii. 7, 48, 62; xxvi. 16; xxvii. 84; xxx. 78, 79.—on ġēare, *some year.* i. 273 (see BTS, III. a, citing Napier); *a year,* xix. 130. [Gender elsewhere sometimes masc. as at CH II. 300/32; here neuter at xviii. 369; otherwise uncertain.]

ġearcian, ġeġearcian, II. *to prepare.* ii. 191; ix. 15, 122, 188; w. prefix, xi. 410, 438, 518; xix. 218.

ġeare, adv. with **witan** and **cunnan**, *well, perfectly, for certain.* xii. 29, 175 (ġearu, v.l. ġeare); xvii. 292(?); xxvi. 101.

ġearu, adj. *prepared, ready.* v. 80, 248; xv. 43; xx. 203.

ġeat, n. *gate.* xix. 214 (ap. **helle** ġata); xxvii. 86. [BTS questions 'helle-ġeat' as a compound.]

Gelboe, Mount *Gilboa* (Vulg. *Gelboe*) in Galilee. (I Reg. xviii. 4). gs. **Gelboes**, xxix. 44.

ġeld, n. *money-payment, tax.* xiii. 69 (v.l. **ġyldan**.) [Cf. **ġyldan**.]

Genesareþ, *Genesareth,* another name for the Sea of Galilee. xiv. 4.

ġeoc, iuc, n. *yoke, collar.* xxi. 261; xxiii. 133; fig., *domination,* xix. 85.

ġeoguþ, f. *youth.* xxx. 103, 110. with def. art., (a) *the younger generation,*

geoguþ (*cont.*)
xx. 370; (b) *the young* (of cattle), xxx. 78.

*geōmrian, II. trans. *to bewail.* xxvi. 91. [This use not illustrated in dictionaries, but see O.E. Bede, I. 27, ed. Miller, I. i. 82/12 and 88/15. Usually intrans. *to sigh, groan, lament,* as in MS. F's emendations at vi. 79, 85.]

geōmrung, geōmerung, f. *lamentation, groaning.* xv. 162; xvii. 32, 135, 138, 143, 146; xxvi. 82.

geond, prep. w. acc. *beyond, through, throughout.* xi. 63; xia. 180; xvii. 5; xviii. 282, 305, 389; xxi. 157, 240, 243, 245, 341, 403, 553, 558.

geong, iung, adj. *young.* xi. 116, 172; xix. 16, 87; xxi. 261, 275. comp., **gingra**, xxii. 73.

geonglic, iunglic, adj. *youthful, young.* vii. 102; xxiii. 7.

(geongling), iungling, m. *young one, child.* xix. 16.

georne, adv. *eagerly, earnestly, carefully.* iii. 182; v. 92; vi. 155; xiii. 195; xviii. 395; xxi. 86, 310; xxiii. 28; xxvi. 99, 114; xxvii. 8; xxx. 9.

geornfull, adj. *zealous, diligent.* xviii. 192.

geornfulnyss, f. *diligence, zeal.* xxv(c). 18.

geornlīce, adv. *earnestly.* viii. 37, 179; xi. 172; xii. 184; xviii. 172; xx. 393.

Gerasenorum, gp. *of the Geraseni,* A. V. *Gadarenes* (Mark v. 1). xvii. 221 (the Lat. gp. to be taken with *lande.*)

gif, gyf, conj. *if.* i. 147, etc. (11 times); ii. 175, 272; iii. 140, 172; iv. 21, etc. (15 times); etc.

gifan, gyfan, 5. *to give.* only as pres. 3s. gyfþ, i. 354, gifþ, iv. 161; x. 15; xi. 68; xia. 185. [Cf. **agifan, forgifan.**]

gīfernyss, gȳfernyss, f, *greediness, gluttony.* iv. 250; v. 237; xix. 128.

gifu, gyfu, f. *gift, grace.* i. 54, 335, 456, 457, 466; ii. 74, 94; iv. 156, 161; v. 18, 130, 131, 212; vi. 277; vii. 218, 222; etc.

gingra, see **geong.**

girnan, I, w. gen. *to ask for, demand.* xxx. 48.

gīt, see **gȳt.**

gītsere, m. *miser.* xi. 375.

gītsung, gȳtsung, f. *avarice, greediness.* iv. 250; v. 203; xix. 128.

gladian, gegladian, II. (1) trans. *to make glad:* (a) of God's action toward men, *to gladden, cheer:* ix. 145; x. 89; xi. 490; *with tō, *to cause to rejoice in:* i. 92; x. 91. (b) of man's action toward God, *to please, appease, propitiate.* iii. 149; vi. 142; xv. 48, 138; xvii. 177; xviii. 52; with dat., *to make pleased with:* i. 255. (c) of one man's action toward another, *to appease, be reconciled to:* xv. 23, 142, 195, 206. (d) the object a feeling (anger), *to placate, mitigate:* xv. 134.—(2) intrans. *to rejoice:* xi. 207. [Only six without prefix: iii. 149; vi. 142; ix. 145; xi. 207; xv. 48; xvii. 177. The use with tō is not in dict.]

glædlīce, adv. *gladly, willingly.* xiii. 115; xv. 208; xxx. 76, 91, 102.

glædnyss, f. *gladness, joy.* xix. 51.

glēawlīce, adv. *wisely, prudently.* xvi. 233.

geglengan, I. *to adorn, decorate.* xvii. 278.

glōwan, 7. *to glow.* part. **glōwende**, xxvii. 35, 43.

gnætt, m. *gnat.* i. 230; iv. 142.

gnagan, 6. *to gnaw.* pret. 3p. **gnōgon**, i. 235.

god, m. *God, a god.* i. 29 (twice), 30, 37, 48, 50, 53, etc.—nap. **godas** (not neuter, though applied in some instances to heathen gods), i. 162, 358, 362, 379, 381; xxi. 80, 82, 86, etc.—spelled **Godd**, xxiii. 31.— **Godes æcer**, see **æcer**; **Godes mann**, *man of God,* xxi. 325, 477 (Daniel). [This word is usually distinguished from **gōd** in the MSS. by having no accent, but the rule is broken on several occasions. In MS. V it is sometimes clearly distinguished by a breve, 'gŏd', xi. 104, etc.]

gōd, gōōd, adj. *good.* i. 130, 191, 192, 198, 252; ii. 209; iii. 63 (twice),

91, 183; iv. 238, 244; v. 134; vi.
294, vii. 88 (gp. gŏddra); etc.—
strong pl. as noun, *good ones*, xiv.
156.—wk. pl. with art. þā gōdan,
etc. *the good.* xi. 348, 353; xviii. 207
(gōōd-), 209 (gōōd-); xxi. 54
(gōōd-). [Frequently accented,
'gód, góód', but see comment under
preceding word.]

gōd, n. (a) *good, benefit, good thing,
wealth.* i. 335, 402; xi. 381; xiii. 13
(twice), 106 (twice), 113; xvi. 6, 89,
154, 168, 214, 273; xix. 162; xxx.
52, 79, 113. (b) *good deed(s), good.*
xxx. 30. (c) moral *good, virtue.* vi.
135; xiₐ. 116; xii. 152; xvi. 109; xxi.
52 (ap. gōōd). (d) tō gōde, *for a
good end.* xiii. 116; xxvii. 9; xxx. 43.

godcund, adj. *divine.* i. 333; iv. 7; xi.
289; xvii. 216; xxi. 6.

godcundlic, adj. *divine.* x. 158.

godcundnyss, f. *divinity, godhead.*
i. 3, 9, etc. (11 times); ii. 291; iv.
168; vi. 239, 248; vii. 209; viii. 104,
187, 195, 210, 226, 246; etc.

gegōdian, II. *to endow.* xxiii. 41.

gōdnyss, gōōdnyss, f. *goodness.* i.
206, 353; vi. 294; viii. 68; x. 64; xi.
152; xiₐ. 8; xiii. 39, 55; xv. 48; xvii.
148; xix. 24, 245, 253; xxi. 92;
xxiii. 9; xxvi. 13; xxx. 48, 51 (ap.
gōdnessa for as. -e?).

godspelbodung, f. *gospel-preaching,
new dispensation.* xix. 36.

godspell, n. *gospel.* i. 2, 17, etc. (9
times); ii. 2, 59, 84, 160; iii. 46, 120;
iv. 56; v. 1, 98, 160, 272; vi. 1, 131,
217, 301; vii. 1, 5; etc.—the word
explicated, viii. 1–11.

godspellere, m. *evangelist.* i. 12, 17,
etc. (8 times); ii. 5, 161; iv. 57; v. 1;
viii. 24; etc.

godspellic, adj. *evangelical.* v. 267;
xi. 62; xiₐ. 179; xvi. 202.

gold, n. *gold.* i. 248; xx. 43, 46, 50;
xxi. 191, 530.

goldhord, m. *treasure.* ix. 44.

gōōd, see gōd.

græfseax, n. *graving tool.* xxi. 207
[BT has only one instance, from a
gloss.]

gram, adj. *angry.* xx. 178; xxix. 39.

grama, m. (a) *anger, wrath.* xx. 221,

309; xxi. 236, 452. *(b) *manifestation of divine wrath, plague.* xx. 273;
xxi. 257. [Meaning (b) is a special
instance of BTS, II.]

gramlic, adj. *fierce, cruel.* iv. 88; xi.
373; xxi. 288, 296; xxix. 39.

grāpian, gegrāpian, II. *to lay hold
of, touch.* vii. 140, 147, 154. [Cf.
gegrīpan.]

grāpiendlic, adj. *palpable, tangible.*
xi. 325. [BT cites one example only,
CH I. 230.]

Gratianus, Roman emperor, A.D.
375–83. xxii. 59.

Grecisc, adj. *Greek.* x. 84. on Grecisc, *in (the) Greek (language)*, v.
208.

Gregorius, *Gregory* the Thaumaturgist, d. A.D. 266. viii. 101, 106; xxi.
575, 605 and 608 (gs. Gregories),
615, 626, 628, 629, 643 (ds. Gregorie).

gremian, gegremian, II (orig. I). *to
enrage, provoke, irritate.* i. 256; xi.
373; xv. 190; xvii. 174, 269; xviii.
56; xx. 40, 80, 104, 235, 265, 358,
394; xxvi. 33.

grētan, I. *to greet.* xxi. 341, 616.

grindan, 3. *to grind.* part. grindende,
xviii. 113; pres. 3p. grindaþ, xviii.
33, 110.

gegrīpan, 1. *to snatch up, carry off.*
pp. np. gegripene. xviii. 207. [Cf.
grāpian.]

gristbitian, II. *to gnash the teeth.* xi.
328.

gristbitung, f. *gnashing of teeth.* xviii.
433.

gegrundweallian, II. *to establish.* ii.
164. [Cf. geweallod.]

grymettan, I. *to cry out.* vi. 79, 85
(Lat. *infremuit, fremens*, where A.V.
has the milder *groaned, groaning*;
MS. F emends; see geōmrian).

grȳtra, wk. adj. (comp. of 'grēat').
greater. xvi. 134.

gyden, f. *goddess.* ns., xxi. 114—inflected as if from 'gydene', wk. f.:
gydenan, ds., xxi. 176; as., xxi.
154; np., xxi. 156. [See S–B 258,
Anm. 2; Cpb 592 (c), (e).]

gyf, see gif.

gyfan, see gifan.

gȳfernyss, see gīfernyss.
gyfu, see gifu.
gyldan, I. *to pay, requite.* xiii. 122
(pres. 3s. gylt; v.l. forgylt); xvi.
21, 128 (v.l. gild-). [Cf. geld and
agyldan, forgyldan.]
gylden, adj. *golden.* xxi. 256, 257, 263,
273; xxvi. 20.
gylp, m. *boasting, pride.* xxx. 61, 72.
sē īdela gylp, *vainglory.* xvii. 192,
194; xxx. 60, 64, 68.
gylt, m. *sin, offence.* i. 204; vi. 216;
ix. 176; x. 54, 193; xi. 225; xiii. 167,
168, 182, 228; xv. 18, 157; xxi. 58,
332; xxvi. 3; xxvii. 13, 110.
gȳman, I, w. gen. *to care for, take
heed to, regard, observe.* xiii. 79; xiv.
74; xviii. 78; xxi. 322.
gȳmelēas, adj. *careless, negligent.* xi.
228; xviii. 192; xix. 140.
gȳmen, f. *care, diligence.* xxi. 54.
gyrd, f. *rod.* xxi. 218.
*gyrle, wk. f. *dress, apparel.* xi. 244
(dp. gyrlum), 342 (gsf. gyrlan).
[BTS records only 'girela', wk. m.,
and str. f. 'girelu'.]
gȳt, gīt, adv. *yet.* (a) marking con-
tinuance, *still, yet.* i. 195, 219; iv. 64;
ix. 171; xi. 154; xiv. 96, 224; xvii.
96, 152; xxi. 54; xxvi. 66; xxix. 118.
(b) as complement to a period of
time or a quantity, *remaining, still,
yet.* v. 78; vii. 24, 187. (c) *in addition, further.* i. 343; xvii. 277; xx.
9; xxi. 572; xxvi. 1; xxvii. 114;
xxx. 30. (d) with negatives, *yet (till
now, till then, even now, even then).*
viii. 32, 38, 158, 206; xix. 6; xx. 183.
(e) with comparatives, *still, yet.* iv.
54, 287, 291; xviii. 180; xxi. 181.—
with other adverbs: eft gȳt, *yet
again.* i. 77.—gȳt æfre, *now (still)
and ever after.* xii. 185.—þā gȳt
(where þā limits the meaning to the
time it points to), (a) marking per-
sistence, *still.* vi. 69; xiii. 213; xx.
101. (b) of consecutive action,
further, besides. ii. 193; x. 204. (c)
with negatives, *as yet, yet, till then.*
i. 142, 193; iii. 134; v. 151, 155;
vi. 178; vii. 24, 78; xii. 70; and reversed at beginning of sentence,
gīt þā, *even then.* xxi. 99.—for forþ

gȳt see forþ.—spelled gytt, viii.
158.
gyte, m. *pouring forth, shedding.* only
in blōdes gyte, *bloodshed.* viii. 126.
gȳtsung, see gītsung.

H

habban, III. *to have.* I, as an independent verb. (a) *to possess, enjoy,
entertain, experience, have* in various
familiar senses: e.g. to have in one's
possession as property, to have the
use or benefit or assistance of, to
have a servant, master, friend, or
relation, to have an attribute, name,
meaning, quality, faculty, power,
to have a feeling, opinion, sentiment, to have a subordinate part or
adjunct, a place, etc. [Cf. BTS, II.
2, IV, V, VI, X; OED, I. 1–4, 9.]
i. 173, 180, 181 (?), 291, 457, 461;
ii. 64, 82; iii. 51, 59, 111, 113;
iv. 35, 78, 84, 184, 252; v. 37 (twice),
72, 114, 220, 227; vi. 199, 248, 322,
343, 348; vii. 49, etc. (11 times);
etc. [For habban cȳþþe tō, see
cȳþþ.] (b) *to hold* in possession,
keep. [BTS, IX; OED, I. 1.] xxi.
239, 251. (In 239 habban, *keep*, is
contrasted with hæfdon in 238: the
Philistines *were holding* the ark as
if they intended to *keep* it.] (c) *to
have, hold* in a relation specified by
a prepositional phrase. [BTS, III;
OED, I. 2. b.]—with mid, *to have
in one's company, enjoy the presence of.*
v. 187; viii. 160; xi. 546.— with
tō, *to have* or *accept* someone *as*
such and such. ix. 163 (to have
the prophets as witnesses); xia. 31 (to
have their Creator as their Lord).—
with on anwealde, *to hold in one's
power.* iv. 189.—with on gewunan,
to be accustomed to, make a habit of.
vi. 200; xiii. 68.—with tō hospe,
tō tāle, tō forsewennysse, *to hold
in scorn, reproach, contempt.* vi. 219;
x. 173; xx. 182, 280. (d) with
object and dat. inf., *to have* as a duty
or thing to be done. [BTS, VII;
OED, I. 7.] vii. 24, 187 ('ic hæbbe

eow to secgenne fela þing'). (e)
with for, *to consider as, regard as.*
[BTS, XII; OED, I. 10.] iii. 45, 167;
xxiii. 163. (f) *to have, hold, carry on*
some proceeding. [BTS, XIII;
OED, I. 11.] viii. 21 (had a talk).
(g) *to come into possession of, have* by
taking or receiving, *obtain, receive.*
[BTS, XV; OED, I. 14.] i. 325,
387; iii. 116, 148, 185; iv. 71; v. 22;
vi. 264; vii. 134; viii. 7, 112; ix.
215; xi. 137, 370, 410, 557; xii. 42,
223, 237; etc. (h) *to possess* a woman
carnally. xv. 96. [Sweet has 'wīf
habban *have intercourse with*'; not
in BT or Hall, though perhaps considered a special instance of (g). An
instance at LS xxx. 162 (non-
Ælfrician).] (i) of parents, *to have*
a child by getting or bearing. [A
special instance of (g): BTS, XV;
OED, I. 14.] xix. 107 (said negatively of a barren wife). *(k) with
willan, *to wish to find present* in
another a quality one approves or
enjoins. [Not in dict. but cf. OED,
I. 18. b.] xvi. 225 ('Crist wile habban
unsceþþinysse on us'). (l) with
tō, intō, *to cause to go* or *come, to
receive, bring, take* to or into a
place or state. [BTS, XVI; OED,
I. 16.] ii. 243; xi. 170; xiv. 70, 184,
187; xvii. 71. II, as an auxiliary
verb. [BT, IV, V; BTS, B. II;
OED, II. 24, 25.] (a) with object
and inflected past participle, once
only: xxi. 465, hæfde rifteras
abedene, almost *had reapers who
had been called in.* (b) with pp. uninflected (or uncertain): present
forms making a compound perfect
tense, ii. 59; iii. 46; vi. 229; viii. 50,
240; xi. 151; xvi. 18, 125; xviii. 43,
222, 259, 270, 382; xx. 1, 49, 319;
xxi. 453, 506; xxvi. 52, 119; xxix.
103.—preterite forms making a compound pluperfect tense, iii. 32, 52;
xvii. 259; xx. 260, 264; xxi. 45;
xxiii. 43; xxvii. 82. [Forms: inf., ii.
243 (49 times); imp. pl. habbaþ, xi.
410; pres. 1s. hæbbe, v. 72 (7 times);
habbe, xxiii. 102; 2s. hæfst, v.
37 (4 times); 3s. hæfþ, i. 291 (45

times); hafþ, xxiii. 34; 1p. habbaþ,
ii. 59 (16 times); hæbbe wē, vi. 264;
xvi. 257; 2p. habbaþ, xxi. 506;
3p., i. 173 (15 times); pres. subj. 1,
2, 3 sing. hæbbe, xvi. 164, 223;
xix. 89 (12 times); 1, 3 p. habbon
-an, i. 325; iii. 185 (11 times); pret.
1s. hæfde, xxiii. 163; 2s. hæfdest,
v. 37; xxvii. 104; subj., xxiii. 19;
3s. hæfde, i. 457 (37 times); subj.,
i. 387 (4 times); 1p. hæfdon, vii.
161; 3p., iii. 59 (16 times); 3p. subj.,
ix. 215; xvii. 76; xxi. 251. For pp.
see next entry. Cf. also æt-, forhabban, and nabban.]

gehabban, III, only as pp. gehæfd.
(a) *possessed* or *afflicted* (by a disease).
ii. 23. (b) vaguely *owned* or *kept in
use, maintained*, but equivalent, with
wæs, to *was situated* or even *there
was.* ii. 10 (see note).

hād, m. (a) *person* (of the Trinity).
viii. 198; xia. 6, 200. (b) *state, estate.*
xix. 86, 88 ('widowhood'), 115 ('layman's estate'). (c) *sex.* xi. 314.

gehādod, adj. (pp. of 'gehādian').
ordained, consecrated. xi. 148, 166;
xxv(a). 16, 17.

gehæftan, I, pret. 3s. gehæfte, pp.
gehæft. *to bind, fetter.* xvii. 224;
xxiii. 81, 92, 131.

hæftling, m. *captive, prisoner.* xxiii.
140, 143, 201.

*hæftnȳd, hæftnēd, f. *captivity,
confinement in bonds*; here in pl. concretely: *bonds* or *shackles.* xxiii. 81,
83, 131. [This meaning not recognized in dict.: see note.]

hæftnyss, f. *captivity*; in pl., *snares?
bonds?* dp. hæftnyssum, xi. 159
(v.l. ēhtnyssum). [Two examples,
not from Ælfric, cited by Hall,
'hæftnes'. Plural not recorded.]

hæl, m. *salvation, health.* ii. 129, 131;
v. 49, 167, 193, 194; vi. 321; xi. 567;
xvi. 180; xvii. 173 (ds. hæle, perhaps rather from hælu).

gehælan, I. (a) *to heal*: ii. 40, 45, etc.
(26 times, including 276, 287, pp.
as wk. adj., gehæleda); iv. 8, 59,
89, 93; vi. 84, 332; etc. (b) *to
castrate*: xix. 62. [Meaning (b) not
in BT; see Hall.]

Hælend, m. *Saviour, Jesus.* i. 2, etc. (13 times); ii. 7, etc. (21 times); iii. 30, 142, 143, 185; iv. 1, etc. (19 times); etc. [Ælfric normally uses def. art., 'se Hælend', but at viii. 62 he points out that the name *Jesus* means 'Hælend'.]

hǣlu, f. *health, salvation.* ii. 109, 140; v. 244; viii. 61, 63, 72; xia. 105; xvii. 100, 111; xx. 356; xxvi. 139; perhaps ds. **hǣle,** vi. 321 and xvii. 173 (see **hǣl**).—in sing. only; oblique cases have both -**u** and -**e**.

hǣman, I *to have intercourse, cohabit.* xv. 90.

hǣmed, n. *cohabitation.* i. 426; xix. 45, 72, 101, 111.

hǣr, n. *a hair.* vii. 160.

hǣr, adv. see **hēr**.

hǣre, wk. f. *sackcloth of hair.* xvii. 63.

hǣs, f. *behest.* ii. 80, 175; xia. 110; xii. 228; xiii. 48; xv. 89; xvii. 217; xviii. 320; xix. 30, 52; xx. 63, 233, 361; xxi. 69; xxii. 92; xxvi. 75, 78, 128; xxx. 19, 28.

hǣte, f. *heat.* xxi. 42.

hǣþen, adj. *heathen, gentile.* i. 113, 146, 348 (contrasting Jews and gentiles); iii. 145 (same); iv. 76, 232; v. 122; viii. 78, 104; xii. 107, 108, 112; xiv. 55, 85, 180 (these three referring to the once-heathen but converted gentiles); xvii. 222; xxi. 145, 211, 283, 286, 581; xxii. 9; xxvi. 13, 22; xxix. 119.—as noun, dp. strong, **eallum hǣþenum,** xxi. 139.—as noun, wk. w. def. art.ʻ *the heathen,* usually in pl. iv. 80; v. 125, 129; xi. 64, 384; xia. 181; xii. 93 (þone hǣþenan); xiv. 93; xviii. 184; xxi. 99, etc. (17 times); xxii. 62, 64, 65, 93; xxiii. 8; xxix. 86.

hǣþengyld, n. (a) *idolatry.* xviii. 288; xxi. 72, 512 (see note), 647 (-gild). (b) *idol, heathen shrine.* xxiii. 18 (dp. -gildum).

hǣþenscipe, -scype, m. *idolatry, paganism.* xviii. 284, 350; xxi. 239; xxiii. 44; xxvi. 10; xxx. 26.

hāl, adj. *whole, sound, well.* ii. 22, 32, 38, 86, 193; vii. 192; xvii. 83; xx. 346; xxiii. 26, 33, 136.—comp.

nsm. **hālre** (v.l. **hālra,** properly), vi. 106.

gehāl, adj. *whole, entire.* xiii. 165.

gehālgian, II. *to hallow, sanctify.* ii. 217, 252; ix. 50; xi. 18; xia. 92; xii. 103, 104; xvi. 141; xxi. 581, 644.

hālig, adj. *holy.* (a) strong dcl., examples of forms: ns., i. 133; asn., viii. 107; gsm. **hāliges,** xxi. 301; dsm. **hālgum,** vii. 112; dsf. **hāligre,** ii. 133; asm. **hāligne,** viii. 100; np. **hālie** (for **hālige**), xxiii. 142; ap. **hālige,** ii. 142; dp. **hālgum,** iii. 56. (b) wk. as adj., examples of forms: nsm. **hālga,** i. 393; nsf. **hālige,** i. 85; nsn., i. 404; asn., i. 2; gsm. **hālgan,** i. 109; dsm., i. 25; asm., i. 21; dsf., i. 320; asf., i. 26; dsn., ii. 2; np., iv. 126; ap., iii. 61; gp. **hāligra,** xi. 258; dp. **hālgum,** i. 201,—**sē Hālga Gāst,** *the Holy Spirit.* variously inflected, i. 88, 92, 159, 397, 401, 471; ii. 179, 291; iii. 179; iv. 135, 152, 160, 162, 167; etc.—similarly with **Frōforgāst,** vii. 57; x. 11, 80; xia. 7.—wk. as noun w. def. art., poss. **Godes** or **his,** *saint.* nsm. **hālga,** xvii. 292; dsm. **hālgan,** xxiii. 121; nap. **hālgan,** viii. 176, 199; xi. 458; xiv. 167, 194; etc. (16 times); gp. **hālgena,** viii. 155; xi. 470, 533, 546; xvi. 82; xxv(c). 7; dp. **hālgum,** i. 133; iv. 155, 161; etc. (15 times).

hāligdōm, m. *(holiness), holy things.* xxi. 222 (the contents of the Ark of the Covenant).

~~**hālsian,** II. *to adjure.* xvii. 230 (Lat. *adiuro per Deum*).~~

hālwende, adj. *healing, salutary.* xvii. 31, 121, 125, 130, 151; xx. 356.

hām, m. *home.* (a) in phrase, **æt hām,** *at home,* with endingless locative. vi. 50; xx. 108, 127; xxi. 264; xxii. 86. (b) as adv., *home, homewards.* v. 218; xvii. 245; xxi. 222, 251, 253, 262, 620; xxiii. 26; xxvi. 79.

*hama, m. *(covering), slough* of a snake. xvi. 235. [Uniquely used for *slough* in this passage; already cited by Napier.]

hand, f. *(u-decl.) hand.* ii. 26, 69, 82,

86, 89; iv. 150, 166; vi. 101; vii. 140, 141, 154; etc. [Forms: nas. **hand**, ii. 82; iv. 150; ds. **handa**, xxvii. 34; nap. **handa**, vii. 154; xxvi. 65; dp. **handum**, ii. 26.]

handbred, n. *palm of the hand*. xxi. 232 (np., -**breda**).

handgeweorc, n. *handiwork, creation*. ix. 63; xia. 147.

handlian, II. *to handle*. vii. 140.

hangian, II, intrans. *to hang*. xix. 246 [Cf. **ahōn**.]

hāt, adj. *hot*. xix. 198.

hātan, 7, pp. **gehāten**. (a) *to bid, order, command*. imp. s. **hāt**, xx. 325; pres. 1s. **hāte**, xxiii. 185; 2s. **hātst**, xxiii. 108; 3s. **hāt**, xiii. 104 (v.l. **hēt**); pret. 2s. **hēte**, xxiii. 85; xxvi. 67; 3s. **hēt**, ii. 48, etc. (6 times); iii. 4, 5; viii. 164; xia. 64; xiii. 54, 104 (v.l. **hāt**), 179; etc. (46 times more); 3p. **hēton**, xix. 168; xxi. 517; 3s. subj. **hēte**, xiii. 211; xix. 46. (b) *to call, name*: pres. 3s. **hǣt**, xv. 16, 150; xxi. 578; 1p. **hātaþ**, xi. 56; xia. 173; xviii. 5; 3p., iv. 14, 24, 74, 117; xix. 46; xx. 28; xxi. 142, 143; xxx. 106; pret. 3s. **hēt**, i. 140, 362; iii. 61; vii. 173; xv. 227; xxi. 673; 3p. **hēton**, iv. 77, 83; xiv. 47; xxi. 194; pp. **gehāten**, *called*. i. 175, 324; ii. 11; iv. 159, 165; v. 4, 57; vi. 183, 231, 262; etc. (c) **hātte**, *is called, was called*. vi. 304; viii. 145; x. 159; xvii. 57; xxi. 124, 126, 150, 224; xxii. 52; xxiii. 53; xxvii. 17. [Cf. **behātan**.]

hātheortnyss, f. *rage*. xxvi. 67.

hatian, II. *to hate*. iv. 105; ix. 206 (twice); xiii. 47, 48, 155, 161; xv. 82.

hatung, f. (a) *hate, hatred*. ii. 202; xiii. 154, 159, 180. (b) *a demonstration of hatred*. dp. **hatungum**, ix. 198.

hē, m., **hēo**, f., **hit**, n., pron. 3d person. i. 3, 4, 5, 6, 7, etc. Prevailing forms include gdsf. **hire**, asf. and nap. **hi**, gp. **heora** (very rarely **hyra**, as at iv. 17, MS. T and xi. 245, MS. U). Substitution of y for i occurs frequently in **hit**, **his**, **hine**, **hire**, and occasionally in **hi**. The dsm. and n. **him** usually retains i

and some MSS. (e.g. L, R, U) tend to distinguish the dp. by spelling it **hym**. Others (e.g. C, E, M, and the interpolated sections of H) have dp. **heom** and **hiom**. Late alterations in the Worcester MSS. (E, P, R, S, T, X^d), not here recorded, give dp. **ham**. Use of **ig** as a spelling for long i leads to an occasional **hig** for **hi** (e.g. vi. 290, 291; xxiii. 106, 108, 155) and even **hyg** (xiii. 115).

hēafod, n. *head*. i. 7; vi. 101 (**hēafud**); xi. 433, 533; xii. 201, 207, 211; xvi. 240, 241, 242, 245; xix. 193; xxi. 231, 550, 552, 558, 566 (ap. **hēafda**); xxii. 35.

hēafodburh, f. *chief city*. xxi. 522; xxvi. 28, 34.

hēadfodleahter, m. *capital sin*. iv. 249, 252, 263; xiii. 159; xvii. 199; xix. 127.

hēafodlēas, adj. *headless*. xxi. 233.

hēafodmann, m. *head man, elder, leader*. xiii. 218; xx. 148, 219.

hēah, adj. *high*. nsn., viii. 108; xxi. 535; nsf., xxi. 531; nsm. wk. **hēaga**, v. 178; asf. wk. **hēagan**, v. 178; dsm. wk. **hēan**, v. 176 (v.l. **hēagan**); dp. **hēagum**, xxi. 138. —sup. **hēhst(a)**, only in wk. decl. for God, *the Highest*. gsm. **Hēxtan**, i. 359 (as noun); **Hēhstan**, xviii. 229 (as adj.); xxi. 671 (as noun).

hēahengel, m. *archangel*. xia. 62.

hēahfæder, m. *patriarch*. iii. 118; v. 4, 256; xx. 146.

hēahgerēfa, wk. m. (*high sheriff*), *prefect*. xxiii. 52.

hēahnyss, **hēannyss**, f. *high place*. v. 182; xii. 40, 221.

hēahset(t)l, n. *throne, judgement-seat*. xi. 362.

hēahþegen, m. *chief minister*. xxi. 301 (Godes h., the prophet Daniel).

healdan, **gehealdan**, 7. (a) *to hold, sustain, govern*. i. 88, 181 (?); x. 118. (b) *to guard, preserve, protect, save*. iv. 202; v. 262; vi. 33; ix. 50, 55; xiv. 194; xviii. 391; xix. 59; xxi. 53; xxv(b). 1;—against (**wiþ**) an adversary, vi. 282; xxi. 283, 326, 348. (c) *to keep* something *in store*. xvi. 162 (w. dat. of pers. for whom);

healdan, ġehealdan (*cont.*)

with extension or complement, *to keep* in a place, xxi. 217; in a place and condition, xxi. 264; in a condition (compl. adj.), xii. 106. (d) *to hold, keep from getting away*, by **(mid)** some specified means, xvii. 223; in **(on)** a restraining medium, xxiii. 52. (e) w. **fæst**, *to hold fast, keep safe*. iv. 34, 183. (f) *to hold in place, hold together*. iii. 143. (g) fig., *to have hold of, possess* a spiritual benefit. i. 332. (h) *to hold* an office. xxi. 644. [BTS, 'healdan', VIII. a.] (i) *to keep, observe faithfully, keep unbroken* or *inviolate* a religious faith, a rite, a designated day or season, a command, a law, a state of purity, etc. ii. 165, 167; iii. 90; iv. 55, 182, 237, 288, 292, 294, 296; ix. 108; x. 4, 7, 30, 58; xi. 2, 105, 137, 148; xiv. 96, 98; xv. 28, 32, 64, 66, 104, 105, 112, 114; xvi. 82, 252; xviii. 395; xix. 7, 46 (twice), 47, 114, 121; xxi. 35, 44;—with **fram**, *keep free from*, xviii. 340. *(k) *to hold* in veneration, *worship* a god. xxi. 658 (apparently an extension of the preceding, glossed *obseruabant*). (l) *to withhold from present use, reserve*. vi. 129. (m) *to hold back, restrain*. xv. 179;—refl., *to restrain oneself* (sometimes also, from sense b, *to be on guard*?), ii. 55 (w. neg. clause, *lest*), 278 (**wiþ**, *from, against*); xiii. 229 (**wiþ**) ; xxi. 55 (**wiþ**). (n) pp. **ġehealden on**, *satisfied with*. xxi. 99 [BTS, 'ġehealdan', XI. a, including this instance, cited from the revised excerpt by Wulfstan.]—[Forms: inf. **healdan**, ix. 50 (11 times); ġeh., iv. 202 (6 times); d. inf. **healdenne**, ii. 165 (4 times); ġeh., xv. 28 (3 times); imp. sg. **heald**, ii. 55; ġeh., ii. 278; imp. pl. **healdaþ**, xxi. 264; pres. 3s. **healt**, iv. 34 (5 times); **hylt**. i. 88 (8 times); ġehylt, i. 332 (3 times); 1p. **healdaþ**, xi. 2 (3 times); 3p., iv. 182 (6 times); ġeh., iv. 55, 288; pres. 3s. subj. **healde**, xix. 46; ġeh., vi. 282; xv. 179; 1p. subj. **healdan**, xvi. 252; xviii. 395; pret. 3s. **hēold**, vi. 129;

xxi. 348; ġeh., xxi. 35 (4 times); 3p. **hēoldon**, iii. 90 (4 times); 3p. subj., xv. 112; pp. **ġehealden**, v. 262 (7 times).—Cf. **behealdan**.]

ġehealdsumnyss, f. (a) (*religious*) *observance*. xv. 80. (b) *moral practice* (or *restraint*?). xvii. 276 (-**healt**-).

healf, f. *side*, always in the phrase, **on . . . healfe** (acc. sg.) or **healfa** (acc. pl.). iii. 112; xi. 407; xiii. 118; xiv. 159, 170; xix. 175; xxvii. 57.

healf, adj. *half*. viii. 81 (**to fēorþan healfan ġeare**, *for three years and u hulf*); xvi. 177; xx. 218, 257 (both **þridde healf hund**, *two hundred and fifty*).

hēalic, adj. (a) physically *high, on high, lofty*. xviii. 239, 265, 309, 409. (b) of spiritual signs, meanings, *lofty, sublime* or *deep, profound*. vi. 322; xii. 39, 220. (c) of honours, adoration, *high, exceptional*. xix. 14; xxvi. 22. (d) of gods or great men, *highly honoured, exalted*. iv. 80; xxi. 114, 128; xxii. 59. (e) of a heretic, *proud* or *notable*. x. 159. (f) of a heresy, *egregious* or *grievous, profound*. xxi. 160, 592.

hēalīce, adv. *loftily, proudly*. xxi. 235.

healt, adj. *lame*. ii. 78. str. pl. as noun, *lame persons, cripples*. ii. 26, 69; xia. 105; xvi. 169.

hēan, adj. *lowly* (in rank and power). i. 214; nsm. wk. as noun, xi. 401.

hēan, see **hēah**.

hēannyss, see **hēahnyss**.

hēap, m. *throng, company*. xi. 153, 435; xxvii. 79.

heard, adj. *hard*. xix. 31, 32; xx. 22.

hearde, adv. *severely, greatly, grievously*. xvii. 140; xxi. 50.

heardheort, adj. *hardhearted*. iii. 168; iv. 31, 132, 258.

heardheortnyss, f. *hardness of heart*. vi. 275, 314.

heardnyss, f. *hardness*. xix. 14.

hearmian, II. *to harm, injure*. xxx. 47.

hearmlic, adj. *harmful, grievous*. xx. 275.

hearpe, wk. f. *harp*. xxvii. 72.

hebban, 6. *to lift up*. pret. 3p. **hōfan**, xxi. 228. [Cf. **ahebban**, **upahebban**.]

hefe, m. *weight, burden.* xxvi. 51.

hefig, adj. *heavy, burdensome.* xi. 253; xiii. 57, 68; xviii. 118; xxvi. 91 (hefeᵹ- last three).

ᵹehefiᵹian, II. *to oppress, burden.* only as pp. np. **ᵹehefeᵹode,** ii. 62; v. 158.

***hefiᵹmōd,** adj. *heavy-hearted.* xi. 559. [Unique in this sense. Cited by Napier.]

hefiᵹtȳme, adj. *grievous.* xxi. 41.

heᵹe, m. *hedge.* iii. 68.

Hēhstan, see **hēah.**

Helias. *Elias (Elijah).* ii. 154 (v.l. **elias);** viii. 79; ix. 67.

hell, f. *hell.* iv. 196; x. 202; xi. 170, etc. (11 times); xia. 51; xii. 112; xviii. 57, 218, 432; xix. 214 **(helle ᵹata,** see **ᵹeat),** 224, 229; xx. 253; xxi. 70; xxvii. 32, 47.

helleᵹrund, m. *abyss of hell.* ii. 176.

hellewīte, n. *hell-torment.* xia. 85; xxvii. 6.

hellic, adj. *hellish, of hell.* iv. 113; xi. 134; xviii. 71; xix. 198, 219, 237; xxi. 201, 291.

ᵹehelpan, 3, w. gen. (as indicated) or dat. *to help.* inf., ix. 215; xiv. 194 (w. gen.); imp. sg. **ᵹehelp,** xvii. 209 (w. gen.); xxvii. 100 (w. gen.?); imp. pl. **ᵹehelpaþ,** xxiii. 104 (w. gen. or dat.); pres. 2s. **ᵹehylpst,** xxiv. 10; 3s. **ᵹehelpþ,** xi. 242; **ᵹehylpþ,** xv. 228; pres. 1p. subj. **ᵹehelpon,** xv. 215; pret. 3s. **ᵹehealp,** xxii. 42 (MS. **ᵹeheolp).**

ᵹehende, adv. and prep. w. dat. *near.* (a) adv., viii. 108; xiv. 81; xxi. 580 (all three w. **þǣr).** (b) prep., ii. 10; v. 183; viii. 107; xiv. 13, 78.— comp. **ᵹehendor,** *nearer.* v. 176; xix. 27 (w. dat.).

henᵹen, f. *rack* (instrument of torture). ds. **henᵹenne,** xxiii. 190.

hentan, I, w. gen. (a) *to capture* an animal. i. 214. (b) *to get at* with a blow, *strike.* xvi. 242.

hēo, see **hē.**

hēofian, II. *to lament.* xi. 293, 328; xxvi. 79, 88, 91.

heofon, m. *heaven.* ns., xxvi. 96 (or f., see next)—all other instances pl. nap. **heofonas,** i. 82, 200, 359; xi.

79; xia. 45, 195; xxi. 368; gp. **heofona, heofena,** iii. 179; xxvii. 10 (both w. **rīce,** normally wk. fem. **heofonan** and so v.l. at iii. 179); dp. **heofonum, heofenum,** i. 89, 435, 443, 453; ii. 92; iii. 126; etc. (52 times more).

heofon, f. *heaven.* ns. **sēo heofon,** xxi. 186, 540, 549; **heofon** (uncertain gender), xxvi. 96. [See note on xxi. 186.]

heofone, wk. f. *heaven.* only in sing. as **heofonan,** gs. v. 197; xviii. 263, 402; and w. **rīce,** iii. 98; iv. 196; v. 150, 262; xi. 142, 151, 370; xv. 6, 57; xvi. 272; xviii. 54, 166, 422, 436; xix. 45, 69; xxv(a). 10; ds. xi. 516; as. i. 72, 280; xi. 510; xviii. 269, 417; xix. 234; xxx. 38.

heofonlic, adj. *heavenly.* i. 91, 146, 405, 471; ii. 19, 233, 244; iii. 52, 117; iv. 59, 164, 167, 180; v. 47, 103, 165, 181; vii. 33, 63, etc.

hēold, hēoldon, see **healdan.**

heonon, heonan, adv. *hence.* ii. 39; x. 201; xi. 436; xii. 209; xxi. 268; xxiii. 137.—**heonon forþ,** *henceforth.* ii. 55; v. 32, 153; x. 24, 185; xiii. 227; xiv. 38, 216; xxii. 47.

heora, see **hē.**

heorcnian, II. (a) *to hearken to,* w. gen., viii. 18. (b) *to give heed to.* xxx. 23 (construction not clear).

heord, f. *herd, flock.* xiv. 206; xvii. 235.

heorte, wk. f. *heart.* i. 94; ii. 78, 144; vi. 286; vii. 11, 39, 223; viii. 95, 247, 254; etc.

hēr, adv. *here.* i. 26, 80, 84, 147, 157, 346, 352, 405; v. 32, 153, 228; vi. 52, 67, 76 **(hǣr),** 215; etc.—**hēr on līfe,** *in this life.* i. 4; ii. 7; v. 2; vii. 128; ix. 1; etc.—**hēr on worulde,** v. 270; vii. 95.—**hēr bæftan,** *after this, immediately after.* i. 343.—**hēr beforan,** *earlier in this (discourse).* vi. 198. [On **hēr** with other adverbs, see OED, 'here', adv. 16. The next entry is similar but seems a little more closely united.]

hēræfter, adv. *hereafter, immediately after.* xiii. 98.

here, m. *army.* ix. 51; xx. 64; xxvi. 34.

herereaf, f. *booty, plunder.* iv. 38, 187, 193; x. 202.

heretoga, m. *general.* i. 70; iii. 57; xi. 25; xia. 99; xii. 227; xx. 141, 236, 369; xxii. 14, 18, 35, 52, 64, 74, 83; xxiii. 46.

gehergian, II. (a) *to overrun with an army, lay waste.* xxii. 92. (b) *to carry off as spoil.* xx. 169.

herian, II (orig. I). *to praise.* ii. 289; iv. 71 (pres. 3s. heraþ), 285, 295; xi. 73, 90, 563; xia. 190; xvi. 29, 193, 204, 207; xvii. 112, 272; xxi. 299. pp. gehered, xiii. 188.

heriendlic, adj. *laudable.* xxvi. 135.

Hermes, (a) *Hermes Trismegistus.* i. 115, 138, 144. (b) *Hermes,* Prefect of Rome and martyr in the time of Pope Alexander I. xxiii. 11-199 (ns. 11, etc., 10 times; ds. Ermen, 74, 83, 87, 91; as. Ermen, 52, 54, 95, 174, 199).

herung, f. *praise.* xv. 79; xvi. 207; xvii. 91.

hetelice, adv. *malignantly, savagely, fiercely.* vii. 100; xix. 192; xxi. 207.

hetol, adj. *hostile, malignant, evil.* iii. 168; iv. 8, 107, 206; vi. 275, 284; vii. 173; xi. 31; xia. 131; xiii. 155; xviii. 184; xix. 237; xxi. 110, 145.

Hextan, see heah.

hi, see he.

hider, adv. *hither.* v. 34, 74, 76, 241; vi. 98; vii. 9; xii. 36, 198; xxiii. 88, 152; xxvi. 108.

Hieremias, *Jeremiah.* ix. 68.

Hieronimus, *Jerome.* xxviii. 7.

Hierusalem, *Jerusalem.* ii. 9; iii. 84; v. 42, 46, 164; vi. 45 (Ieru-); xiii. 192; xvi. 189. [Uninfl. in ds. and as.]

hig, see he.

hiht, hyht, m. *hope, expectation.* ii. 173; xvi. 264, 267; xix. 250.

hihtan, I. *to hope, trust.* xiii. 82; xix. 133.

hihtleas, adj. *hopeless.* ix. 175; xix. 135.

him, hine, see he.

hingrian, II (older 'hyngran', I). *to hunger.* (a) impers. w. dat. of person. ii. 112; xi. 412, 439, 559; xxv(c). 8 (twice). (b) w. nom. of person; perhaps hungrienne, xi. 420, is a de-

based spelling of pres. part. asm. hingriendne, but it may be intended for hungrigne: see hungrig, and the note on xi. 420.

gehiran, see gehyran.

hire, see he.

hired, m. *household, family.* iii. 4, 51, 115, 133; iv. 105; xv. 2; xvi. 180.

his, hit, see he.

hiw, n. (a) *form, appearance.* vii. 47; xii. 128; xviii. 82; xix. 79. (b) *colour.* xvii. 260. (c) *nature.* xii. 137 (hywe).

hiwan, imp. (*members of a*) *household.* xvii. 245; xx. 251 (*households*); xxiii. 159.

hiwere, m. *hypocrite.* iii. 98; xiii. 31, 172 (hywere), 175.

gehiwian, II. (a) *to simulate.* xx. 351; xxix. 29. (b) reflex., *to disguise oneself.* xxix. 66.

hiwræden, f. *family, household.* iii. 76; iv. 20 (twice), 100 (twice); xxx. 85.

hiwung, f. (*false*) *pretence, dissimulation, hypocrisy.* iv. 227, 245; xv. 84, 207; xviii. 97, 102, 109.

hladan, 6. *to draw water.* inf., v. 32, 153.

gehladan, 6. *to load, heap up.* pp. ap. gehladene, xiv. 39, 226.

hlædfæt, n. *vessel for drawing water, pitcher.* v. 22.

hlaf, m. *loaf, bread.* xia. 121, 124; xix. 4 (twice), 5; xx. 312; xxx. 108 (twice).

hlaford, hlafurd, m. *lord.* iii. 12, 15, 25, 106; iv. 105; v. 31, 39, 152; vi. 10, 52, 62, 76, 81, 87; etc.

hlafordscipe, m. *authority, rule.* xia. 36.

hlid, n. *lid, cover.* vi. 91 (stone cover of Lazarus's tomb).

gehlid, see gehlyd.

hlisa, m. *fame, repute.* vi. 167; ix. 76; xv. 79; xvii. 11, 304.

hloh, see hlyhhan.

hlowan, 7. *to low* (as do cows). pres. part. hlowende, xxi. 276.

hlude, adv. *loudly.* i. 453; vi. 97; x. 97; xviii. 418.

hluttor, adj. *pure, unsullied.* xiii. 181.

*hluttrian, II. *to strain out* (an impurity from a liquid). xiii. 168. [This meaning not in dict. See **ahlyttrian,** for which this verb is substituted in a partial repetition.]

ġehlȳd, ġehlīd, m. *noise, tumult.* xvii. 115; xx. 266. [Sometimes fem. but xvii treats as masc.]

hlyhhan, 6. *to laugh.* pret. 3s. **hlōh,** xxi. 417.

hlystan, I. *to listen to* (w. gen.). xix. 25.

hnesce, adj. *soft.* xix. 30.

***hōc,** m. *hook,* here fig., *crafty device.* xvi. 219. [This fig. sense not recorded in BT or BTS, though something similar is cited from CH I. 362/27. Nearest definition in OED is I. 2. b, dating from 1430.]

hōfan, see **hebban.**

hoferode ('hoferede'), adj. *humpbacked.* xxiii. 104.

hogian, II. *to think, consider, be solicitous, take care,* xi. 125, 126; xiii. 175; xvii. 174; xviii. 155, 172, 182; xix. 80, 81; xxii. 3. [Cf. **forhogian.**]

hogu, f. *concern, anxiety.* xi. 271.

hohfull, adj. *anxious, solicitous.* xi. 154.

hol, adj. *hollow.* iv. 227.

hold, n. *dead body, carcase.* xviii. 39, 205, 211.

hold, adj. (a) *gracious.* xxi. 507. (b) *faithful.* xi. 153, 239.

holdlīce, adv. *faithfully.* xvi. 292.

holian, II. *to hollow out.* xxi. 207.

Hon, a rebel against Moses (Num. xvi. 1 sqq.). xx. 220.

hopian, II. (a) w. **tō,** *to look with expectation to, put trust in* (God). xv. 229; xix. 252; xxv(*c*). 11.—*to hope for* (a satisfaction). xvi. 146; xix. 133. (b) w. **on,** *to put trust in* (a thing). xvi. 264.

hordcleofa, m. *treasury, secret chamber.* xxiii. 94.

hors, n. *horse.* i. 272; xxvii. 93; xxix. 28.

hosp, m. *reproach, insult, blasphemy, scorn.* vi. 219, 224, 226, 269; x. 173; xiii. 170; xv. 15, 143, 144, 153; xx. 288; xxi. 558.

***ġehradian,** II, trans. *to make pass*

quickly, accelerate. xviii. 375. [This sense not in dict; cf. BTS, I.]

hraþe, hræþe, raþe, adv. *quickly, immediately, soon.* **hraþe,** ii. 189; viii. 31, 58; xi. 254, 300; etc. (12 times more). **raþe,** iv. 104; vi. 72, 91; xv. 194; xix. 47; xxiii. 129.—**swā raþe swā,** *as soon as.* xi. 194.—**hraþe þæs,** *immediately (after that), thereupon.* xv. 53 (**hræþe**); xix. 200.—comp. **hraþor,** *sooner, more readily.* xi. 340 (with logical force).

hrēam, m. *lamentation, sorrow, cry.* iii. 79; xx. 254.

hrēod, rēod, n. *reed, rush.* iv. 223, 227 (**rēodes, rēod,** v.l. **hrēodes, hrēod**); vii. 101 (**rēodum**).

hrēoflig, adj. *leprous.* xia. 105.

hrēohnyss, f. *rough weather, storm.* xvii. 205 (-ness).

hreppan, I, hrepian, II. *to touch.* xvii. 27, 31, 130 (**hrepode**); xix. 91 (pres. 3s. subj. **hreppe**); xxi. 48 (inf. **hreppan**).

hrepung, f. *touch.* xvii. 82, 152.

hring, m. *ring.* xxi. 256, 272 (ornamental gold), 395 (a seal-ring).

ġehrisian, II. *to shake together.* pp. **ġehrysed,** xiii. 16; **ġehrisod,** xiii. 111. (Lat. *coagitatam.*)

hrōf, m. *roof.* xviii. 239, 240, 309, 310.

hrȳman, I. (a) *to rave.* xvii. 226. (b) *to cry out, wail.* xxi. 248.

hrȳþer, n. *ox* (including *cow, bull*). iv. 81 (ap., -**u**). [Shortened **y**? See OED, 'rother'.]

hū, adv. *how.* (a) in direct questions, modifying a verb. iii. 25; iv. 22, 109; xii. 11, etc. (6 times); xiii. 20, etc. (6 times); xix. 223; xxvi. 65, 119; xxvii. 68. (b) in direct questions, modifying an adj. or adv., *to what extent* or *degree.* xx. 182; xxiii. 178. (c) in an exclamation, modifying an adj. xix. 230 (**hū mycel tōdāl,** *how great a difference!*).—(d) in dependent questions, modifying a verb. i. 18, 120, 430, 435; ii. 124; iii. 43, 165; iv. 112, 207; vi. 82, 109, 206; vii. 131, 141; etc. (55 times more); *(e) elliptically, the verb of the dependent clause omitted. iii. 172 (**gyf hī wiston hū**). [OED, 12, first

hū (*cont.*)

quotation 1200.] (f) in dependent questions, modifying an adj. or adv. i. 180; xi. 287; xvii. 246; xxi. 495, 507; xxii. 83. —(g) as interjection introducing a negative question and calling for an affirmative answer, **lā hū ne**, *what! will not*, etc. v. 77; vi. 25, 83, 89; xxi. 628. **hū ne**, *will not, can it be that . . . not.* xiii. 21, 125. (Lat. *nonne*.)—(h) **swā hū swā**, conj., *howsoever.* xx. 21 [i.e. *in whatever style (of cookery?)*].

gehū, adv. *in some way or other.* i. 199.

hūmeta, adv. *in what way, how.* xx. 183; xxiii. 108.

hund, m. *hound, dog.* i. 233; xiii. 232; xviii. 176 (np. **hundas**, one MS. **hundan** as if from wk. **hunda**); xxiii. 194.

hund, n. *hundred.* xx. 10, 218, 257.

hundeahtatig, num. *eighty.* xvi. 28, 145.

hundfeald, adj. *hundred-fold.* xxx. 15.—**be hundfealdum**, adv. *by a hundred-fold.* xiii. 108; xvi. 159; xxx. 42.

hundred, n. *hundred.* xxiii. 39.

hundseofantig, num. *seventy.* xxi. 389.

hundtēontig, num. *hundred.* xvi. 23, 26, 130, 143.

*hundtēontigwintre, adj. *a hundred years old.* xix. 20. [Cited by Napier from this passage, where it is unique; cf. **þrītigwintre**.]

hundtwelftig, num. *hundred and twenty.* x. 100; xx. 366; xxi. 503 (dp. -**um**).

hungor, m. *hunger.* xxi. 41.

hungrig, adj. *hungry.* xi. 420 (asm. **hungrienne**, v.l. **hungrigne**), 446 (asm. **hungrinne**, v.l. **hungrigne**); xxiii. 182 (nsm. wk. **hungria**). [For an alternative interpretation and discussion of the curious form **hungrienne** see **hingrian** and the note on xi. 420.]

hūru, interj. and adv. marking the emotional and logical force of the neighbouring words, hence to be variously translated. (a) *at least.* xix. 7, 130. (b) *at last.* xi. 198; xix. 151, 253. (c) *indeed.* xii. 50 (**swā hūru**,

though indeed); xix. 93; xxvii. 3 (?). (d) *even.* xvi. 195. (e) *only.* xi. 195. (f) *above all.* xvi. 242.

hūs, n. *house.* (a) an ordinary dwelling. vi. 177; x. 100; xi. 58; xia. 175; xvi. 17, 124, 148, 182; xviii. 28, 239, 241, 309, 311; xix. 174; xxiii. 92, 107; xxix. 91. (b) the house of a god, a temple, a church. xxi. 194, 535; xxvi. 95, 113, 116, 127. (c) a guest-house. xxvi. 105 (ds. **cumena hūse**, see **cuma**). (d) fig., iv. 45, 236); xiv. 121; xix. 68.

hūsel, n. *housel, Eucharist.* xi. 177; xix. 119, 121, 130; xxvi. 69.

hūslian, II. *to administer the sacrament.* xix. 131.

hūsling, f. *administration of the sacrament.* xix. 226.

hūxlic ('hūsc-'), adj. *contemptible.* xi. 341.

hūxlīce, adv. (a) *shamefully, ignominiously*: xiv. 142. *(b) *contemptuously, insultingly*: xiii. 170; xx. 275. [Meaning (b) not in dict. though implicit in 'hūsc'.]

hwā, m. (f.), **hwæt**, n., interr. pron. *who, what.* nsm. **hwā**, v. 18; vi. 114; xi. 143, 157; xx. 85; xxi. 382, 404; gsm. **hwæs**, iv. 26, 119; xxi. 420; asm. **hwæne**, x. 176; xi. 291; xx. 228.—nsn. **hwæt**, ii. 50, 51; vii. 103; ix. 65, 69 (second), 146; etc. (12 more including xxiii. 183, **lōc hwæt**, see **lōc**); asn. **hwæt**, iii. 24, 67, 114, 133; v. 63 (twice), 155; etc. (24 more); gsn. **hwæs**, i. 224; xix. 184; dsn. **hwām**, xxvi. 58; xxvii. 119; isn. **hwī** in **tō hwī**, *for what reason, why*, xvii. 210. [See also **hwī**, adv.]—indef. pron. *someone, anyone, something, anything.* nsm. **hwā**, vi. 224; viii. 48, 91, 243; xv. 173; xvi. 194; xviii. 27, 253, 376; xix. 106; xxi. 539; xxix. 9.— asn. **hwæt**, xxx. 50; gsn. **hwæs**, xxi. 590.—**swā hwā swā**, *whosoever.* nsm., ii. 128; xii. 14, 96; xix. 37; xxiii. 152; xxv(*a*). 2; xxx. 83.— **swā hwæt swa**, *whatsoever.* nsn., xxv(*c*). 2; xxx. 110; asn., v. 91; vii. 27, 207; viii. 95; tc. (5 more). **swā hwæs swā**, gsn., vi. 54.

ġehwā, m. (f.), ġehwæt, n., indef. pron. (a) *each one, everyone.* ġehwā, nsm. vi. 289; ix. 210; xix. 53; ġehwæne, asm. xvi. 256; xvii. (71)?—(b) *someone, something, somewhat.* ġehwā, nsm., xxix. 97; ġehwæt, asn., xxi. 586; xxix. 99.

ġehwæde, adj. *small, slight.* xix. 168.

hwænne, hwenne (v.l. hwanne, hwonne), adv. *when.* (a) in direct questions. xi. 419, 422, 423, 424, 445. (b) in dependent questions. xi. 275; xviii. 45; xxiii. 89.

hwǣr, adv. *where.* (a) in direct questions. vi. 80; xiii. 222; xxvi. 118. (b) in dependent questions. ii. 241; xix. 218.—swā hwǣr swā, *wheresoever.* xviii. 39, 205; xx. 16; xxi. 246 (hwār).

ġehwǣr, adv. *everywhere.* iv. 233; xxvi. 24.—*ġehwǣr and þǣr, *there and everywhere?* xxi. 648. [This idiom not listed in dict.]

hwæt, interj. *what!* occurs only at head of sentence or question. (a) before a question. xiv. 136; hwæt lā, ii. 272; xvii. 213. (b) with adv. þā before another step or phase in a narrative; the combination often to be translated merely by *then, so then, and then.* hwæt þā, iv. 7; viii. 125; xiii. 218; xvi. 29, 204; xvii. 36; xix. 176; xx. 329; xxi. 498; xxiii. 30, 90, 184; xxvi. 124. hwæt þā sōna, xvii. 168, 211; xx. 57. hwæt . . . þā, xxi. 271, 406. hwæt . . . þā þā, iii. 40, 162.

hwæt, ġehwæt, pron., see hwā, ġehwā.

hwǣte, m. *wheat.* xvi. 26, 143.

hwæthwega, pron. *somewhat, a little.* xi. 93.—as adv., xiv. 24, 127.

hwæþer, pron. adj. *which (of two).* as adj. in dependent question, asf. hwæþre, xiv. 170.—swā hwæþer swā, *whichever (of two).* xi. 219.

hwæþer, conj. w. subj. *whether.* (a) introducing a dependent question, no alternative given, *whether (or not), if.* ii. 267; v. 68; xx. 152; xxiii. 123; xxx. 92.—with alternative, hwæþer . . . oþþe, *whether . . . or.* x. 50–51; xxi. 251.—with ellipsis of verb and contrast of two nouns, hwæþer þe. . . þe, *whether . . . or.* xxix. 41.—(b) introducing a direct question, no alternative given, with declarative word-order, approx. *say whether (or not)*; but need not be translated if ordinary form of question is substituted. v. 74; xxi. 415; xxvi. 53.

hwanon, adv. and conj. *whence.* (a) introducing a direct question, v. 22. (b) introducing a dependent question, w. subj., xii. 22, 148; w. ind., xxvi. 58.

ġehwanon, adv. *from everywhere.* xvii. 17.

hwēne, adv. (instr. of hwōn). *somewhat, a little.* xxvii. 109(?).

hwenne, see hwænne.

hwer, m. *pot, bowl.* xxi. 518.

hwī, adv. and conj. (instr. of hwæt). *why.* (a) in direct questions. v. 14; viii. 143; xx. 104, 222, 310; xxi. 364, 601; xxiii. 55; xxv(c). 5 (twice), 6; xxvi. 108; xxvii. 103. (b) in dependent questions. viii. 2; xix. 224; xxi. 603; xxvi. 88. [For tō hwī, see hwā.]

hwider, hwyder, adv. and conj. *whither.* vii. 10; xii. 22, 148; xviii. 38, 204, 207, 208.—swā hwider swā, *whithersoever.* xvi. 185.

hwīl, f. *while, time.* sume hwīle, *for a certain time.* v. 282; vi. 148. lȳtle hwīle, *for a little while.* xi. 229. þā hwīle, *meanwhile.* v. 10; xx. 42; xxii. 89 (hwȳle). þā hwīle þe, conj., *while.* xi. 178, 482; xix. 85; xxi. 35, 44; xxvii. 4 (twice), 7, 104; xxviii. 9.

hwilc, ġehwilc, see hwylc, ġehwylc.

hwīlon, hwīlum, adv. (a) *once, at one time.* i. 322, 430; iv. 75; viii. 79, 103, 139; ix. 64, 72; xii. 3; xiv. 140; xv. 3; xvii. 52; xxii. 79; xxvii. 83. (b) *sometimes.* xv. 148, 166; xxi. 668.—corr. or with a similar expression, *sometimes . . . sometimes.* hwīlum . . . hwīlum, xviii. 315–16; hwīlon . . . on sumne sǣl, xiv. 73.

hwīlwendlīce, adv. *temporarily.* xx. 351.

hwīt, adj. *white.* xxi. 192, 530. See also eallhwīt.

hwōn, adv. *somewhat, a little.* xiv. 12, 77.

hwōnlīcor, comp. adv. *to a slighter extent, less.* xi. 494 (twice).

hwylc, hwilc, adj. and pron. (a) as interr. adj., attributive, *what, what sort of, how much.* i. 180; v. 151; vi. 119; ix. 45, 75, 76; xxi. 287; xxv(*a*). 3; xxvi. 63, 64, 68.—predicative, *what, of what nature.* xv. 131. (b) as interr. pron., neuter, *what, what sort of thing.* xvii. 213. (c) as indef. adj., *any, some, a.* xix. 94, 97. (d) swā hwylc . . . swā, rel. adj. and pron. *whichever, whatever.* as adj., ii. 21, 23; xix. 54; as pron., w. gen., xiii. 215 (nsm. hwylc ēower).

*hwylc-ēower, indef. pron. (*any*) one of you.* gsm. hwylc-ēowres, *of one of you.* ii. 272. [See note.]

gehwylc, gehwilc, indef. pron. and adj. (a) in sing., *each, every, every sort of.* as pron., i. 380; xxvii. 109 (w. gp. manna); as adj., i. 396 (gehwylc mann in neg. sentence, *a man, no matter who*); iv. 158. (b) in pl., *many, numerous.* as pron., np. gehwylce ōþre, *many others,* xix. 111; transposed, xxi. 152; as adj., xiv. 112; xxii. 75.

hwȳle, see hwīl.

hȳ, hyg, see hē.

hyht, see hiht.

hym, hyne, hyra, see hē.

hȳran, I. (a) with tō, *to belong to.* xxx. 96 (þǣr þǣr hē tō hȳrþ, *whereto he belongs*). (b) w. dat., *to serve, obey.* xv. 32. [Cf. gehȳrsumian, and next entry.]

gehȳran, I. (a) trans. or intrans., *to hear.* i. 56, etc. (8 times); ii. 2, 81; iii. 40, 162, 174; iv. 10, 55, 288, 293; v. 96, etc. (7 times); vi. 1, etc. (6 times); vii. 27, 77, 153, 207; etc.; spelled gehiran, xvii. 89. (b) w. dat., *to obey.* xi. 97.

hyrde, m. *shepherd, guardian.* iv. 206; ix. 50.

hyrdrǣden, f. *guard, garrison.* iii. 82 (ds. -a); xv. 182.

hyre, see hē.

hyrne, f. *corner.* iii. 33.

hyrnet(t), f. *hornet.* i. 272.

hyrnstān, m. *cornerstone.* iii. 30, 31, 142, 148.

gehȳrsum, adj. *obedient.* w. dat., iii. 130; x. 208; xv. 89; xix. 56; xx. 355, 361; xxvi. 78; xxx. 1; w. tō, xxx. 16.

gehȳrsumian, II, w. dat. *to obey.* i. 201, 446; ii. 81, 133, 175; iv. 205; ix. 185; xi. 138, 191; xvii. 214; xviii. 51; xx. 418; xxi. 69; xxvi. 128; xxx. 28.

gehȳrsumnyss, f. *obedience.* xvii. 117; xx. 285; xxx. 21, 90.

hyrwan, I. *to slander, blaspheme.* xxi. 399.

hys, see hē.

hysecild, n. *male child.* xx. 113.

hyt, see hē.

hȳwe, hȳwere, see hīw, hīwere.

I

Iacob. (a) *Jacob,* son of Isaac. v. 4, 6, 23; vi. 361 (gs. -es). (b) *James* the Apostle, son of Zebedee. ix. 196; xiv. 34, 208, 210. (c) *James* the Just, head of the church at Jerusalem, author of Epistle, regularly identified at this time with the Apostle, son of Alphæus. ix. 195; xiii. 100 ('Iacob se rihtwisa'). [Cf. Ælfric's account of the martyrdom, CH II. 298, and the note on ix. 195.]

ic, pron. 1st pers., *I.* ns. i. 69 (twice), 290, 358, 463; ii. 34, 36, etc.—mīn, gs. xxi. 479; xxv(*c*). 5, 6; xxvii. 100 (?); xxx. 92; usually as possessive adj., see separate entry, mīn. —mē, ds. i. 290, 440, 445; iii. 65; etc. as. ii. 34, 48 (twice); etc.—wē, np. i. 1, 26, 52, 61, 77, etc.; ūre, gp. i. 134; ii. 203; xi. 393; xi*a*. 169; xvii. 209; xxvi. 61; for possessive see separate entry, ūre.—ūs, dp. i. 37, 51, 63, 96, etc. ap. i. 315, 362; ii. 99; etc.—wyt, n. dual, viii. 190, 194; x. 5; wit, x. 36.—uncer, g. dual as possessive adj., xxiii. 71.

īdel, n. *emptiness, vanity.* only in phrase, on īdel, *in vain.* ii. 119; xiv. 20, 116, 122, 125; xx. 215 (ȳdel).

īdel, adj. *idle, vain.* ii. 210; x. 59;
xv. 185; xvii. 179, 192, 194; xxx.
60, 64, 68.

īdelġylp, n. *vainglory.* iv. 251; xix.
129.

**īdellic, adj. *idle, foolish, vain.* vii.
103. [Cited by Napier from this
passage.]

īdelnyss, f. *vanity, frivolity.* xix. 18,
25.

Ierusalem, see **Hierusalem.**

Iesus, *Jesus.* viii. 59, 62. [Elsewhere
replaced by translation, **Hǣlend** or
se **Hǣlend.**]

īgland, īland, n. *island.* xxi. 104, 111.

ilca, see ylca.

in, inn, adv. *in.* (a) before a verb of
motion or its negative, iii. 99, 100;
xxi. 225, 335, 396, 414, 418, 426,
491; xxvi. 113 (**inn ḡān intō**);
xxvii. 95; and with **tō** after the verb,
xii. 12, 76; xiii. 194. (b) after a verb
of motion, ii. 117; and followed
directly by **tō**, v. 87, 255; xix. 160;
xxi. 459; xxvi. 86; and elliptically
after **mǣg**, xii. 15, 97. [The line
between **in tō** and **intō**, q.v., is not
always clear.]

in, prep. *in.* xxiii. 171; xxx. 114 (**in
ealra worulda woruld**, *for ever*;
v.l. **on ēcnysse**: see note).

inburh, innburh, f. *hall* (entrance
hall or court of a stronghold, translating *atrium*). iv. 34, 183.

inc, see þū.

incund, adj. *inward, heartfelt.* ix. 134
(dsf. **incundre**, v.l. **inweardlicre**).

incundnyss, f. *inward conviction,
sincerity.* xxi. 97.

infær, n. *ingress.* xi. 52; xia. 160; xii.
108 (**innfær**).

ingang, inngang, m. *going in, entrance.* xi. 19; xia. 93; xxvi. 47, 93,
116, 127.

ingehȳd, inngehȳd, n. *consciousness,
mind, intention.* iv. 225; ix. 142, 145;
xv. 206; xviii. 94. [As elsewhere in
Ælfric, the gender is neuter, not
fem.]

inmēde, adj. *close to one's heart, dear.*
xvi. 55. comp., **inmēddre** (for
nsm. **inmēddra**), xx. 135. [Cited
by Napier from the passage in xvi

and from the homily later printed
by Brotanek, p. 15. It occurs also in
Benedictine Rule.]

innan, prep. *within, inside, into.* xvii.
154 (w. acc.); xviii. 16 (w. dat.).

inne, adv. *inside.* xi. 59; xia.
176.

inneweard, adj. *inward, innermost,
sincere.* xv. 44.

innoþ, m. (a) the *inside* of the body,
inwards, vitals: x. 165, 167; xix. 195.
(b) the *belly*: v. 145; vii. 148, 150.
(c) the *womb*: i. 406; ii. 231; iv. 52,
271, 279; xia. 65, 168; xii. 12, 76.

inra, wk. adj. (comp. of **inne**). *inner.*
xviii. 316.

ġeinseġlian, II. *to seal.* xxi. 320, 395,
405, 413.

intinga, m. *cause.* xxi. 602.

intō, inntō, prep. w. dat. *into.* ii. 21,
35, 37, 244; iv. 45, 236, 237; v. 9,
65, 82, 250, 261, 275; x. 111; xi.
437, 452, 462, 467; etc.—elliptically as adv., *into* (*it*), xxi. 485.
[Can sometimes be taken rather as
two words. Cf. **in.**]

Ioab, *Joab*, David's general (II Reg.
x. 7 sqq.). xxii. 19, 24, 35, 43 (gs.
Ioabes).

Iob, *Job.* xvii. 163.

Iohannes, *John.* (a) the Evangelist. i.
4, 21 (as. **Iohannem**); ii. 5; v. 1;
vii. 4; viii. 24; ix. 128 (gs. **Iohannes**), 129; x. 1; xi. 459, 466, 508,
536; xiv. 34, 208, 210. (b) the
Baptist. i. 38, 300, 307, 316 (as.
-em), 437; ix. 67; xi. 15 (ds.
Iohanne); xia. 89 (same).

Iordan, the river *Jordan.* i. 437 (ds.
Iordanen?); xi. 16 (ds. **Iordane**);
xia. 90 (same); xiv. 46 (as. **Iordanen**, v.l. **Iordanem**?).

Iosep, *Joseph*, son of Jacob. v. 5 (ds.
Iosepe).

Iosue, *Joshua.* xx. 170, 189, 200, 360,
368, 372; xxii. 88. [Uninflected in
dat. and acc.]

Iouis, the god *Jove.* xxi. 110, 113, 122,
142, 145, 150 (gs. **Ioues**), 175 (ds.
Ioue).

irnan, see yrnan.

Isaac, son of Abraham. vi. 361; xix.
111 (both gs. **Isaaces**).

Isaias, the prophet *Isaiah.* iii. 64; v.
213; xix. 66 (as. **Isaiam**).

īsen, n. *iron.* i. 247; ix. 133; xxvii. 35,
43.

īsen, adj. *of iron.* xvii. 225; xix. 191;
xxvii. 96.

Israhel, Israel, the land or people of
Israel. xii. 167 (ds. uninfl.); xv. 10,
126 (ds. **Israhele**); xxi. 282; xxii.
39.

Israhela, gp. *of the Israelites* (as if
from np. **Israhele**). iii. 76, 81; xii.
26; xx. 119, 304; xxi. 212, 276, 280;
xxii. 49 (MS. **iørahøra**).

iū, adv. *of old, formerly, already.* i. 113,
228, 364, 464; vii. 94; ix. 158; x.
159; xiv. 1; xvi. 4, 87; xvii. 281 (MS.
iv̄); xviii. 65, 281; xxii. 58.—**iū ǣr,**
long ago, ix. 144; **nū iū,** *even now,
already,* xx. 50; **þā iū,** *even then,
already,* v. 154; xii. 102. [Usually
accented in the MSS., sometimes
on the originally consonantal **i**
rather than **u**; perhaps the pronunciation varied.]

iuc, see **ȝeoc.**

ȝe-iucian ('-ȝeoc-'), II. *to yoke.*
xxi. 275.

Iudas, *Judas* Iscariot. vi. 351.

Iudei, np. *the Jews.* np., ii. 70, 257
(v.l. **Iudeiscan**); iii. 119, 127; vi.
71; dp. **Iudeum,** iii. 80; gp. **Iudea,**
w. **lande, folce:** vi. 20; xiii. 192;
xiv. 42, 54, 92, 112, 183; xvii. 1;
xviii. 237, 307, 339; xxi. 464. [Ex-
cept in gp., an infrequent substitute
for **þā Iudeiscan.**]

Iudeisc, adj. *Jewish.* i. 348; ii. 65,
122; iii. 53, 145; iv. 261; v. 15, 49,
115, 167, 193, 195; vi. 310; vii.
79; xii. 2, 54; xiv. 89; xvii. 253;
xx. 132.—wk. with def. art. as
noun, *the Jew(s).* nsm. **se Iudeisca,**
as epithet of Lazarus, vi. 197;
everywhere else in pl. ii. 16, etc. (7
times); iii. 3, 26, 133; iv. 12, etc.
(7 times); v. 16, 124, 190; vi. 22,
etc. (6 times); vii. 96, 109; ix. 29,
etc. (5 times); xii. 51, 181, 189; xv.
167; xix. 37, 216.

Iulianus, *Julian* the Apostate. viii.
132.

iung, iung-, see **ȝeong, ȝeong-.**

Iuno, the goddess *Juno.* xxi. 114.

K, see **C**

L

lā, interj. *lo.* (a) by itself, calling attention parenthetically to a question.
v. 23; vi. 119; xii. 12, 76; xiii. 20,
24, 124, 146; xvi. 11, 100; xvii.
301; xx. 310; xxi. 325, 371; xxix.
112. (b) reinforced by **hwæt,** interj.,
before a question. ii. 272; xvii. 213.
(c) **lā h̄ū ne,** *is it not true that* (Lat.
nonne), calling for an affirmative
answer. v. 77; vi. 25, 83, 89; xxi.
628. [Cf. **hū.**] (d) with a vocative:
lā lēof, *dear sir, O sir, sirs,* ii. 33;
v. 68; xxi. 471; **lā lēof hlāford** and
lārēow, vi. 10, 21; **lā wīf,** xiii.
222; **lā cyning,** *O king,* xxi. 419.

lāc, n., rarely f. *gift, sacrifice.* usually
neuter plural: iii. 88; xi. 14, 24; xia.
88, 98; xv. 19, 21, 24, 191, 193, 196,
208, 214, 218; xvi. 198 (or as.); xx.
44, 51; xxi. 84, 130, 137, 254, 260,
263, 397, 401, 410 (see note), 444,
591, 597; xxx. 24, 32, 35, 50, 104,
111. once nsf., **lāc,** xix. 50; ds., **lāce**
(gender not indicated), xxi. 256, 373.

ȝelācnian, II. *to heal, cure.* xiii. 3.

-lǣcan, I, verbal suffix. *to cause to be,
become.* Cf. **ȝedyrst-, ȝe-ed-, ȝe-
efen-, ȝenēa-, ȝeriht-, ȝeþwǣr-
lǣcan.**

ȝelǣccan, I, pret. 3s. **ȝelǣhte,** pp.
ȝelǣht. *to seize, attach, grasp.* iii.
12, 23; x. 197; xiii. 202; xxi. 216,
338, 417 (v.l.), 424, 473; xxiii. 189.

lǣce, m. *physician.* xiii. 1.

lǣcecræft, m. *leech-craft, art of healing.* xiii. 3.

lǣcedōm, m. *medicine, healing, remedy.* i. 216; xv. 188; xvii. 108; xxvi.
73, 122.

lǣdan, ȝelǣdan, I. *to lead, take,
bring, convey.* iii. 23, 58; iv. 196; vii.
89 (pres. 3s. **ȝelǣt**); xi. 183; xiii. 20,
124; xiv. 64; xvii. 29, 114; xix. 254;
xx. 145, 174, 310, 372; xxi. 242;
xxiii. 17 (pret. 2s. subj. **ȝelǣddest**),

87, 88, 91, 106 (imp. sg. **lǣd**), 111, 206; xxvii. 47; xxix. 18. [Cf. **a-**, **for-lǣdan**.]

lǣfan, I. *to leave, leave behind, leave remaining.* xi*a*. 125; xxi. 108; xxvii. 2.

lǣg, see **licgan**.

gelǣht(-), see **gelǣccan**.

lǣmen, adj. *of clay, earthen.* xxi. 376.

gelǣndan, see **gelendan**.

lǣne, adj. *transitory.* i. 341; xii. 210.

lǣran, I. *to teach, instruct.* ii. 85; v. 284; vii. 131, 199; ix. 101; xiii. 143, 195; xiv. 14, etc. (9 times); xv. 164; xvi. 274; xvii. 6, 283; xix. 1; xx. 277; xxiii. 155.—pp. **gelǣred**, *learned, well-instructed.* vii. 197; xiv. 231; xv. 62; xix. 208. [Cf. **for-lǣran**, **ungelǣred**.]

lǣs, adv. *less.* ii. 146 (**tō þām twām lǣs fēowertigum**, *to the two less than forty*).—for **þȳ lǣs þe**, **þe lǣs þe**, see **þȳlǣste**.

lǣssa, comp. adj., wk. *lesser, inferior, weaker.* iv. 165 (**lǣsse** for nsm. **-a**); vii. 121; x. 153 (**lǣsse** for **-a**); xi*a*. 223; xv. 105; xvi. 282, 286; xvii. 65. asn. as noun, **lǣsse**, *less, a lesser quantity* (of worldly goods). xvi. 165. pl. as noun, **þā lǣssan**, *the weaker, the poor.* xiii. 59.

lǣst, sup. adj. *least.* vii. 160; xi. 555.

gelǣstan, I. *to carry out, grant.* xi. 526 (pres. 3s. **gelǣst**).

lǣtan, 7. (a) *to let, allow, cause.* iii. 111; vi. 104; xiii. 43, 200; xvi. 256; xxi. 316; xxiii. 150, 173; xxx. 87. (b) *to leave* something (acc.) in (**on**) someone's control. iii. 110. (c) *to leave* some portion (acc.) of an enterprise to the action (dat.) of another. ix. 124. (d) with acc. and complement, *to consider.* xvi. 244. (e) with **ūt**, *to let a ship go out.* xiv. 111 (**lēton ūttor**). (f) with **ēaþe**, *to take easily.* xix. 146 (**lēt him ēaþe embe þæt**, *he took the matter easily*). [Forms: inf., xvi. 244; imp. sg. **lǣt**, xxiii. 150; pl. **lǣtaþ**, vi. 104; pres. 3s. **lǣt**, xiii. 43; xxx. 87; pres. 1p. subj. **lǣtan**, xvi. 256; pret. 1s. **lēt**, xxiii. 173; 3s., iii. 110 (5 times); 3p.

lēton, xiii. 200; xiv. 111.—See also **alǣtan**, **forlǣtan**.]

gelǣte, n. *meeting.* only in **wega gelǣte**, *crossroads.* xxi. 137 (dp. **-um**, v.l. **wegelǣtum**, probably for the compound, 'weg-gelǣtum'); xxix. 118 (dp. **-on**, v.l. **-um**).

lǣwede, adj. *lay, unlearned.* xiii. 129; xix. 115; xxv(*a*). 16, 18;—wk. w. def. art. as noun, dp. **lǣwedum**, xiii. 133.

lāf, f. *what is left.* only in **tō lāfe bēon**, *to be left over.* xi*a*. 122.

lāge, **lāgon**, see **licgan**.

lagu, f. [from ON neuter pl.] *law.* ns., i. 465; ds. **lage**, vii. 201; xiii. 203; xv. 10, 30, 62, 81, 126; as. **lage**, viii. 17; ix. 190; xiii. 208 (MS. H); npn. **lagu**, xv. 35 (?); xx. 34; **laga**, xiii. 208 (MS. U). [See note on xx. 34.]

lama, wk. m. *lame person, cripple.* ii. 33, 85.—as adj., same form, *lame, crippled.* ii. 147; xi. 323.

lamb, n. *lamb.* xxx. 103.

gelamp, see **gelimpan**.

land, n. *land.* i. 20, 259; iii. 8, 58; iv. 140; v. 185, 189; vi. 20, 146; etc.

landlēod, m. or **-lēoda**, wk. m. *inhabitant of a country, native.* xxi. 242 (np. **-an**). [Wk. forms recorded only in pl., but see BTS, 'landleoda' and 'leoda'.]

lang, adj. *long.* i. 147; xi. 229; xiii. 153; xiv. 43; xxi. 483, 557, 610.

Langa Frīgedæg, m. *Good Friday.* xi. 36 (ds. **Langgan**, v.l. **langan**, **langum**).

lange, adv. *long.* ii. 31, 154; xi. 120; xii. 107; xx. 182; xxi. 570, 637; xxvii. 44.—**lange syþþan**, *long after.* vi. 105; xi*a*. 115 (**lange ... syþþan**); xviii. 348. **swā lange swā**, *as long as.* xvii. 164; xxi. 206. **swā lange oþþæt**, *just long enough until.* vi. 330. [Comp. **leng**, q.v.]

gelangian, II. *to summon, send for.* xvi. 7, 90, 94; xxiii. 162 (inf., **-en**). [Cf. **gelencgan**.]

langsum, adj. *long* (in duration). ii. 147; v. 98; vi. 145; vii. 2; viii. 22; xx. 354; xxi. 511; xxii. 80.

lār, f. *lore, teaching, instruction, doctrine.* i. 320; ii. 3, 123, 162, iii. 158

lār (*cont.*)
174; iv. 127; v. 94, 257, 267; vi. 204; vii. 131, 194; etc.

lārēow, m. *teacher, master.* i. 268; iii. 49; v. 71, 226; vi. 21, 67; vii. 206; viii. 102; xi. 399; xii. 4, 26, 56, 89, 167, 169; etc. spelled **lareaw**, xiii. 135, 136.

lārlic, adj. *instructive.* iii. 171.

late, adv. *tardily, late.* viii. 143.— comp., **lator**, *later* (of later origin or action). xia. 223. [Cf. CH I. 284/7: 'þæt þæt lator biþ, þæt hœfþ anginn', where also the adv. is used rather than the adj.]

lāþ, adj. *hateful, grievous.* vii. 40 (**him wæs lāþ**, *it was abhorrent to them, they were very loath*); xia. 84, 135; xx. 115; xxi. 509; xxvii. 58.

laþian, II. *to invite.* v. 229.

gelaþian, II. *to summon, call in.* xvi. 19, 126, 168.

gelaþung, f. *congregation, church.* i. 400; ii. 129; iii. 146; iv. 65, 178, 283; v. 116; vi. 194; xii. 83, 130; xiv. 84, 87, 129, 154, 232; xviii. 146, 190.

Lazarus, the brother of Mary and Martha. vi. 2 (ds. **Lazare**), 16 (as. **-um**), 30, 34 (gs. **-es**), 37, 98, 113, 197, 298, 328, 355.

lēad, n. *lead.* xxi. 196.

lēaf, f. *leave, permission.* xvii. 257; xix. 121; xxi. 440, 608, 616.

gelēafa, wk. m. *faith, belief.* i. 151, 319, 332, 345, 395; ii. 71, etc. (9 times); iii. 88, etc. (6 times); iv. 71, etc. (8 times); v. 117, etc. (6 times); etc.

gelēafful, adj. *faithful, believing, of the true faith, Christian.* x. 123; xi. 3, 13, 70; xia. 87, 186; xvi. 34, 217; xviii. 73, 149; xix. 96, 97, 99; xxi. 464, 511, 610; xxiii. 160 (*Christian*), 195; xxvi. 17.—in pl. as noun, i. 321; xxix. 108. comp., np. **gelēaffulran**, ii. 3.

gelēaflēas, adj. *faithless.* iii. 3 (MS. **geleafsumum** for **geleafleasum**; see note.) [BTS has two quotations from Ælfric's LS.]

gelēaflēast, f. *unbelief, faithlessness.* iv. 275; vii. 121; xx. 71.

lēah, see **lēogan**.

leahter, m. *vice, sin, offence.* ii. 102, 190; iv. 208; v. 239; vi. 168, 203; x. 51; xi. 220; xiii. 130, 177; xvi. 52, 68, 72; xvii. 264, 269; xviii. 323; xxi. 55, 162, 165, 508; xxiii. 146.

leahterfull, adj. *full of sins, vicious.* xiii. 130, 177; xxi. 509.

***lēap**, m. *dead body, corpse.* xxi. 462 (translates *corpora*). [Hitherto cited only as *trunk* of the body from Judith 111: BT, 'leap', II.]

lēas, adj. *false.* xi. 390; xviii. 102, 255, 298, 322, 378, 386 (twice), 388; xxi. 424, 494, 544, 572.

lēasbregdnyss, f. *deception, false-hood.* xxi. 135. [BTS cites LS, xvii. 107, and this passage, from Kemble's ed.]

lēaslīce, adv. *falsely.* xxix. 30.

lēasung, f. *lying, falsehood.* xvi. 76; xvii. 167; xxi. 200; xxii. 101; xxix. 50.

lecgan, I, pret. 3s. **lēde**, pp. **gelēd**. *to lay, place, set, bury.* i. 7; ii. 146 (imp., **lege** . . . **tō**, *lay next to, add to*); v. 201; vi. 80 (pret. 2p., **lēde gē**, *buried*), 102 (pp., *buried*); xxi. 621. [Cf. **alecgan**.]

Leden, n. *Latin:* **on Leden**, *in* (*the*) *Latin* (*language*), i. 117(?); v. 209; x. 84; xv. 149; xxii. 14, 102.—adj. *Latin.* xxii. 16.

Leden-bōc, f. *Latin book.* xxii. 12.

lēdon, see **lecgan**.

gelēfan, see **gelȳfan**.

lege, see **lecgan**.

leger, n. (*a lying sick*), *sickness.* ii. 147.

legerbedd, n. *sick-bed.* ii. 39, 41, 140, 185, 194, 195.

gelencgan, f. *to lengthen.* vi. 367. [Cf. **gelangian**.]

Lencten, Lengten, m. *Lent.* ii. 163; vi. title (as in MS. H); xi. 28, 33; xia. 128, 133.

Lenctenfæsten, n. *Lent.* xix. 122.

Lenctenwuce, wk. f. *a week in Lent.* ii. title (and the titles of iii and v as in MS. H.)

gelendan, gelændan, I. *to land, reach the land.* xiv. 201; xvii. 220. [BTS, 'gelendan', I, records the instance in xvii from CH.]

leng, adv. (comp. of lange). *longer.*
i. 265; vi. 367; x. 187; xi. 161; xvi.
9, 92; xxi. 251, 316.

Lengten, see Lencten.

lengu, f. *length*; of the human or
quasi-human figure, *height, stature.*
xi. 308; xxi. 531.

lēo, m. *lion.* nap., xxi. 326, 338, 460;
gp. lēona, xxi. 313, 329, 475; dp.
lēonum, xxi. 317, 461.

lēod, f. in singular, *people* of a country
collectively, *nation*: ix. 59; xiv. 135;
xxi. 236; xxii. 75; xxvi. 10.—in
plural, (a) *peoples, nations*: iv. 76,
129; viii. 78; xxii. 54, 84, 86; (b) the
people of a country individually: iv.
101, 102; xxi. 125, 283, 341,
538.

lēodscipe, -scype, m. *nation, people.*
iv. 182; v. 117; xiv. 185; xviii. 67;
xx. 391, 411, 416.

lēof, adj. *dear, beloved.* i. 330, 440,
445, 465; v. 71, 226; vi. 10, 21, 87,
209, 264; vii. 2, 40, 91, 128; etc.—
used absolutely in vocative, *dear
(one), (dear) sir,* ii. 33; v. 68 (pl.); viii.
45, 237; xx. 320; xxi. 471; xxix. 23.—
comp. lēofre, *dearer, more to one's
liking, more pleasing.* nsn., xxvii.
2(?); and w. dat. of person, nsf.,
xv. 45; nsn., vi. 207; xix. 48.—sup.
lēofost, *dearest.* wk., voc., pl., ii. 1;
xxi. 6. him lēofost byþ, *is most
to their liking, best pleases them.* xix.
55.

leofa, leofaþ, leofod-, see libban.

lēogan, 2. *to speak falsely, lie.* pret.
3s. lēah, v. 232; 3p. lugon, iv. 14,
74. [Cf. alēogan.]

lēoht, n. *light, a light* (lit. and fig.). i.
34–42, 207, 286–332 (32 times); ii.
77; iv. 71, 226; vi. 27, 29, 345, 346,
348; etc. [Probably not used as an
adj., *bright*; at i. 316 it might be so
interpreted, but the Latin source
favours *a light*.]

lēoht, adj. *not heavy.* (a) *light* in weight.
xi. 252. (b) *minor, trifling.* xi. 225.
(c) *delicate, insubstantial.* xx. 313.
(d) *light* in oppressiveness or
severity. comp., nsn. lēohtre, xv.
139; sup., nsn. wk. lēohtoste, xi.
497.

lēohtfæt, n. *a lantern, lamp, light.* i.
207; xvi. 111, 138; xxii. 49.

lēoma, m. *light, radiance, ray of light.*
i. 15, 295; viii. 231, 235.

lēon(-), see lēo.

leornian, II. *to learn.* ii. 228; xi. 183;
xii. 64; xiii. 141; xvi. 238; xix.
7.

leorningcild, n. *(young) pupil.* xiii.
141. [Cited by BT from one passage
in Ælfric only.]

leorningcniht, m. *disciple.* (a) in
plural, Christ's disciples. iii. 3; v.
60, 70, 207, 225, 229; vi. 19, 21,
334; viii. 22; xvii. 205, 208; xviii.
225, 286; xix. 40. (b) generally, ns.,
xiii. 22, 134.

gelettan, I. *to hinder, stop.* vi. 334;
viii. 144 (pp. gelett); xxi. 417 (pret.
3s. gelette, v.l. gelæhte: see
gelæccan).

Leui, *Levi,* son of Jacob. xx. 58 (gs.
Leuies).

libban, lybban, III (pret. and one
form of pres. part. as from 'lifian,
leofian', II). *to live.* i. 284; ii. 171,
178; iv. 219; v. 270; vi. 59, etc. (11
times); vii. 137; etc.; trans. libban
. . . līf, *to live* (one's) *life,* xviii. 133;
xxv(a). 19; xxx. 9.—pres. part. has
two forms: (a) libbende, lybbende,
with ordinary verbal sense. iv. 154;
vi. 362; xi. 482; xv. 139; xvi. 2
(applied to Christ living as man);
xviii. 237, 307; as noun, þā
lybbendan, xi. 301. (b) lifi-
(g)ende, lyfi(g)ende, as epithet of
the *living* God in one of his three
persons. i. 75, 152, 323, 383; iii.
169, 177; v. 89, 223; vi. 255; vii.
87; etc. (14 more)—falsely claimed
for Bel, xxi. 372. [Other forms: inf.
libban, vi. 364 (3 times); lybban,
xi. 120 (3 times); imp. sg. leofa,
xxi. 327; pres. 3s. leofaþ, vi. 59 (12
times); lyfaþ, xxi. 372, 376; pres.
1p. lybbaþ, i. 284; ii. 178; 3p.
lybbaþ, iv. 219 (6 times); libbaþ,
xia. 24 (5 times); pres. 3s. subj.
lybbe, xv. 51; 1p. lybban, ii. 171;
3p. lybban, vi. 150; lybbon, vi.
300; pret. 3s. leofode, vi. 105 (6
times); lyfode, xi. 122; xxi. 591,

libban, lybban (*cont.*)
638; 3p. **leofodon, xi***a*. 115 (3 times); **leofedon**, xvii. 70; **leofodan**, xviii. 11; xxi. 158; **lyfedon**, xi. 374; **lyfodon**, xviii. 437.]

Liber Regum, the first book of Kings according to the older reckoning, now I Samuel. xxi. 210. [Cf. **Cyninga bōc**.]

līc, n. *body*. x. 175; xx. 192; xxiii. 27, 195, 200.

gelīc, adj. (a) *alike*. iv. 201; xi. 235, 400; xxiv. 9. (b) with dat., *like, similar to*. vii. 99; ix. 113; xi. 534; xiii. 232, 233; xv. 175; xvi. 61; xvii. 271; xxiii. 160; xxvi. 59.

gelīca, wk. m. the *like* or *equal* of another. i. 225.

gelīce, adv. *alike, equally*. vi. 235; vii. 211; x. 115; xi. 87, 201; xiii. 43; xxi. 18.

licgan, 5. *to lie*. (a) of persons, to be in a recumbent or prostrate position. ii. 24, 28, 68, 85, 91; vi. 30, 306; xxi. 226; xxvi. 87; xxvii. 51(?). (b) with predicative complement expressing condition: *to lie* sick, dead, buried, etc. ii. 249; vi. 2, 8, 34, 177, 197; x. 155; xx. 168; xxi. 233; xxvii. 29, 87 (**on forþsīþe**, *at the point of death*); xxix. 121. (c) *to lie* sick. vi. 329; xi. 169; xix. 149. (d) fig. *to be in a state of captivity*. xxiii. 56.—*in a state of indolence*. xix. 211. (e) fig. *to lie* in sins, in lusts, as if in mud or in the grave. ii. 190; iv. 67; vi. 202, 207; xvi. 67. (f) of animals, *to dwell, have their lair?* xxi. 317. (g) of bodies, *to lie* (*lifeless*) in or on the ground. xx. 192. (h) of something material, *to be situated, be contained* in a place. xiii. 153. (i) *to assume a prostrate position, lie* (*down*). xxvi. 130. [Forms: inf., xiii. 153; xx. 192; d. inf. **licganne**, vi. 207; pres. part. **licgende**, vi. 306, 329; xi. 169; xix. 149; xxi. 226 (uninfl. asm., v.l. **licgan**, inf.); pres. 2s. **ligst**, xxiii. 56; 3s. **līþ**, vi. 30; xxix. 121; 3p. **licgaþ**, vi. 202; 3s. subj. **licge**, xvi. 67; 1p. subj. **licgan**, xx. 168; pret. 2s. **lāge**, ii. 190; 3s. **læg**, ii.

28 (17 times); 3p. **lāgon**, ii. 24 (4 times). Cf. **forlicgan**.]

līchama, wk. m. *body*. i. 407, 435; ii. 94, 107, 114, 228, 230, 234; vi. 145, 151, 157, 207; vii. 144, 155, 161; etc.

līchamlīce, adv. *bodily, in the flesh*. ii. 8; x. 75; xix. 124.

līcian, gelīcian, II, w. dat. *to please, be pleasing to*. (a) the subject a person or a thing. i. 440; vi. 290; viii. 86; xvii. 118; xix. 84; xx. 20, 71; xxi. 162; xxvii. 5(?), 80. (b) the subject a clause. xix. 12. (c) the subject undefined. i. 115 (**on þām mō wel līcaþ**, *in whom I am well pleased*). [Cf. **mislīcian**.]

gelīcnyss, f. *likeness*. i. 12, 14; ii. 180; ix. 132; x. 97; xi. 58, 217; xi*a*. 175; xviii. 60 (*analogue*); xxvii. 97; xxix. 59, 67, 121.

līcweorþe, -wyrþe, adj. *pleasing, attractive*. viii. 54; xv. 220.

līf, n. *life* (as vital principle, the life of an individual or of men in general, the present or future life, the divine life, etc.). i. 33, etc. (12 times); ii. 99, etc. (7 times); iii. 114, 132, 185; v. 30, etc. (8 times); vi. 58, etc. (6 times); vii. 63, 134, 204; etc.—gs. **līfes**, as predicate, *alive*. vi. 365.—**on līfe**, *in life, in the world*. i. 19; vii. 161; viii. 119 (**welige on līfe**, *rich in worldly goods*); etc.—**hēr on līfe**, *in this life, in this world*. i. 4; ii. 7; v. 2; vii. 128; etc.—**hāliges līfes mann**, *a man of holy life* (character and conduct). xxi. 301; xxix. 47.—**mæres līfes menn**, *men of distinction*. xxiii. 126.—**bēon of līfe**, *to pass away, die*. xv. 53.

gelīf, see **gelȳfan**.

gelīffæstan, I. *to quicken, endow with life*. pres. 3s. **-fæst**, ii. 228, 234; pret. 3s. **-fæste**, i. 75; vi. 245; xi*a*. 209; pp. **-fæst, -e**, iv. 154; vi. 153; xi*a*. 14; xxi. 19.

lifi(g)ende, see **libban**.

līflēast, f. *loss of life, death*. xxi. 398.

līflic, adj. *living, of life*. i. 279; v. 20, 22, 31, 145, 148, 152; vi. 110, 273; xi. 468; xi*a*. 66; xvii. 55; xxv(*c*). 17.

līg, m. or n. *fire, flame*. xx. 30; xxi. 298.

līget, n. or m. *lightning*. xviii. 8.

lihnian ('lygnian'), II. *to give the lie, contradict.* xxii. 12.

lihtan, I. *to alight, dismount.* xxvii. 95 (pret. 3p. lihton, after lacuna: perhaps alihton; see alihtan).

lihting, f. *lighting, illumination.* i. 326; xvi. 115. [In both, artificial light is meant; in i, with contrast to daylight.]

lim, n. *limb.* iv. 158; vii. 145, 157 (gp. limena); xi. 217, 323, 434; xii. 207; xviii. 388; xix. 61; xxi. 309, 330, 338, 557, 559; xxiii. 191; xxv(*c*). 2; xxvi. 130; xxix. 78.

gelimpan, 3. *to befall.* inf., xxix. 41; pres. 3s. gelimpþ, xxv(*c*) 2; subj. gelimpe, ii. 57, 279; pret. 3s. gelamp, xiii. 196; xviii. 10, 17; xxi. 214, 270; xxiii. 14; xxvi. 30, 43. [Cf. belimpan.]

liss, f. *kindness, mercy.* xiii. 64, 66.

*lissian, II, w. dat. *to be lenient toward, show kindness* or *mercy to.* xiii. 67; xvi. 146. [Not in dict., but see OED, 'lisse'; cf. liþian (a).]

liþ, n. (*fermented*) *drink.* xiii. 164.

liþ, see licgan.

liþe, adj. *gentle, gracious.* vi. 252.—comp., dp. liþran, xix. 7. sup., nsn. wk. liþoste, xi. 497.

liþian, II. (a) w. dat., *to be kind* or *lenient to.* xiii. 65. (b) *to be gentle.* xv. 36.

liþnyss, f. *softness, gentleness, kindness.* xiii. 67, 186, 208; xix. 2, 6, 13.

loc, n. (a) *lock, bolt, bar.* xxi. 395; xxiii. 80. (b) *a locked enclosure, closet.* xvii. 201 (dp. locum, less probably from 'loca', wk. m.).

lōc, interj. *look, look you.* only in lōc hwæt, *whatever,* xxiii. 183.

lōcian, II. *to look, take heed.* ii. 77; xiii. 32, 173; xxx. 9; preceded by on as post-positive prep. w. dat., *to look upon,* xii. 161; xxix. 16; preceded by adverbial on, *to look on, behold,* xxi. 514. [The last three examples might be taken under onlōcian, q.v., though in the last two if on is stressed it improves the alliteration.]

lof, n. *praise, glory.* i. 470; iii. 187; v. 290; vi. 212, 373; xii. 156; xiii.

236; xv. 217; xvi. 79, 83, 200; xx. 429; xxi. 676; xxx. 31, 50, 62, 73.

lofsang, m. *song of praise, hymn.* xi. 3, 13, 29, 76; xi*a*. 82, 87, 129, 183, 190, 192; xxiii. 1; xxvii. 77.

logian, gelogian, II. (a) *to lodge, place.* i. 147; iii. 52; xviii. 131; xxi. 195, 401. (b) *to order, dispose.* v. 238; xviii. 372; xxvii. 27. [All with pref. except i. 147.]

gelōme, adv. *frequently.* ii. 17, 20; iii. 117; viii. 172; xiii. 126; xvii. 110; xix. 33, 145; xxi. 211, 597; xxiv. 1.

gelōmlīce, adv. *frequently, continually.* vi. 306.

losian, II. *to be lost, fail, perish.* xi. 133; xii. 41, 222; xvii. 210; xix. 135, 251; xxi. 612.

lotwrenc, m. *deceitful device.* xvi. 234; xxix. 108.

Loþ, *Lot.* xviii. 17 (gs. Loþes), 20, 61, 64 (ds. Loþe), 65, 73.

Lucas, *Luke* the Evangelist. iv. 57 (ds. Lucam); xiii. 1; xvii. 279.

lufian, II. *to love.* i. 221, 341, 383; ii. 143; iii. 114, 186; iv. 292, 296; v. 179; vi. 10, 14, 82, 312; vii. 135, 175, etc.

luflīce, adv. *lovingly, kindly.* xxi. 341.

lufu, f., with occas. wk. ds. lufan (as if from 'lufe' wk. f.). *love.* strong forms very frequent: (a) as common noun. i. 93, 444; ii. 150, 202, 203, 206; iii. 131; iv. 294; vii. 49, 166, 223; etc. (b) as the divine love equated with the Holy Spirit, the distinction from sense (a) not always clear. vi. 234, 246, 257; vii. 210, 224; viii. 188; ix. 113; x. 41 (ds. lufu, v.l. lufe); xi*a*. 11, 12, 210, 221; xxi. 18.—wk. ds. lufan, xiv. 206 (v.l. lufon); xv. 86; xvi. 245; xviii. 343; xxx. 43, 59; lufon, xviii. 127; xxiii. 196.

lugon, see lēogan.

lūs, f. *louse.* i. 233 (ap. lȳs); xxi. 47 (np. lȳs).

lust, m. *pleasure, desire, appetite.* ii. 170; vi. 207.—on luste, *joyful.* i. 95; mid luste, *with* (*evil*) *desire, lustfully.* xv. 95.

lȳfan, I. *to allow, give leave.* xxi. 628; xxvi. 127. [Cf. alȳfan.]

gelȳfan, rarely gelīf-, gelēf-, I. *to
believe.* (a) alone. i. 40, 305; v. 94,
95, 279, 284, 286; vi. 38, 90; vii.
132; etc. (b) with **on** and acc., *to
believe in* or *on* (a god). i. 48, etc. (8
times); ii. 75; iii. 129, 169, 177; iv.
76, 179, 181, 284; v. 89, etc. (9
times, including 116, where MS. F
has dat.); vi. 58, etc. (7 times); vii.
19, etc. (7 times); etc. (c) with dat.,
to believe in (something). xviii. 295;
xxix. 85. (d) with acc. (or dat.?) of
person, *to believe* someone. xx. 183
(Lat. *credent mihi*); xxi. 394; xxii.
16. (e) with gen. (once acc.), *to believe* something. vi. 61 (acc. þis, v.l.
þises); x. 23, 183; xi. 338; xia. 66;
xii. 33, 187, 196; xviii. 59, 255, 378.
(f) with clause, *to believe that*. . . .
i. 152; vi. 63, 96; viii. 49, 251;
xviii. 47; xxi. 131; xxiii. 22; and
with acc. (dat.?) of person, *to believe*
someone, *that*. . . . v. 44, 162.—
spelled gelif (imp. sg.), v. 44;
gelefan (inf.), xxiii. 98. [See also
next word. Cf. belȳfan.]

gelȳfed, adj. (pp. of gelȳfan). *faithful, believing.* v. 258; xiv. 183; xix.
94; xxiii. 162; swȳþe on God
gelȳfed, *an ardent believer in God*,
xxii. 60.—with art. as noun, *the
faithful.* dp., v. 270.

lyffetung, f. *adulation, flattery.* xviii.
102. [BT, BTS have twelve exam-
ples, seven from Ælfric.]

lyfi(g)ende, see libban.

lyre, m. *loss.* xxiv. 2.

lȳs, see lūs.

lystan, gelystan, I, impers. w. dat.
to please. pres. 3s. lyst, ii. 1; pret.
3s. (ge)lyste, xx. 17, 312.

lȳt, adv. *little.* xiii. 79.

lȳt, n. with part. gen., *few.* xviii.
169.

lȳtel, adj. *little.* i. 84; xi. 225, 229,
429 (lyttl-), 431, 450; xia. 121; xiii.
168; xvi. 165 (wk. as noun), 196,
212, 280, 284; xvii. 210; xviii. 372;
xix. 16, 184; xxi. 44; xxvi. 43; xxx.
32, 36, 45.

lȳtel, n. *little.* as adverb, xvi. 119.

lȳtle, adv. *a little.* ii. 247 (lyttle); iii.
106; xix. 166.

lȳtlian, II. *to diminish, belittle.* x. 160;
pp. gelȳtlod, x. 180.

lȳtling, m. *little one, child.* xix. 17
(lȳtlingc, twice).

lȳtlung, f. *diminution.* xia. 225.

M

mā, indecl. sb. *more.* iii. 16, 145; v.
94; w. gen., xviii. 165 (mā sāwla—
perhaps adj. with ap.); xxiii. 79
(mā wearda).—as adj., iii. 122
(mā þēowan). þō mā þe, conj.
any more than. xiii. 139. [Cf. māra.]

Macharius, *St. Macarius,* a hermit
of the desert. xxix. 11, 18 (ds.
Macharie), 25, 31.

macian, II, pp. gemacod. (a) *to
make, build, bring about, accomplish,
perform.* i. 249; iv. 230; viii. 115,
153; xviii. 365; xix. 44; xx. 266, 328,
329; xxi. 126, 204, 273, 609; xxii.
80; xxvi. 21; xxix. 4. (b) *to prepare*
food. xxi. 382 (w. dat. of person *for*
whom). (c) with compl. adj.,
macodon hī gearwe, *made themselves ready.* xx. 203. (d) with
compl. sb. preceded by tō, *to cause
to become, make* (*into*). xxi. 107, 136.

mǣden, n. *maiden.* (a) with ref. to the
Virgin. i. 414, 416, 419, 459; iv.
289; xi. 10, 11, 22; xia. 60, 63, 79,
80, 96. (b) with ref. to other women.
xvi. 110; xix. 74, 82, 103; xxix. 13,
15, 21, 26, 31; xxx. 12.

mǣg, m., nap. māgas. *kinsman.*
xvii. 101; xxix. 18, 20, 25. [Cf.
māge.]

mǣg, mǣge, see magan.

mǣgen, n. *virtue, power.* ii. 191; xxi.
642.

mǣgenþrymm, m. *power, majesty.*
vi. 249; x. 161; xia. 19, 212, 222.

mǣgenþrymnyss, f. *majesty, magni-
ficence.* i. 160, 411; vii. 226; viii.
195; xvii. 216.

mǣgþ, f. *generation, race, tribe.* iv.
260; xx. 57, 63, 114, 147.

mǣgþhād, m. *virginity.* i. 6, 426;
xix. 47, 51, 67; xxiii. 197 (mǣigþ-);
xxx. 8, 14.

mǣnan, gemǣnan, I. *to mean.* v.

151; viii. 2, 14; xiii. 113; xviii. 328;
xix. 15; xxvi. 74. [Only viii. 2 has
pref. Cf. bemǣnan, *to lament*.]

gemǣne, adj. w. dat. *common to*;
always as pred. in nom. i. 160, 161;
v. 204; vii. 225; viii. 121 (nsm. instead of asm.), 188, 196; x. 72, 93;
xia. 211, 217; xvii. 290; xxi. 258.

gemǣnelic, adj. *common*. xi. 200.

gemǣnelīce, adv. *in common*. i. 213;
vi. 240.

mǣnig, mǣnig-, see **menig,
menig-**.

mǣre, adj. *great, famous, glorious*.
i. 70; iii. 57, 175; iv. 1; v. 94; viii.
73, 153; xi. 25, 554; xia. 99; xv.
109; xx. 287 (asm. wk. **mǣron**);
xxi. 136 (dsm. wk. **mǣran** for str.),
173, 416; xxii. 13, 87; xxiii. 126;
xxvi. 21, 38, 41, 134.—sup. **mǣr-
est, mǣrost**, xxi. 118, 175.

gemǣre, n. *boundary, limit*. xvii. 22,
218.

mǣrlic, adj. *great, magnificent, extraordinary*. iii. 82; xi. 55; xia. 172.
—sup., **mǣrlicost**, vi. 112.

mǣrlīce, adv. *impressively, magnifi-
cently*. xx. 161; xxi. 174.

mǣrsian, gemǣrsian, II. *to glorify*.
i. 102 (pp. np. **gemǣrsode**), 450
(twice, **mēr-, mǣr-**); ii. 289
(pret. 3s. **mǣrsode**, v.l. **ge-**); vii.
29, 219, 221; xi. 55; xia. 172. [Cf.
gewīdmǣrsian.]

mǣrþ, f. (a) *glory*. i. 360; xi. 45;
xia. 33, 152; xv. 117. (b) *mighty
work*. in pl., xia. 22; xvii. 42, 183.

mǣsse, wk. f. *a mass* (service of the
church), *the mass*. i. 252; vii. 1; xi.
212, 241; xvii. 19; xxvi. 133; xxx.
71.

mǣssedæg, m. *mass-day, festival*.
xvi. 82.

mǣsseprēost, m. *mass-priest*. v. 230;
xii. 86; xiv. 203; xviii. 123, 154;
xxiii. 3, 126, 207.

Mǣssias, Messias, *Messiah*. v. 57,
205, 208.

mǣst, adj. (sup. of **micel**). *greatest*.
(a) wk. w. def. art., xix. 7; xxvi. 73.
(b) strong, xxi. 497. (c) elliptically
as sb. w. gen., xiii. 167; xxiv. 13.

mǣþ, f. (a) *measure, degree*. vi. 216.

(b) (*measure* or *extent of*) *ability*. xvi.
163, 164; xxx. 45.

mǣþlēas, adj. *inordinately greedy,
rapacious*. i. 233.

magan, pret. pres. vb. (a) as an independent vb., w. two datives, *to
avail to* (someone) *for* (something).
xix. 162 (ne miht þū mē nānum
gōde ; the same idiom cited by BT
and BTS from Napier's Wulfstan,
p. 151/12, and, w. instr. for second
dat., p. 122/7). (b) with an infinitive,
directly expressed or implied from
a preceding clause, *to be able, may,
can*. i. 9, etc. (24 times); ii. 34, etc.
(12 times); iv. 22, 109, 200, 203;
v. 99, 159, 228; vi. 83, etc. (11
times); vii. 25, etc. (16 times); etc.
(c) elliptically, the infinitive to be
inferred: with sb. object or defining
clause, *can do*. ii. 157 (mæg ealle
þing); viii. 113 (mæg þæt hē
wile). with prep. or adv. giving
direction of motion, *can go*. xi. 483
(mæg of); xii. 15, 97 (mæg inn).
[Forms: 1s. **mæg**, xxi. 601; 2s.
miht, i. 226, etc.; 3s. **mæg**, i. 131,
etc.; pl. **magon**, i. 157, etc.;
magun, xia. 42; **mage wē**, vi.
115; **mage gē**, xxi. 265, 269; 2s.
subj. **mæge**, ii. 196; xvi. 224;
mage, vi. 159; xxi. 419; 3s. **mæge**,
mage, i. 190; ii. 34; etc.; pl. **magon**,
i. 120; etc.; pret. 3s. **mihte**, i. 9,
etc.; pl. **mihton**, i. 265, etc.; pret.
3s. subj. **mihte**, i. 240, etc.; pl.
mihton, i. 145, etc. Inf. rare, not
recorded for Ælfric.]

mǣge, wk. f. *kinswoman*. ap.
mǣgan, xxi. 117 (see note).

mǣgas, mǣgum, see **mǣg**.

man, see **mann**.

gemāna, m. *company* (in sexual intercourse). i. 416; xxi. 13.

mān-āþ, m. *false oath*. xvi. 74.

māndǣd, f. *evil deed*. iv. 204; vi.
297; xix. 142; xx. 62.

māndǣda, wk. m. *evil-doer*. xi. 375.

manega, manegra, manegum, see
menig.

mānfull, adj. *wicked*. i. 410; iii. 16,
122, 127; iv. 195, 209; v. 269; vi.
288; xi. 132; xia. 39; xii. 86; xvi.

mānfull (*cont.*)
52; xvii. 95; xxi. 118, 188; xxiii.
144, 207; xxvi. 73, 120; xxix. 71.
mānfullic, adj. *wicked.* xxiv. 12.
mānfullīce, adv. *sinfully, wickedly.*
xxi. 117 (variant; see **mānlīce**).
mangung, f. *trade, business.* xxx. 100.
manian, II. *to admonish.* ii. 88 (pp.
gemanod); ix. 36; xix. 142; xx.
391; xxx. 75.
mānlīce, adv. *sinfully, wickedly.* xxi.
117 (v.l. **mānfullīce**).
man(n), m., ds., nap. **men(n).** (a)
man, person. i. 18, etc. (23 times);
ii. 1, etc. (24 times); iii. 99, 113,
116, 180; iv. 2, etc. (30 times); etc.
applied to a woman, vi. 302 (**swīþe
fordōn mann**). in generic sense,
ds. **men(n),** i. 42, 328; xi. 313.
Christ's human nature, x. 157. (b)
mannes Sunu, *Son of man.* xii. 37,
41, 199 (interpreted, 200 sqq.), 222;
xviii. 264, 408, 410 (interpreted,
411). (c) as indef. pron., *one,* ns.
only, usually spelled **man.** ii. 14,
15; iii. 49, 150; vi. 214; vii. 87, 104,
164; etc.
manna, wk. m. *man.* only in singular,
i. 42, 328; ii. 34; xv. 11, 127; xvii.
29; xxi. 37.
manncwealm, m. *pestilence.* xxi.
237, 281.
man(n)cynn, n. *mankind.* i. 319; ii.
93, 132, 181; iii. 93, 127, 131; iv.
128, 189, 268; v. 112, 242; vi. 284;
vii. 105, 132, 199; etc.
man(n)hata, m. *man-hater, oppressor
of men.* xiii. 70 (v.l. **mán-** as if
'wicked hater'; see note); xxv(*a*).
19 (ns., glossed *hodiosus hominum*).
Mannichei, mp. *the Manichees.* i.
410.
mannrǣden, f. *dependence, service*
entered into by an act of homage;
fig. applied to service of the devil.
xiv. 133.
man(n)sliht, m. *manslaughter, murder.* viii. 123; xv. 137; xvi. 74;
xxiv. 12 (-**slyht**).
māra, -e, comp. adj. *greater.* ii. 98;
iii. 102, 176; vi. 122; vii. 49, 124;
viii. 84; ix. 34; xiii. 171; xv. 7, etc.
(9 times); xvi. 133, 281, 283; xviii.

164, 296; xix. 8; xx. 234, 363, 403;
xxi. 204.—**māre** for nsm. **māra,**
x. 21, 141, 147.—as sb., **māre,** n.
(*a greater quantity*), *more.* xiii. 142;
xvi. 164, 191. [Cf. **mā, mǣst,**
micel.]
Marcus, *Mark* the Evangelist. xvii.
20.
Maria. (a) the Virgin *Mary.* i. 406;
iv. 289; v. 195; x. 154; xi. 10, 22;
xia. 63, 79, 96, 156, 228. (b) *Mary*
the sister of Lazarus. vi. 4, 5, 15, 47,
50, 70, 71, 74, 108. [The name is
declined with -**u** in gda. sing.]
Mars, the god. xxi. 126, 170 (ds.
Marte).
Martha, the sister of Lazarus. vi. 4,
15, 47, 49, 51, 55, 61, 70, 87, 108,
355. [gda. sing. **Marthan,** spelled
Marðan at 4, **Marþan** at 47.]
martir, martyr, m. *martyr.* viii. 137;
ix. 167; xiv. 142; xvii. 20; xxi. 149.
martirdōm, m. *martyrdom.* xxiii. 3,
181.
gemartirian, gemartyrian, II. *to
martyr.* xviii. 353; xxii. 57.
Matheus, *Matthew* the Evangelist. i.
446; iv. 57 (ds. **Matheum**), 136; ix.
96; xv. 1.
Mathias, the apostle chosen to replace Judas. vi. 353.
mē, see **ic.**
mearcian, II. (a) with reference to
fixing boundaries of land, *to mark
out.* viii. 111. (b) with reference to
signs (lit. or fig.) of a man's allegiance
or servitude, *to mark.* xiv. 133
(almost *brand*); xix. 209 (**gemearcod Gode,** *marked for God:* i.e.,
tonsured?).
mearcung, f. *marking.* viii. 114.
mēd, f. *meed, reward.* ii. 183; v. 81,
249; xvi. 196; xvii. 197; xxx. 73.
gemedemian, II. *to condescend.* vi.
124.
mēder, see **mōdor.**
Mediolana-burh, f. *the city of Milan.*
xxvi. 39, 45 (ds. -**byrig**).
meldian, II. *to inform against, accuse,*
v. 230.
melu, n. *meal* (ground grain). xxi. 358.
men, see **mann.**
gemengan, I. *to mingle, mix.* v. 269

(pp. ģemenced, v.l. ģemenged);
xvii. 94; xxi. 446.

menig, mænig, pl. **manega, -ra,
-um**, pron. adj. *many, many a.* (a)
as adj., nsn. **mænig**, xiii. 141 (v.l.
menig); gsn. **meniges**, xix. 9 (v.l.
menģes); nap. **manega**, i. 222,
260; v. 89; vi. 312, 325; vii. 1; viii.
137; ix. 2; xi*a*. 21; xiv. 221; xv.
228; xvi. 81; xviii. 156; xix. 1; xx.
401; xxi. 117, 155; xxix. 4; gp.
manegra, xiii. 4; xiv. 43; xviii.
334; xxi. 532; dp. **manegum**, viii.
173; x. 47; xi*a*. 58; xiii. 69; xvi. 136,
213; xvii. 15, 146; xix. 115; xxi.
500; xxii. 8, 84; xxvii. 45. (b) as
pron., nap. **manega**, i. 347; iii. 93,
145, 147; v. 200, 223; vi. 46, 107,
121; ix. 34; xi. 545; xii. 183; xiii.
2; xiv. 58; xvi. 275; xvii. 234; xix.
175, 242; xxi. 240; dp. **manegum**,
ix. 33; xi. 160. [These are the usual
forms in Ælfric manuscripts; nap.
'menige', not represented here, is
occasional elsewhere, e.g., CH II.
130/6, 16. The late MS. B has
'moniģæ' for **manega** at viii. 137,
'moniģe' for **manegum** at viii. 173
(Belfour, pp. 16/30, 18/20).]

meniģfeald, mæniģ-, adj. *manifold,
various, numerous.* i. 209; iii. 88; iv.
156, 161; vii. 131; viii. 77, 123;
xviii. 353, 361; xxi. 537, 589; xxix. 5.

ģemeniģfyldan, I. *to multiply, increase* (intrans.). xviii. 332 (pres. 3s.
-**fylt**); xix. 35 (pp. np. -**fylde**).

meni(ģ)u, meni(ģ)o, mæni(ģ)u, f.
crowd, multitude. i. 234; ii. 52; iii.
44, 166, 173, 176; iv. 11, 51, 63,
270; xvii. 29, 114; xx. 142, 157, 185.
[All cases in sing. represented, all
ending in -**u** exc. two, ds., in -**o**, iv.
51, 270.]

menn, see **mann**.

mennisc, adj. *human.* vii. 47; xi. 474;
xvi. 52; xvii. 132; xxix. 17, 26.—
*as noun, n. *portion of the human
race, people* (in any specified division of mankind, as into Jews and
gentiles, believers and unbelievers).
xiv. 58; xvii. 69. [This meaning
differs only slightly from those listed
in BTS.]

menniscnyss, f. *humanity, human
nature* (always with reference to
Christ), *incarnation.* i. 3, 18, 339,
406, 457; iv. 2, 277; v. 107, 211;
vi. 263; vii. 221; viii. 202, 208,
224; ix. 91, 127, 136; x. 147 (on
þǣre **menniscnysse**, *in respect to
[Christ's] humanity*), 150; xi. 8, 89,
351; xi*a*. 74, 77, 156; xii. 212;
xvii. 215; xviii. 213; xxi. 573, 657.

meolc, f. *milk.* xix. 3.

meox, n. *filth, dirt, dung.* vi. 206; xvi.
67; xvii. 265.

Mercurius, the god *Mercury.* xxi.
133, 143 (gs. **Mercuries**), 173 (ds.
Mercurie).

mere, m. *sea, lake.* viii. 120, 129 (a
lake); xi. 462, 467, 473 (the sea of
fire described in Revelation); xiv.
4, 5, 8, 43, 46, 49 (the Sea of Galilee).

mergen, meri(ģ)en, m. *morning.*
only in phrases: (a) **on mergen**,
in the morning. ix. 3; xxi. 230, 609.
(b) þæs **on mergen**, *the next morning.* x. 186; xx. 203, 229; xxix. 92, 98.
[Cf. **tomergen** and **ærnemergen**.
The form **mergen** in these phrases is
probably endingless locative, though
perhaps it had come to be felt as
accusative. See S–B 237, Anm. 2;
Cpb 572.]

mērsode, see **mǣrsian**.

Messias, see **Mæssias**.

ģemet, n. *measure.* xiii. 15, 16, 18,
110, 111, 114, 117, 119.

ģemētan, I, pret. 3s. **ģemētte**, pp.
ģemētt. *to meet, encounter, find.* ii.
276; xi. 301; xviii. 106; xx. 62; xxi.
149; xxiii. 75, 94, 110, 114.

mete, m. nap. **mettas**. *food, victuals.*
i. 234; v. 10, 72, 74, 75, 227, 229,
240, 242; xi*a*. 125; xvi. 136; xix. 5;
xx. 6, etc. (14 times); xxi. 107, etc.
(14 times); xxiii. 182.

ģemeteģian, II. *to regulate, apportion.*
xi. 493.

ģemetlīce, adv. *moderately.* ii. 171.

metsung, f. *feeding, provisioning.* xxi.
358.

miccle, adv., see **micele**.

mic(c)lum, adv. (ds. of **micel**).
greatly, much. i. 424; ii. 213; iv. 11,
63; vi. 312; vii. 47, 214; xi. 165;

mic(c)lum (*cont.*)
xiii. 70; xv. 62; xvii. 213, 234 (*insistently*); xviii. 171; xx. 89, 100, 206 (*vigorously*), 222 (mycclum), 234; xxi. 131.—**swā miclum** . . . **swā**, *by as much . . . as, in proportion as.* xviii. 164.

micel, mycel, adj. *great, large.* i. 116, 180, etc. (12 times); ii. 245, 268; iii. 131; iv. 128, 156, 195; v. 106, 159; vi. 5, 112, 214, 333; vii. 62, 90, 175, 201, 210, 218; etc.—of the voice, *loud.* iv. 51, 270; of quantity, *much.* xxi. 532; etc.—**on micclum and- gyte,** *in largeness of understanding, intellectual power.* xiii. 142.—neuter as sb., *a great number* or *quantity, much, many.* ii. 243; ix. 124; etc.— occas. spelled **mycel,** e.g. xxi. 489. [See separately comp. **māra,** sup. **mǣst**; also **mā.**]

micele, mic(c)le, adv. (is. of **micel**). with comparatives, (*by*) *much.* i. 422; ii. 98; vi. 122; ix. 210; xv. 28, 35, 45, 157; xvi. 33, 216; xx. 363; xxiii. 178 (**mycele**).—w. **mā,** *many more.* iii. 16; v. 94.

micelnyss, mycel-, f. *greatness, size, magnitude.* vi. 293; xi. 309; xiv. 48; xxi. 537; xxvi. 49.

Michael, the archangel. xxvii. 55, 60 (ds. **Michaele**), 62, 67, 78 (gs. **-es**).

miclum, see **micclum.**

mid, prep. w. dat. *with* in its major modern senses, excluding those involving opposition (see **wiþ**); sometimes, with a plural object, *among.* (a) denoting association of some sort: companionship, accompaniment, agreement, combination, addition, etc., *together with, along with, in conjunction with, accompanied by*; *having* (an appearance, an attribute, an accessory, etc.); *accompanying, attending*; *combined with*; etc. i. 4, etc. (17 times, including 217, *and also, besides*); ii. 174; iii. 44, 166, 173, 178, 185; iv. 2, etc. (10 times, including 39, *on the side or party of,* and 48, fig., *in the house or dwelling of,* as guests or lodgers); v. 16 (*in company with*), 187, 204; etc. (over 250 instances in all, including xi. 41,

clothed with; 270, **hwæt ġewyrþ mid ūs,** *what happens among us,* i.e. *to people in our world*; 472, **fram frymþe mid Gode,** *present from the beginning with God,* i.e. *in God's mind*; xia. 69, **mid cilde,** *with child*; xii. 31, **underfōn mid ēow,** *receive among you*; xxi. 416, **mid þē,** *attending* or *dwelling with thee,* i.e. *in thy nature*; and two instances of ellipsis after an auxiliary: xvii. 245 and xxii. 48, where **mid** implies *go with*). (b) denoting, with its object, an accompanying state of mind, action, circumstance, etc., the phrase often equivalent to an adverb of manner; sometimes hard to distinguish from meaning (c). ii. 43, 133, 143, 177, 203; iii. 88; iv. 51, 68, 95, 112, 270, 294, 296; v. 175, 180, 183, 186; etc. (over 130 in all). (c) denoting instrumentality, agency, or causation, *by, by means of, by the use of, in consequence of, by reason of.* i. 13, 25 (**afylled mid,** *filled with,* involving addition as well as agency and means), 54 (twice, **full mid,** *full of*), 105, 199, 212 (*because of* and *in accordance with*), 230, 258, 297, 320, 456 (twice); ii. 13 (**beworhte mid,** *built about with, surrounded by,* involving addition as well as means), 63, 66, 74, 79, 88, 108, 122, 135, 144 (partly sense b), 175, 234, 238, 271, 280; etc. (about 315 in all). (d) *in regard to.* xix. 41; xxix. 19 (**mid þam,** *in regard to that* [*maiden*]?). (e) expressing simultaneous occurrence and association, *at the same time as.* xix. 225, **mid þam wordum,** *as he said these words*; xxvii. 77, **mid þam lofsanġe,** *as they sang the hymn*; xxviii. 12, **mid þæs Hǣlendes tōcyme,** *upon the Saviour's arrival* (the last two involving some sense of causation).—(f) in adverbial and conjunctional phrases: **mid ealle,** adv. *altogether, entirely* (sense a). ix. 180; xi. 187, 357; xiii. 88; xiv. 201; xviii. 23, 261, 400; xxi. 517, 541, 612; xxiii. 178; xxvii. 102; xxviii. 11; xxix. 32.—**mid þam**

adv. *thereupon, meanwhile* (sense e).
v. 60; xiv. 8.—mid þam þe, conj.
while, when, as. ii. 186; iv. 50, 269
(þan); v. 216; vii. 16, 73; viii. 223;
ix. 191; xx. 246; xxvi. 6.
middæg, m. *midday, noon.* v. 8;
xxiii. 25 (-dæig).
middan, see on middan under on,
I. (u).
middaneard, m. *the earth, the world*
(as the dwelling of men, or as all
men on earth). i. 43, etc. (16 times);
v. 97, 112, 288; vi. 27, 64, 261, 345,
347; vii. 16, etc. (10 times); etc.
middaneardlic, adj. *earthly.* xxx. 39.
middanwinter, m. *midwinter, Christmas.* xxvi. 84 (ds. -wintra). [Cf.
middewinter.]
middeweard, adj. *middle,* as noun in
the phrase on middeweardan, *in
the midst.* i. 379 (Lat. *in medio*). [BT
and BTS have a few examples with
genitive, which is here lacking as in
the Latin, though implicitly *eorum*,
'heora'.]
middewinter, m. *midwinter,* (then
the same day as) *Christmas.* xia. 71;
Middewintres Dæg, *Christmas
Day,* xi. 6; xia. 75.
midwunung, f. *fellowship* (in a common dwelling-place). xviii. 53.
miht, f. *might, power, virtue.* i. 83, 109,
180; ii. 115, 121, 157, 289; iv. 7, etc.
(10 times); vi. 106, etc. (6 times,
including 122, *an exercise of power*);
vii. 88, etc. (5 times); etc.—at vii.
185, MSS. have eall . . . miht for
as. ealle . . . mihte.
miht, miht-, see magan.
mihtig, adj. *mighty, powerful.* ii. 88;
vi. 259; vii. 210; x. 152; xi. 87, 286,
348; xia. 207; xxi. 17, 102, 489.
mihtiglice, adv. *mightily, wondrously.* i. 97; ii. 40, 223, 245; v.
211; ix. 120; x. 60 (mihti-); xi. 364
(mihte-); xviii. 213; xxiii. 23
(mihte-).
mil, f. *mile.* xiv. 43, 44.
milde, adj. *mild, gracious, merciful.*
iv. 208; xi. 348; xv. 227; xxvii. 108.
mildelice, adv. *graciously.* xvii. 103.
mildheort, adj. *merciful.* iii. 125; iv.
1, 7; vi. 187; xia. 53; xiii. 9, 38, 42

(twice), 54, 56, 71, 82; xv. 117;
xvii. 250; xxi. 672.
mildheortnyss, f. *mercy.* ii. 82; iii.
103; vi. 288; xiii. 72, 74, 97, 101,
102; xv. 226, 227 (uninflected after
het).
milds, f. *mercy, kindness, favour.*
xiii. 71; xx. 363; xxiii. 149.
mildsian, gemildsian, often milt-,
gemilt-, II. absolute or w. dat. of
person, *to have mercy (on), be
gracious, kind (to).* vi. 274 (pres. part.
miltsiendan, *merciful, forgiving*),
276, 277; xi. 198; xiii. 76, 80, 137
(twice); xv. 44, 49, 160; xvii. 247;
xix. 245; xxvii. 40(?).
mildsung, milt-, f. *mercy.* i. 236; vi.
274; xia. 39; xv. 42; xvii. 72, 273;
xviii. 220; xix. 133, 252; xxvi. 132
(w. gen. of the offence, *a merciful
estimate of, lenience toward*).
min, poss. pron. and adj. *my, mine.*
i. 440, 445; ii. 49; iii. 19, 65; v. 75,
240; vi. 52, 76; vii. 21, 29, 47, 163,
219; etc. [See also ic.]
Minerua, the goddess *Minerva.* xxi.
115.
misdæd, f. *misdeed, evil deed.* vi. 261;
xiii. 171; xviii. 123; xxvi. 81, 132;
xxvii. 7.
misfaran, 6. *to go astray.* pres. 3p.
misfaraþ, xiv. 157. [Cf. faran.]
mislic, adj. *various.* iii. 147; iv. 208;
xiii. 2, 69; xviii. 117, 352; xxi. 101,
519; xxiii. 146.—with sing. noun,
various kinds of, xxi. 193.
mislice, adv. *variously.* i. 222; ii. 25;
iv. 268; xvii. 15; xviii. 131; xxi. 155.
mislician, II, w. dat. *to be displeasing
to.* x. 51; xvi. 72; xx. 191. [Cf.
lician.]
misræcan, I. *to revile.* xv. 176. [BT
and Hall cite one example only,
from CH II. 590. Cf. ræcan.]
misrædan, I. *to advise wrongly.* xxx.
6 (pres. 3s. misræt). [BT and Hall
cite one example only in this sense,
from Ben. Rule. Cf. rædan.]
mistihtan, I. *to persuade or incite
wrongly.* iv. 209; xx. 197.
mistucian, II. *to maltreat.* xxvi. 31.
miswendan, I. *to go bad, decay.* i. 273
(pres. 3s. miswent).

*miswyrcan, I. *to make amiss, mis-create*. xv. 69 (pp., np. **mis-worohte**, v.l. **-worhte**). [Not in dict. OED, 'miswork', illustrated from 1300, but in this sense (3) not till 1626.—Cf. **wyrcan**.]

mitta, wk. m., or **mitte**, wk. f. *a measure, bushel*. xvi. 26, 143.

mōd, n. *mind, heart, spirit, mood*. i. 196, 257, 297; ii. 70, 76, 137; iii. 168; iv. 112, 163, 216, 285; v. 187; vi. 252, 275, 278, 369; etc.

moddra, **mōder**, see **mōdor**.

mōdig, adj. *proud*. xi. 474; xxx. 12.

mōdigian, II. *to take offence (through pride)*. i. 226 (pres. 2s. **mōdegast**). [For this meaning see BT, s.v., II, citing CH II. 170/25.]

mōdignyss, f. *pride*. i. 244; iv. 251; v. 178; xia. 29; xiii. 167; xviii. 370; xix. 127.

gemōdod, part. adj. *minded, disposed*. xviii. 108, 131. [BT and BTS have two examples, both from Ælfric.]

mōdor, **mōder**, f. *mother*. i. 142, 414; ii. 231 (gp. **moddra**), 233 (ds. **mēder**); vi. 184, 187, 194; xi. 11, 22; xia. 63, 80, 96, 168 (gs. **mōder**), 227; xii. 12 (gs. **mōdor**), 76, 81, 130, 192; xiv. 212; xix. 54, 56, 60.

mōdri(ġ)e, **moddri(ġ)e**, wk. f. *mother's sister, maternal aunt*. i. 5; ii. 6; xiv. 212.

molde, wk. f. *(ground)*, *dust*. xi. 521.

mōna, wk. m. *the moon*. i. 208, 280; xi, 285, 288, 514; xviii. 261, 400; xxi. 56, 60, 64, 83, 166, 169, 183.

Mōnandæg, m. *Monday*. xxi. 169.

mōnaþ, m. *month*. v. 78 (np. **mōn-þas**); xia. 71; xviii. 369; xx. 92 (ds. **mōnþe**); xxvi. 81.

mōnaþsēoc, adj. (a) *lunatic*: xvii. 14 (ap. wk. as noun, **-an**, Lat. *lunaticos*). (b) *menstruous*: xix. 113 (**monoþ-**).

morþdǣd, f. *murder, deed of violence*. xvi. 74; xxi. 496.

morþslaga, wk. m. *murderer, homicide*. xi. 375; xxiii. 144.

mot, n. *mote, speck, atom*. xiii. 24, 28, 33, 146, 150, 156, 157, 174.

gemōt, n. *assembly*. ix. 179 (dp. **-um**, referring to synagogues).

[mōtan], pret. pres. vb. (a) with in-finitive (directly expressed, or implied from a preceding clause), *to be permitted, may, must*. pres. 1s. **mōt**, xxi. 607; xxvi. 95; 2s. **mōst**, ii. 46; viii. 67; 3s. **mōt**, xi. 402 (10 more); 1p. **mōton**, i. 218 (7 more); **mōte** **wē**, xv. 120; 3p., **mōton**, xi. 351; xiv. 203; xvi. 276; xix. 54; pres. 1p. subj. **mōton**, xvi. 152, 294; xvii. 275 3p., xiii. 77; pret. 1s. **mōste**, xxvii. 38; 3s. **mōste**, ii. 268; xxi. 49, 53; 3p. **mōston**, x. 146; xv. 81 (subj. ?); xxi. 339 (subj. ?); pret. 3s. subj. **mōste**, xi. 198; xix. 248; xxi. 442, 612; xxvii. 19; 3p. **mōston**, xii. 204; xiv. 145. (b) elliptically with prep., an in-finitive to be supplied: pret. 3p. subj. **mōston intō**, *might go into*, xvii. 236; pret. 3s. subj. **mōste** **mid**, *might go with*, xvii. 245.

mōtian, II. *to hold speech, confer, converse*. xvii. 93, 95; xxii. 89.

moþþe, f. *moth*. xvi. 161.

Moyses, *Moses*. ns., i. 70, 229, 236; ii. 66, 152; iii. 57; xii. 38, 219, 227; xv. 103; xx. 10, 41, 52, 66, 76, 89, 147, 206, 225, 229, 322, 329, 365, 368; xxii. 87, 89; gs., i. 232; ii. 44, 72 (**Moysæs**), 213; iv. 146; vii. 201; ix. 190; xiii. 203; xv. 10, 27, 35, 62, 81, 126; xviii. 66; xx. 63, 245, 298; xxi. 219; ds. **Moysen**, i. 264, 364; xi. 25; xia. 99; xx. 75, 181, 248, 324; **Moyse**, i. 265, 370 (both orig. **-n** ?); xx. 47, 141 (v.l. **-n**), 157, 305, 318; as. **Moysen**, i. 260, 464, 468; iv. 141; xx. 217, 222, 262, 287, 309; xxii. 94.

Mundiu, *the Alps*. xxi. 578. [The nearest approach to this spelling is 'Muntgiu', cited by BTS from a passage by Ælfric in Napier's Wulfstan, p. 152/9.]

munt, m. *mountain, hill*. i. 441; iv. 146; v. 41, 46, 164, 174, 176, 178; viii. 92, 97, 111, 114, 116; xiii. 191; xviii. 238, 308; xx. 28, 30, 41, 47, 48, 52; xxi. 219, 578; xxix. 44.

munuc, m. *monk*. viii. 145, 147, 152 (twice); xi. 171; xix. 62; xxvii. 18, 31, 48, 81, 83, 87, 90.

munuclīf, n. *monastic life, cloister*.

xxix. 13 (**munuclīfes mann**, *man of the cloister*).

murcnian, II. *to complain.* xx. 83.

murcnung, f. *complaint.* xx. 69.

mūs, f. *mouse.* np. **mȳs**, xxi. 240, 257, 273; gp. **mūsa**, xxi. 281, 551, 554.

mūþ, m. *mouth.* i. 83, 131, 233; iv. 285; v. 216; x. 63; xv. 179, 182, 185; xvii. 35, 178, 233; xx. 19; xxi. 40, 97, 329.

myc-, see **mic-**.

gemyltan, I. *to melt* (trans.) xxi. 519 (pp. dp. **gemyltum**).

myltestre, f. *prostitute.* xi. 379; xxi. 153.

gemynd, f. or n. *memory, remembrance.* xi. 239, 469; xv. 163; xix. 206.

gemyndig, adj. *mindful.* ix. 18, 207; xxi. 479; xxvii. 101.

myne, m. *love, regard.* ix. 109.

mynster, n. (a) *monastery.* viii. 115, 118. (b) *church, minster.* xxx. 94.

mynsterlīf, n. (*monastic life*), *monastery.* viii. 107, 109.

mynstermann, m. *monk.* xix. 209.

gemyntan, I. *to intend.* xxi. 427 (pp. **gemynt**).

Myrce or **Myrcan**, mp. *Mercians.* xix. 138 (gp. **Myrcena**).

mȳre, wk. f. *mare.* xxix. 15, 17, 20, 22.

myrhþ, f. *joy, pleasure.* x. 77; xi. 151, 249; xv. 38; xvi. 120, 277; xviii. 53, 104; xix. 46; xx. 400; xxv(a). 7. [No example of ns. but BTS, 'myrigþ, myrhþ', cites an instance from Ælfric without the old '-u' ending, which indeed is not on record.]

myriġe, adj. *pleasing, agreeable.* viii. 109; xiv. 41, 47.

myriġe, adv. *pleasantly, sweetly.* xxvii. 76.

mȳs, see **mūs**.

N

nā, adv. (a) *not.* i. (41), 49, 162, etc. (11 times); ii. 225; iii. 105, 112; iv. 19, 99; v. 233; vi. 12, 231, etc. (8 times); vii. 27, 70, 207, 208; etc. (b) introducing a reply, *no.* xiii. 225.

nabban ('ne habban'), III. *not to have, have not.* i. 142 (pret. 3s. **næfde**), 190 (pres. 3s. **næfþ**), 251, 335 (pres. 1p. **nabbaþ**), 397, 415; ii. 34 (pres. 1s. **næbbe**), 82, 150; iv. 89, 226, 253; v. 22 (pres. 2s. **næfst**), 35, 36, 239; vi. 25, 219; vii. 177; etc. [Forms correspond to those of **habban**.]

nacod, adj. *naked.* viii. 52 (ap. wk. **nacedan**); x. 34; xi. 415, 446; xxvii. 118.

næbbe, see **nabban**.

næddre, neddre, wk. f. *snake, serpent.* i. 242; xii. 39, 220, 228, 229, 230, 233; xvi. 228, 230, 235, 240; xvii. 87; xx. 315–48 (11 times).

næfd-, næfþ, see **nabban**.

næfre, adv. *never.* i. 164, 183; iv. 171, 172; v. 125, 126, 232; vi. 159, 213, 219, 270, 277; etc.

nægl, m. *nail.* xi. 36; xia. 138 (dp. **nægelum**).

nænne, see **nān**.

nǣre, nǣron, næs, see **bēon-wesan**.

nāgan ('ne āgan'), pret. pres. vb. *not to have.* pres. 3p. subj. **nāgon**, xix. 78.

nāht, n. *nothing, naught.* i. 325; xi. 329, 337, 338, 565; xiv. 21, 117; xviii. 59; xx. 88; xxi. 94; xxix. 115.—as adv., *not a whit.* xi. 272; xv. 50; xvii. 298; xxvi. 90; xxx. 47.

nāhwǣr, nāhwār, adv. *nowhere.* i. 193; ii. 229; ix. 183; xi. 391; xviii. 434.

nāhwider, adv. *nowhither, nowhere.* xxi. 579.

Naim, a city mentioned at Luke vii. 11 (Vulgate, *Naim*; A.V., *Nain*). vi. 183.

nama, wk. m. *name.* i. 38, 48, 131, 300, 351; ii. 95; iii. 62; iv. 25, etc (9 times); viii. 30, etc. (14 times); ix. 102; x. 12, 81; etc.

namcūþ, adj. *well-known, celebrated.* xxi. 524; xxvii. 26.

genamian, II. *to name, appoint.* xx. 147.

nān, pron. adj. *not one, no, none.* (a) as adj. i. 142, 183, 184, 190, 249, 415; ii. 34 (asm. **nænne**), 129, 222, 257; iii. 75; etc.—**nān þing**, n. *nothing.* i.

nān (*cont.*)
32, 168, 176; ii. 275; v. 125 (gs. **nānes þinges**); viii. 32, 158; ix. 30, 39, 183; x. 26, 189, 194; xi. 560; xiii. 178; xiv. 37, 215; xv. 209; xvi. 244; xix. 111 (ds. **nānum þinge**), 172, 202; xxiii. 150; xxix. 28. (b) as pron., *no one, none.* asm. **nǣnne**, xiii. 99; w. gen., nsm., vii. 10; xiii. 223, 225; xiv. 166.

nāst, nāt, see **nytan.**

nāteshwōn, adv. *not at all.* i. 136; iv. 201; vii. 177; viii. 46, 238; x. 16, 130; xia. 225; xii 18, 31, 35, 140, 177, 197; etc.

nāþer, nāþor, adj. *neither.* iii. 112 (dsf. **nāþre**).—as pron., xix. 92.— as adv. in correl. constr., **nāþor ne . . . ne,** *neither . . . nor.* ix. 204. reversed, **ne . . . ne . . . nāþor,** v. 105.

Nazareth, the city. xvii. 3.

ne, nē, particle. *not.* i. 45, 46, 131, etc.—as conj., *nor.* i. 49, 50, 163, etc. often in series, as at i. 251–2, 391–4; seldom as correlative, *neither . . . nor,* as at vi. 220.

nēadung, f. *compulsion.* xix. 52.

genēalǣcan, I, pret. 3s. **-lǣhte.** (a) *to draw near, approach* a place or person. absolute, xiv. 50; xvii. 208; w. prep. **tō,** vi. 305; xii. 48; xvii. 67, 84; w. dat. of person, xix. 113 (for sexual intercourse). (b) *to draw near* in time. absolute, iii. 9. (c) impers. w. dat., *to draw near to* a time. xxvi. 83. [Cf. **-lǣcan.**]

nēawist, f. *nearness, presence.* vii. 41 (v.l. **-est-**).

*neb(b)wlita, wk. m. *face, countenance.* xxix. 102 (gs. **nebwlitan**). [Not in dict., though BT has 'wlita' as a variant of 'wlite', and BTS cites Ælfric for 'andwlita'. Cf. next word.]

nebbwlite, m. *face, countenance.* i. 432. [BTS cites Ælfric for this form; BT, for '-wlitu', f.]

neddre, see **nǣddre.**

nellan, nyllan ('ne willan'), anom. vb. *to be unwilling, will not.* elliptically, **nolde ūt,** *would not go out.* xxvii. 58. pres. 1s. **nelle,** xxi.

366; xxvi. 113; 2s. **nelt,** xiii. 29, 151; xxi. 364; xxx. 52; 3s. **nele,** i. 162 (15 more); **nyle,** xiii. 61; xv. 50; pl. **nellaþ,** ii. 81 (14 more); **nyllaþ,** xvi. 53; **nelle ġē,** ii. 272; pres. 3s. subj. **nelle,** xix. 29, 130 (or ind.; v.l. **nele**); xxx. 28; **nylle,** xvi. 78; pret. 2s. **noldest,** xxi. 437; xxvii. (103); 3s. **nolde,** i. 387 (12 more); pl. **noldon,** i. 152 (18 more); **noldan,** xviii. 178; xxi. 99; **nolde ġē,** xi. 442; pret. 3s. subj. **nolde,** xix. 152 (or ind.?), 155 (or ind.?); xxv(b). 4; 3p. subj. **noldon,** iii. 141.

nēod, f. *need.* i. 218; vii. 34; viii. 48, 155, 243; ix. 58; xi. 160; xv. 119; xvi. 45, 247, 266; xx. 389; xxx. 36, 89.—**embe sume** (**his āgene**) **nēode,** *on some* (*his own*) *business,* xxi. 577; xxvii. 85.

genēosian, II. *to visit* (the sick). xi. 416, 424.

nēosung, f. *visitation.* x. 56.

nett, n. *net.* xiv. 9, 18, etc. (18 times).

nēxt, adj. *last, latest,* in phrase **æt nēxtan,** *at last.* i. 262; iii. 18, 124, 155; ix. 59; xix. 148, 213; xxi. 559.

nēxta, nȳhsta, wk. m. (f.). *neighbour.* ii. 145 (MS. F has **cs** for **x**), 196 (see note); xviii. 336.

Nichodemus, *Nicodemus* the Pharisee (John iii. 1). xii. 1, 10, 24, 47, 74, 139 (ds. **Nichodeme**), 165, 218.

nigon, nigen, num. *nine.* xia. 71; xxx. 80, 87.

niht, f. *night.* (a) forms without ending: ns., xii. 69; xviii. 88; as., xiv. 20, 116; ap., xi. 44, 52; xia. 151, 171; and ds.(?) in phrase, **on niht,** *at night,* i. 208, 326; vi. 28; xxi. 594. (b) with ending: ds. **nihte,** vii. 3, 8; ix. 3; xviii. 31, 86; xxi. 322, 408. [Originally athematic, nas. 'neaht' or 'niht', gds. and nap. 'niht'. See S–B 284, Anm. 4; Cpb 628. 3.—With **on niht** cf. **on dæg** under **dæg.**]

nihtes, adv. *by night.* xii. 3, 50, 54, 65, 69; xvii. 226.

nihtlic, adj. *of night.* xii. 48 (**on nihtlicre tīde,** *in the night-time*).

genihtsumian, II. *to suffice.* vi. 320.

genihtsumnyss, f. *abundance, plenty.*
xi. 567; xxx. 94.

niman, geniman, 4. (a) *to take* (*in
hand, up, away, to,* or *from*), *receive,
accept, appropriate, seize.* i. 406; ii.
48, 50; iv. 194; ix. 62; xia. 156; xii.
192; xviii. 32, etc. (17 times); xix.
14, 171, 187; xx. 226, 237; xxi. 261,
316, 445, 453, 477, 619; xxiii. 27;
xxvii. 46, 61, 64. (b) with on and
refl. pron. *to take upon oneself,
assume.* xvii. 259. (c) with tō and
refl. pron. *to take* another *to oneself
as a confederate.* iv. 47, 246. (d)
with tō. *to take as, consider as.* xxi. 82.
e) *to take* a wife. xix. 39, 40, 74, 108.
[Forms: inf. niman, ii. 48, 50; xxi.
316; geniman, ix. 62 (v.l. niman);
xix. 108; d. inf. genimen(n)e,
xviii. 243, 313; imp. sg. nim, xxi.
477; genim, xxvii. 61; pl. nimaþ,
xix. 187; xx. 226; xxi. 261; pres.
2s. nimst, xix. 74; 3s. nimþ, xix.
38; genimþ, iv. 47 (5 more); pres.
1p. subj. genimon, xxvii. 64; 3p.
subj. niman, xix. 14; pret. 3s.
nam, xxi. 445; genam, i. 406 (7
more); 3p. nāmon, xxi. 82; genā-
mon, xix. 171; pp. genumen,
xvii. 259; xviii. 32–204 (12 times);
xxi. 453. Cf. a-, for-niman.]

nis, see bēon-wesan.

nīþfull, adj. *rancorous, malicious.*
ix. 198.

nīwe, adj. *new.* ix. 193; xi. 516 (twice);
xv. 30; xix. 36; xxi. 260; xxx. 76,
107.—*of the new* (*Christian*) *era,*
i. 466 (ūs nīwum mannum).

niwelnyss, f. *abyss, precipice.* xia. 46.

Noe, *Noah.* ns., xviii. 13; gs. Noeys,
xviii. 10 (v.l. Noes), 61 (v.l. Noeis);
Noes, xxi. 73, 75; ds. Noe, xviii.
62.

genōh, adj. *enough.* ii. 192; xx. 23, 92
(np. genōge), 416 (asf. genōge).

nold-, see nellan.

nosu, f. *nose.* xvii. 155, 158 (gs. nosa),
165.

notian, II, w. gen. *to make use of.*
xxi. 520.

nū, adv. *now.* i. 84, 247, 281, 322, 327,
367, 455; ii. 1, 55 (second), 59, 175,
252; iii. 46, 47, 67, 182; iv. 149,
284; etc.—with iū (q.v.), *even now,
already.* xx. 50.—with rihtes (q.v.),
right now, immediately. xxvii. 71.—
with pret., *just now.* ii. 2; vi. 1; ix.
166; xii. 18, 43; xxvi. 67; xxvii. 109.
nū for fēawum dagum (gēa-
rum), *just a few days* (*years*) *ago.*
vi. 22; xxiii. 62.—as conj., marking
a step in an argument or exposition,
now. i. 387, 410, 451; ii. 167, 232,
241; iv. 86; v. 174; vi. 170, 213,
236, 264, 278; etc.—*now that,* ii. 55
(first), 278; xv. 121; xvi. 12, 100;
xxiii. 99, 164.

nȳdan, I. *to compel.* iii. 112.

nȳhsta, see nēxta.

nyle, nylle, nyllaþ, see nellan.

nys, see bēon-wesan.

nytan ('ne witan'), pret. pres. vb.
not to know. pres. 1s. nāt, xxi. 472;
2s. nāst, xii. 21, 27, 147, 167; xxvi.
49; 3s. nāt, xviii. 63; 2p. nyton, v.
48, 72, 166, 227; nyte gē, xxix.
112; 3p. nyton, ii. 243; viii. 1;
pres. 3s. subj. nyte, xxiii. 89; xxx.
57; pret. 3s. nyste, ii. 51; v. 151;
xii. 70; xxvii. 118; 3p. nyston, xxi.
653; pret. 3s. subj. nyste, xii. 169.

nȳten, n. *cattle, beast, animal.* i. 16,
215; ii. 223, 236; v. 25; xvi. 60, 68,
230; xvii. 266.

nytennyss, f. *ignorance.* viii. 1; xii.
70, 74, 78; xiv. 69; xviii. 88.

nyttwyrþe, adj. *useful, profitable.*
xviii. 194.

nyþan, adv. *beneath.* xxi. 541.

nyþer, adv. *downward, down.* xii. 36,
198 (v.l. niþer).

genyþerian, II. *to abase, bring low.*
xix. 201.

genyþerung, f. *abasement, condemna-
tion.* vi. 136.

O

of, prep. w. dat. *of, from, out of, off.*
(a) indicating the thing, place, or
direction, or the situation, condition, or state whence anything goes,
comes, is released, driven, or moved
(literally or figuratively): (*away, out,*

of (*cont.*)

up, down) *from* (OED, 'of', 1 and 3). i. 434, 443, 453; ii. 19, 38, 52, 92, 106, 110, 251; iii. 126; iv. 23, 25, 51, 116, 118, 196, 232, 270; etc. (about 107 more); and with adverbs of direction: **ūt**, iv. 41, 45, 212, 236; xiii. 32, 33, 158, 173, 174; xvii. 29, 114; xviii. 74; xx. 271; xxvii. 59, 77; **aweġ**, viii. 105; xvii. 295; **ufan**, x. 98; **nyþer**, xii. 36, 198; **up**, xiv. 66; **adūne**, xx. 48. (b) indicating a course from which something deviates: *from, away from* (not explicit in OED, but cf. OED, 'off', prep., 1). xxi. 278. (c) indicating a limit *from* which time or space is measured: time, with **syþþan**, xxi. 639 (cf. OED, 'of', 2); space, with correlative **up oþ**, xviii. 269, 417 (not in OED under 'of', 'off'; cf. OED, 'from', prep., A. 2). (d) expressing transformation *from* a former condition (OED, 'of', 20. b; cf. also 3). viii. 191, 193 (**elles of**, *different from*); xii. 137. (e) expressing position by reference to the fixed point (or state) from which one has departed (OED, 4). xv. 53 (**of līfe**, *out of life, dead*). (f) expressing exclusion from a specified class, *distant from, not included in, different from* (cf. OED, 'off', prep., 6). ii. 226; xiv. 102. (g) indicating origin or source, personal or impersonal, *from, of, out of* (OED, 'of', 9, 10, 11). i. 49 (twice), 50 (twice), 133, etc. (28 times); ii. 233 (twice); iv. 16, 91, 95, 130, 181, 182; v. 49, 117, 124, 126, 167, 193, 195 (twice), 199; etc. (about 86 more, including xia. 206, 207, where the sense is probably *emanating from* but verges on *belonging to*, OED, 'of', 49. b). (h) indicating the mental or spiritual source or spring of action, *out of, from, as an expression of* (OED, 'of', 12). vii. 27 and 207 (**of him sylfum**, *out of himself, as an expression of his own independent thought or volition*), 209 (**of þam þe hē is on ānre godcundnysse**, *out of that which he is in* [i.e. *as an aspect of*] *one divinity*).

(i) indicating that which has caused the condition specified by an adjective (OED, 'of', 14. a). v. 7 (**of þam sīþfæte wērig**, *weary from the journey*). (j) indicating that by means of which something is obtained or accomplished (OED, 'of', 18). i. 335 (**of Godes ġyfe**, *by God's grace*); xvi. 36 and 259 (**of þam unrihtan welan**, *out of*, or *by the use of, the unrighteous riches*), similarly 157. (k) indicating the material or substance of which anything is made or composed, (*out*) *of, from*. (OED, 'of', 20). i. 247, 261; iii. 144, 145 (twice, with admixture of the partitive sense next below); xi. 337; xx. 43, 46, 50; xxi. 191, 192 (twice), 518, 519, 528, 529 (twice), 532. (l) *of*, in partitive expressions: where the part is indicated by a word of number or quantity (OED, 'of', 42. a), i. 347, 348 (twice); ii. 134; iii. 93, 119; v. 88; vi. 46, 83, 107; x. 203; xi. 432, 450; xia. 149; xii. 181; xiv. 58, 86; xviii. 101; xx. 55, 185; xxx. 102; by a substantive or adjective used absolutely, or a demonstrative with defining clause (OED, 42. b), xviii. 130, 136, 218; xx. 142; by a superlative (OED. 43), xxvi. 8; without a partitive word, where the phrase is object of a verb and the preposition is equivalent to *some of* (OED, 45), v. 26, 27, 31, 137, 138, 152; xx. 99, 151; xxi. 481. (n) *off* (*from*), expressing separation from attachment, contact, or position on, with verbs signifying *to shake, put, lift, cut*, or (in xxi. 552) with **wæs**, describing the resultant position; followed by a noun as object, vi. 91; xxiii. 130; preceded by a pronoun object, hence emphatic and quasi-adverbial, ii. 189; vi. 86; xxi. 550, 552 (cf. OED, 'off', adv., 3). [Neither BT nor the more precise and detailed OED gives all these meanings with exactness.—Cf. **þǣrof**.]

ofǣte, wk. f. *edible produce, food, fruit*. as. or ap. **ofǣtan**, xx. 156, and by emendation, 379 (MS. **ofǣtum**).

[On this rare and problematical word, easily confused with strong neuter 'ofet, ofæt', *fruit*, see note on xx. 379.]

ofāxian, II. (a) *to learn, find out* (*by asking*). vi. 303; xiii. 90 (pres. 3s. subj. **ofāxxie**); xxvi. 40 (pret. 3s. **ofāhsode**). (b) *to seek out* (*by inquiry*). xxii. 68. [Cf. **āxian.**]

*ofcuman, 4. *to come out, come away.* inf., xi. 489. [This sense not in dict. The compound is hardly distinguishable from **of,** adv., plus **cuman,** unless by weakness of stress on **of.** BT cites 'ofcumende' derivative from Ælfric's Grammar, ed. Zupitza, p. 92/17.]

ofdrǣdd, adj. (wk. pp. allied to 'drǣdan', 7; cf. **ondrǣdan**). *afraid, terrified.* xxiii. 119.

of(e)n, m. *furnace.* xxi. 294.

ofer, prep. w. acc., less frequently dat. (the distinction between motion and rest not always clear). *over.* (a) with idea of descending widely upon, covering, spreading abroad upon, being distributed far and wide upon; w. acc., viii. 232; x. 43, 98; xi. 57; xi*a.* 174; xiii. 44 (twice); xvii. 12; xviii. 14; xx. 30; w. dat., ix. 119; xii. 101 (**gefered ofer wæterum,** Gen. i. 2, though Ælfric's translation in O.E. Hept. has acc. 'wæteru'); xviii. 21, 306; case uncertain, iv. 20, 100. (b) with idea of motion in one direction across a surface or from end to end of a way or course; w. acc., v. 185 (twice); xx. 4, 95, 121; xxi. 483, 578, 610. (c) *above,* with idea of superiority, rule, power to control, guardianship, etc.; w. acc., i. 137; vii. 174, 183; xx. 225; xxi. 9, 30; xxiii. 79; xxvi. 17; w. dat., ix. 49; xvi. 213; xviii. 167; xx. 223. (d) with idea of being maintained above and directed to or bestowed upon; w. dat., i. 353 (where one would normally say *to, towards,* or *regarding*). (e) in comparisons: *in excess of, beyond, more highly than, above the measure or ability of*; w. acc., xi. 557; xxi. 353; w. dat., i. 16.

oferbīdan, 1. *to outlive.* pres. 3s. **oferbīt,** xix. 85. [Cf. **abīdan.**]

ofercuman, 4. *to overcome.* inf., xx. 176. [Cf. **cuman.**]

oferdrīfan, 1. *to get the better of.* inf., xvi. 224 (in competition); pres. 3s. **oferdrīfþ,** i. 154 (in an argument: *refute*). [Cf. **drīfan.**]

oferflōwan, 7. *to overflow, run over.* pres. part. **oferflōwende,** xiii. 17, 112; pres. 3s. **oferflēwþ,** xiii. 118. [Cf. **flōwan.**]

oferflōwednyss, f. *superfluity.* iv. 219.

oferfyll, f. *surfeit, gluttony.* xvi. 77.

ofergān, anom. vb. *to go over, overrun, overspread.* inf., xvii. 219; pres. 3s. **ofergǣþ,** xi. 296; xviii. 77. [Cf. **gān.**]

ofergeweorc, n. (*superstructure*), *ornamental covering* (of a tomb). xv. 77. [In another version of this scriptural passage, CH II. 404/18, Ælfric uses the word to mean simply *sepulchre.* The meaning here is an easy modification of meanings given in BT.]

oferrōwan, 7. *to row over.* pret. 3p. **oferrēowon,** xvii. 220. [This instance already cited in BTS, from CH. BT has one other instance, also Ælfric's.—Cf. **rōwan.**]

oferswīþan, -**swȳþan,** I. *to overpower, overcome.* i. 262; ii. 275; iv. 36 (pres. 3s. -**swīþ**), 139, 143, 185, 278; vii. 111, 138, 144; xi. 32, 176; xi*a.* 132; xxvi. 55.

oferþeccan, I. *to cover over.* xvii. 206 (pp. **oferþeht**). [BT cites this instance from Thorpe's text in CH.]

oferwinnan, 3. *to conquer, subdue.* inf., xx. 380; pret. 3s. **oferwann,** xxii. 26; xxvi. 24. [Cf. **winnan.**]

offeallan, 7. *to fall upon.* pres. 3s. **offylþ,** iii. 39. [Cf. **feallan.**]

offrian, geoffrian, II. *to offer* (in sacrifice). ii. 15; iii. 87; iv. 80; xv. 19, 24, 191, 196, 214, 219; xvi. 198; xix. 51; xx. 44, 51; xxi. 84, 130, 137, 263, 597; xxiii. 179; xxx. 24.

offrung, f. *offering, sacrifice.* ii. 14; iv. 79, 82; xxi. 567; xxvi. 15; xxx. 22.

ofhrēosan, 2. *to overwhelm, cover.*
pp. np. ofhrorene, vi. 203.
ofhrēowan, 2. impers. w. dat., *to grieve.* pret. 3s. ofhrēow, xvii. 140.
[For LWS '-hrēow' instead of '-hrēaw' see S–B 126, Anm. 2.]
oflǣte, wk. f. (*oblation*), *sacramental wafer.* i. 252.
oflyst, adj. (pp. of 'oflystan'). *full of desire.* w. æfter, *lusting after.* xx. 84. w. gen., *desirous of.* xx. 122; xxiii. 182.
ofne, see ofen.
of(o)st, f. *haste, speed.* xxiii. 130.
ofsceamian, II. *to put to shame.* xi. 397; xxi. 569. [Cf. sceamian.]
*ofsetnyss, f. *oppression.* i. 199. [BT and BTS cite two examples classified as 'ofsetenness', *a siege* and *a sitting down* resp. Both 'ofsittan', pp. 'ofseten', and 'ofsettan', pp. 'ofset(t)', can mean *to oppress.*]
ofslēan, 6. *to slay.* inf., iii. 21; vii. 106; xxi. 428; xxii. 41; xxiii. 167; xxvi. 35; d. inf. -ne, xxiii. 47; pres. part. -slēande, xx. 64; imp. sg. -sleh, xv. 11; -slih, xv. 127; imp. pl. -slēaþ, xx. 61; pres. 1s. -slēa, xxi. 441; 3s. -slihþ, xv. 12, 128; pl. -slēaþ, ix. 14, 187; xxi. 456; pret. 3s. ofslōh, iv. 131; xxi. 455; xxii. 43; xxvi. 37; 3p. -slōgon, iii. 13, 24, 119; iv. 81; xi. 291; xix. 216; xx. 65, 213; -slōgan, xxix. 93; pp. -slagen, viii. 150; xv. 136; xviii. 403; xx. 265, 359; xxviii. 12; np. -e, ix. 168; xi. 302; xx. 168, 199; xxiii. 177. [Cf. slēan.]
ofspring, m. *offspring.* i. 203; iv. 194; vii. 182; xi. 106; xia. 52.
ofste, see ofost.
oft, adv. *often.* i. 231, 236, 274, 420; ii. 239, 264; iii. 1, 61; vi. 221; viii. 122; etc.—swā oft swā, conj. *as often as, whenever.* xi. 428, 431, 450; xxi. 129.—comp. oftor, xix. 26, 119.
oftorfian, II. *to stone to death.* iii. 14; ix. 194; xiii. 204, 211; xx. 179; xxvi. 32.
oftrǣdlīce, adv. *frequently.* ix. 92; xv. 66; xxi. 586. [The glosses at ix. 92 show that rǣdlice was taken as

a separate word and interpreted with some plausibility as *certe* (= *iwislice*) or quite wrongly as 'hrǣdlīce', *mox.*]
ofþincan, I. impers. w. dat., *to cause regret to.* ix. 39 (pres. 3s. ofþingþ). [Cf. þincan.]
ofwundrod, adj. (pp. of 'ofwundrian'). *astonished.* xii. 10; xxiii. 136. [Cf. wundrian.]
ōga, m. *terror.* (a) as an emotion in the observer, xvii. 299. (b) as the exciting cause of this emotion, considered as a quality, xi. 204; or concretely as a terrifying phenomenon, xviii. 78.
olfend, m. *camel.* xiii. 165.
Olimpius, an Arian heretic of the fifth century. x. 170.
Oliueti, Lat. gs. with munt, *Mons Oliueti, the Mount of Olives.* xiii. 191.
ōm, m. *rust.* xvi. 161.
*ōme, wk. f. (less probably ōma, wk. m.). *a cask* of uncertain size regarded as a liquid measure. xvi. 23, 130 (ap. ōman). [Cited from this passage, the only recorded occurrence, by Napier. Related to German *Ohm*, m. and n., *Ohme*, f., Dutch *aam* 'a liquid measure' of about 40 gals.; ON *áma*, f. 'a tub'. Holthausen lists as *ōme*, f., and derives from Lat. *āma*, earlier (*h)ama* 'a water-bucket'. See OED, 'aam'.]
on (an, xia. 18), prep. w. dat. (rarely endingless locative) and acc. I. w. dat. (a) of position or location, *on, upon* (above and in contact with, or above and supported by, as on fōtum, on cnēowum); *in, within, among.* i. 4, 5, 8, 10, etc. (50 times); ii. 6, 10, 15, 26, etc. (34 times); iii. 31, 50, 53, etc. (10 times); etc., including instances in which the object designates the part of anything in which it is affected (e.g. ii. 26), or that which covers or clothes (e.g. xi. 244; xvii. 63), or a non-physical substance or abstraction treated as having extension or content (e.g. i. 278; ii. 70, 71); on Gode, *in spiritual union with God,* i. 284, 285,

322 (these three from St. Paul); ii.
4; vi. 193; xvii. 76; denoting continued motion (*on* an errand, *on*
the way), viii. 140, 150; rarely denoting motion *to*, *toward*, or *into* a
position or state, as probably i. 46,
344; xiv. 17, 109; xvi. 214; xxi. 38;
xxiii. 119.—(b) of temporal relations, *on*, *at*, *in* a point of time as
designated by an event or by a particular hour, day, night, etc., i. 1, 30,
64, 65, 72, 78, 148, 150, 155; ii. 121,
126, 174, 179; iv. 128; v. 110, 111,
271; vi. 56, 57, 372; etc.; *in*, *within*,
during a period of time, i. 219, 332;
ii. 158, 182 (twice), 215, 220, 250,
279; iii. 114, 187; iv. 1, 280; v. 232,
274; vi. 327; etc.; indicating any
of a recurrent class of times or
seasons: **on dæge**, *in the daytime*,
by day, i. 207; viii. 181; **on niht**
(old umlauted dative?), i. 208, 326;
vi. 28; xxi. 594; **on ḡeare**, *in some
year* (or *season*), i. 273; (*three times*) *a
year*, xix. 130; on a day of the
week, ii. 251, 253, 256; etc.; **on
ḡewissum tīman**, *at certain times*,
iii. 29, 138; xix. 93; indefinitely, **on
fyrste**, *in time*, xix. 147; see also
sǣl (usually w. acc.), **tīd**, and **tīma**.
—(c) indicating state, condition,
occupation, or engagement, *in.* i. 93,
95, 143, 165, 166, 227, 264, 402, 408,
411, 457; ii. 29, 106, 132, 190, 261;
iii. 146; iv. 2, 19, 35, 66, 67, 99,
184, 219, 229, 254, 277; v. 106,
184, 211; vi. 156, 202, 207, 266,
287, 299, 314; etc.—(d) marking the
object of feeling, trust, etc., *in.*
i. 445; iv. 38, 187; vi. 216; x. 89;
xi. 108; xvi. 263, 264; xxix. 109.—
(e) marking the persons *in* or *through*
whom God receives praise or
suffers, xiii. 188; xxv(*c*). 9.—(f)
marking form, appearance, *in.* i. 12,
14; ii. 180; vii. 71; ix. 132; x. 97;
xi. 58; xi*a*. 175; xxvii. 97; xxix. 26,
59, 67, 121.—(g) marking the language *in* which something is expressed. i. 28, 62 (?), 179; iv. 222; x.
84; xi. 524; xiv. 90; xv. 224; xx. 284,
424; xxii. 16; xxv(*a*). 12.—(h) marking manner, *in*, *with.* i. 455; ii. 209;

iv. 127, 286; v. 52 (twice), 55 (twice),
170 (twice), 173 (twice); vi. 174, 175
(twice); vii. 144; viii. 10 (twice), 11;
etc.—(i) *in*, *according to* someone's
opinion, view, testimony, or a particular mode of interpretation. iii.
35; xiii. 210; xv. 74; xvi. 150; xx.
334.—(j) *in accordance with* God's
will. ix. 23—(k) *in the case of*, xv. 139
(second).—(l) *in respect to*, *in the
matter of.* i. 151, 177, 407; ii. 286;
iv. 164; vi. 203; viii. 171 (twice);
ix. 76, 113, 138, 140 (three times),
141, 142 (twice), 143; x. 147, 161;
xi. 235; xi*a*. 216 (first); etc.—
(m) marking the material or com-
ponents of which a thing is made
or a class of things consists, *in*, *of.*
ii. 236 (three times); xi. 312 (twice);
xi*a*. 47 (twice); xiii. 69 (twice); xvi.
20, 127; xxx. 100 (twice), 101.—
(n) marking the means, instrument,
or cause, *in*, *by*, *in consequence of.*
i. 104, 189, 333 (twice); ii. 155; iii.
43, 165; iv. 13, 32, 133, 138; viii.
34, 35, 49, 167, 168, 173, 251;
ix. 79; x. 47 (second), 207; xi. 124,
186, 192, 366, 455; xii. 73; xv.
41 (twice); xvii. 15; xx. 274; xxx.
31, 44, 50, 112 (twice).—(o) *in* the
name of. iv. 25, etc. (9 times);
viii. 30, etc. (14 times); ix. 102;
x. 12, 81; xxiii. 159; xxv(*c*). 9 (case
uncertain except in **on mīnum naman**, viii. 30, etc.).—(p) *in view of*,
on account of. xx. 184.—(q) marking
end, purpose, *in*, *for.* i. 39, 304; xiv.
18, 110.—(r) marking size, proportion, *in*, *of.* xi. 309; xiii. 18, 119.—
(s) marking the beneficiary *on* whom
something is spent or bestowed. xxx.
34, 45.—(t) marking the place *from*
which something is taken, the persons *upon* or *from* whom a victory
is won. x. 202; xxi. 215.—(u) in
combinations: **on . . . middan**,
prep. w. dat., enclosing its object,
in the midst of. iii. 53–54; xx. 117;
on þam þe, conj., *in so far as*, x.
156; *in that*, *by the fact that*, x. 208.
—**II.** w. endingless locative: **on
Bethania-wīc**, vi. 3; and probably
in certain temporal phrases: **on**

on (*cont.*)

dæg, vi. 26, 344; on æfen, xxi. 413; on mergen, ix. 3; x. 186; xx. 203, 229; xxi. 230, 609; xxix. 92, 98; on ærnemergen, xiii. 193; xxi. 225, 396, 411; xxiii. 88, 93; on dægrēd, i. 306 (?); xxi. 323; though the temporal words may have come to be regarded as accusative (see Introduction, p. 183).— III. w. acc. (a) indicating motion to or towards a position, *upon, on to*; *into, unto, among*. i. 7, 43, 233, 329, 405; ii. 273; iii. 8 (or dat.), 38, 92, 107; IV. 33, 134, 174 (case uncertain in these three; Latin has acc.); vi. 64, 286 (less probably dat.); etc.; w. a verb of throwing, *at*, xiii. 216. —(b) indicating continued motion toward an objective, viii. 146 (faran forþ on þīn ærende, *on thine errand*; cf. I. b).—(c) in certain temporal expressions: on ēcnysse, i. 470; etc. (see ēcnyss; less probably dat.); on ealra worulda woruld, v. 276; xi*a*. 234; on sumne sæl, ii. 266; etc. (see sæl; but w. dat. in on ōþrum sæle, xi*a*. 123); on sumne tīman, vi. 148 (but other phrases with on . . . tīman have dat. or uncertain case); on a specified day, ii. 9, 110, 216, 221; vi. 43; vii. 108, 159; xi. 51; etc. (but more often w. dat.); and perhaps the temporal examples under II above.—(d) after certain verbs: gelȳfan on, *to believe in* or *on* a god, true or false, i. 48, 95, 111, etc. (very common; for further instances see gelȳfan and gelȳfed); truwian on, *to trust in*, xvii. 105 (but usually w. dat.); gefullian on, *to baptize in* (the name of?) the Trinity, ix. 107; hihtan on, *to place hope in*, xiii. 82; xix. 133; gelogian on, *to dispose towards*, xxvii. 27; syngian on, *to sin against*, iii. 152; gewīfian on, *to take* (someone) *to wife*, xxi. 113; gewrecan on, *to avenge on*, xxii. 91; gewyrcan on, *to build* something *into* a position (or *convert into*?), iii. 33 (case uncertain; Latin has acc.).—(e) in

certain set phrases: see the respective nouns or adjectives for examples of on ān, on twā (under twēgen), on eornost, on īdel; indicating this or that side, on , . . hand, on . . . healfe; indicating manner, on . . . wīsan (rarely w. dat.).— (f) *in* or *into* a language in the elliptical form, on Englisc, Ebreisc, Grecisc, Leden. iv. 177; v. 208, 209; etc. (for further instances see Denisc, Englisc, and Leden). [on retains its prepositional character with certain adverbs: see on ǣr, under ǣr, and þǣron.]

on, adv. (elliptical use of the prep.), *on*. i. 205; xxi. 36 (*on it*), 514, 536. [See also onhāwian and onlōcian, in all examples of which on might be treated separately as an adverb. See forþ on under forþ.]

onǣlan, I. *to set on fire, cause to burn*. fig., ix. 133. [Ælfric's qualification here shows that incandescent iron was thought to be burning though unconsumed.]

onbryrdan, I. *to stimulate, incite, stir*. pp. onbryrd, vii. 214; xxi. 630.

onbryrdnyss, f. (a) *pricking of the heart, compunction*. viii. 13. (b) *stimulation, incitation*. x. 111.

onbūtan, adv. of place, *about*. *her onbūtan, vi. 95. [BT gives 'þær onbutan', not 'her o.', and OED dates 'hereabout' from 1225.]

onbyri(g)an, I, w. gen. *to taste, partake of*. xi. 180; xxx. 108, 109.

oncnāwan, 7. (a) *to know, recognize, perceive*. inf., xxvi. 54; pres. 3s. oncnæwþ, xxvi. 51; pl. oncnāwaþ, viii. 199; ix. 146; xi. 233; 3s. subj. oncnāwe, x. 27, 205; pret. 1s. oncnēow, xix. 182; 3s. i. 45, 121, 337; xxix. 56; 3p. oncnēowon, iii. 41, 163, 170. (b) *to acknowledge*. inf., i. 342; ix. 201; pres. 2s. oncnāwst, xxx. 44; 3p. oncnāwaþ, xi. 295; xiv. 86; xvi. 47; 1p. subj. oncnāwan, xxx. 40; pret. 3p. oncnēowon, xvii. 248. [Cf. tocnāwan.]

ondrǣdan, 7. *to dread*. (a) with refl.

dat. pron. and acc. object, imp. sg.
ondrǣd, xiv. 37, 215; pres. 3s.
ondrǣd, vi. 143; **ondrǣt**, xi. 118;
3p. **ondrǣdaþ**, vi. 144; xi. 119.
(b) with acc. object, no refl., pres.
3p. subj. **ondrǣdon**, xxi. 344;
pret. 3p. **ondrēdon**, iii. 44, 166.
(c) with ellipsis of object (**dǣþ**)
and no refl., pres. 2s. subj. **on-
drǣde**, vi. 154 (twice).

onemn, onemm, prep. w. acc. (*next
to*), *on the side of*. xvii. 235.—as adv.
with **þǣr**, *alongside*. viii. 108.

onfeohtan, 3. *to attack*. pres. part.
asm. **onfeohtendne**, ix. 51. [Cf.
feohtan.]

onfōn, 7. (a) w. acc., *to receive*. pres.
3p. **onfōþ**, xi. 246; 3s. subj. **onfō**,
xia. 169; 3p. subj. **onfōn**, xi. 182.
(b) w. gen., *to take, partake of*. pret.
3s. subj. **onfēnge**, xxi. 404. [Cf.
fōn.]

onfōnd, m. (*one who takes another
under his protection*), *protector*. xv.
225. [Used here as elsewhere to
translate *susceptor* in the Psalms.]

ongēan, prep. w. dat. and acc. (a) expressing opposition, resistance, or
hostility in action or feeling, *against,
in opposition to, in contravention of,
contrary to*. w. dat., i. 266; xiv. 102
(v.l. acc.); xvii. 207; xx. 175; w. acc.,
i. 228, 260 (*in contention with*); iv.
210; vi. 218, 269, 285; vii. 110; xia.
29; xiv. 104, 137; xvii. 88; xx. 69,
79, 197, 216, 217, 308, 309, 320
(twice); xxi. 287; xxii. 32, 54
(second); xxiv. 8; xxvi. 42, 110; w.
uncertain case, ii. 123; iv. 39, 198;
xx. 187, 259; xxx. 27. (b) marking
the adverse bearing of something
(an event, a cause for complaint) on
someone, *against*, w. uncertain case,
xv. 21, 193, 203; *to the disadvantage
or detriment of*, w. acc., vii. 115.
(c) indicating motion directed with
hostile intent, *against*. w. acc., xxii.
54 (first); fig., w. dat., xxvii. 12.
(d) indicating opposite motion, *contrary to the course of*. w. acc., xxi.
185. (BTS cites this instance from
Kemble's text.)—as adv., marking
reaction, *in return*, i. 226; with

wiþerian, *to offer resistance*, iii.
130; marking reversal of direction,
with **eft**, *back again*. vi. 24; viii.
148; xxi. 483, 631; xxiii. 88.

onginnan, 3. *to begin*. (a) absolutely,
to have a beginning. pret. 3s. **ongann**, i. 164; xia. 1. (b) w. dat. inf.,
pret. 3s. **ongann**, i. 25; imp. sg.
onginn, xxiii. 183. (c) w. inf., pret.
3s. **ongan**, xx. 262; xxix. 43; 3p.
ongunnon, ii. 49; xx. 83. (d) w.
acc., pres. 3s. **onginneþ**, xv. 111
(*sets* the example). [Cf. **beginnan**.]

onhāwian, II. *to look on, behold*. vii.
38 (pres. part., dp. **onhāwigen-
dum**, v.l. **onlōcigendum**). [Not
in BT or BTS, but Hall cites
the example at LS II (not III).
261.]

oninnan, prep. (*within*), *into*. xxi.
622 (w. acc. in MS. R, dat. in MS.
C); xxvii. 49 (w. dat.).

onlīhtan, I, pres. 3s. **onlīht**, pret. 3s.
onlīhte, pp. **onlīht**: *o enlighten,
illuminate*, always in a spiritual
sense. i. 42, 298, 315, 316, 328, 331;
ii. 138; vi. 252; vii. 218; viii. 254;
x. 109, 115; xii. 151; xiv. 123; xvii.
123, 124, 133; xxi. 500; xxiii. 69.—
w. tō, *to show* (someone) *the way
to, light to*. i. 319; xia. 8.

onlōcian, II. *to look on, behold*. pres.
part., dp. **onlōcigendum**, vii. 64,
193, and a variant at 38 (see **onhāwian**). [BT and BTS record
only the verbal noun, 'onlociend',
but Hall has the verb. It occurs,
e.g., in Cura Past., ed. Sweet,
p. 110–21. Ælfric has the participle
as dat. abs. at CH I. 296/1 (printed
as two words), and at LS xxix. 265,
295; xxxi. 456, 505, 607. The prefix can be treated separately as an
adverb, thus receiving extra stress,
and it has been so treated at xxi.
514; see above under **on**, adv.]

onsǣgednyss, f. *sacrifice, offering*.
xxi. 138 (as. -e, v.l. **onsǣgnysse**);
xxx. 22.

onscunian, II. *to abhor*. (a) xiii. 70,
177; xvi. 219; xxi. 165. (b) *to reject
(with abhorrence), shun*. vi. 291; ix.
198; xxx. 68.

onscuniendlic, adj. *abominable.* xviii. 234, 278 (-scunigend-).

onsīgan, I. *to approach, impend.* pres. part. **onsīgende,** xviii. 344.

onsundron, adv. *separately.* v. 273.

ontendan, I. *to kindle, set fire to.* pret. 3p. **ontendon,** xx. 240.

onwinnan, 3. *to assail, attack.* pres. part. **onwinnende,** nsm., iv. 106; ap. wk. **-an,** xxii. 10, 54. [Cf. **winnan.**]

onwrēon, I, 2. *to reveal.* pret. 3s. **onwrēah,** vii. 202; xii. 145. [Cf. **bewrēon.**]

onwrige(n)nyss, f. *exposition.* ds. **(onwri) genysse** (?), i. 61.

open, adj. *open, exposed to general view or knowledge, public, manifest.* i. 465; vi. 191; xiii. 92, 202.

ge-openian, II. *to disclose, open, expose, expound.* iii. 47 (-opn-), 160; vi. 181, 323; ix. 92; xi. 52; xia. 159; xiii. 35; xv. 187; xvii. 34, 35, 36, 48, 137, 149, 168; xviii. 316; xix. 214; xxi. 414; xxvi. 116, 117; xxvii. 122.

openlīce, adv. *openly, publicly, plainly, clearly.* iv. 143; vi. 36, 165, 178, 189; vii. 136; ix. 20, 27, 32, 80; xii. 32, 186; xviii. 182, 288, 384; xix. 236, 251.

ōra, wk. m. *ore.* i. 250.

ordfruma, m. *beginning, origin, source, author.* ii. 163; vii. 86, 88; xi. 465; xxi. 289.

oreþung, f. *breath.* xvii. 164 (Lat. *halitus*). [Normally 'orþung'; cf. **orþian.**]

orf, n. *cattle.* i. 217 (as. **orfe,** probably for **yrfe,** q.v.); xx. 23 (ds. **orue**) ; xxx. 78 (ds. **orfe**).

orfcynn, n. *cattle.* i. 215.

ormǣte, adj. *immeasurably great, enormous, ponderous.* xi. 286; xvii. 207; xix. 177, 195.

orsorh, adj. *free from care.* ii. 114 (w. gen., *free from care of, untroubled by*); xi. 155; xxi. 33.

ortruwian, II. *to lose faith, despair.* vi. 287, 313; xix. 132, 134.— **geortruwian,** the same, xix. 250; reflex., *to lose hope for oneself,* vi. 293. [Cf. **truwian.**]

orþian, II. *to breathe, blow.* xii. 20, 146, 150 (twice in each). [Cf. **oreþung.**]

orue, see **orf.**

orwēnnyss, f. *hopelessness, despair.* vi. 287; ix. 174; xia. 38; xix. 132, 199, 223, 240.

oþ, prep. w. acc., occas. dat. (a) referring to a temporal limit, *until, till, to.* w. acc., ii. 179; vi. 130; ix. 194 (**oþ dēaþ,** *to death*); x. 208 (**oþ dēaþ,** *till death*); xi. 75; xiv. 190; xviii. 100; xxi. 314, 377; and w. uncertain case but probably acc., v. 268; xia. 71; xii. 185, 208; xviii. 138, 391; xxvii. 106.—**oþ þæt,** *till then.* ii. 87; iv. 9; v. 122; xvii. 70, 150; xxi. 462. **oþ þis,** *till now.* ii. 223, 242. (b) referring to a spatial or quantitative limit, *to.* w. acc., xviii. 9, 269, 417. w. dat., xx. 60; xxx. 92. [Cf. **oþþe, oþþæt,** conj.]

ōþer, pron. adj., strong decl. only. *other, another, second.* as adj., i. 12, 17, 98, 217; ii. 37, 167, 222; iii. 15, 28, 60, 137; iv. 47, 129, 175, 182, 246; v. 156, 234; vi. 36, 137, 352, 359; vii. 93; etc.; including xii. 163 (*different*); xxii. 25 (**on þam ōþran gēare,** *the next year,* where the **-an** of MS. P is perhaps a levelling of **-um** rather than an exceptional use of the wk. declension).—as pron., i. 163; ii. 116, 203; iii. 17, 105, 123; iv. 110, 209; v. 86, 200, 254; etc.; correl., **ōþer . . . ōþer,** *one* (thing or person) . . . *another.* i. 158–9 (3 times); iii. 150–1; v. 84–85, 252–3; viii. 171; xiii. 127; **ōþer . . . se ōþer,** *one . . . the other.* vi. 237; **ōþre . . . ōþre,** *some . . . others.* xviii. 96–97, 109.—*as adj., qualifying a noun in a comparison, a second (exactly similar) sort of, such another, so many.* xx. 164 (**swylce ōþre gærstapan,** *like so many* [or *veritable*] *grasshoppers*). [This last use inadequately treated in BTS. See note.]

Ōþon, the Scandinavian god *Odin* (ON. *Óðinn*), corresponding to the English 'Woden'. xxi. 140, 143. [The same form appears in LS

xxxi. 715 sqq., quoted in BTS under 'Fricg'. BT quotes the Wulfstan revision of the present passage.]

oþþæt, conj. *until.* i. 238, 262; ii. 73, 124, 141; v. 284; vi. 70, 331; viii. 138; xi. 173, 175, 189, 259, 283; etc. [Cf. oþ.]

oþþe, conj. *or.* ii. 273; iii. 72; iv. 84; v. 17, 63; vi. 224, 226; viii. 2, 64; ix. 68, 76, 79, 171; etc.—as correl., *either . . . or.* i. 326, 333; xi. 128, 420–1; xvi. 95–96; xviii. 28; xxx. 100 (3 times).

oxa, wk. m. *ox.* ii. 273.

P

pāpa, wk. m. *pope.* xxiii. 2, 6, 25, etc. (17 times).

paraclitus, Latin spelling of Gk. παράκλητος, *Paraclete*, cited as the Greek name of the Holy Spirit. x. 83.

Paulus, *St. Paul the Apostle.* uniformly nom. sg., i. 107, 285, 321; ii. 168, 198; vii. 206; xi. 538; xv. 169; xvii. 159; xviii. 148; xix. 14, 71, 90; xx. 390, 422; xxv(*c*). 3, 11; xxviii. 5; xxix. 105.

Pentecoste, f., gda. sing. Pentecosten, *Pentecost.* ii. 179; xi. 56; xi*a.* 173, 188; xix. 124. [The regular Latin form, from the Greek, is *Pentecoste*, f., gen. *-es*, but frequently in the Latin of this period as in OE, all the oblique cases have *-en*: e.g. titles of x, xi (gen.) as well as xii–xvi (acc.).]

Petrus, *St. Peter.* ix, 70, 158; xiv. 10, 17 (as. **Petrum**), 19, 29, 36 (ds. **Petre**), 75, 81 (gs. **Petrus**), 91, 109, 115, 195, 214, 217; xxiii. 6 (gs. **Petres**), 18 and 86 (gs. **Peteres**).

Pharao, Farao, the *Pharaoh* who opposed Moses. i. 228, 237, 259, 368 (gs. **Pharaones?**—see note); iv. 140 (ds. **Farao**); xx. 3 (gs. **Faraoes**), 109 (gs. **Pharaoes**), 116.

Phariseisc, adj. *of the Pharisees.* xii. 1.

Philistei, mp. *the Philistines.* xxi. 211, 237 (ap. **Philisteos**), 247 (**Philistheos**), 271, 279; xxix. 43 (ap.

Philisteos), 92 (MSS. have **Philisteos** for np.!).

pic, n. *pitch.* xxi. 445.

pistol, m. *epistle, letter.* i. 107, ii. 168, 198; xi. 538; xiii. 100; xv. 169; xviii. 148, 301; xix. 71; xx. 422; xxi. 340; xxviii. 6; xxix. 105.

plantian, II. *to plant.* xviii. 19.

plega, m. *play.* vii. 102.

plegan, plegian, I, II. *to play, dance.* xx. 45 (dat. inf., **plegenne**); xxvi. 89 (pres. 2s., **plegast**).

plegstōw, f. *playground.* vii. 102.

plēolic, adj. *hazardous.* xix. 28.

pliht, plyht, m. *peril, risk.* xii. 106 (tō plihte, *to (their) peril*); xxii. 48 (þinum fēore tō plyhte, *at the risk of your life*).

portic, m. or n. *portico, porch.* dp. porticon, ii. 13, 91; -um, ii. 20, 24, 63, 68.

prēost, m. *priest.* viii. 133; xii. 91; xxiii. 134, 135.

Publius, a monk who thwarted the emperor Julian by his prayers. viii. 145.

pund, n. *pound* (of money). xvi. 292 (ap., fig., *heavenly riches*).

pūnian, II. *to pound, beat.* xxi. 445.

purpure, f. *purple* (robe of empire). xxvi. 60.

pytt, m. *pit, hole.* ii. 273; v. 24, 110, 136; xxi. 469.

Q

Quirinus, a Roman officer converted by Pope Alexander I and martyred. xxiii. 53, etc. (19 times; gs. **-es**, 92; as., **-um**, 162).

R

rācentēah, f. *chain, fetter.* xvii. 223 (dp. -tēagum), 225 (ap.-tēaga, v.l. -tēagan implying the alternative form, wk. f. '-tēage'). [This passage already cited in BT from CH.]

racu, f. *account, narrative.* xx. 78; xxii. 27, 74.

ġerād, n. *reason, good sense.* xxvi. 55.

rǣcan, I. *to reach* or *hand* (something to someone). xix. 178. [Cf. **mis-rǣcan** and next entry.]

gerǣcan, I. *to reach* (a limit). xxi. 534.

rǣd, m. (a) *advice, counsel, judgement.* vi. 339; ix. 47; xix. 88; xx. 175; xxi. 271, 606; xxii. 33, 96; xxx. 6. (b) *good counsel, wisdom.* ix. 34, 41. (c) *decision, decree.* xi. 278. (d) *purpose, mind.* xxi. 24.

rǣdan, I. (a) *to advise*, intr., w. dat., ix. 33. (b) *to expound, explain.* trans. used absolutely, ii. 217; viii. 204 (see note). (c) *to read* (something written) to oneself. trans., x. 108 (first); xviii. 235 (first), 279 (first).—abs., xix. 168, 178. (d) *to read* (*aloud*), *read out.* trans., i. 1; ii. 2; vi. 1; x. 108 (second); xviii. 235 (second), 279 (second).—abs., xviii. 398. (e) *to learn by reading.* trans., iii. 31; vi. 301; xi. 168; xix. 61; xxi. 72, 144, 210; xxix. 36.—abs., xvi. 157; xviii. 174, 338; xix. 116; xx. 121.—intr., vi. 318. [Cf. **be-, mis-rǣdan.**]

rǣdels, m. or f. *enigma, riddle.* xi. 540.

rǣding, f. *reading, lesson.* x. 113; xi. 34; xia. 134; xii. 216; xvi. 203; xviii. 398; xix. 204.

rǣsan, I. *to rush forth, spring up.* v. 29, 140) pres. part., gsn. **rǣsendes**, translating *salientis*; v.l. **rǣscendes** ; see note on 29).

rǣstendæg, see **restendæg.**

rāp, m. *rope.* xxi. 557.

rāpe, see hrāþe.

rēad, adj. *red*, in **sēo Rēade Sǣ**, *the Red Sea.* i. 374 (. . . **Rēadan Sǣ**); xx. 4, 121 (as. **þā Rēadan Sǣ**).

rēaf, n. *robe, shroud, vestment, clothing.* xi. 249, 339, 340, 341; xviii. 243, 313; xx. 8; xxiii. 172.

rēafere, m. *robber, plunderer.* xi. 377; xxiv. 7.

rēafian, II. *to take unjustly, steal.* xvi. 178. [Cf. **berēafian.**]

rēaflāc, n. or m. *robbery, rapine.* xvi. 73.

rēcan, reccan, I. *to be concerned for.* x. 55 (pret. 3s. **rōhte**).

gereccan, I. *to tell, narrate.* inf., xvii. 203; (pret. 3s. **gerehte** conjectured, xxvii. 94).

gerecednyss, f. *narrative.* xxix. 36. [Cf. **þrȳfeald Gereccednyss.**]

rēcelēas, adj. *reckless.* iv. 218 (dp. as noun, **-um**).

rēcelēast, f. *negligence, lack of consideration.* x. 55; xv. 176.

rēcelsfæt, n. *censer.* xx. 239, 258.

gerēfa, m. *reeve, steward, high official.* xvi. 5, 10, 24, 27, 30, 49, 88, 99, 131, 144, 205; xxiii. 43 (corresponds to *prefect*); xxvi. 32 (Lat. *iudex*).

regol, m. *regulation, rule.* xix. 112.

rēnscūr, m. *shower of rain.* iii. 75; viii. 81, 82; xiii. 45; xviii. 22; xx. 377; xxx. 93.

rēocan, 2. *to reek.* pres. part., dsn. wk. **rēocendan**, vi. 206.

rēod, see hrēod.

gereord, n. *language, speech.* iv. 222; vii. 198; xi. 61, 524; xia. 178; xvii. 38, 170; xviii. 331; xx. 284; xxi. 75; xxii. 16; xxv(a). 12.

gereord, f. *a meal, feast.* xx. 21; xxv(a). 19.

gereordian, II. *to feed, refresh.* v. 158; xi. 412, 439; xia. 120.

rest, f. *rest, quiet.* iv. 43, 214, 218, 224.—esp., the *rest* appointed for the virtuous after death: **tō reste**, xi. 128, 183, 206, 208, 215, 233; xv. 53.

gerestan, I, reflex. *to rest.* iv. 222 (pres. 3s. **gerest**).

restendæg, m. *day of rest.* ii. 45, 247, 256, 259 (**ræsten-**), 263, 274 (**ræsten-**); xvii. 283; xviii. 247, 327, 338.

rēþe, adj. *fierce, savage, cruel, dire.* iv. 114; xi. 128, 168, 267, 377; xiii. 52; xxi. 248, 349; xxiv. 7; xxvii. 91.

rēþnyss, f. *cruelty, ferocity.* iii. 121; ix. 195; xxvi. 50.

rēþra, m. *oarsman, sailor.* xvii. 213. [Hitherto cited only as a gloss for *nauta*, in Ælfric's Grammar and elsewhere. Thorpe omitted this passage from CH.]

riccetere, n. *tyranny, arrogance.* xxvi. 110. [A similar use of the word in LS xxxii. 233.]

rīce, n. *kingdom.* i. 390, 397; ii. 244; iii. 36, 98, 156, 179; iv. 22, etc. (11 times); v. 150, 262; etc.

rīce, adj. *mighty, rich.* i. 214; xi. 401 (wk. as noun); xvi. 173; xxvii. 86.

rīcsian, see rīxian.

rīdan, 1. *to ride.* pres. part., gp. rīdendra, xxvii. 91; pret. 3s. rād, xxi. 577.

riftere, m. *reaper.* v. 260, 263, 271; xxi. 465.

rīhsian, see rīxian.

riht, adj. *right, true, just, lawful.* iii. 103; vii. 168; viii. 5, 10; xi. 401; xiii. 75, 85; xv. 138; xvi. 157; xvii. 171; xx. 34; xxi. 278.—sb., n. *what is right, the right (justice, truth).* ix. 57; xii. 155; xiii. 90; xvi. 256 (mid rihte, *justly*); xviii. 174; xxi. 144.

rihtes, adv. qualifying nū (q.v.), *immediately.* xxvii. 71 (see note).

rihtgeþancod, adj. *right-minded.* dp. asnoun, xiii. 83 (-þanced-); xvii. 105.

rihting, f. *direction, governance.* vi. 299; xii. 182; xv. 45 (MS. rihtinge for ns. rihting); xx. 78.

gerihtlǣcan, I. *to put right, direct.* ii. 74 (pret. 3s. -lǣhte); iii. 118; ix. 77; xiii. 97, 129, 176, 181; xvii. 56; xix. 204 (pp. np. -lǣhte); xx. 405, 427. [Cf. -lǣcan.]

rihtlic, adj. *equitable,* xix. 102.

rihtlīce, adv. *rightly, justly, truly, correctly.* ii. 172; iii. 139; v. 127; vii. 132, 164; xiii. 52; xvii. 38, 170, 171, 172; xviii. 133, 162; xix. 126; xxv(*a*). 18.

rihtwīs, adj. *righteous, just.* (a) as ordinary adj., strong or weak. ii. 286; xiii. 85; xiv. 174; xv. 74; xvi. 265; xviii. 430 (dp. with ellipsis of noun, 'mannum'); xxvii. 21 (nsm. wk. with ellipsis of 'mann'). (b) absolutely, *righteous (persons).* dp. rihtwīsum, xiii. 45. (c) as identifying epithet of James the Just. ix. 195 (þone rihtwīsan Iacob); xiii. 100 (Iacob se rihtwīsa). (d) with def. art., wk., as noun, *the righteous.* np. -an, v. 277; xi. 453; gp. -ra, xvi. 171.

gerihtwīsian, II. *to make righteous, sanctify.* ii. 72; xvi. 181; xix. 96, 99.

rihtwīsnyss, f. *righteousness, justice.* iii. 79; vii. 17, 20, 74, 162, 164, 168 (ūs tō rihtwīsnysse, *for our justification*); viii. 10; xiii. 129; xv. 6, 57, 87, 120; xvi. 63, 255; xxi. 331; xxvi. 102; xxx. 86.

rīnan, I. *to rain.* iii. 75 (pres. 3p. subj. rinon).

gerīp, n. *harvest.* v. 78, 80, 81, 248, 249, 259, 261.

rīpan, 1. *to reap.* d. inf. rīpanne, v. 85 (ripp- MS. D), 253; pres. 3s. rīpþ, v. 81, 83, 85, 249, 251, 253.

gerīpian, II. *to become ripe, ripen.* xxx. 106. [Cf. ungerīpod.]

gerīsan, 1, impers. (a) *to be proper.* pres. 3s. gerīst, xi. 547; xxvi. 55. (b) w. dat. *to be proper for, befit.* inf. ii. 244. [Cf. arīsan.]

rīxian, rīcsian, rīhsian, II, intr. *to reign.* i. 390; ii. 245; iv. 170, 298; ix. 218; x. 190; xi. 86, 525, 534, 572; xviii. 213, 215, 369, 422, 430; xxviii. 10; xxx. 114.

rōd, f. *the cross, rood.* vii. 118, 122; xi. 35, 290; xi*a*. 137; xii. 235; xix. 246.

roder, m. *the heavens* (here esp. the sphere of the fixed stars, or all the heavenly spheres conceived as moving together): xxi. 185 (as. roder, v.l. rodor, roþer).

Rōm. *Rome.* xxiii. 46, 49.

Rōmane, mp. *the Romans.* gp. Rōmana, xxiii. 12; xxviii. 10 (see note). [The nom. occurs elsewhere with '-e' or '-an'.]

rōwan, 7. *to row* or *sail.* pret. 3s., rēow, xvii. 251. [This passage already cited by BT from CH. Cf. oferrōwan.]

rūm, adj. *wide, spacious.* xvii. 12. comp., nsm. rūmra, viii. 110.

rūnung, f. *whispering, secret suggestion* or *advice.* ix. 33, 47. [One example each in BT and BTS, both from Ælfric.]

Ruphinus, a thane of Theodosius I. xxvi. 86, 98.

rȳmet, n. (a) *space, extent* (of a building). viii. 112. (b) *clear space, room* (made for a building). viii. 115.

ryne, m. or n. *running, course.* viii. 232; xvi. 284.

gerȳne, n. *mystery, secret.* xii. 169.

rysel, m. *lard, fat.* xxi. 445 (Lat. *adipem*).

S

sācerd, m. *priest.* xx. 242 (dp. -on), 259 (dp. -um), 276; xxi. 389, 406, 424 (ap. -os, v.l. -as), 588, 591, 596, 605, 609, 619, 624.

sacu, f. *contention, conflict.* iv. 103; xxi. 126.

sǣ, f. *sea.* v. 185; vi. 146; viii. 93; xia. 108; xiv. 47; xvii. 21, 206, 211, 212, 214, 217, 218, 239; xx. 95, 117; xxiii. 203. [Applied to the Sea of Galilee in xiv and xvii.]

sǣd, n. *seed.* v. 268.

sǣdere, m. *sower.* v. 257, 263.

sǣl, m. *time, occasion.* (a) **on sumne sǣl,** *on one occasion, at some time.* ii. 266; iii. 2, 96; v. 3; x. 3; xia. 119; xiii. 51; xiv. 74; xviii. 2; xix. 8; xxi. 214. (b) **on ōþrum sǣle,** *on another occasion,* xia. 123.

sǣland, n. *coast, maritime district.* xvii. 23, 67.

sǣlic, adj. *of the sea.* xia. 108.

gesǣlig, adj. *happy, fortunate, prosperous, blessed.* iv. 53, 272, 281; viii. 218; x. 38; xi. 99; xiv. 163; xviii. 438; xix. 87; xx. 302; xxvi. 1 (perhaps both *virtuous* and *successful*).

gesǣli(g)līce, adv. *blissfully, blessedly.* xi. 251 (or adj., np.?); xviii. 423.

gesǣlþ, f. *happiness, blessing.* ix. 216; xxi. 46; xxx. 74. [No example of ns., but elsewhere Ælfric has it without the old '-u'.]

sǣndon, see **sendan.**

sǣt, gesǣt, see **sittan, gesittan.**

Sǣternes-dǣg, m. *Saturday.* ii. 42, 212, 255.

sǣton, see **sittan.**

sǣwþ, see **sāwan.**

sagol, m. *club, cudgel.* xxvii. 96.

Salomon, *Solomon.* ii. 12, 15; iii. 84.

Samaria, the country. v. 3, 11, 88, 113 (all gs., **Samarian.**)

Samaritanisc, adj. *Samaritan.* v. 15, 16, 119.

sāmlǣred, adj. *half-taught, not fully instructed.* xiii. 34.

samnung, gesamnung, f. *assembly* (applied to the Jewish synagogue). i. 378; ix. 13, 28, 173; xvii. 6, 286.

samod, adv. *at the same time, together.* v. 83, 251, 263; xxiii. 95.

Samuhel, the prophet *Samuel.* xxi. 285 (gs. -es); xxix. 47, 58, 74 (ds. e), 77; xxx. 18, 25 (ns., **Samuel**).

*sāmweaxen, adj. *half-grown.* xi. 311. [Unique in this passage; already cited by Napier.]

sāmworht, adj. *half-wrought, unfinished.* xxi. 206.

sanctus, adj. *Saint.* ii. 61 (interpolation in MS. F; probably not authentic).

sand, f. (a) *mission:* viii. 141. (b) *repast, victuals* (as sent forth or served). xx. 99; xxi. 393 (victuals offered to Bel), 481 (heaven-sent repast).

sang, m. *song, singing.* xi. 43, 66; xia. 150.

sang, vb. see **singan.**

sār, n. *bodily pain, wound.* xix. 195.

sārig, adj. *sad, sorrowful.* xxi. 321, 485 (nsm. with semi-adverbial force); xxiii. 15, 16.

sārlic, adj. *sorrowful.* xxvi. 97.

sārlīce, adv. *sorrowfully, sorely, grievously.* vi. 77; xix. 148; xxi. 324.

sārnyss, f. *pain, grief.* i. 417; vi. 9; xi. 218, 485, 486; xxv(c). 7; xxvii. 64.

Saturnus, the god *Saturn.* xxi. 105, 146 (gs. **Saturnes**), 178 (ds. **Saturne**).

Saul, king of Israel. xxii. 91; xxix. 38, 48 (ds. **Saule**), 56, 88, 90, 93, 98; xxx. 18.

Saulus, the name of St. Paul before his conversion. xxv(c). 3 (ds. **Saule**), 4 and 5 (voc. s. **Saule**). [The vocative in -e implies a nominative in -us as in Latin, matching the OE **Paulus.**]

gesāw-, see gesēon.

sāwan, 7. *to sow.* pres. 3s. sǣwþ, v. 83, 84, 251, 252; pret. 3s. sēow, v. 267; pret. 3p. sēowon, v. 257.

sāwlian, II. *to expire.* xi. 178; xix. 222; xxvii. 57.

sāwol, sāwul, f. *soul.* i. 407; ii. 94, etc. (10 times); v. 244; vi. 137, etc. (14 times); etc. [The spelling sawol occurs at xi. 126; sawul at ii. 105; vi. 139, 140. Variants in xi have sawl, sawel.]

gesceād, n. (a) *distinction.* xxi. 90. (b) *power of distinguishing, reason.* i. 279; xvi. 43, 52, 53, 70; xvii. 132.

sceadu, f. *shade, shadow.* iv. 222, 224.

gesceaft, f. *creature, creation, created thing.* i. 74, 169, etc. (7 times); ii. 220, 222, 225, 235; iv. 151, 154; v. 104; vi. 118, 245; etc.

sceal, scealt, see sceolan.

sceamian, II, impers. w. dat. of pers. *to cause shame to, make ashamed.* xxvii. 111 (twice), 116 [Cf. of-sceamian.]

*sceamigendlic, adj. *causing shame.* wk. pl. as noun, *private parts*: xxvii. 119 (ap. -lican). [Not in dictionary. Cf. BT, 'sceamu', III, and note on xxvii. 112–18.]

sceamlēas, adj. *shameless, immodest.* xxi. 176.

sceamlic, adj. *shameful.* xviii. 69.

sceamu, f. *shame.* xvi. 13, 102.

sceān, see scīnan.

sceanca, m. *leg.* vii. 146.

sceandlic, adj. *wicked, shameful.* iv. 75, 79.

scēap, n. *sheep.* iv. 81; xxi. 356, 462.

gesceap, n., nap. gesceapu. in pl., *genitals.* xix. 61. [Cf. BT, 'gesceap', III.]

gesceapen, see gescyppan.

scear, n. *ploughshare.* xix. 192.

scearp, adj. *sharp, piercing.* i. 13; xxi. 546; xxiii. 185; xxix. 100.

sceatt, m. *property, money;* hence: (a) *payment, bribe.* xiii. 95. (b) *gift.* xv. 46.

sceaþa, m. *criminal, thief.* xix. 246.

scēawere, m. *looking-glass, mirror.* xi. 539. [This meaning otherwise at-tested for OE only by a gloss. Cited from this passage by Napier.]

scēawian, II. *to look at, see, observe, inspect.* i. 13, 15, 280; v. 79, 247; vii. 142; viii. 230; xi. 261; xv. 95; xix. 169; xx. 143, 149, 150, 154, 156, 158, 172, 173, 196; xxi. 396, 412, 569; xxx. 35. [Cf. be-, fore-scēawian.]

scencan, I. *to give drink, pour out drink.* xi. 421, 440.

sceocca, m. *evil spirit, devil.* iv. 21, 108; xvii. 296; xxix. 112.

*sceoccen, adj. *devilish.* xxi. 556. [Unique in this passage. Cited by Napier.]

[sceolan, sculan], pret. pres. vb. *shall.* (a) w. inf., *to be obliged, be destined, shall, must, ought.* i. 111, 243, 369; ii. 67, 203, 259; iii. 55, 62; iv. 127, 163, 205, 256; etc.—(b) pret. (subj.) w. inf., denoting an as-sertion that is matter of report and may be untrue; not to be directly translated. iv. 12 (sǣdon . . . þæt ūre Drihten sceolde . . . wyr-cean, *alleged that our Lord per-formed*), 72, 87; xvi. 6, 89 (þæt hē . . . sceolde . . . aspendan, *on the charge that he was squandering*); xxix. 45, 48 (segþ . . . þæt sēo wicce sceolde arǣran . . . Samuhel . . . and hē sceolde secgan Saule, *alleges that the witch raised Samuel and that it was he who told Saul*).—(c) with tō and ellipsis of infinitive of a verb of motion, *shall go.* xi. 193; xv. 53; xix. 235; xx. 143; xxii. 47.—(d) *to owe* something (acc.) to someone (dat.). xvi. 16, 20, 25, 26, 123, 127, 142, 143.—(e) impers. w. acc. hwæt and dat., *shall avail.* xi. 327 (hwæt sceal him ǣnig wlite?) [Forms: pres. 1s. sceal, xxvi. 123; 2s. scealt, vi. 195 (5 more); 3s. sceal, i. 369; ii. 203; iv. 163; vi. 292, 294, 364; ix. 40; x. 35 (sceall), 62; etc.; pl. sceolon, occas. sceolan, i. 111; ii. 259; iv. 127, 205; v. 180; vi. 278; viii. 14, 252; ix. 32, 75; etc. sculon, xxiii. 179; scylon, xxx. 112; sceole wē, viii.

[sceolan,] sculan (*cont.*)
12 (6 more); **scyle ḡē**, xii. 106;
pres. 2s. subj. **sceole**, xi. 125;
xxvi. 54, 114; 3s. **sceole**, vi. 287
(4 more); pl. **sceolon**, xx. 383 (or
ind.?), 402; pret. 3s. **sceolde**, iv.
114 (14 more); pl. **sceoldon**, i. 243
(10 more); **sculdon**, xxiii. 177;
pret. 3s. subj. **sceolde**, iv. 12 (18
more); pl. **sceoldon**, ii. 67 (8 more);
sceoldan, xxii. 32.]
ḡesceōp, see **ḡescyppan**.
sceort, adj. *short, short-lived.* v. 100;
xvi. ꝺ70; xix. 75.
sceortlīce, adv. *shortly.* ii. 59, 62,
141; iv. 58; viii. 50; xii. 226; xv. 25;
xvii. 46; xviii. 40, 224; xx. 336;
xxx. 29.—sup. **sceortlīcost**, xx. 1.
scēotan, 2. *to shoot, run, rush.* pres.
3s. **scȳt**, xviii. 9; pret. 3p. **scuton**,
xvii. 238; **scutan**, xxi. 551.
sceotian ('scot-'), II. *to shoot* (as with
bow and arrows). vii. 101.
sceotung, f. (*shooting*), *a shot.* vii. 101.
sceþþan, 6. *to injure, hurt.* inf., xxi. 34
(v.ll. **sceþþian, sceaþan, sceaþi-
gean**).
scīnan, 1. *to shine.* inf., xiii. 43; pres.
part. **scīnende**, variously inflected,
i. 295; iv. 228; vii. 71; viii. 231; xi.
284, 324; xviii. 9, 48, 72, 85; xix.
167, 234; xxi. 28 (**scinænd-**), 65,
83, 85; xxix. 107; pres. 3s. **scīnþ**, i.
420; xxi. 61; 3p. **scīnaþ**, v. 277;
xi. 570; pret. 3s. **sceān**, i. 35, 292,
307, 432, 442; 3p. **scinon**, xxi. 187.
xxi. 187. [Cf. **bescīnan**.]
scincræft, m. *sorcery, magic.* xvii. 97;
xviii. 257, 380, 390; xxix. 2, 60.
scip, scyp, n. *ship.* xiv. 5, 11, 12,
etc. (21 times); xvii. 204, 206, 244;
xxiii. 203.
ḡescip-, see **ḡescyppan**.
scipmann, m. *sailor.* xia. 111.
scippend, see **scyppend**.
scīr, f. *district, province, shire.* xiv. 42;
xvii. 2, 5; xxi. 244 (twice).
scīr, adj. (*bright,*) *clear.* xii. 127.
ḡescōp, see **ḡescyppan**.
screadian, II. *to prune.* iii. 71 (pp.
ḡescrēadod).
scrift, m. *confessor.* ii. 166; xviii. 124;
xxvii. 8, 13, 14, 108, 115.

scrīn, n .*chest, coffer, ark.* xxi. 216–74
(16 times).
scrȳdan, ḡescrȳdan, I. *to clothe,
dress.* xi. 415, 423, 442; xvii. 243;
xxiii. 172. [Cf **ymbscrȳdan,
unscrȳdd**.]
sculdon, sculon, see **sceolan**.
scutan, -on, see **scēotan**.
scyfe, m. *pushing, instigation.* xvii. 240.
scyld, f. or m. *guilt, offence.* xv. 131.
scyldiḡ, adj. (a) *guilty.* xiii. 93 (asm.
wk. as noun); xv. 133, 148); xxiii.
176; xxvi. 36. (b) w. gen., *liable to.*
xv. 12, 13, 15, 16, 128, 129, 143, 150.
scyle, scylon, see **sceolan**.
ḡescyndan, I. *to put to shame.* iv. 273
(pp. np. **ḡescynde**).
ḡescyndnyss, f. *shame, humiliation.*
xx. 111.
scyp, see **scip**.
ḡescyppan, -scippan, 6. *to create.*
d. inf. **ḡescyppenne**, xxv(*b*). 3;
ḡescippenne, vi. 122 (v.l. **scip-
penne**); pres. 3s. **ḡescipþ**, ii. 227,
234; pret. 3s. **ḡesceōp**, i. 74, 93,
200, 261, 279; ii. 214, 220, 221,
224, 225; iv. 151; etc. (47 times);
ḡescōp, xxi. 659; subj. **ḡesceōpe**,
vi. 124; xxi. 661; pp. **ḡesceapen**,
variously inflected, i. 31, 167, 169,
170, 174, 191, 192; ii. 229, 230, 242;
vi. 118; xi. 95; xia. 205; xxi. 63.
scyppend, scippend, m. *creator.*
xxi. 95, 664.—esp. *the Creator.*
i. 93, 221, 384; ii. 150 (**scip-**), 243
variant (**scip-**); vii. 169, 176; xi.
80, 261, 266, 550; xia. 31, 196; xii.
122; xiii. 48; xvi. 289; xvii. 112, 218;
xix. 29; xxi. 81, 84, 93, 508; xxvi.
62; xxix. 65, 87.
ḡescyrtan, I. *to shorten.* v. 161; xviii.
250 (pret. 3s. subj. **ḡescyrte**), 252
(pret. 3s. **ḡescyrte**), 366 (pret. 3s.
subj. **ḡescyrtte**), 368.
scȳt, see **scēotan**.
sē, m., **sēo**, f., **þæt**, n., pron. adj.,
def. art. *that one, that, the.* [Forms,
one example each: **sē**, i. 55; **þæs**,
i. 2; **þām**, i. 25 (**þǣm**, xxiii. 35,
etc.); **þone**, i. 21, or **þæne**, i. 294;
fem. **sēo**, i. 85; **þǣre** i. 15 (gen.),
10 (dat.); **þǣræ**, iv. 1 (dat.); **þā**,
i. 26; neut. **þæt**, i. 29; **þæs**, i. 49;

þām, i. 24 (þǣm, xxiii. 202); þæt, i. 31; pl. all genders, þā, i. 17 (nom.), 198 (acc.); þǣra, i. 234 (alt. to þāra) or þāra, xviii. 87; þām, i. 12.]—Special uses: the demonstrative adj. with a proper name, tō þām Nichodeme, to that (this) Nicodemus, xii. 218; se Abbacuc, xxi. 470; se Siba, xxii. 34.—idioms with the neuter pron.: þæt is, that is, i. 28, 86, 179, etc. (before plural nouns, þæt syndon, i. 340, 345; þæt synd, i. 400).—þæs, from that time, xi. 54; xia. 171; and in þæs on mergen (see mergen); þæs þe, conj. after which, ix. 3; after, xi. 46; xia. 153.—hræþe þæs, very soon after that, xv. 53.—tō þām, to that degree, vi. 214.—the old instrumental appears only in set expressions involving the neuter pronoun: þȳ, þē, þe in forþī and þȳlǣste, q.v., and tō þȳ þæt, see tō; unemphatic þe with comparatives, þe gelēaffulran, the more faithful, ii. 3; and similarly ii. 4, 283; viii. 15; xi. 340; xiii. 139 (þe mā þe, see mā); þæs þe leng, all the longer, xi. 161; þæs þe swīþor, all the more, x. 144; xi. 266; xvii. 41, 182; for traces of instr. þan, þon, see forþam and for þan þe under for.—sē þe, etc., rel. pron. who, which, etc. i. 8, 49, 50, 136, 170, etc.—the particle þe is sometimes omitted (e.g. mid þam, i. 66; þurh þone, i. 74; þone, ii. 213), and sometimes treated as a separate relative after the demonstrative (e.g. þā þe, those who, i. 441).

sēac, see sūcan.

geseah, see gesēon.

geseald, (ge)seald-, see syllan, gesyllan.

sealf, f. salve, ointment. vi. 6, 309.

sealm, m. psalm. i. 98.

sealmwyrhta, wk. m. psalmist. i. 79, 98, 375; vii. 94; xiv. 119; xv. 222; xvi. 57.

searucræft, m. artifice, wile. iv. 111, 192; xxix. 104, 114 (seara-).

sēaþ, m. hole, pit, den. xiii. 21, 125

(translating fovea); xxi. 313, 317, 320, 324, 337, 472, 475, 485, 490 (translating lacus).

sēaþ, v., see sēoþan.

sēcan, I, pret. sōht-. to seek. (a) w. acc., to try to find or obtain. iv. 43, 214, 218, 233; v. 52, 170, 185; viii. 11; xiv. 52; xxix. 117. to try to obtain from (æt), xvii. 107; xxii. 96; (tō), xxvii. 108. (b) w. obj. clause introduced by hū, to try to discover. iii. 42, 164. *(c) w. acc. of pers. and dat. inf., to try to do something to someone. vi. 22 (sōhton . . . þē tō stǣnenne). [This idiom illustrated by one example in BTS but inadequately explained. See note.] *(d) absolute, to make search. xxii. 67 (sēce sē þe wylle). [Not recognized in BT but see OED, 'seek', 12, citing WS. Gospels, Luke xv. 8.] *(e) intr. w. prep. tō, to resort (for help) to. xvii. 98 (tō him sēcaþ). [Meaning not recognized in BT though summarily mentioned by Hall. OED dates from 1200. See note on xvii. 98.]

gesēcan, I, pret. -sōht-, trans. (a) to obtain (by seeking). xvii. 111 (with æt, from). (b) to seek out, go to. xix. 228; xxi. 611 (his fēt gesōhte, fell at his feet).

secgan, sæcgan, rarely secc-, III, pret. sǣd-, pp. gesǣd. to say. i. 26, etc. (25 times); ii. 1, etc. (8 times); iii. 1, etc. (13 times); etc.—is gesǣd, is called, means. iv. 85 [Normal forms in pres. ind. sing., ic secge, iii. 35; þū segst, viii. 46; hē segþ, i. 303;—pres. forms with æ for e: sæcgan, xiii. 36; sægest, iii. 205; sægeþ, xiii. 86; sægþ, xiii. 98; xiv. 169, 176; xv. 141, 149, 154; xviii. 253; sæcgaþ, xxx. 30;—pres. 2p. seccaþ, iv. 116, MS. Q; segce gē, iii. 24 (for secge gē, as at v. 77; ix. 69).—Cf. a-, fore-, for-secgan.]

segen, f. speech, utterance. viii. 241; xia. 69; xii. 196.

seldcūþ, adj. unusual, novel. ii. 225 (ap. -e, v.l. selcūþe).

seldon, adv. seldom, rarely. xix. 170.

sēlest, sēlost, adj. sup. *best.* iii. 53; xvi. 248; xix. 68.

sellan, see **syllan.**

sēlra, adj. comp. *better.* ii. 101; iv. 255; xix. 41, 69; xxi. 25; xxx. 46.

sendan, sǣndan, I, pret. **send-.** (a) trans., *to send.* i. 241; iii. 10, 15, 18, 115, 117, 122, 124; v. 85, 253; ix. 116; xviii. 20, 72; xx. 25, 94, 141, 158, 314; xxi. 236, 253, 254, 340, 478; xxii. 74. (b) intr., *to send (a message) to* (**tō**) *a person.* vi. 8; xx. 231.—spelled **sǣnd-** at vi. 8 and in variants, ix. 116 and xxi. [Cf. **asendan.**]

sēo, see **sē.**

sēoc, adj. *sick, ill, diseased.* ii. 111, 188 (as noun), 192; vi. 2, 8; xi. 177, 195; xix. 131, 160 (as noun); xxvii. 29, 33, 50, 98; xxx. 66.

sēocnyss, f. *sickness.* ii. 118; xxi. 42.

seofan, seofon, num. *seven.* iv. 47, 246, 249 (twice), 263; xi. 44, 66; xia. 124, 125, 151, 183; xxiii. 15; xxvi. 37; **syfan, syfon,** xxi. 183, 460.

seofonfeald, adj. *sevenfold.* v. 212; ix. 121, 139; xi. 68; xia. 185; xvii. 122.—**be seofonfealdum, -an,** *by sevenfold,* xi. 514; xxi. 59.

seofoþa, adj. *seventh.* ii. 216, 221; xi. 297; xxi. 178, 484.

seohhe, wk. f. *sieve.* xiii. 164 (ds. **seohhann**).

seolfor, n. *silver.* i. 248; xxi. 192, 530.

seolfren, see **sylfren.**

gesēon, 5. *to see.* (a) w. acc., *to behold, observe, perceive, discern* with the eyes or the mind, naturally or supernaturally. i. 52, 295, 297, 325, 427, 429, 434; ii. 53, 76; iii. 20, 174; iv. 17, 92, 94, 97; etc. (80 times). (b) w. obj. clause, *to observe, perceive, apprehend,* or *discover* (*by seeing*): the clause introduced by **þæt,** stating what is learned, v. 39; vi. 72; vii. 143; xi. 206; xx. 215; xxvii. 31; xxix. 34; or by an interr., stating the question to be answered, vi. 81 (ellipsis of clause), 82, 109; vii. 35; xi. 291; xii. 125, 159; xxi. 450; xxii. 44; xxvii. 19, 88. (c) w. acc. and infin., *to observe, behold* a thing or person

doing something. vi. 77 [first construction; see (d) below]; xiv. 5, 53; xviii. 233, 277.—with passive sense when acc. is obj. of infin., *to behold* a thing or person being acted upon. xii. 127. (d) w. acc. and compl. participle, adj., adv., or adv. phrase, *to observe, behold, notice* a person doing something or in a particular state, situation, or manifestation. vi. 77 [second constr.; see (c) above]; vii. 191 (acc. adj. followed by nom. or uninfl. participles); xi. 155, 350, 419, 445 (series of complements includes a noun); xvii. 242; xviii. 264, 408; xxiii. 98, 99. (e) intr. or ellipt., *to observe, notice.* i. 274, 420; xxvii. 94. (f) intr. *to have the faculty of seeing.* xi. 539, 540. (g) intr. *to have visual illumination* concerning some mystery. xxvii. 24, 82. [Forms: inf. i. 297 (22 more); imp. sg. **geseoh,** vi. 81; pl. **gesēoþ,** v. 66; pres. 1s. **gesēo,** v. 39, xxi. 422; xxix. 26; 2s. **gesihst,** vi. 90; xiii. 25, 147; xxiii. 99; **gesyhst,** xxix. 20; **gesixst,** vi. 82; **gesyxt,** xii. 127; 3s. **gesihþ,** i. 295; vi. 345; xii. 67; xvii. 202; **gesicþ,** vi. 27; pl. **gesēoþ,** i. 325 (21 more); pres. 2s. subj. **gesēo,** xxi. 420; pret. 1s. **geseah,** xxi. 471; 3s., ii. 53 (24 more); pl. **gesāwon,** i. 52 (23 more); **gesāwan,** xxix. 34; **gesāwe wē,** xi. 419, 445; pret. 2s. subj. **gesāwe,** xxiii. 98; 3s., xi. 509; xxix. 58; pp. **gesewen,** xxix. 103; np. **-e,** xxvii. 122; **gesāwen,** xxvii. 82. [Cf. a-, be-, for-, þurh-sēon.]

sēow, sēowon, see **sāwan.**

sēoþan, 2. *to boil, cook.* pret. 3s. **sēaþ,** xxi. 447; 3p. **sudon,** xx. 127.

Seraphis, the Egyptian god *Serapis.* xxi. 524 (v.l. **Serapis**), 545.

sester, m. *a measure* of uncertain quantity. ap. **sestras,** xxi. 357 (of wine, translating *amphoræ*), 358 (of meal, translating *artabæ*).

setl, n. *seat, place.* xix. 218, 224; xxiii. 86.

gesetnyss, f. *a written composition:* (a) *book, treatise, writing:* i. 110, 138. (b) *a portion of a longer piece, here*

GLOSSARY

811

of the Bible: *lesson, scriptural account, scripture*: vii. 31; xxix. 55. (c) a particular *version* of the gospel: ix. 128. (d) *ordinance, law, institute*: xiii. 69, 85; xiv. 95, 99, 101, 102; xx. 278; xxi. 312; xxvi. 112.

settan, ġesettan, I, pret. **sett-, ġesett-,** pp. **ġesett.** *to set, place, set down, establish, appoint.* i. 177, 367, 371, 464; ii. 66, 151, 153, 224, 226; iii. 4, 54, 84; vii. 1; viii. 24; x. 28; xiii. 101; etc. [Cf. **besettan.**]

sēþan, I. *to affirm, testify.* xii. 29, 175. [Cf. **ġesōþian.**]

***ġesēþnyss,** f. *affirmation.* xii. 180, 182. [Unique in this passage, though cited by Napier from MS. U and printed from B by Belfour, p. 8/ 25–27, with the late spellings **ġesæþnysse** and **sæþnysse.**]

ġesewen, see **ġesēon.**

ġesewenlic, adj. *visible.* i. 171; ii. 103, 215; viii. 221; xiᵃ. 3; xii. 119; xxi. 14.

ġesewenlīce, adv. *visibly.* xx. 247, 268.

sī, see **bēon-wesan.**

Siba, *Sheba,* a rebel against David. xxii. 30, 34.

sibb, f. *peace.* iv. 19, 35, 99, 184; x. 14 (twice), 121 (twice), 122, 123, 125, 126; xi. 553, 567; xv. 200, 220; xxi. 285.

ġesibb, adj. *related, akin.* xxiii. 38.

sibling, m. *relative.* iv. 28, 121.

siccetung, f. *sighing, sobbing.* xxvi. 97.

ġesīcelian, II. *to sicken, take sick.* xix. 148.

ġesicþ, see **ġesēon.**

sīde, adv. *extensively.* **wīde and sīde,** *far and wide,* xxix. 104.

sīde, f. *side.* vii. 142, 147, 149; xiᵃ. 139.

Sidon, city of Syria. xvii. 51, 61 and 65 (ds. **Sidone**).

siġe, m. *victory.* vii. 124; ix. 52, 215, 216; xiᵃ. 146; xx. 375; xxi. 215, 284; xxii. 27, 66, 71, 90; xxix. 42.

siġefæst, adj. *victorious.* x. 201; xxii. 83; xxvi. 23.

ġesihst, see **ġesēon.**

(sihþ), syhþ, f. *sight, range of vision.*

xix. 189. [Normally with pref. as next entry.]

ġesihþ, ġesyhþ, f. (a) *faculty* or *act of sight, range of vision, sight, eyes*: ii. 270; iii. 35; iv. 5, 30, 123; vi. 184, 189; vii. 48; etc.—spelled **ġesihthe** (ds.), xxi. 402. (b) *thing seen, vision*: i. 10; xi. 508; xix. 202; xxix. 56, 88, 90.

ġesihþ, vb., see **ġesēon.**

Simeon, Symeon, the old man who blessed Jesus (Luke ii. 25, sqq.). xi. 26; xiᵃ. 100.

Simon, a Pharisee (Luke vii. 40). vi. 304.

Sinagoga, Latinized Greek, introduced by Ælfric as the technical name of the Jewish congregation. xiv. 89 (v.l. **Syn-**).

Sinai, *Mount Sinai.* iv. 146 (ds. **Syna**); xx. 28, 47 (as., ds., **Sinai**).

singal, adj. *continual.* xvi. 48.

singan, 3. *to sing.* inf., xxii. 76; pres. part. **singende,** xiv. 119; xxi. 298; xxvii. 73, 76; pres. 1s. **singe,** xiii. 74; xv. 225; 3s. **singþ,** xii. 156; 1p. **singaþ,** xi. 75; pret. 3s. **sang,** i. 79, 98, 106, 375; vii. 94; xv. 222; xvi. 57. (With acc. at xii. 156; xiii. 74; xxii. 76; otherwise intr. All instances of **sang** characterize the mode of utterance of the psalmist; also **sing- ende,** xiv. 119.)

singian, see **syngian.**

sinscipe, m. *conjugal tie, wedlock.* xix. 106; xxx. 10.

sint, see **bēon-wesan.**

Siria, *Syria.* xvii. 11 (gs. **Sirian**).

sittan, 5. (a) *to sit, be seated, sit down.* v. 7, 110, 281; xi. 59, 347, 355, 358, 362; xiᵃ. 162, 176; xiii. 195; xiv. 13, 78; xxi. 486; xxiii. 117; xxv(ᵃ). 13; xxvii. 57. (b) *to occupy a seat* (of dignity) as one's prerogative, not necessarily continuously. xiᵃ. 162; xviii. 303. (c) w. refl. dat., *to seat oneself, be seated.* x. 171. (d) treating the posture as typical, *to stay, remain, reside.* vi. 50; xxii. 85; xxv(ᶜ). 1; xxvi. 80, 105; xxvii. 26.—of a prisoner, *to be confined.* xxi. 469.—of besiegers, *to be posted.* xix. 175. (e) w. **upp,** *to sit up.* xiii.

sittan (*cont.*)

214, 221. [Forms: inf., xxv(*a*). 13; pres. part. **sittende**, xiii. 195 (twice more); pres. 3s. **sitt**, xi. 347 (twice more); pl. **sittaþ**, xi. 355, 358, 362; pret. 3s. **sæt**, v. 7 (13 more); pl. **sæton**, xi. 59 (4 more).—Cf. **be-sittan** and **ǥesittan** next below.]

ǥesittan, 5. (a) *to take a seat, remain sitting.* pret. 3s. **ǥesæt**, xxvii. 86. (b) *to sit* (*regularly*) *in an official seat.* xxiii. 85.

sīþ, m. (a) *a time, occasion*, with ordinals. **þriddan sīþe**, i. 447; **ōþre sīþe** (instr.), xii. 81; xiv. 151. (b) *lot, fate.* xxi. 611.

sīþ, adv. *afterwards, later.* xxi. 652.— **sīþ and ǣr**, *at any time, ever.* xix. 180. [Cf. **syþþan**.]

sīþfæt, m. or n. *journey.* v. 7.

sīþian, II. *to make a journey, go.* i. 429; vi. 337; vii. 32, 51; x. 201; xi. 208, 458; xv. 122; xviii. 435; xx. 4, 205; xxiii. 204; xxvii. 62; xxix. 53.

siþþan, see **syþþan**.

six, syx, num. *six.* ii. 215, 220; xvii. 249; xviii. 369; xx. 10; xxi. 357, 460.

ǥesixst, see **ǥesēon**.

sixta, syxta, num. adj. *sixth.* v. 110, 111; xi*a*. 61; xxi. 176, 499.

slǣp, m. *sleep.* i. 227; vi. 35; xvii. 208, 215; xxi. 600.

slǣpan, slāpan, 7. *to sleep.* inf. **slāpon**, xxi. 321 (v.l. **slǣpan**); pres. 3s. **slǣpþ**, iv. 225; vi. 30, 32; pret. 3s. **slēp**, xvii. 216.

slaǥa, m. *slayer.* xi. 291.

slēacnyss, f. *slackness.* ii. 189.

slēan, 6. (a) *to strike.* pret. 3s. **slōh**, xxi. 206, 546; 3p. **slōǥon**, xix. 192; xxi. 284 (*strike down, subdue*). *(b) with inanimate subj., to become* (*suddenly, at a stroke*)? pret. 3s. **slōh**, xiv. 23, 126. [Meaning (b) unrecorded: see note on xiv. 23.—Cf. **ofslēan**.]

sleǥe, m. (a) *onslaught*: xix. 194; (b) *slaughter*: xxvi. 49.

ǥeslit, n. *bite, sting* of a snake: xx. 317, 332.

slite, m. *bite, sting* of a snake. xxi. 40.

smǣte, adj. *pure, refined.* xxi. 191.

smēaǥan, II. (a) alone, with **ymbe**

(**embe**), or with a clause, *to ponder, meditate, take thought, deliberate.* ii. 241; iii. 182; x. 45 (pret. 3p. **smēadon**); xi. 478; xii. 158 (pres. 3s. **smēaþ**); xix. 83; xxi. 27, 624; xxv(*c*). 11. (b) with acc., *to meditate, contrive.* xvii. 167. [Cf. **asmēaǥan**.]

*****smēalīce**, adv. *subtly, cunningly.* xxi. 202. [This meaning not recorded; see note.]

smēaung, f. *cogitation, reflection.* xxi. 633.

smiþ, smyþ, m. *smith.* xix. 208, 236; xxi. 202.

smiþþe, wk. f. *smithy, forge.* xix. 211.

smyltnyss, f. *gentleness, mildness, tranquillity.* xv. 221; xvii. 212.

smyrian, ǥesmyrian, II (orig. I). *to anoint.* v. 209, 211; vi. 6, 309; xxix. 32.

snāw, m. *snow.* i. 433; xxi. 579.

snoter ('snotor'), adj. *clever, wise.* iii. 49, 84; xvi. 228, 232, 243; xx. 170, 199; xxi. 361; xxviii. 7.—comp. **snoter(r)a**, xvi. 33, 216 (np. **snoterran**, v.l. **snoterran**).—sup. **snoterost**, xvi. 230.

snotorlīce, adv. *prudently, wisely.* xvi. 31, 206 (v.l. **snoter-**).

snotornyss, f. *prudence, wisdom.* xvi. 218 (**snoter-**).

Sodomitisc, adj. *Sodomitish, of Sodom.* xviii. 68.

sōftnyss, f. *softness.* vi. 208; xi. 218; xiii. 60, 62; xix. 13.

sōna, adv. *immediately, forthwith.* ii. 22, 40, 86, 118, 269; iii. 17, 41, 163, 171; iv. 106; v. 214; vi. 9, 65, 68, 99, 185; vii. 59; etc.—**sōna swā**, conj. *as soon as.* vi. 51, 74; vii. 18, 75; etc.

sorhfull, adj. *sorrowful.* xi. 295, 397; xviii. 250, 366; xxvi. 82.

sōþ, adj. *true.* i. 40, 42, 95, 102, 166, 174, etc.; ii. 94, 150, 206; iii. 146; iv. 2, 66, 68, 127, 277, 278, 286; v. 51, 84, 127, 169, 180, 236, 252; vi. 222, 266, 346 (twice); etc.—wk. neuter as noun, **þæt sōþe**, *the true, what is true.* xiii. 95—as sb., **sōþ**, n., *truth.* ix. 169; xix. 187.—sb. as adv., *truly, verily.* (a) translating *amen*, viii. 29 (twice), 56 (twice),

91; xi. 427, 449; xii. 8 (twice), 14 (twice), 28 (twice), 67 (twice), 96 (twice), 174 (twice); xxv(*a*). 12. [Cf. Bede, In Lucam, VI. 303: 'Amen interpretatur verum.'] (b) in comparable expressions, viii. 244; xv. 5, 56.—adv. phrase, **tō sōþan**, *verily, in truth.* i. 358; v. 287; xi. 481; xv. 13, 129; xvii. 64; xix. 37; xxi. 146; xxix. 51, 60.

sōþfæst, adj. *true, faithful.* i. 63; iv. 267, 286; vi. 230, 272; vii. 205; ix. 169; xi. 197; xi*a*. 11; xv. 210; xix. 233; xxii. 90; xxix. 51.

sōþfæstnyss, f. *truth.* i. 54, 456, 461, 463, 466; iv. 256, 257; v. 52, 55, 170, 173, 183, 222; etc.

gesōþian, II. *to bear witness to, certify.* xii. 179. [Cf. **sēþan**.]

sōþlic, adj. *true.* xviii. 60.

sōþlīce, adv. *truly, in truth, surely, indeed.* i. 52, 121, 427; ii. 9, 151, 201, 206; iii. 14, 76, 104, 140, 158; iv. 5, etc. (15 times); etc.

spātl, n. *spittle.* xvii. 31, 130, 154, 156.

spēd, f. *wealth, riches.* xv. 121; xvi. 186, 267 (all three qualified by **heofonlic**).

speligend, m. *a representative, vicar.* ix. 48; xx. 292.

spell, n. (a) *message.* viii. 6. (b) *sermon, discourse.* ii. title (and the titles of iii, v, vi as given in MS. H); viii. 103; ix. 72; x. 106; xi. 69; xii. 224; xx. 335; xxii. 58, 79.

spere, n. *spear.* xi. 37; xi*a*. 138.

spiweþa, m. *vomit.* xiii. 232.

spræc, f. *speech, (spoken) word(s), saying(s), language, power of speech.* i. 132, 140; iv. 5; v. 95; vii. 2, 194; viii. 22; x. 4, 7, 8 (twice), 30, 58, 64, 65 (twice), 69, 70 (twice); xv. 185, 186; xvii. 285; xxii. 31—**tō þæs Hǣlendes spræce**, *to speak with the Saviour*, xii. 55 (see note); **tō his spræce**, *to speak with him*, xxi. 380.—**on Englisc(e)re spræce**, *in the English language*, i. 28, 179; xiv. 90; xv. 224; xx. 424; **on Greciscre spræce**, x. 84.

sprecan, 5. (a) intrans., *to speak.* i. 69; ii. 256; iii. 159; iv. 10, 188; v.

59, 61, 207, 217; vi. 70, 221; vii. 5, 27 (1st), 151, 197, 207 (1st), 208, 213; etc. (b) trans., *to speak, utter, say.* v. 63; vii. 2, 27 (2nd), 207 (2nd); viii. 4, 205; ix. 12, 18, 30, 172, 207; x. 10, 24, 67, 69, 71, 74, 185; etc. [Forms include inf., xi. 60; pres. 1s. **sprece**, i. 69; 2s. **sprecst**, viii. 45; 3s. **sprycþ**, iii. 159; **sprecþ**, vii. 27; pl. **sprecaþ**, vii. 5; pret. 1s. **spræc**, viii. 34; 3s. iv. 10; pl. **sprǣcon**, ii. 256; **sprǣcan**, xxix. 1; pret. 3s. subj. **sprǣce**, v. 63.]

gesprecan, 5. (a) intrans., *to speak.* pret. 3s. **gesprǣc**, xii. 218; xx. 140, 181. (b) trans., the object a person, *to speak with.* pret. 3s. **gesprǣc**, ii. 287; xvii. 92.

spyrte, wk. f. *basket.* xi*a*. 125. [Lat. *sporta*: defined by Ælfric himself, CH II. 402/6–9.]

stæf, m. (a) *staff.* i. 251; xxi. 441 (ds. **stafe**). (b) *written character, letter.* xix. 179.

stæflic, adj. *literal.* xxx. 58. [BT cites two passages from Ælfric.]

stæmne, see **stefen**.

stǣnan, I. *to stone.* iii. 121; vi. 23.

stǣnen, adj. *of stone.* iii. 83.

stæpe, m. *step.* dp. **stapum**, ii. 210; ap. **stapas**, xxi. 422.

stæppan, 6. *to step, go or come on foot.* pret. 3s. **stōp**, vi. 99 (w. **forþ**; see **forþstæppan**); 3p. **stōpan**, xxi. 229; **stōpon**, xxi. 388; xxvii. 95; pret. 3s. subj. **stōpe**, xxi. 36, 404. [Cf. a-, forþ-stæppan.]

*****staþþig**, adj. *stable.* xiv. 71 (dsf. wk. **staþþian**). [BT has only the meaning *grave, staid*, etc., as applied to moral character; the meaning here is nearer to the basic comparison with 'stæþ', (*firm*) *shore*; but BT has 'gestæþþig', *steadfast*, cited from Alfred's Boethius. See also OED, 'steady'.]

stafe, see **stæf**.

stāh, see **stīgan**.

stalu, f. *stealing, theft.* xvi. 76; xxi. 135.

stān, m. *stone.* iii. 14, 38, 39, 150, 151, 152, 153; vi. 86; ix. 194; xiii. 204,

stān (*cont.*)
211, 216; xvii. 227; xix. 30, 32; xx.
22, 26, 179; xxi. 192; xxvi. 32.

standan, 6. *to stand*. (a) of the posture, position, or situation of persons, images of gods, animals,
objects placed right side up. v. 214;
vi. 95; vii. 146; xi. 345, 407, 436;
xiii. 200, 220; xiv. 3, 5, 11, 14, 49,
53, 76, 79, 81; xv. 198; xvii. 235;
xviii. 233, 277, 300; xx. 272; xxi.
229, 235, 584; xxvii. 97. (b) w.
compl. adj. or part., *to be* or *remain*
in a specified state. ii. 210; iv, 22,
109; xxi. 413. (c) of words, *to be
recorded*. iii. 50; xi. 522; xx. 397;
xxii. 102; xxx. 81. (d) of a decree, *to
remain in force*. xxi. 388. (e) of an
emotion, w. dat. of person, *to
threaten, come upon, assail*. xxi. 208
(**ne stōd him nān ege**, *he stood
in no awe*). (f) w. **on**, *to belong to,
be proper to*. vi. 250. (g) w. **ongēan**,
prep., *to oppose* (*steadily*). xvii. 207
(of a contrary wind). [Forms: inf.,
ii. 210 (8 more); pres. 3s. **stent**, iii.
50 (8 more); pl. **standaþ**, xi. 345,
407; xv. 198; 3s. subj. **stande**,
xxi. 388; pret. 3s. **stōd**, vii. 146
(15 more); pl. **stōdon**, xxvii. 97; 3s.
subj. **stōde**, xxi. 235.—Cf. **æt-,
under-standan, ymbstandend**,
and next entry.]

ġestandan, 6. (a) *to stand, take one's
stand*. pret. 3s. **ġestōd**, i. 378 (Lat.
stetit). (b) trans., *to attend* a service
at which one is required to stand,
stand in one's place during. pret. 3s.
ġestōd, xxvi. 133. [Cf. BTS,
'gestandan', B. II.]

stānweall, m. *stone wall*. xxii. 99.

stap-, see **stæpe**.

ġestaþelfæstan, I. *to confirm*. i.
90.

staþolfæst, adj. *steadfast*. iv. 22, 109
(v.l. **staþel-**); xviii. 107.

staþolfæstnyss, f. *steadfastness*. xiv.
60, 63, 71 (**stoþol-**); xvii. 75.

stēap, adj. *high, lofty*. xx. 48.

stede, m. *place, position*. iv. 252; v.
239; viii. 98, 109.

stef(e)n, stemn, f. *voice*. iv. 51, 270,
273; vi. 134; vii. 153 (**stæm**);

xii. 21, 147, 156, 157; xvii. 229;
xxvii. 36, 67, 74.

stenc, m. *odour*. xvii. 158 (twice: first
time, **þǽre nosa stenc**, *the odour
in the nose?*).

stent, see **standan**.

stēopcild, n. *orphan*. xxx. 97.

stēor, f. *guidance, discipline, correction*. iv. 148; xiii. 85; xiv. 99; xv.
173, 177.

steorra, wk. m. *star*. i. 208; xviii.
262, 401; xxi. 85, 182, 187.

stēorsetl, n. *steering-seat* or *-place,
stern*. xvii. 208.

Stephanus. St. Stephen, protomartyr.
ix. 194 (as. **Stephanum**); xix. 231.

stēran, I. *to burn incense, fumigate*.
xx. 227, 240. [Cf. **stōr**.]

sticca, wk. m. *stick*. i. 251.

sticmǽlum, adv. *to pieces*. xxi. 556.
[Cf. BT, 'styccemælum', I, with
two citations from Ælfric in this
sense; but the gloss *paulatim* shows
that the glossator took the meaning
to be *little by little*.]

sticol, adj. *lofty, steep*. v. 174; xviii.
240, 310; xx. 52.

stīgan, 1. *to ascend, go aboard* (a ship).
pres. 3s. **stāh**, xvii. 204. [Cf.
astīgan.]

ġestillan, I. *to make still, quiet, calm*.
xia. 110; xvii. 217; xx. 229.

stille, adj. (*motionless*), *still*. xvii. 211.

stil(l)nyss, f. *tranquillity*. xviii. 92,
107.

stincan, 3. *to stink*. pres. part. **stinc-
ende**, i. 269 (dsn. **-um**); vi. 113
(asm. **-an**), 198 (nsm.); pres.
3s. **stincþ**, vi. 87, 169, 201.

stīþ, adj. *hard, unfeeling*. iii. 121. comp.
stīþra, *harder*, xv. 28; of food,
solider, xix. 5 (referring to Heb.
v. 12–14, 'strong meat' in A.V.).

stīþnyss, f. *hardness, severity*. xix. 2,
6, 8.

stōd, stōdon, ġestōd, see **standan,
ġestandan**.

stōp, stōpe, stōpon, see **stæppan**.

stōr, m. *incense, frankincense*. xx. 240,
256. [For quantity of vowel see note
on xx. 240.]

stōrcylle, wk. f. *censer*. xx. 226, 272.

stoþol-, see **staþol-**.

stōw, f. *place.* (a) in set phrases: on ǣlcere stōwe, iii. 109; xvii. 162, 305; on ōþre stōwe, iv. 175; vi. 359; ix. 96; xiii. 162; xviii. 329, 424; xxv(*a*). 1; on sumere stōwe, i. 311; xvii. 52; on sum(e)re ōþre stōwe, v. 156; xv. 197; xvi. 279; on þǣre ylcan stōwe, vi. 18, 69, 330. (b) miscellaneous uses: iv. 42, 213, 223; v. 42; xviii. 233, 277, 300; xxi. 607, 614, 617.

strand, n. *shore* of sea or lake. xiv. 63.

strang, adj. *strong.* i. 266; iv. 34, 183, 188; xx. 371 (ful strang, see full, adv.)—comp. strengra, iv. 191; as noun, iv. 36, 185.

ġestrangian, II. *to strengthen, confirm.* i. 90; ix. 147, 153; x. 48.

strēam, m. *stream.* xx. 22.

strengþ, f. *strength.* ix. 141; xia. 21 (both ds. strengþe). [BT records ns. 'strengþ' rather than 'strengþu' for Ælfric.]

ġestrēon, n. (a) *procreation.* i. 394; xix. 112. (b) *gain, treasure.* xvi. 157.

ġestrȳnan, I. (a) *to beget, produce* (children). xi. 319; xia. 202; xxi. 12. (b) *to gain* for someone (dat.) by cultivation. xviii. 156, 168 (fig., of the souls in God's acre).

stunt, adj. *dull, stupid, foolish.* xv. 16, 150, 165 (as noun); xvi. 60, 110; xvii. 69.

stuntnyss, f. *stupidity, folly.* xv. 174, 177; xvi. 222.

stūt, m. *gnat.* xiii. 164, 168.

stȳpel, m. *steeple, tower.* iii. 6, 83; xxi. 74.

stȳran, I. *to correct.* xiii. 131 (twice), 161, 183 (twice), 185; xv. 164.—ġestȳran, the same. xiii. 160.

styrian, II. (orig. I). (a) trans., *to move, stir.* ii. 19, 46; xxi. 127 (*stir up*). (b) intrans., *to move.* i. 284. [Cf. astyrian.]

styrne, adj. *stern, severe.* xv. 173.

styrung, f. *stirring, agitation, movement.* ii. 22, 27, 35, 117, 130; xvii. 205.

sūcan, ġesūcan, 2. *to suck.* pret. 3s. sēac, iv. 280; pret. 2s. ġesuce, iv. 53, 272.

sudon, see sēoþan.

sum, pron. adj. *some, a certain, one;* in pl., *some, certain (ones).* as adj., i. 22, 37, 98, 151, 225, 288, 299, 311, 325, 346, 356; ii. 9, 28, 37, 56, 85, 187, 198, 266 (twice), 279; iii. 2, 4, 96, 182; etc.—qualifying a number, *some, about.* xvii. 239 (sume twā þūsend).—hī sume, sume hī, np., *some of them.* i. 349; ii. 282; iii. 94; iv. 15, 90; etc. ġē sume, *some of you.* xviii. 62.—as pron., (a) sing., with gen., v. 272; vi. 369; viii. 151, 184; etc. (b) pl. with prep. of, vi. 83; xviii. 101. (c) alone or as correl., sing. or pl., i. 454; ii. 283-4 (3 times); iii. 13-14 (3 times), 119-21 (3 times); iv. 77; vi. 126; ix. 66-68 (3 times); xi. 205, 209, 213, 229 (twice); etc. [Forms to be noted: nsf. sum (not 'sumu'), xvi. 187; xxvi. 28; dsm., dsn., dp. sumon, i. 288; vi. 131; ix. 72; xx. 407, 412; xxii. 79; xxvi. 1; xxviii. 6; xxix. 105; otherwise sumum; ism. sume, xx. 27; xxi. 435 (forming traditional phrase with dæg, endingless locative); parasite e in dsf. sumere, i. 311; xv. 197; xvi. 279; xvii. 52; xxvi. 30; (sumre, v. 156); gp. sumera, xi. 202 (frequent in LWS; Cpb 641); npn. sume (not 'sumu'), xiii. 91, 92 (sume þing).—For other examples of sum þing see þing. For LWS levelling in npn. sume see S-B 293, Anm. 3; Cpb 641. The comparable nsf. sum is not documented for LWS, only '-sum' in Vespasian Psalter, see S-B 294, Anm. 2; Cpb 641. Ælfric has 'sum earm wydewe' in CH II. 106/8 = Napier's Wulfstan, p. 287/12.]

sumor, m. *summer.* xvi. 118 (ds. sumera).

sunbēam, m. *sunbeam, sunshine.* i. 432; viii. 233.

ġesund, adj. *uninjured, sound, in good health.* ii. 251; ix. 162; xx. 328; xxiii. 33.—as part of a formula in a vow, *gif ic ġesund bēo, if I have my health.* xxi. 383. [This idiom, though in Warner's text, p. 39/22, is not in BT; but cf. the

gesund (*cont.*)
passage there cited from Apollonius, ed. Goolden, p. 10/3.]

ġesundfulnyss, f. *health.* xxx. 80.

Sunderhālga, Sundor-, wk. m. *a Pharisee.* iii. 41, 90, 97, 163; vi. 304; xii. 47; xiii. 197; xv. 8, 59, 60; xviii. 2, 206, 222.

sunderlic, see **synderlic**.

***sundorrūnung**, f. *private consultation, secret counsel.* iii. 43, 165.

Sunnanǣfen, m. *eve of Sunday, Saturday night.* xi. 75.

Sunnandæg, m. *Sunday.* ii. 251, 252; xl*a*. 189; xvi. 79, 80; xviii. 340; xix. 121, 125; xxi. 168.

sunne, wk. f. *sun.* i. 15, 207, 280, 294, 307, 420; v. 277; viii. 230; xi. 285, 288, 513, 571; xiii. 43; xviii. 260, 399; xxi. 56, 59, 61, 65, 83, 166, 168, 183; xxvii. 102 (fig., the vital energy of one man's life-span); xxviii. 13.

sunu, occas. **suna**, m. (gds. **suna**, nap. **suna**). *son*; esp. the *Son* of God. i. 5, 53, etc. (14 times); ii. 6; iii. 18, etc. (7 times); iv. 26, etc. (7 times); v. 5, 105; vi. 134, 229–80 (11 times); vii. 118, 211, 225; etc.

sūsl, f. or n. *torment.* iv. 113; xi. 134, 269, 326; xiv. 138; xxi. 201. [The reference is always to the torments of hell.]

suwian, II. *to be silent.* ii. 269; xviii. 181. [Cf. **swiġian**.]

swā, adv. and conj. *so, as.* i. 24, 223, 228, 240, etc. (16 times); ii. 70, 154, 166, 201, 205, 231, 267; etc.—**swā swā**, conj. *as.* i. 4, 15, 26, etc. (18 times); etc.—**swā . . . swā**, (a) enclosing adjective or adverb, *so, as . . . as.* iv. 158, 227; etc. (for special combinations, see the interrogatives **hū, hwā, hwǣr, hwæþer, hwider, hwylc**, and **fela, oft, swilc**); (b) correlative, *either . . . or, whether . . . or.* xi*a*. 170; xix. 86, 206.—**swā þæt**, *so that* (expressing purpose, result, or manner). i. 389; ii. 18, 123, 221; v. 133; vii. 182; etc. **swā . . . þæt**, *so . . . that*, enclosing adj. or adv., indicating degree. i. 457; iii. 125, 128; etc.; enclosing a verb, indicat-

ing manner. ii. 207; etc.—**ēac swā**, see **ēac**.

ġeswāc, see **ġeswīcan**.

swæcc, m. *flavour, taste.* xx. 16, 20, 124 (as. **swæc**).

swǣslīce, adv. *kindly.* vi. 186.

swān, m. *herdsman, swineherd.* xvii. 240.

swanc, see **swincan**.

swār, adj. *heavy, oppressive.* xxvi. 115.

swātclāþ, m. *'sudarium'*, a *handkerchief* or small *towel, napkin.* vi. 102 ('napkin' in A.V.).

swāþēah, adv. *however, nevertheless.* i. 254, 408; ii. 62, 109, 187, 192, 281; iii. 108; iv. 94, 291; v. 62, 106; etc.

ġeswearc, see **ġesweorcan**.

sweart, adj. *dark, black.* iv. 225, 257; viii. 182; x. 40; xi. 327; xvii. 260; xviii. 57; xix. 179, 190; xxvii. 37.

swefel, m. *sulphur.* xviii. 22, 71.

swēġan, I. *to sound.* vii. 152; x. 97; xi. 57; xi*a*. 174; xii. 156, 157; xxi. 298.

sweltan, 3. *to die, perish.* inf., vi. 159, 339, 340; xi. 125; xxi. 383, 385; xxix. 98; pres. 3s. **swelt**, xi. 121, 134; **swylt**, ii. 111; vi. 61, 359; pres. subj., 2s. **swelte**, vi. 156; 3s., xxi. 399; 1p. **swelton**, vi. 41; pret. 3s. **swealt**, x. 166; 3p. **swulton**, ii. 104; pret. subj., 3s. **swulte**, vi. 84; xix. 151; pl. **swulton**, vi. 341; xx. 311.

ġeswencan, I. (a) of the effect of a long sermon, *to fatigue, weary, trouble.* vi. 368. (b) of hard or cruel taskmasters, *to afflict, harass, oppress.* i. 199; xiii. 56, 61, 84; xx. 117 (pret. 3s. **ġeswencte**). (c) of disease, pestilence, the wrath of God, *to afflict.* ii. 282 (pp. np. **ġeswencte**); xvii. 15; xxi. 43, 267.

ġesweorcan, 3. *to become dark*; here fig., *to become angry.* pret. 3s. **ġeswearc**, xxi. 378 [BTS, II. 3, cites same metaphor in LS xxv. 329. Cf. **forsweorcan**.]

swerian, 6. *to swear, take oath.* pres. 3s. **sweraþ**, xxiv. 1; pret. 3p. **swōron**, xxii. 46. [Cf. **forsworen**.]

swica, m. *deceiver, traitor.* xxv(*a*). 19.
geswīcan, 1. (a) absolute, with a person as subject, *to cease* from a specified action. ii. 221. (b) absolute, with impersonal subject denoting activity or phenomena of a certain kind, *to cease, come to an end.* ii. 255; xx. 273; xxi. 244, 257, 281. (c) w. gen., *to cease from, desist* or *abstain from.* i. 197; ii. 216, 250; viii. 67; ix. 184; xv. 46; xix. 142; xxvi. 82; xxvii. 8. (d) with dat. inf., *to cease* to do something. vi. 270. [Forms: inf., ix. 184; xxvii. 8; pres. 3s. geswīcþ, vi. 270; viii. 67; pl. geswīcaþ, i. 197; xv. 46; 3s. subj. geswīce, xxi. 257; pret. 3s. geswāc, ii. 216 (6 more); pret. 3s. subj. geswice, xix. 142; xxi. 244.—Cf. beswīcan.]
swicdōm, m. *fraud, deceit.* x. 124; xvi. 201, 232.
geswicennyss, f. *abstention* (from sin). xia. 10 (dōþ geswicennysse, *practise abstention.* [BTS, citing this passage from Assmann, gives the meaning *cessation,* but *abstention* seems at least as good: in fact one must first cease, then abstain.]
swician, II. with prep. embe, ymbe, *to practise deceit with respect to.* xi. 163; xxi. 159. [BT cites latter passage as revised by Wulfstan; BTS gives another passage from Ælfric, to whom the expression seems peculiar. Cf. ge-æswician and syrwan.]
swicol, swicel, adj. *deceitful.* vi. 351; xi. 378; xix. 157; xxi. 134, xxiv. 6; xxix. 96, 114, 127.
swift, adj. *swift, rapid.* xxi. 475.
swiftlīce, adv. *swiftly.* xxi. 474.
swīgdæg, m. *day of silence,* one of the three Swīgdagas preceding Easter Sunday. xix. 122 (dp.). [Ælfric alone is cited in BT for this term.]
swīge, f. *silence.* vi. 66.
swigian, II. *to be silent.* imp. sg. swi(ga)?, xvii. 294. [Cf. suwian, another form of the same verb.]
swilc, swylc, pron. adj. *such.* as adj., i. 145, 371; ii. 91, 156; v. 53, 171; vii. 61, 109; viii. 153, 218; x. 38, 40;

xiii. 40, 205; etc. (17 more). correl., *such . . . as,* asm. swylc . . . swā, i. 53, 428; np. swylce . . . swylce, xviii. 248, 345; ap. swilce . . . swilce swā, xii. 5, 57.—elliptical use of adj., swylc þing, *such a thing* (as they pretend), xxix. 7 (but see note).—as pron., *such* (*a thing, person, matter*). ii. 84; iv. 230; vi. 202, 301; xxx. 26. [Forms are normal, but note parasitic e in dsf. swylcere, xiii. 205 (3 more), gp. swylcera, i. 145.]
swilce, swylce, conj. (a) w. subj., *as if.* ii. 88, 182, 188; v. 176; vi. 189; xi. 44; xia. (151); xiii. 177; xvi. 198; xviii. 22; xix. 29, 76, 77 (twice), 78, 154; xx. 241; xxi. 182, 227, 239, 278; xxvii. 26, 58; xxix. 7, 15, 17, 122. (In only six instances are the subj. forms the same as the ind. See note on i. 162.)—(b) elliptically, w. adv. phrase, *as if.* ii. 271; xi. 539; xii. 231; xviii. 325; xix. 15; xx. 326.—w. noun, *as if, as, like,* but always implying that the resemblance is illusory or inexact. i. 432; vii. 71; xi. 169; xix. 177, 192; xx. 164; xxvii. 43, 91; xxx. 26.—for the adv. see ēac.
swīn, swȳn, n. *swine.* xiii. 233; xvii. 236 (twice), 238 (twice), 241, 257, 260, 262, 265, 271.
geswinc, n. *labour, hardship.* ii. 177; v. 87, 104, 154, 255, 264; vi. 151; viii. 117; xiii. 64, 68; xviii. 118; xx. 70, 308, 417; xxi. 46, 51, 55.
swincan, 3. *to work, labour.* inf., vi. 149; pres. 3s. swincþ, xiv. 125; 3p. swincaþ, vi. 146; xiv. 122; xviii. 145; 3s. subj. swince, vi. 208; 1p. subj. swincon, ii. 182; pret. 3s. swanc, ii. 119; v. 105; xvi. 119; xxi. 314; pl. swuncon, xiv. 20, 116; xx. 70, 215.—geswincan, same meaning. pres. 2p. geswincaþ, v. 157 (but read ealle gē þe swincaþ?). [Cf. beswincan.]
swingel, f. *scourge, affliction.* ii. 240.
swīþe, swȳþe, adv. *very, greatly, strongly, vehemently.* i. 97, 102, 341; ii. 285; iii. 1; iv. 195; v. 101, 218; vi. 146, 213, 214, 295, 302; etc,—

swīþe, swȳþe (*cont.*)

  comp. **swīþor, swȳþor,** *more greatly, rather, more.* i. 267, 422; ii. 136; iv. 211, 291; vi. 115, 368; vii. 176; ix. 186; xi. 92, 126, 495 (twice); xii. 170; xiii. 3; xv. 51; xvi. 149; xvii. 177; xxi. 120, 652; xxiii. 178; xxx. 35.—þæs þe swīþor, *all the more.* x. 144; xi. 266; xvii. 41, 182.—sup. **swīþost, swȳþost, -ust, -est,** *mainly, chiefly, above all.* ix. 128; xi. 212, 241; xiii. 83; xx. 387; xxi. 125.

swīþlic, adj. *great, mighty, strong, intense.* viii. 44, 236; xvii. 138, 285 (?); xx. 94 **(swȳþ-)**; xxi. 42, 105, 156, 639; xxii. 53.

swīþra,-e, comp. adj. (*stronger,* hence) *right* (hand or side). ii. 87; xi. 345, 407; xi*a.* 139; xiv. 159, 167, 168; xxx. 57, 63, 66.—as noun, *right hand or side:* xi*a.* 163; xiv. 175; xix. 234.

swōron, see **swerian.**

swult-, see **sweltan.**

swuncon, see **swincan.**

swura, wk. m. *neck.* xxiii. 133. [On the form see S–B 113, Anm. 4; Cpb 241. 2, note 5. Cf. **swyre** below.]

swurd, n. *sword.* xx. 213; xxi. 441.

swuster, -or, f. *sister.* vi. 15, 66, 108, 355; xxi. 113; xxiii. 199.—np. **ġeswustra,** *sisters* of common parentage. vi. 8, 328.

swutel, adj. *clear.* iv. 92 (ap. **swutele,** v.ll. **swytele, swytela**); vii. 194; ix. 73.

ġeswutelian, -swutol-, II. *to make clear, show, manifest, display.* ii. 280; vi. 333; vii. 137, 149; viii. 16; ix. 160; x. 13, 35, 62, 82; xi. 396; xi*a.* 103; xii. 98; xvii. 143, 215; xix. 220; xx. 195, 228; xxi. 501; xxx. 51, 53.

swute(l)līce, swutol-, adv. *clearly.* vi. 133; vii. 35, 70; viii. 36, 45, 69, 174, 233, 237; ix. 94, 115; x. 184; xi. 268, 350, 535, 537; xviii. 407; xix. 182, 233; xx. 18; xxvii. 18, 24.—comp. **swute(l)līcor,** i. 281; vii. 31; viii. 239; ix. 144; x. 105; xiii. 36; **swutolīcor,** xxix. 2.

swutelung, f. (a) *clarity.* ix. 89. (b) *clarification, explanation.* ix. 104;

xi. 1; xxviii. 6, 7. (c) *manifestation.* viii. 246. (d) *enlightenment.* i. 80.

ġeswutelung, f. *manifestation.* i. 87.

swylc, see **swilc.**

swylian or **swyllan,** II, I (orig. I). *to wash.* xiv. 9, 67, 72 (pret. 3p. **swyledon,** v.l. **swiledon**).

swylt, see **sweltan.**

swȳn, see **swīn.**

***swyre, swȳre,** wk. n.? *neck.* as. (?), xxiii. 132. [The form in the MS. must be either a scribal blunder for **swuran, swyran,** or evidence of a variant word, otherwise unrecorded. Cf. **swura** above and see note on this line.]

swȳþ-, see **swīþ-.**

sȳ, see **bēon-wesan.**

syfan, syfon, see **seofan.**

syferlīce, adv. *purely.* ii. 171.

syfernyss, f. *purity.* iv. 217.

syftan, I. *to sift.* xxi. 402.

ġesyhst, see **ġesēon.**

syhþ, ġesyhþ, see **sihþ, ġesihþ.**

sylen, f. *gift.* xxx. 36.

sylf, pron. adj. *self.* (a) declined strong in agreement w. noun or pers. pron., *myself, thyself, himself,* etc. i. 33, 37, 52, 60, 69, etc. (19 times); ii. 67, etc. (9 times); iii. 99, 135, 140, 143, 180; iv. 18, etc. (10 times); etc.—in ns. agreeing w. subject sometimes preceded by refl. dat. pron., **him sylf,** i. 41, 57, 253, 310, 314, 331; ix. 65; x. 195; **hyre sylf,** i. 277; **mē sylf,** vii. 51; etc.—(b) declined wk. with art.: w. following noun, *that (self)same, very;* or sometimes equivalent to art. and noun foll. by strong form. i. 96; vii. 111; viii. 40, 213 (*the Father himself*); x. 190 (*the devil himself*); xii. 159; xiii. 197; xvii. 14; etc.—without following noun, **þā sylfan,** ap., *the same (ones),* ii. 222; **sē sylfa . . . þe,** *that very one . . . who,* ix. 214; etc.

sylfren, seolfren, adj. *made of silver.* xxi. 203; xxvi. 20. [Cf. **seolfor.**]

sylfwilles, adv. *voluntarily.* iii. 132; vi. 340; ix. 116; x. 210; xv. 124, 156; xix. 228; xxvii. 12; xxx. 2.

syllan ('sellan'), I, pp. **ġeseald.** *to give.* i. 96 (pres. 3s. **sylþ**); ii. 157

(pret. 3s. **sealde**); iii. 37 (twice), 132, 157 (twice); v. 13 (imp. sg. **syle**), 19, 20, 28, 31, 139, 152; vi. 223; vii. 58; etc.—rarely *to sell*, as at xviii. 18.—**s. to gafole**, *to give upon usury, lend at interest.* xxiv. 5, 8.

gesyllan, I. *to sell.* xxi. 203 (pret. 3p. **gesealdon**). [Perhaps not really to be distinguished from **syllan**.]

syllic ('seldlic'), adj. *wondrous, strange.* ii. 138; iv. 15, 90; xiii. 34.

symbeldæg, m. *feastday, festival.* i. 1; ii. 9.

symble, symle, adv. *always, ever, continually.* i. 95; ii. 15, 171, 235, 260; iii. 88; iv. 204, 205, 230; v. 133, 183, 244; vi. 94; vii. 225; etc.

Symeon, see **Simeon**.

Syna, see **Sinai**.

synd, see **bēon-wesan**.

synderlic, sunderlic, adj. (a) *separate, individual.* i. 381; xix. 105. (b) *sequestered.* xxvii. 25 (**sunder-**). [For (b) cf. BT, 'synderlic', I.]

synderlīce, adv. (a) *separately, individually.* i. 380. (b) *specially.* xxi. 588; xxx. 97.

syndon, see **bēon-wesan**.

syndrig, adj. *various.* np. **(syn)drige** (?), i. 274.

synfull, adj. *sinful.* iv. 66; v. 273; vi. 173, 191, 199, 292, 297, 302; xi. 202; xii. 131 (**synn-**), 135; xiv. 32, 198; xviii. 68, 429; xxiii. 148; xxvii. 20.—wk. w. def. art. as noun, vi. 296; x. 190; xi. 191, 265, 293, 349, 352, 444, 451, 456; xv. 50; xviii. 55;—ap. wk. **synfullan** where one expects 'synfulle' or 'þa synfullan', xxiii. 149.

syngian, singian, II. *to sin.* ii. 56, 67; iii. 152 (**on Crīst**, *against Christ*); vi. 140, 149, 166, 173, 189, 192, 210, 313; xi. 98, 99, 102, 104, 388, 494; xia. 27; xiii. 227; xv. 47; xix. 74, 75.—pp. **gesyngod**, xx. 49, 319.

synlic, adj. *sinful.* ix. 176.

synn, f. *sin.* i. 97, 183 (?), 223; ii. 97, 105, 240, 246, 260, 278, 280, 282; iii. 147; iv. 67, 242; v. 238; vi. 139,

etc. (16 times); vii. 17 (10 times); etc.

synt, see **bēon-wesan**.

syrwan, syrwian, I, II. *to plot, scheme.* (a) forms of class I: pres. 3s. **syrwþ**, vi. 284 (w. **embe**; cf. **swician**); pret. 3s. **syrwde**, xxii. 44 (w. **embe**); pret. 3p. **syrwdon**, ii. 124. (b) forms of class II: pres. part. **syrwiend-, syrwigend-**, iv. 17, 97; xi. 163; xxi. 159; pres. 3p. **syrwiaþ**, iv. 111. [Cf. **besyrwan**.]

syrwung, f. *machination, plotting.* vii. 109.

syþþan, siþþan, adv. *afterwards.* i. 441; ii. 53, 111, etc. (15 times); iii. 7, 15, 22, 28, 92, 137; etc.—conj. *after.* i. 434; ii. 287; iii. 107; vi. 65, 88; vii. 81, 129; etc. [Spelling **syþþan** almost universal in principal MSS.; **siþþan** at xxv(a). 18, and in several excluded variants. Cf. **sīþ**, adv.]

syx, syxta, see **six, sixta**.

gesyxt, see **gesēon**.

T

tabule, tabole, wk. f. *table, tablet.* iv. 146, 147; xxi. 219. (All three refer to the stone tablets of the Mosaic Law.)

tācn, tācen, n. *sign, significant form, miracle, prodigy.* i. 260; ii. 138 (as. **tācn**); iv. 15, 90 (as. **tācen**), 92 (ap. **tācna**); vi. 110; vii. 80; x. 47; xii. 5, 39, 57, 220, 231; xiv. 222; xvii. 54, 55; xviii. 256, 298, 357, 359, 379; xx. 326, 330; xxi. 347, 501.

getācnian, II. *to signify, betoken, prefigure.* ii. 120, etc. (7 times); iii. 86; iv. 135, 282; v. 178; vi. 172, 179, 188; xii. 69, 102, 234; xiii. 126, 154, 156; xiv. 53, etc. (10 times); xvii. 85, 122, 156, 158; xviii. 210; xx. 334; xxx. 61.

getācnung, f. *meaning, significance.* ii. 64, 218; v. 114, 220; vi. 199, 322; vii. 202; viii. 171; xii. 44, 82; xiii. 36, 127; xiv. 149, 153, 161; xvii. 50, 68; xx. 128, 338.

tǣcan, I, pret. **tǣht-**. (a) trans. *to*

tǽcan (*cont.*)

teach. vii. 26, 195; ix. 169; x. 12, 81;
xia. 116; xv. 107; xxi. 6, 499; xxiii.
70, 155.—more narrowly, *to enjoin,*
xiv. 102; xvi. 257; *to prescribe,* xxvi.
121, 124. (b) trans. *to designate,*
assign. xi. 184. (c) intr. *to teach* (*in-*
struct, prescribe, enjoin). ii. 166;
iii. 56; ix. 28; xv. 110; xxiii. 76; xxvii.
116. —(d) þone ræd tǽcan þæt, *to*
advise that. vi. 339. **tǽcan tō rǽde,**
to advise. xxi. 606. [Cf. **betǽcan**
and next entry.]

getǽcan, I, trans. (a) *to prescribe.* xiii.
209. *(b) w. compl. adj., *to declare,*
pronounce (innocent or guilty after
trial). xv. 132 (pp. **getǽht**). [No
exact parallel in BT.]

tǽcing, f. *teaching, instruction.* xviii.
124; xix. 102.

tǽlan, I. *to accuse, blame, censure.* iv.
268; vi. 300; x. 176; xiii. 166, 170;
xix. 154; xx. 196, 275, 290 (twice);
xxi. 386; xxiii. 63.

tāl, n. *reproach, calumny, blasphemy.*
vi. 224, 226, 269; xii. 168; xx. 182.
[Usually considered fem. but note
as. **tāl** in vi.—BT and BTS suggest
neuter variant and exhibit both n.
and f. in Ælfric MSS.]

***talian, II,** refl. *to claim to be* such
and such. xviii. 297. [This shade of
meaning not in dict.; see note.—
Cf. **tellan.**]

tāllic, adj. *blasphemous.* vi. 218.

talu, f. *tale, story.* xxii. 80.

tēar, m. *tear.* vi. 307; xvii. 146.

teart, adj. *sharp, severe.* xi. 227.

getel, n. *number, (full) count, reckon-*
ing. ii. 151; vi. 354 (v.l. **getæl**); xi.
257 (v.l. **getæl**); xiv. 186. [Cf.
fēowertig-getel.]

geteld, n. *tent.* xx. 15, 239, 267, 271.

tellan, I, pret. teald-, pp. geteald.
(a) *to count, number.* xia. 126 (pp.).
(b) *to consider* something or someone
(acc.) to be such and such (com-
plem. acc. noun or adj.). xv. 74;
xxiii. 65 (complement ān . . . tō
lufienne, *alone to be loved,* see
note); in passive, w. nom. for acc.:
xv. 133 (mixed constr., see note);
xvi. 284. (c) *to consider* or *reckon*

something *as* (**tō**) such and such
(dat.). xvi. 223; and in passive:
xvii. 249; xxx. 111. [Cf. **talian** and
betellan.]

tempel, n. *temple.* (a) the temple in
Jerusalem. ii. 10, 15, 54, 277; iii.
83; v. 191; ix. 28; xi. 23; xia. 97;
xiii. 193, 198. (b) God's temple,
typically, xviii. 303; applied to a
cathedral, xxvi. 63. (c) various
heathen temples. xxi. 194, 222, 388,
407, 412, 431, 525, 581, 583, 585,
630; xxvi. 12, 21 (ap. **tempel**).

getenge, adj. w. dat. *oppressing.* xvii.
250. [This passage cited from
Thorpe and the word so defined by
BT and BTS; Thorpe, 'weighing
down'.]

teolung, see **tilung.**

tēon, 2. (a) *to draw* (to), *attract.* pres.
3s. **tīhþ,** iv. 204. (b) *to pull, row*
(a boat). pret. 3p. **tugon,** xiv. 39,
226. [Cf. **atēon, forþtēon, þurh-**
tēon.]

tēona, m. *injury, insult, contumely.*
iv. 86; xiii. 104, 231; xxix. 80.

tēonfull, adj. *spiteful.* ii. 197; xiii.
154, 166; xiv. 106.

tēonfullic, adj. *slanderous.* i. 225.

tēonrǽden, f. *contumely.* xv. 153.

tēoþa, wk. adj. *tenth.* xxx. 87, 105.

tēoþian, II. *to pay tithe of.* iii. 101; xv.
102.

tēoþung, f. *tenth part, tithe, tithing.*
xxx. 77–104 (9 times).

teran, 4. *to tear, lacerate.* pres. part.,
np. wk. **terendan,** xx. 343. [Cf.
toteran.]

Theodolus, one of two priests who
suffered martyrdom with Pope
Alexander I. xxiii. 4, 127 (as., -um).

Theodora, sister of Hermes, prefect
of Rome and martyr. xxiii. 200.

Theodosius. (a) *Theodosius* I, the
Great (Roman emperor A.D. 379–95).
xxi. 542 (gs. **Theodosiges**); xxii. 64
(as. -um), 72 (ds., **Theodosige**);
xxvi. 4, 15, 121.—(b) *Theodosius* II,
the Younger (Roman emperor A.D.
409–50). xxii. 73 (**Th. se gingra**).

Thesalonica, the city of *Thessalonica.*
xxvi. 28.

Thomas, the disciple. vi. 39.

tīd, f. *hour, time, season, period.* ii. 166, 224; iv. 1; v. 110; vi. 25, 343, 349; xi. 2, 12, 43, 72, 91; xia. 86, 150, 188; xii. 48; xiii. 6; xiv. 1; xviii. 27; xxvi. 92; xxvii. 45.

tīdsang, m. *canonical hour(s), lauds.* xix. 211; xxx. 71.

getīgan, I. *to tie, tie up* (as an animal). xxi. 264.

tihtan, see tyhtan.

tīhþ, see tēon.

tilia, m. *husbandman.* iii. 7, etc. (12 times); xviii. 163.

tilian, II. (a) where the object of effort is not expressed, with dat. of person (or personified thing) for whom the effort is made, *to toil for.* xi. 120, 121; xvi. 278; xviii. 189.— (b) with refl. dat. and genitive of the object of effort, *to provide oneself with.* xvi. 15, 122, 150; xxi. 51.

tilþ, f. *husbandry, harvest.* xxx. 84.

tilung, teolung, f. (a) (*gainful*) *labour,* esp. work of *cultivation, husbandry.* xi. 281; xviii. 19, 27; fig., of the cultivation of souls, xvi. 209; xviii. 152 (Lat. *agricultura,* v.l. eorþteolung), 155, 168, 190, 242, 312. (b) *gain* from labour, *profit.* viii. 121; xviii. 124; xxx. 100.

tīma, wk. m. *time.* iii. 29, 114, 138; v. 45, 50, 163, 168; vi. 132, 148; viii. 34, 167; ix. 14, 19, 187, 208; xia. 71, 83; xiii. 80; xv. 27, 31; xviii. 89, etc. (11 times); xix. 75, 93; xx. 304; xxi. 542; xxii. 2; xxviii. 8. [Note dp. tīman, iii. 29, 138; xix. 93.]

getimbrian, II. *to build, construct.* iii. 83; xiv. 121; xx. 110.

getimbrung, f. (*act of*) *building, edification.* xviii. 152.

getīmian, II, impers. *to happen.* vi. 296; xiv. 1; and w. dat. of person, xia. 68; xix. 58, 227.

tintreg, n. *torture.* xviii. 353, 364.

tintregian, II. *to torture, torment.* xvii. 230; xviii. 357.

Tirus, see Tyrus.

tīþa, wk. m. *receiver* of something requested (gen.). viii. 94 (þæt hē þæs tīþa bēo, *that what he has asked will be granted to him*).

tīþian, getīþian, II. (a) trans., *to grant.* viii. 211; impers., passive, w. dat. of person, xvi. 118. (b) intrans., *to grant, assent.* v. 283; w. dat. of person, xvii. 103; and gen. of thing, vi. 53; viii. 65.

tō, prep. *to, for, as.* (a) w. dat. noun or pron., i. 18, 37, etc. (36 times); ii. 9, etc. (15 times); iii. 16, etc. (11 times); iv. 3, etc. (29 times); etc. (b) w. dat. inf., i. 25, etc. (6 times); ii. 93, 165, 167; iii. 104, 105, 127; iv. 89; etc. (c) w. endingless locative, tō ... wīc, vi. 44; and originally todæg, here treated as one word. (d) in traditional combinations w. instr. pron., tō hwī, *for what reason,* xvii. 210; tō þȳ þæt, *in order that,* xxx. 80.—as adv. (a) with verb of motion, expressed or implicit, hither, thither. iii. 18, 124; iv. 46, 240; v. 143; etc.—þǣr . . . tō, thither, xi. 171. þyder þe . . . tō, whither, xix. 235. (b) qualifying an adv., adj., or fela, lȳt, *too.* i. 147, 341; ii. 246 (ealles tō fela, *altogether too many*); v. 101; vi. 202, 295; viii. 108; xii. 107; xiv. 107; xvi. 98; xvii. 175 (ealles tō swīþe); xviii. 169, 390; xx. 39, 40, 235, 396; xxi. 27.—for tō sōþan see sōþ.

toberan, 4. *to carry off.* pres. 3s. toberþ, iii. 69. [Cf. beran.]

toberstan, 3. *to burst asunder.* inf., xxi. 541; pret. 3s. tobærst, xx. 249; xxi. 448, 549. [Cf. berstan.]

tobrecan, 4. *to shatter, break, break through, destroy.* inf., xxi. 543; xxvi. 18, 112; pres. 1s. tobrece, iii. 68; pret. 3s. tobræc, iv. 192; xi. 105; xii. 134; xvii. 224; xx. 66; xxi. 45, 430; xxvi. 12; 3p. tobræcon, xia. 50; xxi. 515, 561; pret. 3s. subj. tobræce, xiii. 208; 3p. subj. tobræcan, xxi. 32; pp. tobrocen, iii. 38; xx. 8; xxiii. 203 (dsn. wk. -an). [Cf. abrecan.]

tobrytan, I. *to break in pieces, destroy.* iii. 69 (pres. 3s. tobryt); xx. 66; xxi. 545 (pp. tobrytt).

tocnāwan, 7. *to know, discern.* inf., i. 268; ii. 232; iii. 48; x. 207; xi. 4, 232, 455; xx. 413; xxi. 90, 265, 269,

tocnāwan (*cont.*)
286, 403, 419, 554; xxix. 70, 113;
pres. 1p. subj. **tocnāwon**, i. 223.
[Cf. **oncnāwan**.]

tocwȳsan, I. *to crush utterly*. iii. 39,
154 (pres. 3s. **tocwȳst**); xvii. 225;
xxi. 517.

tōcyme, m. *coming, advent*. i. 308 (?),
342; ii. 27, 120, 121, 125, 126, 173; vi.
143; viii. 6, 105; ix. 90; xi. 67, 154,
512; xia. 184; xv. 30; xvi. 182;
xviii. 3, 75, 284, 404; xxi. 605, 613;
xxvi. 4; xxviii. 12, 13.

todæg, adv. *today* xi. 73; xvi. 180;
xxiii. 19 (**todæig**).

todǣlan, I. *to distribute, divide*. iv. 18,
21, 38, 98, 108, 155, 171, 187, 193;
ix. 118; xi. 70; xia. 186; xviii. 95.
[Cf. **dǣlan**.]

tōdāl, n. *distinction, difference*. xix.
230.

tofēran, I. *to disperse* (intrans.). xxi.
77 (pret. 3p. **tofērdon**). [Cf. **fēran**.]

*toferian, II. *to separate, pull apart*.
xxi. 557 (translates *distrahuntur*, is
glossed *digerebant*). [This sense not
illustrated in BT. Cf. **ferian**.]

toforan, prep. w. dat. *ahead of, beyond, above*. xvi. 44; xix. 69.

tōforlǣtennyss, f. *intermission*. xi.
562.

togædere, adv. *together*. iii. 144; x.
165; xix. 196; xxi. 255, 445.

togēanes, prep. w. dat. of friendly or
hostile encounters, *to meet, towards,
against*. vi. 50; xia. 166; xvii. 222;
xx. 212; xxii. 63, 88; xxvi. 47;
xxvii. 71.

tohēawan, 7. *to hew in pieces*. pret. 3s.
tohēow, pret. 3s. **tohēow**, xxi. 556.
[Cf. **ahēawan**.]

tōl, n. *tool, implement*. xix. 191.

tolȳsan, I. *to release*. vi. 104. [Cf.
alȳsan.]

tomergen, tomerigen, adv. *to-
morrow*. xx. 226; xxix. 69.

tomiddes, prep. w. dat. *amidst,
among, in the midst of*. xvii. 25, 297;
xx. 61, 272; xxi. 560.

tōnama, wk. m. *surname*. iv. 78; vi. 40.

tosc(e)ādan, 7. (a) with plural object,
to judge between or *among*. i. 379.
(b) with indirect question as object,

to distinguish, decide. xv. 131. (Both
have pres. 3s. **toscǣt**.)

toslītan, I. *to rend, tear apart, lacerate,
bite*; describes the action of (a)
snakes. pp. **tosliten**, xii. 229, 232
(np. -e); xx. 327, 331 (np. wk. -an).
(b) sins likened to snakes. inf.
toslīton, xx. 344. (c) lions. pret. 3p.
subj. **tosliton**, xxi. 463.

tosomne, adv. *together, in succession*.
xi. 30; xia. 130.

tostencan, I. *to drive apart, scatter,
disperse*. iv. 207 (pres. 3s. subj. **to-
stencge**, v.ll. **-stence, -stentte**);
xvii. 75 (pp. np. **tostencte**).

getot, n. *pomp*. iv. 239. [Cf. CH II.
52/7.]

toteran, 4. *to lacerate, tear in pieces*.
pret. 3p. **totǣron**, xx. 343 (of
snakes); xxi. 338 (of lions). [Cf.
teran.]

totwǣman, I. *to divide, separate*. iv.
106; xix. 100 (refl.); xxvii. 66.

tōþ, m. *tooth*. vii. 152; xviii. 433; xx.
101.

tōweard, tōwerd, adj. (a) *future,
(that is* or *was) to come*. ii. 160, 182;
v. 198; vi. 220; ix. 209; xii. 102;
xiii. 79; xiv. 60, 64; xv. 17, 151,
155, 159; xx. 137, 301; xxiv. 3.
*(b) with **þyder** to mark reversal of
the ordinary direction, *about to go,
headed, bound*. xix. 238. [Meaning
(b) not in dict. but cf. BTS, II. 2,
quoting Ælfric.]

tōweard, prep. w. dat. *toward*. only
in separated form: **tō . . . werd**,
xxi. 185; **tō . . . weard**, xxvii. 23.
[Cf. **weard, wiþ . . . weard**.]

towurpan, 3. (a) trans. *to destroy,
break down, disperse, scatter*. pres.
1s. **towurpe**, iii. 70; pret. 3s. **towearp**, xxi. 431, 455; pret. 3p.
towurpon, xxi. 512, 515 (-an);
pp. **toworpen**, iv. 19, 99, 104, 172;
xi. 335; xxi. 346; xxviii. 11. (b) intrans. *to scatter*. pres. 3s. **towyrpþ**,
iv. 40, 199; 3p. **towurpaþ**, iv. 211.
[Cf. **wurpan**.]

traht, m. *tract, sermon, commentary*.
v. 161; vi. 367; xii. 82; xvii. 156.

trahtnere, m. *interpreter, expositor*.
ii. 64; xv. 149.

trahtnian, II. *to interpret.* xxviii. 7.

trahtnung, f. *interpretation.* ii. 61; iii. 50; v. 98.

Traianus, *Trajan* (Roman emperor A.D. 98–117). xxiii. 13, 42 (ds. Traiane), 48.

ġetredan, 5. *to tread, tread down.* pp. ġetreden, xiii. 117. [Cf. fortredan.]

trēow, n. *tree.* xvi. 132; xix. 22.

trēowcynn, n. *kind of tree.* xxi. 529.

ġetrēowe, ġetrȳwe, adj. *true, faithful, trustworthy.* xvi. 208, 211, 212, 280, 281, 291; xxii. 99.

trēowen, adj. *of a tree, wooden.* xxi. 547.

ġetrēowlīce, adv. *faithfully.* xvi. 278.

Tripartita Istoria, the history attributed to Cassiodorus, based on three Greek authorities. xxii. 61. [Cf. þrȳfeald Gereccednyss.]

trum, adj. *firm.* comp., np. trumran, xxii. 99.

ġetruma, wk. m. *troop.* as. (ġetru)man (?), xxvii. 90.

trumnyss, f. *strength, firmness.* v. (108), 109 (MS. H).

truwian, II. *to trust.* iv. 38, 187; vi. 216; x. 89; xvii. 105; xxix. 109. [Cf. ortruwian.]

ġetrymman, I. *to confirm, strengthen.* i. 83 (pp. ġetrymmed); ii. 180 (pret. 3s. ġetrymede); ix. 138 (pret. 3s. ġetrymde).

trymming, ġetrymming, f. *confirmation.* ii. 162; viii. 173; xvii. 203 (ġe-), 307.

ġetrȳwe, see ġetrēowe.

*ġetrȳwsian, II. *to make true, faithful.* xvi. 293. [This meaning not in dict. Usually refl., *to prove oneself true.*]

tugon, see tēon.

tunge, wk. f. *tongue.* vii. 114, 116, 151, 152; xvii. 31, 37, 130, 167, 169; xxiii. 185.

tūngerēfa, m. *steward* of an estate. xvi. 4, 39, 87.

tungol, n. or m., wk. nap. tunglan. *star, planet.* xxi. 183 (ap., þā syfan tunglan). [BT and BTS show Ælfric using strong 'tungol'

in sing. and either strong neuter 'tungla' or wk. 'tunglan' in nap.]

tuwa, adv. *twice.* xii. 85; xiv. 147.

twēgen, m., twā, f., n. *two.* nom. acc. m. twēgen, ii. 224; iii. 143; v. 93, 283; vi. 18; viii. 119; xi. 129; xia. 47; xviii. 31, etc. (13 times); xix. 62, 166, 191; xx. 200; xxi. 462, 534; xxiii. 126; xxx. 94.—nom. acc. f. twā, ii. 115; xvi. 94; xvii. 51; xviii. 33, etc. (9 times); xxi. 261.— nom. acc. n. twā, ii. 146; xiv. 5, 53; xv. 144; xvii. 239; xix. 192; xxi. 232, 462; on twā, *in two, into two parts,* xia. 224; xviii. 95.—dat. twām, i. 460; ii. 142, 146; iii. 144; iv. 57; xia. 121; xii. 224; xv. 145, 147; xx. 360; xxi. 534; xxiii. 207; twǣm, xxiii. 3. [Note contrast of m. and f. in xviii. 31–35 and 86 sqq.]

twelf, num. *twelve.* vi. 25, 343, 349 (twice), 354; xi. 354, 355; xia. 81, 122; xx. 114, 147, 148; xxi. 358; xxiii. 39.

twelffeald, adj. *twelvefold.* vi. 354.

twelfta, wk. adj. *twelfth.* xi. 12; xia. 86.

twēntig, num. *twenty.* xx. 65; xxiii. 157 (twēnti).

twēo, twȳ, wk. m. *doubt.* only in phrase, būtan twēon, ix. 156; twȳn, vii. 145; x. 114. [On the form twȳn see note on vii. 145.]

twēonian, twȳnian, II. impers. w. dat. of person, *to cause doubt.* viii. 94; xxiii. 150.

*twēonung, f. *ambiguity, divergence.* x. 72. [BT only approaches this meaning with 'uncertainty' but quotes Ælfric's Grammar, 'Butan twynunge *absque ambiguitate.*']

twīfeald, twȳfeald, adj. *twofold, double.* xi. 255, 569 (wk. as noun, be twȳfealdan).

twȳ, see twēo.

twȳnian, see twēonian.

tyhtan, tihtan, I, pret. tiht-. (a) *to draw* the mind to something, *incite, exhort, urge, persuade.* xii. 144; xvi. 288 (pres. 3s. tiht); xvii. 110; xviii. 373; xix. 145; xxi. 495; xxii. 70. (b) *to draw out, stretch.* xxiii. 192 (pres. 3s. tyht). [Cf. mistihtan.]

tyhting, f. *exhortation.* xxiii. 141.

tӯman, I. *to bring forth, engender, be fruitful.* xviii. 320; xix. 108, 110. [Cf. untӯmende.]

tӯn, num. *ten.* i. 373; iv. 147; viii. 142; xi. 54; xia. 171; xvii. 24, 80 (see next).

Tӯn Burhscīra, *Decapolis,* a district east of Jordan on the Sea of Galilee. xvii. 24(?), 80. (In 24 probably descriptive rather than a place-name.)

tӯrgan, III (var. of 'tēorian', 'tӯrian', II). *to tire, weary, exhaust.* xx. 234 (pret. 3p. tӯrigdon, glossed *exasperabant*).

Tyrus, Tirus, the city of *Tyre.* xvii. 51, 61 (ds. Tyro), 65.

getӯþian, see getīþian.

þ

þā, adv. *then.* i. 20, 23, 388, 438; ii. 24, 28, etc. (35 times in ii–iv); etc.— used correlatively after þā þā and other temporal conjunctions to introduce main clause. ii. 8, 32; iii. 10; iv. 3, 50, 262, 269; etc.—conj. *when,* usually þā þā, *(then) when, since.* i. 442; ii. 7, 30, 85, 264; iii. 9, 40, 162, 180; iv. 17, 97, 141, 194, 264; etc. occas. þā . . . þā, e.g. *(then) . . . when,* ii. 42; or in reversed order, xxiii. 135; confined to sub. clause, *when . . . (then),* vi. 3.—for þā gӯt see gӯt.

þā, pron. adj., see sē.

þæ, see þe.

þæm, þæne, see sē.

þær, þār, adv. *there.* ii. 14, 24, 28, 45, 51, 148; iv. 82, 93; v. 113, 282, 283; etc.—conj. *where.* v. 189, 262, 276; vi. 44, 70; etc.—þær þær, conj. *(there) where.* ii. 85; iv. 113; v. 43, 281; etc.—spelled þar at xi. 551 and xxi. 76, 251, etc. (13 times).

þæra, þæræ, see sē.

þæræfter, adv. *thereafter.* xia. 189.

þære, see sē.

*þærfore, adv. (in payment) *for that, for it.* xxx. 104. [This compound not in dict. For the rule governing its class, see BT, 'þær', IV.]

þærinne, adv. *therein.* iii. 5; xxiii.125; spelled þarinne, xxi. 195.

þærof, adv. *thereof, from there.* v. 24.

þæron, adv. *therein.* xi. 4, 484, 489; xix. 169, 179.

þærrihte, adv. *thereupon, forthwith.* xi. 303.

þærtō, adv. *thereto.* xii. 231 (with besāwon, *looked upon it*); xiii. 35; xviii. 283. spelled þarto, xxi. 196, 198.

þærtoēacan, adv. *besides, in addition to that.* xv. 119; xvi. 44, 177; xx. 363, 389; xxvi. 96 (þār-).

þærtogēanes, adv. *on the contrary, in opposition to that.* xx. 406; xxvi. 136 (þār-).

*þærwiþ, adv. *close by.* xiv. 11, 76. [This meaning not in dict.]

*þærwiþinnan, adv. *within it, therein.* iii. 86. [Not in dict. OED, 'there-within', cites as two words in EME (1200). Here one word (adv. plus prep.) seems a little better than two (two adverbs).]

þæs, see sē.

þæt, conj. *that,* introducing: (a) a substantive clause. i. 21, etc. (122 times in i–vii). (b) a clause of purpose, result, or manner, *(in order) that, (so) that, (in such a way) that.* i. 13, etc. (71 times in i–vii).—for swā þæt, see swā. (c) a causal clause, *in that, because.* iv. 290; vi. 340 (only these two in i–vii).

þæt, pron., see sē.

geþafian, II. (a) *to permit.* with dat. of pers. and clause as obj., xiii. 63; w. þæt as obj., xvii. 237; elliptically, implying infin. obj., iii. 100; w. clause as obj., person unspecified, i. 162; viii. 197; xia. 218; xiii. 28, 150.—(b) *to assent to a request* by somebody (dat.) that one act in a certain way (clause). xxvii. 69. [Meaning (b) approximated in BTS though no exact parallel.]

geþafung, f. *consent.* vi. 174; xviii. 291; xxix. 101.

þām, þan, see sē.

þanc, m. *thanks.* xxiii. 139.

geþanc, n. *thought.* vi. 180; xvi. 121.

þances, adv. *willingly.* xxix. 54.

þancian, II, w. dat. of person. *to thank*. w. gen. of thing, iii. 181; xi*a*. 231; w. clause giving the reason for thanks, vi. 93 (pres. 1s. þanciġe); xi. 266.

þanon, adv. *thence*. ii. 194; vi. 337; xi. 190, 214; xi*a*. 28; xvii. 141; xxi. 229.—conj. *whence*. vi. 45; xiv. 166 (þanan) ; xxi. 291.

þār, þǣr-, see þǣr, þǣr- ; þāra, see sē.

þe, þē, indecl. rel. particle. (a) as substitute for an inflected relative pronoun, *that, who, which,* etc. i. 4, 19, 43, etc.—usually subj. or obj. but may imply a prep., e.g., iv. 1 (time *in which, when*) or be the object of a following prepositional adverb, e.g. ii. 179, 190, 256.—(b) as sign of the relative in combination with the demonstrative, often not to be separately translated. e.g. sē þe, i. 384; þā þe, i. 49, and w. prep., on þam þe, *in which,* i. 8; þurh þone þe, *by whom,* i. 170. (c) as an enclitic element in various compound conjunctions. e.g. for þan þe, mid þam þe, þēah þe, etc.— spelled þæ, i. 50; xviii. 295.

þē, pers. pron., see þū.

þē, þe, instr. neuter pron., with comparatives, see sē and þȳlǣste.

þēah, conj. *though.* ii. 77; vi. 292; xix. 106; xxi. 180; xxvi. 57; xxvii. 3.— þēah þe, i. 159, 267, 349; ii. 81, 107, 239, 282; iii. 94, 168; iv. 130; v. 102, 230; vi. 59, etc. (9 times); etc. —adv. *nevertheless, yet.* i. 206; iii. 170; vi. 266; xi. 134; xxiii. 195.— much more often in conjunction with swā : see swāþēah.

þēah, vb. , see þēon.

þeaht, n. *counsel, advice.* xv. 15, 143 (gs. þeahtes, translating Lat. *concilio*).

geþeaht, n. *thought, consideration, counsel.* ix. 38, 140; xv. 145, 146.

þearf, f. *need.* xix. 117; xxvii. 16, (107?).—in phrase, tō þearfe, *as is needed, for (one's) benefit.* w. dat. of person, viii. 19; xx. 279; xxii. 86; xxx. 90; enclosing gen. of person, xxii. 70.

þearfa, wk. m. *poor man, beggar.* ii. 90; viii. 156; xi. 431; xiii. 113; xvi. 151, 168, 177, 271; xxv(*c*). 9 (twice); xxx. 34, 97.

þearft, see þurfan.

þearle, adv. *greatly, violently, mightily.* xxi. 451; xxvi. 33. [Cf. forþearle.]

þēaw, m. *custom, habit, way* of behaving. only in plural, vi. 203; ix. 76; xiv. 65, 106; xvi. 238, 252; xvii. 118, 262; xviii. 373; xix. 22, 140; xx. 395.

þēawlēas, adj. *incapable of acquiring good habits, incorrigible.* xvii. 266.

þegen, þegn, þēn, m. *minister, noble attendant, thane.* viii. 151; xi. 543; xiii. 188; xvi. 151; xvii. 152; xviii. 65; xix. 12, 140; xx. 221, 407; xxi. 353, 669, 673; xxii. 30, 42, 45, 46; xxiii. 53 (þeign-) ; xxv(*a*). 4, 7; xxvi. 85. [Cf. þēnian, þēnung.]

þegenlic, adj. *befitting a thane, noble, brave.* xix. 156.

þelǣste, see þȳlǣste.

þēn, see þegen.

þencan, I. *to think.* vi. 205 (pres. 3s. subj. þence); xix. 17 (pret. 1s. þōhte). [Cf. beþencan and next entry.]

geþencan, I. *to think of, consider, remember.* vi. 162 (pres. 3s. ġeþengþ, v.l. ġeþencþ) ; xiii. 61; xv. 20, 192.

þēnian, II. w. dat. (a) *to serve, minister to.* xi. 447, 544; xxv(*a*). 2 (twice), 4, 7, 9 (twice), 13, 15. (b) ironically, *to serve* (ill), *treat* (badly). iii. 123. [BTS cites Beow. 560, 'ic him þenode deoran sweorde'. No other example of ironic sense. Cf. OED, 'serve', 47.]

þēnung, f. *service, ministry.* ix. 15, 188; xii. 92 (as. þēnunga for -e); xvi. 141 ; xix. 12; xx. 228; xxv(*a*) 15. [For the form in xii. 92, cf. S–B 255. 1.]

þēod, f. *people, nation, tribe.* i. 348; iii. 37, 53, 60, 157; vi. 310; vii. 198, 206; ix. 101, 106; xii. 26, 167 variant; xiv. 51, 98; xix. 14, 71, 90; xx. 390; xxi. 124, 522; xxvi. 62.

þēof, m. *thief.* xi. 377, xvi. 160.

þēon, geþēon, 2 (orig. 1, 3). *to thrive,*

þēon, geþēon (cont.)
prosper, flourish. inf. geþēon, vi.
195; pres. part. þēonde, xxvi. 6;
pret. 3s. þēah, xxi. 641.—Gode
geþēon, *to prosper in the Lord, advance spiritually in God's service.*
inf., xii. 172; xvii. 276; pret. 3p.
geþugon, iii. 93.—geþogen, pp.
as adj. *advanced* (in moral or
physical development). xxvii. 84.
[Cf. geþungen, ungeþungen.]

þēos, see þēs.

þēostru, fp. *darkness.* i. 35 (twice),
291, 292 (twice, 1st time þystr-),
322; vi. 348; viii. 182; xxviii. 13.

þēow, m., þēowa, wk. m. *servant, slave.*
weak forms, iii. 10, 12, 15, 122
(ap. -an); xi. 400 (ns. -a); xvi. 211
(voc. s. -a); xxiii. 87 (ds. -an); xxx.
108 (ns. -a).—indeterminate, dp.
þēowum, xvi. 271; xxx. 94.—
strong, xxv(a). 17 (np. þēowas).

þēow, adj. *servile.* xxvi. 92.

þēowan, I. (a) w. dat. *to serve.* iii. 60;
xxi. 379, 390. (b) w. acc. and dat.
*to put at the service of, devote
to.* xxi. 170. [See BTS, second
'þeowan', II, citing this passage from
Kemble. Cf. þēowian.]

þēowdōm, m. *service.* viii. 136; xi.
54, 74, 91; xia. 171, 231; xiv. 96;
xviii. 94, 97, 100, 161; xix. 57.

þēowian, II, w. dat. *to serve.* ii. 260;
iv. 216; xi. 5; xviii. 127, 161;
xxiii. 197; xxv(a). 18; xxix. 82;
xxx. 99. [Cf. þēowan.]

þēowot, n. *servitude, enslavement.* ii.
261; xia. 84, 135; xx. 3, 110, 115
(all six ds. þēowte).

þēowtlic, adj. *servile.* ii. 257, 261.

þerrscwald, m. *threshold.* xxi. 232
(ds. -e, v.l. þrexwolde).

þēs, m., þēos, f., þis, n., dem. pron.
and adj. *this.*—prevailing forms, one
example each: sg. masc. þēs, i. 39;
þises, iv. 88; þisum, i. 1; þisne, i.
43; fem. þēos, i. 164; gen. þissere,
viii. 225; dat. þissere, i. 205; acc.
þās, i. 341; neut. nom. acc. þis,
i. 30; ii. 59; þises, iv. 273; þisum,
i. 157; pl. all genders, nom. acc.
þās, ii. 54; iv. 252; gen. þissera,
viii. 182; dat. þisum, i. 455.—

variant forms: gsm. or n. þisses,
x. 188, v.l.; xvi. 85; dsm. or n.
þissum, xxiii. 1, 5, 61; dsn. þyson,
xxv(a). 1; nasn. þiss, xxiii. 65;
xxvi. 40; þyss, vi. 112; gdsf. þisre,
xi. 72, v.l.; xxi. 668, v.l.; þysre,
ii. 170; þisse, xi. 72, v.l.; xxi. 498;
þysse, xviii. 46; dp. þissum,
xxx. 112.—nearly all forms with i
occur also with y.—instr. m. or n.
'þys' does not appear.

þicgan, I (orig. 5). *to partake of, eat,
taste.* xi. 178, 179; xxi. 382, 427
(pret. 3p. þigdon). [This vb. regularly strong in the poetry, weak
in Ælfric and other prose writers.]

þider, þyder, adv. *thither.* ii. 30, 36;
vi. 24, 31, 305; xviii. 39, 205; xx.
31; xxi. 582; xxv(c). 19 (w. þær,
conj.).—þyder þe, conj. *whither.*
vii. 51; xix. 235, 238.

þīn, poss. pron. and adj. *thy, thine.*
i. 103, 104, 105, 225, 369; ii. 39,
etc. (11 times); v. 33, 38, 95, 286; vi.
55, 194; etc. [See þū.]

þincan ('þyncan'), geþyncan, I. (a)
without prefix, w. dat., *to seem to*
(someone). pres. 3s. þincþ, vi. 205;
xxi. 371, 419; xxvi. 89; pret. 3s.
þūhte, xix. 156; xxi. 249; xxix. 16;
subj., i. 147. (b) w. pref. and dat.,
to seem good to (someone). pres. 3s.
subj. geþynce, xxiii. 183. (c) pp.
geþūht, with bēon, without dat.
of person, *to be considered, seem.* vi.
112; xi. 555; xx. 164. [Cf. ofþincan.]

geþincþ, geþingþ, f. *dignity, rank,
office.* i. 360 (np. geþingþu); viii.
102; xviii. 144, 164; xix. 14; xxi.
102; xxx. 14 (as. geþincþe). [EWS
'geþyncþ(u)'. The ns. does not occur
here and is not recorded in BT, but
Ælfric does not retain '-u' in the ns.
of other words of this declension.
Cf. cȳþþ, mærþ, myrhþ, gesælþ,
strengþ, yrhþ, yrmþ.]

þīnen, f. *maid-servant, handmaid.* xia.
67.

þing, n. *thing.* i. 254, 467; ii. 184;
iii. 104; iv. 35, 184; v. 67; vii. 28,
30, 76, 84, 121, 215, 217, 220; etc.—
ealle þing, nap. *all things.* i. 31,

88, 103, 112, 167, 170; ii. 157, 214; v. 58; vi. 228; viii. 47, 211, 242, 245; ix. 38; etc.; gp. **ealra þinga**, xxi. 9; dp. **eallum þingum**, xxi. 24.—**fela þing**, v.l. **fela þinga**, *many things.* vii. 24, 187, 189; x. 24, 185; etc.—**sum þing**, *something.* ii. 56, 187, 279; viii. 166; xiii. 91, 92 (np. **sume þing**); xv. 21, 193, 203; xx. 9; xxix. 2.—**sumera þinga**, gp. as adv., *in some respects.* xvii. 64 (used by Ælfric in CH I. 190/16 and 236/11; see BT, 'þing', 11). [For **ǣnig þing, nān þing**, see **ǣnig, nān**.]

þingere, m. *intercessor.* viii. 212.

þingian, II. *to mediate, intercede.* w. **for**, viii. 39, 207; w. dat. of person, xi. 240; xxvi. 122. [Cf. **foreþingian**.]

þingrǣden, f. *intercession.* xi. 190.

ġeþingþ-, see **ġeþincþ**.

þingung, f. *intercession.* i. 232. [Cf. **foreþingung**.]

þis(s), þis-, see **þēs**.

ġeþogen, see **þēon**.

ġeþōht, m. *thought.* iv. 17, 97; vi. 174, 285, 288, 289; viii. 248; xi. 393, 558; xv. 100; xviii. 116; xix. 181.

þōhte, see **þencan**.

þolian, II. *to suffer, endure, undergo.* xiv. 191; xix. 231.

þon, þone, see **sē**.

þonne, adv. *then* (marking temporal coincidence or sequence or logical consequence). ii. 37, 148, 240; iv. 22, 26, etc. (19 times); v. 277; vi. 115, 169, 190, 227; etc.—conj. *when.* ii. 36, 110; iii. 26; iv. 34, 41, 67, 183, 212, 232; v. 51, 58, 163, 169, 229; vi. 132, 139; etc.—*seeing that, since.* i. 426; v. 15; vi. 120, 259; etc.— conj. with comparatives, *than.* i. 57, 163, 433; ii. 100, 103; iii. 176; iv. 48, etc. (8 times); v. 23; vi. 106, 115, 123, 208; etc.

Þōr, the Scandinavian God *Thor*, corresponding to OE. 'þunor'. xxi. 124, 142.

þorfte, see **þurfan**.

þorn, m. *thorn.* iii. 73.

*****þrafian**, II. *to press accusingly for an answer, keep asking bitterly.* xx. 224.

[Ordinarily *to press* or *rebuke*, but here the reproachful attack is made by an insistent question. Nothing precisely similar in BT.]

þrēagan, II. *to reprove, rebuke.* inf., xv. 165; imp. sg. **þrēa**, xv. 171; pres. 3s. **þrēaþ**, vii. 16, 19, 20, 22, 73, 85, 162, 171; pret. 3s. **þrēade**, vii. 76, 78, 83; xvii. 293. [S–B 415, d; Cpb 759.]

þridda, adj. *third.* i. 447; vi. 196; ix. 159; xi. 371; xia. 6, 143; xx. 218, 257; xxi. 170; xxx. 96.

þrimfealdum, see **þrȳfeald**.

þringan, 3. *to throng.* pret. 3s. **þrang**, xiii. 194.

þrītiġwintre, adj. *thirty years old.* xx. 186.

þrittig, num. *thirty.* ii. 29, 139 (as sb. w. part. gen.); xxi. 303 (as adj., dp. -um).

þriwa, adv. *thrice.* i. 452; xix. 130.

þrote, wk. f. *throat.* vii. 153.

þrōwian, II. *to suffer.* trans., ii. 240; xx. 294, 296; xxiii. 3, 181; intrans., vi. 263; viii. 21, 201 (twice); ix. 3; x. 186, 200; xi. 41, 189, 306, 494, 495 (pres. 3s. subj. **þrōwiġe**), 496; xia. 144; xii. 234; xv. 147, 159; xx. 339; xxiii. 5.

þrōwung, f. *passion, suffering.* i. 447; ii. 131, 219; v. 142, 235; vii. 181; x. 148; xi. 34; xia. 134; xii. 190, 203; xiv. 150, 158; xx. 345; xxi. 149; xxiii. 6.

þrūh, f. *tomb.* vi. 91 (ds. **þrȳh**, v.l. **þrūh**). [An athematic noun: S–B 284; Cpb 628.]

þrȳ, m., **þrēo**, f. and n., num. *three.* nom. acc. m. **þrȳ**, i. 17, 76, 162; iv. 170; vi. 171, 172, 211; viii. 197, 203; xi. 85; xia. 216, 218; xxi. 21, 22, 23; xxix. 94. acc. f. **þrēo**, vi. 173 (**on þrēo wīsan**, v.l. **on þri[m] wīsum**); xi. 111; xiv. 44. nom. acc. n. **þrēo**, ii. 184; xv. 152; xviii. 369; xx. 65. gen. **þrēora**, i. 23; vi. 161 (v.l. **þrīra**). dat. **þrim, þrym**, vi. 318; vii. 84; xia. 200; xviii. 200, 218; xix. 122; xxi. 24, 292.

þrȳfeald, adj. *threefold, triple.* vi. 172 (asm. wk. **þrȳfealdan**); xxiii. 80, 81 (dp. with each member of the

þrȳfeald (cont.)
compound declined, þrimfealdum; see note).

Þrȳfeald Gereccednyss, f. the Historia Tripartita attributed to Cassiodorus. xxii. 61. [Cf. Tripartita.]

þrȳfealdlīce, adv. in three ways, triply. vi. 210.

*þrȳfyrclede, adj. three-pronged. xxvii. 34. [Not in dict. but cf. BT 'twifyrclede', normalized from Ælfric's Grammar, 'twyferclede', ed. Zupitza, p. 288/10, note, and BTS, 'twifyrclian'.]

þrȳh, see þrūh.

þrymlic, adj. powerful, mighty(?). xxi. 110 (v.l. þwȳrlic, q.v.). [BT has no example from Ælfric except this passage, quoted from Kemble. The meaning elsewhere is 'glorious, magnificent'. See note.]

þrymm, m. glory. ii. 19; iv. 167; xviii. 406.

þrymsetl, n. seat of majesty, throne. xi. 347 (ds. -setle), 405 (ds. -settle).

þrymwealdend, adj. modifying God, glory-ruling. i. 85; xi. 85; xxi. 665. [For this adjectival use of a nominal form, cf. eallwealdend.]

þrynnyss, f. trinity. i. 165 (þrym-); xia. 216; the Trinity, i. 85; vi. 266; ix. 90, 107; x. 173; xi. 73, 79; xia. 6, 17 (MS. þrym-), 190, 195; xii. 88, 90; xxi. 20, 26, 28, 665.

þū, pron. 2d. person, thou, etc.— examples of forms: ns. þū, i. 102; gs. þīn occurs only as poss. adj., see separate entry; ds. þē, i. 225; as. þē, i. 227; np. gē, i. 120; gp. ēower, as partitive, vi. 369; vii. 11; xiii. 215; xviii. 63; xx. 226; for the poss. adj. see separate entry; dp. ēow, i. 69; ap. ēow, v. 45; the dual only as acc. inc, xxiii. 75. [See also hwylc-ēower.]

geþugon, see geþēon.

þūhte, geþūht, see þincan.

geþungen, adj. (pp. of geþēon, q.v., as of class 3). distinguished. xviii. 210; xix. 11. comp., ap. geþungen-ran, xix. 10.

þunor, m. thunder. i. 454; xx. 32.

Þunresdæg, m. Thursday. xi. 51; xix. 123.

[þurfan], pret. pres. vb. to need, be required, must, have occasion to. pres. 2s. þearft, xi. 125; 1p. þurfe wē, v. 174; þurfon, v. 185; viii. 249; pres. 1s. subj. þurfe, v. 32, 153; 3s. subj., xv. 159; pret. 3s. þorfte, vi. 339.

þurh, prep. w. acc. through. (a) in a physical sense, xxi. 199, 595. (b) figuratively, indicating the means, instrument, agent, cause, through, by (the action of), by means of, by the aid of, by reason of, in consequence of. i. 11, etc. (21 times); ii. 3, etc. (19 times); iii. 34, 61; iv. 7, etc. (17 times); etc.

þurhgān, anom. vb. to go through, penetrate. pres. 3s. þurhgǣþ, xix. 32.

*þurh-hlynnan, I. to resound through, thunder through (?). pres. 3s. subj. þurh-[hlyn]ne, xv. 179. [Conjectural reading; see note.]

þurhsēon, 5. to see into. inf., viii. 248. [Cf. gesēon.]

þurhtēon, 2. (a) to carry out, accomplish. inf., ii. 156. (b) to perpetrate. pret. 3s. þurhtēah, xi. 500. [Cf. tēon.]

þurhwunian, II. to persevere, continue, remain. i. 402, 416; ii. 106; xviii. 85, 391; xix. 73; xxi. 299; xxiii. 196.

þurst, m. thirst. ii. 112; xi. 560; xxi. 41.

þurstig, adj. thirsty. xi. 421 (asm. þurstine), 440, 446 (asm. þurstigne); xvi. 195.

þūsend, n. thousand. (a) as a pure numeral, undeclined, usually with partitive gen., e.g. fīf þūsend manna, xia. 119; similarly xia. 123; xx. 10; irregularly seofon þūsenda manna, xxvi. 37 (v.l. þūsend); gen. omitted but implicit in sume twā þūsend, xvii. 239 (MS. H perhaps originally þūsenda). (b) declined as a plural substantive, thousands, i.e. more than one set of a thousand individuals each. xia. 21 (manega

þūsenda, ap. or gp.); xvii. 249 (tō
syx þūsendum) ; xx. 65 (þūsenda,
ap.), 270 (the same); xxii. 65 (feala
þūsenda, ap. or gp.).

þus(s), adv. *thus.* i. 138, 155, 375, 446,
452, 455; ii. 164; iii. 30; iv. 260;
v. 71, etc.; vi. 210; etc.

ᵹeþwǣrian, II. *to agree, be reconciled.* iv. 201.

ᵹeþwǣrlǣcan, I, w. dat. *to comply
with, observe.* xi. 91. [Cf. -lǣcan.]

ᵹeþwǣrnyss, f. *fellowship.* xi. 552.

þwēal, n. *washing, bath.* xiii. 233;
xvii. 266.

þwēan, 6. *to wash.* pret. 3s. þwōh,
ii. 14. [See also aþwēan.]

þwȳr, adj. *crooked, perverse.* xv. 165
(ap. wk. as noun, þwȳran).

þwȳrlic, adj. *perverse.* vi. 285; xxi.
110 (MS. S; other MSS. þrymlic,
q.v.).

þȳ, see þȳlǣste, tō, and sē.

þyder, see þider.

þȳlǣste, þelǣste, þȳ lǣs þe, þe
lǣs þe, conj. *lest.* ii. 56; v. 101; vi.
369; xix. 91, 144, 154; xx. 209, 402;
xxii. 49; xxiii. 138; xxvi. 70.
[Originally instr. þȳ with comp.
lǣs, q.v., and particle þe. Alter-
nation of particle þe with te seems
to show that the phrase was beginning to be treated as a single word.]

ᵹeþyld, n. or f. *patience.* ds. ᵹeþylde,
xv. 171. [BTS cites neuter for
Ælfric; elsewhere often fem.]

ᵹeþyldiᵹ, adj. *patient.* ii. 195.

þyllic, adj. *of that sort, such.* i. 154;
xia. 127; xvi. 200.

ᵹeþynce, see þincan.

þyrlian, II. *to pierce.* xix. 31.

þyrstan, I. impers. w. dat. of pers.
to thirst. pres. 3s. þyrst, v. 26, 27,
137, 138, 149; subj. þyrste, v. 32,
143, 153; pret. 3s. þyrste, v. 243;
xi. 413.

þȳstrum, see þēostru.

þȳwan, I. *to rebuke, threaten.* xvii. 211.

U (vocalic)

ufan, ufon, adv. *from above.* iv. 95;
x. 98; xxvii. 36.

ufeweard, adj. *later, the latter part of.*
xi. 33; xia. 133.

unamānsumod, pp. adj. *relieved
from sentence of excommunication.*
xix. 64.

unametendlic, adj. *not to be
measured.* i. 182. [Not in dict. but
see the one instance of the closely
similar 'unametenlic' in BTS.]

unasecᵹendlic, adj. *unutterable, in-
effable.* i. 132, 144; xviii. 439.

unasecᵹendlīce, adv. *ineffably.* vi.
230.

unatēoriᵹende, adj. *untiring;* here
with reference to eyes, *undimmed.*
dp. unatēoriᵹ(endum), i. 16. [The
application here is unrecorded
but the general sense is well attested.]

unbeᵹunnen, adj. *without beginning.*
vi. 232, 256; xxi. 21. [Cf. beᵹin-
nan.]

unbindan, 3. *to unbind.* inf., xxvi.
107, 114; pres. 3s. unbint, vii. 105;
pret. 3s. unband, xxvi. 126; 3s.
subj. unbunde, xxvi. 77, 100; pp.
unbunden, xvii. 37, 169. [Cf.
ᵹebindan.]

*ᵹeunblissian, II. *to make unhappy.*
viii. 125 (pp. ᵹeunblissod).
[Unique in this passage; cited by
Napier.]

uncer, poss. adj., 1st pers. dual. *of us
two.* xxiii. 71. [See ic.]

unclǣne, adj. *unclean.* iv. 41, 70, 212,
242; xvii. 231, 232, 303.

unctus, given as Lat. equivalent of
Messias. v. 209.

uncūþ, adj. *unknown.* vii. 198.

uncūþlīce, adv. *in an unfriendly
manner, unkindly.* viii. 156.

uncyst, f. *niggardliness.* xxx. 53 (as.
uncyste).

uncystiᵹ, adj. *niggardly.* ii. 89.

undēadlic, adj. *immortal.* xi. 250.

undēadlicnyss, f. *immortality.* xi. 42;
xia. 145.

under, prep. w. dat. *under.* (a) of
physical position, xx. 249; xxi. 407,
426, 565. (b) under iuce, *under yoke.*
lit. xxi. 261; fig. xix. 84. (c) of subordination to a person, ix. 53; xxii.
7; xxiii. 13. (d) of subordination

under (*cont.*)
to or inclusion within one of the
two divine dispensations: under
Moyses lage, vii. 201; xv. 10, 62,
126; under Godes gyfe, ix. 192;
xv. 31 (gife); xx. 299.
underbæc, adv. *backwards, back.*
xviii. 243, 313; xxi. 186.
underfōn, 7. *to receive, take, assume.*
i. 35, 46, 47, 292, 344, 350; ii. 174,
183; iii. 11; iv. 261; v. 81, 147, 249;
vi. 263; vii. 30, 37, 57, 220; etc.
[Forms include inf., xxvi. 68; imp.
sg. -fōh, xxvi. 72; imp. pl. -fōþ,
vii. 57; pres. 3s. -fēhþ, v. 81;
-fēcþ, v. 249; pl. -fōþ, ii. 174; pret.
3s. -fēng, iv. 261; pl. -fēngon, i.
35; -fēncgon, xx. 297; pret. pl.
subj. -fēngon, iii. 11; pp. -fangen,
ii. 183 (dsf. -re).—Cf. fōn.]
undergytan, 5. *to understand.* inf., v.
99; pres. 3s. subj. undergyte, xviii.
236, 280. [Cf. be-, forgytan.]
underntīd, f. *the third hour,* about
9 a.m. xxiii. 24.
understandan, 6. *to understand.* inf.,
v. 159; vii. 25, 188, 191; xvi. 64, 86,
149; xviii. 42, 314, 317; d. inf.
-standenne, xi. 430; xxx. 58; imp.
pl. -standaþ, xi. 287; pret. 3s.
-stōd, xii. 59; xvi. 60. [Cf. standan.]
underþēod(d), adj. (pp. of 'under-
þeodan', I). *subservient, subject,
subordinate.* xiii. 63; xv. 174 (dp.
-þēoddum, as noun); xvi. 19, 127;
xix. 126; xxx. 4.
underþēodnyss, f. *submission,
obedience.* ix. 143.
*undīgol, adj. *manifest.* xi. 404 (np.
undīgle). [Not in dict.; cf. BT,
'undigollice'.]
undōn, anom. vb. *to undo, unfasten,
open.* inf., xv. 185; pret. 3s. undyde, xvii. 151. [Cf. dōn.]
unēaþe, adv. *not easily, with difficulty.*
vii. 41.
*unfæderlīce, adv. *in an unfatherly
manner.* xxi. 107. [Only in this
passage; cited in BTS from Kemble,
and in BT from Wulfstan's revision.]
unforht, adj. *fearless, unafraid.* xi.

63; xia. 180; xx. 59 (np. -e, or adv.);
xxiii. 120.
unforhte, adv. *fearlessly.* xx. 59 (or
adj., np.).
unforwandodlīce, adv. *unabashedly;
inconsiderately, without compunction.*
vi. 166; xiii. 58.
ungebētt, adj. (neg. pp. of gebētan).
unatoned, unexpiated. xi. 396 (np.
wk., ungebēttan). [Cf. bētan.]
ungederod, adj. *unharmed.* xxi. 299.
[Cf. derian.]
*ungedwimorlīce, adv. *without taint
of magical illusion.* vii. 38. [Unique
in this passage. Cited by Napier.
Definition adapted from Napier
and Toller.]
unge-endod, adj. *without end.* xxi. 21.
[Cf. ge-endian.]
ungefullod, adj. *unbaptized.* xi. 498.
[Cf. gefullian.]
ungehealtsum, adj. *incontinent.* xix.
87.
ungehȳrsum, adj. *disobedient.* xix.
57, 60.
ungelǣred, adj. *untaught, ignorant.*
xiv. 229. [Cf. gelǣred.]
ungelēaffull, adj. *unbelieving.* i. 345;
iv. 67; xix. 95, 96, 97, 98. as noun,
unbeliever, infidel. i. 296 (np. wk.,
-an).
ungelēaffulnyss, f. *unbelief, in-
credulity.* iv. 95; vii. 86.
ungerīpod, adj. *unripened, prema-
ture.* xi. 114, 116. [Cf. gerīpian.]
ungesǣlig, adj. *unblest, unfortunate,
wretched, unprofitable, accursed* (applied solely to the morally weak or
wicked). iii. 80, 94; xi. 478; xvii. 98
(ap. ungesǣlige, strong for wk.);
xviii. 101; xix. 238.—wk. as noun,
wretch, poor wretch. xii. 196; xxiii.
188.
ungesǣliglīce, adv. (a) *miserably.*
xxvii. 29. (b) *wickedly.* x. 171.
ungesewenlic, adj. *invisible.* i. 172;
ii. 101, 215; viii. 162, 222, 224;
xia. 3, 25; xii. 118, 125, 162; xviii.
304; xxi. 14.
ungetrȳwe, adj. *untrue, unfaithful.*
xvi. 282, 283, 290.
ungetrȳwþ, f. *unfaithfulness, bad
faith.* xiv. 144.

ungeþungen, adj. *undistinguished, base.* comp., ap. -ran, xix. 10. [Cf. geþungen and þēon.]

ungewemmed, adj. *unspotted, unblemished.* xix. 102, 104. [Cf. gewemman.]

ungewiss, adj. *uncertain, in ignorance.* viii. 149. [The gloss *ignominiosus* is cited by BT and yields a cogent meaning in this passage, but Ælfric elsewhere uses the word in the other sense. Cf. CH II. 350/26. Belfour translates, 'in ignorance'.]

ungewunelic, adj. *unwonted, not customary.* xxx. 111.

unhælþ, f. *infirmity, disease.* xii. 62.

unhāl, adj. *diseased.* xxiii. 121.

unhearmgeorn, adj. *inoffensive.* xvi. 251, 252. [Cited in BT from CH II. 44/20; in BTS from Napier's report of this passage, illustrating unhetol.]

*unhetol, adj. *peaceable, kindly.* xvi. 251. [Unique in this passage. Cited by Napier.]

unhlīsa, m. *ill repute.* vi. 201.

unlūcan, 2. *to unlock.* pret. 3s. unlēac, xxiii. 116. [Cf. belūcan.]

unlust, m. *evil desire, sensuality.* xv. 98; xx. 122.

unlybba, wk. m. *poison.* xvi. 77 (ap. -an). [Ælfric elsewhere treats this weak noun as a masc.]

unlybwyrhta, wk. m. *maker of poisons, sorcerer.* xi. 376; xxiii. 145. [This passage already cited in BTS from Napier's quotation of it under unmæþful. Several other instances in BT.]

unmægþlīce ('-mæþ'), adj. *immoderately, out of measure.* xx. 123 (v.l. unmæþe[līce]?).

*unmæþfull, adj. *immoderate, greedy.* xi. 375 (np., -e). [Unique in this passage. Cited by Napier.]

unmihtig, adj. *weak, of little power.* comp., nsm. unmihtigra, i. 163; x. 161 (-e for -a).

ge-unnan, pret. pres. vb., w. dat. of person. *to grant.* (a) w. gen. as obj., pres. 3s. subj. geunne, iv. 297; pret. 3s. geūþe, i. 202; xvi. 42.

(b) w. acc. or indecl. þe as obj., pres. 3s. geann, xii. 122; pret. 3s. geūþe, i. 206; xx. 293. (c) w. clause as obj., pret. 3s., xviii. 354.

unnytt, adj. *useless, unprofitable.* xxi. 520.

unnyttwyrþe, adj. *useless.* xviii. 194.

unriht, adj. *false, unrighteous, unjust.* ix. 170; xvi. 36 (dp. -an), 254, 259, 262.

unriht, n. *wrong, wickedness, injustice.* i. 221; xiii. 96; xviii. 181.

unrihthǣmed, n. *fornication, adultery.* xix. 128.

unrihtlic, adj. *unjust, unrighteous.* xix. 128 (MS P: see unwīslic).

unrihtlīce, adv. *unrighteously, unlawfully, unjustly.* ii. 79; xiii. 59, 84; xv. 90.

unrihtwīs, adj. *unrighteous.* viii. 18; xvi. 173, 263; xvii. 176; xxvi. 66.— absolute as noun, *unrighteous (ones).* xiii. 45.—wk. w. def. art. as noun, i. 296; vii. 174.

unrihtwīsnyss, f. *unrighteousness.* i. 184, 197; iii. 78; v. 274; xia. 117; xvi. 30, 205; xvii. 166; xviii. 173, 332; xx. 193; xxvi. 119.

unrōtnyss, f. *sadness.* iv. 251; xix. 129.

unrōtsian, II. *to be sorrowful.* vii. 11, 39.

unsceþþignyss, f. *innocence, harmlessness.* xvi. 225.

unscrȳd(d), adj. *unclothed, naked.* xi. 423, 442. [Cf. scrȳdan.]

unscyldig, adj. *guiltless, innocent.* x. 200; xiii. 94 (wk. as noun); xv. 132; xx. 340; xxi. 305; xxvi. 36.

unsīþ, m. *misfortune, time of trouble.* xxix. 38.

unsnotor, adj. *unwise.* xxix. 3 (ap. wk. as noun, unsnoteran).

unstæþþignyss, f. *instability, inconstancy.* xvii. 69.

unsynnig, adj. *without sin.* xi. 17; xia. 91, 137; xii. 234.

*untīma-ǣt, m. *eating at improper times.* xvi. 77. [Not in dict. but the same in sense and formation as 'untīdǣt', BTS. The spelling indicates a compound of two nouns rather than adj. plus noun.]

untodæledlic, adj. *inseparable, indivisible.* vi. 247; xxi. 23.

untrum, adj. *infirm, weak, ill, sick.* ii. 21, 25, 31; vii. 116; xi. 416, 424, 443, 447; xvii. 8; xxvi. 60; xxx. 66 (nsf. **untrum**, not '-u').—as noun, np. **-e**, *the infirm*, ii. 281; dp. with def. art., ii. 134.

ǥe-untrumian, II. *to make ill or infirm, deprive of health or strength.* only as pp., **ǥeuntrumod**. (a) in passive construction implying God as agent, ii. 283; vii. 114. (b) predicatively, agency indefinite, *(taken) ill or sick*, vi. 11, 17; xx. 7; **wearþ ǥeuntrumod tō dēaþe**, *became mortally ill*, xix. 213.

untrumlic, adj. *feeble.* vii. 103.

untrumnyss, f. *sickness, infirmity, weakness.* ii. 23, 29, 186; v. 108, 109; vi. 12; xia. 113; xvii. 9; xix. 155, 159.

untwȳlīce, adv. *indubitably.* iv. 282; vi. 267; viii. 31, 58, 65; x. 28, 206; xii. 17, 117; xxiv. 1. [Cf. **twēo, twȳ.**]

untȳmende, adj. *barren, unfruitful.* xix. 107, 110, 114. [Cf. **tȳman.**]

unþanc, m. *an ill turn, offence.* xv. 204, 211.

unþances, adv. *unwillingly, against one's will.* xix. 229; xxi. 425; xxvi. 2; xxix. 54.

unþearfes, adv. *without a cause, needlessly.* xx. 104. [BT has one citation only, from Paris Psalter.]

unþēaw, m. *evil custom, vice.* x. 39; xiii. 132, 179, 187; xvii. 196; xviii. 371; xix. 212.

unþēawfæst, adj. *disorderly, dissolute.* xv. 175.

unwær, adj. *incautious, unwary.* ix. 177. wk. as noun, ap. **unwaran**, xviii. 324; xxiv. 6.

unwæstmbǣre, adj. *unfruitful.* ii. 83.

unwæteriǥ, adj. *dry, without water.* iv. 42, 213, 217.

unwīslic, adj. *irrational.* xix. 128 (MS C: see **unrihtlic**).

unwīslīce, adv. *unwisely.* xia. 37; xix. 163.

unwittiǥ, adv. *without understanding, unknowing, ignorant* (here used

without reproach to describe little children). xi. 147, 498; xx. 190.

unwrenc, m. *a wicked trick.* xviii. 324.

unwurþ, adj. (a) w. dat. of pers., *ignominious for, dishonouring to.* i. 411. (b) *worthless.* xvi. 71. [Cf. BT, 'unweorþ', IV, IVa, V. The construction and meaning in (a) are not exactly illustrated.]

unwurþian, II. *to dishonour, degrade.* xii. 90 (pp. **ǥeunwurþod**); xvi. 66. [Cf. **wurþian.**]

unwurþlīce, adv. *ignominiously.* xxi. 431.

up, less frequently **upp**, adv. *up.* i. 306, 438; ii. 193, 273; iv. 196; vii. 21, 36, 163; viii. 223; etc. (22 more).

upahebban, 6. *to lift up.* pp. in dat. absolute construction, **upahafenum ēagum**, vi. 92. [Not in BT but in Hall. Same dat. abs. used by Ælfric at CH II. 516/31; LS III. 449, 451; XXXI. 304. See also BTS 'ahebban' with adv. 'up'.]

upflōr, f. *upper chamber* or *storey.* ix. 131 (ds. **-flōra**, v.l. **-flōre**); x. 99 (same); xxi. 308 (ds. **-flōre**, v.l. **-flōra**). [Orig. *u*-stem with later variations. Cf. **flōr.**]

uppan, uppon, prep. w. dat. and acc. *upon, against.* (a) w. acc., iii. 150, 151, 152, 153. (b) w. dat., i. 431; xxix. 95. (c) uncertain, xia. 108.

upplic, uplic, adj. *upper, on high, heavenly.* i. 220; iii. 74; vii. 50; viii. 232; xvi. 199; xvii. 157; xx. 15.

upstiǥe, m. *ascension.* viii. 74; xi. 53; xia. 161; xii. 194; xxi. 512.

ūre, poss. pron. and adj., 1st pers. pl. *our.* i. 97, etc. in predicate, *ours* (e.g. iii. 22). usually inflected (e.g., gp. **ūrra**, ii. 103), but uninfl. **ūre** at i. 97; iii. 181; vi. 265; etc. [For pers. pron. see **ic.**]

urne, see **yrnan.**

ūs, see **ic.**

ūt, adv. *out.* iv. 41, 45, 212, 236; v. 69; vi. 98; viii. 93; x. 165; etc.

ūte, adv. *out, outside.* xi. 485.—**ūttor**, comp. *further out.* xiv. 111.

ǥe-ūtlaǥian, II. *to outlaw, banish.* ix. 13, 173, 180; xii. 52.

*ūtlīce, adv. *remotely? utterly, com-*

pletely? xvii. 142. [Not in dict. See note.]

uton, hortatory auxiliary (1p. subj. of 'wītan', *to go*, weakly stressed) with infin. *let us.* iii. 21, 182; iv. 295; vi. 20, 39, 41, 370; xv. 188; xvi. 84, 237; xvii. 272; xx. 167; xxvii. 6, 8, 62. [BT lists under older forms, 'witon', 'wuton'.]

ġe-ūþe, see **ġe-unnan.**

U (cons.) (= V)

Uenus, the goddess *Venus.* ns., xxi. 115, 150 (v.l. **uena**), 177 (v.l. **uena**).

Uerbum Perfectum, title of book attributed to Hermes Trismegistus. i. 118.

Uita Patrum, the title regularly used by Ælfric for the work now called *Vitæ Patrum* (Migne, PL LXXIII). xix. 62; xxvii. 17. [See note on xix. 62.]

W

wā, interj. w. dat. *woe* (to). iii. 97; xvii. 59 (twice); xviii. 244, 318; xxvii. 5.

wāc, adj. *weak, degraded, base.* xvi. 71; xxiii. 55.

wāce, adv. *weakly, laxly.* xiv. 98.

wacian, II. *to stay awake, watch.* xiv. 20, 116.

wāclīcor, comp. adv. *more cheaply.* xxi. 205. [BT, 'waclice', illustrates this meaning from Ælfric, though not with specific application, as here, to buying and selling.]

ġewǣde, n. *a garment,* pl. *clothes.* xviii. 30 (gp. or ap. **ġewǣda,** v.l. ap. **ġewǣdu**).

wǣfersȳn, f. *a spectacle.* xxi. 566.

wǣgan, I. *to deceive* (intrans.). viii. 227. [For another use of this word by Ælfric see ONT, line 842, cited by BTS. Cf. **awǣgan.**]

wælhrēow, adj. *cruel.* iii. 25; xia. 146; xiii. 210 (**wælrēow**); xvii. 275; xxi. 105.

wælhrēownyss, f. *cruelty, ferocity.* ix. 56; xiii. 58 (**wælrēow-**).

wǣn, m. *carriage, waggon.* xxi. 259, 273, 275, 279.

ġewǣndon, see **ġewendan.**

wǣpen, n. *weapon.* iv. 37, 186, 192; xx. 59; xxi. 443; xxix. 95. [All forms inflected, **wǣpn-,** once **wēpn-,** iv. 192.]

wǣpmann, m. *male, man.* xi. 282, 313 (both times pl. in contrast to **wīfmenn**).

wǣps, m. *wasp.* i. 271. [BT cites glosses only.]

wǣre, wǣron, see **bēon-wesan.**

wǣrlīce, adv. *cautiously, warily.* xxi. 50.

wǣrscipe, m. *caution, prudence.* xv. 123.

wǣs, see **bēon-wesan.**

wǣstm, m. (a) *produce, fruit* (often fig.). i. 217, 273; iii. 9, etc. (12 times); v. 82, 250; viii. 83; xiii. 46; xv. 113; xvi. 104; xix. 23; xx. 149, 151, 378; xxx. 15, 77, 93, 109. (b) *growth, stature.* xvi. 133.

wǣstmbǣre, adj. *fruitful.* xx. 152.

wǣter, n. *water.* i. 396; ii. 19, 21, 37, 130; v. 12, etc. (15 times); xi. 333; xia. 112; xii. 15, 97, 101, 103, 127; xiv. 9, 44, 45, 72; xvi. 195; xix. 30, 31; xx. 22; xxi. 37, 49, 88.

wǣterfæt, n. *water pot, vessel, jug.* v. 64, 214, 220.

wǣterpytt, m. *well.* v. 6, 8, 21 (**-pyt**).

wǣterscipe, m. (*piece of water*), *pool, pond, water* (collectively, as contained in a well or pool). ii. 11, 12, 17, 35, 63, 115; v. 12; viii. 122, 127.

wǣtersēoc, adj. *dropsical.* ii. 266, 270.

wǣterstrēam, m. *stream of water, river.* xi. 19; xia. 93. [This passage cited in BTS from Napier. An instance from the psalms in DT.]

wana, m. *want, deficiency.* xx. 138 (w. substantive vb., dat. of person, gen. of thing).—as adj., *wanting, lacking.* xi. 565 (as complement w. substantive vb. and dat. of person).— in mixed construction, vii. 156, **ne mihte nān wana bēon þam ...**

wana (*cont.*)

Hǣlende ǣniġ his limena, where if wana is an adj. one expects nā; if a noun, ǣniġes. [BT cites Ælfric's Grammar for both uses of 'wana', as noun and as adj.]

wandian, II. *to neglect, omit.* xiii. 178. [Cf. forwandian.]

wanhāl, adj. *sick, infirm, maimed.* ii. 70; xi. 321; xxx. 45.—abs. as noun, pl. *invalids, cripples.* ii. 91; xvi. 168 (wann-).

wanian, II, pp. ġewanod, trans. *to diminish.* x. 168, 169; xi. 264.

wānian, II, intrans. w. refl. dat. *to lament* (for oneself). xix. 219. [The same expression at LS xi. 223.]

wann, see winnan.

wānung, f. *wailing, lamentation.* v. 276; xviii. 433.

warnian, II. (a) trans. *to warn, caution.* ix. 178, 209, 214. (b) reflex., *to warn oneself, take warning, take heed.* ix. 22; xviii. 259, 382; xx. 393. (c) intrans. *to take warning, take heed.* vi. 155 (v.l. refl.); xxi. 49 (v.l. refl.); xxvi. 125 (hēt hine warnian, perhaps elliptical).

ġewarnian, II, trans. *to warn, caution.* xviii. 393. [Like warnian, (a).]

waru, f. *protection, care, defence.* ix. 59; xxii. 75, 84, 95.

wāt, ġewāt, see witan, ġewītan.

wāwa, m. *woe.* xxi. 127. [BT cites Genesis B, Wulfstan, and several examples in Ælfric.]

wē, see ic.

wealcan, 7. *to turn over* in the mind; on mōde wealcan þæt, *to entertain the idea that.* inf., iv. 163.

ġeweald, n. *control.* iii. 110; xxi. 182; xxvi. 9.

wealdan, 7. intr. *to rule, govern.* pres. part., dsm. wk. wealdendan, i. 135. [Cf. next entry and ġewyldan.]

ġewealdan, 7. *to rule, govern, have control of.* (a) w. acc., pres. 3s. ġewylt, i. 135, 359; xi. 79; xia. 195. (b) w. gen., pres. 3s. ġewylt, xia. 163; xxi. 666; xxviii. 9; pret. 3s. ġewēold, viii. 135 (with his sylfes, *was his own master*—Belfour's trans-

lation). [BT cites Ælfric for both acc. and gen. after 'ġewealdan'.]

wealdend, m. *Ruler, God.* iv. 297; ix. 118; xia. 1.

weall, m. *wall.* iii. 33, 70, 143; xx. 109; xxi. 534.

ġeweallod, pp. adj. *walled.* xx. 161. [BT cites two occurrences of this word, one in the corresponding passage of Ælfric's version of Numbers, O.E. Hept., p. 316, Num. xiii. 29. Cf. ġeġrundweallian.]

weallweorc, n. *work on a wall, wall-building.* xx. 112. [BT cites only one example, CH II. 166/14 and 25.]

weallwyrhta, wk. m. *wall-builder, mason.* iii. 32.

wēamōdnyss, f. *anger, impatience.* xix. 128.

weard, m. *watchman, guard.* xxiii. 79.

weard, f. *guardianship, protection.* xv. 183.

weard, adv. in combination wiþ . . .

weard, prep. w. gen. *towards.* xiv. 6. [For tō . . . weard, see tō-weard, prep.]

weardmann, m. *watchman, guard.* vii. 119.

wearp, see wurpan.

wearþ, ġewearþ, see wurþan, ġewurþan.

weaxan, 7, pp. ġeweaxen. *to wax, grow, grow up, increase.* imp. pl. weaxaþ, xix. 35; pres. 3s. wyxt, v. 268; xii. 120; xvi. 132; 3p. weaxaþ, iii. 73; pret. 3s. wēox, viii. 131; xix. 159; xxi. 78; pp. ġeweaxen, xx. 371. [Cf. full-weaxan, sāmweaxen.]

webb, n. *web.* xxiii. 192.

wecġ, m. (a) *a mass* or *casting of metal*, perhaps *piece of money.* i. 249. (b) *metal.* xxi. 529.

wēdan, I. *to be mad, rage.* iv. 6; xviii. 363 (pres. 3s. wēt). [Cf. awēdan.]

wedloġa, m. *violator of agreement, traitor.* xi. 378.

weġ, m. *road, way* (lit. and fig.). i. 463; iv. 256; vi. 273; viii. 148, 150; xiv. 105; xvii. 119, 227; xxi. 266, 278, 483, 610.—for weġa ġelǣtum, see ġelǣte.

wel, adv. (a) *well* (properly, skilfully,

virtuously, fittingly, excellently, thoroughly, satisfactorily, abundantly). i. 440, 445; iv. 10; v. 36; xi. 122, 547; xia. 120; xii. 215; xiii. 117; xv. 65 (swā wel swā), 77; xvi. 211; xvii. 43, 44, 184, 185, 243; xviii. 160; xix. 120; xx. 112; xxvi. 74; xxx. 67. (b) with willan, to have good will, be kindly disposed, benevolent. viii. 154 (well); xvi. 197; w. dat., xiv. 218; xvii. 104; xx. 81. (c) very in wel fela, a great many. xia. 102; xiv. 143. (d) fully, quite in wel twenti. xxiii. 157. *(e) as pred. adj. well off, well provided. xx. 86. [OED, 'well', adj., 3, first quotation 1386.]

wela, m. prosperity, wealth, riches. xvi. 36, 41, 49, 259, 262, 270. [welan, in 36, 259, may be ds. but probably dp. as indicated by 262.]

weldǣd, f. good deed, beneficence. xi. 235; xvi. 152, 196.

weldōnd, m. well-doer. v. 188.

weler, m. or f. (a) lip. xv. 183; xvii. 166. *(b) what one can take with the lips, a ball or cake the right size for a mouthful, a morsel (?). xxi. 446 (translates massas, is glossed by ME balles; the conjectured meaning not in dict.; see note).

welig, adj. well-to-do, rich, prosperous. viii. 119; xvi. 4, 39 (nsm. wk. welega), 87.

welwillende, part. adj. benevolent. ii. 238; v. 186; vii. 156; xi. 144 (nsm. wk. -a, v.l. -e); xvii. 306 (wel- not in MS.; see note); xviii. 157.—as noun, xiii. 83; xiv. 218.

wēman, I. (a) to allure, persuade, win over (to)—in a good sense. xviii. 159. (b) to entice, win away (from)—in a bad sense. xxx. 7.

gewemman, I. to besmirch, defile. xxi. 117. [Cf. ungewemmed.]

wēn, f. expectation. wōn is þæt, it is likely that. v. 19.

wēnan, I. to ween, believe, imagine. iii. 134; iv. 163; vi. 35; ix. 15, 188, 189; xiv. 172; xv. 26; xix. 88; xxix. 27, 57, 77.

wendan, gewendan, I, pret. gewend-. (a) intrans., to turn, go. viii.

128, 148, 152; xiv. 82 (-wǣnd-); xvii. 244; xviii. 218; xxiii. 71; xxvi. 58, 79, 110; xxvii. 23, 81; xxix. 91. (b) trans., to convert. xxiii. 8. [Cf. a-, mis-wendan.]

gewenian, II (orig. I). to accustom. pres. 3s. subj. gewenie, xx. 428.

wēofod, n. altar. iii. 86 (wēofud); xv. 19, 22, 191, 194; xvi. 189; xxi. 565.

gewēold, see gewealdan.

wēop, see wēpan.

weorc, n. work, labour, deed. i. 103, 283; ii. 79, 82, 175, 209, 216, 257, 261; iii. 91, 103, 161, 183; iv. 158, 210, 239, 244; v. 77, 106, 134, 241; vi. 129, 247, 268; vii. 99, 180; etc.

weorcstān, m. hewn stone. ii. 13.

weorld-, see woruld-.

weorþ-, geweorþ-, see wurþ-, gewurþ-.

weoruld-, see woruld, woruld-.

wēox, see weaxan.

wēpan, 7. to weep. inf., vi. 73, 77; pres. part. wēpende, vi. 78, 185, 306; xxvi. 80, 87, 131; pres. 3p. wēpaþ, xi. 293; pret. 3s. wēop, vi. 81.

wēpna, see wǣpen.

wer, m. man, husband. i. 50, 392, 394, 416; v. 33, 35, 36, 37, 38; viii. 100, 118; xi. 147, 316, 318, 356; xviii. 128, 212, 437; xix. 41, 84, 85 (twice), 96, 97, 98, 100, 107; xxi. 504, 594; xxiii. 79, 132, 191; xxvii. 26.

werd, see tōweard, prep.

wered-, see werod-.

werian, II (orig. I). to wear. pres. 2s. subj. werige, xxvi. 60. [Cf. bewerian.]

wērig, adj. weary. v. 7, 102, 106, 110.

wērignyss, f. weariness. xi. 563.

werlic, adj. manly, of a man. xix. 18.

werod, n. multitude, host. ii. 245; xi. 290 (np. werod, as at CH II, 548/10), 365, 371, 394, 547; xviii. 218, 405 (np. werodu); xix. 174; xx. 74; xxii. 26; xxvii. 113 (twice, wered-).

werodnyss, f. sweetness, pleasantness (of taste). xx. 17 (wered-), 125, 138 (wered-).

wesan, see bēon-wesan.

westdǽl, m. *western quarter, western part.* xviii. 9.

wēsten, n. or m. *desert, wilderness.* ds. wēstene, xi. 30; xia. 130; xii. 38, 219, 227; xx. 25, 38, 193, 311, 347, 359, 364, 370, 396; xxvii. 18, 31, 81; xxix. 12.

wēt, see wēdan.

wīc, f. *village.* endingless locative, vi. 44. [Cf. Bethania-wīc.]

wicce, wk. f. *witch* (probably never wicca, wk. m. *wizard*). (a) certainly fem., xxix. 40, 45, 67, 91, 118. (b) probably fem. but grammatically uncertain, np. wiccan, xi. 376 (paired with m. wīgleras); xvii. 96 (with drȳmen); dp. wiccan, xxix. 1 (paired with drȳmannum).

wiccecræft, m. *witchcraft.* xvi. 75; xxix. 53, 72, 124.

wīce, wk. f. *office, function.* xiv. 204; xvi. 9, 18, 92, 125.

wīcian, II. *to encamp, lodge.* xx. 16, 252; xxi. 594.

wīcnere, m. *steward, bailiff.* xvi. 208.

wīcstōw, f. *place to camp.* xxi. 580.

wīd, adj. *wide.* xxi. 535.

wīde, adv. *widely.* ix. 118; xiv. 114, 181; xvii. 304; xviii. 282, 305.— wīde and sīde, *far and wide,* xxix. 104.

gewidere, n. *weather.* ap. gewideru, xxx. 93.

wīdgil, adj. *widespread, wide, extensive, spacious.* v. 186; viii. 129; xi. 467; xia. 46; xviii. 431; xxi. 553.

gewīdmǽrsian, II. *to spread abroad.* vi. 167; xvii. 304. [Cf. mǽrsian.]

wīf, n. *woman, wife.* i. 394; iv. 50, 269, 273, 282; v. 12, etc. (27 times); vi. 302, 305; xi. 147, 316, 319; xia. 120; xiii. 198, etc. (9 times); xv. 91; xviii. 12, 320; xix. 38–41, 74–113 (20 times); xx. 12, 169, 252; xxi. 13, 150, 336, 406, 423, 504; xxiii. 24, 38; xxx. 11.

wīfian, gewīfian, II. *to take a wife, wive.* xi. 282, 318; xviii. 12; xix. 41, 92, 103; xxi. 113 (on hys swustor gewīfode, *married his sister*).

wīfmann, m. *woman.* i. 412; v. 61;

xi. 282, 313; xia. 126; xiii. 204; xv. 95; xviii. 437.

wīg, n. *war.* xx. 371.

wīgende, part. adj. *fighting.* xx. 11.

wīglere, m. *soothsayer, wizard.* xi. 376.

wīglung, f. *soothsaying, augury.* xvi. 75; xxix. 124.

gewildan, see gewyldan.

wilde, adj. *wild.* i. 211; iii. 73; xi. 333; xxii. 62.

wildēor ('wilddēor'), n. *wild beast.* xxi. 39, 459 (dp. wilderon, v.l. wildēorum).

wilia, wk. m. or wilie, wk. f. *basket.* xia. 122.

gewill, n. *will, wish, desire.* ix. 35; xvi. 223.—mid gewille, *willingly,* xiii. 93.

willa, wk. m. *will, desire; Will* (of the Father and the Son, the Holy Spirit). i. 49, 50, 130, 185, 391, 392; iii. 111; v. 76, 134, 240, 245; vi. 234; vii. 210; viii. 55; ix. 23; x. 46; xi. 257, 406; xia. 13, 43, 210, 214, 221; xii. 164; xiii. 235; xiv. 97; xv. 101, 134, 218; xvi. 54, 197, 208, 294; xviii. 137, 179, 188; xix. 82, 109; xx. 259, 374, 428; xxi. 18, 94; xxii. 55; xxv(a). 8; xxvii. 39; xxx. 5, 23, 27, 33.

willan, wyllan, anom. vb. (a) w. infinitive, expressed or implied; normally, *to desire, wish, be willing, intend, be disposed to.* i. 240, 450; ii. 8, 32, 60, 98, 136, 243; iii. 47, 100, 116, 118, 172, 180; iv. 44, 58, 94, 142, 235; v. 12, 14, 20, 123, 154; vi. 23, 31, 73, 127, 160, 162, 164, 332, 334, 336, 338, 340; vii. 6, 32, 105, 106, 127; etc.; sometimes approaching simple futurity, *to be going to, be sure to,* e.g., iii. 19; iv. 202, 203; *to be accustomed to,* e.g., in pret., v. 40; xxi. 127. (b) w. acc. or clause, *to desire, wish.* iv. 15, 90; v. 63, 181; xxix. 19; etc. (c) hū wylt þū, *how wilt thou do* (or *have done*), *what is thy will,* xxvii. 68. (d) elliptically, w. adverbs giving direction, *will go,* xxi. 129; xxvii. 74. (e) w. clause, *to maintain, 'want to make out';* in pret., xv. 68. [BT, 'willan', VIII, cites Ælfric alone for this meaning, LS xxvII. 28, 33. The definition here chosen is in OED, 'will', v.¹, 24, first quotation 1500.—Forms include pres. 1s. **wille**, vi. 31; 2s. **wylt**, ii. 32; **wilt**, v. 14; 3s. **wylle**, iv. 44 (perhaps subj.); **wyle**, iv. 202; **wile**, ii. 243; pl. **willaþ**, ii. 60; **wyllaþ**, iii. 19; 2s. subj. **wylle**, xxiii. 167; 3s. **wylle**, vii. 106; pret. 3s. **wolde**, i. 240; pl. **woldon**, iv. 15; **woldan**, xxix. 19; pret. 3s. subj. **wolde**, v. 20; **woldon**, iii. 100.—Cf. **nellan**.]

wilnian, II. *to wish, desire*. w. obj. clause, xi. 254 (**will-**); xviii. 341.

gewilnian, II. *to wish, wish for, desire*. (a) w. gen., i. 224; vii. 50; viii. 71; xi. 143, 556; xv. 98; xvii. 144(?); xxix. 83 (**þæs** followed by clause); probably also, though forms may be acc., v. 119, 244; xvii. 157; xx. 100. (b) w. dat. inf. as object, xxiii. 180. (c) absolute, viii. 117; xxvii. 82.

gewilnung, f. *desire*. v. 221; xvii. 148; xx. 93; w. **tō**, vii. 62.

wīn, n. *wine*. xia. 112; xvi. 132; xx. 25, 379; xxi. 357, 409.

wīnbōh, m. *vine-shoot, vine*. ap. **wīnbōgas**, xx. 155.

wincel ('wencel'), n. *child*. dp. **winclum**, xia. 126.

wind, m. *wind*. xia. 109; xvii. 206, 211, 214; xx. 94; and in phrase, **fram þām fēower windum**, *from the four winds (quarters)*, xviii. 268, 416.

wīneard, m. *vineyard*. iii. 4–137 (21 times).

gewinn, n. *conflict, strife*. ix. 215; x. 145; xxii. 8, 84.

winnan, 3, intrans. *to fight, contend, strive*. pres. 3s. **winþ**, iv. 101; xx. 216; pret. 3s. **wann**, i. 228; viii. 138; 3p. **wunnon**, iv. 141; ix. 189; xxii. 54, 62, 94. [Cf. **ofer-**, **on-winnan**, and next entry.]

gewinnan, 3. trans. *to win*. pret. 3s. **gewinþ**, iv. 17, 186; pret. 3p. **gewunnon**, xx. 374; pp. **gewunnen**, dp. **-um**. vii. 124; xia. 146.

winter, m. *winter, year*. ii. 29, 139; xvi. 117; xviii. 246, 326 (ds. **wintra**),

328; xx. 364; xxi. 577, 583; xxiii. 15 (perhaps for 'seofon-wintre'). [Cf. **hundtēontigwintre, þrītigwintre**.]

wīnwringe, wk. f. *wine press*. iii. 6, 86.

wīpian, II. *to wipe*. vi. 7, 308.

wīs, adj. *wise*. ii. 12; iii. 89; vi. 243; viii. 16; xia. 206; xix. 26; **se wīsa** as epithet of **Augustinus**, i. 55; xxix. 50.

*****wiscere, wischere**, m. *diviner*? (Skeat), *wizard*? (BT). np. **wisceras** (v.l. **wischeras**), xxix. 6. [Unique in this passage, though already printed by Skeat and recorded from his text as 'wischere'. Etym. unknown, but see note.]

wīsdōm, m. (a) *wisdom*, sometimes God's *Wisdom*, equated with the *Son*. i. 86, 87, 104, 106, 109, 116, 132, 140, 174, 278, 282, 333; vi. 244, 279; ix. 36, 40, 44, 140; xia. 3, 4, 206; xii. 153; xiii. 184; xv. 135, 186; xvi. 116, 222, 223, 288; xvii. 157; xix. 25 (twice), 27; xx. 230; xxi. 20, 82; xxii. 82. (b) *a wise thought or act*. i. 334.

wīse, f. *manner, way, condition*. iv. 49, 248, 266; xix. 159.—in phrases, (a) **on . . . wīsan** (as.), *in* (a specified) *manner*: **āne**, xviii. 191; **ǣlce**, xviii. 374; **ǣnige**, xxv(a). 9; **þā**, xiii. 228; **þā ealdan**, ii. 14; iii. 87; xx. 245; **þǣra Iudeiscra**, ii. 16; **heora**, xv. 63; **myltestrena**, xxi. 153; **Abrahames**, xxi. 213. (b) **on . . . wīsan** (ap.), *in* (so many) *ways*: **þrēo**, vi. 173; xi. 111; **twā**, xvi. 94; xviii. 108, 131; **seofonfealde**, ix. 138; **manega**, xv. 228; xix. 1. (c) **on manegum wīsum** (dp.), x. 47; xia. 58.

wīsian, II. *to direct, instruct*. pres. 3s. subj. **wīsige**, xxvii. 8. [This passage probably not by Ælfric, who seems ordinarily to use **wissian** or **gewissian**, q.v., in this sense.]

wīslic, adj. *wise, sagacious*. ix. 140.—sup. **wīslīcost**, nsn., xxi. 249. [For comp. see next.]

wīslīce, adv. *wisely*. xii. 59; xxi. 644. —comp. **wīslīcor**, vi. 155 (but

wīslīce (cont.)
should properly be comp. adj., nsn.
'-līcre').

gewislīce ('gewiss-'), adv. certainly,
surely, clearly, explicitly. vi. 315 (v.l.
gewi's's-); xi. 292, 455; xii. 225.

gewiss, adj. certain, sure, unhesitating.
xxi. 96.—on gewissum tīman, at
appointed times. iii. 29, 138; xix. 93.
—tō gewissan, for certain, clearly.
xiii. 24, 146.—comp., np. gewissran, xxvii. 16.

*gewiss, adv. assuredly, for certain.
vii. 59, 116; viii. 1; xii. 195, xv. 53;
xvi. 106; gewis, xvi. 276. [The adv.
is not listed in OE dictionaries.
First quotation in OED, 'iwis',
dated 1160. See note on vii.
59.]

wissian, II. to instruct, direct. w. dat.,
xiv. 15, 80; xviii. 16, 121; xxx. 17
(pres. 3s. wissaþ, MS. wissiaþ); w.
acc., to direct. vii. 130. [Cf. wīsian,
and next entry.]

gewissian, II. (a) to direct, govern,
instruct. w. acc., ii. 238; v. 133; ix.
56; x. 79; w. uncertain case, xiii.
178, 235; w. dat., xvi. 53; xxv(b). 2.
(b) to inform, enlighten. ix. 135 (passive). (c) passive, impers. w. dat.
of person, him wæs gewissod
þæt, it was made clear to him that.
xxvii. 23.

wissung, f. guidance, instruction. xvii.
90; xviii. 122; xxii. 82, 95; xxvii. 14;
xxx. 7, 19.

gewissung, f. information, enlightenment. i. 22.

wist-, see witan.

wit, pron. 1st pers. dual, see ic.

gewit, see gewitt; gewīt, see
gewītan.

wita, wk. m. wise man, councillor,
elder. ix. 32, 40, 46; xii. 53; xiii. 88,
184; xiv. 103; xv. 61, 165, xxi. 249,
252, 302.

gewita, wk. m. witness. ix. 163, 167,
170; xxi. 504.

witan, pret. pres. vb. to know. inf.
vi. 258 (7 more); dat. inf. witenne,
vi. 213 (3 more); imp. sg. wite,
xix. 164; pl. witaþ, xviii. 153; pres.
1s. wāt, v. 56 (5 more); 2s. wāst,

viii. 47, 242; 3s. wāt, viii. 245 (3
more); pl. witon, v. 48 (13 more);
wite ge, xviii. 62; pres. 2s. subj.
wite, xxvi. 56; 3s., vi. 289; xix. 53;
pret. 3s. wiste, ii. 31; vii. 4; xii.
178; xxvi. 74; xxix. 97; pl. wiston,
v. 198; pret. 2s. subj. wistest,
v. 18; pl. wiston, iii. 140, 172; ix.
22. [Cf. next entry, bewitan, and
nytan.]

gewitan, pret. pres. vb. to get to know.
inf., xi. 270 (v.l. witan).

gewītan, 1. (a) to go, depart, with adv.
or prep. phrase stating whence or
whither. inf., xiv. 200; xix. 196; imp.
sg. gewīt, xiv. 32, 198; xvii. 231,
295; xxvi. 70 (twice); imp. pl.
gewītaþ, xi. 436; pres. 3s. gewīt,
xi. 207; 3 p. gewītaþ, xi. 451; xvii.
303; pres. 3s. subj. gewīte, xxvii.
69; pret. 3s. gewāt, xix. 200, 225;
xxvii. 76; xxix. 95; 3p. gewiton,
xvii. 237; xix. 189; pret. 3s. subj.
gewite, xxvii. 21.—absolute (whence
understood), pret. 3s. gewāt, xxiii.
113.—(b) unqualified, to depart
from life, pass away, die. pres. 3s.
gewīt, xix. 79; 3p. gewītaþ, xi.
194; pret. 3s. gewāt, xi. 175, 311;
xxiii. 48; pp. gewiten, xi. 37, 180;
xia. 139.

wīte, n. punishment, torture. iii. 154;
iv. 114; vi. 158; xi. 128-497 (16
times); xia. 52; xiv. 142; xv. 16,
146, 150, 152, 155; xvii. 65; xviii.
434; xix. 188, 200, 215, 237, 239;
xx. 295, 297, 301, 403; xxi. 71, 258;
xxiii. 124, 189; xxiv. 3; xxvii. 10,
44; xxix. 128. [Among forms note
nap. wīta, xix. 237; xxiii. 189; xx.
403 (emend., MS wite); gp.
wītena, xi. 465.]

wītega, wk. m. prophet. i. 146, 369,
468; ii. 154 (wītiga); iii. 45, etc.
(8 times); iv. 157; v. 40, 198, 212,
256; vii. 67, 94, 98, 115, 212; viii.
79; ix. 68, 164; xia. 57, 199; xiii.
72; xv. 160, 180; xviii. 177, 236, 280,
386; xix. 19, 66; xxi. 300-476 (8
times); xxiv. 4; xxix. 46-79 (7
times); xxx. 91.

wītegian, II. to prophesy. i. 468 (pp.
np. gewītegode); iv. 157, 265; v.

198; vii. 68, 212; ix. 164; xi. 27; xi*a.* 101.

wītegung, f. *prophecy.* ii. 155; v. 213; vii. 216.

gewītendlic, adj. *transitory, perishable.* x. 128.

witlēas, gewit(t)lēas, adj. *foolish, mad.* xi*a.* 106 (**gewittlēasan,** ap. wk. with art. as noun); xix. 165 (**ge-**); xxi. 458.

gewitlēast, f. *folly, madness.* x. 168; xvi. 66.

gewītnian, II. *to torment, afflict.* xviii. 363.

wītni(g)endlic, adj. *tormenting, punishing.* xi. 226; xv. 17, 151. [BT cites Ælfric alone for this word.]

gewitnyss, f. *witness, testimony.* i. 116, 145, 451; ix. 9, 88, 125; xi. 403; xiii. 210.

witodlīce, witud-, adv. *assuredly.* i. 34, etc. (8 times); ii. 105, 155; iii. 19, 51, 101, 142; iv. 32, 133, 152, 174, 260; v. 190, 260; vi. 62, 129, 209, 243; etc.

witsēoc, gewitsēoc, adj. *insane.* iv. 4; xvii. 241, 244 (**ge-**).

gewit(t), n. *understanding, right mind, sanity.* xi*a.* 106; xvii. 129; xix. 164, 165.

gewittig, adj. *sane, in one's right mind, endowed with reason.* iv. 10; xvii. 243; xxi. 278.

gewittlēas, see **witlēas.**

wiþ, prep. w. acc. (for use w. gen., *in the direction of,* see **weard,** adv.). (a) marking juxtaposition, *next to, beside, against.* v. 8; xiii. 192; xiv. 3, 5, 49, 111; xxi. 235, 620. (b) marking combination (where there is a sense of disparity), *with.* v. 269. (c) *in comparison with.* xvi. 285; xx. 164. (d) marking conflict *with;* hostility, opposition, transgression *against.* i. 237, 372; iv. 101, 102, 141; viii. 138; ix. 189; xi. 104, 149; xv. 14, 40 (twice), 130, 200; xx. 262, 263, 313; xxi. 212, 332; xxii. 19, 39, 62, 64, 94; xxix. 43, 115. (e) marking defence, precaution, or warning *against;* deliverance or preservation *from.* i. 227; ii. 278; vi. 282; ix. 22, 51, 170, 177, 178, 209; xiii. 229;

xvi. 232; xx. 393; xxi. 49 (twice), 55, 283, 296, 315, 326, 349; xxvi. 125; xxvii. 10; xxix. 116. (f) marking conversation or conference *with.* viii. 22; x. 71, 187; xvi. 3; xvii. 93, 95; xxii. 87, 89. (g) marking sexual intercourse *with.* xv. 91. (h) marking action affecting a person, *towards.* xvi. 31, 206. (i) marking one's dealings *with* a person where terms are come to. xv. 190; xx. 303. (j) marking one's relations with a person from whom one gets or expects favour or disfavour, *with, in relation to, in the eyes of.* xvii. 271; xx. 419; xxx. 54. (k) marking action directed by a third party *to* a person with whom one has dealings. xvi. 5, 88 (**forsǣd wiþ his hlāford,** *accused to his lord,* with some sense of being discredited *with* him; cf. the definition and the similar quotation in BT, 'wiþ', III. 11). [Cf. **mid,** prep.]

wiþæftan, prep. w. dat. *after, behind.* xxvii. 2 (?).

wiþcweþan, 5. w. dat. of person or thing, *to speak against, contradict, oppose.* inf., xxi. 457; pres. 3s. **wiþcwyþ,** xxix. 50; 3p. **wiþcweþaþ,** xviii. 294; pret. 3p. **wiþcwǣdon,** ix. 203. [Cf. **cweþan.**]

wiþercoren, adj. *rejected, reprobate, wicked.* xviii. 132; wk. w. art. as noun, xi. 326, 346; xviii. 139 [Cf. **gecēosan.**]

wiþerian, II. intrans., *to strive, contend.* iv. 102, 210; xxx. 27 (pres. 3s. subj. **wiþrige**); w. **ongēan,** adv., *to offer resistance.* iii. 130.

wiþerrǣde, adj. *contrary, perverse, rebellious.* xx. 39, 175, 357.

***wiþerrǣdlīce,** adv. *perversely, rebelliously.* xx. 396. [The adv. not in dict.; the adj. in '-lic' cited once, in BT and Hall, from Ælfric's Grammar.]

wiþersaca, wk. m. *adversary, apostate.* iv. 274; viii. 132; xxix. 126.

wiþerwinna, wk. m. *adversary, enemy.* xxvi. 24.

wiþinnan, prep. and adv. *within.* as prep., w. dat., ii. 91; vi. 163 (semi-adv. by position), 180; as adv., iv.

wiþinnan (*cont.*)
228; x. 132; xii. 105; xv. 69; xvi.
239; xxi. 376. [Cf. **þǣr-wiþinnan.**]
wiþmetan, 5, w. dat. *to measure
against, compare to, equate with.* pp.
wiþmeten, xvi. 61 (*made equal to,
comparable to*); xviii. 115 (*compared
to*). [At xvi. 61 Ælfric is translating
comparatus, which can bear the
same sense according to Lewis and
Short, A Latin Dictionary, first
'comparo', II. A. 1. BT gives only
compare, but cites Ælfric at CH II.
456/13, Job's 'Ic eom lame wiþmeten', where Thorpe translates
compared to, but one might better
say *comparable to* or *made equal to.*]
wiþrige, see **wiþerian.**
wiþsacan, 6. (a) w. dat. (gen.), *to renounce, reject* (the authority and
practices of someone). pres. 3s.
wiþsæcþ, ii. 153; 3s. subj. **wiþ-
sace,** xxiv. 13; pret. 3s. **wiþsōc,**
iv. 131; 3p. **wiþsōcon,** iv. 264,
267; xiv. 144; pret. 3s. subj.
wiþsōce, iv. 239 (MS. Q has both
gen. and dat.). (b) w. acc., *to deny,
renounce* a superior. pres. 1p. subj.
wiþsacon, xvi. 247; xviii. 396;
pret. 3s. **wiþsōc,** xvii. 253. [The
distinction of meaning between (a)
and (b) is doubtful. See BT, V and
III.]
wiþstandan, 6, w. dat. *to withstand,
resist.* inf., i. 265.
wiþūtan, prep. and adv. —prep. w.
dat., *outside of, out from.* xviii. 104;
xxvii. 25.—adv., *without, outwardly,
outside.* iv. 228; xiv. 125; xv. 76;
xvi. 114; xviii. 139, 199, 217; xix.
175; xxi. 320, 375.
*****wlatian,** II, impers. w. dat. of per-
son. *to feel nausea, loathing.* (a) the
object of loathing in acc. after **wiþ,
ūs wlataþ wiþ þysne mete,** *we
feel loathing against (for) this food.*
xx. 313.(b) the desire which has bred
loathing in gen. or dat., **him
wlatode þǣre gewilnunge,** *they
felt loathing of (for?) that desire.*
xx. 93. [BT has the word but not
these constructions. The examples
from Leechdoms have acc. of per-

son; the others, from Alfred and
Ælfric, have ambiguous forms better
taken as dat. BT has a variant of
(a) from Ælfric's trans. of Numbers,
xxi. 5, with 'for' instead of 'wiþ';
but the exact construction with
'with' appears three times in OED,
'wlate', v., def. 1, in passages dated
after 1300. Construction (b) not on
record.—Cf. **awlǣtan.**]
wlite, m. *brightness, beauty of aspect.*
i. 216; xi. 327.
wlitig, adj. *beautiful, comely.* xxiii.
103.
wōd, adj. *insane, mad.* iv. 93; xvii.
221, 242, 286, 295.—wk. w. def. art.
as noun, *the madman, the mad.* iv. 60;
vii. 184; xia. 106; xvii. 14, 233.
wōdlīce, adv. *madly, furiously.* xx.
179.
wōdnyss, f. *madness.* iv. 60; xx. 74,
230, 234; xxix. 116.
wō(h), n. *crookedness, wrong.* ds. **wō,**
xiii. 94; xvi. 224.
wō(h), adj. *crooked, perverse.* np. wk.
wōgan, xvi. 75.
wō(h)līce, adv. *perversely, wrongly,
unjustly.* xv. 102; xviii. 134; xx. 357;
xxi. 80, 663; xxii. 94.—spelled **wo-**
except in MS. S, **woh-,** xxi. 80, 663.
wōhnyss, f. *crookedness, wickedness,
perversity.* ix. 79; xii. 155; xxvi. 103.
wolcn, n. *cloud.* iii. 74; vii. 37 (v.l.
weolcn); xviii. 265, 409, 412.
wold-, see **willan.**
wōp, m. *weeping, lamentation.* v. 276;
xvii. 263; xviii. 433; xxvi. 89, 97.
word, n. *word, speech, sentence, command; the Word.* i. 28, etc. (35
times); ii. 54, 135, 197, 277; iv. 55,
136, 147 (**tȳn word,** *ten commandments*), 282, 288, 292, 294; v. 84,
252; vi. 36, 218; vii. 6, 77; etc.—
words of advice, counsel. ap., ix. 32.—
(*good or bad*) *name, reputation.* as.,
ix. 75; xv. 190.
geworden, see **gewurþan.**
wordsnoter, adj. *expert in speech,
eloquent.* i. 55.
*****geworht,** adj. (pp. of **gewyrcan**).
fabricated, artificial, man-made. xxi.
366 (ap. wk. **-an,** translating *manufacta*). [This disparaging sense not

in BT. Cf. OED, 'wrought', 1. b;
2; 4. a; but no exact parallel.]

worht-, ġeworht-, see wyrcan,
ġewyrcan.

wōrian, II, pres. part. wōriġende.
(a) *wandering*. iv. 42, 213. (b) as adj.
characterizing waves, *fluctuating,
inconstant*. xvii. 68. [BT gives
sense (b) only in the gloss 'woraþ
fluctuat'.]

worpan, see wurpan.

worþ-, see wurþ-.

woruld, f. (a) *world*, usually this
world: i. 171, 205, 341, 405, 469;
ii. 170, 238; iii. 54; v. 111, 268,
270, 271; vi. 121, 130; vii. 95, 199;
etc.; this world and the next, vi.
220; xx. 137; the next world, xiv.
71; xv. 17, 151; xx. 301; xxiv. 3.
(b) *age*, in expressions meaning *for
ever*. ā to worulde, ii. 262; v. 290;
vi. 153, 373; vii. 226; xiv. 234; xv.
230; xx. 429; xxi. 11, 676; ǣfre to
worulde, xviii. 58; on weorulde,
xxi. 345; on ēcere worulde, iii.
187; on ealra worulda woruld
v. 276; xiↄa. 234; xxx. 114 (MS. V,
in for on).—occasionally spelled
weoruld, e.g. xiii. 236; xviii. 377.
[No ending in acc. sg.; see Cpb
610, n. 2.]

woruldcaru, f. *worldly anxiety, care*.
xviii. 93, 99, 115, 129.

woruldcund, adj. *worldly, secular*.
xvi. 218, 286.

woruldlic, adj. *worldly*. iv. 101; v.
221; xi. 357; xvi. 263 (weoruld-);
xviii. 341 (worold-); xxi. 102;
xxiii. 58 (weorld-); xxvi. 56.

woruldmann, m. (a) *man* (*upon
earth*). xi. 281. (b) *man engaged in
worldly pursuits, man of the world,
layman*. ix. 65; xi. 365; xvi. 32,
215, 218; xviii. 114, 130, 136.

woruldþing, n. *worldly affair,
worldly thing*. xvi. 290; xviii. 114;
xix. 81, 84; xxi. 640.

wōrung, f. *wandering, roving*. v. 186.

wræcsīþ, m. *journey of exile, journey
abroad*. (a) literally, in the parable,
iii. 92, 107. (b) fig. of life on earth,
i. 219.

ġewrecan, 5, trans. *to take ven-*

geance for, *avenge*. pret. 3s. ġewrǣc,
xx. 289; xxii. 91.

wrēgan, I. *to accuse, impeach*. xiii.
222; xxi. 311, 335; xxvii. 13. [Cf.
forwrēgan.]

wringan, 3. *to squeeze, press*. pres. 3s.
wringþ, xvi. 134.

ġewrit, n. (a) *writing, scripture,
written testimony*. v. 144; xi. 81, 108;
xvi. 27, 144; xviii. 393; xxi. 6. (b)
written message or *command*. xx. 406;
xxi. 615, 619, 621, 631.

wrītan, 1. *to write, record*. d. inf.
wrītenne, i. 25; pret. 3s. wrāt, i.
138; v. 213; vi. 320. [Cf. awrītan.]

ġewrīþan, 1. *to tie, fasten*. pret. 3s.
ġewrāþ, xxvi. 100. [BT includes
several examples from Ælfric.]

wrōht, f. *blame, accusation, contention*.
xiii. 207; xxi. 127.

wrohton, see wyrcan.

wuce, wk. f. *week*. ds. wucan, xi. 72,
74; xiↄa. 188. [Cf. Gang-, Lenctenwuce.]

wudu, m. *wood, forest*. ds. wuda,
xx. 149, 378; dp. wudum, i. 211.

wuduwe, wudewe, wydewe, wk. f.
widow. xi. 27; xiↄa. 101; xvi. 187;
xix. 72, 86, 88; xxx. 97.

wuldor, n. *glory*. i. 52, 53, 93, 427,
428, 451, 470; ii. 290; iii. 187; v.
290; vi. 13, 90, 373; viii. 177, 255;
ix. 154, 217; x. 145, 210; etc.

wuldorfull, adj. *glorious*. xi. 348, 471.

ġewuldrian, II. *to glorify*. pp. ġe-
wuldrod, vi. 14; x. 149; np. -e, xi.
549, 569.

wulf, m. *wolf*. iv. 206.

ġewuna, wk. m. *habit, custom, practice*. vi. 175, 201; xiↄa. 70; xiii. 196;
xiv. 15, 80; xvii. 116; xxi. 307, 409.
—hæfþ him on ġewunan, *makes
a practice of*, vi. 200; habbaþ on
ġewunan, *are accustomed to per-
forming*, xiii. 68.

wund, f. *wound*. vii. 99; xi. 292; xxvi.
120.

ġewundian, II. *to wound*. pp. ġe-
wundod, xi. 37; xiↄa. 138.

wundor, n. *wonder, miracle*. i. (19),
(430); ii. 17, 88, 98, 100, 101, 103,
122, 137, 250, 284; iii. 174; iv.
3, 13, 30, 64, 73, 94, 123; vi. 111,

wundor (*cont.*)

112, 119, 319, 333; vii. 90, 93; etc. [nap. **wundra**, ii. 17, etc.; gp. **wundra**, ii. 250, etc.]

wundorlic, adj. *wonderful, wondrous.* i. 109; ii. 11, 115; iii. 34, 85; v. 102; xia. 46; xiv. 222; xvii. 43, 184, 284, 301; xx. 375; xxi. 74, 526; xxii. 40.

wundorlīce, adv. *wondrously, remarkably, strangely.* iv. 4; ix. 135; xx. 165, 178; xxvi. 88.

wundrian, II. (a) absolute, *to wonder, be astonished.* vi. 115; xvii. 213. (b) with a clause, *to wonder that* (**þæt**), v. 61, 123; xii. 18, 140; *to wonder how* (**hū**), xxix. 97. (c) w. gen., *to wonder at.* iv. 11, 63; viii. 228; xvii. 248; xxvi. 134. [Cf. **ofwundrod**.]

wundrung, f. *wonderment, wonder.* i. 436; vii. 124; xvii. 41, 182.

ġewunelic, adj. *customary, usual, ordinary.* vi. 100, 310; viii. 170; xii. 111; xx. 107; xxi. 614.

ġewunelīce, adv. *habitually, customarily, regularly.* vi. 166 (**-wuno-**, v.l. **-wune-**); xi. 339; xviii. 328.

wunian, II. *to dwell, remain.* i. 5, etc. (13 times); ii. 8, 139; iii. 179; iv. 2, 19, 48, 99, 113, 172, 247; v. 93 (twice), 133, 148, 182, 282, 283; vi. 3, 17, 271, 329; vii. 53, 67, 77, 80, 82, 128, 139, 179, 222; etc.— w. dat. of person, *to remain in store for, await.* xxiv. 3. [Often **wunig-** for **wuni-** before **e**.—Cf. next entry and **þurhwunian**.]

ġewunian, II. *to dwell*; with **tō**, *to dwell next to, make a home near.* iv. 82.—pp. **ġewunod**, as adj. *domiciled, settled.* xxi. 432 (**þær wæs on þære byriġ ġewunod ān draca**, *there was a dragon that lived in that city*). [For two other examples of this use see BTS, 'gewunian', B. I.]

wunnon, see **winnan**.

wunung, f. (a) (*the act of*) *dwelling,* (*continued*) *presence.* x. 50, 56. (b) *a dwelling-place, habitation, abode.* i. 200, 202, 220; iv. 215, 230, 233, 234, 253; vii. 50; viii. 8; xi. 184, 368; xvi. 199, 272; xvii. 144, 222; xix. 68; xxi. 554, 604; xxv(*a*). 6; xxvii. 25, 39; xxix. 52, 69, 73, 74.—

(c) as a philosophical term, *separate abode, substantial existence* (substances, even if incorporeal, being thought of as capable of local existence apart from other substances). i. 173, 190. [See BT, III for other examples of sense (c) in Ælfric.]

wurm, wurmcynn, see **wyrm, wyrmcynn**.

wurpan, worpan, wyrpan ('weorpan'), 3. *to hurl, cast.* inf., xxi. 317 (**wurp-**); xxiii. 194 (**worp-**); xxvii. 13 (**wyrp-**); pres. 3p. **wurpaþ**, v. 275; pret. 3s. **wearp**, xvi. 187; pret. 3p. **wurpon**, xiv. 22; xvi. 188; **wurpan**, xxi. 459. [Cf. **a-, to-wurpan**.]

wurþ, ('weorþ'), n. *worth, value, price.* v. 201; xxi. 204, 205.

wurþan ('weorþan'), 3. *to become, be.* (a) with compl. past part., i. 24, 412, 430; ii. 40; iv. 106, 273; etc. (80 more). (b) with compl. noun or adj., ii. 22, 86, 219, 231; v. 28, 139; viii. 135, 152; xi. 99, 101, 106, 299; xia. 51; xii. 137; xiii. 210; xvi. 290, 291; xx. 178, 357; xxi. 321, 352, 423, 551; xxii. 66; xxiii. 15, 160; xxvii. 108, 118. (c) with compl. prep. phrases: **tō nāhte**, *to be annihilated*, xi. 329; **mid cilde**, *to become pregnant*, xia. 69; **on slǣpe**, *to go to sleep*, xvii. 208. (d) without compl., *to come about, take place, come.* ii. 17; viii. 122; xvii. 299. [Forms: inf., xi. 329, 331; pres. 3s. **wyrþ**, v. 28, 139 (v.l. **wyrcþ**), **wurþ** (v.l. **wyrþ**), xvi. 285, 290, 291 (v.l. **wyrcþ**); 3p. **wurþaþ**, ii. 231 (3 more); pres. 3s. subj. **wyrþe**, xxvii. 108; 3p. **wurþon**, xi. 189; xx. 169; pret. 1s. **wearp**, viii. 144; 3s., i. 24 (63 more); 3p. **wurdon**, ii. 17 (29 more); **wurdan**, xxi. 164, 336, 662; pret. 3s. subj. **wurde**, i. 412; xi. 99, 101, 335; xii. 103; xiii. 210; xix. 47; xxvii. 118; 3p. subj. **wurdon**, v. 129; xvii. 35, 60. For pp. see next entry. Cf. **for-wurþan**.]

ġewurþan ('-weorþ-'), 3. (a) w. compl. adj. or noun, *to become.* ii. 111; iii. 180 (**wæs ġeworden,**

became); xii. 120; xxi. 454 (**is
geworden**, *has become*); xxiii. 170.
(b) with **tō**, *to turn to, prove a
source of.* xxvi. 70. (c) expressing
movement, with **oninnan** and acc.
(v.l. dat.), *to become present within,
enter into.* xxi. 621. (d) without
complement, *to come to pass, happen, come into being, be.* ii. 42 (**wæs
geworden**, *was done, occurred*);
vii. 28, 215; viii. 96, 99; x. 22, 182;
xi. 270, 532; xi*a.* 41, 58; xii. 24,
165; xviii. 249, 258, 346, 381, 397;
xxii. 39 (**wæs geworden**, *was
brought about*); xxix. 99.—w. dat.
of persons affected, iv. 260; xvi. 180
(**is geworden**, *has come to*).—
wearþ geworden, *was brought
about, was established,* xvii. 212.
(e) impers. w. dat. of person, *to be
fitting for, agreeable to, to please.*
i. 382; iv. 162; ix. 122. [Forms: inf.,
xii. 24 (4 more); pres. 3s. **gewyrþ**,
i. 382 (9 more); 3p. **gewurþaþ**, vii.
28 (3 more); pres. 3s. subj. **ge-
wurþe**, x. 22 (2 more); pret. 3s.
gewearþ, viii. 99; xxi. 621; 3p.
gewurdon, xxiii. 170; pret. 3s.
subj. **gewurde**, xi. 532; xi*a.* 58;
pp. **geworden** with aux. **is, wæs,
wearþ** as cited above (often
translating Lat. *factum est,* etc.), 6
times.]
wurþfull, adj. *worthy.* xxii. 73.
**wurþian, weorþ-, worþ-, wyrþ-,
II.** *to honour.* ii. 43, 143, 213, 254,
267; iii. 55, 161, 175, 184; v. 122,
190; vii. 166; etc.—spelled **weorþ-**
at xi. 2, 33; **worþ-** at xi. 6; **wyrþ** at
xi*a.* 75, 128. [Cf. **ārwurþian, unwurþian.**]
wurþig, m. *homestead, farm.* v. 4, 5.
wurþlīce, adv. *honourably, fittingly,
splendidly.* vii. 37; xi. 43, 50; xi*a.*
150, 158; xxi. 259, 526.
wurþlicor, comp. adv. used as uninflected adj. *more to be valued.* xx.
126.
wurþmynt, wyrþ-, m. *honour.* i.
381, 419, 470; ii. 16, 254; iii. 85; vi.
352; viii. 255; ix. 217; xi. 55, 144,
381, 566; xi*a.* 81, 172, 233; xii.
239; xiv. 234; xv. 230; xvi. 59, 64,

67, 78; xvii. 129, 314; xviii. 297;
xxi. 156, 175, 672; xxv(*a*). 4, 5;
xxvi. 22; xxx. 41, 89.
wurþscipe, m. *honour, worth, dignity,
glory.* xi. 549; xxiii. 56, 58.
wydewe, see **wuduwe.**
gewyldan, I, pret. **gewyld-.** *to conquer, subdue, control, handle.* i. 230,
243; iv. 191; xix. 8 (pres. 3s. subj.
gewylde), 117; xx. 98; xxii. 10, 55
(**-wild-**). [The form **gewylt** is
probably always pres. 3s. of **gewealdan,** q.v.]
gewylde, adj. *adapted, subject to control.* iv. 158.
wyle, wyll-, see **willan.**
wylspring, m. *fountain, spring.* v. 29,
140, 148.
wylt, see **willan.**
gewylt, see **gewealdan.**
wynstra, -e, adj. (appearing only in
wk. decl.). *left.* xi. 346, 436; xiv.
171; xxx. 57, 61, 65, 67. as noun w.
possessive, wk. f., *left hand.* xiv. 172.
asm. **nænne wynstran (dæl** understood?), *no part that is left,* xiv. 174.
—spelled **winstr-** only in variants,
MS. H, xiv. 171, 172.
wynsum, adj. *pleasant, delightful.*
viii. 127; xi. 143, 252; xi*a.* 112; xxi.
57; xxv(*a*). 15.
wynsumlīce, adv. *pleasantly, delight-
fully.* viii. 131; xvi. 139.
wynsumnyss, f. *loveliness, joyous-
ness.* xxi. 67.
wyrcan, gewyrcan, I, pret.
-worht-, trans. (a) *to make, create,
produce, fabricate, build.* i. 32, etc.
(13 times); iii. 6, 62; iv. 142; v. 6;
vi. 116, 243, 283; viii. 118; xi. 337;
etc. (altogether 48, 25 with **ge-**). (b)
to perform, work, do, commit. i. 19,
260, 283, 430; ii. 100, 250, 257; iii.
77, 78, 79; etc. (altogether 64, 15
with **ge-**). (c) with compl. noun, *to
make the object such and such.* i. 31,
381, 403 (all with **ge-**). (d) w. acc.
and **tō**, *to change* or *make* the object
(*into*) such and such. viii. 127; xi.
313 (**ge-**); refl., xx. 241 (**ge-**), 259.
*(e) w. acc. and **on** plus acc.(?), *to
build into* a particular position? or
convert into?* iii. 33 (**sē is geworht**

wyrcan, ġewyrcan (*cont.*)
　on þæs wealles hyrnan). [Not
　illustrated in BT.] (f) absolute or
　elliptical, *to produce*. x. 61; *to do
　or earn by deeds*, xi. 210 **(ġe-)**.
　[Spelled **wyrceaþ** for **wyrcaþ**, vi.
　268; xxvii. 121. **wroht-** for **worht-**,
　iv. 123. Cf. **be-, mis-wyrcan**, and
　ġeworht, adj.]
wyrcend,m. *worker, maker*. ii. 262 (ap.
　wyrcendras); *the Maker*, xxi. 347.
wyrdwrītere, m. *historian, chroni-
　cler*. xxii. 1; xxix. 45.
ġewyrht, f. or n. *deed, desert*. xi. 127,
　184; xxi. 58.
wyrhta, wk. m. *maker, builder*. xxi. 76.
wyrm, wurm, m. *worm, snake, ser-
　pent*. i. 173, 274; xx. 332; xxi. 434,
　443.
wyrmcynn, wurm-, n. *species of ser-
　pent*. xxi. 39 (**wurm-**, v.l. **wyrm-**).
wyrpan, see **wurpan**.
ġewyrpan, I. *to recover from illness,
　get better*. pret. 3s. **ġewyrpte**, xi.
　174; xix. 153.
wyrsa, -e, comp. adj. *worse*. ii. 57,
　279; iv. 48, 49, 247, 248, 266; xi.
　484; xiii. 234 (nsm. **-e** for **-a**); xiv.
　136, 146; xvii. 254; xviii. 180.
wyrsian, II. *to get worse*. pres. part.
　wyrsiġende, xix. 159.
wyrst, sup. adj. *worst*. iv. 260; vi. 315.
wyrt, f. *herb*. i. 216; iii. 101; xv. 102;
　xx. 107, 126.
wyrþ, see **wurþan; wyrþ-,** see
　wurþ-.
wyrþe, adj. (a) *worth*. xxx. 105. (b)
　w. gen. or defining clause, *worthy*.
　i. 224; xxix. 73.
wyt, pron. 1st pers., dual, see **ic**.
wyxt, see **weaxan**.

Y

ȳddisce, n. *household stuff, possessions*.
　xviii. 241, 311 (glossed *familiam* but
　it renders *aliquid de domo sua*). [See
　BT, BTS, 'idisc'; BTS admits
　'-isce' as a nom. form, and the as.
　ȳddisce here confirms it. Holt. has
　'īedisc'.]
ȳdel, see **īdel**.
yfel, n. *evil*. i. 184, 190, 193, 195, 197;

vi. 136, 162 (twice), 164 (twice), 167,
　271; viii. 67, 69, 71; xia. 117; xii.
　163; xv. 46; xvi. 51; xviii. 173, 325;
　xxvii. 9, 27.
yfel, adj. *evil, wicked*. ii. 170; iii. 27,
　136; iv. 78, 130; vi. 167, 174 (twice),
　175 (twice), 180, 181, 200, 201, 285,
　289, 342, 366; etc.—strong pl. as
　noun, *evil ones*, xiv. 156.—wk. as
　noun, **sē yfela**, *the evil one* (the
　devil), vii. 186; **þā yfelan**, *the
　wicked*, nap., xiv. 171; xviii. 208; dp.
　þām yfelum, xviii. 209.
yfeldǣde, adj. *of evil deeds*; absolute
　as noun, *malefactor*, esp. *magician*.
　np., xxiii. 145. [See BT for the
　magical implications of this word,
　which is here suggested by the
　Latin *malefici* in the same sense. Cf.
　CH I. 22/31, where Thorpe's 'evil-
　doing' is surely inadequate.]
yfele, adv. *evilly, with evil, in an evil
　manner*. iii. 27, 136; vi. 156, 165;
　viii. 144; xvi. 50, 69; xviii. 359.
yfelnyss, f. *evilness, wickedness*. ii.
　204, 239; viii. 80 (concretely in pl.,
　wicked ways or *deeds*); xix. 240;
　xxv(*a*). 20; xxx. 54 (**-nes**).
ylca, ilca, -e, pron. adj., always decl.
　wk. *same*. as adj., i. 77, 202, 261, 364,
　448; ii. 247; iv. 64; vi. 18, 69, 238,
　280, 325, 330; vii. 54, 224; etc.—as
　pron., ii. 28; iv. 78, 125; vi. 152;
　etc. [Spelled **ilc-** at xxi. 330, 631;
　and occasionally elsewhere. See
　variants of xi. 38, 48, 156, 459.]
yld, f. (a) *age, old age*. ii. 237; xi.
　305, 306, 307; xii. 111, 122; xix. 18,
　19, 21, 114; xx. 366. (b) *older
　generation, seniors*. ns., xx. 359.
　(c) *age* of the world. **on þære
　syxtan ylde**, v. 111; xia. 61; xxi.
　499. [For Ælfric's use of the form
　'yld' rather than 'yldu' see xx. 359
　and BT, 'ild'.]
yldest, yldost, adj. (sup. of **eald**).
　eldest, chief. xii. 53; xxi. 180; xxiii.
　11.
yldra, -e, wk. adj. (comp. of **eald**).
　older, elder. xix. 5; xxi. 650, 651.
ymb, ymbe, more often **embe**, prep.
　w. acc. (a) *about, concerning* an object
　of speech, thought, inquiry, etc.

i. 57, 275; ii. 256; iii. 59; iv. 188, 265, 276; etc. (b) indicating the object with which an action is concerned, *with regard to, about, with.* iii. 17 (twice), 25; xxi. 250; xxvii. 68; and w. **swician,** q.v., xi. 163; xxi. 159; w. **syrwan,** vi. 284; xxii. 44. (c) of worldly care, compared to a mill-wheel, **gǣþ abūtan ymbe,** *revolves about.* xviii. 116 (w. both acc. and dat.; see note). (d) indicating the object of a journey, *with concern for, on* some business. xxiii. 577; xxvii. 85. (e) w. **bēon-wesan,** *to be about, occupied with.* xviii. 27, 242, 312; **sǣton ǣt hām ymbe,** *stayed home, occupied with,* xxii. 86. (f) temporally, *after* a stated interval, e.g. viii. 142; xi. 54; xi*a.* 171; *at* or *about* a stated time, e.g. xxiii. 24, 25. (g) elliptically as adv., *about it.* xviii. 182. [Spelled **ymbe,** v. 215, 233; xi. 54; xiii. 175; xviii. 1, etc. (8 times); xxii. 86; xxiii. 25; xxv(*c*). 10; and occasionally in variants; **ymb,** xxiii. 24; elsewhere **embe.** Forms with **y** prevail in most of the compounds below. Combinations of **embe** with forms of **sprecan** and **secgan** (as at ii. 256; iv. 188; v. 259; vii. 5; xiv. 41; xx. 263; xxi. 472) might be taken as compounds with weakly stressed prefix, but see note on xxi. 472.]

ymbgang, ymbegang, m. *going about, circuit, (cyclical) course,* as part of a revolution. xi. 5, 12, 90; xi*a.* 86.

ym(b)hwyrft, emb-, m. (a) *circuit,* in phrase, w. gen., **on embhwyrfte,** *around.* xvi. 241 (MS. **emn-,** v.l. **ymb-).** (b) *(curved) surface, extent.* i. 105 (**eorþan, ymhwyrft**). (c) with **eorþan** understood, *surface of the earth, sphere of the earth.* vii. 179 (**emb-**). [For (b) and (c), cf. Lat. *orbis terræ, orbis terrarum.*]

Ymbrenfæsten, n. one of the four periodical *Ember-fasts.* xix. 126. [On the etymology see OED, 'ember', 2.]

ymbryne, m. *circuit, course.* xviii. 329.

ymbscrȳdan, I. *to clothe.* pp. np. **ymbscrȳdde,** xvi. 239. [Cf. **scrȳ-dan.**]

ymbstandend, m. *bystander.* dp. -**um,** vi. 86, 103. [Cf. **standan.**]

ymhwyrft, see **ymbhwyrft.**

yrfe, n. *cattle.* i. 217 (? MS. has as. **orfe,** but regular forms are either **orf** or **yrfe.**]

yrfenuma, m. *heir.* iii. 21.

yrfweardnyss, f. *heritage.* iii. 22.

yrhþ (EWS 'ierhþu'), f. *cowardice.* ds. **yrhþe,** xix. 154. [The ns. not recorded in BT but it would probably have lacked the old '-u' in Ælfric's speech. Cf. **cȳþþ, myrhþ, gesǣlþ, strengþ, geþincþ,** and **yrmþ.**]

geyrman, I. *to afflict, make wretched.* pp. **geyrmed,** xviii. 171.

yrmþ, f. *misery.* as. **yrmþe,** xxvi. 90. [The ns. **yrmþ,** not **yrmþu,** in Ælfric's Grammar, p. 207/15. Cf. **yrhþ** above.]

yrnan, 3. *to run.* inf., xxvi. 98; pres. part. **yrnende,** xxi. 553; pres. 3p. **yrnaþ,** xiv. 51; pret. 3s. **arn,** xvii. 221, 227; xx. 22; 3s. subj. **urne,** xxi. 38.

yrre, n. *anger.* iv. 250; xiii. 160; xv. 137, 144, 153; xx. 194, 199; xxi. 267, 270; xxiii. 119, 184.

yrre, adj. *angry.* xxi. 423.

yrsian, II. *to be angry.* xv. 14, 130, 140.

yrsung, f. *anger.* xiii. 156; xv. 135.

ytt-, ge-ytt, see **etan, ge-etan.**

ȳþ, f. *wave.* xi*a.* 108; xiv. 59; xvii. (68), 206.

ȳþian, II. *to fluctuate;* pres. part. asf. wk. **ȳþiendan,** *turbulent.* xvii. 217.

Z

Zacheus, *Zacchæus,* a man visited by Jesus (Luke xix. 8). xvi. 173, 175, 181.

Zebedeus, *Zebedee,* father of the apostles James and John. ns., xiv. 211; gs. **Zebedees,** xiv. 34, 208.

Zebub, surname forming second member of **Beelzebub,** q.v. iv. 79, 85.

EARLY ENGLISH TEXT SOCIETY

THE Subscription to the Society, which constitutes full membership for private members and libraries, is £3. 3s. (U.S. and Canadian members $9.00) a year for the annual publications, due in advance on the 1st of JANUARY, and should be paid by Cheque, Postal Order, or Money Order made out to 'The Early English Text Society', to Mr. R. W. Burchfield, Hon. Secretary, Early English Text Society, 40 Walton Crescent, Oxford. Individual members of the Society are allowed, after consultation with the Secretary, to select other volumes of the Society's publications instead of those for the current year. The Society's Texts can also be purchased separately from the Publisher, Oxford University Press, through a bookseller, at the prices put after them in the List, or through the Secretary, by members only, for their own use, at a discount of 2d. in the shilling.

The Early English Text Society was founded in 1864 by Frederick James Furnivall, with the help of Richard Morris, Walter Skeat, and others, to bring the mass of unprinted Early English literature within the reach of students and provide sound texts from which the New English Dictionary could quote. In 1867 an Extra Series was started of texts already printed but not in satisfactory or readily obtainable editions.

In 1921 the Extra Series was discontinued and all the publications of 1921 and subsequent years have since been listed and numbered as part of the Original Series. Since 1921 nearly a hundred new volumes have been issued; and since 1957 alone more than a hundred volumes have been reprinted at a cost of £40,000.

In this prospectus the Original Series and Extra Series for the years 1867–1920 are amalgamated, so as to show all the publications of the Society in a single list. In 1963 the prices of all volumes down to O.S. 222, and still available, were increased by one half, and the prices of some texts after O.S. 222 were also increased, in order to obtain additional revenue for reprinting.

LIST OF PUBLICATIONS

Original Series, 1864–1968. Extra Series, 1867–1920

O.S. 45. King Alfred's West-Saxon Version of Gregory's Pastoral Care, ed., with an English translation, by Henry Sweet. Part I. (*Reprinted* 1958.) 45s.   1871
    46. Legends of the Holy Rood, Symbols of the Passion and Cross Poems, ed. R. Morris. (*Out of print.*)   "
    47. Sir David Lyndesay's Works, ed. J. A. H. Murray. Part V. (*Out of print.*)   "
    48. The Times' Whistle, and other Poems, by R. C., 1616; ed. J. M. Cowper. (*Out of print.*)   "
E.S. 12. England in Henry VIII's Time: a Dialogue between Cardinal Pole and Lupset, by Thom. Starkey, Chaplain to Henry VIII, ed. J. M. Cowper. Part II. (*Out of print*, Part I is E.S. 32, 1878.)
    13. A Supplicacyon of the Beggers, by Simon Fish, A.D. 1528–9, ed. F. J. Furnivall, with A Supplication to our Moste Soueraigne Lorde, A Supplication of the Poore Commons, and The Decaye of England by the Great Multitude of Sheep, ed. J. M. Cowper. (*Out of print.*)   "
    14. Early English Pronunciation, by A. J. Ellis. Part III. (*Out of print.*)   "
O.S. 49. An Old English Miscellany, containing a Bestiary, Kentish Sermons, Proverbs of Alfred, and Religious Poems of the 13th cent., ed. R. Morris. (*Out of print.*)   1872
    50. King Alfred's West-Saxon Version of Gregory's Pastoral Care, ed. H. Sweet. Part II. (*Reprinted* 1958.) 45s.
    51. Þe Liflade of St. Juliana, 2 versions, with translations, ed. O. Cockayne and E. Brock. (*Reprinted* 1957.) 37s. 6d.   "
    52. Palladius on Husbondrie, englisht, ed. Barton Lodge. Part I. (*Out of print.*)
E.S. 15. Robert Crowley's Thirty-One Epigrams, Voyce of the Last Trumpet, Way to Wealth, &c., ed. J. M. Cowper. (*Out of print.*)   "
    16. Chaucer's Treatise on the Astrolabe, ed. W. W. Skeat. (*Out of print.*)   "
    17. The Complaynt of Scotlande, with 4 Tracts, ed. J. A. H. Murray. Part I. (*Out of print.*)   "
O.S. 53. Old-English Homilies, Series II, and three Hymns to the Virgin and God, 13th-century, with the music to two of them, in old and modern notation, ed. R. Morris. (*Out of print.*)   1873
    54. The Vision of Piers Plowman, ed. W. W. Skeat. Part III. Text C. (*Reprinted* 1959.) 52s. 6d.   "
    55. Generydes, a Romance, ed. W. Aldis Wright. Part I. (*Out of print.*)   "
E.S. 18. The Complaynt of Scotlande, ed. J. A. H. Murray. Part II. (*Out of print.*)   "
    19. The Myroure of oure Ladye, ed. J. H. Blunt. (*Out of print.*)   "
O.S. 56. The Gest Hystoriale of the Destruction of Troy, in alliterative verse, ed. D. Donaldson and G. A. Panton. Part II. (*See* O.S. 39.)   1874
    57. Cursor Mundi, in four Texts, ed. R. Morris. Part I. (*Reprinted* 1961.) 25s.   "
    58, 63, 73. The Blickling Homilies, ed. R. Morris. Parts I, II, and III. (*Reprinted as one volume* 1967.) 63s.   "
E.S. 20. Lovelich's History of the Holy Grail, ed. F. J. Furnivall. Part I. (*Out of print.*)   "
    21, 29. Barbour's Bruce, ed. W. W. Skeat. Parts II and III. (*Reprinted as Volume II* 1968.) 84s.   "
    22. Henry Brinklow's Complaynt of Roderyck Mors and The Lamentacyon of a Christen Agaynst the Cytye of London, made by Roderigo Mors, ed. J. M. Cowper. (*Out of print.*)   "
    23. Early English Pronunciation, by A. J. Ellis. Part IV. (*Out of print.*)   1875
O.S. 59. Cursor Mundi, in four Texts, ed. R. Morris. Part II. (*Reprinted* 1966.) 42s.   "
    60. Meditacyuns on the Soper of our Lorde, by Robert of Brunne, ed. J. M. Cowper. (*Out of print.*)   "
    61. The Romance and Prophecies of Thomas of Erceldoune, ed. J. A. H. Murray. (*Out of print.*)
E.S. 24. Lovelich's History of the Holy Grail, ed. F. J. Furnivall. Part II. (*Out of print.*)
    25, 26. Guy of Warwick, 15th-century Version, ed. J. Zupitza. Pts. I and II. (*Reprinted as one volume* 1966.) 55s.   1876
O.S. 62. Cursor Mundi, in four Texts, ed. R. Morris. Part III. (*Reprinted* 1966.) 37s. 6d.   "
    63. The Blickling Homilies, ed. R. Morris. Part II. (*See* O.S. 58.)   "
    64. Francis Thynne's Embleames and Epigrams, ed. F. J. Furnivall. (*Out of print.*)   "
    65. Be Domes Dæge (Bede's *De Die Judicii*), &c., ed. J. R. Lumby. (*Reprinted* 1964.) 30s.   "
E.S. 26. Guy of Warwick, 15th-century Version, ed. J. Zupitza. Part II. (*See* E.S. 25)   "
    27. The English Works of John Fisher, ed. J. E. B. Mayor. Part I. (*Out of print.*)   1877
O.S. 66. Cursor Mundi, in four Texts, ed. R. Morris. Part IV. (*Reprinted* 1966.) 25s.   "
    67. Notes on Piers Plowman, by W. W. Skeat. Part I. (*Out of print.*)   "
E.S. 28. Lovelich's Holy Grail, ed. F. J. Furnivall. Part III. (*Out of print.*)   "
    29. Barbour's Bruce, ed. W. W. Skeat. Part III. (*See* E.S. 21.)   1878
O.S. 68. Cursor Mundi, in 4 Texts, ed. R. Morris. Part V. (*Reprinted* 1966.) 30s.   "
    69. Adam Davie's 5 Dreams about Edward II, &c., ed. F. J. Furnivall. 9s.   "
    70. Generydes, a Romance, ed. W. Aldis Wright. Part II. 7s. 6d.   "
E.S. 30. Lovelich's Holy Grail, ed. F. J. Furnivall. Part IV. (*Out of print.*)   "
    31. The Alliterative Romance of Alexander and Dindimus, ed. W. W. Skeat. (*Out of print.*)   "
    32. Starkey's England in Henry VIII's Time. Part I. Starkey's Life and Letters, ed. S. J. Herrtage. (*Out of print.*)   1879
O.S. 71. The Lay Folks Mass-Book, four texts, ed. T. F. Simmons. (*Out of print.*)   "
    72. Palladius on Husbondrie, englisht, ed. S. J. Herrtage. Part II. 9s.   "
E.S. 33. Gesta Romanorum, ed. S. J. Herrtage. (*Reprinted* 1962.) 80s.   "
    34. The Charlemagne Romances: 1. Sir Ferumbras, from Ashm. MS. 33, ed. S. J. Herrtage. (*Reprinted* 1966.) 50s.   1880
O.S. 73. The Blickling Homilies, ed. R. Morris. Part III. (*See* O.S. 58.)   "
    74. English Works of Wyclif, hitherto unprinted, ed. F. D. Matthew. (*Out of print.*)   "
E.S. 35. Charlemagne Romances: 2. The Sege of Melayne, Sir Otuell, &c., ed. S. J. Herrtage. (*Out of print.*)   "
    36, 37. Charlemagne Romances: 3 and 4. Lyf of Charles the Grete, ed. S. J. Herrtage. Parts I and II. (*Reprinted as one volume* 1967.) 50s.   "
O.S. 75. Catholicon Anglicum, an English-Latin Wordbook, from Lord Monson's MS., A.D. 1483, ed., with Introduction and Notes, by S. J. Herrtage and Preface by H. B. Wheatley. (*Out of print.*)   1881
    76, 82. Ælfric's Lives of Saints, in MS. Cott. Jul. E VII, ed. W. W. Skeat. Parts I and II. (*Reprinted as Volume I* 1966.) 60s.   "

3

4

O.S. 103. **The Legend of the Cross, &c.,** ed. A. S. Napier. (*Out of print.*) 1894
E.S. 65. **Sir Beves of Hamtoun,** ed. E. Kölbing. Part III. (*Out of print.*) „
66. **Lydgate's and Burgh's Secrees of Philisoffres** ('Governance of Kings and Princes'), ed. R. Steele. (*Out of print.*) „
O.S. 104. **The Exeter Book** (Anglo-Saxon Poems), re-ed. I. Gollancz. Part I. (*Reprinted* 1958.) 45s. 1895
105. **The Prymer or Lay Folks' Prayer Book,** Camb. Univ. MS., ed. H. Littlehales. Part I. (*Out of print.*) „
E.S. 67. **The Three Kings' Sons,** a Romance, ed. F. J. Furnivall. Part I, the Text. (*Out of print.*) „
68. **Melusine,** the prose Romance, ed. A. K. Donald. Part I, the Text. (*Out of print.*) „
O.S. 106. **R. Misyn's Fire of Love and Mending of Life** (Hampole), ed. R. Harvey. (*Out of print.*) 1896
107. **The English Conquest of Ireland,** A.D. 1166–1185, 2 Texts, ed. F. J. Furnivall. Part I. (*Out of print.*) „
E.S. 69. **Lydgate's Assembly of the Gods,** ed. O. L. Triggs. (*Reprinted* 1957.) 37s. 6d. „
70. **The Digby Plays,** ed. F. J. Furnivall. (*Reprinted* 1967.) 30s. „
O.S. 108. **Child-Marriages and -Divorces, Trothplights, &c.** Chester Depositions, 1561–6, ed. F. J. Furnivall. (*Out of print.*) 1897
109. **The Prymer or Lay Folks' Prayer Book,** ed. H. Littlehales. Part II. (*Out of print.*) „
E.S. 71. **The Towneley Plays,** ed. G. England and A. W. Pollard. (*Reprinted* 1966.) 45s. „
72. **Hoccleve's Regement of Princes, and 14 Poems,** ed. F. J. Furnivall. (*Out of print.*) „
73. **Hoccleve's Minor Poems, II,** from the Ashburnham MS., ed. I. Gollancz. (*Out of print.*) „
O.S. 110. **The Old-English Version of Bede's Ecclesiastical History,** ed. T. Miller. Part II, 1. (*Reprinted* 1963.) 45s. 1898
111. **The Old-English Version of Bede's Ecclesiastical History,** ed. T. Miller. Part II, 2. (*Reprinted* 1963.) 45s. „
E.S. 74. **Secreta Secretorum,** 3 prose Englishings, one by Jas. Yonge, 1428, ed. R. Steele. Part I. 36s. „
75. **Speculum Guidonis de Warwyk,** ed. G. L. Morrill. (*Out of print.*) „
O.S. 112. **Merlin.** Part IV. Outlines of the Legend of Merlin, by W. E. Mead. (*Out of print.*) 1899
113. **Queen Elizabeth's Englishings of Boethius, Plutarch, &c.,** ed. C. Pemberton. (*Out of print.*) „
E.S. 76. **George Ashby's Poems, &c.,** ed. Mary Bateson. (*Reprinted* 1965.) 30s. „
77. **Lydgate's DeGuilleville's Pilgrimage of the Life of Man,** ed. F. J. Furnivall. Part I. (*Out of print.*) „
78. **The Life and Death of Mary Magdalene,** by T. Robinson, c. 1620, ed. H. O. Sommer. 9s. „
O.S. 114. **Ælfric's Lives of Saints,** ed. W. W. Skeat. Part IV and last. (*See* O.S. 94.) 1900
115. **Jacob's Well,** ed. A. Brandeis. Part I. (*Out of print.*) „
116. **An Old-English Martyrology,** re-ed. G. Herzfeld. (*Out of print.*) „
E.S. 79. **Caxton's Dialogues,** English and French, ed. H. Bradley. (*Out of print.*) „
80. **Lydgate's Two Nightingale Poems,** ed. O. Glauning. (*Out of print.*) „
80A. **Selections from Barbour's Bruce** (Books I–X), ed. W. W. Skeat. 20s. „
81. **The English Works of John Gower,** ed. G. C. Macaulay. Part I. (*Reprinted* 1957.) 60s. „
O.S. 117. **Minor Poems of the Vernon MS.,** ed. F. J. Furnivall. Part II. (*Out of print.*) 1901
118. **The Lay Folks' Catechism,** ed. T. F. Simmons and H. E. Nolloth. (*Out of print.*) „
119. **Robert of Brunne's Handlyng Synne,** and its French original, re-ed. F. J. Furnivall. Part I. (*Out of print.*) „
E.S. 82. **The English Works of John Gower,** ed. G. C. Macaulay. Part II. (*Reprinted* 1957.) 60s. „
83. **Lydgate's DeGuilleville's Pilgrimage of the Life of Man,** ed. F. J. Furnivall. Part II. (*Out of print.*) „
84. **Lydgate's Reson and Sensuallyte,** ed. E. Sieper. Vol. I. (*Reprinted* 1965.) 42s. „
O.S. 120. **The Rule of St. Benet in Northern Prose and Verse,** and Caxton's Summary, ed. E. A. Kock. (*Out of print.*) 1902
121. **The Laud MS. Troy-Book,** ed. J. E. Wülfing. Part I. (*Out of print.*) „
E.S. 85. **Alexander Scott's Poems,** 1568, ed. A. K. Donald. (*Out of print.*) „
86. **William of Shoreham's Poems,** re-ed. M. Konrath. Part I. (*Out of print.*) „
87. **Two Coventry Corpus Christi Plays,** re-ed. H. Craig. (*See under* 1952.) „
O.S. 122. **The Laud MS. Troy-Book,** ed. J. E. Wülfing. Part II. (*Out of print.*) 1903
123. **Robert of Brunne's Handlyng Synne,** and its French original, re-ed. F. J. Furnivall. Part II. (*Out of print.*) „
E.S. 88. **Le Morte Arthur,** re-ed. J. D. Bruce. (*Reprinted* 1959.) 45s. „
89. **Lydgate's Reson and Sensuallyte,** ed. E. Sieper. Vol. II. (*Reprinted* 1965.) 35s. „
90. **English Fragments from Latin Medieval Service-Books,** ed. H. Littlehales. (*Out of print.*) „
O.S. 124. **Twenty-six Political and other Poems** from Digby MS. 102, &c., ed. J. Kail. Part I. 18s. 1904
125. **Medieval Records of a London City Church,** ed. H. Littlehales. Part I. (*Out of print.*) „
126. **An Alphabet of Tales,** in Northern English, from the Latin ed. M. M. Banks. Part I. (*Out of print.*) „
E.S. 91. **The Macro Plays,** ed. F. J. Furnivall and A. W. Pollard. (*Out of print;* see 262.) „
92. **Lydgate's DeGuilleville's Pilgrimage of the Life of Man,** ed. Katherine B. Locock. Part III. (*Out of print.*) „
93. **Lovelich's Romance of Merlin,** from the unique MS., ed. E. A. Kock. Part I. (*Out of print.*) „
O.S. 127. **An Alphabet of Tales,** in Northern English, from the Latin, ed. M. M. Banks. Part II. (*Out of print.*) 1905
128. **Medieval Records of a London City Church,** ed. H. Littlehales. Part II. (*Out of print.*) „
129. **The English Register of Godstow Nunnery,** ed. A. Clark. Part I. 18s. „
E.S. 94. **Respublica,** a Play on a Social England, ed. L. A. Magnus. (*Out of print. See under* 1946.) „
95. **Lovelich's History of the Holy Grail.** Part V. The Legend of the Holy Grail, ed. Dorothy Kempe. (*Out of print.*) „
96. **Mirk's Festial,** ed. T. Erbe. Part I. (*Out of print.*) „
O.S. 130. **The English Register of Godstow Nunnery,** ed. A. Clark. Part II. 27s. 1906
131. **The Brut, or The Chronicle of England,** ed. F. Brie. Part I. (*Reprinted* 1960.) 45s. „
132. **John Metham's Works,** ed. H. Craig. 27s. „
E.S. 97. **Lydgate's Troy Book,** ed. H. Bergen. Part I, Books I and II. (*Out of print.*) „

5

6

7

Forthcoming volumes

Other texts are in preparation including three further English versions of the Ancrene Riwle.

Supplementary Texts

The Society proposes to issue some Supplementary Texts from time to time as funds allow. These will be sent to members as part of the normal issue and will also be available to non-members at listed prices. The first of these, Supplementary Text 1, expected to appear early in 1970, will be *Non-Cycle Plays and Fragments*, ed. Norman Davis (about 42s.). This is a completely revised and re-set edition of the texts in Extra Series 104 with some additional pieces.

May 1968

Publisher: LONDON · THE OXFORD UNIVERSITY PRESS, ELY HOUSE, 37 DOVER ST., W. 1

ILLUSTRATIONS

VOLUME II